FOURTH EDITION
PERSPECTIVES ON
INTERNATIONAL
RELATIONS

≫ Power, Institutions, and Ideas

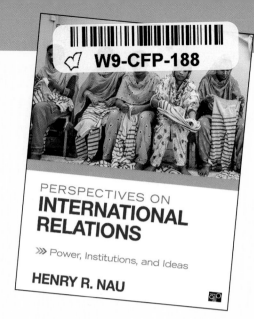

PERSPECTIVES ON
INTERNATIONAL
RELATIONS

≫ Power, Institutions, and Ideas

HENRY R. NAU

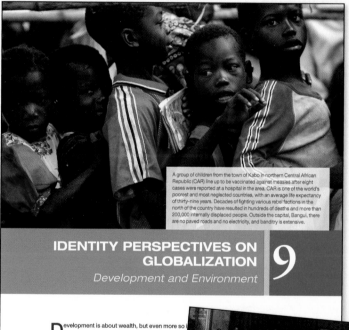

A group of children from the town of Kabo in northern Central African Republic (CAR) line up to be vaccinated against measles after eight cases were reported at a hospital in the area. CAR is one of the world's poorest and most neglected countries, with an average life expectancy of thirty-nine years. Decades of fighting various rebel factions in the north of the country have resulted in hundreds of deaths and more than 200,000 internally displaced people. Outside the capital, Bangui, there are no paved roads and no electricity, and banditry is extensive.

IDENTITY PERSPECTIVES ON GLOBALIZATION
Development and Environment

9

≫ *Perspectives on International Relations*—an even-handed presentation of realism, liberalism, constructivism, and critical theory—expertly applies these perspectives in every chapter, training students to think critically about the world's most urgent issues

Development is about wealth, but even more so i[...] the environment. In this chapter, we focus on the [...] ronment. There are four aspects to development: Wh[...] the human measures of development and change in [...] the consequences for the environment? And, finall[...] and what constitutes social justice in the age of glo[...]

Demonstrating the successful rise of collective security from the liberal perspective, the United Nations Security Council votes on November 29, 1990, to adopt a resolution authorizing the use of military force against Iraq beginning in January 1991.

LIBERAL PERSPECTIVES ON TODAY'S WORLD
Collective Security, International Negotiations, Institutions, and Law

6

On August 2, 1990, Iraq invaded Kuwait. In contrast to the world's response when Japan invaded Manchuria in 1931 or Hitler annexed the Sudetenland in 1938, international organizations responded to Iraq's actions promptly and decisively—the way they were supposed to. The United Nations immediately condemned the attack, and the United States, supported by all the great powers, mobilized a UN-blessed military force to eject Iraq from Kuwait. As that unprecedented global action took place, President George H. W. Bush proclaimed to Congress a "new world order . . . in which the rule of law supplants the rule of the jungle" and expressed to the UN General Assembly what appeared to be the fulfillment of liberal hopes to replace the balance of power with a collective security system.

Karim Muhammad poses with his two new smartphones after waiting in line overnight to be among the first to purchase the latest generation of the smartphone in Glendale, California, September 2013. Do the economic policies that make his purchases possible make the countries of the world increasingly interdependent—and more vulnerable?

REALIST AND LIBERAL PERSPECTIVES ON GLOBALIZATION
Trade, Investment, and Finance

8

How does globalization actually work? What policies and institutions govern it? Too many scholars and commentators write about globalization without saying anything about how the actual economic mechanisms of globalization work.

Pedagogy that lets your students really see the root causes of world events

as "victors' justice." Reconciliation may be promoted, they argue, if past leaders are not openly tried and prosecuted. After its revolution against apartheid, for example, South Africa decided not to prosecute individuals responsible for the racist policies of the apartheid government. Instead it celebrated the heroic actions of the new leaders and government, especially its first president, Nelson Mandela. On the other hand, other countries have decided that they cannot clear the decks for future peace until they settle accounts for past atrocities. The ad hoc tribunal for Rwanda, for example, is engaged in such an effort. It has completed fifty trials and convicted twenty-nine defendants, and the trials of eleven more are ongoing.

CAUSAL ARROW: PERSPECTIVES

Help or hinder reconciliation?	Punish atrocities	Tribunals
IDENTITY	REALIST	LIBERAL

>>> International Economic Institutions

Liberal perspectives strongly promote world trade and economic development. Wealth, although not a pure collective good because growth can be distributed unequally, is nevertheless a prerequisite of greater economic justice and political opportunity. The United Nations, through its Economic and Social Council, nominally superintends the global economic institutions, but the three main international economic institutions— the International Monetary Fund, World Bank, and World Trade Organization—are

 Perspectives and Levels of Analysis features give students a visual for tracking how each perspective interprets events from the individual, domestic, and systemic levels

TABLE 6-1			
Collective Security in Today's World: The Liberal Perspective and Levels of Analysis			

Level of analysis	Liberal perspective		
Systemic	Structure	Success of UN collective security in first Persian Gulf War and then its failure in Somalia
	Process	Path dependence leads to Osama bin Laden's declaration of war against West
Foreign policy		President Clinton, caught between international and domestic pressures, decides to pull troops out of Somalia
Domestic		Domestic conflict makes it difficult for UN to intervene impartially
Individual		Saddam Hussein defies UN resolutions despite defeat

MAP 4-2

Laos, Cambodia, North and South Vietnam

CHINA

Dien Bien Phu
Hanoi
Haiphong

LAOS

NORTH VIETNAM

Gulf of Tonkin

Hainan (CHINA)

Demilitarized zone

Demarcation line, July 195-

THAILAND

Da Nang
My Lai

KAMPUCHEA (CAMBODIA)

SOUTH VIETNAM

Phnom Penh

Saigon

Gulf of Siam

Mekong Delta

South China Sea

North Vietnam
South Vietnam

0   100 Mi
0   100 Km

A vigorous U.S. rebound and a preci
the balance of power and ended the
only mi

U.S. Re
United
and th
it exite
confide
projecte
landma
the Sov
governn
States h

Then in
dent Jin
econom
Washin
in Euro
to elim
based
Defen
Under
cuts,
from
per y

SDI
to k
of
depend

destruction with no effective ABM
Now Reagan's plans suggest
weapons built down. The **Stra**
focus to reducing, not just lin
grams invested greater resource
increase instability, because w
sis, launch a first strike agains
defeat whatever offensive mis
offered to share SDI technolog
from MAD to **mutual assured p**
able to protect itself against lo
humana than the specter of M
it scan
defens

Strategic Defense Initiative (SDI): the space-based antimissile systems that formed the core of Reagan's program to enhance U.S. missile defenses.

Strategic Arms Reduction Talks (START): U.S.-Soviet talks held in the 1990s to reduce offensive weapons systems.

A marginal glossary defines every key term in the book and chapters end with a Summary, a Key Concepts list, and a robust set of Study Questions

SUMMARY

Realist perspectives emphasize power. At the systemic level, bipolarity and a power vacuum caused the Cold War, and U.S. power outcompeted Soviet power to end the Cold War. At the systemic process level, Western alliances proved superior. At the domestic level of analysis, either the Soviet Union caused the Cold War because it was aggressive militarily or the United States did because it was aggressive economically; the Cold War ended either because the United States revived its military and economic power or because the Soviet economy collapsed.

Liberal perspectives emphasize institutions, diplomacy, and interdependence. At the systemic structural level of analysis, the Cold War started because the United Nations failed and collective security could be achieved within the Western region only under NATO and the EU. At the systemic process level, it started because the Marshall Plan threatened the Soviet Union, while the spread of Marxist-Leninism in west-

government bure
coalitions; and at
NGOs emerged a
in European coun

Finally, identity p
tion and constru
structural level,
Cold War. And at
ological zealotry
your pick—that o
perspective, the C
tural level becaus
the systemic proce
ologies converge
Gorbachev was
despite the skept
domestic level bec
at the individual

KEY CONCEPTS

Afghan War, 000	containment, 000	iron curtain, 000
Anti-Ballistic Missile (ABM) Treaty, 000	decolonization, 000	Korean War, 000
arms race, 000	détente, 000	long telegram, 000
balance of terror, 000	domino theory, 000	Marshall Plan, 000
Baruch Plan, 000	extended deterrence, 000	massive retaliation, 000
Berlin Blockade, 000	freedom fighters, 000	maximum deterrence, 000
Cold War, 000	Helsinki Accords, 000	

STUDY QUESTIONS

1. How would you line up the following causes of Soviet behavior in Kennan's analysis in the long telegram: security, ideology, and international institutions?

2. In what way do realist and liberal interpretations of deterrence differ, especially as they relate to the use of force and diplomacy?

3. What led to a resolution of the Cuban Missile Crisis as seen from liberal and realist perspectives?

4. What does *Finlandization* mean, and how did different perspectives interpret it?

5. Do the following arguments about the causes of the end of the Cold War differ in terms of perspectives or levels of analysis: information revolution, emergence and outreach of peace research and other nongovernmental groups in Germany and elsewhere, and détente?

Dramatically expanded graphics program and new full-color interior help students better visualize concepts, data, and information

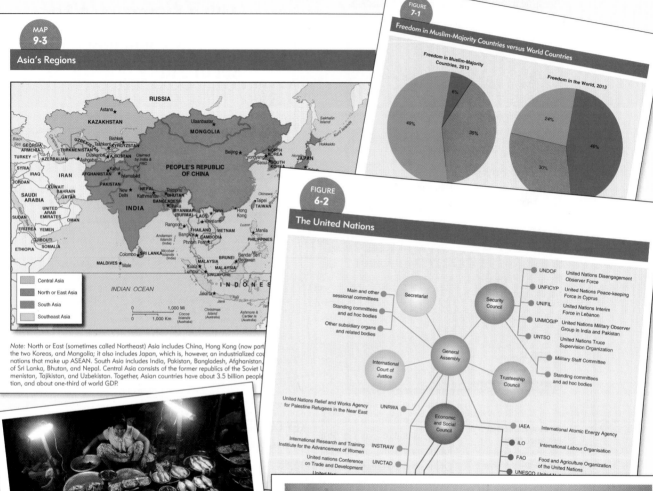

MAP 9-3

Asia's Regions

Note: North or East (sometimes called Northeast) Asia includes China, Hong Kong (now part of the two Koreas, and Mongolia; it also includes Japan, which is, however, an industrialized country nations that make up ASEAN. South Asia includes India, Pakistan, Bangladesh, Afghanistan, of Sri Lanka, Bhutan, and Nepal. Central Asia consists of the former republics of the Soviet Union, menistan, Tajikistan, and Uzbekistan. Together, Asian countries have about 3.5 billion people tion, and about one-third of world GDP.

FIGURE 7-1

Freedom in Muslim-Majority Countries versus World Countries

Freedom in Muslim-Majority Countries, 2013

Freedom in the World, 2013

FIGURE 6-2

The United Nations

onomy. Again, the United States has the largest share of
-G-5 countries control 37 percent, and the G-7 countries
gave China the third-largest share at 4.4 percent, behind
The Bank has more than ten thousand employees and is run
lected by the United States.

ription to the World Bank just as in the IMF. IDA increases
hments) every four years. But the World Bank itself, unlike
noney by selling World Bank bonds on private financial
ts back World Bank bonds, these bonds have the highest
sell at a higher price or lower interest rate. The World Bank
rates to developing countries. If the latter were to borrow
al markets, they would have to price their bonds at lower
terest rates.

A fishmonger uses battery-powered portable lamps as she waits for customers at a night market in Yangon, Myanmar, in September 2013. The World Bank recently approved aid for a power plant project in Myanmar aimed at boosting electricity production in one of Asia's poorest countries.

The Jin Mao Tower (center left) and the Oriental Pearl Tower (background center right) stand among

interest is driving the news coverage? Jobs changing on a massive scale is the mark of a growing and robust economy. The former communist countries tried to save jobs by not participating in free international trade—and they did save jobs. They saved the same old jobs in the same old industries that became obsolete and uncompetitive and

FOURTH EDITION

PERSPECTIVES ON
INTERNATIONAL
RELATIONS

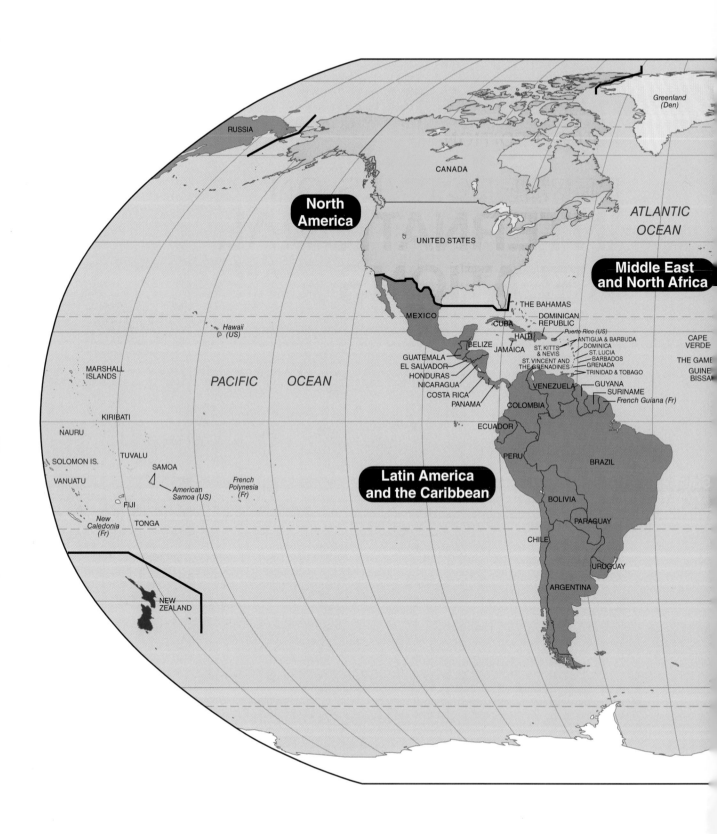

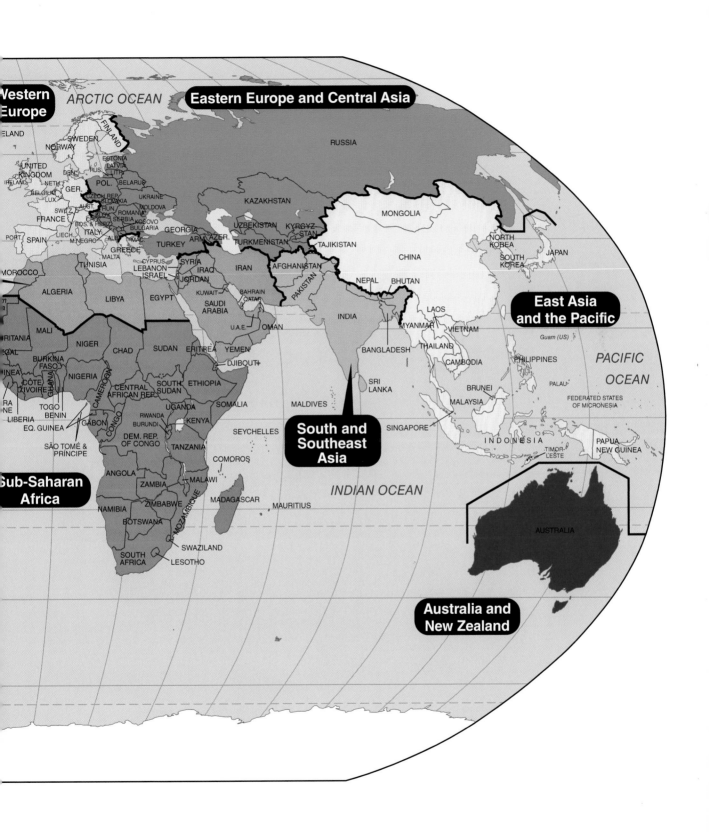

FOURTH EDITION

PERSPECTIVES ON INTERNATIONAL RELATIONS

≫ Power, Institutions, and Ideas

HENRY R. NAU

George Washington University

SAGE | CQPRESS

Los Angeles | London | New Delhi
Singapore | Washington DC

Los Angeles | London | New Delhi
Singapore | Washington DC

FOR INFORMATION:

CQ Press

An Imprint of SAGE Publications, Inc.

2455 Teller Road

Thousand Oaks, California 91320

E-mail: order@sagepub.com

SAGE Publications Ltd.

1 Oliver's Yard

55 City Road

London, EC1Y 1SP

United Kingdom

SAGE Publications India Pvt. Ltd.

B 1/I 1 Mohan Cooperative Industrial Area

Mathura Road, New Delhi 110 044

India

SAGE Publications Asia-Pacific Pte. Ltd.

3 Church Street

#10-04 Samsung Hub

Singapore 049483

Acquisitions Editor: Charisse Kiino

Developmental Editor: Elise Frasier

Production Editor: Libby Larson

Copy Editor: Judy Selhorst

Typesetter: C&M Digitals (P) Ltd

Proofreader: Wendy Jo Dymond

Indexer: Kathy Paparchontis

Cover Design: Scott Van Atta

Interior Design: Scott Van Atta

Marketing Manager: Amy Whitaker

Printed in Canada

Library of Congress Cataloging-in-Publication Data

Nau, Henry R., 1941–
Perspectives on international relations : power, institutions, and ideas / Henry R. Nau, George Washington University. — Fourth edition.

pages cm
Includes bibliographical references and index.

ISBN 978-1-4522-4148-7 (pbk. : alk. paper) —
ISBN 978-1-4833-1203-3 (web pdf : alk. paper)
1. International relations. 2. World politics. I. Title.

JZ1305.N34 2015
327.101—dc23   2014000237

This book is printed on acid-free paper.

14 15 16 17 18 10 9 8 7 6 5 4 3 2 1

To all my former students, especially Alan, Ann, Gabriel, Jim, and Roy

ABOUT THE AUTHOR

 **Henry R. Nau** has taught political science for forty years. He is currently professor of political science and international affairs at the Elliott School of International Affairs, George Washington University. He taught previously at Williams College and held visiting appointments at Johns Hopkins School of Advanced International Studies, Stanford University, and Columbia University. Since 1989, he has directed the U.S.–Japan–South Korea Legislative Exchange Program, semiannual meetings among members of the U.S. Congress, the Japanese Diet, and the South Korean National Assembly.

Nau also served in government twice, once from 1975 to 1977 as special assistant to the undersecretary for economic affairs in the U.S. Department of State and again from 1981 to 1983 as a senior staff member of the National Security Council under President Reagan, responsible for international economic affairs. He was the White House aide, or sherpa, for the annual G-7 economic summits in Ottawa (1981), Versailles (1982), and Williamsburg (1983), and for the special summit with developing countries in Cancun (1982). He is a former member of the UN Committee for Development Planning and the U.S. Department of State's Advisory Committee on International Investment. From 1977 to 1981, Nau served on the Board of Editors of the journal *International Organization*. He has received research grants from, among others, the Woodrow Wilson International Center for Scholars, the National Science Foundation, the Council on Foreign Relations, the Smith-Richardson Foundation, the Century Foundation, the Japan-U.S. Friendship Commission, the Hoover Institution, and the Lynde and Harry Bradley Foundation. From 1963 to 1965, he served as a lieutenant in the 82nd Airborne Division at Fort Bragg, North Carolina.

Nau's published books include *Conservative Internationalism: Armed Diplomacy under Jefferson, Polk, Truman, and Reagan* (Princeton University Press, 2013); *At Home Abroad: Identity and Power in American Foreign Policy* (Cornell University Press, 2002); *Trade and Security: U.S. Policies at Cross-Purposes* (American Enterprise Institute, 1995); *The Myth of America's Decline: Leading the World Economy into the 1990s* (Oxford University Press, 1990); and *National Politics and International Technology: Peaceful Nuclear Reactor Development in Western Europe* (Johns Hopkins University Press, 1974). His most recent edited book is *Worldviews of Aspiring Powers: Domestic Foreign Policy Debates in China, India, Iran, Japan, and Russia*, coedited with Deepa M.

Ollapally (Oxford University Press, 2012). His recent articles and chapters in edited books include "The Jigsaw Puzzle and the Chess Board: The Making and Unmaking of Foreign Policy in the Age of Obama," *Commentary* 133, no. 5 (May 2012): 13–21; "Ideas Have Consequences: The Cold War and Today," *International Politics* 48 (July/ September 2011): 460–81; "No Alternative to 'Isms,'" *International Studies Quarterly* 55, no. 2 (June 2011): 487–91; "Ronald Reagan," in *US Foreign Policy and Democracy Promotion: From Theodore Roosevelt to Barack Obama*, edited by Michael Cox, Timothy J. Lynch, and Nicolas Bouchet (Routledge, 2013); "Scholarship and Policy-Making: Who Speaks Truth to Whom?," in *The Oxford Handbook of International Relations*, edited by Christian Reus-Smit and Duncan Snidal (Oxford University Press, 2008); and "Iraq and Previous Transatlantic Crises: Divided by Threat, Not Institutions or Values," in *The End of the West? Crisis and Change in the Atlantic Order*, edited by Jeffrey Anderson, G. John Ikenberry, and Thomas Risse (Cornell University Press, 2008).

BRIEF CONTENTS

CONTENTS

Conclusion. Applying Perspectives and Levels of Analysis: The Case of the Democratic Peace 475

FIGURES, MAPS, PARALLEL TIMELINES, AND TABLES

Figures

Maps

Parallel Timelines

Tables

PREFACE

Confucius, the Chinese philosopher, once said, "To learn without thinking is in vain; to think without learning is dangerous." Learning or knowing anything requires both thought and investigation, theory and facts.

I confirmed Confucius's insight when I took a break from teaching to serve in government from 1975 to 1977 and again from 1981 to 1983. At that point, having spent a decade in the classroom, I thought I would learn at last about how policy was really made. I would have access to all the facts, even the secret ones kept by intelligence agencies, and I would understand the logic behind how those facts relate to policy choices. My first awakening came when an officer from one of the intelligence agencies paid me a visit, not to give me the facts I so wanted, but to ask me which facts I might be interested in. Oh, I suddenly realized, "the facts" depend on which theory or set of ideas I might wish to test. Now I had to do some thinking. What did I really want to know? Well, of course, I wanted to know what was happening. But I didn't have time to learn about what was happening everywhere, so I had to focus on certain areas and issues. And I wanted to know not just facts but what caused these facts. I learned subsequently that intelligence officers often do not agree on the facts, let alone on the interpretation or the causes of those facts. There is no one theory that explains policy, no one set of facts that defines any given situation objectively. There are many theories and many facts—far too many for me to take them all into account.

When I left the government, I understood better than ever that the policy world is not all that different from the classroom. Both require theoretical commitment. You have to decide what you want to learn, what interests you. And that's a function of your thinking—or perspective—and your values. And both require empirical effort. You assemble and investigate as many facts as you can, then you test your ideas against the facts. But, in the end, you make judgments about which questions and which answers are most important. The one big difference is that you have more time to deliberate and choose in the classroom. In government, you have to act quickly because events move quickly and you lose the opportunity to influence outcomes if you wait too long. As one colleague said to me, you consume thought in government; you accumulate it in the classroom.

The idea for this textbook began to emerge the day I left government. I wanted to demonstrate for students the relationship between perspectives and facts for understanding international relations. It was a long way from there to here, but ultimately the book emerged through happenstance and history.

The happenstance part occurred when I began teaching a large introductory course in international relations a few years after leaving the government. I was eager to do this, but it also coincided with efforts at George Washington University's Elliott School of International Affairs to design a more coherent interdisciplinary introductory course for undergraduate majors in international affairs. My task was to come up with a course that not only shepherded students through the nuts and bolts of world politics but also taught them how to look at world problems through different disciplinary lenses. I knew a lot about economics and loved history, and I had always considered my strengths to lie more on the conceptual than the methodological side of political science, but was I ready for such a demanding task?

The history part had to do with waiting until I was fully prepared to write this book. My academic research interests progressed over the years from a relatively narrow focus on the technological aspects of U.S. foreign policy and international affairs to broader economic aspects and finally, in the 1990s, to strategic and military aspects. As I broadened my focus, I taught the introductory course in increasingly bolder strokes, exposing students to alternative theoretical perspectives—the realist, liberal, and constructivist approaches in particular—as well as hefty doses of historical narrative and how economic policy mechanisms work. I worried initially that the design expected too much of students. But I refused to underestimate young people and worked hard to simplify and illustrate complex issues, especially the role of perspectives. The text is full of examples that illustrate how perspectives influence both scholarly discourse and everyday debates about world politics. To my joy, the students really cottoned to this approach. They grasped the big ideas and applied them, often bringing me newspaper articles to illustrate the different perspectives and levels of analysis. After fifteen years of teaching the introductory course and thirty years of broadening my research interests, happenstance and history came together and I put pen to paper. Happily for me, and hopefully for students too, this book is the fruit of that labor.

≫ Approach of the Book

The purpose of this book is to teach students how to think critically about the subject matter of international relations. To that end, I introduce readers to the principal conceptual tools used by students of politics, namely, the main theoretical perspectives of international relations, the levels of analysis from which we analyze global problems, and the crucial idea of causality. Throughout the book I apply the perspectives and levels of analysis as evenhandedly as possible, including the most recent constructivist perspectives, and I integrate the disciplines of history, economics, and political science into the presentation. Knowing that this material is both intrinsically interesting and challenging, I do my best to write in an uncomplicated and engaging style.

First, the book uses the concepts of perspectives and levels of analysis to address all aspects of international affairs. While most textbooks introduce theories in an opening chapter, they seldom apply or even mention those theories in subsequent chapters.

Some start with a history chapter before they introduce theory, as if there is only one objective account of history. By contrast, I start with theories but simplify them using the student-friendly concept of perspectives. Perspectives focus on certain facts and emphasize certain causes. For example, realist perspectives point toward powerful actors and emphasize the distribution of *power* as the primary cause of world events, liberal perspectives focus on interactions and emphasize the rules and roles of *institutions* as primary causes, and constructivist perspectives highlight *ideas* and how actors identity themselves and others as the principal causes.

Similarly, the book addresses multiple levels of analysis within each perspective. While perspectives highlight the causes of events, the levels of analysis highlight the levels or sources from which these causes come: the *individual* or decision-making level; the *domestic* level, or the characteristics of countries as a whole; the *foreign policy* level, which links internal and external causes; and the external or *systemic* level, which highlights the relative position and external interactions among countries. I then use these two analytical devices of perspectives and levels of analysis to discuss and illuminate the different conclusions that scholars and students of international affairs draw concerning historical events as well as contemporary issues.

All serious study of international affairs addresses simultaneously all perspectives (power, institutions, and ideas) and all levels of analysis (individual, domestic, and systemic). The perspectives and levels of analysis constitute alternative hypotheses about the nature and direction of the causes of international events. Critical thinking demands that we apply at least two or more hypotheses to assess empirical evidence. But the point of including multiple hypotheses at the outset is to weigh the *relative* importance of each variable and assess the causal relationship between the variables in drawing conclusions. Thus, the book gives special attention to the *direction* of causality (using a device I call *causal arrows*) among the principal variables of the different perspectives and levels of analysis. The realist perspective, for example, does not ignore ideas; it just concludes that power is the primary cause or source of ideas—big powers think one way, small powers another. Liberalism does not ignore the balance of power; it just sees diplomacy and international institutions as the primary means to constrain and eventually reduce the role of the balance of power in world affairs. And constructivism does not diminish practices/institutions or material power; it just sees identities and discourse as interpreting and giving meaning to material and institutional realities. A fourth perspective, critical theory, critiques the other perspectives by casting doubt on whether we can actually isolate the primary causes of events. It argues instead that events must be understood in the broadest historical context and are often caused by deep-seated forces that we can master only, if at all, by achieving new forms of self-consciousness, not by manipulating individual variables. Critical theory is a reminder that we may not be able to slice and dice reality into separable causes as our Western positivist or rationalist methods prescribe.

Second, the book treats the principal realist, liberal, and constructivist or identity perspectives evenhandedly. I avoid organizing the topics primarily around one perspective or level of analysis. Scholars often have a preference for one perspective or level of analysis. Some textbooks, for example, treat realism primarily at the systemic level of analysis, focusing on states, and liberalism primarily at the domestic level of analysis, focusing on democracy. This shortchanges realism and loads the dice in favor of liberalism. Other texts start with "problems," such as the problem of cooperation or of war and peace, assuming we can know what a problem is before we have a theory or perspective of the world that tells us why it is a problem. Problems don't just exist objectively, so this approach winds up hiding rather than highlighting perspectives. Students should confront and learn about all perspectives in as balanced a manner as possible. They will encounter opinions throughout their lives that differ from their own, and they need conceptual equipment to help them appreciate other opinions. One frightful piece of information from the American Institutes for Research tells us that only 38 percent of college graduates can successfully perform tasks such as comparing viewpoints in two newspaper editorials (see Thomas Toch and Kevin Carey, "Where Colleges Don't Excel," *Washington Post*, April 6, 2007, A21). Somewhere, we as instructors are dropping the ball.

Thus, this book does not start with the presumption that one perspective is best or that topics or problems can be listed without an understanding of the perspective from which these topics are considered to be important. Rather, I lead the student into different worlds, looking at the same reality from different angles. This approach, I believe, is the essence of a liberal arts education, equipping students to think critically—that is, by alternatives—and to make their own intellectual choices. I have my own preferences, to be sure, as does any other instructor, but I believe that all perspectives have a coherent logic and are supported by important evidence from history and contemporary world affairs. Thus, I strive to present the alternative perspectives not only accurately but also sympathetically.

Third, by taking into account more recent constructivist perspectives on international relations, the book updates the field. It includes the ideational or identity perspective. This perspective emphasizes the causal role of ideas, belief systems, norms, values, speech acts, and social discourse in international affairs, particularly as these factors affect the identities of actors and thus define their material interests as well as their behavior in interactions and institutions. The identity perspective revives the study of ideas in international affairs, which was neglected for several decades when realist and liberal perspectives were favored.

Fourth, the book is genuinely interdisciplinary. It includes a good deal of history and economics. Too often in international affairs we do not sufficiently understand other disciplines, or we simply append them to our instruction in a multidisciplinary rather than interdisciplinary fashion. In this book, the student learns history and economics through the relevant political science concepts. For example, the student explores the major wars of the twentieth century through the realist concept of German unification and the balance of power (World War I), the liberal concept of collective security and the League of Nations (World War II), and the identity concept of relative political ideologies—communism and capitalism (the Cold War). Economics is also presented practically and historically. The student sees the underlying concepts at work in day-to-day practices of globalization—for example, when an American consumer uses domestic tax cuts to purchase imports or borrows money to refinance a mortgage from capital made available by China's purchases of U.S. Treasury securities. Policies (including fiscal and monetary) and concepts such as comparative advantage and strategic trade are explained through historical examples and disputes rather than through abstract formulas.

Fifth, this book reinforces an emerging trend toward less encyclopedic, more focused texts, but it does more than that by tying the discussion together with a coherent and central theme about how the world works from the vantage points of different perspectives. The book, in short, has a pedagogical "plot"; it is not just a series of "one-act plays" or topics. I hope that students will experience this book as an adventure, like a good novel or historical biography: inviting, evolving, and delivering insights that move the reader forward toward greater and greater insight. If that happens, the book succeeds in educating as well as instructing and becomes potentially a reference work that students retain and revisit as they pursue international studies in more advanced courses and throughout their lives.

Sixth, and to this end, I employ a direct and engaging writing style that avoids professional jargon and textbook ennui. Students are easily bored by concepts and topics presented in an obligatory fashion, much like an endless list of addresses in a telephone book. They sense the difference between professional and pedantic instruction. The prose in this book is professional yet light and, I hope, occasionally humorous. It seeks to reach a generation raised on the Internet by enticing and entertaining as well as by teaching.

>>> New to the Fourth Edition

Earlier editions of this book have long been admired for their evenhanded presentation of perspectives and levels of analysis to train students to think critically about the world's most urgent issues. This hallmark hasn't changed with this new edition; in fact, it has been enhanced by the further development and presentation of the causal arrows feature, which helps students to see graphically the impact of specific causes from the different perspectives and levels of analysis on historical and current controversies in world affairs.

Adopters of the previous editions will notice that the big differences between this edition and previous ones are length and focus. The fourth edition is shorter. It eliminates (much to my regret, because I love history) a good deal of the early history of the world, mostly because students get that material in history courses and this is a book about modern international affairs. This edition retains the deep historical coverage of World War I, World War II, and the Cold War, not only because that history is still so relevant today but also because these make such rich and illuminating cases for the comprehensive application of the book's framework of perspectives, levels of analysis, and causal arrows.

I have also reorganized and focused the middle chapters of the book in Part II on the contemporary international system. Here I devote a single chapter to each perspective's view of the contemporary world from the different levels of analysis. This approach reduces the number of moving parts that the student has to consider. He or she can see the world today primarily from a realist perspective, then jump to the next chapter to see it primarily from a liberal perspective, and so on. By the end of this middle section, the student has a clear idea of how the perspectives differ in terms of what they emphasize when examining the contemporary world.

The globalization section (Part III) has also been shortened and focused. It separates the economic aspects of growth, the relative and absolute gains that realist and liberal perspectives emphasize, from the normative aspects of growth (growth for whom and for what) that identity perspectives emphasize. This division helps the student see the continuing relevance of perspectives in the economics section of the course. The book retains the chapter on critical theory perspectives on development, which is an essential counterpoint to the rationalist focus on Western and material aspects of development.

The other major difference previous adopters will notice is that the book is now published in a beautiful full-color, eye-catching design that showcases the relevance of its contents for today's students, with more than seventy photos and visually appealing maps, tables, and graphs that display important concepts and key data and empirical findings. Happily, this new design comes at no additional cost to students.

≫ Organization of the Book

Perspectives on International Relations sticks with the theme of perspectives and levels of analysis in every chapter—including the sections on the world economy and global forces. There is some variation, however. Some chapters concentrate on a single perspective; others include all perspectives but start from different perspectives, to show that there is no favored perspective; and provided throughout all chapters are repeated marginal references back to the main perspectives, concepts, and levels of analysis of the book.

The introduction is, in effect, an argument for the book's approach, why we have to select and make judgments to understand international affairs. It shows students immediately, in the case of reactions to the terrorist attacks of September 11, 2001, how perspectives and levels of analysis are evident in almost everything they encounter about international affairs. It also explains the need for methods, judgment, history, and ethics and morality to understand world events. Chapter 1 then walks students through the details of the causal logic of the different perspectives and levels of analysis. It starts with the story of the prisoner's dilemma to show how different perspectives view the same game differently because of their contrasting assumptions and logic. But the prisoner's dilemma story can be skipped, if the instructor prefers. The bulk of the chapter lays out in straightforward terms the main logic and concepts of each perspective, defining concepts that appear over and over again in the actual history and debates in later chapters.

Part I of the text covers historical issues and controversies. Chapters 2–4 review world history from World War I through the end of the Cold War. Chapter 2 shows, for example, that after one hundred years and all of the evidence that probably exists, scholars still disagree about the causes of World War I. There must be elements at work in addition to the facts, and these are perspectives and levels of analysis.

Part II addresses contemporary issues and controversies. Chapters 5–7 illuminate the contemporary world from specific perspectives. These chapters help students see the world from one perspective at a time. By the end of this part, they will better understand why scholars and citizens see the world in many different ways and disagree about many aspects of the contemporary world system.

Part III looks at global forces for change in the contemporary international system. Chapter 8 focuses on the realist and liberal aspects of the world economy, the way domestic economic policies, trade, investment, and finance interact globally to produce greater wealth and distribute it. This chapter helps students understand the practical aspects of how the global economy works, the ways in which an open global economy increases overall wealth (absolute gains) and allocates it across nations and regions (relative gains), creating the various controversies about free trade, inequality, and infringement of national sovereignty. Chapter 9 addresses the identity aspects of development, surveying the development experience since World War II across four regional groups of countries: Asia, Latin America, the Middle East and North Africa, and sub-Saharan Africa. This chapter brings out the various external (e.g., outside intervention) and internal (e.g., different development strategies) causes of the differentiated growth experiences of developing countries and highlights the cultural and environmental aspects of development. Chapter 10 retains the analysis from earlier editions of the world economy from a critical or neo-Marxist perspective. It serves as a healthy reminder that the world of development since the 1500s has been largely a Western world and that any attempt to learn from that experience may also be interpreted as an imperialist project to perpetuate it.

Finally, the conclusion wraps up with a vivid demonstration of the usefulness of perspectives and levels of analysis for understanding international relations. It applies these tools to sort out the various explanations of one of the most significant phenomena in contemporary world affairs, the democratic peace. It shows how these explanations differ based on the causal arrows that run from different perspectives and levels of analysis. Each one of these explanations is backed by scholarly evidence, but the evidence is not conclusive. The various explanations motivate further examination and testing of the major theories (perspectives) by which we try to understand international relations.

Students finish the book with newfound knowledge of the complexity and limits of good social science research, in part, because they have mastered by this point some simplified tools and can use them to dissect complicated controversies. Above all, the conclusion warns students to be modest about what they can know with certainty and to prepare to spend the rest of their lives with open minds, learning even as they act without complete knowledge to fulfill their obligations as good citizens of their countries and their world.

⟫ Key Features

Each of the book's pedagogical features contributes directly to the balance and coherence of the volume by helping students keep track of the different perspectives and levels of analysis and allowing students to see how these are applied in contemporary debates:

- The book's **causal arrows** appear where there is explicit discussion of the interactions among perspectives and levels of analysis. The arrows help students to hone their ability to see which perspective or level of analysis a scholar or world leader is emphasizing as the cause of a particular problem or world event. Students see, for instance, whether power struggles (realist), weak institutions (liberal), or cultural differences (identity) weigh more importantly in explaining ethnic conflicts. The causal arrows have been significantly redesigned in this edition so that they do more than just point to instances of causality in the text; now they explicitly lay out the order of causality by coordinating ideas and concepts, as in this example:

CAUSAL ARROW: PERSPECTIVES

Create New Thinking	Decrease security dilemma	Helsinki Accords
IDENTITY	REALIST	LIBERAL

- "Perspective and Levels of Analysis" **tables** appear throughout the book to help students summarize and keep track of the various explanations of events covered from the different perspectives and levels of analysis.
- Graphic **Parallel Timelines** appear in the historical chapters, offering simultaneous chronologies of major historical events and movements and placing the different events under the particular perspectives that would most likely emphasize them.
- A **marginal glossary** provides succinct explanations of key concepts, with a definition in the margin the first time each term (in boldface) is discussed at length.
- Seventeen unique **maps** help students absorb important geopolitical, demographic, and thematic information.
- More than seventy full-color **photos** greatly enhance the book's art program and help students visualize important events and issues.
- **Key concepts** appear in boldface when first discussed in the book and are listed at the ends of chapters with their page reference for ease of review.
- Thought-provoking **study questions** at the end of each chapter provide a basis for in-class discussions and help gauge student comprehension.
- A complete **glossary** at the end of the book fully defines each key term and helps students prepare for exams.

⋙ SAGE edge for CQ Press

This book comes with a full range of high-quality, class-tested instructor and student ancillaries. The Instructor Resources, including PowerPoint lecture slides, a test bank, instructor manual, and sample syllabi, were prepared by Michael J. Struett, North Carolina State University. Markian Romaniw, The George Washington University, prepared the Student Resources: chapter summaries with learning objectives, quizzes, multimedia content, and internet exercises. Elise Frasier selected the SAGE journal articles featured in the Student Resources. Each ancillary is specifically tailored to *Perspectives on International Relations*.

SAGE edge offers a robust online forum featuring an impressive array of tools and resources for review, study, and further exploration. SAGE edge content is open access and available on demand at **http://edge.sagepub.com/nau4e**

SAGE edge for Students helps enhance learning and offers a personalized approach to coursework in an easy-to-use environment.

- Mobile-friendly **eFlashcards** strengthen understanding of key terms and concepts.
- Mobile-friendly practice **quizzes** allow for independent assessment by students of their mastery of course material.
- A customized online **action plan** includes tips and feedback on progress through the course and materials, which allows students to individualize their learning experience.
- **Chapter summaries** with **learning objectives** reinforce the most important material.
- EXCLUSIVE! Access to full-text **SAGE journal articles** that have been carefully selected to support and expand on the concepts presented in each chapter.

SAGE edge for Instructors supports teaching by making it easy to integrate quality content and create a rich learning environment that helps students perform at a higher level. Go to **http://edge.sagepub.com/nau4e** and click on "instructor's resources" to register and begin downloading resources.

- A comprehensive **test bank** provides more than 900 multiple-choice, fill-in-the blank, and short- and long-essay questions, as well as the opportunity to edit any question and/or insert personalized questions to effectively assess students' progress and understanding. The test bank is available in Word and fully loaded in Respondus, a flexible and easy-to-use test-generation software that allows instructors to build, customize, and even integrate exams into course management systems.
- **Sample course syllabi** for semester and quarter courses provide suggested models for structuring one's course.
- Editable, chapter-specific **PowerPoint slides** offer complete flexibility for creating a multimedia presentation for the course.

- An **instructor's manual** features chapter overviews and objectives, lecture starters, ideas for class activities, discussion questions.
- A set of all the **graphics from the text,** including all of the maps, tables, and figures, is available in PowerPoint, .pdf, and .jpg formats for class presentations.
- EXCLUSIVE! Access to full-text **SAGE journal articles** that have been carefully selected to support and expand on the concepts presented in each chapter to encourage students to think critically.
- A **common course cartridge** includes all of the instructor resources and assessment material from the student study site, making it easy for instructors to upload and use these materials in LMS such as Blackboard, Angel, Moodle, Canvas, and Desire2Learn.
- **Transition Guide** provides a chapter-by-chapter outline of key changes from the third edition to the fourth.

≫ Acknowledgments

I dedicate the book to all of my former students, both graduate and undergraduate, who inspired me to teach better. I mention five in particular: Alan D. Buckley, who teaches at Santa Monica College; Ann Becker, who runs her own consulting firm in Chicago; Gabriel Szekely, who taught at El Colegio de Mexico and served in past years as chief of staff to the Mexican minister of tourism; Jim (or James P.) Lester, who taught at Colorado State University until his untimely death; and Roy H. Ginsberg, who teaches at Skidmore College. Their friendship and success are the true rewards of teaching.

Colleagues who have helped are far too numerous for me to mention them all. Several, however, were particularly encouraging and read the whole or portions of the manuscript and contributed comments. One even volunteered to use an early draft of the manuscript in his undergraduate class; that was especially helpful. I am deeply grateful to all of them: Alan D. Buckley, Santa Monica College; Colin Dueck, George Mason University; Marty Finnemore, George Washington University; David Forsythe, University of Nebraska–Lincoln; Roy Ginsberg, Skidmore College; Jolyon Howorth, Yale University; Aida Hozic, University of Florida; Bruce Jentleson, Duke University; Peter Katzenstein, Cornell University; Stuart Kaufman, University of Delaware; Bob Keohane, Princeton University; Charles Lipson, University of Chicago; John Mearsheimer, University of Chicago; Scott David Or, Texas Lutheran University; Robert Paarlberg, Wellesley College; Thomas Risse, Free University of Berlin; Randy Schweller, Ohio State University; David Shambaugh, George Washington University; Janice Stein, University of Toronto; and J. Ann Tickner, University of Southern California.

Other colleagues who offered helpful advice at various stages include Christine Barbour, Indiana University; Larry Berman, University of California–Davis; Bruce Bueno de Mesquita, New York University and the Hoover Institution; Dan Caldwell, Pepperdine University; Gary Jacobson, University of California–San Diego; Sam Kernell, University of California–San Diego; Robert Lieber, Georgetown University; Mike Sodaro, George

Washington University; C. William Walldorf, Wake Forest University; and Steve Wayne, Georgetown University. I had a string of research assistants to help me on this project. I thank, in particular, Mark Romaniw, Bethany Remely, and Jordyn Cosmé. For earlier editions, I owe a special debt to Jamie Kebely, Sandy Snider-Pugh, David Tarre, and Ikuko Turner, and for this fourth edition, to Michael Wain and Alex Forster, who helped me balance this project with other obligations and thus preserve my sanity through very intense months of work.

I have never worked with a more professional and pleasant staff than the one at CQ Press. And they have been with me throughout the life of the book. Charisse Kiino was my first contact with CQ Press about this book. I never thought negotiating a contract could be done without stress, but it was with Charisse. Elise Frasier made so many contributions to the original book and subsequent editions that it would not be what it is without her. She and Charisse not only solicited numerous detailed and thoughtful critiques of the manuscript from outside reviewers, but they also dived into the details of the project, drafted summaries and tables of issues raised, and discussed these issues with me during numerous extended brainstorming sessions. I was astonished at their profes-sionalism—they must have had good instructors in international relations—and deeply grateful, even when they pinned my ears back on many needed adjustments. Brenda Carter was enormously supportive throughout, and Judy Selhorst did the copyediting of the fourth edition with splendid aplomb, building on the work of Julie F. Nemer, who copyedited previous editions as well as another of my previous books with unparalleled skill and patience. Gwenda Larsen, the production editor for many of the book's edi-tions, moved mountains each time to see the book through production in a timely way, somehow never losing sight of the most important and intricate details. In this edition, Libby Larson has taken the reins with equal assurance. I was warned that a textbook writer's nightmare is to have editors interfere either too much or not enough. I lived a dream because the CQ Press touch was absolutely perfect.

I can't thank my past and current reviewers enough. They were the most thorough and tough I have encountered in any peer-review process. Some have consented to be men-tioned here:

Richard Anderson, *University of California–Los Angeles*

Marc Genest, *U.S. Naval War College*

Amy Gurowitz, *University of California–Berkeley*

Kathleen Hancock, *University of Texas–San Antonio*

Eric Hines, *University of Montana – Missoula*

Matthew Hoffmann, *University of Toronto*

Ian Hurd, *Northwestern University*

Nathan Jensen, *Washington University in St. Louis*

Peter Katzenstein, *Cornell University*

Stuart Kaufman, *University of Delaware*

Alan Kessler, *University of Texas at Austin*

John Masker, *Temple University*

Heather Elko McKibben, *University of California–Davis*

Patrice McMahon, *University of Nebraska – Lincoln*

Waltraud Morales, *University of Central Florida*

Travis Nelson, *University of Wisconsin – Platteville*

Richard Nolan, *University of Florida*

Timothy Nordstrom, *University of Mississippi*

John Owen, *University of Virginia*

Rita Peters, *University of Massachusetts – Boston*

Robert Poirier, *Northern Arizona University*

Richard Price, *University of British Columbia*

Randall Schweller, *Ohio State University*

James Scott, *Indiana State University*

Nicole Simonelli, *Purdue University*

Michael Struett, *North Carolina State University*

Nina Tannenwald, *Brown University*

Clayton Thyne, *University of Kentucky*

Michael Touchton, *Boise State University*

Ronald Vardy, *University of Houston*

Jim Walsh, *University of North Carolina at Charlotte*

Patricia Weitsman, *Ohio University*

Dwight Wilson, *University of North Georgia*

I also thank five other reviewers who chose to remain anonymous. The advice of all these colleagues was so pertinent and penetrating that it was taken into account in almost every single case.

No one gave more to this project, just by letting me do what I do, than my wife and best friend for now almost fifty years. Marion—or, as I call her, Micki—has always been there for me, even when I was so often absent from her, physically present perhaps but lost in my thoughts about this or some other book. Kimberly, my daughter, is another source of inestimable joy and pride, which sustains me in everything I do. They give me my life in the small, which is the nurturing bedrock of my life in the world at large.

A Free Syrian Army fighter opposed to the government of President Bashar al-Assad takes a position close to a military base in northern Syria in December 2012. What has caused Syria's bloody civil war, and what can be done to end it?

INTRODUCTION
Why We Disagree about International Relations

In the spring of 2011, countries across the Middle East from Tunisia to Turkey erupted in unprecedented political and social upheaval. By 2013 some countries, such as Tunisia, had managed to avoid military violence, whereas others, like Egypt, had succumbed to military coups. But none experienced the degree of strife that Syria has, with a full-blown civil war taking place, more than one hundred thousand civilians dead, and a dictator who uses chemical weapons against his own people and remains unwilling to cede power. Why is Syria experiencing such a terrible conflict? What causes a conflict of such magnitude? And what can be done about it? As students of international relations, we might consider the following facts.

Syria is situated in a geographically strategic region. It is an Arab Muslim country in the Middle East that borders the Mediterranean Sea, Lebanon, Israel, Jordan, Iraq, and Turkey. Both Eastern and Western empires have occupied it. Christian crusaders invaded in the eleventh and twelfth centuries, and it was part of the Ottoman Empire headed by a Muslim caliph and then, after World War I, a colonial territory under French administration. It became independent in 1946.

Syria is ethnically and religiously diverse, and power is shared unevenly within the country. Muslims in Syria are divided between Sunni and Shiite sects and between moderate and radical groups. The majority population (74 percent) is Sunni, but the government has been controlled since 1970 by a minority Shiite sect known as the Alawites (with Druze and other Shiite groups, 16 percent). Other minorities include Christians (10 percent) and small numbers of Jews.

In today's civil war, foreign nonstate actors support various domestic groups. Both local (Muslim Brotherhood) and foreign (Al Qaeda) Sunni fighters support the rebels seeking to depose the Alawite-led government of Bashar al-Assad. Shiite groups supported by militia from Lebanon (Hezbollah), Iraq, and Iran back the government.

Foreign states have a stake in the war. Russia supplies arms to the government; Saudi Arabia, Qatar, and Turkey, all led by Sunni governments, arm the rebels. Since 1967 Israel has occupied Syrian territory in the Golan Heights, patrolled by a United Nations peacekeeping force until it was asked recently to leave. The United States, having withdrawn its forces from Iraq, has stayed out of the military conflict, although it provides nonlethal aid (medical supplies and the like) and light arms to the rebels, says the Assad government must go, and warns the Assad government not to use chemical weapons, which Assad did in the summer of 2013.

Those are some of the facts—but what do they mean? What is the primary cause of the Syrian conflict? Is it the colonial powers that created arbitrary countries in the Middle East? Is it religious and ethnic rivalries that lead groups to impose oppressive governments on one another? Is it the Arab Spring, the outbreak of democratic sentiment in the Middle East to end oppressive regimes? Is it terrorist and radical Islamist groups that seek to reestablish the Muslim caliphate of the old Ottoman Empire? Is it Israel, which, backed by the United Nations, established and maintains a Jewish state in Palestine on what Arab peoples considered to be Muslim lands? Is the conflict just another power struggle over land and wealth among various local and, because the region is strategic and contains vast amounts of oil, foreign powers? Maybe all of these factors play roles. If so, how do you end the war and prevent the problem from arising again? You can't address all of these causes at once. So what do you do first?

That raises a second critical question. Where does the cause of the conflict come from? Does it come primarily from a single individual or group of individuals? If Assad were replaced, would that end the war and ensure future peace? Or does the cause come from the religious divisions within Syria and the region as a whole, in which case replacing Assad would not matter that much? Or maybe the cause comes from outside the region—the meddling of former colonial powers, the military rivalry between the United States and the Soviet Union during the Cold War and now between Russia and the Persian Gulf Sunni states of Saudi Arabia and Qatar, and the failure of the United States to negotiate an equitable and lasting peace between Israel and its Arab neighbors. Again, it may come from all of these directions, but which do you address first?

You have just encountered the two most critical aspects of learning about international relations. International relations do not start with a priori facts about what is happening in some part of the world such as Syria. They start with theories or judgments about what facts are significant and therefore may be causing other facts to happen. This first aspect of international relations we call in this book perspectives. A **perspective** is a theory or hypothesis that explains why something happens. For example, if war is happening in Syria, it may be due to a power struggle. President Assad wants his regime to survive, and so he has acquired the military and economic resources he needs to defend it, which includes maintaining relations with Russia and competing against forces that oppose him within Syria. That, as we will see, is a realist theory or hypothesis about international relations. Without a perspective, we have nothing but a description of what is happening, and any description is always partial because it cannot possibly include everything that is going on. We describe only what we consider significant, and what we consider significant is already determined by some prior theory or hypothesis rumbling around in our heads even if we are not conscious of it. As one wise political scientist, Professor Robert Jervis at Columbia University, said, "Without a theory, we're just lost. We just have all these random phenomena we can't make any sense of."[1]

perspective: a statement or a hypothesis that explains the primary cause of what is happening—for example, a struggle for power causes conflict and sometimes wars.

Perspectives or theories tell us about the content of causes—for example, a power struggle rather than religious conflict or misunderstandings in negotiations. But in order to understand fully what is causing a problem, we need to know where the cause is coming from. This is what we call the **level of analysis** problem in international relations. If we know what the primary cause is, do we know where it is located? If Russia and the Persian Gulf Sunni states could be persuaded to stop arms shipments to belligerents in Syria, would that do more than anything else to end the conflict? If so, we say the primary level of analysis is systemic (outside the country), not domestic (inside the country). Or would the conflict continue because the power struggle between Shiites and Sunnis lies primarily inside Syria—that is, at the domestic level—and if arms shipments from abroad stopped, the belligerents would just find new ways to acquire arms?

level of analysis: the direction, or "level," from which the primary cause of events is coming.

Notice that in talking about perspectives and levels of analysis, we emphasize *primary* causes and levels of analysis. That is because a host of causes and levels of analysis are present in any international situation. Reality is endlessly complex. In the Syrian case, for example, a realist perspective identifies the struggle for power as the primary cause. But that does not mean that a negotiated settlement (an approach emphasized by a liberal perspective, as we shall see) is not possible. Nor does it mean that ethnic or religious ideas (emphasized by an identity perspective) do not matter. It simply means that from a realist perspective the competition for power to survive comes first and will determine in large measure how much and what kind of negotiation takes place and how the actors identify themselves and others. So, in the Syrian case, if power causes are primary, the competition for arms will create more and more distrust between the belligerents and limit the degree to which they can cooperate. And this competition will reinforce the image of the belligerent groups as enemies rather than as partners or friends. In other words, power factors are stronger (primary) influences on the negotiations and identities of the actors than the latter are on power factors. Similarly, causes will always come from all levels of analysis. But the individual level is primary if the individual or small group involved has a stronger influence on the factors coming from the domestic and international (systemic) levels of analysis than those factors have on the individual or small group. In the Syrian case, if the individual level is primary, Assad is creating—not just responding to—domestic religious and other differences and is inviting intervention from international sources rather than being the victim of such intervention. In this book, we'll use the term **causal arrow** to point out the perspective and level of analysis that is primary—that is, which cause or perspective dominates and from which direction that cause comes.

causal arrow: an indicator of which perspective or level of analysis influences the other perspectives and levels of analysis more than the reverse.

Our objective in this book is to develop these tools of analysis—perspectives and levels of analysis and how the causal arrows run between them—which you need to understand international situations like the one in Syria. Along the way, you will learn many facts about world history and contemporary events. But facts alone are not sufficient, because we can never know all the facts. As the historian Charles Tilly tells us, we seldom do more than skim the surface when we gather facts: "I must deal with historical facts like a rock skipping water. . . . I do not know all the history one would need to write this book fully."[2] And the facts do not interpret themselves. Think about the newspapers you read or the television news programs you watch. Do front pages give you all the news that is fit to print, or TV newscasters all the news for that day? No, they don't and they can't. Someone decides what goes on the front page of a newspaper or is covered in a twenty-minute TV broadcast, and those decisions involve selecting and emphasizing certain facts over others. Before you read or watch the news, someone has already narrowed down the coverage on the basis of some perspective. You need to be alert as to what perspective that might be, so you can evaluate the news you are being given critically from an *alternative* perspective. In the social sciences and in a healthy democracy, we call that critical thinking, and it is the essence of a good liberal arts education.

Thus, this textbook is not like others that begin with a key problem or single theory of international relations, such as focusing on how groups achieve their "collective interests" or privileging a single framework of "interests, interactions, and institutions" that reflects a rational choice theory. Both of those approaches start with assumptions that are characteristic of a liberal perspective, as we shall see, and inevitably de-emphasize problems such as the security dilemma, which is more important from a realist perspective, or the role of ideas and actors' identities, which is more important from an identity perspective. We will look at history differently, too, through the lens of perspectives and levels of analysis. That means that we approach, say, World War II as the different perspectives from the various levels of analysis explain it, rather than simply present facts for you to memorize, as though history did not already involve theoretical choices about what events are most significant and cause other events. In this way we cover *more*, not *fewer*, facts, because each perspective and level of analysis emphasizes different facts. So you will encounter and memorize many facts, and it is important that we know the major events of European, Asian, African, Middle Eastern, and Latin American history and contemporary life if we are going to be serious students of international affairs. But that is not the ultimate payoff of this exercise. The payoff is the strengthening of your intellectual tool kit and your ability to think critically about and understand world affairs. We will be working mostly on your central processor rather than on your memory storage—although we hope to fill up the latter as well.

The rest of this introduction outlines the most important tools or ingredients for understanding international relations, which we will be using throughout this book—perspectives and levels of analysis, history, contemporary foreign policy disputes, methods, conclusions based on causal arrows, judgment, and ethical values.

≫ The Roles of Perspectives, Levels of Analysis, and Causal Arrows

We see and understand international relations through different perspectives and levels of analysis. Perspectives help us decide what the primary cause of an event is. We consider three principal perspectives in this book. The first claims (hypothesizes) that a struggle for power is the primary cause of what happens in international affairs; this we call the realist perspective. The second, the liberal perspective, argues that interactions, interdependence, and institutions exert the primary influence on world events. The third, the identity perspective, asserts that ideas are more important than power or institutions in shaping international outcomes. These three principal perspectives capture the main causes of international events—power, institutions, and ideas—which make up the subtitle of this text. From time to time, we'll take note of a fourth perspective, the critical theory perspective. We'll do so because this perspective questions the basic Western, rationalist assumption used by the principal perspectives, that we can break up reality, separate specific causes and effects from historical circumstances, and use this knowledge of the past to engineer the future. Critical theory, such as Marxism, emphasizes deep-seated causes of human events that unfold within historical processes and obscure vast inequalities that marginalize weak and minority peoples. It seeks to expose these deep roots of injustice in past political life and encourage more radical, maybe even revolutionary, solutions to bring about social justice and change.

Levels of analysis tell us the direction from which different causes come. We consider three principal levels of analysis. The individual level, sometimes called the decision-making level, emphasizes the leaders and decision-making institutions within a country. The domestic level focuses on the internal characteristics of countries as a whole, such as their cultural, political, and economic systems. And the systemic level highlights the way countries are positioned (e.g., their relative power) and interact (e.g., unilaterally or multilaterally) with respect to one another. At times we consider other levels intermediate between the domestic and systemic levels. For example, the foreign policy level of

Perspectives and Levels of Analysis: A Synopsis

		Perspectives are ideal types that reflect primary but not exclusive emphasis on the following causes:			
		Realist perspective emphasizes struggle for power	**Liberal perspective** emphasizes interdependence and institutions	**Identity perspective** emphasizes ideas	**Critical theory perspective** emphasizes embedded historical change
		At a specific level of analysis, each perspective focuses on			
Levels of analysis are the directions (levels) from which causes emerge	**Systemic level** emphasizes relative position of one country versus another (structure-systemic) and interactions between countries (process-systemic)	The balance of power between states, anarchy in the interstate system	Negotiations and international organizations	Shared or conflicting ideas	Denies possibility of separating perspectives and levels of analysis
	Foreign policy level links domestic and systemic (process) concerns	Leaders use war to survive in office	Leaders use diplomacy to alter relations among domestic institutions	Leaders use ideological alignments abroad to strengthen or weaken ideological groups at home	
	Domestic level focuses on internal cultural, political, and economic characteristics	Aggressive or revisionist states	A country's institutions	A country's political culture or ideology	
	Individual level focuses on leaders and decision-making groups	Human nature	A leader's bureaucratic role	A leader's ideologies or strategies	

analysis links domestic politics and international relations when, for example, leaders try to use foreign wars to get reelected or domestic events to invite foreign intervention. The transnational level of analysis involves the interactions of nongovernmental groups across national boundaries, such as multinational corporations and labor unions, that operate to a significant extent independent of relations among governments (see Figure Intro-1).

Each of the three mainstream perspectives—realist, liberal, and identity—operates at all of the levels of analysis. For example, while the realist perspective emphasizes power at all levels, it singles out human nature (lust for power) at the individual level, aggressive or revisionist states at the domestic level, leaders seeking to survive in office at the foreign policy level, and the balance of power and anarchy at the systemic level. The liberal perspective emphasizes institutions at all levels but singles out a leader's bureaucratic role at the individual level, the country's institutions at the domestic level, and negotiations and international organizations at the systemic level. And the identity perspective emphasizes ideas at all levels but zeroes in on shared or conflicting ideas at the systemic level, a country's political culture at the domestic level, and leaders' ideologies or strategies at the decision-making (individual) level. The critical theory perspective emphasizes all the primary causes and levels of analysis at once and adopts a holistic interpretation of reality, one that cannot be broken down into separate causes and effects or tested by rationalist means against alternative hypotheses.

Both perspectives and levels of analysis are what we call **ideal types**. They help boil down a complex reality, allowing us to see certain features of international relations more readily than others. Think of it this way. A theory interprets international relations the way a portrait interprets a face. Some portraits emphasize noses over eyes and mouths; others emphasize the eyes or mouths. Group together all the portraits that emphasize noses, and you have a perspective. Group together all the portraits that emphasize eyes, and you have another perspective. That's how the perspectives used in this book group together the various theories of international relations. All theories of international relations include power, institutions, and ideas, just as all portraits of faces include noses, eyes, and mouths. But some theories emphasize one of these factors, just as some portraits emphasize noses.

ideal types: perspectives or simplified characterizations of theories that emphasize the most important aspects of reality, not all of its intricacies and variations.

Standing in front of the damaged Askariya shrine in Baghdad, an Iraqi policeman views the world from this Muslim country. How others see the world and how we see others are matters of perspective.

Similarly, to understand the level of analysis concept, think of a baseball analogy. Imagine trying to hit a pitch. Perspectives tell us what kind of pitch is coming: fastball, curveball, or changeup. Levels of analysis tell us the direction from which the pitch is coming, whether it is thrown overhand, sidearm, or underhand. Unless we know both the kind and the direction of the pitch, we'll probably miss the ball—or, in international affairs, we'll fail to understand the events we are interested in.

⫸ The Role of History

History is the laboratory of international relations. We use historical examples to gather the facts and test the perspectives that enable us to explain and anticipate how the world works. Students often ask why we have to study history. That was then, they say; this is now. Everything changes and is new under the sun, right? Well, if that's the case, how do we recognize when something is new under the sun? Don't we have to know what is old in order to determine what is new? Take globalization, for example. Is it new? Many commentators say it is. But globalization existed before World War I at levels that were not surpassed again until after the mid-1970s. That makes globalization today different but not unprecedented. We need to recognize patterns from the past to identify the trends of the future.

History is also fun. Perhaps you like to read novels. They contain all the elements of human tragedy, triumph, mystery, adventure, and romance. Well, so does history. After all, it is the *real* story of human triumph and tragedy. History is also personal. Think of where you come from. Where was your family when the Berlin Wall came down or your grandparents during the Vietnam War? Do you know from what part of the world your family comes? If you live in the United States, unless you are Native American, your family came from someplace else. All these personal stories are part of the historical narrative. As we go through the book, I'll share some snippets of my family's history. I do this not to focus on my life but to help you discover how your life, too, is linked with history.

This book therefore covers more history than most international relations textbooks. It shows that although we have most of the facts about these events, we still disagree about them. For example, what caused World War I? Scholars do not agree. History therefore gives us a chance to explore the role of perspectives and levels of analysis in sorting out disagreements when the facts are pretty much the same. This exercise primes us to understand contemporary disagreements. Often we attribute these disagreements to facts. One side has more facts than the other. And, when we are dealing with contemporary issues, we should always opt to gather more facts. The perspectives help us in this regard, because they prompt us to look for and consider facts from multiple perspectives rather than just one. But why, if facts are the most critical ingredients, do we disagree about historical events when most of the facts are already known? Something else is going on, and that something else is the influence of perspectives and levels of analysis. The history covered here is cursory, so be sure to take history courses to explore the details. We are looking only for patterns that illuminate contemporary events. For example, Germany was a rising power before World War I; China is a rising power today. Are there similarities? We will see that there are, not identical but analogous. That's why we need to know at least the rough outlines of history in order to understand international relations today.

>>> Contemporary Foreign Policy Disputes: The 9/11 Attacks

Perspectives and levels of analysis do not just affect scholarship; they also affect everyday disputes about foreign policy. All serious students of international affairs respect the facts. But they emphasize different facts and draw conclusions that point the causal arrows in different directions among the major facts. Let's take a first look at how our four different perspectives help sort out the reactions of various analysts to a relatively recent policy event, the terrorist attacks of September 11, 2001, against the World Trade Center in New York and the Pentagon in Washington, D.C. The analysts are working from the same facts, but they interpret them differently because they emphasize different perspectives and levels of analysis.

Realist: Weak versus Strong

Three days after 9/11, Ronald Steel, a professor at the University of Southern California, characterized the attacks in the *New York Times* as "a war in which the weak turned the guns of the strong against them . . . showing . . . that in the end there may be no such thing as a universal civilization of which we all too easily assume we are the rightful leaders."[3] Steel interprets the attacks by Al Qaeda as weak actors rebelling against strong actors, with the weak actors rejecting the notion that the strong ones can dictate what is right and therefore universally valid in international affairs. Steel is applying the **realist perspective** emphasizing the struggle for relative power, which in turn limits the universality of what is right. It sees the world largely in terms of strong actors seeking to dominate weak ones and weak actors resisting strong ones to preserve their interests and independence. Notice that when he emphasizes relative power he does not ignore ideas. He simply argues that relative power limits the role of ideas, that there "may be no such thing as a universal civilization" that might prevent such conflicts. The struggle for power precludes the existence of a universal civilization in which the strong may claim they are the rightful leaders. Steel is making the realist point that the struggle for power has a greater impact on ideas than ideas have on power. The causal arrows run from the realist perspective to the identity perspective, with power factors determining for the most part what we can expect from the role of ideas or values.

realist perspective: a perspective that sees the world largely in terms of a struggle for relative power in which strong actors seek to dominate and weak actors seek to resist.

The struggle for power goes on at all levels of analysis. In the case of the 9/11 attacks, the Al Qaeda terrorists represent nonstate actors coming from the individual level of analysis. However, if we emphasize the Taliban government in Afghanistan, where Al Qaeda trained, we might be thinking of weak or failed states that have been taken over internally by terrorists and conclude that the cause is coming from the domestic level of analysis. Or, if we think more broadly still and argue that Al Qaeda is a product of the weak Muslim countries dominated in the Middle East and elsewhere by the strong

Why did Al Qaeda attack the United States on September 11, 2001? Was it the weak balancing the strong, a reaction to U.S. diplomacy in the Middle East, or a rejection of Western values? Realism views the attacks as the weak turning the weapons of the strong against them.

liberal perspective: a perspective that emphasizes repetitive relationships and negotiations, establishing patterns or institutions for resolving international conflicts.

Western powers, we might decide the cause is coming from the distribution of power in the international system as a whole, or the systemic level of analysis. At each level, the cause is the same—namely, the struggle for power between the weak and the strong. But depending on which level of analysis we emphasize, we respond differently to the attacks. At the individual level, we focus our attention on specific terrorists. At the domestic level, we react to the problems of a country as a whole, whether it is a weak or failed state. And at the systemic level, we address problems in broader international relationships between Muslim and Western countries (see Table Intro-1).

Liberal: Failed Negotiations

Writing two days after Steel in the *Washington Post,* Caryle Murphy, a journalist, saw the attacks quite differently. September 11, 2001, was not a result of the weak striking back against the strong but of unresolved diplomatic disputes, such as the Israeli-Palestinian conflict, that created unfairness and grievances between the feuding parties. She argued that "if we want to avoid creating more terrorists, we must end the Israeli-Palestinian conflict in a way both sides see as fair."[4] Murphy is using the **liberal perspective**. It emphasizes relationships and interdependence among actors in international affairs, how groups

TABLE Intro-1

The Causes of the 9/11 Attacks: From the Realist Perspective	
Level	**Perspective** Realist: Struggle for power between the "weak" and the "strong"
Systemic	Muslim countries opposing U.S. oppression in the region/world
Domestic	Taliban takeover of the weak Afghan state
Individual	Individual terrorists plotting against the United States

interact, communicate, negotiate, and trade with one another. She is saying that the cause of the 9/11 attacks stems from the absence of a negotiated agreement that includes all parties—terrorists and nonterrorists, Palestinians and Israelis—one that is considered fair and legitimate. An outcome decided by a power struggle (realist) or by the imposition of one side's ideas on the other (identity) would not be considered fair or legitimate and would probably just create more terrorists. On the other hand, a fair and inclusive agreement might actually reduce the threat of terrorism. Note how diplomacy and cooperation trump power. The liberal perspective holds out the prospect that solutions to international conflicts are not determined primarily by a balance of power but derive instead from common rules and institutions that include all actors regardless of their relative power or ideas.

Palestinian (Yasser Arafat, left) and Israeli (Shimon Peres, right) leaders meet in late September 2001 to discuss an end to the conflict between Israel and Palestine. Liberalism emphasizes international cooperation and interdependence and views unresolved misunderstandings between the two states as a critical factor precipitating 9/11.

Murphy is emphasizing the systemic level of analysis because international negotiations are a more important cause of and, therefore, solution to the problem of terrorism than the internal characteristics of countries (domestic level) or the specific behavior of individual leaders (individual level). From the liberal perspective, actors at any level—systemic, domestic, or individual—behave not so much on the basis of their relative power, whether they are weak or strong, but on the basis of the way the other party behaves, how the parties interact and negotiate, the patterns of reciprocal behavior they create, and the roles and rules they establish in institutions that regularize their relationships (see Table Intro-2).

TABLE
Intro-2

The Causes of the 9/11 Attacks: From the Liberal Perspective	
Level	**Perspective** Liberal: Failed negotiations, absence of Israeli–Palestinian agreement
Systemic	Exclusion of weak or aggrieved actors
Domestic	Ineffective domestic governments impeding international negotiations
Individual	Specific leaders opposing international negotiations

Identity: Democratic Reform of Governments

Writing a year after the 9/11 attacks, as prospects of war against Iraq loomed, Jim Hoagland, a columnist for the *Washington Post,* suggested still a third way to think about the attacks. He was skeptical of finding a solution to terrorism through a better balance of power between the weak and strong or through negotiations of the Arab–Israeli dispute. He felt that the problem was one of nondemocratic governments in the Middle East: "The removal of Saddam Hussein [then Iraq's leader] and Yasser Arafat [then leader of the Palestinian Authority] are necessary but not sufficient conditions for stabilizing the Middle East. . . . The administration cannot rely . . . on a now discredited peace process. . . . Only a level and clarity of American commitment to democratic change . . . will calm an ever more deadly conflict."[5] Note how Hoagland de-emphasizes the negotiation process, which a liberal perspective would emphasize, by describing it as a "discredited peace process" and says that the mere removal of Saddam Hussein and Yasser Arafat from power, which the realist perspective would emphasize, is not enough. Instead, what is needed, he maintains, is a change in the nature of Arab governments. They need to reform and, with U.S. help, become more democratic, in short, change their basic political ideas and identities.

identity perspective:
a perspective that emphasizes the causal importance of the ideas and identities of actors, which motivate their use of power and negotiations.

Hoagland is employing the **identity perspective.** This perspective emphasizes the importance of ideas that define the identities of actors and motivate (cause) their use of power and negotiations in international affairs. He is suggesting that democratic reforms at the domestic level of analysis are more important than removing individual leaders—the individual level—and may subsequently change the way Middle East states behave toward one another at the systemic level. If actor identities remain divergent, some democratic and others nondemocratic, negotiations are more

TABLE Intro-3

The Causes of the 9/11 Attacks: From the Identity Perspective

Level	Perspective Identity: The ideas that define actors and guide their use of power and institutions
Systemic	Divergent identities generating conflict; converging identities generating cooperation
Domestic	Democratic reforms in Arab governments, making them less adversarial toward Israel and others in the region
Individual	Removing individual leaders and thus changing the identity of actors

difficult to achieve and power balancing is more likely to occur. If, on the other hand, actors converge toward democratic identities, cooperation is more likely. Hoagland argues that until Arab identities become more democratic and their identities converge with that of Israel, negotiations (the liberal solution) will remain discredited and shifts in power such as removing Hussein and Arafat (the realist solution) will not change much (see Table Intro-3).

Fires burn in and around Saddam Hussein's Council of Ministers during the first wave of attacks in the "shock and awe" phase of Operation Iraqi Freedom on March 21, 2003, in Baghdad, Iraq. From the critical theory perspective, America's imperialistic behavior and use of force are the causes of international conflict, not responses to it.

Critical Theory: Pervasive Violence

From a **critical theory perspective**, the cause of 9/11 is the pervasive and deep-seated violence in the present international system, reflected in the behavior of the United States. As the preeminent power, the United States contributes to if not creates terrorism through its military presence and imperialism throughout the world and the suppression of alternative cultures and political ideas. It invites radicalism and apocalyptic outcomes. As one radical critic puts it, "The probability of 'apocalypse soon' . . . is surely too high . . . because of Washington's primary role in accelerating the race to destruction by extending its historically unique military dominance."[6] American power, ideas, and institutions permeate the system at all levels of analysis, systematically excluding minority groups and driving the system toward violent upheaval and change (see Table Intro-4).

critical theory perspective: a perspective that focuses on deeply embedded forces from all perspectives and levels of analysis.

TABLE
Intro-4

The Causes of the 9/11 Attacks: From the Critical Theory Perspective

Level	Perspective Critical theory: Events are deeply embedded in historical context, driving the world toward social justice and change
Systemic **Domestic** **Individual**	Pervasive and deep-seated violence in the international system at all levels of analysis

⫸ The Role of Methods

The perspectives and levels of analysis thus help illuminate contemporary foreign policy disputes as well as historical disagreements. They do not substitute for facts; they compel us to collect the facts from different perspectives and levels of analysis. We then make judgments on the basis of the facts (evidence) as to which perspective or level of analysis seems to be most persuasive. Because we can never consider all the facts, our judgments remain open to further facts.

In this sense, all knowledge starts with theories. Even the natural sciences use theories to select and interpret facts. Before Galileo, scientists thought about motion only in linear terms, in straight lines from one point to another. Galileo was the first to think about motion in periodic terms, that is, as the back-and-forth motion of a pendulum or the movement of the Earth around the sun. As a result, he discovered and emphasized new facts such as inertia, a precursor to Isaac Newton's discovery of the force of gravity. The difference between the natural and social sciences is not that social sciences like political science depend on theories and natural sciences do not. They both use scientific methodology, or what we call rationalist methods. The difference lies in the kinds of facts they deal with. The natural sciences deal with facts that do not have minds of their own. Atoms are not self-conscious actors. The social sciences deal with human beings, who do have minds of their own and often change them, and that is what makes social science facts somewhat more elusive. Moreover, in the social sciences we study ourselves. We like and dislike the things we study, such as the political parties we belong to. Natural scientists do not like or dislike atoms. All this means that we need to be more conscious of our perspectives when we deal with social science subjects. We are dealing with people whose perspectives may differ from our own and may change in response to the information we provide. If we ask them questions, they may not understand or answer our questions in the way we expect. And they could always change their minds the minute after they answer a question.

methods: the formal rules of reason (rationalist) or appropriateness (constructivist) for testing perspectives against facts.

Scholarly theories seek to *describe, explain,* and *predict* events. **Methods** provide rules for testing theories against facts. They allow us to conclude whether our theories or perspectives are consistent with the world out there. But methods are not miracles. They cannot tell us the way the world out there actually is. They can tell us only that the way we are thinking about that world is not falsified by what is out there. The scientific method in the natural sciences faces these same limitations. Newtonian physics, which helps us reach the moon, assumes the universe is made up of fixed bodies, time, and space. Quantum physics, which helps us explode the atom, tells us it is made up of probabilities and relative time and space. Which world is the real world? We don't know. Physicists search today for a unified theory that subsumes both Newtonian and quantum mechanics. But even if they find it, a rival theory may always be possible.

Rationalist versus Constructivist

In the social sciences, we speak of two general types of methods: rationalist and constructivist.[7] Realist and liberal perspectives of international affairs generally employ rationalist methods. Identity perspectives use both rationalist and constructivist methods.

Both methods start by naming or labeling facts. Before we can test whether sunlight causes plant growth or power balancing causes war, we need definitions of *sun, sunlight, plants,* and *growth* or *power* and *war.* **Rationalist methods** assume that such labeling can be done in a reasonably objective way; **constructivist methods** pay more attention to the discourse or subjective language game that produces labels. For example, when U.S. policy makers named the first atomic weapon, they called it Little Boy. Did that reflect a subjective discourse that discriminated against women and fostered male predilections for war?

More important, the two methods differ over whether facts or events *cause* or *constitute* one another. Rationalist methods see **causation** as sequential. One fact or event exists independent of another and precedes or comes before it. The preceding event is cause; the subsequent event is consequence. For example, the sun exists before a plant and drives plant life. Sunlight initiates photosynthesis, producing carbohydrates, the fuel of plant growth. Plants grow and reproduce as a result of the sun's light. Rationalist methods apply this kind of sequential causation to international affairs. For example, various types of power balances, whether two great powers or multiple great powers exist, precede and cause different types of interactions between states, ranging from cooperation to war. Realist perspectives argue that polarity, the number of great powers in the system, causes or determines the prospects of war.

Unlike rationalist methods, constructivist methods see events as bound together in context, not as separate and sequential occurrences. They fit together not because one causes another but because they *mutually* cause one another. Social relationships often have this constitutive characteristic. Take, for example, the relationship between a master and a slave. One status does not precede and cause the other. The master, unlike the sun, does not exist before the slave; instead, the master is defined by acquiring a slave, and the slave is defined by succumbing to a master. The two entities appear together chronologically, and one has no meaning without the other. They mutually cause or constitute one another and, in that sense, explain one another. Two things fit together in a given context or situation because they are appropriate to that context. Constructivist methods rely on a logic of appropriateness, whereas rationalist methods rely on a logic of consequence by which one event precedes and causes the other or a logic of argumentation by which one point of view prevails over another.

Sovereignty: Caused or Constituted

For one quick example, let's explore the question of what facts caused the rise of the legal concept of sovereignty among states in international relations. Social scientists using rationalist methodologies hypothesize that sovereignty was caused by an independent and preceding event, namely, the Treaty of Westphalia in 1648. Monarchs who existed

rationalist methods: methods that disaggregate and explain events sequentially as one event preceding and causing a second event.

constructivist methods: methods that see events as mutually causing or constituting one another rather than causing one another sequentially.

causation: explaining events in terms of one another rather than just describing them.

in Europe prior to Westphalia gathered together to assert their independence from the universal Catholic Church, represented by the pope in Rome and the Holy Roman Emperor in Vienna. In the treaty, they established (caused) the practice of sovereignty, legal recognition of their rights to decide all matters domestically and their responsibilities to respect similar rights of other monarchs. Social scientists using constructivist methodologies hypothesize that sovereignty emerged from a network of developments taking place over the course of an earlier historical period and, most important, "a change . . . in the basic *structure* of property rights," which came about through a newly interdependent international society.[8] Before the seventeenth century, monarchs held property in common as local members of a single universal community known as the Holy Roman Empire. By the end of the seventeenth century, they possessed territory separately and exclusively. How did this change in the understanding of property rights come about? Not by one prior thing causing another subsequent one, but by a combination of factors—population pressures, diminishing returns to land, a widening of trade, and institutional innovations—that accelerated the growth of international social relationships. Notice how constructivist methods explain things in terms of broad context and appropriateness (at some point, sovereignty and states seemed appropriate to the situation) and how, in this example, ideas—a new conception of property rights—altered institutions and power, rather than the reverse (identity over liberal and realist perspectives).

Correlation, Causation, and Process Tracing

Rationalist methods separate events from context and examine many cases to find patterns of correlation among them. Some rationalist methods become formalistic and mathematical. Because statistical studies show that wars seldom, if ever, occur among democracies, rationalist methodologies conclude that democracies do not go to war with one another. **Correlation** is not the same as causation, however. Correlation tells us only that democracy and the absence of war appear together across many cases. It does not tell us whether democracy causes no war (an identity explanation) or no war causes democracy (a realist explanation if no war is a result of successful balancing and peace; a liberal explanation if no war is a consequence of cooperation and international institutions). Nor does it tell us that the two variables appearing together, such as democracy and no war, may not be caused by a host of other factors or variables that we have not considered. Called **exogenous variables**, these omitted variables lie outside the theoretical framework. They contrast with **endogenous variables**, which are included in the framework.

What is more, all these factors may be interrelated with one another, creating what methodologists call **multicollinearity**. To move from correlation to causation requires a method known as **process tracing**, which examines events historically and in context to trace how different variables interact with one another. Does one variable appear in time before the other and thus can be said to cause it? Constructivist methods assume that we cannot separate variables in sequence or time. We have to substantiate all the

correlation: a situation in which one fact or event occurs in the same context as another fact or event but is not necessarily linked to or caused by it.

exogenous variables: autonomous factors that come from outside a theoretical model or system and that cannot be explained by the system.

endogenous variables: causal variables that are included in a theoretical model or framework.

multicollinearity: a statistical situation in which multiple variables are all highly correlated with one another.

process tracing: a method of connecting events in sequence to identify cause and effect.

facts through a thick description or narrative of the repetitive practices and interactions through which they emerge. Constructivist methods offer plausible, rather than predictive, explanations. They call attention to how situations might be interpreted rather than replicated and sensitize us to future possibilities rather than make precise predictions. Thus, constructivist studies might conclude that the peace among democracies is hard to separate from the deeply embedded structure of American and British culture in the contemporary world and may be a consequence of unique rather than replicable factors that can be applied to future situations.

Counterfactual Reasoning

Both rationalist and constructivist methods use what we call **counterfactual reasoning.** The counterfactual of the claim "Event A caused event B" is to ask, "If event A had not happened, would event B have happened?" History appears to have a single outcome because we look back on events that have already occurred. It appears to be factual. But we know that along the way many choices were made. With each choice, history took one path and abandoned others. Maybe a war of some sort was going to happen in the early twentieth century. But it did not have to begin in July 1914, and it did not have to cost twenty million lives. How do we determine what choices or paths were *not* taken and use that knowledge to judge the present circumstances? We ask *counter*factual questions. What if Archduke Franz Ferdinand of Austria-Hungary had not been assassinated in Sarajevo in June 1914, the triggering event for the start of World War I? What if Germany had not had a military plan to fight a war at the same time against both Russia and France? What if the United States had given United Nations weapons inspectors more time in 2003 to do their work in Iraq? We make educated guesses about alternative paths that history might have taken, and that helps us to look for missing facts and test alternative explanations.

counterfactual reasoning: a method of testing claims for causality by asking what might have happened if one event had not occurred.

≫ Is One Perspective or Method Best?

Is one perspective or method better than another? Perhaps, but there is no general consensus among specialists and, like all other analysts and even professors, you will eventually have to make a judgment for yourself.[9] This book will familiarize you with the arguments of each perspective and method and thus help you decide which one works better for a given set of facts and circumstances.

The realist perspective may have certain advantages in situations of greater threat. When someone draws a gun on you, you tend not to ask what that person believes (an identity approach) or whether you can refer the dispute to a court or institution (a liberal solution). You duck or fight back to even up the balance of power if you can. But how do you determine situations of greater threat? Often a threat is not obvious. It depends on what you are looking for. So the realist perspective, it is sometimes argued, may exaggerate threat.

The liberal perspective may be better at finding ways to cooperate. Long before someone draws a gun on you, you try to find out what is aggravating that person and negotiate a compromise or alleviate the circumstances, such as poverty or lack of education, that may be driving him or her to violence. But what if the individual intends all along to harm you, not because of anything you do or he or she doesn't have but just because this person doesn't like you (an identity cause)? You may be compromising with someone who will take advantage of you later (a realist possibility). How do you protect yourself? So the liberal perspective, it is sometimes argued, may risk exposure to unanticipated dangers.

The identity perspective may be best at distinguishing between potential allies and enemies. It looks for similarities or differences in collective and individual self-images and asks how these self-images get constructed. If identities can be brought closer together, you might be more willing to risk cooperation (for example, if it's your brother who pulls the gun on you). If identities diverge, you might prefer to protect yourself. But how do you manage relations with an enemy country to avoid war and maybe mutual destruction? Don't you have to risk cooperation, even or especially with enemies? And what about friends? Don't they sometimes change and become enemies? Maybe the identity perspective is too categorical—some would say ideological—and leads to more fear or more complacency than power disparities or opportunities for compromise might otherwise prescribe.

This book presents and discusses the different perspectives (and methods) evenhandedly. Through this approach each perspective, in effect, critiques the others. What the realist perspective relatively de-emphasizes—for example, the roles of institutions and ideas—the liberal and identity perspectives emphasize. What the liberal perspective de-emphasizes—for example, the roles of power and ideas—the realist and identity perspectives emphasize. And so on. Thus, when we discuss the Cuban Missile Crisis or terrorist attacks from the four different perspectives, we will see the strengths and weaknesses of each perspective. We can keep an open mind toward each perspective rather than being told at the outset that this or that perspective is best.

Many studies of international affairs deliberately exclude alternative explanations. Professor Sean Wilentz, for example, places the burden of judgment on the reader: "I reject . . . the now fashionable claim that objectivity involves reporting all views or interpretations equally. Objectivity instead involves judging validity for oneself, fairly, and then inviting others to consider and argue the evidence, logic, and fairness on which that judgment is based."[10] This textbook will help you develop that capacity to judge validity for yourself, first, by making you aware that you have a preferred point of view and, second, by keeping you open to alternative points of view. This is healthy. Too much contemporary debate about international affairs is personalized and vitriolic. People label one another wicked or stupid instead of listening carefully to one another. Once we are used to thinking in terms of alternative perspectives, we may become more patient and generous in our debates with fellow citizens. We may concede that they are just as well meaning and smart as we are but may be judging the world from different perspectives or levels of analysis.

⟫ The Role of Judgment

There will always be differences and controversies in international affairs. As noted above, scholars still disagree about the causes of World War I. Contemporary controversies are no different. Take the war in Iraq in 2003. Did Saddam Hussein have weapons of mass destruction (WMDs)? At the time the United States invaded Iraq in March 2003, the major intelligence services around the world in the United States, France, Russia, China, Great Britain, and Australia thought he did, particularly biological and chemical weapons.[11] UN inspectors thought so as well. After the invasion, however, no weapons were found. Was that simply a case of bad intelligence? To some extent, no doubt it was. On the other hand, decision makers never act on the basis of perfect information. They have to rely on conjecture and judgment. As the *Washington Post* columnist Jim Hoagland writes: "Most of the time you are not going to have perfect knowledge for making decisions. If you look at the way Saddam Hussein acted, any reasonable person would have concluded that he was hiding those weapons, just from what he said and did. The key point is always going to be the judgment you then make from what is almost always imperfect intelligence."[12]

After we have assembled all the facts and done all the testing of perspectives we have time for, **judgment** comes into play. This is especially true in policy making, where time is always a pressing factor. We make decisions on the basis of some broader judgment about what we think makes sense. What is judgment? Is it instinct? Is it experience? Is it character? It is probably all of these. Whatever it is, it is different from facts and tested knowledge, yet it does not substitute for them. The best judgment, we say, is informed judgment—judgment enriched by facts and accumulated knowledge.

judgment: the broader assessment of what makes sense after one accumulates as many facts and tests as many perspectives as possible.

Thus, judgment is indispensable for good statesmanship as well as good scholarship. Oliver Wendell Holmes, the Supreme Court justice, once described President Franklin D. Roosevelt as a man with "a second-class intellect but a first-class temperament."[13] Many said the same thing about President Ronald Reagan. Neither man had a brilliant mind, yet, arguably, these two men were the greatest American presidents of the twentieth century. They had first-class personalities and instincts; they were excellent judges of people and events. As *The Economist* observed on Reagan's death in June 2004, Reagan knew "that mere reason, essential though it is, is only half of the business of reaching momentous decisions. You also need solid-based instincts, feelings, whatever the word is for the other part of the mind. 'I have a gut feeling,' Reagan said over and over again, when he was working out what to say or do."[14] A gut feeling without facts is ignorance, but incomplete knowledge without a gut feeling is often useless, especially under time constraints.

>>> The Role of Ethics and Morality

ethics and morality: standards of good conduct for human behavior.

Judgment is part of character, and character in turn is guided by **ethics and morality**. Because judgment plays a role in decision making, personal honesty is very important in intellectual and human affairs more generally—which is why we emphasize it in academic and other activities. What are our obligations to one another as human beings and to the world we inhabit? Ethics and morality deal with standards of right conduct and behavior—what we ought to do, not what we need, can, or prefer to do. Thus ethics and morality go beyond mere facts and perspectives. They involve what we believe, not what we want, have, or know. Belief often delves into intangible, maybe religious, worlds that we cannot access or test through logical or scientific means. But that does not mean that ethics and morality are incompatible with the material world. Indeed, ethical and moral beliefs are essential guides for directing contemporary scientific and technological debates. The question of what we do with nuclear technology or with the technology used to clone human beings involves moral and ethical dilemmas. In international affairs, we can distinguish three broad views about ethics and morality: relativism, universalism, and pragmatism.[15]

Relativist Values

relativism: a position that holds that truth and morality are relative to each individual or culture and that one should "live and let live."

Relativism holds that all truth is relative. There are no universal moral principles that apply to all people under all circumstances. Each culture or religion is entitled to its own view of truth. Because relativists do not believe in an ultimate truth, they are willing to tolerate multiple truths. Their attitude is "live and let live"—respect all views of ethics, morality, and religion. This became the moral view, at least within Christendom, in the seventeenth century. Protestants and Catholics who had been fighting one another for more than a hundred years decided to tolerate one another and agreed in the Treaty of Westphalia in 1648 to respect the right of each sovereign to choose the religion for his or her own country. Sovereignty meant that each sovereign, and subsequently each state, agreed not to interfere in the domestic life—meaning, at that time, religion—of other sovereigns. This principle of nonintervention in the domestic affairs of other states remains enshrined today in the Charter of the United Nations. It now accommodates a world of diverse religions, going beyond Christianity. But such moral relativism, taken to an extreme, could also accommodate genocide—the purposeful slaughter of human beings because of their race, religion, or ethnicity—because there are no moral absolutes or prohibitions to condemn it. Shouldn't it be possible to proscribe morally the slaughter of Jews in Germany, Muslims in Bosnia, and Tutsis in Rwanda under all circumstances at all times?

Universal Values

Universalism rejects relativism and argues that some absolute moral principles apply to all people in all countries at all times. After World War II and the murder of six million Jews in Europe, many decided that genocide should never happen again, that the world community has a moral obligation to prevent or stop it. Thus, the United Nations has evolved a standard of humanitarian intervention that directly contradicts the organization's charter. Kofi Annan, then secretary-general of the United Nations, framed the contradiction this way: even though the UN Charter rules out intervention in the domestic affairs of states, "is it permissible to let gross and systematic violations of human rights, with grave humanitarian consequences, continue unchecked?"[16] The international community may be moving beyond Westphalia's relativist morality and insisting that there are universal standards of basic human rights that all states, whatever their cultural or moral beliefs, must follow. But where do we draw the line? Saddam Hussein grossly violated the human rights of the citizens of Iraq, yet neither the United Nations nor the North Atlantic Treaty Organization (NATO) authorized the U.S. invasion of Iraq in March 2003. Was the United States nevertheless right to intervene based on universal standards of human rights? If so, how do we know whose standards are the universal ones?

universalism: a position that holds that truth and morality are universal and cannot be adjusted to specific circumstances.

Pragmatic Values

Pragmatism offers a third point of view. Pragmatists answer the question of whether to intervene based on certain practical requirements, such as preserving stability or not setting a precedent. That is, they ask, will an intervention create disproportionate consequences that actually reduce world solidarity, and will an intervention set a standard that encourages repeated future interventions? U.S. intervention in Iraq, pragmatists might argue, increased rather than reduced the scale of violence. Moreover, the U.S. action sanctioned the doctrine of preemption, attacking another state *after* you see it preparing to attack you, or, worse, the doctrine of prevention, attacking another state *before* you see any preparations because you fear it may attack you at some point in the future. Whether Iraq was an imminent threat was much disputed at the time. But some pragmatists might conclude that the threat was not imminent and that America's intervention encouraged further repeated interventions in the future. Pragmatists look to the immediate circumstances surrounding the action and ask whether intervention minimizes instability in that situation while at the same time securing whatever just outcome is possible. Pragmatism does not abandon a notion of universal morality but opposes the application of a single morality at all times in all places. It is willing to compromise, even though compromise, repeated too often, risks slipping into relativism.

pragmatism: the idea that morality is proportionate to what is possible and causes the least harm.

Moral Choice

A simple story illustrates the differences among these moral views.[17] An officer and a small group of soldiers involved in war enter a village that enemy forces recently occupied. Overnight, one soldier is killed by a single shot. The next morning, the officer assembles the village residents and asks who shot the soldier. The villagers remain silent. The officer then announces that he will randomly select and kill three villagers in retaliation for this atrocity. You are a member of the officer's group. What should you do?

If you are a relativist, you will not object. Each side has its own standards of morality. If the other side can justify killing you, certainly you can justify killing them. Killing three people instead of one sets an example in a situation where force is the only arbiter of order because there is no common morality.

If you are a universalist, you will object. No one can kill innocent villagers under any circumstances at any time. To do so may be committing a war crime. So you say to the officer, "This is wrong; you can't do it." At this point, the officer turns to you and says, "OK, you shoot one, and I'll let the other two go." As a universalist, you still have to say no because it is wrong to kill innocent people, whether the number is one or three. You may go on to report the incident as a war crime if you are not arrested for disobeying an order.

If you are a pragmatist, however, you might accept the officer's offer and shoot one villager, thereby saving the lives of two others. For the pragmatist, killing three villagers would be disproportionate because only one person on your side was killed and the disproportionate retaliation might encourage further arbitrary killing. Killing one innocent villager is still immoral, but the pragmatist minimizes the violence and sets a standard—tit for tat, not triple tit for tat—that potentially limits a chain of future retaliations.

SUMMARY

Figure Intro-2 shows how the various elements covered in this introduction about how we study and understand international affairs fit together. We start with perspectives because we could not start at all if we tried to consider all at once the many facts that make up world affairs. We theorize about what causes events and select or consider as many facts as we can from the different levels of analysis. Then we test our perspective against other perspectives using rationalist or constructivist methods or some combination of the two. Finally, we draw conclusions based on how the causal arrows run and which perspective and level of analysis seems to be primary, relying on judgment, ethics, and morality to fill in the gaps that analysis inevitably leaves.

FIGURE
Intro-2

How One Thinks about International Relations

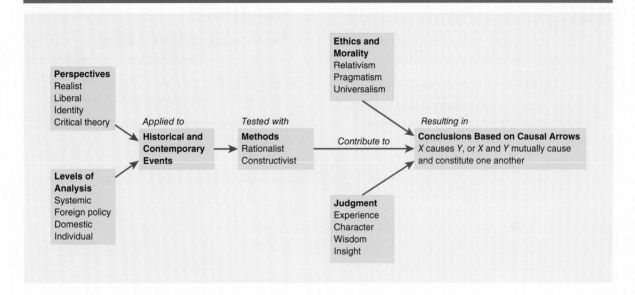

Sharpen your skills with SAGE edge at **edge.sagepub.com/nau4e.**
SAGE edge for students provides a personalized approach to help you
accomplish your coursework goals in an easy-to-use learning environment.

KEY CONCEPTS

causal arrow, 4

causation, 15

constructivist
methods, 15

correlation, 16

counterfactual
reasoning, 17

critical theory
perspective, 13

endogenous
variables, 16

ethics and morality, 20

exogenous
variables, 16

ideal types, 7

identity perspective, 12

judgment, 19

level of analysis, 3

liberal perspective, 10

methods, 14

multicollinearity, 16

perspective, 3

pragmatism, 21

process tracing, 16

rationalist
methods, 15

realist perspective, 9

relativism, 20

universalism, 21

STUDY QUESTIONS

1. Why is one event considered front-page news but not another?

2. Do you think terrorism is caused by American military dominance or American diplomacy? Which answer reflects the realist perspective? Which reflects the liberal perspective?

3. How would you test the perspective that American military dominance is the cause of terrorism—by measuring relative power over different periods or by examining the social purposes of American foreign policy embedded in specific historical circumstances? Which method is rationalist, and which is constructivist?

4. Do you believe the U.S. invasion of Iraq was wrong because it violated Iraq's independence or right because it ended genocide in Iraq? Which argument is relativist, and which is universalist?

5. Why is history relevant to what is new even though it deals with what is old?

We study the world together from many different analytical perspectives and social settings.

HOW TO THINK ABOUT INTERNATIONAL RELATIONS

Perspectives and Levels of Analysis

What are the differences among the following statements?

1. The rise of German power caused World War I.

2. Kaiser Wilhelm II's clumsy diplomacy caused World War I.

3. Germany's militarist ideology, which glorified aggressive war, caused World War I.

4. Capitalist class conflicts caused World War I.

The statements offer different explanations of the causes of World War I, which we explore more fully in Chapter 3. The purpose of examining them here is to help you see that these explanations come from different perspectives and levels of analysis. As already noted, we cannot describe everything in international affairs. Perspectives on international relations help us make selections. They point us in certain directions to find facts, and they order these facts differently to explain events. One fact becomes the cause or independent variable; a second fact becomes the effect or dependent variable. Or, in the case of constructivist methods, two facts mutually cause or constitute one another. Some political scientists like to say we start with a puzzle, but in truth perspective comes first, because we do not have a puzzle until we cannot explain something, and that requires an already existing perspective. The occurrence of war, for example, is not a puzzle unless we expect peace. So we formulate hypotheses from the different perspectives, and then we look at the facts to test our hypotheses. Often we go back and forth between the hypotheses and the evidence many times, refining our analysis. Then we make judgments drawing the causal arrows as to which perspective and level of analysis make most sense. As Professor Thomas Risse says, we see "how far one can push one logic of action [perspective and level of analysis] to account for observable practices and which logic [causal arrows] dominates a given situation."[1]

The realist perspective focuses on separate actors and military conflict and the role that state-based actors play in it, and argues that the relative distribution of power among actors in international affairs is the most important cause of war. When one actor becomes too powerful, the other actors feel threatened. They form alliances to counterbalance the first actor, and that can lead to tension and war. Did this happen before World War I? The realist perspective says it did. The rise of German power (see statement 1) upset the relative distribution of power among states in Europe and set in motion a security competition that eventually caused World War I. The liberal perspective focuses on global society and international institutions and argues that the reciprocal process and quality of interactions and negotiations among actors have more to do with peace and war than does the relative power of separate actors. If actors lack sufficient social and economic connections to enable them to build trust, or institutions do not provide clear rules and sufficient information for communicating effectively, war may result. This perspective looks at the facts before World War I and finds that the German monarch, Kaiser Wilhelm II, was not an effective diplomat and caused the war by provoking unnecessary rivalries, especially with Great Britain (see statement 2). The identity perspective focuses on ideas and norms and argues that the way actors think about themselves and others—their identities—influences international behavior more than do specific institutions or power disparities. This perspective holds that countries with aggressive self-images are more inclined to go to war and finds that prior to World War I Germany had just such a domestic ideology of military aggressiveness, which caused conflict with its neighbors (see statement 3). The critical theory perspective focuses on deep-seated forces driving history and, in the case of Marxist-Leninism, sees World War I as rooted in the capitalist forces of economic production, which generate social conflicts between capitalist and proletariat classes (see statement 4).

Explanations also differ in terms of the levels of analysis at which they operate. Perspectives tell us what the substance of the cause is—power, institutions, or ideas; levels of analysis tell us where the cause is coming from. Statement 1 sees the cause of war as coming from the level of the state system as a whole. The rapid rise of German power relative to that of all other states in Europe caused instability and war. Germany's position in the system was the source of instability. The specific characteristics of Germany and its leaders did not matter; any country rising in power relative to other countries would have caused the same instability. This is why some realists today worry about the rise of China. This type of explanation we call a systemic level of analysis.

Statement 2 sees the cause of war as coming from a specific leader: Kaiser Wilhelm II's bad diplomacy caused the war. If someone else had been in charge of Germany under the same historical circumstances, war might not have occurred. This is a more specific level of analysis. We call it the individual or, alternatively, decision-making level of analysis. Sometimes, however, leaders decide to exploit international events to stay in power at the decision-making level—for example, a leader may choose to go to war to rally the country around the existing government. In that case, the decision-making level connects foreign and domestic causes and becomes the foreign policy level of analysis. Now, Kaiser Wilhelm's incompetence at the individual level of analysis is less the cause than was his desire at the foreign policy level to use war to shore up domestic support for his monarchy.

Statement 3 argues that Germany's militarist ideology, which caused war, came from the nature of Germany's domestic system, not the relative rise of German power or Kaiser Wilhelm II's inept diplomacy. In such a domestic system any leader would have behaved in the same way, regardless of individual and decision-making factors or international conditions. This type of explanation comes from the domestic level of analysis. Finally, statement 4 sees the cause of war coming not from any specific level of analysis but from deep-seated historical forces that tie together leaders, classes, states, and international developments.

Our task in this chapter is to explain these differences. They are a function of the different perspectives, levels of analysis, and the ways the causal arrows run between perspectives and levels of analysis. At the end of the chapter, after we have developed these tools for understanding international affairs, we will revisit the statements about the causes of World War I.

We start by using the story of the prisoner's dilemma and various modifications of this story to highlight the different ways the three core perspectives—realist, liberal, and identity—view the same facts. The perspectives look at the same story but make different assumptions about it—what the situation is, how much the prisoners can interact, and who the prisoners are. As we will see, the realist perspective places primary emphasis on the external situation in which the prisoners find themselves and over which they have no control. This environment in turn dictates how they relate to one another (liberal perspective) and their respective images (identity perspective). The liberal perspective places more emphasis on how the prisoners relate to one another and expects that their repeated interactions in turn eventually override the influences of external (realist) and internal (identity) factors. The identity perspective draws primary attention to who the prisoners are rather than the situation they face or the interactions they undertake. Their identities determine how they evaluate the situation (realist) and behave toward one another (liberal).[2]

⟫⟫ Prisoner's Dilemma

prisoner's dilemma: a game in which two prisoners rationally choose not to cooperate in order to avoid even worse outcomes.

The basic **prisoner's dilemma** story is simple. Two individuals are caught with illegal drugs in their possession. Police authorities suspect that one or both of them may be drug dealers but do not have enough evidence to prove it. So the warden in the prison where the individuals are being held creates a situation to try to get them to squeal on one another. The warden tells each prisoner separately that if he squeals on the other prisoner he can go free; the accused prisoner will then be put away as a drug dealer for twenty-five years. If the other prisoner also squeals, each prisoner gets ten years in prison. On the other hand, if both prisoners remain silent, each will get only one year in prison because there is no further evidence to convict them. The prisoners do not know one another and are not allowed to communicate. Table 1-1 illustrates the choices and outcomes.

Now, let's look at how each perspective analyzes this situation. In this case, as in many real-world cases, the perspectives consider more or less the same facts, but they focus on different facts and order them differently in terms of causal arrows.

The Prisoner's Dilemma from the Realist Perspective

The individual prisoner's dilemma is the following. If actor A remains silent, in effect cooperating with his fellow prisoner, he gets either one year in prison if the other prisoner also remains silent (see upper left box in Table 1-1) or twenty-five years if the other prisoner squeals (lower left box). On the other hand, if actor A squeals, he may either go free if the other prisoner remains silent (see upper right box) or get a sentence of ten years in prison if the other prisoner also squeals (lower right box). Assuming the prisoner's top priority is to go free, it would be logical for him to squeal. But if both squeal, they get ten years each in jail, a worse outcome than if both remained silent (one year in jail for each) but not as bad as the outcome for one prisoner who remains silent while the other squeals (twenty-five years). The point of the story is that each prisoner cannot achieve either his preferred outcome of going free or his second-best goal of

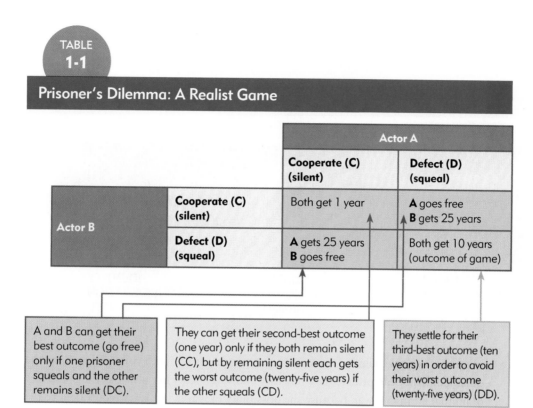

TABLE 1-1

Prisoner's Dilemma: A Realist Game

		Actor A	
		Cooperate (C) (silent)	**Defect (D) (squeal)**
Actor B	**Cooperate (C) (silent)**	Both get 1 year	**A** goes free **B** gets 25 years
	Defect (D) (squeal)	**A** gets 25 years **B** goes free	Both get 10 years (outcome of game)

A and B can get their best outcome (go free) only if one prisoner squeals and the other remains silent (DC).

They can get their second-best outcome (one year) only if they both remain silent (CC), but by remaining silent each gets the worst outcome (twenty-five years) if the other squeals (CD).

They settle for their third-best outcome (ten years) in order to avoid their worst outcome (twenty-five years) (DD).

Notice how the outcomes are ordered for each actor: DC > CC > DD > CD. If this order changes, the game changes. See subsequent tables.

only one year in prison because circumstances outside the control of the prisoner—the various consequences or payoffs of the different choices set up by the warden—make squealing the less risky alternative. Each settles for a second-worse outcome (ten years) to avoid the worst one (twenty-five years).

The realist perspective argues that this sort of dilemma defines the logic of many situations in international affairs. Countries desire peace (analogous to cooperating) and do not want to arm or threaten other countries (analogous to squealing). They prefer less risky or more peaceful strategies such as mutual disarmament (analogous to cooperating and staying only one year in prison). But one country cannot disarm (cooperate) without risking the possibility that the other country may arm (defect) and perhaps seize territory or take away the first country's sovereignty, eliminating its independence and, if it is a democratic state, its freedom as well (analogous to the maximum penalty of twenty-five years). In the case of territory, the situation is what political scientists call zero-sum. What one country gains, the other loses. Notice that the country that arms is not aggressive. It is just looking for the best outcome, and if it arms and the other country does not, it is safer than it would be otherwise. The situation is set up such that each party cannot have peace (going free or spending one year in prison) without risking loss

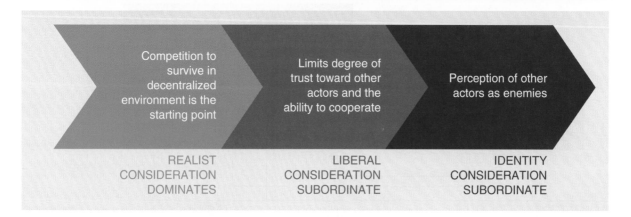

FIGURE 1-1

Causal Arrows: The Realist View

Competition to survive in decentralized environment is the starting point → Limits degree of trust toward other actors and the ability to cooperate → Perception of other actors as enemies

REALIST CONSIDERATION DOMINATES — LIBERAL CONSIDERATION SUBORDINATE — IDENTITY CONSIDERATION SUBORDINATE

of territory or sovereignty (twenty-five years in prison). If both countries arm, on the other hand, they can protect their territory and sovereignty but now risk the possibility of mutual harm and war. Because the possibility of war is less risky (equivalent to ten years in prison) than the actual loss of territory, let alone sovereignty (or democracy), they squeal or defect.

Thus, from the realist perspective much of international relations is about mutual armaments and conflict. *The causal arrows run from competition to survive (go free) in an environment that is decentralized and largely outside the control of the actors to increasing distrust and inability to cooperate to self-images of one another as enemies.*

The Prisoner's Dilemma from the Liberal Perspective

The liberal perspective argues that situations described by the prisoner's dilemma do exist in international affairs but that these situations are not the only or even most prevalent ones and can be overcome. Three factors that realism de-emphasizes help surmount these situations and change the prisoner's dilemma to a more cooperative game: repeated reciprocal interactions or communications, common goals, and technological change. In the original game, the prisoners are not allowed to communicate and build trust; they play the game only once. What if they were allowed to play the game over and over again, the equivalent of meeting regularly in the prison yard to exchange moves and perhaps make small talk? It's not so much the content of what they say that produces trust (after all, familiarity may breed contempt, not cooperation, as a realist perspective would argue) but, rather, the mere fact that they play the game over and over again. In game theory, this is called creating the shadow of the future, that is, the expectation that the prisoners will have to deal with one another again and again—tomorrow, the day after, and every

TABLE 1-2

Situation of Prisoner's Dilemma from Liberal Perspective: Repeated Communications

		Actor A	
		Cooperate (C) (silent)	**Defect (D)** (squeal)
Actor B	**Cooperate (C)** (silent)	Both get 1 year (outcome of game)	**A** goes free **B** gets 25 years
	Defect (D) (squeal)	**A** gets 25 years **B** goes free	Both get 10 years

A and B gain one another's trust and choose to cooperate. They both get one year.

In this game, the prisoners face the same payoffs and goals as in the original game, but we assume A and B can communicate repeatedly. They meet for one hour in the prison yard each day. This interaction becomes patterned and institutionalized and establishes a "shadow of the future."

day in the future. As long as the prisoners can avoid the expectation that they will not meet again—what game theory calls the last move, equivalent to playing the game only once—they might gain enough trust in one another over time to discount significantly the possibility that the other prisoner will defect if the first prisoner remains silent. Now, as Table 1-2 shows, they end up in the upper left box—the second-best outcome of a one-year sentence—rather than the lower right one. The liberal perspective expects that if countries develop habits of regular interaction and communication through diplomacy, membership in common institutions, trade, tourism, and other exchanges, they can overcome the security dilemma that drives mutual armament and conflict.

What is more, according to the liberal perspective, many goals in international relations are common and mutually beneficial, not self-interested and conflicting, such as territory as depicted in the prisoner's dilemma. Countries seek to grow rich together or protect the environment together. These goals are non-zero-sum. Both sides gain, albeit perhaps not equally.

So, what if we change our assumptions about the goals of the prisoners in the original version of the prisoner's dilemma? Let's say the prisoners are less interested in going free than they are in frustrating the warden by reducing the total number of years the warden

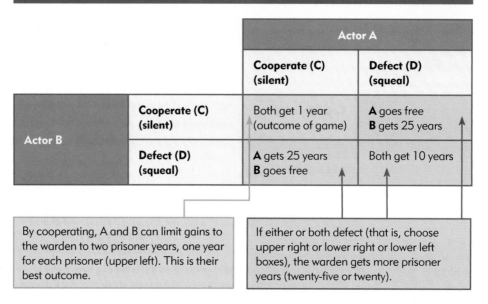

TABLE 1-3

Situation of Prisoner's Dilemma from Liberal Perspective: Change Goals (Frustrate the Warden)

		Actor A	
		Cooperate (C) (silent)	**Defect (D)** (squeal)
Actor B	**Cooperate (C)** (silent)	Both get 1 year (outcome of game)	**A** goes free **B** gets 25 years
	Defect (D) (squeal)	**A** gets 25 years **B** goes free	Both get 10 years

By cooperating, A and B can limit gains to the warden to two prisoner years, one year for each prisoner (upper left). This is their best outcome.

If either or both defect (that is, choose upper right or lower right or lower left boxes), the warden gets more prisoner years (twenty-five or twenty).

In this game, the prisoners face the same payoffs as in the original game, but the goals have changed. Notice that the new goal of frustrating the warden rather than going free is non-zero-sum because both prisoners can now get their best outcome simultaneously.

is able to hold the prisoners in jail. Now the prisoners have a common goal, not a self-interested one. Nothing else in the situation changes, but notice how the outcome of the game changes. As Table 1-3 shows, the logical choice that now meets the goal of both prisoners is to remain silent (upper left box). That gives the warden only two prisoner-years (one year for each prisoner), while squealing by one or both prisoners gives the warden twenty-five or twenty (ten years each) prisoner-years, respectively. The prisoners still can't influence the warden. He is outside their control. But now both prisoners can get their second-best outcome simultaneously by cooperating.[3]

An example of this situation from the real world may be two countries trading to increase wealth for both (non-zero-sum) rather than fighting over territory that only one can gain (zero-sum). Look at how the countries of the European Union have overcome historical disputes over territory by building a common trade and economic union (liberal), which reduces the significance of relative military power (realist) and engenders a common European identity (identity).

Further, what if the warden changes the payoffs, or consequences, of the original game? For example, if both prisoners squeal, that should give the warden enough evidence

TABLE
1-4

Situation of Prisoner's Dilemma from Liberal Perspective: Change Payoffs (Increase Costs of Defection/Conflict)

		Actor A	
		Cooperate (C) (silent)	**Defect (D)** (squeal)
Actor B	**Cooperate (C)** (silent)	Both get 1 year	**A** goes free **B** gets 25 years (outcome of game)
	Defect (D) (squeal)	**A** gets 25 years **B** goes free (outcome of game)	Both get death

A or B gets the best outcome only if one defects (squeals and goes free) and the other actor cooperates (remains silent). Each has a greater tendency to cooperate but still prefers to defect, because that is the only way he can go free, assuming the other cooperates.

If both A and B defect, they risk getting their worst outcome (death).

The warden increases the cost of defection and hence changes the order of preferences for each of the prisoners: DC > CC > CD > DD (different from the original order: DC > CC > DD > CD).

to convict them both as drug dealers and now, let's say, put them to death. Table 1-4 shows the new game. All we have done is increase the worst possible cost of defecting from twenty-five years to death. That might be the equivalent in international affairs of a technological change, such as developing nuclear weapons, that raises the penalty of arms races and war. Nuclear weapons increase the dangers of mutual armament by states just as the death penalty increases the cost of mutual defection by the prisoners. Now the actors no longer have a dominant strategy to defect, as in the original game. Each knows that defecting carries the risk of death, the worst outcome; both would prefer to cooperate. But each still wants most to go free (remain independent), and he can achieve that only by defecting. So the actors are torn between the two strategies depicted by the upper right and lower left boxes: defecting if the other actor cooperates (and going free) or cooperating if the other actor defects (and getting twenty-five years). Much depends on what each actor thinks the other will do. While the prospects of both cooperating and ending up in the upper left-hand box are not assured, they have improved somewhat over the original game. The scale tips toward cooperation. The cost of twenty-five years in prison if the other prisoner does not cooperate is still less than that of death.[4]

TABLE
1-5

Situation of Prisoner's Dilemma from Liberal Perspective: Change Payoffs (Reduce Costs of Cooperation)

		Actor A	
		Cooperate (C) (silent)	**Defect (D)** (squeal)
Actor B	**Cooperate (C)** (silent)	Both get 1 year	**A** goes free **B** gets 5 years (outcome of game)
	Defect (D) (squeal)	**A** gets 5 years **B** goes free (outcome of game)	Both get 10 years

A or B gets the best outcome (freedom) if one defects and the other cooperates. Each has a greater tendency to cooperate but still prefers to defect, because that is the only way he can go free, assuming the other cooperates.

If both A and B defect, they risk getting their worst outcome (ten years).

The warden reduces the costs of cooperation and hence the order of preferences for each actor: DC > CC > CD > DD (different from the original order: DC > CC > DD > CD).

Technological change may work the other way, of course. It may reduce the costs or increase the benefits of cooperating rather than increase the costs of defecting. Let's go back to the original game and reduce the cost of remaining silent if the other prisoner squeals, from twenty-five to five years. Now, as Table 1-5 illustrates, the prisoners risk less if they cooperate (five years) than if they squeal (ten years). Their preferred strategies again are the upper right and lower left boxes. But now, because they risk only five years in prison if they guess wrong about what the other party will do, the prospects of cooperating are better than in the original game. A real-world example of reducing the costs or increasing the benefits of cooperation might be technological advances that make the prospects of ballistic missile defense more feasible. If all countries possessed such defenses, they may be more willing to cooperate in a nuclear crisis. If the other country defects and attacks, the first country can defend itself and not lose as much (the equivalent of getting five years) as it might if it also attacked (the equivalent of getting ten years).

In all these ways—repeated communication and diplomacy, focusing on common rather than conflicting goals, and exploiting technological changes that alter payoffs in favor of cooperation—the liberal perspective argues that realist logic can be overcome.

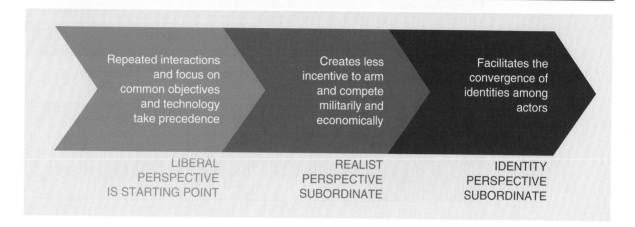

FIGURE 1-2

Causal Arrows: The Liberal View

Repeated interactions and focus on common objectives and technology take precedence

Creates less incentive to arm and compete militarily and economically

Facilitates the convergence of identities among actors

LIBERAL PERSPECTIVE IS STARTING POINT

REALIST PERSPECTIVE SUBORDINATE

IDENTITY PERSPECTIVE SUBORDINATE

The causal arrows run from repeated interactions and a focus on common objectives and technology to less incentive to arm and compete in terms of relative military and economic power to increasing trust and converging identities among the actors.

The Prisoner's Dilemma from the Identity Perspective

The identity perspective takes still another tack on the situation described by the original prisoner's dilemma game. It challenges the implicit assumption that the prisoners have independent identities and receive payoffs that are exclusive of one another. If the identities and payoffs were more common and interdependent, the two prisoners would seek to maximize joint scores. What if, for example, the two prisoners knew that they were both members of the Mafia? Members of the Mafia, an underground criminal organization, take a blood oath that they will never squeal on other members of the organization or reveal anything about its criminal activities. This oath becomes part of their identity. They remain silent because of who they are. They may also remain silent, of course, because they fear that someone else in the Mafia will kill them if they squeal. But, in that case, the scenario mimics a realist situation because their behavior is determined by external circumstances they cannot control. In the case as seen from the identity perspective, they do not squeal because their obedience to the Mafia code has been internalized and is now part of their identity. If each prisoner knows that the other prisoner is also a member of the Mafia, he is unlikely to squeal on the other. No feature of the game has changed except that the prisoners now know they have similar or shared identities. Yet, as Table 1-6 shows, the outcome of the game changes substantially. It is now logical for the two prisoners to remain silent and get off with only one year each in prison.

TABLE
1-6

Situation of Prisoner's Dilemma from Identity Perspective: Change Identity

		Actor A	
		Cooperate (C) (silent)	**Defect (D)** (squeal)
Actor B	**Cooperate (C)** (silent)	Both get 1 year (outcome of game)	**A** goes free **B** gets 25 years
	Defect (D) (squeal)	**A** gets 25 years **B** goes free	Both get 10 years

Because of their shared identity, the prisoners both know that the other will not squeal. Hence, they can choose to cooperate without fear that the other will defect.

In this game, the prisoners are back to the original payoffs and goals and share no communications except knowledge of the other's identity. Assume that A and B are not self-interested actors but members of a common organization—such as the Mafia—and know that about one another.

In the same way, the identity perspective argues that two countries may behave differently depending on their identities. They may see one another as enemies, rivals, or friends, depending on the way their identities are individually and socially constructed. Or their identities may converge or diverge with one another depending on how similar or different these identities are independently. Thus, democracies behave more peacefully toward one another than they do toward autocracies, and countries that identify with common international norms and ideas behave differently than those that see themselves struggling over the balance of power. *The causal arrows in the identity perspective run from converging or conflicting self-images (identity) to more or less cooperation (liberal) to the need or lack of need for military and economic power (realist).*

Let's leave the game metaphor and develop these three perspectives in the real world. The sections that follow introduce numerous concepts, many of which will be new to you. Don't despair. We will revisit these concepts again and again and use them throughout the rest of the book to help you see them at work in our discussion of historical and contemporary international affairs.

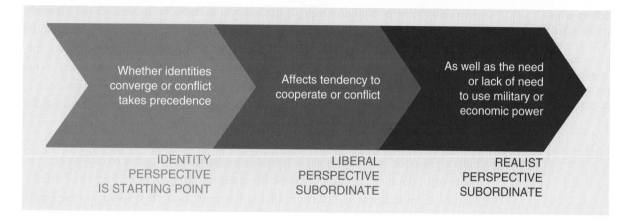

FIGURE 1-3

Causal Arrows: The Identity View

Whether identities converge or conflict takes precedence

Affects tendency to cooperate or conflict

As well as the need or lack of need to use military or economic power

IDENTITY PERSPECTIVE IS STARTING POINT

LIBERAL PERSPECTIVE SUBORDINATE

REALIST PERSPECTIVE SUBORDINATE

>>> The Realist Perspective

The realist perspective focuses on conflict and war, not because people adopting this perspective favor war or believe war is necessary but because they hope by studying war to avoid it in the future. War, according to the realist perspective, is a consequence of *anarchy,* the decentralized distribution of power in the international system. In anarchic situations, actors have to rely on *self-help* to defend themselves; *unilateralism or minilateralism* is necessary because there is no effective central, multilateral power they can appeal to. So, throughout history, wherever anarchy existed, individuals, tribes, clans, villages, towns, and provinces provided for their own security. Today the *state* is the principal actor authorized to use military and other forms of *power* to protect security. The state enjoys *sovereignty,* meaning no other actor can exert legitimate power over it or intervene in its domestic affairs. In pursuing power and sovereignty, however, states inevitably threaten one another. Is one state arming to defend itself or to attack another state? States cannot be sure about other states' intentions. They face a *security dilemma* similar to the prisoner's dilemma. If one state arms and another doesn't, the second one may lose its security. To cope with that dilemma, both states defect and pursue a *balance of power.* They form *alliances* against any country that becomes so strong it might threaten the survival of the others. The number of great power states or alliances involved in the balance of power constitutes the *polarity* of the system. Two great powers or alliances form a bipolar system, three form a tripolar system, and four or more form a multipolar system. Different system polarities produce different propensities toward *war.*

Let's look a little closer at these key (italicized) concepts of a realist perspective on world affairs. (The concepts appear in boldface where they are most succinctly defined.)

Anarchy and Self-Help

From a realist perspective, the distribution of power is always decentralized. This fact of international life is referred to as anarchy. The word means no leader or center, as opposed to monarchy (or empire), which means one leader or center, and polyarchy, which means several overlapping leaders or centers, such as the shared authority of the pope and the Holy Roman Emperor in medieval Europe. In the world today, **anarchy** means there is no leader or center of authority that monopolizes coercive power and has the legitimacy to use it. The United States may be the only world superpower, but, as the Iraq War suggests, the rest of the world does not recognize its legitimacy to use that power as a world government, not in the same sense that citizens of a particular country recognize the legitimacy of the domestic government to monopolize coercive power. There is no world government with the authority of a domestic government and no world police force with the authority of a national police or military force. In short, there is no *world 911*. If you get in trouble abroad, there is no one to call for help, no one except your own clan, tribe, or state. If a student from the United States is arrested in Singapore, for example, the student calls the U.S. embassy in Singapore, not the United Nations in New York. Similarly, if a country is attacked, it provides its own defense or calls on allies. It is not likely to depend on international organizations.

Anarchy places a premium on **self-help**, which means that whatever the size or nature of the actor in any historical period—whether it is a tribe, city-state, or nation-state—it has to provide for its own protection or it risks succumbing to another actor. The size or nature of the actor may change over time. Some states unite like the European

anarchy: the decentralized distribution of power in the international system; no leader or center to monopolize power.

self-help: the principle of self-defense under anarchy in which states have no one to rely on to defend their security except themselves.

The realist perspective emphasizes military power, on display here in a parade celebrating the sixty-fifth anniversary of the North Korean Workers' Party in Pyongyang, October 2010.

Union, while others collapse like the Soviet Union. But the condition of anarchy and the need for self-help do not change. Unless the world eventually unites under a single government that all the peoples of the world recognize as the sole legitimate center of military power, decentralized actors will be responsible for their own security. Realist approaches therefore often favor **unilateralism or minilateralism,** action by one or several states, rather than action by all states (multilateralism).

State Actors and Sovereignty

Because the realist perspective is especially interested in conflict and war, realist scholars find it more important to study states than nonstate actors. **States** command the greatest military and police forces to make war. Corporations, labor unions, and human rights groups do not. Where groups other than states use military-style force—for example, private security forces defending corporate properties overseas—these groups are not recognized by domestic authorities or international institutions as having the right or legitimacy to do so. Only states have that right. They possess what is called sovereignty. **Sovereignty** means that there is no higher authority above them abroad or beneath them at home. It dictates *self-determination* at home and *nonintervention abroad*—that is, agreeing not to intervene in the domestic affairs or jurisdictions of other states.

How do actors acquire sovereignty? When territorial states emerged in Europe during the period from 1000 to 1500 C.E.,[5] they had to demonstrate that they could establish and defend their borders. Once a state monopolized force within its borders and mobilized that force to defend its borders, it was recognized by other states. As power changes, therefore, the principal actors in international politics change. Nonstate actors can become state actors, and state actors can dissolve or evolve. For example, the Muslim population in Kosovo, formerly a minority nonstate actor in the country of Serbia, became independent, recognized by the United Nations and more than one hundred other states. Conversely, the Soviet Union disappeared, and the former republics of the Soviet Union, such as Ukraine, became independent. The European Union has already replaced independent European states in certain specific areas of international negotiations, such as trade and monetary policy, and if it develops an integrated security policy it will become a fully sovereign, new state actor. However actors change, from a realist perspective they remain separate and independent and therefore subject to the same imperatives of anarchy and self-help.

Power

States monopolize power, but what is power? For the most part, **power** from the realist perspective is concerned with material capabilities, not influence or outcomes. Normally, we define power and influence as getting others to do what they would not otherwise do. Power does that by coercion, influence by persuasion. But how do we know what others might intend or otherwise do in the absence of our attempt to influence them? Their intentions may be manifold and hard to discern. And outcomes that might have occurred if we had not sought to influence them are part of that counterfactual history we can only speculate about. As the realist perspective sees it, it is too difficult to measure power and

unilateralism or minilateralism: action by one or several states but not by all states.

states: the actors in the contemporary international system that have the largest capabilities and right to use military force.

sovereignty: an attribute of states such that they are not subordinate to a higher power either inside or outside their borders and they agree not to intervene in the domestic jurisdictions of other states.

power: the material capabilities of a country, such as size of population and territory, resource endowment, economic capability, and military strength.

influence in terms of intentions or outcomes. It is better to measure power in terms of material capabilities. Military and economic capabilities are paramount. It is then assumed that these capabilities translate roughly into commensurate influence and outcomes.

How does the realist perspective measure capabilities? Kenneth Waltz, the father of what is known in international political theory as neorealism or structural realism—a realist perspective based primarily on the systemic structure or distribution of power—identifies the following measures: "size of population and territory, resource endowment, economic capability, military strength, political stability and competence."[6] Population, economics, and military might are obvious elements of state power. Territory and resource endowment are too. They involve geography and contribute to what realist perspectives call more broadly **geopolitics**. Some countries have more land than others, some have more natural resources, and some have more easily defended geographic borders. For example, Switzerland is protected on all sides by mountains, while Poland sits in the middle of the great plains of northern Europe and, as a result, has been more frequently invaded, conquered, and even partitioned. Island nations have certain power advantages by virtue of being less vulnerable to invasion. England was never defeated by Napoleon or Hitler, while states on the European continent succumbed to both invaders.

geopolitics: a focus on a country's location and geography as the basis of its national interests.

Other nations, such as the United States and Russia, occupy the heartlands of vast continents. They have geographic depth that aids their defense. When Napoleon invaded Russia, the czar's forces did not directly engage Napoleon's forces but instead conducted a scorched-earth retreat and drew Napoleon's army deeper and deeper into Russia, farther and farther away from its supply lines and lines of communication. Eventually Napoleon's army ran out of supplies, and the Russian winter destroyed it. The United States has similar geographic depth. It felt safe enough in its continental sanctuary surrounded by two oceans to stay out of World War I until nearly the end and might have stayed out of World War II, even after Britain was almost defeated, if the Japanese had not attacked Pearl Harbor.

Notice, however, that Waltz also mentions capabilities such as political stability and competence, which are not, strictly speaking, material capabilities. These political capabilities involve institutional and cultural or ideological factors that are more important in liberal and identity perspectives, what some analysts call "soft power." The neorealist perspective does not emphasize such political capabilities. It focuses more on material power than on the domestic political institutions and ideologies that mobilize that power. Realists may care about prestige and reputation, which are elements of soft power, but they value such factors mostly in terms of how they derive from or are caused by the credibility to use force.[7] The direction of the causal arrows is decisive: the use of force creates reputation, not the reverse. Another version of the realist perspective, known as classical realism, pays more attention to domestic values and institutions. Power is used to protect American democracy or Russian culture. But at the international level realists pursue relative power, not common values such as the spread of democracy or culture. As Professor Hans Morgenthau, the father of classical realism, tells us, "The main signpost . . . through the landscape of international politics is the concept of interests defined in terms of power."[8]

The realist perspective emphasizes military and economic power over institutions or ideas. It differentiates states in terms of great powers, middle powers, and small powers. States acquire different interests or goals depending on the size of their capabilities, not the characteristics of their institutions or the political ideas (identities) they espouse. Great powers have the broadest interests. They have a concern for the well-being of the international system as a whole because they make up a good part of the whole system. When states fade from great power to middle power status, as Austria did after the seventeenth century, their interests shrink. By the time of World War I, Austria was interested only in its immediate surroundings in the Balkans. Small powers often remain on the sidelines in realist analysis or succumb to the power of larger states, as happened to Poland through repeated invasion and conquest.

Security Dilemma

When states pursue power to defend themselves, they create a security dilemma from which the possibility, although not the inevitability, of war can never be completely excluded. The **security dilemma** results from the fact that, as each group or state amasses power to protect itself, it inevitably threatens other groups or states. Other states wonder how the first state will use the power it is amassing: Will it use its power just to defend its present territory, or will it use that power to expand its territory? (This is analogous to the possibility that the other prisoner will squeal in the prisoner's dilemma.) How can the other states be sure what the first state intends? If it is only seeking to defend itself, other states have nothing to worry about. But if it has more ambitious aims, then the other states too must arm. Exactly how much power is consistent with defense, and at what point does the accumulation of power signal aggressive or offensive intent?

security dilemma: the situation that states face when they arm to defend themselves and in the process threaten other states.

States may signal their intentions by diplomatic means. Defensive realists of the rational choice school emphasize this possibility. For example, a state acquires defensive military capabilities, not offensive ones. But military technologies may have both defensive and offensive uses (think of machine guns). It may be hard to read such signals. When do states become revisionist or greedy—that is, seek more power than they need to defend themselves? And who decides what amount of power is defensive or offensive? Because no state can be sure, other states arm too, and in this process of mutual armament states face all the uncertainties of what exactly constitutes enough power to be safe. Ronald Reagan once said that the United States was seeking a "margin of safety" vis-à-vis the Soviet Union, which to the Soviet Union probably meant that the United States sought "superiority." Scholars who emphasize the realist perspective have never agreed on whether states seek just "security"—that is, enough power to balance and defend themselves—or whether they seek "maximum power," on the assumption that more power always makes the state more secure. Theories of defensive realism say states seek security and manage most conflicts by diplomacy without using force directly; theories of offensive realism say states seek maximum or dominant power and often use diplomacy to disguise their aggressive use of force.[9] Notice how the realist perspective

FIGURE
1-4

The Realist Worldview

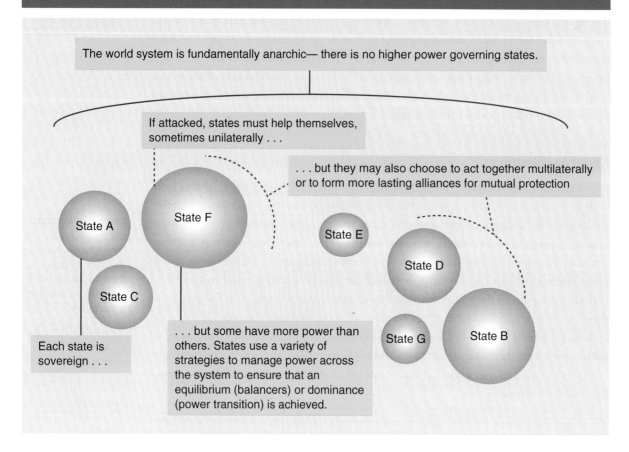

The world system is fundamentally anarchic— there is no higher power governing states.

If attacked, states must help themselves, sometimes unilaterally . . .

. . . but they may also choose to act together multilaterally or to form more lasting alliances for mutual protection

State A

State F

State E

State D

State C

State G   State B

Each state is sovereign . . .

. . . but some have more power than others. States use a variety of strategies to manage power across the system to ensure that an equilibrium (balancers) or dominance (power transition) is achieved.

does not exclude diplomacy, but the causal arrows run from power (realist) to diplomacy (liberal), not the other way around.

Balance of Power

The best states can do then, according to the realist perspective, is to pursue and balance power. The **balance of power** is both a strategy by which states seek to ensure that no other state dominates the system and an outcome that provides a rough equilibrium among states. In balancing power, it does not matter what the rising state's intentions are. Does the United States today seek to dominate the world? Many would say no. But the European states, Russia, or China may have reasons for concern. From the realist perspective, they cannot worry about America's intentions; they have to worry about America's power.

As a strategy, the balance of power focuses on the formation of alliances and requires that states *align against the greatest power* regardless of who that power is. The greatest power is the state that can threaten another state's survival. So it does not matter if

balance of power: the strategy by which states counterbalance to ensure that no single state dominates the system, or an outcome that establishes a rough equilibrium among states.

that greater power is a former ally or a fellow democracy, the smaller state must align with others against that power. After all, a growing power may change its institutional affiliations or values. Hence, states do not align against the greatest threat, which may be a function of a state's institutions and values, but against the greatest power, whatever its institutions and values. Realism does not rule out other strategies, such as bandwagoning, that is, aligning *with,* rather than against, the greatest power to share the spoils of conquest; or buckpassing, that is, avoiding alliances and letting other states do the fighting. It just warns that these strategies are dangerous, as Stalin learned after he bandwagoned with Hitler in 1939 and Hitler turned around and attacked him in 1941.

As an outcome, the balance of power may involve equilibrium or hegemony. Defensive realists argue that states seek equilibrium or **power balancing**, that is, relatively equal power that offsets the power of other states and thus lessens the risk of attack and war. They see danger when one state moves away from equilibrium toward hegemony, dominating other states. Offensive realists argue that states seek empire or **hegemony** because it is desirable (more power is always better than less) and increases stability (other powers have no chance of defeating the dominant power). The danger comes, as Robert Kagan writes, "when the upward trajectory of a rising power comes close to intersecting the downward trajectory of a declining power."[10] This is the moment of **power transition** when war is most likely to occur. As we shall see, that may have been the case when Germany passed Great Britain at the beginning of the twentieth century (Chapter 2), and, according to some realists, it may be the case in the twenty-first century if China surpasses the United States as the world's dominant power (Chapter 5).

In subsequent chapters, I will refer to the power balancing and power transition schools to capture this difference among realist perspectives on which configuration of power—equilibrium or hegemony—is most conducive to stability.

Polarity and Alliances

How do states balance power? It depends on how many states there are. We call the number of states holding power in a system the **polarity** of the system. If there are many states or centers of power, the system is multipolar. In a multipolar system states balance by forming **alliances** with other states to counter the state that is becoming the greatest power. These alliances have to be temporary and flexible. Why? Because the balance of power is always uncertain and shifts, sometimes quickly. States must therefore be ready to shift alliances. Remember that the purpose of alliances is to balance power, not to make permanent friends or permanent enemies. Winston Churchill, Britain's prime minister during World War II, once said that "if Hitler invaded Hell, I would at least make a favorable reference to the Devil in the House of Commons."[11] Alliances in a multipolar realist system are expedient, not emotional attachments.

What if there are only two great powers? After World War II, the United States aligned with western Europe and Japan, while the Soviet Union aligned with eastern Europe and, until the 1960s, China to create a bipolar system. Now the two superpowers could not align with other states because there were none, except small and inconsequential

power balancing: a school of realism that sees hegemony as destabilizing and war as most likely when a dominant power emerges to threaten the equilibrium of power among other states.

hegemony: a situation in which one country is more powerful than all the others.

power transition: a school of realism that sees hegemony as stabilizing and war as most likely when a rising power challenges a previously dominant one and the balance of power approaches equilibrium.

polarity: the number of states—one (unipolar), two (bipolar), three (tripolar), or more (multipolar)—holding significant power in the international system.

alliances: formal defense arrangements wherein states align against a greater power to prevent dominance.

ones that could not contribute much to the balance of power. The superpowers had to balance internally. They competed by mobilizing internal resources to establish a balance between them. Once China broke away from the Soviet Union, the system became tripolar. Now the United States maneuvered to bring China into the western coalition because whichever superpower captured China would have an advantage. The contest before World War II may have also been tripolar. Hitler, Stalin, and the United States/Great Britain competed to control Europe. Because in a contest of three powers a coalition of two powers wins, some scholars believe that tripolarity is uniquely unstable.[12]

Polarity determines the propensity of different international systems for war. Here again, realist scholars don't agree on what distributions of power or numbers of powerful states—polarities—contribute to greater stability. Kenneth Waltz and John Mearsheimer argue that bipolar worlds are the most stable because two bigger powers, such as the United States and the Soviet Union, have only each other to worry about and will not make many mistakes.[13] But Dale Copeland, a professor at the University of Virginia, contends that multipolar systems are more stable because a declining power, which is the one most likely to initiate war, has more partners to ally with and is therefore more inclined to deter than fight the rising power.[14] So far, the statistical evidence from large-scale studies of war has yielded no definitive answer to this disagreement.[15]

War

No state seeks war, but the possibility of war is always inherent in the situation of anarchy. Although the costs of war are always high, the costs of losing sovereignty or freedom may be even higher. Diplomacy and other relationships help clarify *intentions* but never enough to preclude the possibility of military conflict. Ultimately, states have to base their calculations on *capabilities,* not intentions. That is why the realist perspective notes that even democracies, which presumably are most transparent and accessible to one another and best able to know one another's intentions, still cannot fully trust one another. Many European countries opposed U.S. intervention in Iraq, and some European leaders call for a united Europe to become a counterweight or military counterbalance to the United States, despite the fact that Europe and the United States share the same democratic institutions and values. As the realist scholar Charles Kupchan concludes, "Even if all the world's countries were democratic, . . . democratic powers may engage in geopolitical rivalry [and] . . . economic interdependence among Europe's great powers did little to avert the hegemonic war that broke out in 1914."[16] Notice how the causal arrows run in a realist perspective; power competition (realist) limits the influence of interdependence (liberal) even among countries that share democratic values (identity).

Wars result from the dynamics of power balances or polarity and especially from shifts in power balances. Technological change, especially military innovations, and economic growth produce such shifts.[17] Because realist perspectives focus more on relative than absolute gains, they worry more about the zero-sum effects of technological change than they do about the non-zero-sum effects. Military innovations may alter the balance between offensive and defensive technologies, which might give one side a crucial military advantage. Free trade, while it benefits both partners, may benefit adversaries more. Rising powers such as the United States in the nineteenth century, Japan after World War II, and China today have generally favored protectionist policies toward trade. Technological change and modernization offer many benefits, but realist perspectives worry about how these benefits will be distributed, especially if they fall into the hands of opposing powers.

Defensive realist perspectives concentrate on **defense**, the use of force after an attack, and **deterrence**, the use of threatened retaliation through force to deter an attack before it occurs. More offensive realist versions envision the use of force to initiate attacks: compellence and preemptive and preventive war. **Compellence** is the use of force to get another state to do something rather than to refrain from doing something. The threat of force to get Iraq earlier or Iran today to give up its nuclear program is a case of compellence. The strategy to get Iran to refrain from using nuclear weapons once it has acquired them is a case of deterrence.

defense: the use of force to defend a country after an attack.

deterrence: the use of threatened retaliation through force to deter an attack before it occurs.

compellence: the use of force to get another state to do something rather than to refrain from doing something.

Preemptive war is an attack by one country against another that is preparing to attack the first. One country sees the armies of another country gathering on its border and preempts the expected attack by attacking first. Israel initiated a preemptive war in 1967 when Egypt assembled forces in the Sinai Peninsula and Israel attacked before Egypt might have. Preventive war is an attack by a country against another that is not preparing to attack it but is growing in power and is likely to attack at some point in the future. War is considered to be inevitable. And, so, a declining power, in particular, may decide that war is preferable sooner rather than later because later it will have declined even further and be less powerful. It attacks at the point when its power peaks or has not yet declined that much. As we note in Chapter 2, some realists believe that was why Germany attacked Russia in 1914.

It is often difficult to distinguish between preemptive and preventive wars. In the Iraq War in 2003, if you believed—based on imperfect intelligence—that Saddam Hussein had WMDs and might use them or pass them on to terrorists, the war was preemptive, even though Iraq's WMDs may not have been as visible and hence as verifiable as armies massing on the border. If you believed Saddam Hussein did not have WMDs but would surely get them in the future, the war was preventive, because the United States decided to attack before Iraq actually had the weapons. If the United States had waited, it would have been relatively less powerful because Iraq, once it had the weapons, might deter a U.S. attack by threatening to retaliate with such weapons. For realists, this same dilemma faces U.S. policy makers today in Iran. Do you stop Iran's nuclear program before (preventive) or after (preemptive) it becomes imminent? Or do you let it emerge and deter it through the threat of mutual nuclear retaliation?

One thing is certain: the balance of power does not prevent war. Over the past five centuries, there have been 119 major wars in Europe alone, where most of the great powers have been located. (A major war is defined as one in which at least one great power was involved.) Many of these wars were horrendously destructive. How do we defend a way of thinking about international relations that accepts such destructive wars? Well, remember, realist scholars are trying to see the world as it has been and, in their view, remains. They don't favor or want war any more than anyone else. But if any leader anywhere in the world intends war, the quickest way to have war is to assume that it cannot occur. Antiwar advocates made such assumptions both before and after World War I, and the world paid a heavy price for it.

Wars within states, or *intrastate* wars, are more common today than wars between states, or *interstate* wars. So far, intrastate wars, such as the war in Syria, have not ignited global interstate wars. But there is no guarantee they won't do so in the future, and intrastate wars have caused devastation and suffering on a scale comparable to the damage done by interstate wars, although not as concentrated. Thus, the realist perspective advocates constant vigilance regarding power and power balancing as the only path to peace. As Morgenthau explains, the transformation of the world system into something else "can be achieved only through the workman-like manipulation of the perennial forces that have shaped the past as they will the future."[18]

⟫ The Liberal Perspective

The liberal perspective is interested in the problem of cooperation, but not because it is naive and does not recognize the prevalence of violence and conflict. Rather, it is more impressed by the extent to which villages, towns, provinces, and communities have been able, over time, to overcome violence and conflict by centralizing and legitimating power in institutions, always at higher levels of aggregation. The state is just the most recent level at which groups of people have been able to overcome the balance of power and centralize authority. Why could this kind of consolidation not happen eventually at the regional (EU) and international (UN) levels?

The liberal perspective, therefore, focuses on the causes of cooperation and finds them in the ways in which states interact with and relate to one another through repetitive processes and practices. It assumes that individuals and groups behave more on the basis of how other groups behave toward them than on the basis of how much relative power they possess (realist) or what their initial cultural or ideological beliefs are (identity). Just as anarchy is a central concept in the realist perspective, *reciprocity*, or how states respond to one another, is a central concept in the liberal perspective.[19]

States have increased chances to reciprocate if they interact frequently. Thus, in contrast to the realist perspective, the liberal perspective pays more attention to interdependence than to independence or self-help. *Interdependence* links groups and countries together through trade, transportation, tourism, and other types of exchanges and makes countries mutually or equally dependent and hence interdependent on one another. As this happens, they get used to one another and develop habits of cooperation that facilitate the formation of international regimes and institutions. Institutions (liberal) help resolve disputes despite diverse ideologies (identities) and without the use of force (realist). Notice again how the causal arrows run from institutions to ideas and power, not the reverse.

Modernization and *technological change* increase interdependence and the number of *nongovernmental organizations (NGOs)*. Liberal perspectives, therefore, are generally optimistic about change. The agricultural, industrial, and information revolutions steadily expanded the scope and intensity of human contacts and created new nonstate actors at the levels of both domestic *civil society* and *global governance*.

The liberal perspective emphasizes diplomacy and getting together repeatedly to solve problems. During one of several groundbreaking trips to China, Henry A. Kissinger, then national security adviser to President Richard Nixon, toasts with Premier Chou Enlai of China at a state dinner in Beijing in February 1972.

Private multinational corporations (MNCs) and cross-national nonprofit organizations, such as the International Red Cross, proliferated, contributing to the thickening of *transnational relations*, or international relations among nongovernmental actors outside the immediate control of national governments. Partly to control these developments, national governments established *intergovernmental organizations (IGOs)*; the International Telecommunication Union, for example, was founded in 1865 to regulate the ballooning telephone and telegraph traffic. Compared to the realist perspective, the liberal perspective places more emphasis on NGOs and IGOs than it does on states and the balance of power.

In a world of accelerating interdependence and proliferating actors, liberal perspectives place heavy emphasis on cooperation and bargaining. *Cooperation* facilitates the achievement of better outcomes for one or more actors without harming other actors. It is a *non-zero-sum* game. For example, a national or global economy may be operating at a level of less than full employment. If public policy can generate more employment without harming the people who are already employed, the national or global society as a whole is better off. Economists talk about this in terms of moving the society toward a Pareto optimum or frontier, in honor of the Italian economist Vilfredo Pareto, who developed this idea. Cooperation also facilitates the provision of *collective goods,* or common goals that actors can achieve only together or not at all. Collective goods include environmental protection such as clean air, which all or none can enjoy, but also increasingly, in a nuclear and globalized world, security and wealth, which have to be achieved for everyone or no one will benefit for long.

When outcomes cannot be improved for some without harming others, bargaining becomes essential. *Bargaining* arises when actors have to choose among options that make some better off but others worse off. Bargaining is a zero-sum game—that is, what one actor gains the other loses—and can lead to conflict and war. So liberal perspectives do not exclude coercion and the use of force. They simply see such action as determined more by interactive factors that affect bargaining (liberal) than by geopolitical (realist) or ideological (identity) realities that constrain bargaining. For example, rational choice theory, which emphasizes bargaining, pays relatively less attention to the causal forces of anarchy or domestic culture, which lie outside the bargaining context, and more attention to the causal forces of signaling, information, and other factors that lie inside the bargaining context.

Institutions facilitate cooperation and bargaining. *International regimes*, such as the Group of 20 (G-20), which deals with global economic issues, coordinate the expectations and behavior of countries without necessarily incorporating them into a single institution, while *international institutions*, such as the United Nations, formalize interdependence, promote specialization by enabling certain groups or countries to carry out specified roles (for example, the veto rights of great powers in the UN Security Council), and implement common rules and regulations (such as those spelled out in the UN Charter). Regimes and institutions enhance efficiency both by lowering transaction costs, the extra expenses incurred to carry out long-distance business exchanges, and by increasing information, which reduces uncertainty and bargaining asymmetries in diplomacy.

Once created, institutions tend to evolve through feedback and reinforcement, a process called *path dependence*, whereby actions taken initially lead down a path of subsequent interactions to unintended consequences and new challenges that were not predicted or foreseen at the outset. One of the best examples of path dependence, as we will see, is the spillover process in the European Union.

Finally, the liberal perspective expects that, over a long enough time, *diplomacy* among multiple powers and *multilateralism* among multiple ideologies will foster a habit of compromise and pluralism that will eventually consolidate the *legitimacy* or right to use force at the international rather than the state level. The liberal perspective, as deployed in the Western tradition, envisions that such global legitimacy will ultimately reflect liberal values, a world of the so-called democratic peace. But other perspectives that also emphasize interactions over power and ideas envision nondemocratic outcomes. Marxism, for example, emphasizes the dialectical interactions between capitalist and proletariat classes and sees these interactions ending not in democracy, as liberal perspectives expect, or in equilibrium, as realist perspectives expect, but in the eventual triumph of the proletariat over the capitalist classes and, thus, of communism over democracy. (Marxism also sees these interactions as coming from deep-seated historical circumstances that cannot be changed. For this reason, we treat Marxism later in this chapter as a critical theory perspective.)

What distinguishes the liberal perspective from other perspectives, therefore, is not the end state of democracy but how one arrives at that end state. Process, not power or ideology, determines outcomes. Some versions, such as classical liberalism, start with a domestic commitment to democracy but at the international level emphasize economic, social, and institutional interactions, not the spread of democracy.[20] Other versions, such as neoliberalism, focus more exclusively on international interactions. Some realist perspectives too, such as classical realism, emphasize democracy at the domestic level but then rely primarily on balancing power at the international level to produce stability and peace. Identity perspectives reverse the causal arrows. They see ideological commitments to democracy creating the democratic peace at the international level, which in turn facilitates institutional cooperation and the reduction of military and economic competition. Thus, all mainstream perspectives support democracy. We should not bias our choice of perspectives by identifying democracy with only one of them. As Robert Keohane, a liberal scholar, suggests, we should separate our preference for democracy from our analytical perspective:

> Liberalism associates itself with a belief in the value of individual freedom. Although I subscribe to such a belief, this commitment of mine is not particularly relevant to my analysis of international relations. One could believe in the value of individual liberty and remain either a realist or neorealist in one's analysis of world politics.[21]

Let's look more closely at the key (italicized) concepts that provide the logic of the liberal perspective. (Again the concepts appear in boldface below where they are most succinctly defined.)

Reciprocity and Interdependence

From the liberal perspective, reciprocity and interdependence among states matter more than self-help (independence) and anarchy. **Reciprocity** means that states behave toward one another largely on the basis of mutual rather than individual calculations of costs and benefits. Outcomes depend not only on the choices of one state but on how those choices interact with the choices of other states. The focus on reciprocal behavior places greater emphasis on how countries communicate, negotiate, trade, and do business with one another than on how much power they have or what they believe. It also places great emphasis on compromise—swapping or logrolling objectives (for example, trading territory for peace in the Arab–Israeli dispute) or splitting the difference between objectives (drawing territorial borders halfway between what disputants claim).

Interdependence refers to the frequency and intensity with which states interact. How often states interact with and interdepend (that is, mutually depend) on one another increases the opportunities for reciprocity and, hence, cooperation. Cooperation is not automatic. It requires repetition and time to emerge. But, in the end, it is not a product of relative power or shared ideas; it is a product of the cumulative practice through which power and ideas are reshaped. How countries relate to one another changes the ways they perceive one another and use their relative power toward one another. Interactions are doing the heavy lifting, acting as primary causes changing ideas and power relationships.

reciprocity:
the behavior of states toward one another based largely on mutual exchanges that entail interdependent benefits or disadvantages.

interdependence:
the mutual dependence of states and nonstate actors in the international system through conferences, trade, tourism, and the like.

From a liberal perspective, therefore, international relations is more about *relational* (interactive) power than it is about *positional* (relative) power. Authority and hierarchy become more important than anarchy. As Professor David Lake explains,

> Because [in realism] there is no law superior to that of states themselves, there can be no authority over states in general or by one state over others. Through the lens of relational authority, however, we see that relations between states are not purely anarchic but better described as a rich variety of hierarchies in which dominant states legitimately rule over greater or lesser domains of policy in subordinate states. The assumption of international anarchy is not only ill suited to describing and explaining international politics but also can be positively misleading.[22]

Technological Change and Modernization: Nongovernmental Organizations

The imperative from the liberal perspective, then, is not to balance power but to increase interdependence. Two forces, in particular, accelerate interdependence. The first is **technological change**, the application of science and engineering to increase wealth and alter human society; think of the consequences of technological change for communications and transportation alone. The second force is **modernization**, the transformation of human society from self-contained autarchic centers of agrarian society to highly specialized and interdependent units of modern society that could not survive without coordinated exchanges at the national and now international levels.

As the liberal perspective sees it, technological change and modernization bring more and more actors into the arena of international affairs. This pluralization of global politics broadens and deepens the context of international relations. **Nongovernmental organizations (NGOs)** are nonstate actors, such as student, tourist, and professional associations, that are not subject to direct government control. They include economic actors such as MNCs, international labor unions, private regulatory bodies, and global financial markets. They also involve international humanitarian, foreign assistance, and environmental activities. In all these areas, nonstate actors expand the nongovernmental sector or **civil society** of international relations and engage in what are called **transnational relations**—that is, relations outside the direct influence of national governments and international institutions set up by governments.

According to the liberal perspective, the broadening and deepening of international relations through nonstate actors also expand and change the nature of security. International relations are no longer just about the security of states; they are also about the security of people within states. **Human security** focuses on weak actors, not just the strongest or most capable ones emphasized by the realist perspective, and is concerned with violence caused by wars and oppression within states as well as among them. Such intrastate violence includes family violence, especially against women and children; genocide; diseases; pollution; natural disasters; and large displacements of

technological change: the application of science and engineering to increase wealth and alter human society.

modernization: the transformation of human society from self-contained autarchic centers of agrarian society to highly specialized and interdependent units of modern society.

nongovernmental organizations (NGOs): nonstate actors such as student, tourist, and professional associations that are not subject to direct government control.

civil society: the nongovernmental sector.

transnational relations: relations among nongovernmental, as opposed to governmental, authorities.

human security: security concern that focuses on violence within states and at the village and local levels, particularly violence against women and minorities.

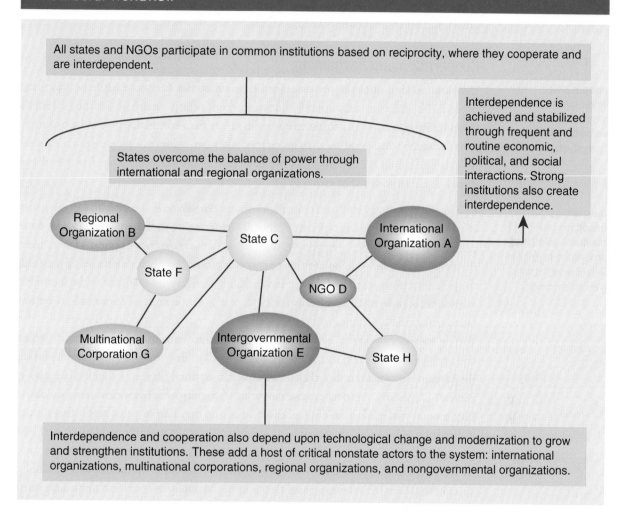

FIGURE 1-5

The Liberal Worldview

All states and NGOs participate in common institutions based on reciprocity, where they cooperate and are interdependent.

States overcome the balance of power through international and regional organizations.

Interdependence is achieved and stabilized through frequent and routine economic, political, and social interactions. Strong institutions also create interdependence.

Regional Organization B

State C

International Organization A

State F

NGO D

Multinational Corporation G

Intergovernmental Organization E

State H

Interdependence and cooperation also depend upon technological change and modernization to grow and strengthen institutions. These add a host of critical nonstate actors to the system: international organizations, multinational corporations, regional organizations, and nongovernmental organizations.

populations. Since the end of the Cold War, liberal perspectives point out, human security issues have become more prevalent than great power or traditional national security issues. Nonstate actors or NGOs play a bigger and more effective role in human security issues.

Diplomacy

Diplomacy is the business of communications, negotiations, and compromise and thus weighs big in the liberal perspective. From this perspective, talking is always better than not talking, especially with adversaries. Whatever the differences among countries, whatever their relative power or beliefs, they can profit from discussions. Discussions encourage cooperation and bargaining, which produce trade-offs and compromises. Compromise consists of splitting the difference between interests in an issue area, while

diplomacy: discussions and negotiations among states as emphasized by the liberal perspective.

trade-offs involve the swapping of interests in one issue area for interests in a second. To reach arms control agreement with the Soviet Union, for example, the United States backed off its interest in promoting human rights in the Soviet Union. An identity perspective, which emphasizes values over institutions and power, might oppose this type of compromise, whereas a liberal perspective, which emphasizes cooperation over power and ideas, might approve it.

Cooperation and Bargaining

cooperation:
working to achieve a better outcome for some that does not hurt others.

Cooperation facilitates the provision of better outcomes for some while not harming others. The idea is to focus on absolute gains, not relative gains. As in the prisoner's dilemma story, if countries focus on common rather than conflicting goals (the prisoners frustrating the warden rather than going free), they can achieve non-zero-sum outcomes in which all gain. One country does not have to win and the other lose. The overall pie grows, and everyone's slice grows in absolute terms.

bargaining:
negotiating to distribute gains that are zero-sum (that is, what one side gains, the other loses).

Of course, one country may gain more than another. **Bargaining** is necessary to sort out issues of relative gains. Liberal perspectives generally assume that such bargaining can be done peacefully. From a liberal perspective, war is always the most costly option. Hence, given the chance, countries will look for lower-cost ways to resolve their differences. If they fail, the primary causes are to be found in the bargaining process (liberal), not in the inevitable constraints of power balances (realist) or types of regimes (identity). For example, countries fail to make credible commitments to signal their interests and intentions, they misread the shifting balance of power, they bluff, or they have inadequate information about the other country's intentions. They are not compelled (caused) to do these things by factors outside the bargaining context; rather, they make less-than-optimal choices within the bargaining context. Bargaining approaches raise questions of cognitive bias as well as miscalculation. Leaders may make less-than-optimal choices because they harbor prior beliefs that distort information or because they are paranoid and psychologically unstable. Saddam Hussein, for example, failed to signal credibly that he had no weapons of mass destruction either because he worried about exposing his weakness to Iran or domestic opponents or because he thought the United States was a paper tiger and would not intervene.[23] Such impediments to rational bargaining may be handled best by psychological theories (see the later discussion).

Collective Goods

collective goods:
benefits, such as clean air, that are indivisible (they exist for all or for none) and cannot be appropriated (their consumption by one party does not diminish their consumption by another).

Cooperation also facilitates the provision of collective goods. **Collective goods** have two properties: they are indivisible (they exist for everyone or for no one) and they cannot be appropriated (they do not diminish as one party consumes them). The classic example of a collective good is clean air. It exists either for everyone or for no one. And breathing by one person does not diminish the air available for another person. The prevention of global warming is another example. It will be accomplished for all countries or for none. And if the benefits of preventing global warming are enjoyed by one country, that does not subtract from the benefits available to other countries.

The liberal perspective sees peace and security in large part as collective goods, especially in today's nuclear and globalized world. If peace and security exist for one member of a society, they exist for all members, because the use of nuclear weapons would destroy peace for everyone; and the benefits to one member do not diminish the amount of peace and security available to other members. **Collective security** does just what it says—it collects military power together in a single global institution, such as the United Nations, that provides peace and security for all countries at the international level, just as national governments do for all citizens at the domestic level. This global institution sets up rules that states must follow to resolve disagreements and then creates a preponderance of power, a pooling of the military power of all nations, not a balance of power among separate nations, to punish aggressors who violate the rules. Because the global institution monopolizes military power, it can reduce military weaponry to a minimum. Arms control and disarmament play a big role in the liberal perspective, just as the opposite dynamics of mutual armament and competitive arms races play a key role in the realist perspective. Collective security becomes an alternative way to organize military power compared to the balance of power.

collective security: the establishment of common institutions and rules among states to settle disputes peacefully and to enforce agreements by a preponderance, not a balance, of power.

Wealth is another collective good. It is not quite as pure a collective good as clean air because it may be appropriated and consumed unequally by one party compared to another, and, unlike air, does not exist in infinite supply. But the liberal concept of comparative advantage and trade, which we examine in detail in Chapter 8, makes it possible to increase wealth overall and therefore, at least theoretically, increase it for each individual or country, although some individuals and countries may gain more than others. Trade is a classic non-zero-sum relationship in which two parties can produce more goods from the same resources if they specialize and exchange products than if they produce all goods separately. The liberal perspective emphasizes such absolute rather than relative gains because these relationships shift the focus away from conflicting goals and demonstrate that, even under conditions of anarchy, cooperation is not only possible but profitable.

International Institutions

The liberal perspective sees the pursuit of diplomacy, cooperation, bargaining, and collective goods as culminating in international institutions. **International institutions** include **intergovernmental organizations (IGOs)** as well as NGOs. IGOs are set up by national governments (hence the label *intergovernmental*) to increase efficiency and control. They help states lower transaction costs, the extra costs involved in managing interactions over longer and longer distances. Unlike trade among village neighbors, international trade takes place between strangers separated by wide distances. IGOs develop and spread information to help determine prices and settle contracts. Greater information reduces asymmetries in the bargaining process generated by secrecy, uncertainty, and miscommunications and misperceptions.

international institutions: formal international organizations and informal regimes that establish common rules to regularize international contacts and communications.

intergovernmental organizations (IGOs): formal international organizations established by governments.

global governance: the system of various international institutions and great powers groups that in a loose sense govern the global system.

Governments create international institutions to serve their common interests, defined as areas where their national interests overlap. But once these institutions exist, they take on a life of their own and constitute a system of **global governance**, or network of IGOs, that may override national interests and make up a kind of nascent world government. In some cases, these institutions make decisions and undertake activities that compromise national interests or supersede them by defining and implementing broader supranational interests, as in the European Union. To the extent that such institutions are not completely under the control of national governments, they become quasi-independent actors in the international system.

Institutions do not always arise by design; trade relationships, for example, cluster into markets, and diplomatic treaties and conferences form a body of international law. Nor do institutions always coincide with physical organizations. For example, global financial relationships are regularized but not incorporated in any overarching organization. The International Monetary Fund (IMF) affects only a small part of global finance; commercial banks and private investment houses provide the bulk of international finance. Yet global finance depends on common rules. The annual economic summits held by the major industrialized countries (Group of 8, or G-8) and now also those held by industrialized and emerging market countries (G-20) represent another type of institution without specific central organization. A network of institutions come together to form an **international regime** that creates a set of rules, norms, and procedures around which the expectations of actors converge in a particular issue area, such as finance or trade policy.[24] The United Nations, for example, might be considered an international institution for the purpose of dispatching peacekeeping forces to manage ethnic conflicts, but the International Atomic Energy Agency, a UN body, might be part of an international regime to stop the spread of nuclear weapons, along with U.S.–Russian bilateral agreements and the Proliferation Security Initiative, an independent multinational effort to interdict nuclear materials and equipment on the high seas.

international regime: a network of international institutions or groups not under the authority of a single organization.

path dependence: a process emphasized by liberal perspectives in which decisions in a particular direction affect later decisions, accumulating advantages or disadvantages along a certain path.

International institutions evolve through feedback and **path dependence**, a process in which later outcomes are shaped by previous outcomes and unintended consequences. Institutions grow through feedback, reinforcement, and learning.[25] This does not always lead to progressive outcomes.[26] It can also lead to the last move or defection. As we discuss in Chapter 2, that may have happened in the case of World War I. War in this case is accidental and can be avoided the next time by better understanding the path of interactions.

A prominent example of path dependence, institutional learning, and growth is provided by the European Union. When European integration was launched, the founders insisted on creating one organization that would focus not on national but on community-wide interests; that was the European Commission. As we learn in Chapter 6, it is the only institution in the EU that has the right to initiate legislation independently. The idea was that individual states would be forced to react to community needs and, in this reciprocal process, would get used to taking into account community as well as national needs. In time, they might begin to think differently about their own needs and identify more with the European Union.

Thus, like the European Union, international institutions alter the relationships through which people interact and pursue common interests. Through repeated interactions, participants acquire different habits and change their perceptions as they exchange better information and their trust in one another increases. They get caught in the labyrinth of cooperation and can't get out or remember the original purposes (entrance) for which they started the process. As Professor John Ikenberry writes, "Conflicts would be captured and domesticated in an iron cage of multilateral rules, standards, safeguards, and dispute resolution procedures."[27] Over the longer run, countries may even change their material interests and identities. Notice how, in this case, process influences thinking and eventually loyalty. States identify with supranational rather than national goals. Eventually they identify more with Europe than with France or Germany. But identities are not the cause of this development; they are the result. Habitual and routine contacts do the heavy lifting in the liberal perspective and cause material power and self-images to adapt. The liberal perspective does not ignore power or identity; it just concludes that these variables are shaped more by institutions than institutions are shaped by them. The direction of the causal arrows that originate in institutions distinguishes the liberal perspective from realist and identity perspectives.

International Law

International regimes and institutions create **international law,** the customary rules and codified treaties under which international organizations operate. International law covers political, economic, and social rights. Historically it developed to protect the interests of states and the rights of sovereignty and self-defense. Increasingly, however, it addresses the rights of citizens and individual human beings to protection from mistreatment and the responsibility of international institutions to intervene in sovereign affairs to prevent genocide, starvation, and the like. **Human rights** involve the most basic protections against physical abuse and suffering. International law and human rights are more controversial than national law. Democratic countries emphasize how the law is made by free institutions and champion political and human rights. Nondemocratic countries emphasize how the law is enforced and, in the case of socialist countries, champion economic and social rights. But the liberal perspective argues that the more treaties and international law there are, the better, because states are acquiring the habit of obeying central norms and guidelines and will eventually move toward greater consensus on the making and enforcement of law.

From the liberal perspective, the essence of international law is **multilateralism,** to include all actors, often nonstate participants as well, and to encourage compromise regardless of the ideologies or beliefs participants hold. All countries and points of view are respected. Tolerance and coexistence are the most important virtues. As Michael Steiner, a UN representative in Kosovo, has argued, "The United Nations wields unique moral authority *because* its members represent a wide spectrum of values and political

international law: the customary rules and codified treaties under which international organizations operate; covers political, economic, and social rights.

human rights: rights concerning the most basic protections against human physical abuse and suffering.

multilateralism: the inclusion of all states in international diplomacy.

systems. Most of the world trusts the United Nations more than it trusts any single member or alliance, . . . not because of the inherent virtue of any individual member but because the United Nations' temporizing influence imposes a healthy discipline on its members."[28] Notice how **legitimacy,** or the right to use power in international affairs, derives from participation by actors of widely differing values in a common universal system, not from any specific actor's values, such as democracy. There is an implicit faith that participants will learn from one another and that, whatever results emerge, all participants will be better off. Diplomacy ultimately produces the same outcome as trade: everyone gains.

legitimacy: the right to use power in international affairs.

In many situations, according to the liberal perspective, international institutions, regimes, law, and diplomacy become the most important facts determining outcomes. They are the independent variables that cause other events (the dependent variables) to occur. Over time, international actors may gradually become more important than states.

≫ The Identity Perspective

The identity perspective is more interested in the ideas that guide institutions and the use of power than it is in the influence of institutions and power on ideas. *Ideas* define the *values, norms,* and *beliefs* that governments and international institutions hold and for which they pursue and apply power. Taken together, these ideas define or construct the *identities* of actors, and these identities in turn interpret or give meaning to the material capabilities (realist) and institutional interactions (liberal) of actors. Interests are not defined just by anarchy or geopolitical circumstances, as the realist perspective highlights, or by institutional relationships and rules, as the liberal perspective argues. They are also defined by independent and collective identities.

How are identities constructed? Just as anarchy is a key concept in the realist perspective and reciprocity is a key concept in the liberal perspective, *construction of identities* is a key concept in the identity perspective. Identities are not given or exogenous—that is, taken for granted—as in realist or liberal perspectives, but are themselves aspects of reality that have to be accounted for. Realist and liberal perspectives spend little time worrying about how the identities of states come about or whether states develop friendly or adversarial self-images of one another. Whatever the identities are, actors behave mostly in response to interests, interactions, and institutions (liberal) or fixed conditions of anarchy (realist). Identity perspectives, by contrast, focus on how actors acquire identities, which shape interests, interactions, and institutions and change material circumstances. Identities, in short, cause or give meaning to institutional and material realities. Interests are defined by beliefs, not by relative power or reciprocal bargaining. Power and institutions are not objective but subjective or intersubjective realities. They have no meaning on their own; their meaning depends on the interpretations that actors (subjects) confer on them.

For some identity perspectives, identities are collective or shared, not autonomous and individual, and can be constructed only through repetitive social interactions.

FIGURE
1-6

The Identity Worldview

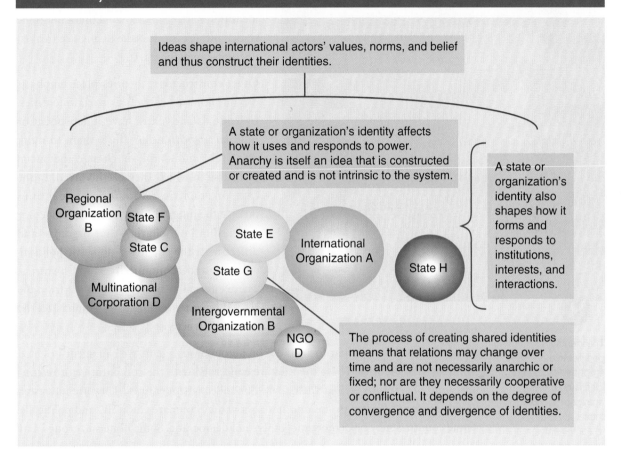

Ideas shape international actors' values, norms, and belief and thus construct their identities.

A state or organization's identity affects how it uses and responds to power. Anarchy is itself an idea that is constructed or created and is not intrinsic to the system.

A state or organization's identity also shapes how it forms and responds to institutions, interests, and interactions.

Regional Organization B

State F

State C

State E

International Organization A

State G

State H

Multinational Corporation D

Intergovernmental Organization B

NGO D

The process of creating shared identities means that relations may change over time and are not necessarily anarchic or fixed; nor are they necessarily cooperative or conflictual. It depends on the degree of convergence and divergence of identities.

Different colors represent separate identities.
Different size circles represent different amounts of power.

Known as *social constructivism,* this constructivist theory sees identities emerging from *communicative action,* social discourse, and the shared knowledge that participants develop. Actors engage in speech acts, essentially substantive communications, to determine what is factual—so-called truth claims—and seek to influence, persuade, and learn from one another.[29] In this process, they shape *shared identities* that define them and their counterparts. Thus, social constructivists argue that anarchy in international affairs is not a fixed material condition. Rather, *anarchy is what states make of it,* meaning states' behavior is not defined by the position states hold in the relative distribution of power or by reciprocal interactions in international institutions but, instead, by the shared or external identities they construct. These identities may be adversarial and distrustful, or they may be friendly and cooperative. In contrast to realist perspectives, identity perspectives see

The identity perspective emphasizes shared ideas and truthful opinions, such as those, according to some analysts, exchanged between Ronald Reagan and Mikhail Gorbachev while they were in office in the 1980s. They are shown here later, in 1992, upon the arrival of Gorbachev and his wife, Raisa, for a two-week tour of the United States.

states as shaping anarchy and institutions, not just responding to them. And in contrast to the liberal perspective, identity perspectives view states as focusing on the content, not just the process, of communications. Words and identities matter and are sometimes not to be traded off just for the sake of alliance (realist) or compromise (liberal).

Other constructivist theories place emphasis on autonomous as well as social identities. Individuals and states have independent or *internal identities* that allow them to think creatively and shape or change the social discourse in which they are involved. In the case of countries, autonomous identities involve the internal ideas, such as democracy or Muslim law (sharia), that organize and differentiate the countries' domestic political, cultural, and economic lives and histories. These internal identities are distinct from the shared or *external identities* emphasized by social constructivists.

Constructivist theories that focus more on autonomous agents we call agent-oriented constructivist theories. These theories are concerned with the comparative or *relative identities* of actors as well as their shared or collectivist identities. They are interested in the different types of groups and states, how they compare culturally and politically. Some countries may be democratic, others nondemocratic. Some domestic groups may be liberal, others conservative. At the domestic and transnational levels of analysis, these actors interact based on their relative similarities and differences, or the "ideological distance" between them.[30] Before World War II, for example, communist parties in France preferred to cooperate with the Soviet Union, which was also communist, while conservative parties in France preferred to cooperate with Italy, which was fascist. The split made it difficult for France to cooperate with either the Soviet Union or Italy (see Chapter 3). At the systemic level of analysis, similarities and differences of identity aggregate to form a *distribution of relative identities*. Relative identities, not relative power or institutional roles, determine whether countries behave as friends, rivals, or enemies toward one another. Converging relative identities create a common international culture that moderates behavior.[31] The Christian monarchs of eighteenth-century Europe shared both religious and political similarities that moderated the balance of power. Diverging relative identities create more competitive balances of power. The more dissimilar fascist, communist, and liberal governments of Europe in the 1930s pursued a more virulent balance of power.

Identity perspectives may include other approaches that emphasize ideas but are less concerned with the construction of identities. Briefly, we consider studies that focus on *soft power, belief systems, psychology,* and *gender (feminism).* Thus, identity perspectives come in multiple variations, just like realist and liberal perspectives.

Once again, we explore the concepts italicized above in the subsections that follow. (The terms are in boldface where they are most clearly defined.)

Ideas and the Construction of Identities

Ideas come in many forms. **Values** reflect deep moral convictions, such as individual freedom and equality. **Norms** guide how groups and states interact and what they jointly prefer; there are procedural or regulatory norms, such as sovereignty, and substantive norms, such as human rights. **Beliefs** constitute comprehensive views about how the world works, such as communist or capitalist ideologies. Ideas, norms, values, and beliefs are not physical entities, as capabilities and some institutions are. We cannot touch sovereignty the way we can a tank or a building. But it is still real. Sovereignty exerts a powerful influence on international behavior and outcomes. Other ideas do so as well. Democracy, capitalism, fascism, and human rights—all play powerful roles in shaping history and international affairs.

Idealists—those who emphasize ideas over material realities—have always argued that ideas matter. Fifty years ago, idealism and realism were the two main schools of thought in international studies. Idealism posited the notion that reasoning or ideas preceded and could be made to shape specific realities. After the horrendous destruction of World War I, idealism was popular. The "passionate desire to prevent war" contributed to the idea of a League of Nations. This idea, President Woodrow Wilson said, "must be made to work."[32] The idea, of course, did not work—or, some would say, was never implemented—because the United States never joined the League. The failure of the League and the disastrous results of World War II discredited idealism. Realism became the preeminent theory of international relations. By the early 1970s, however, some scholars "became increasingly concerned that the postwar aversion to idealism . . . had gone too far [and] . . . was responsible for the discipline's poor grasp of the role of ideational factors of all kinds in international life—be they collective identities, norms, aspirations, ideologies, or ideas about cause-effect relations."[33]

Two decades later, **constructivism** emerged as an approach to international relations that revived the primary causal or constitutive role of ideas. It argues that actors behave on the basis of how they identify themselves and others. The **construction of identities** involves a process of discourse by which actors define who they are and how they behave toward one another. This approach follows in the idealist tradition because it is ideational, seeing ideas as more influential causes than institutions or power. But it also emphasizes cumulative practices such as repetitive communications. These practices are not primarily procedural, however, as the liberal perspective emphasizes. Rather, they are verbal practices or substantive narratives to substantiate and construct identities. Such

values: ideas that express deep moral convictions.

norms: ideas that govern the procedural or substantive terms of state behavior, such as reciprocity and human rights.

beliefs: ideas about how the world works as emphasized by identity perspectives.

constructivism: a perspective that emphasizes ideas, such as the content of language and social discourse, over institutions or power.

construction of identities: a process of discourse by which actors define who they are and how they behave toward one another.

verbal practices constitute who the actors actually are, which in turn defines how they express their interests, whether in terms of power or reciprocity, and how those interests play out through institutional processes.

Some political scientists do not consider constructivism to be a perspective on the same level as the realist or liberal perspectives.[34] They see it as a method, not as a perspective. As discussed in the introduction to this volume, the realist and liberal perspectives rely primarily on causal reasoning: *X* causes *Y*. Many constructivist approaches rely on constitutive reasoning: *X* and *Y* constitute or mutually cause one another rather than one factor causing the other sequentially. In constitutive reasoning, causes emerge from cumulative practices and narratives, not from independent and sequential events.

But other constructivists consider their approach to be a theory. They seek to explain and interpret events. They don't try to predict specific outcomes by a logic of consequences: *Y* is a consequence of *X*. They seek, instead, to elucidate structures of discourse that make certain events possible by a logic of appropriateness. An event occurs because it fits a particular narrative, not because it is caused by a specific preceding event. Today, for example, it is considered increasingly appropriate that when countries intervene to protect human rights, they do so multilaterally.[35] No specific event caused this fact, but one hundred years ago unilateral intervention was much more common. Similarly, constructivists do not try to predict the future in terms of one event causing another. Instead, they project future scenarios that make certain outcomes possible and plausible.

In this book, we treat constructivism as a perspective equivalent to the realist and liberal perspectives. Constructivism comes in different varieties, as we explore next: social constructivism and a more individualistic or agent-oriented constructivism. And we include constructivism under the still broader identity perspective because it is only one of several approaches, along with studies of philosophy and psychology, that give priority to what people and countries say and believe and, hence, to the ideas by which they define themselves and act.

Constructivism

Ideas play the dominant role in constructivism, but they operate at different levels of analysis in the two types of constructivism. Social constructivism operates at the system structural level, what Professor Alexander Wendt, one of the fathers of social constructivism in international affairs, calls "structural idealism." The joint dialogue, not individual participants, shapes and changes identities. Agent-oriented constructivism operates more at the domestic and individual levels of analysis, where an individual or group can come up with ideas based on internal reflection and imagination and change the external social discourse.

Social constructivism stresses social or collective identity formation. According to Wendt, "Structures of human association are determined primarily by shared ideas rather than material forces," and these ideas are social—that is, not reducible to individuals.[36] Thus, as noted in the introduction, the master and the slave are defined by their relationship;

social constructivism: an identity perspective in which states and other actors acquire their identities from intersubjective discourses in which they know who they are only by reference to others.

one cannot be recognized without the other. Similarly, states recognize one another only by association. A state does not exist separately in an objective condition of anarchy, as realist perspectives argue, but defines the condition of anarchy by subjective or intersubjective dialogue with other states. This dialogue between states creates structural social categories, such as friends or enemies, that cannot be reduced to the existence of two or more separate states. States, in short, construct anarchy.

Agent-oriented constructivism allows for greater influence on the part of independent actors. As Professor Thomas Risse tells us, actors "are not simply puppets of social structure" but "can actively challenge the validity claims inherent in any **communicative action**."[37] Through "pure speech acts," meaning a discourse free of material power or institutional constraints, actors persuade one another that their ideas are valid. They change their interpretations of reality by a logic of argumentation, not a logic of appropriateness, as social constructivists argue, or a logic of consequences, as realist and liberal perspectives argue.

Some constructivist accounts see this happening at the end of the Cold War, when Mikhail Gorbachev changed his mind in the middle of a meeting about German membership in NATO after being persuaded by the arguments of other participants. In this case, according to constructivists, negotiations between the Soviet Union and Western countries were not just instrumental in the sense that they facilitated a compromise of interests. Compromise would have probably meant reunifying Germany, the Western preference, but keeping it neutral, the Soviet preference. Instead, Germany was reunited and stayed in NATO. Gorbachev changed his mind on the spot and accepted a united Germany in NATO because he no longer saw NATO as an enemy and believed that Germany had the right to make alliance decisions for itself.[38] A logic of argumentation and persuasion prevailed over a negotiating logic emphasized by liberal perspectives.

Anarchy Is What States Make of It

Thus ideational structures and agents interact continuously to shape international realities. Anarchy, or the decentralized distribution of power, is not a given or fixed. States define it depending on how they think about and engage rhetorically with other states. If we learn to see one another as friends, we act one way; if we see one another as enemies, we act another way. Hence, in challenging the realist and liberal perspectives, social constructivists argue that "anarchy is what states make of it."[39] International relations can be either competitive and full of conflict, as the realist perspective contends, or cooperative and institutionalized, as the liberal perspective argues. It depends, says the social constructivist, on how the actors imagine or construct these relations socially. In short, it depends on shared and collective identities.

Social constructivists emphasize the shared or social elements of communications and identity. For some, such as Professor Wendt, almost all identity is collective or shared, not autonomous or sovereign. These constructivists speak of "ideas all the way down,"

agent-oriented constructivism: an identity perspective that allows for greater influence on the part of independent actors in shaping identities.

communicative action: an exchange of ideas free of material and institutional influence to establish validity claims.

meaning that there is little role for autonomous contributions by separate individuals or states. Notice here how the causal arrows run between levels of analysis as well as between perspectives. In social constructivism, the structural level dominates over the domestic and individual levels. States and all actors constitute their identities socially, not individually. A state's **external identity** is primary. This external identity is a function of historical dialogue and interaction with other countries, shaping images through trade, alliances, and other international associations. For many years, France and Germany shared a history of enmity and war. Over the past sixty years, however, they developed another history of friendship and peaceful integration. Crucial to this convergence was the evolution of common democratic self-images and of external associations with one another and other democracies, such as the United States, as they aligned to confront the totalitarian Soviet Union.

external identity: the identity of a country that is determined by its historical and external dialogue with other states.

Relative Identities

More agent-oriented constructivists emphasize the separate or individualistic, not just social, aspects of identity. They insist that "actors' domestic identities are crucial for their perceptions of one another in the international arena."[40] After World War II, for example, the Soviet Union insisted that eastern European countries be communist internally, not just allies externally. The Soviet Union did not see these countries as friends unless they had domestic identities similar to its own. As Michael Barnett observes, "States apparently attempt to predict a state's external behavior based on its internal arrangements."[41] In other words, independent domestic identities influence the way states perceive one another and socially construct their external identities. This independent or **internal identity** of states creates different types of regimes, which converge or diverge in terms of their domestic experience and national memory.

internal identity: the identity of a country that derives from its unique national self-reflection and memory.

Professor John Owen shows, for example, how domestic identities influence the historical behavior of states as much as power balances and institutional evolution. States intervene to change the domestic regimes in other states, not just to balance power or expand trade with them. Historically, there have been four waves of forcible regime intervention reflecting ideological polarization and conflict in the system: the conflict between Catholicism and Protestantism set off by the Reformation; the conflict among republicanism, constitutional monarchy, and absolute monarchy set off by the French Revolution; the conflict among communism, fascism, and liberalism set off by World Wars I and II and the Cold War; and today, according to some analysts, the conflict among Christian, Muslim, Confucian, and other civilizations and between secular and religious worldviews.[42]

These internal ideas or identities of states differ, and the "ideological distance" between identities may create a threat, either because one state fears that the other's ideology may spread or because the ideologies of the states impose impediments to their communicating with one another.[43] Thus, after World War II, France and Britain did not see the United States as threatening because they shared a democratic ideology with it, even though the United States was very powerful and American troops were stationed on their soil. On the other hand, they did see the Soviet Union as threatening because its domestic identity was different, even though Soviet forces were not physically located on their territory.

Actors therefore have both internal and external identities, one shaped by discourses at home and the other by discourses in the international arena. As Professor Peter Katzenstein concludes, "The identities of states emerge from their interactions with different social environments, both domestic and international."[44] Individuals and nations reflect critically on their experiences and come up with new ideas that society has never known before. That's how the slave stops being a slave or the master a master. Someone in society comes up with an alternative idea about the relationship. Even if the alternative ideas are ultimately also social, they have to originate somewhere. For example, Gorbachev allegedly got his idea that NATO was no longer an enemy from peace research institutes in western Europe.[45] Social constructivists would say such ideas originate in repetitive social practices; more individualistic constructivists insist on tracing them back to agents, norm entrepreneurs or self-reflective individuals, and their capacity for critical thinking and independence.[46]

Distribution of Identities

Just as the realist perspective focuses on the distribution of power and the liberal perspective highlights the division of organizational roles and specialties, the identity perspective emphasizes the **distribution of identities**. This distribution of identities includes both internal and external identities.

These identities distribute themselves across the international system to establish relative and shared identities among actors. They define the "ideological polarity" of the system, the number of separate ideological poles in the system (analogous to poles of power in the realist perspective). At one level, **relative identities** position actors' self-images with respect to one another as similar or dissimilar, just as relative power positions actors' capabilities with respect to one another as bigger or smaller. But at a higher level, identities overlap and fuse to constitute **shared identities**, or norms and images that cannot be traced back to specific identities or their interrelationships. The degree of convergence or divergence of identities defines the prospects of cooperation and conflict. Professor Alastair Iain Johnston explains:

> The greater the perceived identity difference, the more the environment is viewed as conflictual, the more the out-group is viewed as threatening, and the more that realpolitik strategies are considered effective. Conversely, the smaller the perceived identity difference, the more the external environment is seen as cooperative, the less the out-group is perceived as fundamentally threatening, and the more efficacious are cooperative strategies. Most critically, variation in identity difference should be independent of anarchy.[47]

distribution of identities: the relative relationship of identities among actors in the international system in terms of their similarities and differences.

relative identities: identities that position actors' self-images with respect to one another as similar or dissimilar.

shared identities: identities that overlap and fuse based on norms and images that cannot be traced back to specific identities or their interrelationships.

epistemic communities: communities of individuals or countries that share a broad base of common knowledge and trust.

Some constructivist theories speak about **epistemic communities** among individuals or countries that share a broad base of common knowledge and exhibit a great deal of common trust and purpose. One such community among states may be the security community that prevails among democratic states known as the democratic peace (discussed later in this chapter).[48] Another may be the community of scientific experts that cuts across national bureaucracies and defines a secular worldview for solving the world's problems.[49]

Mapping Identities

Table 1-7 offers one example of how we might map the convergence or divergence of relative and shared national identities. In this example, the internal dimension of identity is measured in terms of domestic political ideologies, whether countries are democratic or not. In other examples, it might be measured in terms of cultural or religious similarities and differences. The external dimension of identity is measured in terms of how cooperative or conflictual historical relations have been among the countries. Again, in other cases, it might be measured in terms of trade or common membership in international organizations. Identity is multifaceted, so measuring it, at least in rationalist studies, presents difficulties.

Based on Table 1-7, countries that have strong democracies and historically close relations, such as the United States, France, the United Kingdom, and Canada, cluster in the upper left-hand box. In this box, identities converge so strongly they take on a collective character and common culture that we call the democratic peace. As discussed in the next section, strong democracies, even though they remain separate, seem to escape anarchy altogether and do not go to war with one another. In the lower left-hand and

TABLE 1-7

Relative and Shared National Identities

		Internal dimension of identity (measured in terms of political ideologies)	
		Democracy	**Nondemocracy**
External dimension of identity (measured in terms of historical memories)	**Cooperative**	Strongest convergence: U.S.–UK U.S.–Canada U.S.–France	Weak convergence: U.S.–China (Cold War) U.S.–Russia (today?)
	Conflictual	Strong convergence: France–Germany U.S.–Japan	Weakest convergence: U.S.–China (today?) U.S.–Russia (Cold War)

upper right-hand boxes, countries converge on one dimension of identity but diverge on the other. For example, in the lower left-hand box, France and Germany, and the United States and Japan are now strong democracies, but they have been enemies of one another more recently than have the United States, United Kingdom, France, and Canada. Given that history, their relationships with one another may not be as strong or as intimate as those of countries in the upper left-hand box. Similarly, in the upper right-hand box, China during the Cold War was not a democracy like the United States, but China did have friendly historical ties with the United States before it became communist, and after it became communist it worked closely with the United States against the Soviet Union in the later stages of the Cold War. In the lower right-hand box, countries diverge on both dimensions of identity, and the common culture is weakest. This box constitutes the situation of anarchy, such as that characterizing U.S.–Soviet relations during the Cold War and, as some might argue, U.S.–Chinese relations today.

Democratic Peace

A powerful example of how identities influence international relations is provided by the phenomenon of the democratic peace. Studies show that as countries become stronger and stronger democracies, they appear to escape the security dilemma. They do not go to war with one another or engage in military threats. If this behavior is a result of converging or shared democratic identities, it suggests the importance of looking at identities as well as at power and institutions. It may be that other shared identities— for example, between Muslim states or fascist states—also produce behavior different from what would be predicted from liberal or realist perspectives. As Professor Michael Barnett observes, "A community of Saddam Husseins is unlikely to father a secure environment, while a community of Mahatma Gandhis will encourage all to leave their homes unlocked."[50]

We refer to the democratic peace several times in the following chapters. It was a key factor that played into the "end of history" debate and President Bill Clinton's policies of democratic enlargement as the Cold War ended, and it showed up again in President George W. Bush's thinking about his Greater Middle East Democratic Initiative. Studies of the democratic peace are complex and ongoing, but they offer us a great way to see how different perspectives and levels of analysis influence our thinking about international relations. So, in the conclusion to this text, we use the democratic peace as an example to summarize and pull together the various concepts developed throughout this book. We'll see that it's not completely clear that democracy or ideas cause the phenomenon of peace. The cause could be economic relationships, contract or bargaining factors, or alliance legacies. And if it is democracy, it's not clear exactly what it is about democracy that is most important: institutions, civil liberties, elections, or something else. Social science research is always burdened by questions of how the causal arrows run between perspectives and levels of analysis and whether we can even establish causality at all or have to settle for constitutive narratives or critical theories that consider all understanding as historically bound.

Other Identity Approaches

Other identity approaches emphasize the causal role of ideas but are less concerned with how ideas construct identities. Some scholars might not include these approaches under identity perspectives. But remember that identity perspectives share one big thing in common—they focus on the causal or constitutive role of ideas more than the causal role of institutions or power. In this sense, the approaches described below are identity perspectives.

soft power: the attractiveness of the values or ideas of a country as distinct from its military and economic power or its negotiating behavior.

Professor Joseph Nye has popularized the concept of **soft power**, by which he means the attractiveness of the values or ideas of a country as distinct from its military and economic power or its negotiating behavior.[51] Countries influence one another not so much by force (the realist perspective) or compromise (the liberal perspective), but, often, by just being who they are and attracting other countries to accept their policies through the magnetism of their values and moral standards. A good example may be the way the prospect of membership in the democratic communities of the European Union and NATO encouraged the countries of eastern Europe and the former Soviet bloc to reform their domestic systems—military, economic, and political institutions—to meet the ideological requirements of joining the EU and NATO (such as civilian control of the military). While this process involved lots of negotiations to modify regulations and institutions, it may have been motivated in the first instance by the attractiveness of the values and institutions of the western democratic countries. The negotiations did not split the difference between eastern European and western regulations; rather, they moved the former communist countries decisively toward the standards of the western democracies. All the prospective members, for example, had to privatize industries and create mixed markets where previously state firms dominated. Relative identities converged and shared identities deepened, all toward democratic ideals, not communist or socialist ones.

belief systems: ideas about how the world works that influence the behavior of policy makers.

Still other identity studies focus on countries' **belief systems** and worldviews as ideas that influence their behavior as much as do power and institutions.[52] In this case, ideas do not cause or constitute identities, which then cause behavior, but, instead, suggest to leaders how the world works and point them in particular policy directions. Leaders embrace certain ideas as "road maps" telling them, for example, what causes prosperity, such as free-market economic policies. Or they conclude agreements that elevate certain ideas as focal points to help interpret issues when multiple outcomes are possible, such as the principle of mutual recognition that facilitated the creation of a single European market under the then European Community (more in Chapter 6). Or institutions themselves embody ideas that regulate state behavior, such as the laws of the European Union, which any state seeking EU membership must adopt. Ideas, in short, are pervasive throughout the international system, and they are not just reflections of material and institutional power. Rather, they guide or, in some cases, alter the use of power and institutions.

psychological studies: studies that emphasize ideas that define actor personalities, although the ideas may not be conscious but subconscious and sometimes irrational.

Finally, **psychological studies** of international affairs emphasize ideas that define actor personalities, although the ideas in this case may not be conscious but subconscious and sometimes irrational. Many psychological studies focus on cognitive or rational factors that emphasize the many ways in which our perceptions may mislead us.[53] Two leaders in the same situation may act differently not because they have different information but because they process the same information differently. One may associate a piece of information about the behavior of another state with a generally favorable view of that state and discount any possibility that the behavior indicated hostile intent. The second leader, with a different view of the other state, may be inclined to view the behavior as hostile. Psychologically, we like our views of others to be consistent, and we tend to avoid what psychologists call cognitive dissonance. Thus, in 1941, Stalin refused to believe British warnings that Hitler was preparing to attack Russia because Russia had just signed a nonaggression pact with Germany and the idea that Germany would attack Russia was inconsistent with Stalin's broader view of Germany.

Psychological factors may also explain why some actors behave like defensive realists while others behave like offensive realists. Defensive realists, for psychological reasons, fear losses more than they value gains; hence, they settle for security rather than conquest. Offensive realists do the reverse.[54] Other psychological studies focus on personality development and subconscious factors. Leaders had different formative experiences as children or young adults. Hitler and Stalin had abusive parents, and even Woodrow Wilson, some argue, was constantly trying to counter feelings of inadequacy branded into him as a child. There is also the psychological phenomenon known as groupthink, in which a group of decision makers reinforce a single way of thinking about a problem and rule out alternatives because they want to remain part of the group.

Feminism

Feminism is another important identity-based perspective on international relations. It focuses on gender as the primary determinant of an actor's identity. It argues that the field of international relations has been dominated by men and therefore has a masculine content and form. As Professor J. Ann Tickner writes, "The discipline of international relations, as it is presently constructed, is defined in terms of everything that is not female."[55] By that she means that all mainstream perspectives, but the realist perspective in particular, place too much emphasis on military struggle and war, on sovereignty and self-help, and on environmental exploitation. Relatively, they neglect the feminine virtues of peace, community, and environmental preservation. Mainstream studies celebrate differences and disaggregation. They emphasize individualism and competition. They underplay the exploitation and abuse of natural resources. And they privilege system and statist solutions while downplaying the local and private spheres of activity, especially those where more women than men are involved, such as homemaking, child rearing, caregiving, and community service.

Feminist perspectives, and there are many, call for more attention to comprehensive rather than national security, to protecting women and children in homes where they are often exposed to domestic violence and not just safeguarding states. They emphasize the practices of mediation and reconciliation, peacemaking, and community building,

feminism: a theory that critiques international relations as a male-centered and -dominated discipline.

as well as the nurturing of trust and goodwill in the private as well as the public sector. Instead of large-scale corporate and state-run institutions, some prefer small-scale and often self-reliant and self-sufficient economic solutions that demonstrate as much concern for reproduction and preservation as they do for growth and disruptive change. They assert that states may overcome past tragedies of war and violence by recognizing that they took place in a particular time and place when women did not enjoy full equality and social justice.

Some feminist outlooks see male domination as deeply rooted in the language and culture of international affairs and may be classified as critical theory. They note how diplomacy exalts masculine and denigrates feminine attributes. Alexander Hamilton accused Thomas Jefferson of a "womanish attachment to France and a womanish sentiment against Great Britain"; Walt Whitman talked about the "manly heart" of democracy; atomic bombs were given male names, such as Little Boy and Fat Man; and success in testing the first hydrogen bomb was reported as "It's a boy" rather than "It's a girl," as if the birth of a girl implied failure. These feminist accounts see men and women as fundamentally different, in some sense biologically hardwired, and they seek a qualitative, not just quantitative, change in international life. It's not just a matter of adding a few more women to the military or diplomatic establishments; it's a matter of revolutionary change that converts a male-centered world of international affairs to the virtues of female culture.

Other feminist theories are rationalist. They seek simply equal rights and participation for women across the broad spectrum of domestic and international life. They note that women have played key roles in history since the beginning of time, and prominent women such as Cleopatra, Joan of Arc, Elizabeth I, and Catherine the Great have not so much changed the fundamental character of international relations as added to its diversity and richness. They acknowledge that men may act the way they do because of circumstances, not gender, and that once females are allowed to act in similar circumstances, they may act similarly. If women had been the hunters and men the homemakers, would there have been no conflicts over scarce food and territory? Women add talent, not magic, to human affairs. A world that subjects half its population to inferior status is a world that moves at half speed or achieves only half a loaf. Women need to be given a fair chance, and then the world will see not that women are inherently more virtuous or peace loving but that they are different and add immeasurably to the talents and treasure of the world community.

⟫ Critical Theory Perspectives

Critical theory perspectives offer broad critiques of international relations and generally advocate radical solutions such as revolution. They deny that we can study international relations by abstracting from historical circumstances and separating the observer from the particular time and period of which the observer is part. To critical theorists, all ideas, institutions, and power are historically bound and contingent. The individual, including the observer or social scientist, is never truly free, and thought as well as behavior are consequences of specific historical structures. Notice how critical theories refuse to separate ideas, power, and institutions; for them reality is a seamless web. This is also true for many constructivists who capture reality as narratives rather than as causal sequences. But critical theories do more than reconstruct the past; they also focus on the future. They look for the forces of change and evolution in history that define a future, usually more desirable, outcome. As Robert Cox, a well-known critical theorist, tells us, "Critical theory . . . contains an element of utopianism," but "its utopianism is constrained by its comprehension of historical processes."[56] Critical theory often has a teleological aspect to it; it tells us the direction in which history is moving and therefore what likely, although not certain, futures we may contemplate.

Let's look briefly at two critical theories: Marxism and postmodernism. We'll consider these theories from time to time throughout the rest of this book, especially when we examine deep material and social divisions in the contemporary international system.

Marxism

Karl Marx was a refugee from revolution in Germany when he met and collaborated in London with Friedrich Engels, another radical son of a German merchant. In 1845, Engels published a scathing critique of British industrial society, *The Condition of the Working Class in England in 1844.* In 1848, Marx and Engels together wrote *The Communist Manifesto,* and in 1867 Marx produced the first volume of his monumental work, *Das Kapital.*

Marx, whose work became known as **Marxism**, foresaw permanent revolution on behalf of the oppressed working class until the last remnants of bourgeois industrial society were destroyed and bourgeois politics and its political superstructure, the state, faded away. He based his understanding of this historical outcome on three factors: the underlying material forces shaping industrialization; the dialectic that these forces ignited between social classes, specifically between the working classes, or proletariat, manning the factories of industrialization and the managerial classes, or bourgeoisie, directing and financing industrialization; and the superstructure of states and interstate imperialism that the struggle between social classes generated. The forces of production ensured that capitalism would expand. Industrialization exploited workers by limiting their wages, in the process ensuring that new markets would have to be found because workers could not consume all of the products produced. Capitalism thus built up pressures to export surplus products and colonize other parts of the world. Here the superstructure of states and interstate competition played a role, inviting aggression and wars of imperial expansion. Wherever capitalism expanded, however, it built up its antithesis of working classes that resisted and rebelled against exploitation. Through this dialectic, the workers of the world would unite and eventually break the chains of capitalism. Capitalism would gradually give way to communism, a future state of relations in which workers would control their own lives and destinies, and the state and traditional interstate relations would wither away.

Marxism: a theory that emphasizes the dialectical or conflictual relationship between capitalist and communist states in the international system, leading to the triumph of communism, not democracy.

Marxism evolved subsequently under Vladimir Ilyich Lenin in Russia and Mao Zedong in China. Lenin saw workers or the proletariat as the vanguard in the struggle against capitalism. Mao saw peasants, not workers, in this role. Today, after the collapse of the Soviet Union and the embrace of capitalism by China, the future envisioned by Marx and his followers seems unlikely. Still, Marx's diagnosis of global economic divisions retains its relevance for many analysts, even if his solutions have been overtaken by events. Globalization, while it has created an ever-larger middle class and spread economic gains to millions over the past century, has also carved deep divisions in the world between the upper and middle classes and the poorest classes, even in developing countries such as China and India. The new information era exacerbates these inequalities with the so-called digital divide. In Chapter 10 we examine the critical theory perspective on globalization. How does one explain such persisting injustice? World systems approaches that borrow heavily from Marxism explain it in terms of country categories—core countries, such as those in the advanced world, that exploit semiperipheral (for example, the Middle East) and peripheral (for example, Africa) parts of the world. Other Marxist-related accounts, such as one developed by Antonio Gramsci, an Italian Marxist, explain it in terms of hidden social purposes that exercise a hegemonic grip on social consciousness and perpetuate material divisions.[57] Critical theorists argue that the historical dialectic that Marx discovered is still at work, spawning inequalities and tensions that increase the need for a radical restructuring of the future global system.

Postmodernism

Some critical theories argue that all attempts at knowledge involve the exercise of power, particularly of words, language, texts, and discourses. They assert that commonplace dichotomies in the study of international relations—sovereignty and anarchy, war and peace, citizen and human—mask a power structure that marginalizes many peoples. Sovereignty, for example, legitimates state power and serves the agenda of state elites while delegitimating domestic opposition by minorities, the poor, and indigenous peoples. Anarchy justifies war and imperialism, marginalizing the weak and non-Western cultures, all in the name of establishing world order and civilizing the "backward." The citizen or state is privileged over the human being or society because citizens gain authority to murder human beings, or go to war, in the name of the state. Economic modernity is portrayed as politically neutral when, in fact, it legitimates Western economic oppression.

postmodernists: theorists who seek to expose the hidden or masked meanings of language and discourse in international relations in order to gain space to imagine alternatives.

Much of this discriminatory language originates with modernization and the ascendance of Western elites to the apex of global power. Hence, critical theories that seek to unmask the rhetorical dominance of Western thought are often called postmodern. **Postmodernists** are associated with French theorists such as Jacques Derrida and Michel Foucault, who seek to expose the underlying meanings and hierarchies of power imposed by Enlightenment language and concepts.[58] They hope to find a more socially just form of discourse, and many of them hold a belief in causality, albeit a causality that is constructed rather than objective. However, other postmodernists want to go no further than to demonstrate that all social reality disguises power. They seek to deconstruct that power wherever they find it and show that all politics conceals oppression.

⫸ Levels of Analysis

Perspectives deal with the substantive content of the cause that makes something happen in international relations: power, institutions, or ideas. Levels of analysis deal with the origin of that cause: an individual, a country, or the international system as a whole. And just as we cannot describe everything of substance in the world, we also cannot describe everything from all levels of analysis. And even if we might, we would still have to decide which level to emphasize, or we would not know where to act to change the outcome. Levels of analysis interact, just as perspectives do. But the decisive question is which way the causal arrows run. Until we can say that the domestic-level forces are driving the systemic forces, we do not know that the systemic factors may not be driving the domestic ones. And if we say everything is equally important, again we have an overdetermined outcome, which means we don't know what really caused it.

The struggle for power may be the cause of war (a realist perspective). But the struggle for power may originate in the individual human being's lust for power, the aggressive characteristics of a particular state, or the uncertainties of a decentralized system of power.[59] The individual's lust for power represents an *individual* level of analysis, an aggressive or warlike state represents a *domestic* level of analysis, and the uncertainties of the balance of power represent a *systemic* level of analysis. The systemic level of analysis is often broken down further into a *process* level, involving interactions among states, and a *structural* level, involving the relative positions of states before or independent of interactions. So, for example, war may originate from the failure of alliances (a process level) or the relative rise of a new power (a structural level).

There are, of course, unlimited numbers of levels between these three primary ones. A *regional* level falls between the systemic and domestic levels. For example, a cause may originate in the way power is exercised within the European Union rather than within a single state or the global system as a whole. Another intermediate level, as we see in the following, is the *foreign policy* level of analysis. A leader tries to maneuver between the struggle for power among partisan groups domestically and the struggle among powerful countries internationally. In all these examples, the substance of the cause is the same—namely, power—but in each case the cause comes from a different level of analysis. Can we conclude that causes from all these levels matter? Sure, but which level matters most? If the individual level is more important than the domestic level, we might change the leader; but if the domestic or systemic level is more important, changing the leader won't have much effect.

Systemic Level of Analysis

The systemic level of analysis explains outcomes from a systemwide level that includes all states. It takes into account both the position of states (structure) in the international

This pro-Germany political cartoon from 1914 captures a view of the balance of power in Europe at the outset of World War I from the systemic level of analysis. It shows German military might tipping the scales in Germany's favor, outweighing other European states. The caption reads, "Germany in the 'European balance.'"

system and their interactions (process). The position of states constitutes the systemic structural level of analysis. This involves the relative distribution of power, such as which states are great, middle, or small powers, and geopolitics, such as which states are sea or land powers. The interaction of states constitutes the systemic process level of analysis. At this level, we are concerned with which states align with which other states and which states negotiate with which other states. Thus, we might explain World War I in terms of the absence of systemwide institutions, such as the League of Nations. That would be a liberal explanation from a systemic *structural* level of analysis. Or we might explain World War I in terms of a loss of moderation in the practices of international diplomacy. That would also be a liberal explanation, but from a systemic *process* level of analysis. Another way to think about the difference between the structural and process levels of analysis is the analogy of a card game. The cards you hold constitute the structural level of the game; you can't win the game without a decent hand. This level is equivalent to the relative power states hold. Playing the cards constitutes the process level. You can blow a good hand if you don't play your cards right. This level equates to a state that forms an alliance with another state and either succeeds or fails in enhancing its security.

The systemic level of analysis is the most comprehensive. If we emphasize this level of analysis, we are unlikely to leave out a significant part of the international situation we are looking at and therefore omit a particular cause. On the other hand, this level is also the most general; we will come up with explanations that lack specificity. For example, we may conclude that the relative rise of German power caused World War I, and it may well have. But now we wonder, why did the relative rise of American power not cause World War I? The United States had surpassed Britain at the end of the nineteenth century and was more powerful than Germany. Maybe we have to look just at Europe, the regional level of analysis, because the United States did not see itself as part of Europe. But why, then, did it not feel part of Europe? Perhaps because the United States had fewer interactions with Europe than Britain did—less trade and tourism. Now we are at the systemic process level of analysis. But it might have also been America's ideology of isolationism. Now we are at the domestic level of analysis. And so on. It is hard to be very specific at the systemic level.

Just because causes are remote, that does not mean they do not affect outcomes. More generally, structural-level studies predict outcomes, not behaviors. Neorealists, for example, say that bipolarity decreases the likelihood of war, but they cannot say that bipolarity causes a specific country not to go to war. On the other hand, a structural distribution of power can widen or narrow the options a country faces. In a bipolar world, for instance, neither major actor can find additional allies that will be of much help. Hence, in a bipolar world, states compete through internal competition, not external balancing. In a unipolar world, the hegemonic country may not be able to withdraw, regardless of its domestic preferences. Structural studies help us see the things we take for granted. That's why, as we have already discussed, critical theories are often deeply structural—they are trying to show us alternatives that no one has considered because the hegemonic structure dominating discourse precludes considering them.

Certain perspectives emphasize the systemic level of analysis. Social constructivism, for example, sees identity shaped more by international relationships (systemic process level) and shared knowledge or culture (systemic structure level) than by separate country histories (domestic level) or specific leaders (individual level). Neorealism emphasizes the systemic level of relative power almost to the exclusion of domestic and individual factors.

Domestic Level of Analysis

The domestic level of analysis locates causes in the character of the domestic systems of specific states. Thus, war is caused by aggressive or warlike states (domestic level), not by evil, inept, or misguided people (individual level) or the structure of power in the international system (systemic level). War may also be caused by the failure of domestic institutions. In the case of World War I, the internal collapse of the Austro-Hungarian Empire and the brittle coalition inside Germany of agricultural (rye) and industrial (iron) interests are often cited as important causes. These are also explanations from a domestic level of analysis but now from a liberal perspective: the breakdown of institutional relationships at the domestic level led to war.

Domestic-level causes are more specific than systemic-level causes but not as specific as individual-level factors. We can point to a specific domestic political coalition, such as the iron and rye coalition in Germany, which led to the expansion of German power and caused World War I, rather than the relative rise of German power, which occurred over a longer time and does not tell us exactly when that power became sufficient to precipitate war. On the other hand, at the domestic level we now downplay causes that might come from other countries or the structure of international power. What if the buildup of military power in another country, such as Russia, was the principal cause of German armament, and the need to arm Germany brought together the iron-rye coalition? Now the iron-rye coalition is not a cause of World War I but a consequence of systemic factors and an intervening, not independent, variable causing war. Similarly, the iron-rye coalition had existed for some time, and war did not occur. Was there an even more specific cause that came from the individual level of analysis, such as the brinksmanship of German chancellor Theobald von Bethmann-Hollweg during the critical month of July 1914?

Domestic-level causes may come from various characteristics of the domestic system. Capitalist and socialist economies generate different attitudes and behaviors. The

Muslim and Christian religions or democratic and nondemocratic political ideologies do as well. Stable and failed institutions are domestic-level factors affecting state behavior. A great worry today is the existence of failed states, meaning states whose domestic institutions have broken down, such as Somalia. Another worry is the existence of rogue states, such as North Korea, that may pass nuclear weapons on to terrorists. Both types of states come from the domestic level of analysis, but a failed state usually means an institutional breakdown, a liberal cause, whereas a rogue state often implies evil intentions, an identity cause.

Individual Level of Analysis

The individual level of analysis locates the causes of events in individual leaders or the immediate circles of decision makers within particular countries. Now the cause of World War I comes not from some general characteristic of the German domestic system as a whole—the iron-rye coalition—but from the particular leaders in power at the time. Kaiser Wilhelm II is considered to be the level from which the cause originated. It may have been his need for power to hide a sense of inferiority; this is a realist explanation. Or it may have been his inability to understand the intricacies of statecraft as did Otto von Bismarck, the German chancellor until 1890; this is a liberal explanation. Or it may have been his ideas about the monarchy and German destiny; this is an identity explanation. But all three of these explanations are drawn from an individual level of analysis.

The individual level of analysis is the most specific level. Now we can see the proximate or most immediate cause of some action. According to some analysts, President George W. Bush and a small group of neoconservative advisers made the decision to invade Iraq and cause war in 2003. This level of analysis has great appeal, especially among historians and the media. Much of history is written as the work of great men (and a few great women). The stories of Napoleon, Frederick the Great, Samurai families in Japan, and the strongmen of Africa who led their countries to independence after World War II resonate with human interest and human tragedy. Newspapers sell when they report personal peccadilloes or more serious evils that leaders are alleged to have caused. And the individual level of analysis is important, especially in democratic countries, where accountability is at the heart of domestic politics.

Nevertheless, this level of analysis is the least general level of analysis. It soft-pedals all the domestic- and international-level factors that may have set up the situation in which the American president or other leaders acted. Working at this level of analysis is akin to concluding, after watching an entire baseball game, that a home run in the bottom of the ninth inning caused the final outcome without considering how the rest of the game set up the situation in the bottom of the ninth that made the home run decisive. Would World War II not have occurred if Hitler had not been in power? Or would domestic and international circumstances have produced another leader similar to Hitler? It may stir our human imagination to exaggerate the role of an individual or small group, but that's not the same as proving it is so.

Foreign Policy Level of Analysis

Another important level of analysis, as we have noted, is the foreign policy level of analysis. This level captures the interplay between domestic politics and international politics. As Peter Trubowitz explains, it focuses on "how political leaders manage conflicting geopolitical [systemic] and partisan [domestic] pressures in making grand strategy. . . . geopolitics and domestic politics [are] two faces of the same coin: the president could not respond to one threat without weighing the impact on the other."[60] The foreign policy level of analysis involves a "two-level game."[61] Sandwiched between the systemic process and domestic levels, foreign policy officials mediate between the two, as when a leader goes to war abroad to preserve or increase his or her power at home (Hitler?) or when a leader sacrifices domestic power rather than lead the country to war (Gorbachev?). At the foreign policy level of analysis, the primary causes come from the intersection of domestic and systemic factors, not from the individual leaders themselves. Individuals are intervening, not causal, variables. If the primary causes come from the individual leader, let's say the leader's personality, the level of analysis is individual.

A well-known foreign policy–level perspective in international relations is the rational choice approach. From this approach, as Professor Bruce Bueno de Mesquita tells us, "international relations is the process by which foreign policy leaders balance their ambition to pursue particular policy objectives [security, economic prosperity, and so on] against their need to avoid internal and external threats to their political survival."[62] In short, foreign policy leaders seek to survive in office; they implement this preference through the pursuit of power, they calculate the costs and benefits of various policy options based on their perceptions of relative capabilities abroad and political risk at home, and they decide which option maximizes their chance of political survival. Notice how leaders operating at the foreign policy level make connections between the domestic and international levels and act on the basis of these connections, not on the basis of factors that are purely internal to them, such as their dislike for a particular country.

SUMMARY: CAUSES OF WORLD WAR I

Now, by way of summarizing this chapter and antici-pating the next one, we can revisit the four statements made at the beginning of this chapter about the causes of World War I and show how they reflect the differ-ent perspectives, levels of analysis, and causal arrows involved in understanding this event.

Statement 1: The rise of German power caused World War I. This is a realist explanation from a systemic level of analysis. It attributes the cause of war to a shift in the distribution of power away from equilib-rium within the system as a whole. The shift toward Germany is disruptive and dictates a more ambitious

FIGURE
1-7

Causal Arrows: Realist Explanations for World War I

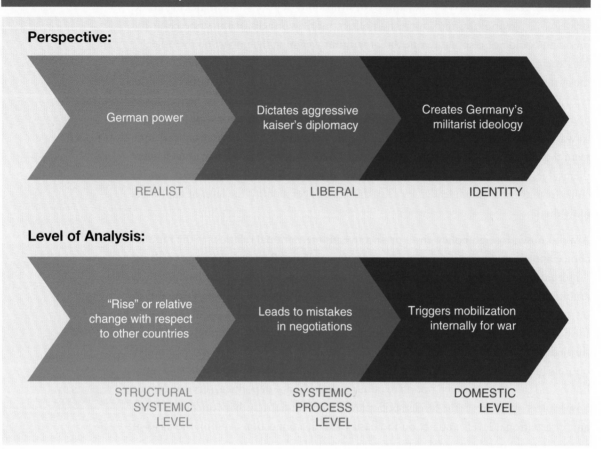

Perspective:

German power	Dictates aggressive kaiser's diplomacy	Creates Germany's militarist ideology
REALIST	LIBERAL	IDENTITY

Level of Analysis:

"Rise" or relative change with respect to other countries	Leads to mistakes in negotiations	Triggers mobilization internally for war
STRUCTURAL SYSTEMIC LEVEL	SYSTEMIC PROCESS LEVEL	DOMESTIC LEVEL

foreign policy by the kaiser, which in turn mobilizes and stirs up the country to adopt a more militant ideology. Figure 1-7 shows the causal arrows in this explanation.

Statement 2: Kaiser Wilhelm II's clumsy diplomacy caused World War I. This is a liberal explanation from an individual level of analysis. The cause now comes from the kaiser himself, from his lack of bureaucratic skills. If someone else had been in power, that person might have acted differently. And there was no

inherent reason the shift in the balance of power had to cause war. Figure 1-8 shows the causal arrows for this liberal explanation.

Statement 3: Germany's militarist ideology, which glorified aggressive war, caused World War I. This is an identity-based account from a domestic level of analysis. It is identity based because it sees the cause of the war in the German militarist ideology or self-image, how the German people thought about themselves, particularly in relation to the aggressive use of force

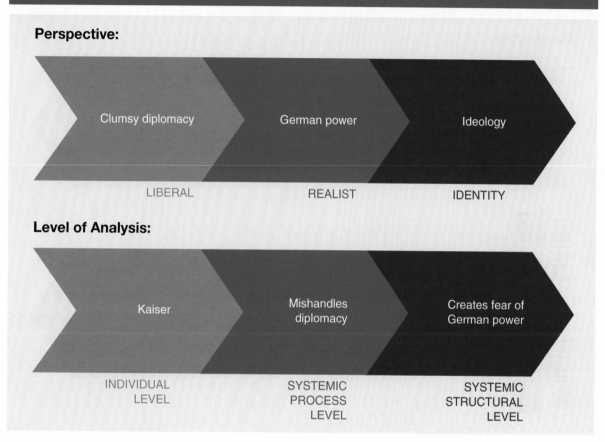

FIGURE 1-8

Causal Arrows: Liberal Explanations for World War I

Perspective:

Clumsy diplomacy	German power	Ideology
LIBERAL	REALIST	IDENTITY

Level of Analysis:

Kaiser	Mishandles diplomacy	Creates fear of German power
INDIVIDUAL LEVEL	SYSTEMIC PROCESS LEVEL	SYSTEMIC STRUCTURAL LEVEL

and heroism of war. The explanation comes from the domestic level of analysis because the cause derives from a characteristic of the domestic political system as a whole, not the foibles of a particular leader or unbalanced relationships with external powers. Figure 1-9 shows the causal arrows for this identity explanation.

Statement 4: Capitalist class conflicts caused World War I. This statement explains World War I from a critical theory perspective that emphasizes the

inseparable and deep-seated forces combining all perspectives and levels of analysis, in this case identifying those forces with capitalism.

This chapter has introduced a lot of concepts. The rest of the book illustrates how these concepts work in the real world, and I will remind you of them as we see them at work in explaining historical and contemporary events.

FIGURE 1-9

Causal Arrows: Identity Explanations for World War I

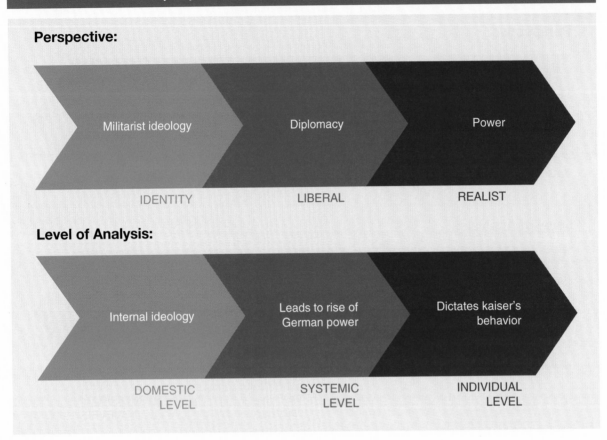

Perspective:

Militarist ideology → Diplomacy → Power

IDENTITY   LIBERAL   REALIST

Level of Analysis:

Internal ideology → Leads to rise of German power → Dictates kaiser's behavior

DOMESTIC LEVEL   SYSTEMIC LEVEL   INDIVIDUAL LEVEL

Sharpen your skills with SAGE edge at **edge.sagepub.com/nau4e.** **SAGE edge for students** provides a personalized approach to help you accomplish your coursework goals in an easy-to-use learning environment.

KEY CONCEPTS

agent-oriented constructivism, 61

alliances, 43

anarchy, 38

balance of power, 42

bargaining, 52

beliefs, 59

belief systems, 66

civil society, 50

collective goods, 52

collective security, 53

communicative action, 61

compellence, 45

construction of identities, 59

constructivism, 59

cooperation, 52

defense, 45

deterrence, 45

diplomacy, 51

distribution of identities, 63

epistemic communities, 64

external identity, 62

feminism, 67

geopolitics, 40

STUDY QUESTIONS

1. How do ideal types, perspectives, and theories differ?

2. What does the realist perspective relatively emphasize? The liberal perspective? The identity perspective?

3. Can any perspective apply at any level of analysis?

4. Is constructivism both a theory and a method?

5. Do perspectives exclude each other or simply draw the causal arrows between power, institutions, and ideas differently?

We are interested in history because it provides a baseline for understanding what is the same and what is different in today's world. History reveals three broad patterns of historical behavior. The first, reflecting the realist perspective on international relations, spotlights repeated cycles between empires and equilibrium, between a distribution of power that features dominant powers and one that features multiple and roughly equal powers. Recorded history begins about five thousand years ago in Mesopotamia. The Akkadian Empire linked Babylonian cities located near modern-day Baghdad and in southern Iraq with Assyrian cities located in northern Iraq and parts of what are now Turkey and Syria. Babylonian, Egyptian, Assyrian, Greek, and Persian empires followed, eventually superseded by the Roman Empire, which stretched across the entire Mediterranean region. But the Roman Empire too gave way to decline, and the Islamic empire ushered in the Golden Age of Islam, covering an area roughly equal to Rome but centered in the Middle East. The same patterns of empire and equilibrium prevailed in other regions. In India, Aryans, an Indo-European people, settled and brought the Hindu religion but eventually succumbed to the followers of Siddhartha Gautama, known as the Buddha, who established an empire under the Mauryan king Asoka. In China, dynasties succeeded one another interrupted by periods of warring states and equilibrium. The Ch'in dynasty united the country around the time of the Roman Empire and built the Great Wall to protect it. But it too succumbed and was followed by other dynasties—Sui, T'ang, Sung, Yuan (Genghis Khan), Ming, and Qing. Africa too saw empires rise and fall, in Ghana, Mali, Congo, Ethiopia, and Swahili-speaking regions of the southeastern part of the continent. In Latin America, the Mayan Empire in southern Mexico, Guatemala, and northern Honduras, the Aztec Empire in central Mexico, and the Andean Empire from Ecuador to central Chile displayed similar patterns. Fueled by the scientific and industrial revolution, European states, and especially Britain, skyrocketed onto the global scene in the seventeenth and eighteenth centuries, establishing colonial empires throughout much of the world that in many cases lasted into the nineteenth and twentieth centuries. In Chapters 2, 3, and 4, we follow this historical thread into the twentieth century, looking at the origins and ends of World Wars I and II and the Cold War and paying close attention throughout to the balance of power between world states—the primary locus of analysis for realists.

The second pattern of historical behavior, reflecting a more liberal interpretation of history, highlights the gradual but inexorable expansion of international interdependence and society among the peoples of the world. From the isolated villages of ancient agrarian societies to the coastal towns of the Mediterranean, the city-states of Greece, and the provinces of Rome and Islam, social units expanded and fostered a division of labor among societies. Trade provided benefits for all parties and eventually forged the "Silk Road" between Europe and China. River commerce helped consolidate feudal estates in Europe to form modern, contiguous territorial states, and the Old World discovered the New World and colonized the whole world, installing an economy based on global trade. Chapters in this part pay especially close attention to the role that interdependence and institutions (both state based and nonstate) played in shaping the world of the twentieth century.

The third pattern, featuring identity aspects of history, traces the primacy of ideas through history. Mythology and religion shaped identities in early societies. Greek philosophy brought rationalist thought to the West, while Confucianism cultivated hierarchical traditions in the East. The great religions—Buddhism, Judaism, Christianity, and Islam—forged distinctive civilizations that persist to the present day. Roman and Orthodox Christianity dominated the late Roman

Empire as well as medieval life throughout Europe. Christianity and Islam squared off in the Crusades, and the Reformation divided Europe bitterly between Catholics and Protestants. Culture reinforced linguistic and ethnic differences and eventually forged secular nation-states in Europe and, through Western imperialism, in the rest of the world as well. We will explore how identity perspectives explain major events of the twentieth century, focusing especially closely on the role of nationalism.

History, of course, consists of all these patterns, but scholars and statespersons cannot emphasize them all. Listen to historian Paul Kennedy, who admits in his discussion of the rise and fall of great powers that he ignores "a complex mixture of motives—personal gain, national glory, religious zeal, perhaps a sense of adventure— . . . because many societies in their time have thrown up individuals and groups willing to dare all and do anything to make the world their oyster." "What distinguished the captains, crews, and explorers of Europe," he concludes, "was that they possessed the ships and the firepower with which to achieve their ambitions and . . . came from a political environment in which competition, risk, and entrepreneurship were prevalent."[1] Can you see in Kennedy's account the realist emphasis on the causal role of power (ships and firepower) and anarchy (competition) as opposed to the identity perspective's emphasis on ideas (motives)?

Or listen to Paul Schroeder, another historian, who writes that "the history of international politics is not one of an essentially unchanging, cyclical struggle for power or one of the shifting play of the balance of power, but a history of systematic institutional change—change essentially linear, moving overall in the direction of complexity, subtlety, and capacity for order and problem-solving."[2] Can you see the liberal perspective's emphasis on institutional changes having a greater causal influence on outcomes than the realist focus on shifting balances of power?

Finally, consider the conclusions of political scientist John M. Owen IV: "I certainly agree that rulers seek to gain, hold, and extend their states' power; but I maintain that the ways they pursue power are constrained by ideas and the transnational networks that carry them."[3] Now, ideas influence power and interactions more than power and interactions influence ideas. Here is the identity perspective front and center.

These disagreements pervade history and remind us that history should not be presented before an introduction to perspectives (theories) as if history exists independent of perspectives. For that reason the following accounts in Chapters 2 through 4 of World War I, World War II, and the Cold War consider all of the main theoretical perspectives and show how they disagree in terms of the judgments they make about whether power, institutions, or ideas are most important. History presented in this way warms us up for understanding why scholars, statespersons, and citizens disagree today about the major issues in international affairs (covered later, in Part II).

There are always parallels between the past and the present. History never repeats itself exactly, but it often rhymes. For example, the rise of Germany in the late nineteenth century unified central Europe and helped ignite World War I. Realists who emphasize such shifts in the distribution of power worry that the rise of China today may ignite similar instabilities. The failure of the League of Nations contributed to World War II. Liberal perspectives worry that the United Nations may suffer a similar fate today and deplore the dangerous drift toward unilateralism and nationalism. The clash of communist and capitalist ideologies dominated the Cold War between the United States and the Soviet Union, and identity perspectives worry that the clash of civilizations between the West and Islam may be equally serious today or, alternatively, blown way out of proportion. Remember, as we examine the great wars of the twentieth century, our goal is not to learn the history for its own sake—that you will get in your history courses—but to understand the differing perspectives on that history and what each perspective takes away from that history to make sense of modern-day events.

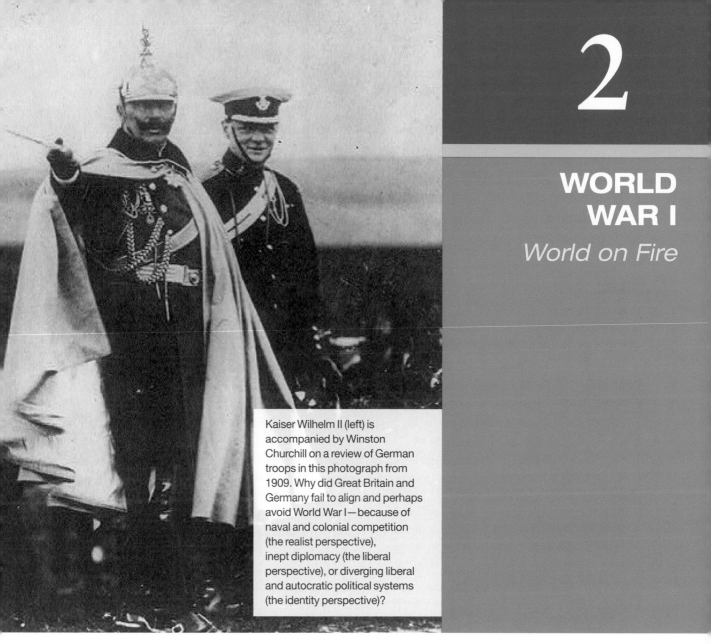

WORLD WAR I
World on Fire

Kaiser Wilhelm II (left) is accompanied by Winston Churchill on a review of German troops in this photograph from 1909. Why did Great Britain and Germany fail to align and perhaps avoid World War I—because of naval and colonial competition (the realist perspective), inept diplomacy (the liberal perspective), or diverging liberal and autocratic political systems (the identity perspective)?

W orld War I was a catastrophe. More than fifteen million people died. The world had not experienced such a level of butchery at least since the Thirty Years' War, which ravaged Europe in the seventeenth century. How did this disaster occur? We still do not know; historians and scholars disagree. Undoubtedly there were many causes. Perhaps it was a "perfect storm," with multiple causes coming together at the same time. But which causes were more important than others? That, we will see, is a matter of perspective and level of analysis.

>>> Europe in 1914

On June 28, 1914, the heir to the Austrian throne, Archduke Franz Ferdinand, was assassinated while on a visit to Sarajevo in Bosnia-Herzegovina, then provinces of Austria. This incident touched off World War I. But if you think history has only one outcome, consider the tragic comedy of the assassination itself. A bomb-wielding Serbian nationalist agent had attempted earlier that morning to kill the archduke. The attempt failed, but several people were wounded, including an army officer in the car trailing the archduke. The archduke went on to City Hall, where he was welcomed, and then later he set out to visit the wounded officer in the hospital. His driver made a wrong turn and stopped the vehicle in front of a shopping area. There, by coincidence, another one of the seven agents involved in the earlier plot was standing. Given an unexpected second chance, this agent stepped forward and succeeded in killing the archduke. So a good counterfactual question is: What if the assassination had never occurred?

Austria considered Serbia responsible for the attack and had to retaliate. The next month brought the world, step by step, closer to war. Now another scene emerges. On the morning of July 28, 1914, Austria-Hungary declared war on Serbia. But before war actually began and before Russia, Germany, Britain, and France joined the hostilities, the monarchs of Germany and Russia exchanged frantic telegrams. The two monarchs were cousins. Kaiser Wilhelm II of Germany was the son of Victoria Adelaide Mary Louise, the first child and daughter of Queen Victoria of Great Britain. Victoria Adelaide had married Prince Frederick, the son of Kaiser Wilhelm I. The second daughter of Queen Victoria, Alice, had married the German duke of Hesse-Darmstadt. Their daughter, Alix, went on to marry Nicholas II, the czar of Russia in 1914. (She became the famous czarina who had a hemophiliac son, befriended the mad monk Rasputin, and was subsequently killed with Nicholas and her five children by Bolshevik executioners in 1918.) So, by marriage Czar Nicholas and Kaiser Wilhelm, known to each other as Nicky and Willy, were cousins. Their frantic exchanges became known as the "Willy-Nicky telegrams." George V, the king of England in 1914 and another grandson of Queen Victoria, was also a cousin. These family members were about to declare war on one another. (And you thought your family had problems?)

Russia had vital interests at stake in Serbia and had pledged to come to its aid in the event of war, so Nicholas II was under great pressure to mobilize Russian forces to support Serbia. His last chance was to get Germany, an ally of Austria, to pull Austria back from its declaration of war against Serbia. On July 29, he telegraphed Willy, "An ignoble war has been declared on a weak country. . . . I beg you in the name of our old friendship to do what you can to stop your allies from going too far." In reply, Willy warned his cousin that "military measures on the part of Russia, which would be looked upon by Austria as threatening, would precipitate a calamity." For three days, Willy and Nicky talked past one another—in English, which was their common language—and on August 1 the world plunged into the abyss of total war.[1]

Could the cousins have changed the course of history even if they had wanted to? Many students of history would say no. Applying levels of analysis tools, they would argue that systemic and domestic forces overrode individual influences. Germany felt encircled and devised a war strategy in 1913 to break out before Russia became too powerful. In addition, monarchs no longer had the absolutist power of Louis XIV or Frederick the Great. Kaiser Wilhelm was not really in full control of his military. But when, then, did events veer out of control? Here the three principal perspectives on international affairs offer different answers. Let's summarize the answers and then explore them in more detail.

CAUSAL ARROW: LEVELS OF ANALYSIS

| Caused czar and kaiser behavior | Empowered military | Encirclement |
| INDIVIDUAL | DOMESTIC | SYSTEMIC |

Realist perspectives argue that the crucial event was the unification of Germany in 1871. German unification created a new power in the heart of Europe that had a larger population and, in short order, a more powerful economy than any other European power. Such a central power inevitably threatened its neighbors, so these neighbors, in response, allied against Germany. Now surrounded by enemies, Germany felt even more threatened.

Notice here the security dilemma at work. How could Germany be sure that its neighbors intended only to defend themselves, and how could its neighbors be sure that Germany would not use its dominance to attack them? No country was being particularly aggressive. The problem, as realist perspectives see it, "was Germany's growing economic and military power, not its aggressive behavior."[2]

Ultimately, the problem could be resolved only through the reduction of German power, which the victors attempted to accomplish after World War I, or the integration of German power into western Europe and then into the whole of Europe, which was done after World War II and the Cold War. History, realist perspectives argue, bears out the fact that a freestanding Germany in the center of the European balance of power is destabilizing. Europe is stable today only because a united and once again powerful Germany is part of a new supranational actor known as the European Union.

Liberal perspectives see it differently. It was not a shift of power due to German unification that made countries insecure; rather, it was the lack of adequate institutions and diplomacy to make commitments openly and to develop information about who was complying with those commitments and who was not. It was, in short, the secrecy and manipulation of European diplomacy from the late nineteenth century onward that created the uncertainty, not the situation of unbalanced power driven by the security dilemma. Notice here the problems of inadequate information, miscommunication, and lack of institutions to enforce compliance that liberal perspectives emphasize. Interestingly, European diplomacy and institutions failed just as powerful new forces of economic and political interdependence emerged that might have overcome distrust. Industrialization was creating new linkages among banks and corporations that opposed war. International institutions, such as the Hague Conferences started in 1899, were being set up to reduce arms and regulate other relationships. When the war ended, liberal perspectives proposed an entirely new system of collective security to manage international military relations. The League of Nations was their hope to replace the balance of power.

Identity perspectives focus on yet another primary force leading to World War I—that of shared and competitive identities. Nationalism, ignited by the French Revolution, grew out of different cultures and, in its most virulent form, was associated with different races. Different cultures and races struggled to survive in world politics, much as different species struggled to survive in the natural world. Social Darwinism, drawn from Charles Darwin's new theory of natural evolution, became the shared mind-set among European nations and drove them to conflict and war. It constructed a particularly virulent form of anarchy, which drove nations apart and eventually proved a stronger force than peace movements, the Hague Conferences, and international trade and investment, which drove nations together. European countries raced off into the inferno of World War I eager to prove that their culture was the superior one. Notice here how ideas, which identity perspectives emphasize, shaped conflicting identities that, in turn, generated military competition and overrode the cooperative opportunities offered by common institutions and trade.

CAUSAL ARROW: PERSPECTIVES

Idea of Social Darwinism	Military competition	Prevented cooperation
IDENTITY	REALIST	LIBERAL

Let's take a deeper look at these three explanations of World War I and then assess their relative validity. As we go along, we take special note in the text's margins of the way the causal arrows work from the different perspectives or levels of analysis, pointing out explicitly in which direction causality runs. We also then summarize in matrix tables the explanations from each perspective at the different levels of analysis. Finally, Parallel Timeline 2-1 will help you remember key historical events and sort them out in terms of which perspective might emphasize them. Remember, historical events always involve all three principal causes of international behavior—ideas, institutions, and power. But realist perspectives highlight the power struggles underlying events, liberal perspectives the interdependence factors, and identity perspectives the ideas.

If you still doubt that this history has much relevance today, consider the many similarities between the world before 1914 and the world today. A dominant power existed (Great Britain then, the United States today), a rising power threatened the status quo (Germany then, China today), failed states proliferated (Balkan states and Turkey then, Somalia, Yemen, Mali, Syria, and Afghanistan today), competition over trade and resources intensified (colonial territories then, commodities and high-tech trade today), and anti-Western doctrines inspired militants (Marxism and anarchists then, jihadism and terrorists today). There are, of course, also many differences; the existence of nuclear weapons is but one of them. But we cannot know what is the same or what is different about today unless we know about the past.

≫ Realist Explanations

From a systemic structural level of analysis, Germany's unification in 1871 significantly altered the balance of power in Europe. Germany, as well as Italy, had been divided for more than a thousand years. The central part of Europe, known as the Holy Roman Empire (the weak successor to the Roman Empire, nominally under the auspices of the Roman Catholic Church), contained more than three thousand separate units at the time

Parallel Timeline 2-1

Events Leading to World War I from Different Perspectives

Realist		Liberal		Identity	
				Nationalism unleashed by French Revolution	1790s
				Liberal nationalism in Britain, France, and United States	1800s
		Prussian Zollverein (economic customs union)	1830s		
		Demise of Concert of Europe	1860s–1870s	Militant nationalism in Germany	1860s
German unification by war	1864–1871				
				Marxist socialism	1870s
		Three Emperors' League	1873		
		Berlin Conference	1878		
German–Austro-Hungarian secret alliance	1879				
German–Italian alliance, creating Triple Alliance	1882	German–Russian Reinsurance Treaty (not renewed in 1890)	1887		
				Social Darwinism	1890s
Franco-Russian Alliance	1894				
		Krüger telegram	1895		
		Hague Conferences	1899 and 1907		
German–British naval rivalry	1900s			Cult of the offensive	1900
French–British Entente Cordiale	1904				
Russo-Japanese War	1905	Moroccan crises	1905 and 1911		
Triple Entente	1907				
		Balkan crises	1908–1909 and 1912–1913		
Schlieffen Plan	1913				
German naval program completed	1914	"Blank check" of July 5	1914		

of Charlemagne in 800 C.E., 300 or so at the Treaty of Westphalia in 1648, and still more than thirty at the Congress of Vienna in 1815. As Map 2-1 shows, this fragmentation provided a kind of buffer as other great powers emerged and contended for power in Europe. At times, the European balance of power functioned in two parts, a major rivalry between France and Great Britain in the west and another among Prussia, Austria, and Russia in the east. And even though western and eastern powers participated in wars across the continent—for example, Russia's role in the Napoleonic Wars in the early 1800s or Britain's role in the Crimean War in the 1850s—their priority interests remained somewhat separate. Britain was concerned primarily with the Low Countries of Belgium and the Netherlands, Russia with the countries of Prussia and Austria-Hungary. Once Germany was united, the European balance of power became a single whole, and it was more likely now that a disruption in one part would trigger a wider war among all great powers. This was especially true because Germany occupied the northern plains of Europe, which offered few geographic obstacles to invasion. A united country in this part of Europe would feel vulnerable, just as Poland, which also occupies the northern plains, was historically vulnerable and indeed subject to repeated partition. Geography matters, a realist perspective would point out; a united Germany would have to be either very strong and threaten its neighbors or very weak and become the potential prey of its neighbors.

The Rise of German Power

Zollverein: a customs union created by Prussia involving other German states that lowered barriers to trade and ignited rapid industrial development beginning in the 1830s.

As it turned out, a united Germany was going to be very strong. Already in the 1830s, Prussia had created the **Zollverein**, a customs union with other German states that lowered barriers to trade and ignited rapid industrial development. Through this trade community, which a liberal perspective might emphasize, Prussia between 1850 and 1870 increased sixfold the number of steam engines driving its industry and tripled its railway capacity. Germany was changing so fast that Karl Marx, visiting Berlin in 1859, said, "Whoever last saw Berlin ten years ago would not recognize it again."[3] (Many visitors see the same rapid change today in the cities of China.) By 1870, Prussia/Germany had pulled ahead of France in both population and gross national product (GNP, the total income of the residents of a country) and had eight times the relative wealth of Russia. And by 1900, Germany had pulled even with Great Britain, the preeminent power in Europe, and was three times wealthier than France or Russia. In 1913, one year before the war broke out, German wealth exceeded that of Great Britain by 40 percent.[4]

Germany was also able to convert its wealth into military power. Countries do this with differing degrees of efficiency, and power conversion becomes one of the factors complicating the assessment of power in balance-of-power politics. Remember from Chapter 1 how realist perspectives include political competence and stability as measures of power capabilities—not something we can touch but clearly something vital for mobilizing and converting resources into military arms. Russia, for example, had substantial wealth, particularly natural resources. But it did not have an efficient bureaucracy and could not support its military the way Germany did. By 1900, Germany, with less than half the population of Russia, had an army (including reserves) bigger than Russia's and was building a navy to challenge British dominance on the high seas.[5] During World War I

MAP 2-1

Europe prior to German Unification in 1871

Legend:
- Major balance-of-power players
- German kingdoms, duchies, principalities, and city-states

itself, Germany massively outproduced Russia across the whole range of military equipment: airplanes, machine guns, artillery pieces, and rifles.[6] This administrative capacity to convert wealth into military power was also one of the strengths displayed by the United States as it rose to the status of a great power around the time of World War I.[7]

Power conversion reflects one of the ways in which the levels of analysis interact in the realist perspective and in international affairs more generally. Different *domestic* capacities to convert resources into power affect the relative *systemic structural* balance of power. Germany and earlier Poland were both affected by vulnerable strategic positions. The one survived while the other succumbed, in part because of domestic factors. But both too were driven by structural vulnerabilities, Germany to aggression and Poland to submission (partitioned by Prussia, Austria, and Russia in the late eighteenth century and not reconstituted until after World War I).

CAUSAL ARROW: LEVELS OF ANALYSIS

Influences policy choices	Affects relative shifts in power	Power conversion
INDIVIDUAL	SYSTEMIC	DOMESTIC

Power Balancing: Triple Entente and Triple Alliance

What was Europe going to do with this efficient colossus sitting across the strategic northern plains? Balance it, the realist perspective says. And that's exactly what Germany's neighbors proceeded to do. For a while, through the masterful but secretive diplomacy of Bismarck, Germany was able to reassure its weaker neighbors and keep them from aligning against Germany's greater power. But in 1894, four years after Bismarck left the scene, the two countries most directly affected by Germany's power, France and Russia, formed an alliance. Now, with the Franco-Russian Alliance, Germany had potential adversaries on both borders. As Map 2-2 shows, Poland did not exist at the time, so Germany and Russia shared a border. A lot now depended on what Great Britain did.

For two decades prior to World War I, Britain and Germany had flirted with the idea of alliance. Remember that Kaiser Wilhelm's uncle, Edward VII, and cousin, George V, were the English monarchs during this period. In the 1890s, Willy spent his summer vacations in England participating in yacht races with his relatives and admiring the British naval fleet. A British–German alliance might have avoided the encirclement that Germany feared from France and Russia. From a realist perspective and systemic level of analysis, alliances tend to develop in a checkerboard rather than a domino pattern. Threatened countries leapfrog their neighbors to counterbalance bordering rivals. An alliance with Great Britain might have offset the threat from France and made sense for Britain as well. By 1900, the United States had surpassed Great Britain in terms of total wealth and power. Britain and the United States did not share a border, but they competed increasingly on the high seas. The American navy was expanding rapidly under the influence of Admiral Alfred Mahan and the leadership of President Theodore Roosevelt. Thus, Germany and Britain might have acted to check the growing specter of American power. But geography matters as well as total power, realist perspectives argue, and Germany

MAP
2-2

Europe and Germany in 1914

was closer to Great Britain and hence a more proximate threat than the United States. Great Britain had long defended the neutrality of the Low Countries of Belgium and the Netherlands, and Germany's new power potentially threatened these countries, just as French power had in the eighteenth and nineteenth centuries.

CAUSAL ARROW: PERSPECTIVES

Shape alliances and behavior — Override culture — Proximate threats

LIBERAL   IDENTITY   REALIST

Observe that, from the realist perspective, it does not matter that the United States and Britain shared similar cultural and political systems. This factor is important from an identity perspective and a domestic level of analysis. Some identity-oriented analysts attribute the eventual alliance between the United States and Great Britain primarily to the shared Anglo-Saxon culture of the two countries.[8] In contrast to realist analysts, they conclude that domestic and dyadic-level (systemic process between two countries) forces of culture and democracy ultimately override the systemic structural-level forces of power competition.

Thus, in 1904, Britain turned to counterbalance Germany, not align with it against the United States. Britain and France signed the **Entente Cordiale**, an agreement that settled colonial disputes between them (they had almost come to blows at Fashoda in the Egyptian Sudan in 1898) and, although not explicitly directed against Germany, ended a century of "splendid isolation" for British policy, during which it had avoided specific commitments on the continent. That the Entente Cordiale had broader purposes became evident within a year. In 1905, Russia suffered a major naval defeat in the Russo-Japanese War. Japan was another rising power in Russia's neighborhood, in this case in Asia. Worried that Russia was now seriously weakened vis-à-vis Germany, Great Britain and France expanded their alliance in 1907 to include Russia. The Entente Cordiale became the **Triple Entente**.

Sir Eyre Crowe, permanent secretary of the British foreign office, wrote a famous memorandum in 1907 that summed up the realist logic driving British policy. He noted that Germany might have two intentions, "aiming at a general political hegemony and maritime ascendance" or "thinking for the present merely of using her legitimate position and influence as one of the leading Powers in the council of nations." However, as he noted, "there is no actual necessity for a British government to determine definitely which of the two theories of German policy it will accept." Either way, "the position thereby accruing to Germany would obviously constitute . . . a menace to the rest of the world."[9] Regardless of German intentions, the Crowe memorandum argued, German power had to be balanced.

And the balance of power seemed to be working. Many scholars estimate that German power reached its peak around 1905. Just as it did so, Germany's major neighbors came together in the Entente Cordiale and Triple Entente to check that power. In 1913, the Triple Entente had about 50 percent of European wealth. The other 50 percent was accounted for by the **Triple Alliance**, an alliance first formed between Germany and Austria-Hungary in 1879, then joined by Italy in 1882. In 1914, the two alliances offered a near-perfect offset.[10] According to the power balancing school of realism, equilibrium existed and should have prevented war. What went wrong?

Here realist perspectives split in explaining the breakdown of the balance of power. Some argue that the offsetting alliances became too rigid and converted a flexible multipolar

Entente Cordiale: an agreement signed in 1904 between Great Britain and France that settled colonial disputes between them and ended a century of British isolation from conflicts on the continent.

Triple Entente: an agreement signed in 1907 in which Great Britain and France expanded the Entente Cordiale to include Russia.

Triple Alliance: an alliance formed first between Germany and Austria-Hungary in 1879, then joined by Italy in 1882, that accounted for 50 percent of all European wealth in the early twentieth century.

balance of power into a rigid bipolar balance. This tense standoff eventually precipitated a preemptive war, an attack by one country on another because the second country is getting ready to attack the first. Others argue, as observed in Chapter 1, that a bipolar distribution is the most stable but that the problem was not the current balance of power but the potential future balance of power. By this account, Germany saw Russia as a rising power in the future and therefore launched a preventive war to avoid Germany's decline at a later date. Still others argue that hegemony or unipolarity is the most stable configuration of power and that Britain, whose hegemony ensured the long peace of nineteenth-century Europe, was now a declining power, leading to a multipolar scramble to decide which country would be the next hegemon. Let's look further at each of these realist arguments.

Rigid Alliances and Preemptive War

preemptive war: an attack by one country against another because the second country is preparing to attack the first.

Schlieffen Plan: Germany's mobilization plan that called for an attack on France first, by way of Belgium, followed by an attack on Russia.

How could countries balance against German power and still preserve flexibility? As we have noted, if Germany had aligned with Britain to avoid encirclement, it would have created an even more powerful grouping, accounting for about two-thirds of Europe's wealth in 1913. And France and Russia would have felt even more threatened. So, the balance of power required Britain to align against Germany. In that sense, encirclement and confrontation of the two alliance arrangements may have been unavoidable. It was a consequence of Germany's superior power *and* its position at the center of the European continent. It was, in short, an outgrowth of the security dilemma. Any effort to counterbalance Germany within Europe would necessarily have involved encirclement, and encirclement meant that Germany had to plan to fight a war on two fronts.

This logic led Germany as early as the 1890s to consider a **preemptive war**, a lightning strike or *Blitzkrieg*, against one neighbor so that German forces could then turn and concentrate against the other neighbor. The **Schlieffen Plan** (named for General Alfred von Schlieffen, who first developed it) called for an attack on France first, by way of Belgium—undoubtedly bringing Britain into the war—followed by an attack on Russia. It became official policy in 1913.

CAUSAL ARROW: PERSPECTIVES

Geopolitics — Dictated military mobilization strategy — Created war fever

REALIST — LIBERAL — IDENTITY

Notice that, in the realist argument, the strategic situation dictated the military strategy and was the primary cause of war. Some scholars say that geopolitics is a necessary but not sufficient explanation for war. They want to emphasize more specific factors at the foreign policy, domestic, and individual levels of analysis. Later we consider liberal arguments, for example, that bureaucratic factors, such as military and mobilization plans, not strategic imperatives, such as geopolitics, were the primary cause of war.

But why must bipolarity of alliances be unstable? The common argument is that each side is supersensitive to any gains by the other side because there are no other allies to turn to for balancing. But a counterargument is that the two powers have only one another to consider and therefore focus "like a laser beam" on each other, so that neither side can gain advantage. Perhaps the balance was unstable in 1914 because both sides believed that military technology favored offensive strategies—machine guns, motorized vehicles, and other attack weapons. In a balanced bipolar situation, offensive technology would give the advantage to the attacker and therefore place a premium on preemption. As it turned out, however, technology actually favored defensive strategies; World War I was a stalemate for most of its duration, involving stagnant trench warfare.

An explanation that hinges on whether weapons are offensive or defensive slides into liberal and identity explanations of the outbreak of World War I (see the subsequent discussion). Such an explanation depends on bureaucratic and cognitive factors that influence perceptions and cause misperceptions. In this case, military leaders had incorrect information about weapons (an argument from the liberal perspective and domestic level of analysis) or saw only the facts they wanted to see based on their ideas or beliefs (an argument from the identity perspective and individual level of analysis). From a strictly realist perspective, perceptions are not a primary variable. Power realities speak for themselves.

Future Balances and Preventive War

A more consistent realist argument is that the balance ultimately broke down not because of current imbalances but because of fears of future imbalances. This argument hinges on Germany's fear of Russian power and whether that fear was reasonable. If the fear was not reasonable, liberal or identity factors were at work, distorting the perception of material balances. According to this argument, Germany feared that Russia would surpass Germany in military and industrial power by 1916–1917. Theobald

In this 1916 photograph from the Battle of the Somme in northern France, British troops ascend from trenches to no-man's land, the devastated landscape between battle lines that changed little during World War I.

von Bethmann-Hollweg, the German chancellor, visited Russia in 1912 and observed "Russia's rising industrial power, which will grow to overwhelming proportions."[11] Russia was rapidly developing a railroad network that would permit it to move forces more quickly to the front. This would give Germany less time to deal with France before it would have to turn and confront Russian forces as well.

But why then didn't Germany attack before 1914? Its power peaked in 1905, when Russia was weak after the disastrous naval defeat by Japan and when Britain and France had just concluded the Entente Cordiale, which was not strictly an alliance against Germany. From 1905 on, there were plenty of occasions for war. Germany and other European powers were involved in a series of diplomatic crises in Morocco (1905 and 1911) and the Balkans (1908–1909 and 1912–1913) that were at least as serious as the assassination of the Austrian archduke in June 1914.[12] One answer to why Germany waited is that its naval program was not completed until July 1914, and Germany relied on this program to either deter Great Britain or hold it at bay while Germany attacked France. Thus, all the pieces for a **preventive war** were in place by the July crisis. Germany knew that Russia was not getting ready to attack it. Hence, the war was not preemptive—that is, it was not initiated in anticipation of an imminent Russian attack. In fact, Germany had to goad Russia into war. Now foreign policy–level factors become important. According to this account, Bethmann-Hollweg and military leaders such as Helmuth von Moltke, the German army chief of staff, used diplomacy "with Machiavellian dexterity" to provoke Russian mobilization and bring about a war to unite domestic groups, even delaying for twelve hours the transmission of the kaiser's instructions to settle the dispute peacefully so that Austria had time to declare war (see more discussion later).[13] Notice how at the foreign policy level of analysis individuals connect systemic (preventive war) and domestic (social unity) factors to cause outcomes. The individuals themselves are not the cause; they are responding to larger forces both beneath and above them.

preventive war: a war by one country against another that is not preparing to attack the first country but is growing in power and may attack in the future.

In this realist account, notice how diplomacy plays a role, but as an intervening, not independent, variable. The projection of future relative Russian predominance drives the diplomacy, not the other way around. And this projection of future balances is systemic as long as it is reasonable. If it is unreasonable, then other factors at the diplomatic, domestic, and individual levels of analysis must be distorting leaders' perceptions. At the time, some believed this fear of Russian power was reasonable.[14] But in retrospect, historians know that Russia was not much of a match for German military forces. Russia eventually capitulated in 1917 to a German force that represented only half of Germany's capabilities (the other half of the German force was fighting against France). And Russia disintegrated into civil war in 1917 and did not emerge to play a role in European politics for the next fifteen years. So, perhaps, identity factors distorted perceptions.

CAUSAL ARROW: PERSPECTIVES

Future Russian power	Creates reasonable fear	Drives diplomacy
REALIST	IDENTITY	LIBERAL

Power Transition and Hegemonic Decline

A final realist perspective is that World War I was caused not by the rising power of Germany or the projected future dominance of Russia but by the declining hegemony of

Great Britain. According to this version, it is not present or future balances that produce stability but hegemony. The dominant power has interests that span the system as a whole and, therefore, more than any other country, looks after the maintenance of the balance of power. Britain played this role during the Pax Britannica, the long century of peace in the nineteenth century. It exercised naval superiority around the globe and kept watch on the European continent so that no power gained ascendance. By the end of the nineteenth century, however, Britain no longer had that kind of power. The United States had surpassed Britain, but the United States was not yet powerful enough to play a global role. It was only beginning to assert its foreign policy presence and did not see its interests affected yet by the larger system or balance of power in Europe.

Thus, in the early twentieth century, the world experienced a dangerous interregnum in which Germany faced no leading power to temper rivalries. British diplomacy was not specifically at fault because it was a product of British power, and British power was simply declining. The same was true for the United States, but for the opposite reason: its diplomacy was not at fault because the United States was not yet powerful enough to direct events in Europe. Notice that, in this explanation from the systemic structural level of analysis, diplomacy is an intervening, not primary, variable. Structural power shifts explain diplomacy, not the other way around.

The absence of a hegemonic power to stabilize the situation draws from the power transition school of realism, which alerts us to dangerous periods of transition when a declining power falls and a challenging power closes in. Moving toward balance from this school's perspective is viewed as destabilizing, whereas moving toward balance from the power balancing perspective is viewed as stabilizing. This difference stems in part from a focus on different actors and different assumptions about goals. Power transition perspectives focus on the declining power and assume that it seeks to preserve the status quo. Thus, the loss of hegemony threatens stability. Power balancing perspectives focus on the rising power and assume that it would like to change the status quo. Hence, the emergence of hegemony threatens stability.

Cartelized Domestic Politics and German Aggression

Realist explanations of World War I also operate at the domestic level of analysis. One domestic-level explanation argues that World War I was caused by German aggression and that German aggression, in turn, was caused by German domestic politics. According to this explanation, Germany's domestic politics was cartelized or united among various elite groups, all of which had independent interests in one or another aspect of German belligerence and expansion. The agricultural landowners of large estates in East Prussia, or Junkers, were interested in high tariffs to protect grain prices; military elites were interested in offensive war plans and military weaponry; and industrial leaders advocated high tariffs to develop industry and military arms, including a naval fleet. As political scientist Jack Snyder explains, "These groups logrolled their interests, producing a policy outcome that was more expansionist and overcommitted than any group desired individually."[15] Thus, grain tariffs antagonized Russia, a large grain exporter;

heavy industry and naval plans antagonized Great Britain; and military leaders and their offensive war plans alienated France and Russia. These cartelized domestic interests "embroiled Germany simultaneously with all of Europe's major powers."[16]

CAUSAL ARROW: LEVELS OF ANALYSIS

Logrolling	Created expansionist foreign policy	Exploited international circumstances
DOMESTIC	INDIVIDUAL	SYSTEMIC

Snyder does not ignore international factors: "International circumstances did affect German expansionist policy, but only by influencing the domestic political strength of imperialist groups."[17] He simply judges that domestic expansionist forces were primary and exploited systemic factors to go to war. (See Table 2-1 for a summary of realist explanations.)

>>> Liberal Explanations

Liberal accounts of World War I focus on diplomatic miscalculations and institutional deficiencies, both in the international system and in the domestic politics of key players such as Germany, Austria-Hungary, Russia, and the Ottoman Empire.

TABLE 2-1

The Causes of World War I: The Realist Perspective and Levels of Analysis

Level of analysis	Realist perspective		
Systemic	*Structure*	Rise of German power engenders threat of empire (power balancing school)	
		Decline of British power signals end of Pax Britannica (power transition school)	
		Loss of flexibility, rise of rigid alliances—Triple Entente versus Triple Alliance—that intensifies bipolarity, which is unstable and increases incentives for preemptive war	
		Future rise of Russian power—bipolarity is stable in present but not in future, leads to preventive war	
		Power vacuum—disintegration of Austro-Hungarian and Ottoman Empires, which sucked in great powers	
	Process	Alliances: Interactive formation of Triple Entente and Triple Alliance, causing rigidity at structural level	
Foreign policy		German leaders use Machiavellian diplomacy to provoke war and unite domestic interests	
Domestic		German bureaucratic efficiency; Russia not so efficient (causing shift in power at structural level)	
		Cartelized German domestic interests combine expansionist aims and provoke other major powers	
Individual		Weak leaders: Emperor Franz Joseph (tired, old man), Czar Nicholas II (isolated autocrat), Kaiser Wilhelm II (weak ruler)	

International diplomacy had been developing since the Congress of Vienna, which ended the Napoleonic Wars in 1815, toward a more multilateral and open system for settling disputes. The Concert of Europe, created at Vienna, convened numerous international conferences during the nineteenth century and for the most part preserved peace among the great powers. But Bismarck's diplomacy to unite Germany dealt this emerging liberal systemic structure a damaging blow. Although Bismarck tried to replace the Concert of Europe with an intricate series of offsetting alliances, his secretive style of diplomacy bred suspicion. Once Bismarck was gone, Kaiser Wilhelm II proved less capable at navigating the system. Notice here the causal effect of the individual level of analysis—Bismarck was able to offset domestic and systemic factors to make diplomacy work to preserve peace; the kaiser was not.

CAUSAL ARROW: LEVELS OF ANALYSIS

Overturned Concert of Europe	Pursued secret diplomacy	Bismarck
SYSTEMIC STRUCTURAL	SYSTEMIC PROCESS	INDIVIDUAL

As the liberal perspective sees it, the kaiser blundered his way into a naval competition with Great Britain and military strategies toward France and Russia that ultimately produced rigid alliances and self-initiating mobilization plans. The explanation thus far emphasizes diplomatic mistakes at the individual level of analysis. Wilhelm was not being pressured to do what he did by domestic or systemic forces. In the crisis of July 1914, German and European diplomacy then got caught up in a spiral of action and reaction, compounding the march to war. Each decision narrowed the options of the next decision in what liberal perspectives call path dependence. Eventually, the process led to the last move of the prisoner's dilemma, in which war seemed to be inevitable. Now the explanation draws on the interactive or systemic process level of analysis. Meanwhile, other liberal causes at the systemic structural level, such as expanding trade and the Hague Conferences called in 1899 and 1907 to resolve disputes peacefully through multilateral consensus, proved too weak to head off war.

Diplomatic miscalculations were abetted by domestic institutional weaknesses in most of the major continental powers. At the domestic level of analysis, Germany's political system was sharply divided between royalist and socialist factions, and its parliament, the Reichstag, had minimal controls over military plans and spending. The czar in Russia was a weak leader with a crumbling imperial administration, and nationalism was eating away at the vital organs of the once mighty Austrian (after 1867, Austro-Hungarian) and Ottoman (remnant of the Golden Age of Islam) Empires. A closer look at these diplomatic and institutional developments illustrates how liberal perspectives emphasize interactions and institutions, rather than power balancing or ideologies, as the primary causes of war and peace.

Secret Diplomacy: Bismarck

After weakening, if not effectively destroying, the Concert of Europe system through wars with Austria and France, Bismarck in 1873 reconstituted the Three Emperors' League, a faint reproduction of the old Holy Alliance. (Identity-based explanations might give more weight to the "Holy" or religious aspect, whereas Bismarck was more interested in the realist "Alliance" aspect.) Germany, Austria-Hungary, and Russia were still led by traditional monarchs. Unlike the emerging constitutional monarchs in Britain and France, they resisted liberal politics and pledged to oppose rebellion in other countries. The Three Emperors' League was immediately tested in the Balkans, a region that produced most of the crises after 1870 and eventually war in 1914. In 1876, Bulgaria, which for centuries had been under Turkish rule, revolted. Russia proclaimed support for its Orthodox religious brethren in Bulgaria. The czar was either genuinely motivated to protect Christians in the Balkans or used this identity factor for realist expansionist aims. Austria-Hungary and Great Britain suspected the latter—suspicions that had led them earlier to block Russia's advance toward the Balkans in the Crimean War in the 1850s. Britain feared Russia's dominance of the Dardanelles, as well as its relentless push through central Asia toward India, then Britain's prize colonial territory. Thus, when Russian and Bulgarian forces reached the gates of Constantinople in 1878 and announced the Treaty of San Stefano, creating a Bulgarian state and drastically weakening Turkey, Bismarck with British support called a conference, the last major conference of the Concert of Europe era. Britain and Russia solved the most contentious issues before the conference, leading to significant Russian concessions. Hence, the Berlin Conference in 1878 left a bad taste in the mouth of the Russians, and Russia thereafter blamed Germany.

Over the next fifteen years, Germany and Russia grew apart, creating one of the fault lines that contributed to World War I. In 1879, Bismarck concluded a secret alliance with Austria-Hungary against Russia. Austria, in turn, gave Germany veto power over its policies in the Balkans. This was the basis for the crucial role that Germany played in Austrian diplomacy in 1914 (see the following discussion). Bismarck renewed the Three Emperors' League in 1881, but its purpose was now purely defensive. Each country pledged to remain neutral if one of them went to war against a fourth country. Russia would stay out of a war between Germany and France, and Austria-Hungary would stay out of a war between Russia and Great Britain. In 1882, Bismarck concluded still another alliance with Italy. This one pledged Italian assistance to Germany against a French attack and to Austria-Hungary against a Russian attack. One of the rigid alliances, the Triple Alliance—Germany, Austria-Hungary, and Italy—was now in place. Another Bulgarian crisis in 1885 shattered the Three Emperors' League for good. Bismarck made one final effort to maintain ties with Russia, the Reinsurance Treaty of 1887. But when Bismarck left office—essentially fired—in 1890, Kaiser Wilhelm II did not renew the treaty.

Although Germany rose rapidly in power from 1870 to 1890, Bismarck's diplomacy preserved the peace. Could his successors have replicated that virtuoso performance? Some prominent realists think so.[18] They judge that systemic factors were driving Bismarck's policy, not individual-level factors. Hence, someone else as adept as Bismarck might have been able to continue his success. But the liberal and identity perspectives might argue that that is expecting too much from any individual. Indeed, even by realist logic, Bismarck's performance was lacking. For example, he did relatively little to reassure France except to avoid rivalry in colonial disputes. Instead, he was the principal architect of annexing Alsace-Lorraine after the Franco-Prussian War of 1871 (the last of three wars leading to the unification of Germany), even though he knew this policy would poison French–German relations thereafter. He did it to weaken France, expecting France to be an enemy for good: "An enemy, whose honest friendship can never be won, must at least be rendered somewhat less harmful."[19] Bismarck apparently considered France a permanent enemy and contaminated the realist logic of a flexible balance of power with identity factors. Realism says to never regard a country as either a permanent enemy or a permanent friend and to be ready to align with any country, regardless of friendship or animosity, to counter greater power. Even if Bismarck had followed that rule, could he have reassured France any more than he was able to reassure Russia? After all, Russia made the first alliance with France relatively soon (four years) after Bismarck left office. Would that not have happened eventually, whoever succeeded Bismarck? From realist perspectives, diplomacy can do only what the balance of power allows. And from the liberal and identity perspectives, the balance of power in Europe before World War I was flawed either because it relied too much on secrecy and manipulation or because it demanded perfect—we might say angelic—statesmanship, which even Bismarck was unable to deliver. Thus, realist perspectives enthrone Bismarck as the master statesman, while liberal and identity perspectives counter that only a godlike statesman could have pulled it off.

Clumsy Diplomacy: Wilhelm II

From a liberal perspective, Kaiser Wilhelm II was clearly a less capable diplomat than Bismarck and quickly stoked further antagonism between Germany and Russia, contributing to the Franco-Russian Alliance of 1894. He also initiated a colonial and naval rivalry with Great Britain, something that Bismarck had astutely avoided. In 1895, the kaiser sent a famous telegram to President Paul Krüger of the independent Boer states, settled by Germans in the South African Transvaal. Krüger's army had just defeated a raid into the Transvaal supported by British colonialists. The so-called Krüger telegram congratulated the Boer leader for the victory. It was a gratuitous slap at the British. The kaiser carried the insult further and launched a major shipbuilding program to challenge British naval supremacy. Envious of the British ships he saw on his summer vacations in England, he launched an arms race that witnessed the production of more and bigger battleships, culminating in the famous Dreadnought competition.[20] The secret and rapid buildup of the German navy under the determined leadership of Admiral Alfred von Tirpitz was a key factor contributing to growing rivalries before World War I.

Other colonial conflicts followed. German and French interests clashed in the Moroccan crises in 1905 and 1911. Russia and Austria-Hungary almost went to war in a Balkan crisis in 1908–1909 after Austria-Hungary annexed Bosnia-Herzegovina (where Sarajevo is located, the site of the assassination of Archduke Ferdinand, which triggered World War I, and, by the way, the central city in the Bosnian crisis of 1992–1995). Balkan wars broke out again in 1912–1913. In October 1912, Montenegro, another small Balkan state, declared war on Turkey and was quickly supported by Bulgaria, Serbia, and

Kaiser Wilhelm II signed this mobilization order, which amounted to a German declaration of war against Russia, in August 1914. Chancellor Theobald von Bethmann-Hollweg countersigned the document. Liberal views fault Wilhelm II's diplomatic failures for the onset of war.

Greece. After this crisis was settled, Bulgaria attacked Serbia and Greece in June 1913. In both crises, Austria and Russia stood eyeball to eyeball, fearing that the other might gain an advantage. Germany supported Austria and had significant influence over Austrian policy, as called for by the Treaty of 1879. Great Britain, which sent its war minister, Richard Haldane, to Berlin in 1912, sought to ensure that Germany would not threaten Belgium. Suspicions were mounting for the final drama of war.

Misperceptions and Mobilization Plans

Why did war break out in 1914 and not in 1912 or 1913? From a liberal perspective, diplomacy had prevented war in earlier crises. Why didn't diplomacy do so again in 1914? For three reasons, liberal accounts suggest. First, Germany expected Britain to remain neutral in 1914 as it had in previous crises, thus permitting a local settlement. Second, mobilization plans—such as the Schlieffen Plan—were finalized in 1913 that called for an automatic escalation to war. Now the slightest spark could ignite a firestorm. And third, civilian institutions in various countries broke down, contributing to a last-move situation familiar in game theory, when the only choice remaining is to go to war. Notice that all these factors are contingent on interactive factors (misperceptions, bureaucratic plans, and policy failures); they are not consequences of unbalanced alliances (power) or conflicting identities (ideas). A primary focus on interrelationships is typical of liberal explanations of international events.

On July 5, a week after the assassination of the archduke, the kaiser met the Austrian ambassador in Germany and told him that Germany would back Austria against Serbia "whatever Austria's decision." The German chancellor, Bethmann-Hollweg, confirmed this commitment the next day in what became known as a "blank check," giving Austria a free hand to start a war.[21] The kaiser did not expect Russia, Serbia's ally, to go to war and did not even discuss the possibility that Britain might intervene. Kaiser Wilhelm left town for his regular summer North Sea cruise. Austria sent an ultimatum to Serbia on July 23. The Serbs replied on July 27 and appeared to concede to Austria's demands. The kaiser, who had just returned from his cruise, ordered negotiations, proposing that Austria "halt in Belgrade"—meaning occupy Belgrade temporarily—until Serbia met other demands. But the kaiser's instructions did not arrive in Vienna until July 28, after Austria had declared war against Serbia—perhaps deliberately delayed, according to some realist accounts that we have discussed, to start a preventive war.

Now the issue hinged on whether the war could be localized between Austria and Serbia without involving their allies, Germany and Russia. British neutrality was key. If Britain did not support Russia, an ally under the Triple Entente, a wider war might be avoided. As already noted, some German officials did not expect Britain to intervene. But on the evening of July 29, a telegram from London warned firmly that Britain would support Russia if war occurred. Germany now tried to rein in its Austrian ally. Early in the morning of July 30, Bethmann-Hollweg fired off his famous "world on fire" telegrams urging Vienna to implement the kaiser's instructions to negotiate—just a smoke screen, as some realist accounts see it, to shift blame for war onto Russia.

Military plans and mobilization, however, now made diplomacy difficult. War plans were based on quick strikes, and Germany's Schlieffen Plan, as we have noted, called for an attack first on France and then on Russia. Military plans relied on precise time-tables and the complex movements of troops. In response to Austria's declaration of war against Serbia, Russia had already partially mobilized on July 29, and the czar actually ordered full mobilization that same evening but canceled the order two hours later when he received another telegram from his cousin Willy. Under intense pressure from his generals, however, Nicholas went ahead the next day with full mobilization. In response, Germany sent an ultimatum to Russia on July 31 and declared war on August 1. When the kaiser met with his generals to order them to limit the war to Russia and not attack France, von Moltke, the German army chief of staff, protested:

> Your Majesty, it cannot be done. The deployment of millions cannot be improvised. If Your Majesty insists on leading the whole army to the East, it will not be an army ready for battle but a disorganized mob. . . . These arrangements took a whole year of intricate labor to complete and once settled they cannot be altered.[22]

The Last Move

The kaiser won the argument, and German troops in the west were pulled back. Although a German infantry unit had already crossed into Luxembourg, another unit went in and, following the kaiser's instruction, ordered the first unit out.[23] France mobilized the same day, even though it positioned its troops ten kilometers from the border to avoid accidents. Nevertheless, German military and political leaders doubted that France would stay out of the war, and on August 3 Germany declared war on France. The next day, German troops invaded Belgium, and Britain entered the war. A general European war was under way.[24]

From the liberal perspective, no one sought a general war, but rational behavior ultimately led to it. Why? The process of interaction broke down. In iterative game theory—which is the liberal perspective, illustrated by the example of the prisoners interacting regularly in the prison yard in Chapter 1—actors count on being able to play the game again tomorrow. This expectation, or shadow of the future, encourages cooperation. But if they come to believe that they are playing the game for the last time, the so-called last move, they face the static prisoner's dilemma or realist situation and defect. In a sense, liberal accounts argue, this is what happened to ignite World War I. Listen to the conclusions of political scientist Marc Trachtenberg: "[Bethmann-Hollweg] had not set out to provoke a great war. . . . He had made a certain effort to get the Austrians to pull back. But war was almost bound to come eventually, so he would just stand aside and let it come now."[25] No one wanted war, but by a process of action-reaction the great powers became dependent on a path that eventually resulted in war.

Notice the language of the pending last move ("almost bound to come eventually"). Under these circumstances, it was rational for Bethmann-Hollweg to behave the way he did. Now compare this argument to the previous, realist one that Germany sought a general war to avoid the future dominance of Russia. In the realist argument, Germany always intended war because future relative power projections required it. In the liberal argument, Germany did not reach that conclusion until late in the process of diplomatic action and reaction. In the realist case, relative power projections at the systemic structural level caused the war; in the liberal case, negotiating dynamics at the systemic process level brought it about. Observe that in neither argument are Germany's intentions the primary cause of the war. Germany's intentions are the result of either power requirements (realist) or interactive factors (liberal).

CAUSAL ARROW: PERSPECTIVES

Mobilization plans	Create suspicion and distrust	Lead to last move and war
LIBERAL	IDENTITY	REALIST

But the debate goes on because, as Professor Kier Lieber notes, World War I "appears to offer at least some empirical support for practically any theory or explanation."[26] Lieber sees a larger role for intentions and identity factors. On the basis of new materials obtained from former East German archives after the Cold War, he concludes that the war was neither unintended, as power balancing (defensive) realists might argue, nor a consequence of diplomatic blunders, as liberal accounts might suggest, but "that German leaders went to war in 1914 with their eyes wide open."[27] The war, in short, was intended. For Lieber, the intentions were caused primarily by hegemonic aspirations. He is a proponent of the offensive realist school, which assumes that countries always seek more power, not just enough power to balance. For others, the intention may derive from ideational or identity factors such as Germany's heroic self-image and militant ideology, as we examine below in the section on identity perspectives.

CAUSAL ARROW: PERSPECTIVES

Intention to go to war	To increase hegemonic power	Leads to diplomatic crisis
IDENTITY	REALIST	LIBERAL

Weak Domestic Institutions

The last-move argument assumes that diplomats are in control of institutions, especially the military, and act rationally. But other liberal explanations suggest that diplomats may not be in control and that institutions malfunction. In the case of World War I, institutional weaknesses contributed to fragmentation and faulty coordination of policy. German diplomacy, for example, was weakened by "an astonishing lack of coordination between the political and the military authorities."[28] Political interests that sought to avoid war, or at least to shift the blame for war, worked at cross-purposes with military strategies that counted on precise timetables and a two-front war to achieve victory.

CAUSAL ARROW: LEVELS OF ANALYSIS

Leads to war	Leads to out-of-control diplomacy	Institutional weakness
SYSTEMIC STRUCTURAL	SYSTEMIC PROCESS	DOMESTIC

German domestic institutions were also divided. The conservative coalition that ran the German government consisted of landed agricultural interests (rye) and industrial leaders (iron). Known as the **iron-rye coalition**, it excluded for the most part the growing working class and its socialist leaders who held the majority in the Reichstag. The only way this growing division could be overcome was by war. A policy of war diverted resources to the military, which the Reichstag did not fully control, and co-opted socialist opponents through appeals to patriotism and nationalism. As one historian concludes, reflecting a foreign policy level of analysis, Germany "sought to consolidate the position of the ruling classes with a successful imperialist foreign policy."[29]

> **iron-rye coalition:** a domestic coalition of military and agricultural interests that dominated German politics before World War I.

Domestic cleavages were even stronger in the other monarchies. Austria-Hungary was disintegrating from within, the Russian czar was in a precarious position, and the Ottoman Empire was barely surviving. Within four years of the outbreak of war, all three of these institutions would cease to exist.

Elsewhere domestic institutions were becoming more popularly based and representative. Representative government made it more difficult to conduct foreign policy in a timely and coherent way. In the United States, President Woodrow Wilson campaigned for reelection in 1916 on a promise to keep the United States out of war; nevertheless, by April 1917 Germany's policy of unlimited submarine warfare and the sinking of the American ship *Lusitania* led the United States to enter the war. American involvement may have been decisive, and German diplomacy blundered by alienating the United States. Germany defeated Russia in early 1918 just as American doughboys arrived to counter the additional German forces moved from the Russian to the western front. Germany may well have worn down the western allies if fresh American troops had not entered the battle.

Insufficient Interdependence: Trade and the Hague Conferences

International commerce and banking had expanded dramatically in the last quarter of the nineteenth century. Not only colonial trade but also trade among the industrial powers reached levels before World War I that would not be reached again until the 1970s. Britain had led an effort to liberalize trade unilaterally, and some countries followed, such as France. But there were no effective multilateral institutions to coordinate and expand this effort, and other countries, such as Germany and the United States, did not liberalize their trade policies. Still, the growing numbers of bankers and merchants opposed war and called for the peaceful resolution of political disputes. A best-selling book published just two years before the outbreak of World War I proclaimed that war was a "great illusion" because the costs of war from the breakup of lucrative trade and investment now far exceeded its benefits. War had become obsolete, its author, Norman Angell, declared.[30] Multilateral diplomacy was a better way to resolve disputes. The Hague Conferences, convened in 1899 and 1907 by initiative of the Russian czar, brought small as well as large states into the diplomatic process (twenty-six states in 1899, forty-four in 1907). Although these conferences solved no major issues, they reformed the rules and methods of diplomacy and started discussions to control arms races.

From the liberal perspective, trade and law were becoming more important aspects of international affairs than power and secret diplomacy. William Gladstone, who became British prime minister in 1880, foresaw this development and observed that

> a new law of nations is gradually taking hold of the mind, and coming to sway the practice, of the world; a law which recognizes independence, which frowns upon aggression, which favours the pacific, not the bloody settlement of disputes, which aims at permanent not temporary adjustments: above all, which recognizes, as a tribunal of paramount authority, the general judgement of civilized mankind.[31]

Notice Gladstone's emphasis on classic liberal themes—law, practice, pacific settlement of disputes, permanent solutions, and universal participation—which he terms the "general judgement of civilized mankind." Gladstone's insights became the banner of another great statesman in the next century. The American president Woodrow Wilson championed worldviews that emphasized open markets, the rule of law, and collective rather than national security. From the liberal point of view, these factors were too weak to head off World War I. But after the war, they formed the edifice of a whole new approach to managing military relations in international politics, which we discuss more fully in the next chapter. (See Table 2-2 for a summary of the liberal explanations of the causes of World War I.)

>>> Identity Explanations

Identity perspectives on World War I emphasize the ideas and norms that motivate prewar diplomacy and military rivalries. These ideas are both shared and autonomous, rational and psychological. The dominant ideology in prewar Europe was nationalism. Three broad varieties emerged in the nineteenth century. **Militant nationalism** focused on cultural and ultimately racial differences and advocated a kind of aggressive, heroic approach to international relations. **Liberal nationalism** focused on political ideologies and called for wider participation and the rule of law in both domestic and international politics. **Socialist nationalism** sought greater economic equality and social justice, especially among social classes and with colonial territories. Each variety of nationalism also had an international or collectivist dimension. Militant nationalism, for example, embraced Social Darwinism, a collectivist norm of political and military struggle to

militant nationalism: a form of nineteenth-century nationalism that focused on cultural and racial differences and advocated an aggressive, heroic approach to international relations.

liberal nationalism: a form of nineteenth-century nationalism that focused on political ideologies and called for wider participation and the rule of law in both domestic and international politics.

socialist nationalism: a form of nineteenth-century nationalism that sought greater economic equality and social justice, especially in class and colonial relationships.

TABLE 2-2

The Causes of World War I: The Liberal Perspective and Levels of Analysis

Liberal perspective		
Systemic	*Structure*	Weakness of common institutions initiated by Hague Conferences
		Collapse of Concert of Europe conference system
	Process	Interactions and path dependence: • Secretive German diplomacy: Drops treaty with Russia, antagonizes Britain • Automatic mobilization plans—"last move" • Growing but insufficient trade, social, and legal interdependence
Foreign policy		German elite use imperial expansion to unify domestic society
Domestic		Cartelized domestic politics in Germany result in overexpansion
		Divisions between Congress and presidency in the United States delay entry into war to counterbalance threats in Europe
		Domestic disintegration of Ottoman and Austro-Hungarian empires/institutions invites aggression
Individual		Some individuals (Bismarck) more effective than others, who are clumsy (Kaiser Wilhelm II)

Level of analysis

preserve and promote cultural superiority. Liberal nationalism supported the Hague legal process and later collective security under the League of Nations, while socialist nationalism embraced a series of international meetings known as the Second International, which advocated the solidarity of the working classes. Let's look more closely at these different types of nationalism.

Militant and Racist Nationalism

Rising nationalism in the nineteenth century weakened the solidarity or collective identity of the European conference system, the Concert of Europe. Bismarck contended that there was no higher principle or purpose than service to one's country. This kind of nationalism exalted the culture and language of each nation, which did not change much and could not be shared easily with other nations.

It was a short step from this type of cultural nationalism to the virulent militarist and racist doctrines that spread in Europe in the late nineteenth century. Militarism reflected the imperative to organize and train a citizen army, often including extensive reserves. Prior to the eighteenth century, armies consisted mostly of nobles, peasants recruited for each campaign, and mercenaries. Wars were fought among tens of thousands, not millions, and direct casualties were relatively low (most soldiers died of diseases). In the eighteenth century, Prussia began to change this model for armies by introducing "limited military conscription, intensive tactical training, efficient artillery barrages, and skillful generalship." Napoleon accelerated these developments. As Robert Osgood and Robert Tucker write, he "created a 'nation in arms' . . . [and] transformed warfare into a national crusade, involving not just tactical maneuver and attrition of the enemy's supply lines but annihilation of the enemy's forces, occupation of his territory, and even political conversion of his people."[32] War now had the objective of regime change. The industrial revolution completed this transformation. It created not only new technologies of military power but also a whole new arms industry that promoted and thrived on accelerating arms races, such as the Dreadnought battleship competition mentioned earlier.

Military technological changes contributed to a widespread belief among European military establishments that offensive strategies would hold the advantage in the next war. This belief led to the need for rapid mobilization plans and secret military planning.

Across Europe, World War I was greeted with nationalistic enthusiasm. Here German citizens rally in late July 1914 in front of the kaiser's palace (right) in Berlin.

In this way, ideas created the mobilization spiral that caused World War I, not the mobilization process itself, which liberal perspectives emphasize. A militarist mentality created the **cult of the offensive**.[33] This belief in the advantage of using military power offensively was the reason rapid mobilization plans were developed in the first place; the mobilization plans and their interaction at the end of July 1914 were simply a consequence. Notice again how arguments are differentiated in terms of the way the causal arrow runs, in this case from ideas (cult of the offensive) to both interactions (mobilization plans) and power (relative military capabilities), rather than the reverse.

CAUSAL ARROW: PERSPECTIVES

Shifts relative military capabilities → Drives mobilization plans → Cult of the offensive

REALIST　　　LIBERAL　　　IDENTITY

cult of the offensive: a belief in the advantage of using military power offensively.

Liberal Nationalism

The second type of nationalism that emerged in the nineteenth century was more ideological and political than racial. It too emphasized culture and military struggle. But it offered political rather than racial visions of the way the world was unfolding. Liberal nationalism saw a trend toward increased individual freedom, fundamental human rights, and the rule of law. It emphasized equality of opportunity, especially the possibility of education and participation of all members of society in the political life and institutions of the country.

The United States and Great Britain led the development of liberal nationalism. By 1830, the United States had enfranchised all white male citizens. Through two major reform laws in 1832 and 1867, Great Britain also extended the franchise. Britain first and then the United States, after a bloody civil war, eliminated slavery, although political and economic, as opposed to legal, emancipation of black citizens took another century or more to achieve. Women too waited another century. Still, these countries planted the seed of expanding individual freedom and developed some of the early international movements for human rights and international law—for example, the British campaign against the international slave trade in the early nineteenth century.

More utopian versions of liberal ideology proclaimed universal peace. Immanuel Kant, the eighteenth-century German philosopher, wrote an *Idea for a Universal History and Perpetual Peace,* in which he predicted that democracy would spread and lead to a federation of peaceful states.[34] This type of thinking may have contributed to a complacency before World War I that war was increasingly obsolete and that international organizations, law, and trade could resolve disputes, as Gladstone and Angell had envisioned.

Socialist Nationalism

Socialist nationalism focused more on the social and economic equality of individuals and advocated that state institutions restrict economic freedoms and redistribute economic wealth from the capitalist to the working classes. While communism, a more radical version of socialism, did not yield political fruit until 1917, when Vladimir Ilyich Lenin installed it in Russia, many European and other societies—for example, India—adopted socialist programs well before World War I.

Socialist parties emerged and sharpened conflicts with liberal and conservative parties. Socialist parties met in international conferences in 1907, 1910, and 1912, known as the Second International, and denounced militarism and war. In the end, however, nationalism proved stronger than internationalism. Although Social Democrats, representing the interests of the working class, held the majority in the German parliament in 1914, they voted on August 4, 1914, unanimously for war. In the 1860s, Bismarck had used war to co-opt the liberal nationalists and unify Germany. Now in 1914 conservatives in Germany, Russia, and other countries used war to co-opt the social nationalists and forge ideological unity through conservative and militant nationalism.

Social Darwinism

Social Darwinism: a nineteenth-century worldview that saw a struggle among nations for survival of the fittest.

Militant, liberal, and socialist spirits came together at the end of the nineteenth century in the worldview of **Social Darwinism**. Charles Darwin, an English scientist, published in 1859 his theory of evolution in *The Origin of Species*. Darwin identified a process of competition and natural selection that accounted for the evolution and survival of biological species. In *The Descent of Man,* published in 1871, Darwin applied his theory to the origins of human beings. Many nineteenth-century political leaders concluded that it must also apply to the survival and evolution of human societies and, indeed, nation-states. Bismarck, for example, said that "without struggle there can be no life and, if we wish to continue living, we must also be reconciled to further struggle."[35] President Teddy Roosevelt once famously mused, "Unless we keep the barbarian virtues, the civilized ones will be of little avail."[36] Thus was born the idea of a struggle among nations for the survival of the fittest. Only strong nations survived, and the strength of a nation involved its military power and its cultural cohesion.

Race inevitably became a measure of cultural cohesion for Social Darwinists. It linked culture to biology and seemed to follow from Darwinist logic. It affected all countries during this period. The United States openly discriminated against Chinese immigrants and continued to disenfranchise black Americans. But German leaders were particularly blunt about race. Kaiser Wilhelm II suggested on more than one occasion that the issue for him was race: "Now comes . . . the Germanic peoples' fight for their existence against Russo-Gallia [Russia and France]. No further conference can smooth this over, for it is not a question of high politics but of race . . . for what is at stake is whether the Germanic race is to be or not to be in Europe."[37] His army chief of staff, von Moltke, agreed: "A European war is bound to come sooner or later, and then it will be, in the last resort, a struggle between Teuton and Slav." And so did his foreign minister, Gottlieb von Jagow: "The struggle between Teuton and Slav was bound to come."[38]

CAUSAL ARROW: PERSPECTIVES

These comments reflect an identity perspective. The kaiser explicitly rules out the possibility that liberal factors might resolve the problem ("no further conference can smooth this over") and says the question is not one of "high politics," a frequent reference to relations among great powers or realist factors. Moltke's and Jagow's comments suggest

TABLE 2-3

The Causes of World War I: The Identity Perspective and Levels of Analysis

Identity perspective		
Systemic	*Structure*	Social Darwinism—shared mentality of international struggle
	Process	Spread or alignment of ideas and ideologies: • Loss of moderation—spread of militarism, cult of the offensive drive mobilization plans • Britain and United States align as democracies even though they are the two largest powers
Foreign policy		Domestic racist clique hijacks German foreign policy
Domestic		Hypernationalism (mixture of race and militarism in Germany as a whole) drives Germany to war
		Liberal nationalism in the United States and Great Britain—precipitates alliance of democracies that isolates Germany
Individual		Evil or emotionally unstable leaders: • Bethmann-Hollweg? • Kaiser Wilhelm II?

Level of analysis (vertical label along left side of table)

that identity differences are bound to override diplomatic efforts for peace and lead to the last move ("war is bound to come sooner or later"). In each case, ideas are driving diplomacy and conflict, not the other way around.

Here was a witch's brew of culture and race stirred together in a kind of hypernationalism that would afflict world politics for the next century. Some historians see German war aims as the direct cause of World War I. Others agree that hypernationalism was present but came to the fore much more virulently in World War II. (See Table 2-3 for a summary of identity explanations of the causes of World War I.)

≫ Critical Theory Explanations

Lenin saw World War I as a product of capitalist dynamics. The capitalist countries would fight one another for markets, and communist countries would be left to pick up the pieces. As soon as Lenin seized control in Russia in 1917, he pulled the Russian forces out of the capitalist war between Germany and the west. He concentrated on building communism in a single country, believing that the historical dialectic of class conflict was on his side. Critical theories, such as Marxism, emphasize the deeper material forces propelling history toward its predetermined end. In the case of Marxism, the predetermined end is communism; in other cases of critical theory, it might be emancipation of marginalized voices or simply deconstruction of all power relationships. Critical theories remind us that attempts to understand history through perspectives are always selective and therefore biased. Social forces are holistic. They drive social science researchers no less than do the political, economic, and military events that researchers try selectively to understand.

Critical theories are skeptical of rationalist explanations. Realism, for example, points to a famous statement by Lord Palmerston, a British prime minister in the nineteenth century. Speaking for Britain, Palmerston said, "We have no eternal allies and no permanent enemies." This statement became realism's mantra—countries should not align with one another based on domestic ideological sentiments but, instead, solely on the basis of relative power considerations to confront the greater power. Yet Lord Palmerston also said that "the independence of constitutional states . . . never can be a matter of indifference to the British parliament, or, I should hope, to the British public. Constitutional states I would consider to be the natural allies of this country."[39] Now, Palmerston is saying that in making foreign policy, the domestic political identities of countries matter more than the countries' relative power. He is hinting at the tendency of democracies (he calls them constitutional states) to align and not go to war with one another, thereby creating the "democratic peace." Which statement is correct?

Critical theories make us skeptical of all these efforts to select and emphasize specific factors to understand international relations, whether power or identity factors. Realist scholars writing about the past do not tell the whole story, not because they are devious but because they can't. Neither, of course, can scholars writing from liberal or identity

TABLE 2-4

The Causes of World War I: The Critical Theory Perspective and Levels of Analysis[a]

Level of analysis	Critical theory perspective		
Systemic	Structure	Historical materialism drives clash between capitalist and communist states; once Russia becomes communist, it pulls out of World War I to let capitalist states fight it out	
	Process	Dialectic drives history through class conflict	
Foreign policy		—	
Domestic		Russia becomes vanguard of the proletariat	
Individual		Lenin builds communism in one country	

a. Factors identified at the various levels of analysis are not causes but parts of a holistic explanation.

perspectives. No single perspective or level of analysis suffices. Reality is holistic, not fragmented or capable of being decomposed piece by piece.

Critical theories, on the other hand, face a comparable limitation. Even though they insist on studying history as a whole, not by selecting and focusing on specific hypotheses, they have to concede that they can never tell us the whole story of history. History is too gargantuan, which is why mainstream scholars turn to selective perspectives in the first place. Critical theory can tell us the story of history only from the social vantage point of a particular critical theory scholar. As we see in this book, the social vantage point that critical theorists often select is that of the poor, oppressed, and disenfranchised peoples of the world, whose interests, in these theorists' view, are systematically de-emphasized in mainstream perspectives. (See Table 2-4 for a summary of critical theory explanations of the causes of World War I. Bear in mind, however, that critical theories do not actually distinguish among the various levels of analysis for causal purposes.)

SUMMARY

Our discussion of World War I shows how the concepts emphasized by each perspective play out in the actual course of historical events. Realist perspectives emphasize material factors such as anarchy and the security dilemma (self-help), rising (Germany) and declining (Great Britain) states, power conversion through more and less efficient bureaucracies, imperialistic domestic interest groups (cartelized politics in Germany), and weak leaders (Czar Nicholas II and Kaiser Wilhelm II). Liberal perspectives emphasize the absence or demise of common international institutions (Concert of Europe), the depth or shallowness of interdependence (the Hague Conferences), the misperceptions and accidents of diplomacy (secret diplomacy and path dependence, leading to the last move), and the breakdown of domestic policy coordination and institutions. Identity perspectives emphasize the variety of nationalist ideologies and their accompanying international discourses. Social Darwinism and the spread of hypernationalist ideologies glorifying the cult of the offensive won out over Kantian liberal and Marxist socialist discourses. Evil or emotionally unstable leaders may have also contributed.

The principal perspectives emphasize these concepts from different levels of analysis. The kaiser may have been a uniquely weak leader (individual level), Germany an aggressive militarist state (domestic level), the leadership manipulative in using war to overcome domestic fissures (foreign policy level), or Germany just too powerful to contain (systemic level).

Critical theories weave all these causal factors from different perspectives and levels of analysis into a single historical drama, such as dialectical materialism in the case of Marxist theories. This drama is driven by factors beyond the control of theorists and thus not subject to rational manipulation. We cannot understand or make the future by applying tested propositions from the past to policy prescriptions for the future.

The variety of explanations is bewildering. But our analytical tools help us distinguish and organize them. Then, as scholars and students, we have an obligation to keep testing and evaluating the explanations. We may never obtain definitive answers, but we can know more, especially about how and why we disagree.

 Sharpen your skills with SAGE edge at **edge.sagepub.com/nau4e.**
SAGE edge for students provides a personalized approach to help you
accomplish your coursework goals in an easy-to-use learning environment.

KEY CONCEPTS

STUDY QUESTIONS

1. Do you believe that the two cousins, Willy
    and Nicky, could have prevented World War
    I? What level of analysis does your answer
    reflect?

2. Why is Bismarck's diplomacy, which included
    the Berlin Conference in 1878, considered to be
    realist rather than liberal?

3. What are the differences among the following
    domestic-level explanations of World War I:
    imperialistic cartels, poorly coordinated military
    and political institutions, and nationalist political
    ideologies?

4. Can you give three explanations, one from each
    perspective, of why World War I started in 1914
    and not earlier?

5. Which perspective is reflected and which
    rejected in the following argument about
    World War I from John Mearsheimer's *The
    Tragedy of Great Power Politics?* Explain your
    conclusion.

    Even if Bismarck had remained in power
    past 1890, it is unlikely that he could
    have forestalled the Franco-Russian
    alliance with clever diplomacy. . . . France
    and Russia came together because they
    were scared of Germany's growing
    power, not because Germany behaved
    aggressively or foolishly.[40]

6. What level of analysis is Professor Jack Levy
    emphasizing when he writes, "It is certainly
    plausible that the July crisis might have ended
    differently if other individuals had been in positions
    of power at the beginning of July 1914"?[41]

7. What level of analysis is Professor Jack Snyder
    using when he concludes that "Germany's
    expansionism was compelled by its position in
    the international system . . . is fundamentally
    unconvincing [because] [e]ven a cursory look at
    Germany's international position will show that
    the nation's vulnerability and insecurity were
    caused by its own aggressive policies"?[42]

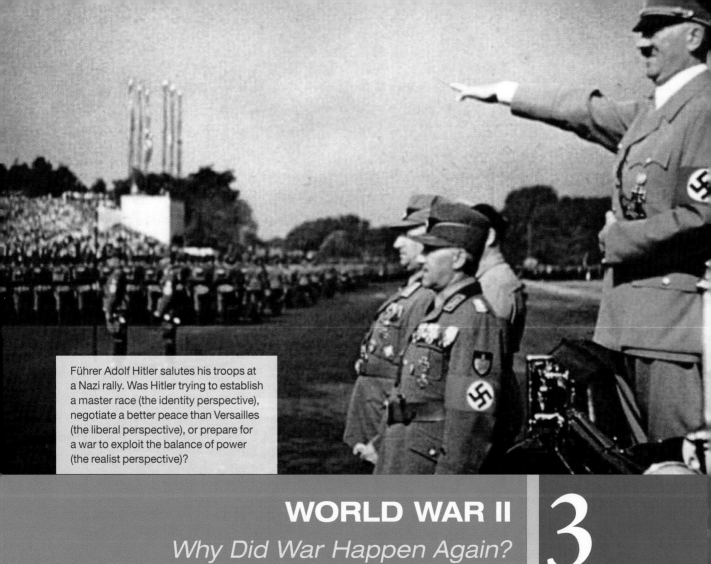

Führer Adolf Hitler salutes his troops at a Nazi rally. Was Hitler trying to establish a master race (the identity perspective), negotiate a better peace than Versailles (the liberal perspective), or prepare for a war to exploit the balance of power (the realist perspective)?

WORLD WAR II
Why Did War Happen Again?

3

On November 5, 1937, Adolf Hitler summoned his generals to a meeting in Berlin. The meeting was expected to be routine, but once it began Hitler swore the participants to secrecy and proceeded to outline his plans for war. According to minutes drafted from memory a few days later by an army adjutant, Colonel Friedrich Hossbach, Hitler said that the aim of German policy was to secure a larger living space—*Lebensraum*—for the German racial community. This expansion could be accomplished only through war, which had to occur before 1943–1945, when German power would peak. The first steps would be to seize Czechoslovakia and Austria. Hitler believed that France, England, and Poland had already written off the Czechs and had too many problems of their own to offer any resistance. But if they did, Germany must counter with lightning strikes. The deck would then be cleared for the final strike against the primary enemy, Russia.[1]

Lebensraum: Hitler's expansionist ideology that proposed a larger living space for the German racial community.

Is this the explanation for World War II? Did the war result from a premeditated plan by a single racist man (notice the identity perspective and individual level of analysis) who had written two books ten years earlier—the two-volume *Mein Kampf* in 1925–1926 and a secret, unpublished book in 1928—that not only laid out a strategy for conquering territory in the east but also hatched his horrific plans for the extermination of the Jews? The war followed this plan pretty closely. As Professor John Mueller concludes, "The Second World War . . . was almost single-handedly created by one man, Adolf Hitler."[2] The explanation seems convincing, right? Case closed. We can go straight to the next chapter.

≫ Causes of Madness

Not so fast. How did a man like Hitler ever come to power in the first place? What domestic-level factors facilitated his rise, and what systemic factors permitted another colossal catastrophe so soon after the death trenches of World War I? What about causal forces from the liberal perspective? Hadn't European diplomats abandoned the balance of power and built a bold new international institution called the League of Nations to settle disputes peacefully? Massive mistakes that set the conditions for war must have been made long before Hitler came to power in January 1933. Did Hitler just exploit these mistakes? Could someone else have started World War II even if he had not? Or would Germany have gone to war eventually because realist factors, such as Germany's unity and exposed central location, continued to fuel the security dilemma, even if Germany and other countries had done almost everything right? We have to try to answer these questions, because World War II killed three times as many people, approximately thirty-five to fifty million, as World War I, six million of them Jews in the Holocaust. What could have caused such madness?

Once again, there is disagreement. Realists ask if World War II wasn't really just a continuation of World War I. The basic problem was the same: anarchy, the security dilemma, and an unstable balance of power. After World War I, Germany was not occupied or destroyed. It remained intact and potentially a looming menace again in the exposed center of the European system (remember the open plains). True, Germany was much weaker. It had lost about 13 percent of its prewar territory, the monarchy had ended, and runaway inflation and economic depression had followed. The Versailles Treaty limited Germany's arms and stripped it of its colonies, but it continued to have the largest population in Europe and one of the most resilient, talented, and efficient societies in the world. The major powers in Europe did not see this problem in the 1920s, distracted, as realists see it, by utopian liberal schemes of collective security centered on the League of Nations. When they did see it in the late 1930s, it was too late. Germany had gathered momentum, as it had before World War I, and the security dilemma intensified with renewed force. Germany was too big to contain without encirclement and too little to feel safe with encirclement.

From the liberal perspective, the balance of power itself was the problem. As the dilemmas with German encirclement suggested, such a balance could never be stable. It had to be replaced by new institutional arrangements. Liberal advocates led by the U.S. president, Woodrow Wilson, proposed a whole new scheme for managing military relations in international politics. The concept of collective security organized force on a different principle, one based on common institutions and the preponderance of power rather than on separate national interests and the balance of power. The League of Nations embodied this imaginative new approach, but it didn't work at the time. Why? Liberal accounts lay the blame largely at the door of the United States. It refused to play its role as a new, leading great power. After helping win World War I, the United States did an about-face, left Europe, refused to join the League, and retreated into isolationism during the 1920s and 1930s. Without the leading power, the League could not muster a preponderance of power, and the world marched off into another nationalist struggle for power.

But why does nationalism have to lead to war? How do nationalities or identities get constructed so as to lead to war? If all nations were satisfied with the status quo, no state would seek to upset it. What kind of nationalism leads to aggression? Identity perspectives have an answer—the kind that derives from revanchism (the desire for revenge), irredentism (the desire to regain territories), racism, and xenophobia. German nationalism after World War I had all these characteristics. Many Germans felt that they had been unjustly blamed for World War I and humiliated by the Versailles Treaty that ended the war.[3] They considered it only reasonable that Germany should regain territories where Germans lived, such as Alsace-Lorraine, which France had seized in World War I (and which, of course, Germany had seized in 1871). Many Germans also indulged in a racism of Aryan superiority and murderous anti-Semitism, and they dehumanized foreigners not of their superior race. This was the extreme nihilistic nationalism that German nationalism unleashed in the 1860s. Otto von Bismarck, the German statesman who unified Germany thorough war, predicted it in conversations with his conservative mentor, Leopold von Gerlach: "I can even think out the idea that some day 'unbelieving Jesuits' will rule over the Mark Brandenburg [core of Prussia] together with a Bonaparte absolutism."[4] Aggressive missionaries (Jesuits) without any beliefs (unbelieving) ruling over Berlin with a Napoleon-like absolutism—not a bad description of the Nazis who controlled Germany from 1933 to 1945.

This time let's start with liberal explanations of the war. President Wilson and the League of Nations may have failed to prevent a second world war, but they left a powerful example of collective security through universal international institutions that was later realized in the UN intervention in 1990–1991 in the first Persian Gulf War (see Chapter 5). Liberal perspectives argue that if there is hope that the world community might someday go beyond the balance of power and domesticate military force—that is, convert it to police power, as in domestic society—this hope will have to grow out of the seed of institutional arrangements in which all nations and people participate. As we will see, other perspectives disagree. Realist perspectives say it still matters more who holds power within those institutions, while identity perspectives argue that the values these institutions promote matter more than the rules or power they employ. Parallel Timeline 3-1 helps organize events leading to World War II by perspectives.

Parallel Timeline 3-1

Events Leading to World War II from Different Perspectives

Realist		Liberal		Identity	
				Nationalism	1900s
Versailles Treaty	1919	League of Nations	1919		
				American exceptionalism/ isolationism	1920s
				Weimar (democratic) Republic struggles and fails in Germany	1920s
				Fascism takes power in Italy; communism in the Soviet Union	1920s
Rapallo Pact	1922	Washington Naval Conference	1922		
France occupies and leaves Ruhr Valley (next to Rhineland); forms alliance with Little Entente	1923				
Locarno Pact	1925	Germany joins League	1925		
		Kellogg-Briand Pact	1928		
				Hitler's idea of a German Third Reich	1930s
Japan invades Manchuria	1931			Japan's idea of a Greater East Asia Co-Prosperity Sphere	1930s
Hitler takes power	1933	Germany and Japan leave League	1933		
		Soviet Union joins League	1933		
		German nonaggression pact with Poland; German-British naval agreement	1934	Spanish Civil War	1934
Italy invades Ethiopia	1935				

Germany occupies Rhineland; signs Axis powers alliance with Italy	1936				Japan and Germany sign Anti-Comintern Pact	1936
Japan invades China	1937					
Germany annexes Austria	March 1938	Appeasement at Munich	September 1938			
Germany occupies Sudetenland	September 1938					
Germany invades Czechoslovakia	March 1939					
Molotov-Ribbentrop Pact	August 1939					
Germany attacks Poland; World War II begins	September 1939					
Germany, Japan, and Italy sign Tripartite Pact	1940					

⟫⟫ Liberal Accounts

In asking Congress to declare war on Germany, Woodrow Wilson emphasized that "the world must be made safe for democracy."[5] Subsequently, in January 1918, he laid out for Congress his famous Fourteen Points, a plan to restructure the world order after the war. Consider the emphasis in this plan on liberal themes of relationships, negotiations, interdependence, and peaceful pursuits (non-zero-sum goals). Wilson advocated open diplomacy, freedom of the seas, general disarmament, removal of trade barriers, impartial settlement of colonial claims, internationalization of the Dardanelles, and establishment of the League of Nations. The program also contained realist elements. It called for territorial and military adjustments: restoration of Belgium, return of Alsace-Lorraine to France, evacuation of Russian territory, readjustment of Italy's frontiers, evacuation of the Balkans, and creation of Poland (actually re-creation—it had been partitioned among Prussia, Russia, and Austria at the end of the eighteenth century) with access to the sea. And there was an important identity element as well, the granting of autonomy or **self-determination** to the national minorities of the Austro-Hungarian and Ottoman Empires. Wilson expected that self-determination would lead to democracy, hence his theme of "making the world safe for democracy." But the plan relied overwhelmingly on the expectation that repetitive practices of trade and diplomacy would condition state behavior to preserve the peace and prepare the way

self-determination: nations' right to autonomy in deciding their own domestic identities.

for democracy to spread and the balance of power to recede. Liberal procedures would steadily trump identity and power disparities.

Collective Security, Not Balance of Power

What was this new approach? Collective security started with a fundamentally different configuration of power. From the liberal perspective, the decentralization or balance of power had failed disastrously. Wilson was an unrelenting critic of the secret treaties, arms races, colonial rivalries, and great power maneuvering that he believed drove the balance of power toward war before 1914. Restoring that system after World War I, as the Congress of Vienna did after the Napoleonic Wars, was out of the question. Wilson wanted "no odor of the Vienna settlement" at Versailles.[6] The new approach of collective security would centralize, not decentralize, military power. It would require all nations to join together in a single universal institution and pool their military power to create an overwhelming central military force. This central force would be so powerful it could reduce the overall level of force through disarmament and operate largely on the basis of economic, not military, sanctions. Now if a particular country threatened another country, the common institution would order the offending power to desist and, if necessary, threaten it with economic sanctions. Overpowered, the offending country would be deterred or, if it persisted, defeated. No country could withstand the centralized power of the entire global community. Protection for all countries would be achieved not through the balance of power but through the preponderance of power.

CAUSAL ARROW: PERSPECTIVES

Institutional rules — Define threat — Isolate enemy

LIBERAL   REALIST   IDENTITY

How would the central institution decide which country was threatening the system? In the balance-of-power system, countries aligned against the country with the greatest power, which constituted the greatest threat. But in the collective security system, all countries belonged to the same common institution (one great big alliance). How would this institution define and measure threat, as the realist perspective did in terms of relative power? It would do so by creating a set of common institutional procedures that states would have to follow in resolving international disputes peacefully. If a state violated these rules, it was the threat. From the liberal perspective, common institutions and rules defined threat, not relative power. Intentions were more important than capabilities.

League of Nations: a universal institution, founded after the Paris Peace Conference in 1919, that embodied the collective security approach to the management of military power.

unanimity: a principle in international affairs that all nations, regardless of size or identity, participate in global institutions and decision making.

The League of Nations

The **League of Nations** was the first international institution to embody the collective security approach to the use of military power. The Covenant of the League spelled out the various provisions of collective security.

Article 5 of the Covenant established the principle of **unanimity**. All nations, great and small, participated in the League and decided collectively what constituted a threat to international peace and security. Remember Gladstone's appeal in the nineteenth century to the "general judgement of civilized mankind"? The League was, as Woodrow

The League of Nations meets in Geneva, Switzerland, in 1921 to resolve disputes peacefully under the auspices of collective security.

Wilson said, the "general judgment of the world as to what is right."[7] Consequently, all countries, regardless of relative power or domestic ideologies, made decisions on an equal basis. The League of Nations buried the old Congress of Vienna system, in which great powers had special responsibilities.

Article 2 created the two main institutions of the League: the Council, composed initially of nine members, and the Assembly, composed of all members. Article 4 made the five great powers that had just won the war (the United States, which of course never joined; Great Britain; France; Italy; and Japan) permanent members of the Council. But these members did not have any special privileges. Each Council member, great or small, had a veto. Unanimity was required to act. Moreover, the Council had no special responsibilities. The Assembly, on which all members sat and also made decisions by unanimity, had exactly the same responsibilities. Indeed, Articles 3 and 4, establishing the responsibilities of the Assembly and Council, respectively, used the same language: either body "may deal at its meetings with any matter within the sphere of action of the League or affecting the peace of the world." There was no hierarchy between the Council and the Assembly.

Articles 10 and 11 of the League Covenant established the collective commitment to deter or defeat aggression. Article 10 committed members to "respect and preserve as against external aggression the territorial integrity and political independence of all Members of the League." Article 11 committed members to consider "any war or threat of war, whether immediately affecting any of the Members of the League or not, . . . a matter of concern to the whole League." Now a threat to any member was a threat to all members, regardless of whether that threat immediately affected a particular country. Conflict anywhere was a threat everywhere. Peace was indivisible; it was a collective good, hence, collective security. It existed for all or none, and its enjoyment by one did not diminish its enjoyment by others.

How was this possible? As realists argue, don't countries have separate geopolitical interests and see threats differently? Think of the differences between the United States and some of its allies in the 2003 war on Iraq. True, but the hope in the League was to channel these differences through a process, a discussion of disputes, a set of rules and procedures that would lead to compromise and define the aggressor as any country that stood in the way of compromise.

Articles 12–15 set out the League's rules that countries had to follow to resolve disputes peacefully. They created a path of procedures that would identify the aggressor. Notice how this liberal approach defines threat by iterative interactions, reciprocity, and path dependence, not by power disparities or ideological differences. Article 12 said members must submit disputes to peaceful arbitration, judicial settlement, or the Council—which in turn could submit disputes to the Assembly. Countries must then refrain from war until after the League made a decision. If the issue was suitable for arbitration or judicial settlement, Articles 13 and 14 set up the Permanent Court of International Justice to render judicial decisions. If the dispute went to the Council, Article 15 required the Council to settle the dispute or issue a report with its recommendations. If the Council issued a unanimous report except for the parties to the dispute, the members agreed that they would not go to war with any party to the dispute that abided by the Council's recommendations. This provision was intended to isolate the aggressor party and make it feel the full condemnation and power of the common community of nations.

Article 16 then said that if any member went to war in disregard of Council or judicial recommendations as prescribed in Articles 12–15,

> it shall, ipso facto, be deemed to have committed an act of war against all other Members of the League, which hereby undertake immediately to subject it to the severance of all trade or financial relations, the prohibition of all intercourse between their nationals and the nationals of the Covenant-breaking state, and the prevention of all financial, commercial or personal intercourse between the nationals of the Covenant-breaking state and the nationals of any other State, whether a member of the League or not.

The word *immediately* implied that these sanctions would be automatic.

Presto, the world had a new system to define threat and deal with it. But didn't such a system risk turning every dispute, however minor, into a global war? After all, everyone had to confront the aggressor. That made a local dispute a global one, just the way the balance of power turned a local clash between Austria and Serbia into World War I. The League had an answer. As Article 16 said, League members would use economic sanctions, not military force. Because everyone would be participating, economic sanctions would suffice to deter the aggressor. The aggressor would be isolated and would relent or starve to death if it did not. Military force would not be necessary, except as a backup or last resort should sanctions fail—for example, if the aggressor attacked out of desperation. Military power, in fact, could be reduced. Article 8 called for "the reduction of national armaments to the lowest point consistent with national safety and the enforcement by common action of international obligations."

Here is the classic liberal solution to conflicts (at any level of analysis, but in this case at the systemic structural level). Get everyone to participate, negotiate peacefully, use economic sanctions if necessary, and maintain military power only to the extent necessary to implement economic sanctions and serve as a last resort should sanctions fail. Do you think this approach is utopian or irrelevant today? Think again—it worked like a textbook case in the first Persian Gulf War in 1990–1991. And it inspired critics of U.S. policy in the second Persian Gulf War in 2003 who argued straight from the collective security rule book: the United Nations was the only legitimate institution to make the decision to go to war because it included everyone (the general judgment of the world), negotiations were the only way to facilitate inspections and resolve the issue of WMDs, economic sanctions were sufficient to convince Iraq to come clean, and military force was necessary only to support economic sanctions—that is, to get the UN weapons inspectors back into Iraq by positioning an invasion force in the Persian Gulf, but not by invading the country. Under both Presidents Bush and Obama, the United States has pursued exactly the same collective security strategy to stop the acquisition of nuclear weapons by Iran. The idea of collective security is alive and well today, even if it failed under the League of Nations.

Why the League of Nations Failed

What went wrong with the liberal solution of the League of Nations? Several things. First, the United States, the leading world power, did not join. Nor did the Soviet Union until 1933, by which time two other major powers, Germany and Japan, had withdrawn. The League of Nations never achieved the preponderance of power it required to work effectively. Second, the League never organized effective security guarantees. It failed to provide credible military commitments to defend all countries and establish the indivisibility of peace as a collective good. Eventually countries scrambled to protect their security outside the League through alliances. Third, although it made some progress in reducing arms, disarmament without credible security commitments led to more, not fewer, security fears. Fourth, unanimity proved to be the League's Achilles' heel. The aggressor country also had a veto. The League could issue a report without concurrence of the parties to the dispute, but the report was toothless unless the League either followed it up with specific actions, which the aggressor could veto, or implemented Article 16 sanctions automatically, which might mean war. When the League condemned Japan's invasion of Manchuria, Japan vetoed the report and withdrew from the League. When the League imposed economic sanctions on Italy, it eventually backed off because France and Britain feared this action might mean war with Italy, and they were more concerned at the time with the threat from Germany. Peace in this case proved not to be indivisible. One threat (Germany) was not considered to be the same as another threat (Italy). And given different perceptions of threat, the veto for everyone became a loophole that enabled inaction.

Let's see how American isolationism, utopian disarmament agreements, unanimity, and Japanese and Italian aggression undermined the League.

American Isolationism. Woodrow Wilson literally died trying to persuade the U.S. Congress and American people to join the League. In July 1919, he returned from the peace negotiations in Paris to campaign nonstop across the country for Congress to approve the Treaty of Versailles and the League of Nations. But in early October he collapsed and suffered a massive paralytic stroke. When the treaty came up for votes in November and again in March 1920, the League's greatest champion was still seriously ill.

A favorite counterfactual question from the liberal perspective is whether different leadership (for example, someone like Franklin Roosevelt, who deftly guided an isolationist country into World War II) or a healthier President Wilson might have persuaded Congress to approve the League. The country was not of one mind on the League issue. One group opposed the League and any American military entanglement abroad. It was led by William Jennings Bryan, a frequent Democratic presidential candidate and Wilson's first secretary of state, and by Senator William E. Borah of Idaho. This group harked back to George Washington's warning in his farewell address to stay out of foreign alliances. A second group, led by former president Teddy Roosevelt and Senator Henry Cabot Lodge, did not oppose military commitments per se, but preferred specific ones and recoiled at the automatic sanctions under Article 16 to act without congressional deliberations. Finally, a third group led by former president William Howard Taft supported the League.

In order to win the confirmation battle in the Senate, Wilson had to win over the second group, the one that demanded reservations on Article 16 preserving the constitutional power of Congress to declare war. He failed, and analysts still argue about the causes. Was it because the constitutional structure of the American government prevented Congress from giving up its power to declare war—a liberal argument from the domestic level of analysis? Or was it Wilson's high-mindedness and ideological inflexibility? Identity factors at the individual level of analysis outweighed institutional ones at the domestic level. Or maybe it was simply a political struggle for domestic power between Wilson and his foes—a realist explanation from the domestic level of analysis. Notice again how our analytical tools of perspectives and levels of analysis help sort out a sometimes bewildering array of conflicting arguments explaining a historical event.

The result, in any case, was a League of Nations that was supposed to mobilize preponderant power but lacked from the outset the world's then most important power, the United States. Another soon-to-be great power, the Soviet Union, also went into isolationism. The October 1917 Russian Revolution toppled the czar, and Vladimir Ilyich Lenin, whom the Germans had transported into Russia in 1916 in a secret railroad car, seized power with his Bolshevik faction and pulled Russia not only out of the war—which is why the Germans helped him—but also out of world diplomacy. Russia slipped into civil war and then, under Stalin after 1925, concentrated on the transformation of its domestic society to communism. Marxist-Leninist ideology—an identity factor—convinced some communist leaders that the state would wither away and that diplomacy, at least as conventionally understood, would not require much of their time.

CAUSAL ARROW: LEVELS OF ANALYSIS

Enfeebled League	Tied Wilson's hands	American constitution
SYSTEMIC STRUCTURAL	INDIVIDUAL	DOMESTIC

Disarmament Agreements: The Washington Naval Conference and Kellogg-Briand Pact. Compared with realist perspectives, liberal perspectives tend to downplay military power. As we have noted, Article 8 of the League Covenant called for disarmament. Other international agreements at the time similarly restricted military capacity. The Treaty of Versailles imposed stringent arms control measures on Germany. The Washington Naval Conference of 1921–1922 set ceilings on sea power, placing the United States on a par with Great Britain and holding Japan to three-fifths of the U.S. level. Disarmament talks continued episodically throughout the 1920s and 1930s. Even after Germany left the League in 1933, Hitler concluded a naval pact with Great Britain in 1935 that limited the German surface fleet to 35 percent of Britain's.

CAUSAL ARROW: PERSPECTIVES

Increase trust	Marginalize military power	Disarmament treaties
IDENTITY	REALIST	LIBERAL

The idea of getting rid of arms and war itself was behind the Kellogg-Briand Pact, signed in 1928. Originally proposed as a U.S.-French agreement, the pact called on all signatories "to condemn recourse to war for the solution of international controversies, and renounce it as an instrument of national policy."[8] Practically all the nations of the world signed it, including Germany, Japan, and Italy. As a statement of moral and legal sentiment, the Kellogg-Briand Pact was unsurpassed. But as a practical matter, it barely survived its signing. Immediately, countries, especially the United States, entered reservations based on self-defense, regional security, and sovereignty that gutted the commitment. The pact became meaningless. When asked why the United States should be interested if another nation broke the treaty, U.S. secretary of state Frank Kellogg replied, "There is not a bit of reason."[9]

Japanese Aggression in Manchuria. The first real test for the League came in 1931. Japan invaded Manchuria, a northern province of China. China appealed to the League, and the League called on Japan to withdraw its troops. But Japan voted against the resolution. Here was the core problem of collective security, as seen from a realist or an identity perspective. Unanimity, and the veto, let the big and the bad guys hold the world community at bay.

When the Qing dynasty fell in 1911 and China lapsed into civil war, Japan had increased its military position along the Manchurian railroad, where it had already stationed troops under agreements stemming from the Russo-Japanese War in 1905 (brokered by U.S. president Theodore Roosevelt, one of America's first forays onto the stage of world diplomacy). In September 1931, the Japanese military, with or without orders from Tokyo (this is still disputed), staged an incident and invaded the rest of Manchuria, creating the puppet state of Manchukuo.

After Japan blocked League action, the League established a commission to investigate the incident. The Lytton Commission (named for its chairman, Lord Lytton of Great Britain) issued a report in September 1932 that asked League members not to recognize Manchukuo. But the report did not invoke Article 16. When the League voted in February 1933 to accept the Lytton report, Japan cast the lone dissenting vote and then abruptly withdrew from the League. The League was exposed as a paper tiger. It was not long before European powers, Italy and Germany, dealt the finishing blow to the League.

Italian Aggression in Ethiopia. In the nineteenth century, Italy acquired colonies in Eritrea, an African territory at the mouth of the Red Sea. It tried at the time to colonize neighboring Ethiopia as well but failed. In October 1935, the Italian government, under fascist dictator Benito Mussolini, invaded Ethiopia again. This time, the League got around the unanimity requirement. It convened a special conference. Fifty members attended and defined Italy as the aggressor. They invoked specific but not complete sanctions—an arms embargo, the cutoff of loans to Italy and imports from Italy, and an embargo on certain exports to Italy, such as rubber and tin. But they did not embargo steel, coal, and oil exports to Italy, break off diplomatic relations, or close the Suez Canal, through which Italy supplied its forces in Eritrea. The League seemed to be working, at least partially and certainly better than in the case of Japan and Manchuria.

By December 1935, however, Britain and France were having second thoughts because they needed Italy to balance power against an increasingly resurgent Germany. Here was the problem with collective security arrangements. These arrangements considered every threat to be of equal concern to all League members, regardless of where the conflict occurred or which countries it involved. Peace was assumed to be indivisible, or a collective good. But in this case, Britain and France did not consider the threat from Italy to be as great as that from Germany. Thus, the British and French foreign ministers met and came up with the Hoare-Laval plan, which divided Ethiopia into two parts, awarding one part to Italy and the other to the League. When word of the plan leaked, the British minister, Samuel Hoare, had to resign. Public opinion was outraged, as were the representatives of small nations, one of whom warned, "Great or small, strong or weak, near or far, white or colored, let us never forget that one day we may be somebody's Ethiopia."[10]

The fate of the weak in this case was nevertheless sealed. When Hitler marched into the Rhineland in March 1936, Britain and France met with Italy in Stresa and gave the green light to Italy's conquest of Ethiopia. The balance of power prevailed over collective security. Would the balance of power now work better than it had in 1914? Don't hold your breath. (See Table 3-1 for a summary of liberal explanations of the causes of World War II.)

TABLE 3-1

The Causes of World War II: The Liberal Perspective and Levels of Analysis

	Liberal perspective		
Systemic	*Structure*	Collective security problems and the failure of the League of Nations: • Major powers not involved to create preponderance of power • Centralized commitments too weak to establish security as a collective good and provide incentives to disarm • Aggressor states not members of League and hence not subject to institutional constraints	
		Economic depression reduces interdependence	
	Process	Misperceptions of threat: • United Kingdom sees France as stronger than Germany • France thinks defense dominant and "chain-gangs" with United Kingdom and Poland (leaving initiative to Hitler) • United Kingdom appeases instead of balancing Hitler at Munich (1938) and fails to align with Soviet Union after Hitler invades Czechoslovakia in March 1939	
		Spread of immoderate goals: Germany and Japan are revisionist states, seeking to overturn the Versailles Treaty and create Greater East Asia Co-Prosperity Sphere	
Foreign policy		British foreign minister tries to finesse domestic opposition to plan to divide Ethiopia	
Domestic		Divided domestic interests lead United States to reject League	
		Economic collapse in Germany	
Individual		Ineffective leadership of Congress by a dying President Wilson	

Level of analysis (left vertical label)

⟫⟫ Realist Accounts

From the realist perspective, the problem was always Germany. As Map 3-1 shows, its unity and location in the center of Europe upset the balance of power. Germany was either too small, and thus vulnerable to neighbors on both sides, or too big, and thus threatening to neighbors on either side. This reality triggered a virulent security dilemma of encirclement and fear. So, Germany had to be either weakened or divided again, as it was before 1871. The Versailles Treaty tried the first solution. It weakened Germany.

Germany before World War II, 1938

But then Germany scratched its way back. It aligned with Russia, joined the League, and accepted border guarantees with France and Belgium in the west but not with Poland and Czechoslovakia in the east. Hitler systematically reclaimed territories and German populations in the east that Germany had lost in World War I. By 1939, Germany faced the prospect of another two-front war. This time it defeated France outright and occupied Russia to the outskirts of Moscow. Germany now dominated a weakened Soviet Union on one side (Map 3-2), and Japan threatened the Soviet Union on the other side (Map 3-3). The United States became concerned. It tightened the noose on Japan, and Japan attacked Pearl Harbor. The United States joined Great Britain and the Soviet Union and eventually destroyed German and Japanese power. After World War II, the allies tried the second solution—they divided Germany again. But we save that story for the next chapter; here we take up the tragedy of Versailles and the interwar period.

Versailles Treaty

After World War I, the victorious allies met in the Versailles Palace outside Paris to conclude the peace treaty. The Versailles Treaty gutted the former German empire. Germany lost territory and its colonies. Alsace-Lorraine went back to the French. The Rhineland

MAP 3-2

Germany and Occupied Territories, 1942

Legend:
- Greater German Reich
- Territories controlled by Germany
- German allies

was permanently demilitarized and administered for fifteen years by an international authority. Poland was restored with a corridor to the sea and the port of Danzig, which became a "free city" under League supervision (see Map 3-1). The Polish corridor split East Prussia from the rest of Germany, in the same way that Kaliningrad, a Russian province in former East Prussia, is separated today from Russia. Versailles cut Germany's army to one hundred thousand volunteers and its navy to six cruisers and a few smaller vessels. The German navy was interned by the British and then scuttled by its own officers pending the outcome of the Versailles negotiations. Germany was forbidden to have a general staff and any offensive weapons such as submarines, aircraft, tanks, or heavy artillery. Most punitively, Versailles pronounced in Article 231, the famous "war guilt" clause, that Germany was solely responsible for the outbreak of World War I (adopting a domestic level of analysis explanation of World War I), and Germany was required to pay massive reparations (then about $33 billion; in today's dollars, some $300–$400 billion) that subsequently burdened the German economy and international trade.

Problem solved, right? Not quite. France knew that Germany would not remain weak permanently. Like the victorious powers at Vienna in 1815, France wanted a military alliance to subdue the defeated power should it rise again. Britain, however, saw France

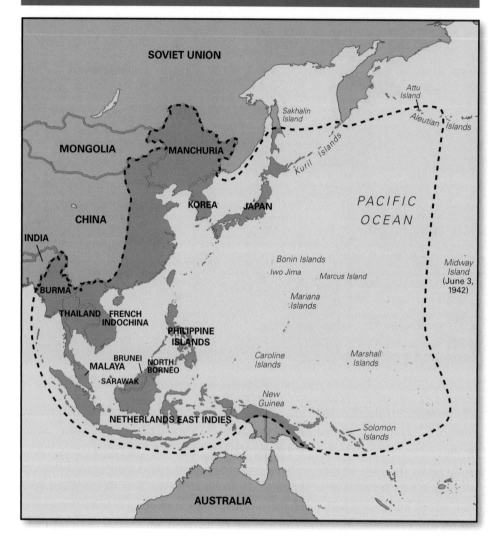

MAP 3-3

Japan and Japanese-Controlled Territories, 1942

as the more powerful country. In the 1920s, France had a smaller share of European wealth than Britain, but it had an army of around six hundred thousand men, double or triple the size of Britain's and six times Germany's allotted number.[11] Neither Wilson and the U.S. Congress nor a Bolshevik and isolated Russia was ready to make a military commitment to defend France. So France turned to keeping Germany weak as long as possible and finding smaller allies. It occupied the Ruhr Valley—the heart of Germany's industrial establishment next to the Rhineland—in January 1923 to extract reparations. And it concluded alliances with the small states of eastern Europe—Poland and the "Little Entente" of Czechoslovakia, Romania, and Yugoslavia—to serve as a substitute, it hoped, for the Franco-Russian Alliance before World War I.

Rapallo and Locarno

Excluded and humiliated by the Versailles Treaty, Germany responded to encirclement by meeting in April 1922 with the Russians at Rapallo, a seaside resort in Italy. Both countries nurtured grievances against the west (Russia because of western involvement in its civil war from 1918 to 1920) and agreed to establish full diplomatic relations. Over the next fifteen years, Russia helped Germany evade some of the Versailles restrictions on its military forces and training. Think of it. Here was a classic realist alignment. Even then ideological foes, the two countries (one recently monarchist going fascist—Hitler's failed barroom putsch occurred in 1923—the other already communist) shared a common interest in radically revising the established order coming out of World War I.

Seeing the dangers of alienating Germany, the western powers rushed to reassure Berlin. France ended the Ruhr occupation in fall 1923, and Great Britain proposed the alliance that France had always wanted. But Britain did not want to isolate Germany further, so it proposed an alliance to guarantee French and Belgian borders as part of a broader agreement under the League, which would also admit Germany as a new member. The Locarno Pact, signed in 1925 (and for which the French, British, and German foreign ministers won the Nobel Peace Prize), guaranteed Germany's western borders with France and Belgium. As a member of the League, Germany now also undertook general obligations to settle disputes peacefully with its eastern neighbors—Poland, Czechoslovakia, and Romania. Significantly, however, arbitration agreements with these countries did not guarantee borders in the east as the Locarno Pact did in the west. Nor did other League members guarantee the eastern borders.

So, here was a huge hole in the commitment to collective security. In the west, where France and Great Britain were relatively strong, the League guaranteed borders. In the east, where small states had replaced Russia and Austria-Hungary and the balance of power was relatively weak, the League did not guarantee borders. All that existed in the east were a few frail alliances that France had set up with Poland, Romania, Yugoslavia, and Czechoslovakia. This vulnerability only got worse with the Kellogg-Briand Pact, which promised peace without any alliances or use of power whatsoever. Without firm security commitments, countries were nevertheless encouraged to disarm. From the realist perspective, the stage was set for German aggression well before Hitler showed up, especially in the east, where World War II started.

Germany Expands

If Germany had ever intended to accept a weakened role in the postwar Versailles order, Hitler emphatically rejected that option. But he disguised his plans masterfully for several years. In October 1933, nine months after coming to power, Hitler pulled Germany out of the League and immediately broke the restrictions on German rearmament. At the same time, however, he concluded a nonaggression pact with Poland that weakened Poland's commitment to France if Germany attacked France and signed a naval treaty with Great Britain that avoided the kaiser's mistake of competing with Britain on the high seas. He also started a major propaganda campaign to promote the notion that Germany sought only to reclaim what an unjust Versailles Treaty had taken away—once Germany had united all Germans again, it would have no further designs on its neighbors.

Thus, when German troops marched into the "permanently demilitarized" Rhineland in March 1936 to liberate German residents, no western power resisted, even though this step violated German as well as League guarantees. The next target was the German people in Austria. Germany signed an alliance with Italy in 1936 to create the Axis powers and wean one of Germany's perennial rivals for control of Austria away from the west (remember how France and Britain had backed off on sanctions in the Ethiopian affair to court an alliance with Italy?). With Italy on board, Hitler then annexed Austria in March 1938. His last target, presumably, was the German population in the Sudetenland—Germans, living on the Czechoslovakian side of the border, who had been separated from Germany by Versailles. Hitler demanded the annexation of the Sudetenland. In late September 1938, Neville Chamberlain, the British prime minister, met Hitler in Munich, together with the French and Italian heads of government. The western allies agreed to return the Sudetenland to Germany, and the Munich Conference went down in history as the classic symbol of **appeasement**, a policy of making concessions to a stronger foe because one is unwilling to consider the use of force. Now that Germany was whole, the allies hoped, Hitler would surely cease to upset the status quo.

appeasement: a policy of making concessions to a stronger foe because one is unwilling to consider the use of force.

Another Two-Front War

Unfortunately, not so! From a realist perspective, whatever Hitler's intentions, Germany still faced a security dilemma. Was that why Hitler did not stop after Munich? By 1939–1940, Germany was again superior. It controlled 36 percent of Europe's wealth, compared to 9 percent for France, 24 percent for Great Britain, and 28 percent for the Soviet Union.[12] It was too big for its neighbors to deal with individually, but if those neighbors got together, Germany was too small to deal with them collectively.

Germany faced the same situation of superiority and encirclement as it had before World War I. The security dilemma still dominated. And Germany followed roughly the same strategy to deal with this situation. It strengthened its position in the east, turned west, eliminated one adversary, and wheeled around for the final stroke against Russia. Some realists find it uncanny that this strategy repeated itself. It's too easy, they argue, to attribute the war simply to Hitler's megalomania. Larger structural forces had to be at work.[13]

CAUSAL ARROW: PERSPECTIVES

Security dilemma	Breeds distrust	Leads to national conflict
REALIST	LIBERAL	IDENTITY

Germany invaded the rest of Czechoslovakia in March 1939. Now Germany's neighbors knew it was not just trying to unite Germans, and Britain immediately signed defense guarantees with Poland and Romania. Counterbalancing was happening, but it was happening late. Why? Some realists argue that it was because Germany's power, especially military power, did not peak until 1939–1940, unlike before World War I, when it peaked already in 1905.[14] In addition, this time Germany had disguised its military buildup as well as its intentions. But the chess pieces were now moving into place. Both Britain and France had defense commitments with Poland and Romania. The Triple Entente (remember, Britain, France, and Russia before World War I) was struggling to reemerge. The missing piece was the Soviet Union.

Joseph Stalin succeeded Lenin in 1925 and brutally yanked his country into the twentieth century. Massive state-driven industrialization raised the Soviet Union to the great power ranks. But Stalin imprisoned and murdered millions of farmers and opponents in the process.[15] The Soviet Union joined the League in 1933 and played a cat-and-mouse game—realists call it **buckpassing**—with France and Britain; each was trying to get the others to stop Hitler. By summer 1939, however, the cat-and-mouse game was over, and the cat was about to jump into the fire.

Stalin had to decide whether to work with France and Great Britain or to throw in his lot with a fellow dictator. He negotiated with both sides and, to the surprise of the world, announced in August 1939 a nonaggression pact with Hitler, the famous Molotov-Ribbentrop agreement, named for the two countries' foreign ministers. Stalin gambled on **bandwagoning** and joined the stronger rather than the weaker side in the hope that the Soviet Union might benefit from the spoils of war between Germany and the west. German and Russian leaders agreed once again to partition eastern Europe, including the Baltic states of Lithuania, Estonia, and Latvia. In September 1939, they implemented this agreement. Germany invaded Poland, the Soviet Union occupied the other half of eastern Europe, and World War II was under way.

Finishing off Poland, Germany turned west. It took Norway in the winter of 1939–1940 and invaded the Low Countries and France in spring 1940. An all-out air war against Great Britain followed, and Britain came perilously close to defeat. But the British air force bested the German Luftwaffe, and Hitler, frustrated, wheeled east in June 1941 and attacked the Soviet Union. Now, as the realist school warns, the dangers of bandwagoning came home to roost. Stalin reportedly couldn't believe the perfidy of his Nazi ally—who was only following, of course, the realist proscription against permanent alliances—and went into a depression for several weeks.[16]

Japan and the Pacific War

All the while, America slept. The United States had long since become the wealthiest country in the world. By 1941, its wealth constituted 54 percent of the combined wealth of the United States plus Germany, the Soviet Union, Great Britain, and Italy.[17] But it was not using this wealth to exert a great power military role. Why? Some realist perspectives explain America's isolationism in geopolitical terms. America enjoys "strategic immunity."[18] As long as it stays out of foreign military commitments, it is relatively invulnerable to attack. Two oceans thwart successful invasion, and the country's vast size enables greater economic independence. Thus, it was rational for the United States to stand aside from Europe's wars. Britain eventually repulsed German air power, and the Soviet Union would shortly emasculate German land power. All the United States

buckpassing: a free-riding strategy wherein a country allows other countries to fight conflicts while it stays on the sidelines.

bandwagoning: the aligning of states with a greater power to share the spoils of dominance.

had to do was buckpass and wait for other countries to do the balancing. Notice that this version of realism expects balancing to take place automatically, like the classic balance-of-power system in eighteenth-century Europe. No one power has to seek overall balance; rather, overall balance results from the work of an invisible hand.

Other realist perspectives aren't so sure. For them, Hitler's success in Russia would have been intolerable for Americans because German and Japanese power would have then dominated the Eurasian landmass. The United States would have faced a fascist juggernaut alone. If the European war was not enough to draw America in, certainly a global war including Asia was. Russia's fate linked the European and Asian balance of power. Someone had to take charge of balancing the overall system, and America was the only remaining great power to step in.

In 1936, Japan signed the Anti-Comintern Pact with Germany. This was a declaration of opposition to communism and Soviet sale of arms to China. From its base in Manchukuo, Japan then invaded China in 1937. It declared its intent to create a Greater East Asia Co-Prosperity Sphere. In 1940, after Hitler attacked France, Japan seized French colonies in Southeast Asia, Vietnam, and Cambodia. And in September 1940, Japan, Germany, and Italy signed the Tripartite Pact, which committed each country to go to war if any other country came to the defense of England. The pact was aimed primarily at the United States, but Stalin had reason to worry about an alliance between the two great powers on either side of the Soviet Union. In April 1941, he countered and signed a neutrality pact with Japan. Fortunately for Stalin, Japan was preparing to attack the United States, not the Soviet Union. When Germany finally attacked the Soviet Union in June 1941, Stalin was able to concentrate all his forces against the Nazi onslaught. Even then, he just barely survived.

So, the fact that Japan struck against the United States rather than the Soviet Union may have saved the Soviet Union. Did the United States play a role in this outcome? President Franklin Roosevelt tightened oil deliveries to Japan in 1939, either to deter Japan from striking the Soviet Union or perhaps to prod it to strike south toward the oil fields of southeast Asia. As Roosevelt put it, "The United States would slip a noose around Japan's neck and give it a jerk now and then."[19] While Roosevelt did not expect an oil embargo to lead to war, Japan began to see the situation it faced as the last move in a prisoner's dilemma game. If war was coming, Japan had better make a preemptive strike first.

And it did. Japan bombed the American fleet at Pearl Harbor on December 7, 1941, and the United States declared war. Four days later, Germany, drawing on the Tripartite Pact, declared war on the United States. The world was off for its second encounter with Armageddon, this one three times more deadly than the first.

Why Don't Hegemons Stop?

Realist perspectives do not predict that balancing will always prevent war. The power transition school, in fact, predicts that balancing causes war when the challenger creeps up on the declining power. Nor do realist perspectives predict that states will always balance. States, like the Soviet Union in 1939, often buckpass or try to get others to balance for them. Realist perspectives predict only that balances will result. By war or other means, hegemons do not endure. That prediction seems solid enough. Hitler, like Louis XIV (who waged a hegemonic war against other European powers in the late 1600s and early 1700s) and Napoleon before him, ultimately went too far, and other states counterbalanced and beat him back.

Soldiers at Ford Island Naval Air Station watch in horror—as did all Americans—on December 7, 1941, as Japan bombs Pearl Harbor, Hawaii, drawing America into World War II.

An interesting question is, Why don't hegemons stop when they are ahead? Hitler did not have to attack the Soviet Union, and he certainly held a commanding position in 1942 after driving the Soviet Union back to the outskirts of Moscow. Look again at Map 3-2. He dominated the entire continent, in effect ending Germany's encirclement and security dilemma. Britain, even if it could not be beaten, posed no threat of invasion, and Russia might have been encouraged to sue for peace. But Hitler, like others before him, could not resist the temptation to keep going.

Realists give multiple explanations for this behavior: offensive imperatives, domestic cartels, polarity, and preventive war. Let's look briefly at each.

Offensive Imperatives. Offensive realists, such as John Mearsheimer, argue that states always seek more power because more power brings more security.[20] In Germany's case, Russia was still a looming menace on its border, and Germany was more secure if it controlled Russia than if it didn't. But was it more secure? Liberal perspectives might respond that conquering and holding territory costs more than it returns. No, the **offensive realism** school replies, conquest pays.[21] Thus, it was rational for Hitler to attack Russia. So far, the argument is pure realist.

offensive realism: a school of realism that says states seek dominant power.

But Mearsheimer goes on to argue that states that achieve conquest and hegemony on land cannot achieve hegemony across large bodies of water. The reason is the "stopping power of water," by which Mearsheimer means that geography does not permit the projection of land power across large bodies of water. And hegemons cannot conquer and hold territory with naval and sea power alone. Thus, Hitler, like Napoleon, did not succeed in conquering Great Britain. And if Hitler could not subdue Great Britain across the English Channel, he certainly could not invade North America across the Atlantic Ocean. The United States was dominant in its region and relatively safe behind two large oceans. True, Japan did attack a territory of the United States, but it did not attack the mainland, and it did so by air, not by land. And although Japan did invade China across a body of water, it had already established a foothold in China in 1905 on the basis of the treaty ending the Russo-Japanese War. In the 1930s, it expanded that position while possessing complete air and sea superiority, something Hitler never achieved against England.

The United States used a similar foothold in England to stage the successful D-Day invasion of Europe in 1944. With such a foothold, a land invasion across a smaller body of water may be possible, especially if the invader enjoys air and naval superiority, as the United States and Japan did in their respective assaults. Thus, technological constraints, not geography, may explain the stopping power of water. And technology can always change. The realist perspective tends to give the nod to geography (stopping power of water) over technology.

Domestic Cartels. Defensive-oriented realists consider expansion beyond what is needed for security unnecessary from a systemic structural point of view. More power is not always better than less, and balancing suffices to achieve stability. Thus, when states cannot stop expanding, **defensive realism** looks for explanations at other levels of analysis. Some attribute the inability of hegemons to stop their expansion to domestic political factors. As noted in Chapter 2, Professor Jack Snyder argues that because of its late industrialization Germany had many diverse social groups with narrowly defined interests; remember the iron (industry) and rye (agriculture) coalition before World War I. These groups could not achieve their objectives independently, but they could logroll, or combine, to implement them through coalitions. In the process, their cumulative goals committed the state to overexpansion.

Hitler faced similar domestic cartels prior to World War II. He did not stop because he was backed by a wide domestic coalition that supported the need for *Lebensraum*. According to Snyder, "The Nazis won power . . . by promising incompatible payoffs to every group in Weimar society: labor, industry, farmers, clerks, artisans. . . . Hitler saw conquest as the only alternative to a politically unacceptable decision to cut consumption."[22] But this explanation, Snyder concludes, is not enough, because Hitler eventually did cut consumption to finance the war effort. Now Snyder appeals to pure ideology. Hitler held the country together with strategic myths such as *Lebensraum*.

Notice how this explanation, while remaining realist at its foundation (domestic interests compete for power), takes on some liberal (an emphasis on political logrolling and coalitions) and identity (myths) aspects. The explanation also drops to the domestic level of analysis. The competition for power as well as the logrolling and strategic myths all come from the country's political system at home rather than from systemic factors such as the relative distribution of power abroad.

defensive realism:
a school of realism that says states seek enough power to be secure.

It is worth quoting Snyder's conclusions in full to show how a sophisticated analyst considers all perspectives but ultimately weighs them differently. When you read books or articles, these are the kinds of passages you cannot afford to miss and, hopefully, with the help of this text, will detect:

> Domestic explanations for German overexpansion must look not only at the interests of groups, but also at the process by which those interests were reconciled [logrolling] and at the unintended ideological consequences [path dependence] of the strategic myths used to promote those interests.[23]

Interests (power) and hence realist factors are still the primary causal variables. Logrolling is now the "process by which those interests were reconciled," and "strategic myths" are "unintended ideological consequences . . . used to promote those interests." Logrolling and myths are instruments or consequences of interests, not causes of them. If they become independent variables and dominate interests (become primary), the argument is no longer a realist one.

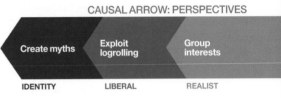

CAUSAL ARROW: PERSPECTIVES

Create myths | Exploit logrolling | Group interests

IDENTITY | LIBERAL | REALIST

Polarity. Still another realist perspective, neorealism, explains Hitler's attack on Russia in purely systemic terms. For political scientist Randall Schweller, the explanation lies in the peculiar distribution of power that preceded World War II.[24] This distribution was tripolar: the United States, Germany, and the Soviet Union. In a tripolar world, no pole can allow the other two to come together, for that would constitute a dominating coalition. Hence, the tripolar distribution of power is uniquely unstable. Either Germany and its allies would dominate Russia or the United States and its allies would. Roosevelt understood that fundamental fact, and this knowledge prompted his intervention to weaken Japan.

Preventive War. For Dale Copeland, the factor that drove German policy in World War II was the same as that in World War I—not the present power balances but Germany's fear of Russian superiority in the future. At the meeting that Hossbach recorded, Hitler said that Russia was the ultimate target and that it had to be attacked before 1943–1945, when Germany's power relative to Russia's would peak. After that, Russia would have the advantage. So Germany undertook a preventive war to keep Russia from becoming more powerful as Germany became less powerful. As long as this assessment of power shifts was reasonable, and Copeland thinks it was, the realist perspective explains Germany's behavior from a systemic structural level of analysis.[25] Copeland, unlike Snyder (and Mark Haas; see the "Identity Matters" section later in this chapter), minimizes the role of race and ideology in Nazi decision making. He sees systemic power factors dominating and allows a role for identity only in the possibility that a country's leadership might change in the future and become more belligerent.

If the assessment of power shifts is not reasonable—meaning not warranted by the systemic evidence available to the observer—then the assessment is being influenced by other factors, namely, institutional (lack of information) and identity (misperception) factors. For example, German leaders may not have had enough information to make an accurate assessment of Russia's future power. Or they may have been affected by their racist or ideological (for example, anticommunist) prejudices toward Russia. When the perceptions of decision makers matter, the level of analysis often drops from the systemic structural level to the foreign policy level. The foreign policy level, as noted in Chapter 1, links systemic process factors such as German perceptions of Russia's rise in power with domestic-level factors such as insufficient or inaccurate information in the German bureaucracy and intentional variables such as German leaders seeking to stay in power. An example, discussed next, is when decision makers misperceive the power realities because they lack information or indulge their biases.

Role of Misperceptions in Realist Accounts

Realist perspectives expect assessments of power to be accurate because material forces dominate. When such assessments are inaccurate, as Professor Snyder's analysis shows, realist explanations appeal to liberal and identity factors that apparently distort material forces. Professor Stephen Walt developed a realist line of reasoning that includes judgments about additional factors such as whether offensive or defensive weapons dominate in a particular historical period as well as nonmaterial factors such as whether leaders' intentions are aggressive or not.[26] Threat is no longer just a function of capabilities, as in neorealist analysis, but also of military strategies (offensive or defensive, since most weapons can be used for both) and ideological intentions. As Walt's critics point out, however, the analysis remains realist only if material factors still account for more of the explanation than does strategy or ideology.[27]

One liberal factor distorting realist behavior is misperception. Stalin, for example, judged French and British power to be much greater in 1939 than it actually was. He thought those two countries would hold out against Germany and drain its resources, allowing Russia to enter the conflict later as the decisive power. Thus, he buckpassed, but in this case he misperceived the realities. He lacked accurate information.

Another realist, the historian A. J. P. Taylor, concludes that the war was the consequence of a long series of such misperceptions and mistakes. Rejecting identity arguments that the war was intentional, he writes, "The war of 1939, far from being premeditated, was a mistake, the result on both sides of diplomatic blunders."[28] Hitler, he argues, bears unique responsibility for domestic horrors such as the Holocaust, but he does not bear any more responsibility than other powers for foreign policy mistakes. He sought to restore German power and exploited other countries' mistakes to do so, especially Britain's failure to negotiate an alliance with Stalin in 1939. "Human blunders," Taylor concludes, "usually do more to shape history than human wickedness."[29] Notice how Taylor discounts motives or identity factors (wickedness) and emphasizes liberal factors (negotiations and blunders). Taylor believes the balance of power should work, and when it doesn't, he blames inept diplomacy, which overrides balancing imperatives.

States also misperceive the advantage of offensive versus defensive military power. France thought a defensive strategy dominated and buckpassed in 1938, when it still had an advantage over Germany. It waited for Britain to commit. When Britain finally did commit in 1939, France expected the defense to dominate and chain-ganged with Britain and Poland. This **chain-ganging**, or creation of a rigid defensive alliance (the opposite of buckpassing), left the initiative to Hitler. Hitler seized it and neutralized Russia while attacking Poland and France. Offensive power proved dominant. France had misperceived the offensive-defensive balance.[30]

chain-ganging: the creation of a rigid defensive alliance.

Identity factors may influence perceptions when realists assess risks. Copeland acknowledges, for example, that even if Russia became more powerful than Germany in the future, Germany would still have to assess whether Russia was more or less likely to attack in the future compared to the present. That assessment might depend to some extent on the identity or nature of the political regime in Russia. A declining authoritarian regime, such as Germany, might remain suspicious of a rising authoritarian power, such as Russia, as was the case in the 1930s, when Germany feared rising Russian power in the future. But a declining democratic state, say Great Britain, might not worry too much about a rising state that was also democratic, say the United States.[31] As noted in Chapter 2, before World War I, Britain worried more about Germany's rise than about America's.

In all these cases, realists draw on other factors to supplement relative power explanations. Liberal factors, such as domestic processes and institutions, distort perceptions. And identity factors, such as the ideology of *Lebensraum* and the nature of domestic political regimes, affect risk taking. When information is missing or misleading, institutions and ideologies fill in the gaps. (See Table 3-2 for a summary of realist explanations of the causes of World War II.)

≫ Identity Matters

World War I decisively ended the common Christian and monarchic community that had provided a shared identity for Europe since the time of Charlemagne. The old Europe functioned on the basis of substantive religious beliefs (Holy Roman Empire) and the equal rights of sovereign monarchs (the Treaty of Westphalia, which ended the religious wars in 1648). The new Europe functioned more on the basis of secular norms (nationalism and self-determination) and international institutions (League of Nations). Self-determination encouraged the proliferation of new nations from the remnants of old empires—Poland, Czechoslovakia, Hungary, Yugoslavia, Lithuania, Estonia, and Latvia, among others—and nationalism pushed nations further and further apart, making institutional agreement based on unanimity more and more difficult.

British nationalism and French nationalism were vindicated by World War I, but German nationalism was humiliated and Russian nationalism was revived by communism. Many of the new nations in eastern Europe became irredentist. Irredentism, a virulent form of nationalism exploited also by Hitler in Germany, demanded changes in national

TABLE 3-2

The Causes of World War II: The Realist Perspective and Levels of Analysis

	Realist perspective		
Systemic	*Structure*		Distribution/balance of power: • Relative rise of German and Japanese power • Germany alienated instead of restored as a great power • Power vacuum caused by many new, weak states in eastern Europe and a weak China in Asia • Major powers such as the United States and Soviet Union do not balance • Tripolarity sets off scramble among Germany, Russia, and the United States to ally with third country
	Process		Failure of United Kingdom, France, Poland, Russia, and United States to align against the greater power (Germany); they buckpass: • German diplomacy adept (compared to clumsy, as before World War I)—Hitler's pact with Poland, naval treaty with Britain, and alliance with Italy • Threats based on different national (geopolitical) interests, not common institutional procedures—peace not indivisible • France forms alliances with Poland, Yugoslavia, Czechoslovakia, and Romania—all weak states—instead of the Soviet Union
Foreign policy			German leaders use aggressive domestic interests to wage expansionary war
Domestic			Aggressive interests of various domestic groups in Germany cause leaders to go to war
Individual			Hitler's war
			Roosevelt's embargo

(Left margin label: Level of analysis)

boundaries to bring together peoples sharing historical memories and speaking the same languages. Liberal nationalism in Britain and France encouraged public indifference and in the United States isolationism. Fascist nationalism engulfed Italy and, after a brief democratic interlude, Germany and Japan as well. The Spanish Civil War in the 1930s showcased the fierce battle between fascism and communism. And anti-Semitism, which had erupted periodically in Europe since the time of Christ, reached its zenith with Nazi racism. Jews became the scapegoats for practically every grievance, from World War I to the Great Depression.

Outside Europe, self-determination did not apply. Colonialism persisted and suppressed nationalist sentiment. The League of Nations created mandates to legitimate colonial rule and carved up Africa, the Middle East, and other parts of the developing world to satisfy colonial rivalries with little regard for the ethnic or national identities of local populations. Resentment and simmering revolutions built up in many mandated territories. The League was trying to hold countries together using rules that liberated nationalities inside Europe and stifled them outside Europe. From an identity perspective, it might be argued that the League sought to hold together too many substantive differences with too little procedural glue.

How much did these ideological differences matter? Identity perspectives say they mattered a lot. They shaped or, as it were, weakened and incapacitated the institutions, such as the League of Nations, that liberal solutions depended on. And they drove the competition for power, weakening the capacity of states to balance power and preserve stability that realist solutions relied on. Consciously or subconsciously, competitive or diverging identities propelled nations toward the abyss. As before World War I, nations constructed identities that exacerbated differences and conflicts, creating an atmosphere of xenophobia and racism. Because realist alliances continued to form among ideological adversaries—the Soviet Union and Germany in 1939 and then the Soviet Union and the western powers after 1941—most historians hesitate to attribute the primary causes of World War II to ideological factors. Identity factors become more prominent in the Cold War, after World War II. Nonetheless, capitalism, fascism, and communism were powerful identity factors driving events before World War II.

CAUSAL ARROW: LEVELS OF ANALYSIS

| Undermined League of Nations | Created competition for power | Social Darwinism |
| LIBERAL | REALIST | IDENTITY |

Cultural Nationalism

Cultural nationalism, the glorification of one national culture over others, hit its high-water mark in the period right after World War I. Romania and Bulgaria had become independent already in 1861 and 1908, respectively. Now Versailles created further new nations out of the collapse of the German, Ottoman, and Austro-Hungarian Empires. Self-determination both justified and contradicted this process. The new countries comprised peoples that shared common languages and cultures, but they also included minorities that did not. And the presence of these minorities triggered resentment, irredentism, and perpetual grievances throughout the interwar period.

The new democracy of Czechoslovakia had a population of fifteen million, which included three million Germans, one million Hungarians, and one-half million Poles. We saw how that mix played into the irredentist demands of Hitler when he claimed that he wanted only to reunite Germans in the new Third Reich. Romania became home to millions of Hungarians, and Poland included millions of Germans. Hungary, created in 1918, was embittered two years later by the Treaty of Trianon, which left five million Hungarians, or one-third of the Hungarian population, outside its national borders. The Baltic states of Lithuania, Latvia, and Estonia gained nationhood but contained significant Russian minorities. Yugoslavia brought together at least six national groups: Serbs, Croats, Slovenes, Macedonians, Montenegrins, and Bosnians. In the process, Yugoslavia became the epicenter of cultural fault lines between Catholic Croatia and Orthodox Serbia on one hand and these Christian groups and Bosnian Muslims on the other. Turkey emerged as the rump or residual Ottoman state and immediately fought terrible wars of ethnic and nationalist fury with Greece and Armenia, resonating to the present day with animosities and charges of genocide. Not only did new nations contain minorities that felt betrayed by the process of self-determination, but other nations also effectively disappeared as the Soviet Union put together its empire and subdued the Caucasus countries of Armenia, Azerbaijan, and Georgia.

What did all this mean? Which peoples should have a nation, when should they have one, and how should they govern it? In particular, how should a nation treat minorities? Nationalism based on language and culture inherently discriminates against other cultures. So, by this standard, minorities either acquired autonomy, which threatened national unity, or were oppressed, which negated their right of self-determination. President Wilson hoped that democratic political ideas would temper and eventually integrate diverse ethnic and national differences. Democracy protects minorities and celebrates cultural diversity. Unfortunately, Wilson was fifty or more years ahead of his time.

Liberal and Social Democracy

Liberal democracy emerged most prominently in the United States. It built a community ethos around the constitutional rights of individuals instead of around the homogeneous culture of the nation (although American folk culture and the English language remained powerful pressures to assimilate) and promoted a free-market economic system based on private property and competition. Social democracy was more prominent in Europe. It put more emphasis on community than on individual rights and favored state regulation and ownership of key sectors of the economy to manage the class struggle between management and labor. Socialist parties were already strong in Europe before World War I, controlling, as previously noted, the German parliament in 1914.

Britain and France became exemplars of social democracy. Both suffered traumas in World War I and in the interwar period confronted virulent enemies of freedom from domestic fascist and communist movements. Liberal forces in the middle were weakened, and inflation and later economic depression undermined enthusiasm for free markets. By the mid-1930s France was so divided that conservatives seemed more fascist than nationalist. "Better Hitler than Blum" was the conservative slogan, referring to the French socialist leader Léon Blum, who came to power in 1936. Ideologies were beginning to transcend national feelings, and this affected foreign policy. As Professor Mark Haas notes, conservative groups in Britain and France preferred to align with fascist countries, such as Italy, to counterbalance Germany, while socialist groups preferred to align with communist countries, such as the Soviet Union, to counterbalance Germany. The unintended consequences of these ideological divisions were indecision and the failure to counterbalance Germany at all.[32]

American Exceptionalism

The United States suffered economic crisis but, because of leadership and national experience, avoided the violent class and cultural cleavages of Europe. The United States began as a conventional nation with a homogeneous culture. Its population was mostly

Anglo-Saxon, except for the enslaved black minority. Despite slavery, it was one of the leading democracies of its day, at least in terms of the number of white male citizens who could vote and the rights of that group to ownership and protection of property.[33] Other countries, such as Britain, had smaller white male franchises during the nineteenth century but abolished slavery before the United States.

Subsequent waves of immigrants slowly transformed America into a multicultural country. The country was tied together less and less by a common culture—although a single language prevailed—and more and more by a common ideological creed of political and economic freedom. Slaves gained legal freedom in the Civil War, a private enterprise system took hold in the late nineteenth century (compared to the state-run industries of fascist and socialist governments in Europe), the Progressive Era (1900–1930) broadened suffrage and regulatory reform, and Franklin Roosevelt introduced a national social security system and broader concern for economic equality.

No fascist or socialist party of any consequence ever developed in the United States. While Europe armed, America's military establishment remained minuscule. In June 1940, America had only 267,767 men under arms. Britain had 402,000, and France and Germany more than 2.2 and 2.7 million, respectively.[34] And Roosevelt's deft leadership during the economic crisis of the Depression preempted more radical socialist and communist economic alternatives that might have nationalized industries or eroded economic freedoms.

Altogether, the United States, even with its continuing faults, such as political and economic constraints on the freedom of blacks and the poor, was the leading example of liberal democracy in the interwar world. In this sense, it acquired an identity of **exceptionalism**, a country set apart from the rest of the world by its progressive, freedom-loving, and pacifist nature.

exceptionalism: the view that a particular state, and especially the United States, is distinct from others because of its specific history and unique institutions.

But the United States indulged this sense of exceptionalism too much and shunned Europe, and while it remained uninvolved, the lights of liberal democracy went out in Europe as well as across the rest of the world. After 1922, as Samuel Huntington observes, liberal democracy disappeared from one country after another:

> In a little over a decade fledgling democratic institutions in Lithuania, Poland, Latvia, and Estonia were overthrown by military coups. Countries such as Yugoslavia and Bulgaria that had never known real democracy were subjected to new forms of harsher dictatorship. The conquest of power by Hitler in 1933 ended German democracy, ensured the end of Austrian democracy the following year, and eventually of course produced the end of Czech democracy in 1938. Greek democracy . . . was finally buried in 1936. Portugal succumbed to a military coup in 1926. . . . Military takeovers occurred in Brazil and Argentina in 1930. Uruguay reverted to authoritarianism in 1933. A military coup in 1936 led to civil war and the death of the Spanish republic in 1939. The new and limited democracy introduced in Japan . . . was supplanted by military rule in the early 1930s.[35]

Why did the United States not care? Some identity perspectives might argue that it was the country's self-image, not its institutions or geography, that kept it out of the League of Nations. American democracy was unique or exceptional and did not apply to other countries in the world. And even if the United States had joined the League, it would not have been prepared to use force. The United States needed more than procedural rules of self-determination or alliance prescriptions of the balance of power to justify its participation in world affairs. As we see in the next chapter, when it finally entered World War II, it came up with another set of universal ideas to run the world. The United Nations was somewhat more realistic perhaps, but it was still pretty high-minded in the tradition of American exceptionalism.

CAUSAL ARROW: PERSPECTIVES

American exceptionalism	Prevented United States from joining League	Created reluctance to use force
IDENTITY	LIBERAL	REALIST

Communist Nationalism

The communist movement brought a radical edge to socialism. In Germany right after the war, communists battled conservatives in Berlin.[36] Whites (conservatives) fought Reds (Bolsheviks) in Russia. Eventually, Lenin and then Stalin consolidated communism in Russia. Whereas socialist parties struggled for the rights of workers through the parliamentary system, communism eradicated the party system. It designated the Communist Party as the sole vanguard of the proletariat or workers' movement and used state institutions to uproot reactionary forces—conservative nobility and peasants—and commandeer the nation's property and industry. Stalin forced Russian industrialization through state ministries and planning and displaced and starved millions of peasants to create collectivized farms. He also purged the military officer corps, a last bastion, as he saw it, of aristocratic nobility and fascist predilections.[37] Stalin's decimation of the officer corps suggests that his decisions were driven more by psychological or identity factors than by national security concerns.

CAUSAL ARROW: PERSPECTIVES

Communism	Purged military	Led Stalin to bandwagon with Hitler
IDENTITY	REALIST	LIBERAL

Fascist and Racist Nationalism

Radicalization on the left was matched by radicalization on the right. Fascist parties rallied conservative forces to recall old glories of national triumph and merge militaristic virtues with heroic symbols borrowed from ancient Greece and Rome. Benito Mussolini's fascist party seized power in Italy in 1922. Fascist and military groups subsequently dominated in Germany and Japan. Both countries had had parliamentary systems in the 1920s. Germany created the Weimar Republic and had, some believe, a moderate foreign policy leadership under Gustav Stresemann that might have brought Germany back peacefully into the European fold.[38] Japan had political parties that struggled to control the military from the late nineteenth century on. By the early 1930s, however, both countries had chosen fascist futures.

Racism became a big part of nationalism in Germany and Japan. While prejudice is hardly unique to these two countries, the maniacal extremes it reached there remain the ultimate examples of human brutality and depravity. The Holocaust, of course, stands out by any standard, with more than six million Jews, plus other minorities such as Roma (often called Gypsies), systematically exterminated. It epitomizes **genocide**, the extermination of an entire people based on their race or ethnicity. Is there any way to explain it? Probably not to everyone's satisfaction. How much blame do the masses of people share? How much do the leaders deserve? Could it have happened elsewhere? Is this a darkness that lurks in every society? The United States is not blameless. It has its own legacy of slavery and then race-based vigilantism. And the United States did not help the international cause of equal rights when it rejected a Japanese appeal at Versailles for a declaration of racial equality. Japan, of course, indulged in its own racism, alienating many of its Chinese and South Korean neighbors and raising issues, such as its use of "comfort women" or sex slaves, that fester to the present day. Suffice it to note that atrocities happened. They cannot be denied, as a few still do in Germany and perhaps more in Japan. And the explanation may not be as important as the process of forever searching for an explanation. Otherwise, such atrocities may happen again.

genocide: the systematic persecution and extermination of a group of people on the basis of their national, ethnic, racial, or religious identity.

Ideological Constructions and Chasms

Social constructivists emphasize the collective identities constructed in the interwar period that glorified nationalist traits and military exploits. More agency-oriented constructivists emphasize the relative identities or chasms that erupted among the self-images of different societies.

The ideological struggles going on in Europe came to the fore vividly during the Spanish Civil War. In 1936, the Spanish people elected a radical socialist government similar to the one in France under Blum. The rightist groups—monarchists, militarists, and fascists—rebelled and started a civil war. Fascism and communism went head-to-head. The battle fascinated the world, including Ernest Hemingway, who covered the war and wrote his classic novel *For Whom the Bell Tolls* to describe it. Italy and Germany aided the fascist rebels. Russia aided the republican government. For reasons of weakness and ideological divisions of their own (as we have noted), France and Great Britain stayed out of the conflict. After two years, the republican government lost the battle it probably would have won with modest help from the democracies. General Francisco Franco seized power but then did not join the fascist alignment during World War II.

So how relevant were ideological struggles to the outbreak of World War II? Did identities really have an effect on behavior, or were states responding largely to material and institutional forces? Clearly the Axis powers shared an ideological affinity. Germany, Italy, and Japan were tied together by similar militarist and fascist politics rather than by the monarchist systems that had united Germany, Austria, and Italy before World War I. On the other hand, Spain, another fascist system, did not join their cause, and for two years Germany allied with its ideological archenemy, the Soviet Union. That alliance did not last, to be sure, but then the Soviet Union joined up with its other ideological archenemies, the liberal democracies of Britain, France, and the United States. Hence, it cannot be said very easily that the war was about conflicting identities and ideologies.

Did Germany's Nazi identity cause World War II, or did Germany's geopolitical circumstances cause the war? Was identity or power more important overall? As we learned in the introduction to this volume, scholars ask counterfactual questions to tease out the answers to such questions.

Professor Copeland writes, "If one imagines a Germany in 1939 with superior but declining military power, but led by military leaders lacking the racist ideology of Nazism, would these leaders have gone to war?" He answers no, they would not:

> Given that to a man senior [German] generals were holdovers from the First World War, and given that the military pushed for war in 1914 because of a rising Russia, . . . racism appears to be neither a sufficient nor even a necessary condition . . . to explain why Germany initiated world war for a second time in a generation. . . . German geopolitical vulnerability and the desire to eliminate the Russian threat would have existed with or without Nazi ideology.[39]

Hitler Youth parades, such as this one taking place in 1936 in Germany, stoked hypernationalism in Germany.

Professor Haas asks the same question and concludes "that Germany's international decisions in the 1930s would have been very different if the Nazis had not been in power." He emphasizes the fact that a group of German generals led by Ludwig Beck, the army chief of staff, "viewed Britain and France as Germany's ideological allies against the greatest ideological threat in the system: the Soviet Union."[40] Before the German attack on France, this group risked treason by communicating Hitler's battle plans to Britain and France. The dissident generals, Haas contends, would not have put their lives on the line merely to disagree with Hitler about the tactics or timing of Germany's attack, which is Copeland's conclusion. Hitler subsequently purged the Beck group, but Haas concludes that it was not geopolitical factors that predetermined Hitler's policies but an ideological struggle within the German leadership that the Nazis won. Thus, for Haas, Nazi ideology played a more important role than existing or future power balances in explaining

<table>
TABLE
3-3
</table>

The Causes of World War II: The Identity Perspective and Levels of Analysis

Identity perspective		
Systemic	*Structure*	Change in individual and collective identity: • Shared norms of self-determination not uniformly practiced or applied create many small, weak states (rather than weak states themselves being the cause, as realist perspectives emphasize) • National identities diverge—different nationalisms drive security dilemma (not geopolitics, as realist perspectives emphasize)
	Process	Spread of fascism, socialism, and racism
		Retreat of democracy
Foreign policy		German decision makers stir the witch's brew of domestic racism and foreign threat
Domestic		Bolshevism/communism in Russia
		Racism/militarism in Germany and Japan
		Exceptionalism in the United States
Individual		Stalin's communist beliefs that Germany and other capitalist countries would fight one another and that the Soviet Union could stay out of it

(Level of analysis — left side label)

the outcome of war. (See Table 3-3 for a summary of identity explanations of the causes of World War II.)

When do identity differences matter and when do power differences matter? Careful analysts consider all factors and try to determine the circumstances under which one variable matters more than another. Professor Haas concludes, for example, that power matters more when identity differences among the major powers are roughly equal distances from one another—that is, when the major powers are equally alienated from one another or have no ideological affinities toward one another. That was the case, some might argue, before World War II. Liberal, fascist, and communist nationalism were equally distant from one another ideologically. Thus, power factors dominated alignments. Fascist Germany allied with communist Russia to concentrate power against liberal France and Britain, and democratic Britain, France, and the United States allied with communist Russia to concentrate power against fascist Germany. Notice that identities still matter, but power prevails and influences identities more than identities influence power. Indeed, that is what realists mean when they tell us that nations pursue different values, but they all pursue power to defend those values.

⟩⟩⟩ Critical Theory Perspective

We can't do justice in this small space to the rich literature that offers critical perspectives on the origins of World War II. Marxism, as amended by Lenin and Stalin, foresaw, as noted in previous chapters, the advance of capitalism, which in turn created its antithesis—communism. Lenin introduced the idea that in the last stages of capitalism, capitalist states pursued colonialism or imperialism as a means to get rid of surplus production and wage war against one another for world markets. The Great Depression of the 1930s seemed to confirm this diagnosis. The capitalist powers suffered economic collapse at home and in turn accelerated the scramble for export markets abroad. Both fascist and liberal states were capitalist and hence in need of foreign markets. They would clash and ultimately hasten the rise of communism. Undoubtedly this expectation influenced Stalin and contributed to his decision to buckpass and ally with Hitler in the hope that Hitler and the other capitalist countries would fight each other to the death and hasten the demise of capitalism altogether. Moscow created the Communist International, or Comintern, to work with communist parties in other countries and foment the revolutionary cause.

The revisionist school of American history known as the Wisconsin School (because of the location of some of its leading adherents at the University of Wisconsin) applied the Leninist thesis to the United States, the leading capitalist country in the twentieth century. Charles A. Beard and William Appleman Williams interpreted America's rising power and influence in the world as the country's quest for markets on behalf of the capitalist class. In a book published in 1930, Beard and his wife, Mary, argued that the Civil War was not an ideological war about human rights but an economic class war between capitalist and agrarian economic systems. The capitalist system won, and American foreign policy after that was one of steady expansion. "As the domestic market was saturated and capital heaped up for investment," the Beards wrote, "the pressure for expansion of the American commercial empire rose with corresponding speed."[41] The "open door policy" followed, in which the United States pressed for economic access to one part of the world after another: China, Europe, and the colonial territories. In a later book, Charles Beard placed the blame for World War II squarely on the policies of the United States. These policies were not only imperialist but deceptive

In this Russian poster from 1920, Vladimir Lenin is depicted wielding the broom of history to sweep the world clean of aristocrats and bourgeoisie. The text reads "Comrade Lenin cleans the world of filth."

ТОВ. ЛЕНИН ОЧИЩАЕТ ЗЕМЛЮ ОТ НЕЧИСТИ.

TABLE
3-4

The Causes of World War II: The Critical Theory Perspective and Levels of Analysis[a]

Critical theory perspective			
Systemic	*Structure*		Capitalist states war against one another while communist states pick up the spoils
	Process		Depression weakens capitalism
Foreign policy			—
Domestic			United States adopts open door policy to dump export surpluses on world markets
Individual			Lenin modifies Marxism to include imperialist phase of capitalist expansion

(Left vertical label: **Level of analysis**)

a. Remember that critical theories consider levels of analysis to be inseparable. Factors identified at the various levels of analysis are not causes but parts of a holistic explanation.

and degenerate, a blatant attempt to saddle the American people with the profit plunder of the arms industry.[42]

William Appleman Williams, who spent his academic career at the University of Wisconsin, picked up on this theme about the dark side of U.S. foreign policy and established the Wisconsin School as one of the most influential and controversial interpretations of international relations in general. We'll have occasion to visit with Professor Williams and some of his critical theory successors again in a later chapter. (See Table 3-4 for a summary of critical theory explanations of the causes of World War II.)

SUMMARY

In this chapter we have revisited numerous concepts laid out initially in Chapter 1 and examined how these concepts work in regard to the history of World War II. The security dilemma figures prominently in realist accounts, collective goods (security) and institutions in liberal accounts, and identity construction and differences in identity perspectives.

Realist arguments often dominate the historical record. Was World War II, then, mostly a struggle for power? Perhaps, but liberal and identity factors were becoming more important. Ironically, one great power, the Soviet Union, joined the League of Nations just as the two aggressor powers, Germany and Japan, withdrew. The United States never joined. In that sense, the

League never got a fair test. Moreover, by the mid-1930s domestic political systems had diverged to such a large extent that trust was increasingly in short supply. When Britain negotiated with the Soviet Union in summer 1939 to form an alliance against Hitler (an exercise that ultimately failed when the Soviet Union aligned with Hitler), here is what Neville Chamberlain, the British prime minister, wrote:

> I must confess to the very most profound distrust of Russia. I have no belief whatsoever in her ability to maintain an effective offensive, even if she wanted to. And I distrust her motives, which seem to me to have little connection with our ideas of liberty, and to be concerned only with getting everyone else by the ears.[43]

Diplomacy—the liberal perspective—cannot bridge unlimited ideological chasms. Nor can alliances—the realist perspective. The United States and the Soviet Union allied in extremis to defeat Nazi Germany, but once that menace was vanquished the wartime allies had a severe falling out that became the Cold War. Ideology ultimately severed the alliance and undermined the United Nations, a body that the allies had intended to lead the world. That's at least an identity perspective on the topic of our next chapter.

 Sharpen your skills with SAGE edge at **edge.sagepub.com/nau4e.** **SAGE edge for students** provides a personalized approach to help you accomplish your coursework goals in an easy-to-use learning environment.

KEY CONCEPTS

appeasement, 130	chain-ganging, 137	genocide, 143	offensive realism, 133
bandwagoning, 131	defensive realism, 134	League of Nations, 118	self-determination, 117
buckpassing, 131	exceptionalism, 141	*Lebensraum*, 114	unanimity, 118

STUDY QUESTIONS

1. If Hitler planned and predicted war at the meeting with his generals in 1937 recorded by Hossbach, how can anyone argue that this was not a premeditated war reflecting the identity perspective from the individual level of analysis?

2. Contrast the way balance-of-power and collective security systems work.

3. Explain why the League of Nations failed from the three different perspectives.

4. What are three realist arguments why hegemons, such as Nazi Germany, France under Louis XIV, and France under Napoleon, cannot stop once they have achieved superiority?

5. Distinguish the following questions in terms of the perspectives they reflect. Did the norm of self-determination create weak states in eastern Europe, did weak states emerge from a vacuum of power, or did the Locarno Treaty concluded by the League of Nations fail to protect weak states?

President Kennedy and Soviet Foreign Minister Andrei Gromyko meet in the middle of the Cuban Missile Crisis as the world watches intently. Also shown in this photograph, taken at the White House on October 18, 1962, are Secretary of State Dean Rusk (seated on the couch, left) and Llewellyn Thompson (seated on the couch, right), special adviser on Soviet affairs.

THE ORIGINS AND END OF THE COLD WAR 4

In mid-February 1946 a young, relatively obscure U.S. Foreign Service officer lay feverish and ill in bed in Moscow. An aide brought him a cable from the State Department in Washington asking why the Soviets seemed unwilling to support the World Bank and International Monetary Fund, two institutions the United States sought to create to manage postwar international economic relations. The query was routine and even trivial. But the sick diplomat, George Kennan, used the occasion to compose his famous long telegram outlining the nature of the conflict the United States faced with the Soviet Union and the diplomatic solution to it.[1]

long telegram:
George Kennan's
diplomatic telegram
of 1946 outlining
the U.S.–Soviet
conflict and arguing
for the policy of
containment.

 # The Long Telegram

Kennan's telegram hit Washington like a thunderbolt and made Kennan an instant diplomatic rock star. In typical telegram shorthand, it made the following six points:

First, the Soviet Union is confrontational. Kennan warned that the leadership of the Soviet Union had adopted an outlook of "antagonistic 'capitalist encirclement,'" expecting a global confrontation between capitalism and socialism. Stalin, Kennan quoted, had stated as early as 1927 that "there will emerge two centers of world significance: a socialist center, drawing to itself the countries which tend toward socialism, and a capitalist center, drawing to itself the countries that incline toward capitalism. Battle between these two centers . . . will decide fate of capitalism and of communism in entire world."

Second, Marxism expresses Russian insecurity. This confrontational

> Soviet party line is not based on any objective analysis of the situation beyond Russia's borders. . . . At the bottom of the Kremlin's neurotic view of world affairs is traditional and instinctive Russian sense of insecurity . . . insecurity of a peaceful agricultural people trying to live on vast exposed plain in neighborhood of fierce nomadic peoples. To this was added, as Russia came into contact with economically advanced West, fear of more competent, more powerful, more highly organized societies in that area. . . . Marxist dogma . . . became a perfect vehicle for [this] sense of insecurity.

Third, the Soviet Union will expand its power. Russia will increase

> in every way strength and prestige of Soviet state; intensive military-industrialization, maximum development of armed forces, great displays to impress outsiders, continued secretiveness. . . . [And] whenever it is considered timely and promising, efforts will be made to advance official limits of Soviet power . . . for the moment . . . restricted to certain neighboring points . . . such as Iran, Turkey, possibly Bornholm [an island in the Baltic Sea south of Sweden]. However, other points may at times come into question . . . a port on Persian Gulf . . . Soviet base at Gilbraltar [*sic*] Strait.

Fourth, the Soviet Union leads a worldwide communist effort. Kennan foresaw that the Soviet Union would work "closely together" with leaders of communist parties in other countries "as an underground operating directorate of world communism, a concealed Comintern [Communist International] tightly coordinated and dominated by Moscow." It would also steer the rank and file of communist parties "through front organizations" and use national associations such as labor unions, youth leagues, and women's organizations, as well as international organizations, the Russian Orthodox Church, pan-Slav and other movements, and willing foreign governments "to undermine general political and strategic potential of major Western powers . . . to disrupt national self-confidence, to hamstring measures of national defense, to increase social and industrial unrest, to stimulate all forms of disunity."

Fifth, the United States must contain the Soviet Union and let communism fail. Perhaps most famously, Kennan argued for resistance to Soviet power but not overreaction to Soviet ideology:

> How to cope with this force is undoubtedly greatest task [U.S.] diplomacy has ever faced. . . . Soviet power does not work by fixed plans. . . . Impervious to the logic of reason, it is highly sensitive to the logic of force. For this reason it can easily withdraw—and usually does—when strong resistance is encountered at any point. . . . if situations are properly handled there need be no prestige-engaging showdowns. . . . Soviet system, as form of internal power, is not yet finally proven . . . never since the termination of the civil war [1921] have the mass of Russian people been emotionally farther removed from doctrines of the Communist Party than they are today. . . . Thus, internal soundness and permanence of movement need not yet be regarded as assured.

Sixth, the United States will win by improving its own society, not by spreading freedom. Kennan warned that the United States must not

> be emotionally provoked or unseated by [the communist movement]. . . . Much depends on health and vigor of our own society. . . . Every courageous and incisive measure to solve internal problems of our own society, to improve self-confidence, discipline, morale, and community spirit of our own people is a diplomatic victory over Moscow worth a thousand diplomatic notes and joint communiqués. . . . We must . . . put forward for all nations a much more positive and constructive picture of the sort of world we would like to see. . . . It is not enough to urge the people to develop political processes similar to our own. Many foreign peoples . . . are less interested in abstract freedom than in security. . . . Finally, we must . . . cling to our own . . . conceptions of human society. . . . the greatest danger that can befall us . . . is that we shall allow ourselves to become like those with whom we are coping.

Long by the standards of a telegram, Kennan's analysis was succinct by the logic of diplomacy. It was also eerily prescient.

>>> Snapshot of the Cold War

Within two years of the end of World War II, the two wartime allies faced off against one another, just as Kennan had highlighted. They used "the logic of force" to checkmate and contain one another. From 1949 to 1955, two massive military alliances, the **North Atlantic Treaty Organization (NATO)** in the west and the **Warsaw Pact** in the east, emerged

North Atlantic Treaty Organization (NATO): western alliance in the Cold War.

Warsaw Pact: communist alliance in the Cold War.

Cold War: the global, putatively bloodless (hence cold, not hot) conflict between the United States and the Soviet Union that resulted in massive arms buildups, international conflicts, and proxy wars.

to divide Berlin, Germany, and the rest of Europe not just politically but physically. By 1961, an ugly wall ran down the center of Berlin, and barbed wire, guard towers, and a barren no-man's land cut a gash across the landscape of Europe, turning eastern Europe effectively into a concentration camp.

The two superpowers engaged one another with considerably more ideological fervor and saber rattling than Kennan had advised, and which he later sharply criticized. An intense series of worldwide crises followed. Berlin, Korea, and Cuba brought the superpowers to the brink of war. Nevertheless, in the end the superpowers ended the confrontation without firing a shot directly at one another. They engaged in a **Cold War** of deterrence and diplomatic crises that, although it included plenty of "hot" wars waged through proxy governments as in Vietnam, did not involve the use of force in direct battles between the superpowers. Deterrence sublimated the use of force to a psychological rather than physical level. The superpowers played out the scenarios of war in their imaginations, testing the credibility of threats against capabilities and resolve and ultimately pulling back from the brink and easing disputes before war began. And all the while, as Kennan anticipated, the United States and the Soviet Union fought the real battle at home through domestic competition. Forty-five years later, the United States and its allies won that competition decisively. In November 1989, the Berlin Wall came down, and in December 1991, the Soviet Union ceased to exist.

Does Kennan's picture offer the best explanation of the start of the Cold War? Possibly, but first, what kind of explanation is it—realist, liberal, or identity? What is driving Soviet behavior in Kennan's analysis? At first glance, it might seem to be Marxist ideology (identity). After all, as he points out, the Soviet party line of "capitalist encirclement" was "not based on any objective analysis" but was, instead, a "neurotic view of world affairs." Moreover, in contact with the advanced west, Russia felt less

FIGURE 4-1

First Page of George Kennan's Long Telegram

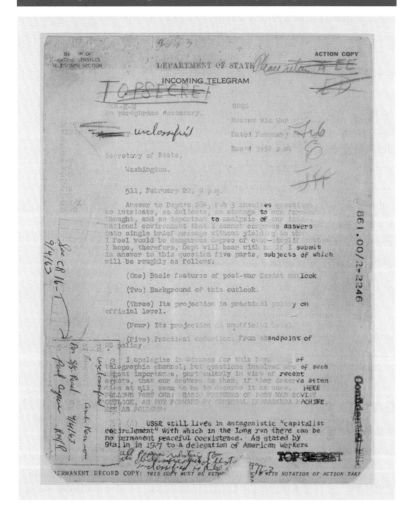

competent, less powerful, making "Marxist dogma" a "perfect vehicle" to express its inferiority. But now geopolitics slips into the picture. This neurotic view was not itself the cause of Soviet behavior but a result of a "traditional and instinctive Russian sense of insecurity." Russia lived on a "vast exposed plain" in a "neighborhood of fierce nomadic peoples" and had suffered three bloody invasions—by Napoleon, Kaiser Wilhelm II, and Hitler—in just over a hundred years. It was geopolitics and security (realist), not ideology, that explained Russia's paranoia.

The real tip-off comes when Kennan suggests that "Soviet power does not work by fixed plans." Moscow might have an ideology, but in the end that ideology bends to "the logic of force." The Soviet Union can "easily withdraw—and usually does—when strong resistance is encountered at any point." The balance of power works. How so, if the Soviet Union's ideology calls for "drawing to itself the countries which tend toward socialism"? Because in determining Soviet behavior, Kennan judges, strategic and geopolitical realities ultimately trump ideology. They also trump liberal factors. Notice that the Soviet Union uses international organizations and transnational actors—for example, the Russian Orthodox Church—to advance the purposes of Soviet ideology. But institutions are instruments, not determinants, of Soviet behavior. Thus, when all is said and done, ideology and institutions bend to the logic of power.

Kennan's analysis is realist, and that's why he can be relatively complacent about the ideological component of Soviet policy. The Soviet people do not really believe it: "never since the termination of the civil war [1921] have the mass of Russian people been emotionally farther removed from doctrines of the Communist Party than they are today." This is why he later criticized other analysts who made too much of ideological or identity factors.[2]

CAUSAL ARROW: PERSPECTIVES

Uses diplomacy instrumentally	Exploits communist ideology	Geopolitical insecurity
LIBERAL	IDENTITY	REALIST

This chapter addresses arguments about what caused the Cold War to begin and what caused it to end. As before, there are realist, identity, and liberal explanations of these historical events from different levels of analysis. And along the way critical theories offer their insights as well. The parallel timeline on page 154 assembles the events of the Cold War period chronologically.

⟫ Realist Explanations

Three main realist arguments explain the origins of the Cold War. All of them trace events back to power factors, but they come from different levels of analysis. One domestic-level explanation suggests that the Soviet Union caused the Cold War because its society was aggressive. A second domestic-level argument says the United States caused the Cold War because its capitalist economic system was expansionist. A third explanation, perhaps the most influential, comes from the systemic level. It argues that neither the United States nor the Soviet Union was responsible for the Cold War; rather, the Cold War was a consequence of the security dilemma. The two countries faced one another across a power vacuum in central Europe and had to compete to fill that vacuum whether they were aggressive or not.

Parallel Timeline 4-1

Events Leading to the Origins and End of the Cold War

Realist		Liberal		Identity	
		Yalta Conference	1945		
		United Nations	1945		
		Potsdam Conference	1945		
		Baruch Plan	1946		
				Truman Doctrine	1947
Berlin Blockade	1948	Marshall Plan	1948		
North Atlantic Treaty Organization (NATO)	1949				
Korean War	1950			Rollback Doctrine	1950s
				Decolonization/ national liberation	1950s and 1960s
		European Coal and Steel Community	1951		
Warsaw Pact	1955	Nonaligned movement	1955		
		European Atomic Energy Community	1958		
		European Economic Community	1958		
Vietnam War	1961–1975				
Cuban Missile Crisis	1962				
		European Communities	1968		
		Détente	1970s		
		Strategic Arms Limitation Talks (SALT I and II)	1970s		
		Helsinki Accords	1970s		
		Anti-Ballistic Missile (ABM) Treaty	1972		
Freedom fighters	1980s	Strategic Arms Reduction Talks (START I and II)	1980s	New Thinking	1980s
				Revitalization of American exceptionalism	1980s
Strategic Defense Initiative (SDI)	1983				

The principal realist explanation for the end of the Cold War also comes from the systemic level. It holds that the United States eventually won the competition by successfully containing the Soviet Union, while domestic developments outside the influence of diplomacy led the Soviet Union to discard its communist ideology. Kennan predicted this outcome in a famous article published a year and a half after the long telegram. By confronting "the Russians with unalterable counterforce at every point where they show signs of encroaching upon the interest of a peaceful and stable world," he wrote, the United States would "promote tendencies which must eventually find their outlet in either the break-up or the gradual mellowing of Soviet power."[3]

How the Cold War Started

In the sections that follow, we examine the three realist explanations about how the Cold War started; then how realist mechanisms such as atomic weapons and nuclear deterrence, crises such as the Cuban Missile Crisis, and alliances/proxy wars expanded the Cold War; and finally the realist explanation of how the Cold War ended.

Soviet Aggression—Historical Expansionism. "Russia on the march," Henry Kissinger writes, "rarely exhibited a sense of limits." It "seemed impelled to expand by a rhythm all its own, containable only by the deployment of superior force, and usually by war."[4] This had been the case since the time of Peter the Great, long before the arrival of communism. So, according to this explanation of the Cold War, Soviet aggression was not a consequence of communist ideology or the sense of historical insecurity that Kennan stressed. It was an outgrowth of the aggressive nature of the domestic society that demanded aggrandizement and empire. As Stalin saw it, "Everyone imposes his own system as far as his army can reach."[5] He was, according to this explanation, an offensive realist, seeking to maximize power rather than just provide security. And the cause of aggression came not from Stalin himself or the individual level of analysis, because every Russian leader since Peter the Great had been aggressive. Nor did it come from the systemic structural level of analysis or the sense of historical insecurity bred by the security dilemma. Rather, it came from the domestic society as a whole, and it was not the communist ideology or institutions but the aggressive nature of that society that caused the expansionism.

Stalin's army had reached quite far when World War II ended. Soviet divisions occupied Lithuania, Latvia, and Estonia; all of eastern Europe; half of Germany; and northern Iran. Meanwhile, U.S. troops withdrew from Europe, reduced from 12 million down to 1.5 million by mid-1947. Stalin also pressed for a naval advantage, looking for warm-water ports in the Mediterranean and modes of access to the Atlantic Ocean, perhaps as a way to challenge, if not encircle, Britain and the United States on the high seas. Finally, when a million Soviet troops maneuvered in Romania and stayed in Iran beyond the end of 1945, Harry S. Truman saw a threat of aggression and became alarmed: "There isn't a doubt in my mind that Russia intends an invasion of Turkey and the seizure of the Black Sea Straits to the Mediterranean. Unless Russia is faced with an iron fist and strong language another war is in the making."[6]

РЕАЛЬНОСТЬ НАШЕЙ ПРОГРАММЫ
—ЭТО ЖИВЫЕ ЛЮДИ, ЭТО МЫ С ВАМИ,
НАША ВОЛЯ К ТРУДУ, НАША ГОТОВНОСТЬ
РАБОТАТЬ ПО-НОВОМУ,
НАША РЕШИМОСТЬ ВЫПОЛНИТЬ ПЛАН.
И. Сталин

This propaganda poster features one of Stalin's five-year plans (1946–1950). Soviet aggression, realists think, prompted Washington to react with containment policies designed to keep Russia at bay.

containment: the policy of the United States during the Cold War that checked aggressive Soviet actions through military alliances.

Although these crises passed, the impression of Soviet aggression lasted, and, by some accounts, the "policy of containment, as it came to be called, was adopted at the beginning of 1946."[7] Aggressive Soviet actions convinced Washington policy officials that they had to draw a line of **containment** around the periphery of the territories Soviet armies occupied and defend that line, if necessary, by military force. No wonder Kennan's telegram, which arrived about this time, set off such a furor. Policy makers had decided "the Soviet Union was an expansionist power, and . . . only countervailing power could keep her in line."[8]

In the same month, British prime minister Winston Churchill declared in Fulton, Missouri, that an **iron curtain** had descended on Europe, "from Stettin in the Baltic to Trieste in the Adriatic."[9] Churchill characterized the impending division of Europe in a political sense. But two years later, in 1948, the iron curtain became a physical barrier when the Soviet Union cut off access routes to the western occupied parts of Berlin located inside the Soviet-occupied zone (see Map 4-1). And two years after that, in 1950, it became a military division when North Korea, a client state of the Soviet Union, invaded South Korea and sparked a buildup of alliances in Europe.

As was assumed then and is known now, the Soviet Union approved the North Korean invasion beforehand.[10] The attack set off alarm bells in Europe and sparked an **arms race** to prevent a Soviet-sponsored invasion from happening there. From this realist argument, Soviet aggression was clearly the culprit. And now Moscow had allies in Asia as well. In 1949, the communists under Mao Zedong won the civil war in China. The Cold War was in full swing.

U.S. Aggression—Capitalist Expansionism. But wait a minute, you say. What about American or Western aggression? Weren't Western armies also ensconced in Europe, even if they were being reduced? Didn't American and British fleets dominate the Mediterranean and Baltic Seas, in effect "encircling" the Soviet Union? Hadn't the Soviet Union, not the United States, recently been invaded by Nazi hordes, and didn't the United States and Great Britain delay for almost three years before establishing a second front to help Russia fight off the Nazi invaders? For every one American who died in World War II, fifty-three Russians died.[11] Might Stalin have had reasons to wonder whether the United States and Great Britain were happy watching Germany and the Soviet Union eliminate or at least drastically weaken one another?

When the war ended, Russia was powerful militarily, but the United States possessed the atom bomb. And, with the Soviet economy in ruins, the United States was by far the most powerful country economically. It was the only major combatant in World War II to escape entirely any damage to its homeland industrial base. So the Soviet Union had good reason to feel that it was the weaker power and to expect and probably deserve substantial economic help from its Western allies, as well as reparations from Germany and conquered eastern European countries.

What did it get? Not much. First, as soon as the war was over in both Europe and Asia, the United States cut off Lend-Lease assistance to the Soviet Union, the supply of all kinds of military and economic assistance during the war to countries fighting Germany and its allies. Then, at the **Potsdam Conference** in July 1945, the allies concocted a reparation plan that assumed Germany would remain unified. But the Soviet Union preferred a division of Germany and rejected the plan.[12] When the Western powers decided in the spring of 1946 to go ahead and rebuild their own zones, the Soviet Union saw the Western powers reconstructing Germany not only without it but against it. The battle for Germany was joined.

One year later, in the spring of 1947, the United States announced the **Marshall Plan**. This plan proposed to integrate the western zones of Germany into a larger program of European economic cooperation. The Soviet zone and other eastern European states were invited to join. But let's think about this proposal now from the point of view of the Soviet Union. Economically ravaged and weak, its satellites were being asked to join a Western market system that was not only more powerful, given the backing of the United States, but that also operated on the basis of free trade. Quite understandably, Moscow saw this move as Western aggression, a plan to penetrate economically, and eventually take over politically, the protective band of countries in eastern Europe that the Soviet Union needed as a security buffer and had just sacrificed so many lives to establish. The U.S. action wasn't military aggression as such, but it could be seen as capitalist imperial aggression. And it threatened the heart of Soviet interests in Europe, whereas alleged Soviet aggression challenged only peripheral Western interests in places such as Greece and Turkey.

When the Western powers announced in spring 1948 that they would unify the currency of the Western zones of Germany, Moscow reacted by shutting down the land routes to Berlin. As Map 4-1 shows, the city of Berlin was located inside the Soviet-occupied part of Germany (East Germany) and was itself divided into Western (U.S., British, and French) and Soviet zones. Thus, the Soviet Union controlled land access to Berlin. When Stalin blockaded the road and railway routes, the Western powers responded with the massive Berlin airlift. Over fourteen months, the allies made 277,804 flights to Berlin, delivering 2.326 million tons of supplies. The **Berlin Blockade** of 1948–1949 was the first physical confrontation of the Cold War. According to the United States-is-the-aggressor argument, however, Russia was not responsible. It was provoked. Moscow could not permit Western economic forces to expand and weaken its control of the Soviet zone.

The argument that the United States caused the Cold War is called a **revisionist interpretation** because it revises the traditional argument that the Soviet Union was the

iron curtain: a metaphor for the political, ideological, and physical (no-man's land) separation of the Soviet Union and Western countries during the Cold War.

arms race: the competitive buildup of weapons systems.

Potsdam Conference: the meeting among wartime allies in July 1945 that produced no agreement on the unification of Germany and other issues.

Marshall Plan: the Western plan to rebuild Germany and the rest of Europe after World War II.

Berlin Blockade: the first physical confrontation of the Cold War, taking place in 1948–1949, in which Stalin blocked the land routes into Berlin.

revisionist interpretation: an interpretation of the origins of the Cold War that emphasizes American ideological or economic aggression against the Soviet Union and its allies.

MAP 4-1

The Division of Berlin

aggressor. To the extent that it emphasizes military causes of U.S. aggressive policy, it is clearly a realist argument. But to the extent that it draws on deeper historical forces of capitalist expansion, it slides into a critical theory perspective, which we address later in this chapter.

Power Vacuum and Spheres of Influence. A third influential realist argument holds that the Cold War was nobody's fault but was a consequence of the anarchic situation that the United States and the Soviet Union faced after World War II. In April 1945, the two massive allied armies met in the middle of Germany, at Torgau on the Elbe River.[13] Because the allies had agreed in 1943 to pursue the war until the unconditional surrender of the enemy, there was nothing left of Germany when they finished. The entire country lay in ruins.

How was Germany going to be rebuilt? Would it be rebuilt as a Western ally, a Soviet ally, or a neutral country? One thing was sure. As we know, Germany was the center-piece of the old European state system. It had been divided for centuries, then it was united for nearly seventy-five years. Now it was destroyed. If it were united or divided again, it would matter greatly whether Germany added to Western power or Soviet power. The distribution of power at the time, some realists argue, was tripolar.[14] And, as discussed in Chapter 1, a tripolar balance may be uniquely unstable. The third country, in this case a reconstructed Germany (or Japan in the case of Asia), could tip the balance. Whoever won this prize would control the center of Europe (or Asia, in the case of Japan). Thus, the stakes were very high. No one had to be an aggressor in this situation. It was a matter of security, not aggression, for each side to seek the best outcome.

So systemic structural forces were driving events. Essentially two great powers (and their smaller allies) sat astride a strategic piece of territory and faced the security dilemma of whether and how much to trust one another. The classic balance-of-power solution was to "split the difference": divide the territory and power evenly and create two **spheres of influence**, one in which the Soviet Union dominated and the other in which the United States dominated. That way, the relative balance of power would not be affected. Roughly, that is what happened. By 1950, two German governments existed and two alliances divided up the rest of Europe.

CAUSAL ARROW: PERSPECTIVES

Prevent a hot ideological war	Minimize interdependence	Create spheres of influence
IDENTITY	LIBERAL	REALIST

spheres of influence: areas of contested territory divided up and dominated by great powers, which agree not to interfere in one another's areas.

The balance of power worked better than it had before World Wars I and II. There was no hot war in Europe for the next forty years. But there was a cold war. Why did it occur? Realist perspectives expected a spheres-of-influence solution, not a cold war. Each superpower would exert dominance in its half of Europe and respect the other's dominance in the other half. That was the solution George Kennan favored. At best, realists might say that spheres of influence made the balance of power rigid once again, as before World War I. The bipolar confrontation left little room for error and thus provoked a deep security dilemma that made the two superpowers enemies instead of rivals. But identity perspectives (examined later in the chapter) might say that it was the ideological divide that prevented an accommodation, not rigid bipolarity and the security dilemma.

Churchill was an avid proponent of the spheres-of-influence solution. In October 1944 he met with Stalin in Moscow and, on a famous half sheet of paper, proposed a breakdown of relative influence in the Balkans.[15] The Soviet Union would have predominant influence in Romania and Bulgaria; Great Britain and the United States would have predominant influence in Greece. Both sides would split influence in Yugoslavia and Hungary. Deal done, right? Why not do the same for Germany and eastern Europe? Well, now think how you would administer such a spheres-of-influence arrangement, especially when the two partners already suspect one another. After the war, Soviet troops occupied Poland, Romania, Hungary, Bulgaria, and Czechoslovakia. How could Britain and the United States know, let alone defend against, what might go on in those countries? At the **Yalta Conference** (held at a Russian resort of that name on the Black Sea) in February 1945, Roosevelt tried to reach an agreement with Stalin about what would happen in Poland. The United States would concede Soviet influence, since Soviet armies already occupied the country, if the Soviet Union would hold free and fair elections and create

Yalta Conference: a wartime conference held in February 1945 where the United States, Soviet Union, and Great Britain agreed on the unconditional surrender of Nazi Germany and postwar occupation of Europe, including a Soviet sphere of influence in eastern Europe.

more transparency. But who then would ensure that the elections were free and fair? Yalta specified few details. In the end, no such elections were held. The Soviet Union installed a puppet government in Warsaw that Moscow manipulated. Later, in 1948, the Soviet Union staged another coup in Czechoslovakia. To this day, the conference at Yalta stands in the minds of eastern Europeans as a callous sellout of small powers by the great powers.

How the Cold War Expanded

So the Cold War divided Europe. But why did it divide the globe? The answer, according to realist perspectives, is that a balance of terror replaced the balance of power and made the segregation of regional conflicts more difficult. Nuclear weapons introduced such a high level of terror that the mere threat to use them would deter all wars, both conventional and nuclear. But to be effective that threat would have to be credible, and superpowers would have to make clear commitments to defend their interests both outside as well as inside Europe. Alliances sprang up, and crises spread. The superpowers dueled through proxy wars in Korea and later Vietnam and Afghanistan, and came close to a direct nuclear war in the Cuban Missile Crisis. The costs of deterrence were high, and eventually the Soviet Union went bankrupt and the United States prevailed. From a realist perspective, competition and relative material capabilities decided the outcome. There was no direct war, but the persistent terrifying threat of nuclear war produced an equivalent psychological result.

The Atomic Bomb and the Balance of Terror. On July 16, 1945, the first nuclear bomb (called Little Boy) was tested in the deserts of New Mexico, an event Truman reported to Stalin at Potsdam. Stalin was not surprised. Klaus Fuchs, a Soviet spy at Los Alamos, the center of U.S. weapons research in New Mexico, had been supplying Russia with atomic secrets for years. After his conversation with Truman, Stalin instructed V. M. Molotov, his foreign minister, and Lavrenty Beria, the head of the Soviet atomic program, "to hurry up the work" on the Soviet bomb.[16] In 1949, the Soviet Union exploded its own nuclear weapon. According to realist logic, the Soviet Union could not depend on the United States or anyone else for security against this type of weapon.

balance of terror: a situation in which two or more countries use the threat of nuclear weapons to deter conflicts.

Now a kind of **balance of terror** superseded the balance of power. If either side attacked, the other side might use nuclear weapons. As these weapons became more powerful— by 1951, hydrogen bombs were developed that were many times more powerful than atomic weapons—no country could risk nuclear war and survive. Yet conventional war might still be possible. If no one could risk nuclear escalation, then the struggle for power might be decided by regular armies with tanks, artillery, and aircraft or even by guerrilla forces engaged in wars of liberation. Each country had to worry about its capabilities to fight wars at all levels of potential conflict—guerrilla, conventional, and nuclear—and its resolve to escalate the use of force to higher levels to contain conflicts. Each country formed alliances to demonstrate such resolve, and **proxy wars**, in which superpowers tested each other's capabilities and resolve in peripheral areas, became more likely. By such logic, according to the realist perspective, the Cold War spread both horizontally to the rest of the globe and vertically to include all levels of military arms.

proxy wars: conflicts in peripheral areas in which nuclear powers tested each other's military capabilities and resolve.

An arms race began even before the Korean War started in June 1950. In early 1950, the White House drafted the famous National Security Council document NSC-68. Under this document, the United States boosted its defense budget in one year from $13.5 billion to $48.2 billion. The number of U.S. troops in Europe ballooned from 80,000 in 1950 to 427,000 in 1953. NATO, created in 1949 to reinforce political ties among the Western allies, now developed into an integrated military force under a U.S. supreme commander. The military occupation of Germany by the Western allies ended, a West German government was established, and West Germany eventually rearmed and joined NATO. Meanwhile, the Soviet Union established a separate government in East Germany and created the Warsaw Pact alliance to counterbalance NATO. In 1955, NATO included, in addition to the United States and West Germany, the United Kingdom, France, Belgium, the Netherlands, Luxembourg, Portugal, Italy, Norway, Denmark, Iceland, Greece, Turkey, and Canada. The Warsaw Pact included, in addition to the Soviet Union and East Germany, Poland, Hungary, Czechoslovakia, Romania, Bulgaria, and Albania.

The **Korean War** globalized the Cold War alliances. Korea had been divided at the end of World War II between a Soviet-dependent government in the north and a U.S.-dependent government in the south. In June 1950, North Korea, with permission from Moscow, invaded South Korea. The United States led a United Nations force to drive the North Koreans back. When UN forces threatened to cross the Yalu, a river dividing China and North Korea, China entered the war, and the fighting seesawed back and forth across the peninsula until an armistice was signed in 1953 along the original dividing line, the 38th parallel. A peace treaty was never signed, and U.S. forces remain to the present day in South Korea. In the course of the 1950s, the United States signed a security treaty with Japan and created the Southeast Asia Treaty Organization (SEATO) with Great Britain, France, Australia, New Zealand, Pakistan, the Philippines, and Thailand to defend allies in the rest of Asia. The United States also concluded bilateral alliances with Australia, New Zealand, South Korea, the Philippines, Thailand, and Taiwan. In the Middle East, the United States established the Central Treaty Organization (CENTO), which included Iraq, Iran, Pakistan, Turkey, and the United Kingdom. And in Latin America it signed the Rio Treaty with twenty other nations.

Korean War: a proxy war on the Korean Peninsula in the early 1950s between Soviet-backed North Korean and Chinese forces and a United Nations force led by the United States.

Nuclear Deterrence and Escalation. How does nuclear deterrence work? Deterrence is the use of the threat of force to stop an attack *before* it occurs, in contrast to defense, which is designed to counter an attack *after* it occurs. If it works, deterrence substitutes the threat of the use of force for the actual use of force. One state threatens to retaliate against a second state that is preparing to attack with enough force that the second state will lose more than it might gain if it attacks, and therefore, it does not attack in the first place.

How much and what kind of capabilities are needed to provide effective deterrence? The debate has produced no conclusive answers. Some analysts argue that all a state needs to deter an attack are a few nuclear weapons that can survive the initial attack by the other side and be launched against the attacker's civilian population and industry. Given the

minimum deterrence: a strategy of deterrence that relies on a few nuclear weapons to retaliate and inflict unacceptable damage on the adversary.

maximum deterrence: a strategy that relies on many nuclear weapons to deter both conventional and limited nuclear attacks.

extended deterrence: a strategy of deterrence in which one country uses nuclear weapons to deter an attack on the territory of an allied country.

destructive power of nuclear weapons, this strategy of **minimum deterrence** makes any war too costly, and states will be very reluctant to build up and use arms at any level of violence. Other analysts argue that minimum deterrence is not enough. One state may acquire a conventional capability that another state cannot stop without threatening to use nuclear weapons first. Now the state threatened by overwhelming conventional forces has to "think the unthinkable" and develop a variety of nuclear responses, or **maximum deterrence**, not only to forestall a conventional attack but also to deter limited nuclear engagements without immediately igniting an all-out nuclear war.

The debate is illustrated by the strategy of **extended deterrence**, in which a country extends the threat of retaliation to defend other countries, not just itself. The United States employed this strategy to defend the territories of its allies in Europe during the Cold War. The scenarios went something like the following.

If Moscow threatened to use its larger conventional armies to invade western Europe, the United States and its allies would threaten to use nuclear weapons to deter the invasion. The threat to use nuclear weapons would deter the Soviet Union from using conventional forces first. But the threat to use nuclear weapons might not be credible because it would mean an immediate all-out nuclear war. So, initially, the allies might threaten to use only tactical nuclear weapons. In the 1950s, NATO deployed nuclear land mines as well as artillery shells in central Europe. But what if the Soviet Union then said it would retaliate against tactical weapons by using short- or intermediate-range nuclear missiles stationed in eastern Europe to attack western Europe but not the United States? Would the United States, even though its territory had not been attacked, still launch intercontinental missiles from the United States on the Soviet Union? That would automatically involve the United States in a global war with the Soviet Union, so the threat might not be considered credible. The Soviet Union and even America's European allies might wonder if the United States would really risk the destruction of New York to retaliate for an attack on Paris. Thus, when the Soviet Union deployed SS-20 intermediate-range ballistic missiles in eastern Europe in the 1970s, western European leaders and then NATO as a whole called on Western nations to station their own intermediate-range nuclear forces (INFs)—Pershing and cruise missiles—on western European territory. Now a threat from Soviet intermediate-range missiles could be counterbalanced by a threat from intermediate-range missiles located in western Europe. An attack from the Soviet Union on Paris would be met by an attack from France on the Soviet Union. The conflict would not immediately escalate to the global level, and the threat from Europe would be considered more credible.

But now wouldn't western Europe be concerned that the United States might be more willing to start a nuclear war in Europe if it did not involve the United States? Yes, but that was one of the reasons the United States placed some American forces in western Europe from the outset. Now, if the Soviet Union attacked western Europe, using conventional or nuclear arms, U.S. troops would be killed and America would be involved in the war. What if the Soviet Union was still not deterred by intermediate-range missiles in Europe and the United States had to launch missiles from the United States? Wouldn't it be better if these missiles were aimed at Soviet missiles, not Soviet cities, to minimize collateral damage and avoid a wider nuclear holocaust? Such missiles, called counterforce weapons, were designed to destroy specific military targets, as opposed to countervalue weapons, which were designed to destroy Soviet industries and cities. The threat of counterforce weapons led to the hardening of missile sites to ensure that some of these missiles would survive a first strike by the other side and thus be available to retaliate in a second strike at the next level of escalation.

First-strike capability is the capacity to use nuclear missiles preemptively to destroy most or all of the missiles of the other side. Second-strike capability involves protecting nuclear missiles so that enough survive a first-strike attack to be available to retaliate and ensure a level of unacceptable damage in a second strike, thereby deterring the first strike to begin with. Missiles were hardened in underground silos and dispersed on submarines, where they were virtually invulnerable and could be launched from unknown locations. In addition, a strategic bomber force armed with nuclear weapons was kept in the air around the clock to ensure that these weapons would not be destroyed on the ground in a preemptive first strike. The combination of land-, sea-, and air-based retaliatory weapons became known as the **nuclear triad.**

nuclear triad: the combination of nuclear land-, sea-, and air-based retaliatory weapons.

The strategy of nuclear deterrence thus sought to slice the stages of escalation finer and finer so as to avoid the last move to all-out nuclear war. The superpowers would move up the various stages, or rungs of the ladder, of escalation in an incremental and controlled fashion until one eventually achieved what was called escalation dominance—that is, the point at which the adversary was convinced not to go any farther up the ladder and was forced to choose between unacceptable escalation and compromise. Nuclear strategies might also be deployed offensively. In a compellence strategy, one state uses the escalation of threat to compel another state to do something the first state wants, whereas in a strategy of deterrence, one state seeks to dissuade the other state from doing something the first state does not want. From the Soviet point of view, was the placement of Soviet missiles in Cuba a strategy of compellence to extract U.S. concessions in Berlin or a strategy of deterrence to discourage a U.S. attack on Cuba? We'll see the different points of view when we take up that crisis later.

Deterrence strategies evolved during the Cold War. For the first decade, the United States had the capacity to strike the Soviet Union but the Soviet Union could not strike the United States. The United States relied on a strategy of **massive retaliation,** or the threat of unleashing a general nuclear war if the Soviet Union attacked western Europe. After the Soviet Union launched the first space satellite, Sputnik, in 1957, thus demonstrating that it could strike the United States, the United States adopted a deterrence strategy of flexible response, or retaliating selectively to fight wars at conventional levels without immediately risking nuclear war or, if the nuclear threshold was crossed, engaging in limited nuclear war.

massive retaliation: the strategy of threatening to unleash a general nuclear war.

mutual assured destruction (MAD): the nuclear deterrence strategy that called for the dominance of offensive over defensive weapons.

Eventually, as both sides acquired increasingly equivalent capabilities, the deterrence strategy settled on what became known as **mutual assured destruction,** or **MAD** (as critics thought it was). If each side could retaliate and assure an unacceptable amount of

Strategic Arms Limitation Talks (SALT): U.S.–Soviet talks held in the 1970s to limit offensive weapon systems.

Anti-Ballistic Missile (ABM) Treaty: a 1972 treaty between the United States and Soviet Union limiting antiballistic missiles.

destruction to the other side, neither side would risk escalation. The strategy involved an emphasis on offensive weapons and a de-emphasis on defensive weapons. The **Strategic Arms Limitation Talks (SALT)** agreements signed in 1972 and 1979 (the latter never ratified by the U.S. Congress) set ceilings on (but no actual reductions of) offensive weapons, while the **Anti-Ballistic Missile (ABM) Treaty**, signed by the United States and the Soviet Union in 1972, prevented the development of antiballistic missile defenses except for two installations on each side (later reduced to one). The idea was to preserve the vulnerability of populated centers to offensive missile strikes and thus maintain the fear of massive civilian casualties that nuclear deterrence depended on.

As you can imagine, all of this nuclear war gaming and buildup provoked massive disagreements. Realist perspectives felt it was imperative to have capabilities at every level of potential escalation and that it was possible to use diplomacy to manage nuclear threats even in heated crises. Liberal perspectives felt that only a few second-strike nuclear weapons were necessary and that diplomacy could not control nuclear crises and should aim to reduce nuclear weapons to this minimum level.

CAUSAL ARROW: PERSPECTIVES

Use of force	Facilitates diplomacy and deterrence
REALIST	LIBERAL

CAUSAL ARROW: PERSPECTIVES

Diplomacy	Reduces need for force
LIBERAL	REALIST

In this debate, realist perspectives see diplomacy as the instrument for projecting credible force; liberal perspectives see it as a cause for reducing the role of force. The difference between realist and liberal perspectives on deterrence again is a matter of how the causal arrows run between force and diplomacy, not the exclusion of one factor. Realist perspectives worry that if only one country in the world decides that something is worth the risk of nuclear war, other countries had better be prepared to deter that country. Liberal perspectives worry that deterrence itself increases the risk of nuclear war.

Cuban Missile Crisis. No crisis illustrates the dynamics of deterrence between the superpowers better than the Cuban Missile Crisis. Soviet leaders risked nuclear war, but in the end superpower diplomacy avoided it. Here we consider realist perspectives, but compare this account carefully with the liberal perspectives presented later in this chapter.

In the summer and fall of 1962, the Soviets moved medium- and intermediate-range nuclear-armed ballistic missiles into Cuba. What induced them to do that? And why did the United States risk nuclear war to get the missiles removed? Here's the calculus according to realist perspectives.

In the 1960s, the United States had a substantial superiority of nuclear weapons and missiles over the Soviets, with roughly 3,000 nuclear warheads, 180 intercontinental ballistic missiles (ICBMs) with a range of 5,000 miles, 630 long-range bombers, and 12 nuclear submarines. The Soviet Union had 300 warheads, 20 ICBMs, 200 long-range bombers, and 6 nuclear submarines. U.S. bombers were deployed at forward bases in Europe and Asia, and American submarines could patrol waters within range of Soviet targets. In addition, the United States had placed intermediate-range ballistic missiles (IRBMs) with a range of 2,200 miles in Britain and medium-range ballistic missiles (MRBMs) with a range of 1,100 miles in Italy and Turkey. All these missiles could reach the Soviet Union. Soviet bombers had no forward bases or refueling capacity, and Soviet IRBMs and MRBMs could hit Europe but not the United States. Soviet submarines operated from bases 7,000 miles from the U.S. mainland and could not patrol in U.S. waters within the range of Soviet missiles, which was only 600 miles.[17]

Why did the United States have such an advantage? As we have noted, the realist argument is that it needed this advantage to provide extended deterrence to its allies in western Europe. If the Soviet Union launched missiles at Europe, Britain and later France might have had a few missiles to retaliate. But the United States would also have to respond; otherwise, a Soviet attack might not entail sufficient risk of retaliatory damage to deter the Soviet Union in the first place, and the Soviet Union might try to divide Europe from the United States. Of course, it made little difference to the Soviet Union why the United States had more missiles. The Soviet Union saw them as an offensive threat, a first-strike capability that could destroy Soviet missiles on the ground before they were launched, thus leaving the Soviet Union defenseless. Might that be why Nikita Khrushchev, the Soviet premier, put missiles in Cuba, to give the Soviet Union an offsetting capability to destroy U.S. missiles before they left the ground?

Perhaps. Missile accuracies were not yet that precise. But once the communist revolutionary Fidel Castro overthrew the U.S.-backed dictatorship in Cuba in 1959, Khrushchev had his own distant ally to defend by extended deterrence. Castro turned to Moscow for help, and the Soviet Union started selling arms to Cuba in fall 1959. In April 1961, the United States backed an invasion of Cuba by anti-Castro exiles. Known as the Bay of Pigs invasion, the attack failed, in part because the United States dropped crucial air support at the last minute. But the United States continued covert activities to support an invasion of Cuba and tried several times to assassinate Castro.[18] Now Khrushchev wondered, as he later wrote in his memoirs, "what will happen if we lose Cuba?"[19] If the United States could defend Turkey by installing missiles, why couldn't the Soviet Union install missiles to defend Cuba?

The credibility of both the Soviet Union and the United States was at stake. This credibility had just been tested in Berlin. From 1958 to 1961, the Soviet Union tried again to deny Western access to West Berlin by threatening to turn over controls to the East German government. East German citizens were fleeing in increasing numbers to the West. Khrushchev felt he had to do something to solve the Berlin problem. After renewing his threat to President John F. Kennedy at Vienna in June 1961, Khrushchev built the Berlin Wall in August. Now he saw another opportunity to get the Western allies out of Berlin altogether—trade a Soviet departure from Cuba for a Western departure from Berlin.

Berlin was the epicenter of the superpower conflict. If either superpower backed down on this issue, it would undermine its European alliances as well as its own security. That might explain the superpowers' willingness to march to the brink of nuclear disaster over the Cuban missiles.[20]

In May 1962, the Soviet Union made the decision to deploy to Cuba 48 MRBMs capable of striking Dallas, St. Louis, Cincinnati, and Washington; 32 IRBMs capable of striking all U.S. cities except Seattle; nuclear weapons for coastal defense; cruise missiles; surface-to-air missiles (SAMs); 42 light Ilyushin-28 bombers; MIG fighter aircraft; and bases for 7 nuclear submarines. It then proceeded to lie to the United States and other nations as the deployment took place. Moscow, of course, believed the United States was doing the same thing as part of plans to invade Cuba. Notice here the realist problem of not being able to trust the other party—for good reason, realists point out, because the other party lies. Nevertheless, Khrushchev's decision to deploy nuclear missiles in Cuba was bold and breathtaking, not to mention deadly. The Soviet premier had either lost his mind or believed he had taken the measure of Kennedy and could get away with it. Here is a case, realist perspectives remind us, when someone was willing to risk nuclear war. Khrushchev expected to complete the installation by early fall and, as Kennedy himself later noted, "face us [that is, the United States] with a bad situation in November at the time he was going to squeeze us on Berlin."[21] With the missiles installed in Cuba by November, Khrushchev would be in a much stronger position to demand a Berlin withdrawal for a Cuban one.

In October 1962, Kennedy reacted. He ordered a naval quarantine, not a blockade, of Soviet ships going to Cuba. A quarantine was a less belligerent act under international law and, in accordance with deterrence logic, initiated the crisis at a lower rung on the escalation ladder. Kennedy then demanded the removal of the missiles already there. He also prepared to escalate the use of force by mobilizing a major invasion force to storm Cuba if the Soviet Union refused. The superpowers were eyeball to eyeball. On Saturday, October 27, Kennedy, according to his own account, decided to schedule air strikes for the following Tuesday, October 30.[22] We now know that 9 MRBMs had already been assembled in Cuba, and 36 nuclear warheads were also on the island. More important, and unknown to American officials during the crisis, Soviet combat troops in Cuba, altogether some 42,000 (many more than U.S. policy makers thought), were equipped with tactical nuclear missiles with a range of 60 kilometers to resist the invasion. Soviet generals later said they were prepared to use the missiles to hit American ships 10–12 miles offshore when they were grouped together for landing and, hence, most vulnerable to attack. The generals had advance authorization to use the missiles if for some reason they could not reach Moscow for instructions, although that authorization was reportedly rescinded once the crisis began.[23] Nevertheless, earlier on October 27, Soviet generals in Cuba had acted on their own authority, after failing to reach Moscow, to shoot down a U.S. reconnaissance plane over Cuba. Thus, on that Saturday night, the world was very possibly only a couple of days away from Armageddon.

On Sunday, October 28, however, the Soviet Union blinked and the crisis ended. Khrushchev agreed to stop deployments and take out the weapons already there. On the surface, it looked like a complete U.S. victory. But in fact Kennedy had secretly traded in return two substantial concessions: a pledge not to invade Cuba and another to withdraw the Jupiter missiles in Turkey. The secrecy protected alliance relations as well as President Kennedy's own legacy.[24] Moreover, Soviet forces and tactical nuclear weapons stayed in Cuba for several years. Some of the delivery systems, although not the warheads, were never withdrawn.[25]

Why did the Soviet Union back down in the Cuban Missile Crisis? According to realist perspectives, it did so because the American threat to escalate and use force was credible. As Graham Allison and Philip Zelikow conclude, "Khrushchev withdrew the Soviet missiles, not because of the blockade, but because of the threat of further action." Khrushchev believed "he faced a clear, urgent threat that America was about to move up the ladder of escalation."[26] The threat of escalation was decisive, at least according to this account.

CAUSAL ARROW: PERSPECTIVES

Caused Soviet Union to back down	Threat of invasion
LIBERAL	REALIST

Alliances and Proxy Wars. As realist perspectives see it, alliances and proxy wars were central to the operation of deterrence and the eventual outcome of the Cold War. Deterrence worked in the Cuban Missile Crisis because alliances stood firm, but in other crises deterrence placed enormous stress on alliances. To work, alliances had to be tight to preserve credibility. But no country could feel completely comfortable relying on another country to defend it with nuclear weapons. America's European allies, for example, feared the alliance might not be tight enough and that they would be abandoned, as the Berlin crises suggested. Or they worried that the alliance might be too tight and they would be entrapped or drawn into wars that they did not want, as the Vietnam crisis suggested. Partly because of these concerns, France withdrew from the NATO military command in 1966 and initiated a policy of détente with the Soviet Union before the United States did. The United States had concerns as well. In Suez, the United States stopped Britain and France from supporting an Israeli invasion of the Suez Canal because it feared being drawn by its allies into a Middle East war with the Soviet Union.

The Soviet Union had even bigger troubles with its allies. It used force in 1956 to crush a revolution and possible "abandonment" of the Warsaw Pact by Hungary and again in 1968 to terminate the anticommunist revolt, called the Prague Spring, in Czechoslovakia. In 1968–1969, it also fought a border war with China, terminating that alliance and providing the opening that President Richard Nixon exploited in 1972 when he visited China and forged a common alignment against the Soviet Union.

Proxy wars highlighted the tendency of deterrence to push disputes into peripheral areas. The Soviet Union supported **national wars of liberation** against Western colonialism, while the United States backed **freedom fighters** against communist revolutions. The superpowers probed one another's intentions in the Middle East, Central America, Africa, Vietnam, and Afghanistan. Some realists such as George Kennan never accepted the necessity of extending U.S. commitments to peripheral areas in the third world and advocated containment only in strongpoint or central areas such as Europe.

After World War II, **decolonization** under the United Nations created more than fifty new nations in the Middle East, Africa, and Asia. As colonial powers retreated from these areas, the competing superpowers moved in to fill the vacuum. When Britain left Greece and Turkey in 1947, the United States stepped in to provide the two countries with economic and technical assistance. In the Middle East, the United States helped create the state of Israel and overthrew a communist government in Iran (1953). In Asia, it fought wars in Korea (1950) and Vietnam (1961). And in Latin America, it intervened

national wars of liberation: Soviet term for proxy wars against Western colonialism in developing countries.

freedom fighters: U.S. term for local forces resisting communist revolution in developing countries.

decolonization: the UN-led process by which former colonies in the third world gained their independence.

in Guatemala (1954), Cuba (1961), the Dominican Republic (1965), Chile (1973), and other places.[27] The Soviet Union intervened in Cuba (1962), Egypt (1973), Angola (1975), Mozambique (1976), Afghanistan (1979), and other places.

The superpowers exacerbated but also contained many of these conflicts. They competed to establish friendly governments but cooperated to control the spread of nuclear weapons. From a realist perspective, the problem was less one of spreading democracy or communism than one of losing bases or allies to the other side. To use a metaphor common at the time, the **domino theory** haunted the superpowers. Leaders feared that if a key country in a particular region went over to the other side, their side would lose momentum and credibility in the larger global struggle. Other countries in that region would fall to the other side like dominoes. This fear, justified from some realist perspectives (not Kennan's) but heavily criticized from other perspectives, led to numerous interventions by both superpowers in third-world conflicts. As realists see it, the issue often came down to a choice between a communist and an authoritarian regime. An authoritarian regime was to be preferred, particularly if it bolstered U.S. and Western credibility to maintain deterrence and protect freedom in western Europe and Japan. President Kennedy captured the dilemma in his comments about U.S. intervention in the Dominican Republic in 1963:

> There are three possibilities in descending order of preference: a decent democratic regime, a continuation of the Trujillo [then the dictator in the Dominican Republic] regime, or a Castro regime. We ought to aim at the first, but we can't really renounce the second until we are sure we can avoid the third.[28]

Many third-world countries sought refuge from the superpower competition by forming a nonaligned movement. Led by India, Yugoslavia, and Egypt, the **nonaligned movement** stressed nonintervention in the domestic affairs of newly independent nations and international aid for third-world development. The movement tempered somewhat the political impact of the Cold War on developing countries and focused attention on economic development.

Wars in Vietnam and Afghanistan marked the apogee of Cold War rivalry in the third world. Both wars ended in defeat for the superpowers. The **Vietnam War** was a traumatic experience for the United States. It cost fifty-eight thousand American lives and some three million Vietnamese lives. When France abandoned Indochina in 1954 (see Map 4-2), Laos and Cambodia became independent, but Vietnam, like Korea, was provisionally divided between a communist north and an authoritarian south. Elections to unite the country were contemplated but never held. The United States backed a fragile military government in the south, while the Soviet Union supported the Viet Cong revolutionaries in the north. After fifteen years of fighting with no significant gains to show for it, the United States packed up and left Vietnam in 1973. Two years later the South Vietnamese government collapsed, and the communists in North Vietnam reunited the country. Then in 1979, the Soviet Union established a naval base in Vietnam and invaded Afghanistan.

domino theory: a theory held by the superpowers that if one country in a developing region went over to the other side, other countries in the region would follow, falling like dominoes.

nonaligned movement: a coalition led by India, Yugoslavia, and Egypt that stressed neutrality in the Cold War.

Vietnam War: costly war fought by the United States in Southeast Asia to contain communism.

The **Afghan War** had even more fateful consequences for the Soviet Union and the United States. Fundamentalist Muslims called mujahideen battled Soviet forces in a long war of attrition. The United States armed and supported the mujahideen as freedom fighters. Eventually, the Soviet Union withdrew and shortly thereafter collapsed. In the process, however, the United States helped radicalize Muslim zealots who later formed the Taliban government in Afghanistan and who today threaten stability in both Afghanistan and Pakistan.

Afghan War: costly war fought by both the Soviet Union in the 1980s and the United States in the 2000s.

As realist perspectives see it, such wars were necessary at the time. When the United States entered Vietnam, the Cold War rivalry in Europe and Asia was intense. The Soviet Union had just put missiles in Cuba, and the eventual collapse of the alliance between the Soviet Union and China was unforeseen. Similarly, Soviet interventions in Africa and Afghanistan signaled Moscow's recovery from the humiliation of the Cuban Missile Crisis and its ability now to compete with Washington in the projection of power worldwide. Constant vigilance in peripheral areas maintained deterrence in central areas where war may have caused a nuclear holocaust. Other perspectives, of course, disagree. They see the wars in Vietnam and Afghanistan as symbols of the folly of domino theory and deterrence outside Europe and a dark legacy for both superpowers. Defensive realists such as Paul Kennedy predicted the decline of the United States due to imperial overstretch, the squandering of resources in conflicts such as Vietnam.[29] In the end, the Soviet Union declined, not the United States, but both superpowers suffered from imperial overstretch in Vietnam and Afghanistan. (See Table 4-1 for a summary of realist explanations for the start and expansion of the Cold War.)

Under siege, the United States leaves Vietnam. Here, a U.S. Marine Corps helicopter lifts off the rooftop of the U.S. embassy during the evacuation of Saigon on April 30, 1975.

How the Cold War Ended

As some realists like Kennan see it, the Cold War ended because the U.S. contained Soviet power until the Soviet Union mellowed. Realists did not predict, however, that the Soviet Union would disappear. They expected the two superpowers to remain rivals and to compete over spheres of influence, as Churchill had advocated right after World War II. Other realist causes from the domestic level of analysis may have been at work.

MAP
4-2

Laos, Cambodia, North and
South Vietnam

A vigorous U.S. rebound and a precipitous Soviet collapse in the 1980s decisively shifted the balance of power and ended the Cold War, with the United States remaining as the only military and economic superpower.

U.S. Rebound. The 1970s was not a good decade for the United States. Its economy fell on hard times, racial tensions and the Watergate scandal rocked its political system, it exited Vietnam with a significant loss of face and self-confidence, and it faced a Soviet Union that for the first time projected its military forces into areas beyond the European landmass, such as Angola and Mozambique. By 1979, when the Soviet Union invaded Afghanistan and a revolutionary government in Iran seized American hostages, the United States hit bottom.

Then in 1980 Ronald Reagan defeated incumbent president Jimmy Carter and launched a massive military and economic buildup. Defense expenditures rose precipitously. Washington galvanized the NATO alliance to deploy INFs in Europe. And Reagan announced major new programs to eliminate offensive nuclear weapons and build up space-based defensive missile systems, known as the **Strategic Defense Initiative (SDI)**, dubbed Star Wars by its critics. Under Reagan's policies of deregulating and supply-side tax cuts, the American economy roared back and grew steadily from 1980 to 2007 at unprecedented rates above 3 percent per year.[30]

SDI was more than satellites, rockets, and lasers in space to knock down ballistic missiles. It changed the calculus of deterrence. As already noted, deterrence under MAD depended on offensive missiles threatening mutual assured destruction with no effective ABM defenses permitted to protect civilian populations. Now Reagan's plans suggested that defensive systems might be built up and offensive weapons built down. The **Strategic Arms Reduction Talks (START)** agreements shifted the focus to reducing, not just limiting, offensive weapons, while SDI and Soviet ABM programs invested greater resources in defensive systems. In the short run, this change might increase instability, because whoever got effective defensive systems first might, in a crisis, launch a first strike against the other side, confident that its defensive systems would defeat whatever offensive missiles survived on the other side. For this reason, Reagan offered to share SDI technology with the Soviet Union. His idea was to shift deterrence from MAD to **mutual assured protection (MAP)**. Each side would deter the other by being able to protect itself against low numbers of offensive missiles.[31] It was certainly more humane than the specter of MAD killing millions of innocent civilians, but at the time it scared a lot of people, including Soviet leaders, and almost thirty years later missile defense has still to be realized operationally.

Strategic Defense Initiative (SDI): the space-based antimissile systems that formed the core of Reagan's program to enhance U.S. missile defenses.

Strategic Arms Reduction Talks (START): U.S.–Soviet talks held in the 1990s to reduce offensive weapons systems.

MAP
4-2

Laos, Cambodia, North and South Vietnam

CHINA

Dien Bien Phu

Hanoi

Haiphong

NORTH VIETNAM

LAOS

Gulf of Tonkin

Hainan (CHINA)

Demilitarized zone Demarcation line, July 1954

Mekong River

THAILAND

Da Nang

My Lai

KAMPUCHEA (CAMBODIA)

SOUTH VIETNAM

Phnom Penh

Gulf of Siam

Saigon

Mekong Delta

South China Sea

North Vietnam
South Vietnam

0   100 Mi
0   100 Km

TABLE 4-1

The Causes of the Origins and Expansion of the Cold War: The Realist Perspective and Levels of Analysis

Level of analysis	Realist perspective		
Systemic	*Structure*	Bipolarity: no flexibility; balance of terror replaces balance of power
		Power vacuum: Germany and Japan surrender unconditionally; reconstructed Germany/Japan could tip balance
	Process	Dynamics of deterrence spreads conflict to third world
Foreign policy		U.S./Soviet leaders manipulate diplomatic and domestic pressures in Cuban Missile Crisis
Domestic		Soviet Union aggressive militarily in eastern European, Baltic, and Balkan states
		U.S. expansionist economically in western Europe and Asia
Individual		Khrushchev takes measure of Kennedy and deploys missiles in Cuba

mutual assured protection (MAP): nuclear strategy, proposed by Reagan, to build up defensive systems and reduce offensive weapons.

Soviet Collapse. While the United States was rebounding under Reagan, the Soviet Union fell on hard times. A series of aging Soviet leaders died in rapid succession: Leonid Brezhnev in 1982, Yuri Andropov in 1984, and Konstantin Chernenko in 1985. Soviet forces bogged down in Afghanistan, and the Soviet economy plummeted. The Soviet economy had never been as strong as U.S. officials thought. It peaked in 1970 at only 57 percent of the U.S. GNP. Reagan's buildup and the advent of the information age hit the Soviet Union at precisely the wrong time. When the younger, more technically sophisticated Mikhail Gorbachev succeeded Chernenko in 1985, his primary goal was to revitalize the Soviet economy and avoid another arms race with the United States, which SDI threatened. In a Politburo meeting in October 1985, he told his colleagues:

> Our goal is to prevent the next round of the arms race. If we do not accomplish it, the threat to us will only grow. We will be pulled into another round of the arms race that is beyond our capabilities, and we will lose, because we are already at the limits of our capabilities. Moreover, we can expect that Japan and the FRG [West Germany] could very soon join the American potential. . . . If the new round begins, the pressure on our economy will be unbelievable.[32]

Here, from a realist perspective, were the material forces driving the Soviet Union to defeat in the Cold War. Figure 4-2 shows the buildup of nuclear weapons in the Soviet Union from the early 1970s through the 1980s. During this time, the number of Soviet warheads quadrupled, and Soviet defense expenditures climbed as a percentage of GNP from 13.5 percent in 1976 to almost 18 percent in 1988 (before dropping for the first time in 1989).[33] Under the pressure of these expenditures, as we now know, the Soviet economy stagnated from 1971 on. The cause of change in the Soviet Union, therefore, was not any new ideas that Gorbachev brought to the table, the New Thinking that identity accounts emphasize (see discussion later in the chapter). Nor was it U.S.-Soviet negotiations, which had been in the deep freeze since Reagan took office. It was, pure and simple, an arms race coupled with the information revolution (notice how technology serves zero-sum, not common, goals in a realist perspective) and the coherence of Western alliances (notice Gorbachev's reference to America's two principal allies, Japan and West Germany). These material pressures affected old thinkers as well as new thinkers in the Soviet Union, showing that it was not a debate won by new thinkers that decided Soviet policy but material circumstances that neither old nor new thinkers could ignore.[34] A hard-liner and critic of Gorbachev's New Thinking, Soviet chief of the general staff Sergei Akhromeyev made the point emphatically: "The Soviet Union could no longer continue a policy of military confrontation with the U.S. and NATO after 1985."[35]

FIGURE
4-2

Number of Nuclear Warheads, United States and Russia, 1945–2013

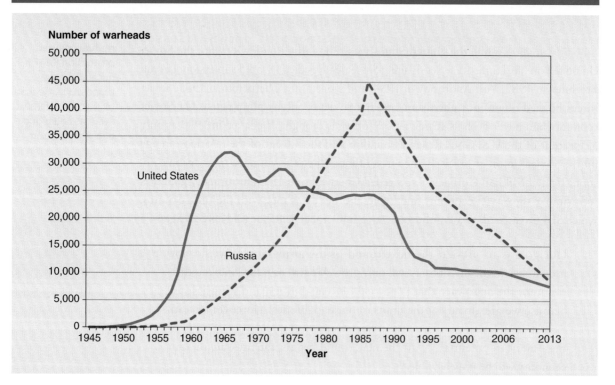

Source: Data are from Robert S. Norris and Hans M. Kristensen, "Global Nuclear Stockpiles, 1945–2013," *Bulletin of the Atomic Scientists*, January–February 2013, 76.

So, from the realist perspective, the Cold War ended without a shot being fired but not without a psychological and material struggle, which the United States ultimately won. Because of nuclear weapons, crises such as those in Berlin and Cuba substituted for war, and conflicts were fought and won virtually through arms races and economic competition rather than violently through battlefield deaths and destruction. The historian John Lewis Gaddis sorts out these realist causes from an individual level of analysis:

> Reagan saw Soviet weaknesses sooner than most of his contemporaries did; . . . he understood the extent to which détente was perpetuating the Cold War rather than hastening its end; . . . his hard line strained the Soviet system at the moment of its maximum weakness; . . . his shift toward conciliation preceded Gorbachev; . . . he combined reassurance, persuasion, and pressure in dealing with the new Soviet leader; and . . . he maintained the support of the American people and American allies.[36]

Notice how the causal arrows run: material pressures (realist), not détente (liberal), strained the Soviet system, and Reagan's actions (individual level of analysis), not responses to Gorbachev (systemic process level of analysis), initiated reconciliation. (See Table 4-2 for a summary of realist explanations for the end of the Cold War.)

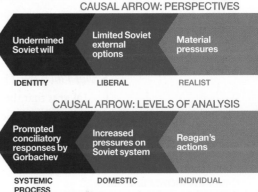

Identity Explanations

Identity perspectives take a very different cut at nuclear deterrence and the Cold War. They doubt that anyone would risk nuclear war for nothing more than a cynical struggle for power for which no one is responsible. They see the Cold War as shaped by values and common humanity. For some identity perspectives, it was a struggle between good and evil, the free world versus totalitarian societies, democracy versus communism. For others, it was a struggle for common human survival, regardless of political philosophy, a quest to save the Earth and human civilization from nuclear winter, the long dark devastation that would follow a general nuclear war.

How Ideas Started the Cold War

Three arguments explain the origins of the Cold War from an identity perspective. Two come from the domestic level of analysis and focus on internal ideological factors: Marxist-Leninism (not Russia's historical insecurity) caused the Cold War, or, conversely, American democracy (not military or economic expansionism) caused the Cold War. The third comes from the systemic level of analysis and focuses on collective identity, on why the United States and the Soviet Union saw themselves as enemies rather than just rivals.

TABLE
4-2

The Causes of the End of the Cold War: The Realist Perspective and Levels of Analysis

	Realist perspective		
Systemic	*Structure*	United States outcompetes Soviet Union materially	
	Process	Information revolution bolsters U.S. advantage	
Foreign policy		Gorbachev adopts conciliatory diplomacy to accommodate domestic weaknesses	
Domestic		United States revives its military and economic power	
Individual		Reagan devises strategy to exploit Soviet weaknesses	

Level of analysis

Soviet Ideology. The first domestic-level identity explanation for the causes of the Cold War is that the Soviet Union genuinely believed its Marxist-Leninist ideology that communism was the wave of the future and would eventually vanquish capitalism. In this case, Marxist-Leninist ideas acted as a belief system that caused Soviet behavior. Now, contrary to Kennan's view, ideology trumps insecurity or geopolitics. From this point of view, the Soviet Union was not likely to back down when confronted by superior force. It saw history as on its side and expected the correlation of forces (the Marxist-Leninist term for balance of power) to move steadily in its direction. That's why Moscow made aggressive moves in the 1970s even though its economy was in decline.

CAUSAL ARROW: PERSPECTIVES

Belief system	Caused Soviet behavior	Generated military conflict
IDENTITY	LIBERAL	REALIST

The Soviet Union did support, as Kennan projected, a worldwide campaign to promote communism. It established Cominform in 1947 (a replacement for the old Comintern, which was disbanded in 1943) to assist communist parties in France, Italy, and elsewhere. Communists led the resistance in France against the Nazi occupation and the Vichy regime (the pro-Hitler puppet government in France that nominally controlled part of the country during the war) and participated after the war in a coalition government. Communists also formed coalition governments in Italy and competed for power in eastern Europe, Greece, and Turkey.

When China fell (or, as it was said, "was lost") to the communists in 1949, the event set off a virulent fear of communist conspiracies, especially in the United States. Senator Joseph McCarthy of Wisconsin held hearings and developed lists of communist spies and sympathizers throughout the U.S. government who he said threatened American freedom. Richard Nixon, then a young member of Congress, gained notoriety when he accused (correctly, as it turned out) Alger Hiss, a highly respected government official and president of the Carnegie Endowment for International Peace, of lying about his earlier membership in the Communist Party. Ronald Reagan, at that time a young actor and president of the Hollywood Screen Actors Guild, testified before the House Un-American Activities Committee that communists were infiltrating Hollywood, saying, "I abhor their philosophy," while adding that he believed they had the right to express it.[37]

American Ideology. Looking at it from the Soviet direction, perhaps anticommunism or America's ideology of democracy caused the Cold War. The United States too made ideas or belief systems the centerpiece of the struggle. Announcing the eponymous **Truman Doctrine** on March 12, 1947, the president had this to say:

> At the present moment in world history nearly every nation must choose between alternative ways of life. . . .
>
> One way of life is based upon the will of the majority, and is distinguished by free institutions, representative government, free elections, guarantees of individual liberty, freedom of speech and religion, and freedom from political oppression.
>
> The second way of life is based upon the will of a minority forcibly imposed upon the majority. It relies upon terror and oppression, a controlled press and radio, fixed elections, and the suppression of human freedoms.[38]

Truman Doctrine: U.S. policy that defined the Cold War in ideological terms.

rollback: John Foster Dulles's policy in the 1950s of liberating the eastern European countries from Moscow's control.

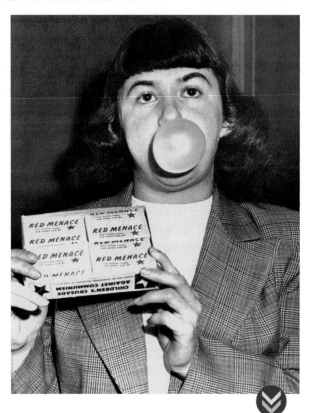

NSC-68, the document that in 1950 called for a big boost in defense expenditures, also laid out the case for the spread of democracy. For realists like Henry Kissinger, it went too far. It abandoned a policy based on material interests and "opted for the alternative vision of America as a crusader."[39] In a speech in April 1950, Secretary of State Dean Acheson echoed the Truman Doctrine: "We are the children of freedom. We cannot be safe except in an environment of freedom. . . . We believe that all people in the world are entitled to as much freedom, to develop in their own way, as we want ourselves."[40]

John Foster Dulles, secretary of state under President Eisenhower, was perhaps the most ardent advocate of spreading American freedom. He labeled the eastern European countries "captive nations" and called on the United States to go beyond the defensive policy of containment and make "it publicly known that [the United States] wants and expects liberation to occur."[41] Dulles favored a policy of **rollback**, or the recovery of the eastern European countries from Moscow's control.

A woman poses in 1951 with a box of chewing gum labeled "Red Menace," a term applied to the purported threat of communism in the United States during the period known as McCarthyism, when Senator Joseph McCarthy instigated anticommunist congressional hearings.

Were Truman, Acheson, Dulles, and others just trying to scare the American public into supporting a balance-of-power policy? Was Stalin also manipulating Soviet public opinion for realist ends? Were public opinion and ideology merely instruments of realist aims, or were they the driving forces of the Cold War?

Here is where judgment comes in. Take Kennan, for example. On one hand, he says the contest is an international struggle for power and discounts Soviet ideology; yet, on the other, he expects the contest to be determined mostly by a political struggle of ideas at the domestic level. Kennan is a classical realist. He, like Hans Morgenthau, judges that values matter more at the domestic level while power matters more at the international level. Every country has values, but all countries need power to protect their values. Kennan warned his superiors in Washington, D.C., that other countries worry less about abstract freedom, at least as Americans understand it, than they do about security. Thus, even if Soviet domestic politics mellowed, as he projected, the United States and the Soviet Union would continue to compete for power (a security concern). But, because communism and anticommunism would be less intense, they would compete more as nationalist rivals than as ideological enemies.

Constructing Cold War Identities. The third identity explanation of the origins of the Cold War addresses more directly the social construction of national identities and argues from the systemic level that the Cold War superpowers saw one another as deadly enemies rather than as less dangerous rivals.

As we have noted, realism expected the great powers to compete across a political vacuum but ultimately to be able to manage their competition through a spheres-of-influence policy. They would become rivals but not all-out enemies. Unlike enemies, rivals compete without trying to change or eliminate one another. They also cooperate. As Walter Lippmann, a famous realist author and commentator of the period, said, "For a diplomat to think that rival and unfriendly powers cannot be brought to a settlement is to forget what diplomacy is all about."[42]

Enemies, on the other hand, threaten one another because of who they are, not just because they compete or cooperate with one another. Opposing ideologies make them mutually unacceptable, and each seeks to convert or eliminate the other side. For constructivist scholars, these identity factors account for the alignments after World War II better than do relative power factors. According to realist logic, Europe should have aligned with the Soviet Union against the United States, since the United States was supremely dominant over both Europe and the Soviet Union after the war. Moreover, U.S. forces occupied western Europe, not Soviet forces. Yet western European countries aligned with the United States because they feared the Russian army more than they did the American one. Why? The answer, constructivists say, has to do with *who* the armies were, not how *big* they were or *where* they were located. The ideology of the Russian army led it to impose its will by force. The ideology of the American army called for free elections. Both armies wanted to expand their ideologies, but for western Europeans the content of the ideology based on consent was less frightening than the one based on coercion.

How domestic identities related to one another was key. As Professor Thomas Risse argues, "Had Stalin 'Finlandized' rather than 'Sovietized' Eastern Europe, the Cold War could have been avoided."[43] Stalin let Finland keep its own domestic system as long as it cooperated with Moscow on foreign policy. In eastern Europe, however, Stalin "Sovietized" domestic politics and imposed Moscow's domestic system. And in western Europe, communist parties tried to exploit domestic disorder to impose communist governments. Thus, as Risse concludes, "Soviet power became threatening as a tool to expand the Soviet domestic order."[44] Domestic identity made power a threat; identity was not simply a rationalization of power (realist).

Some realists argue that Stalin behaved with restraint in eastern Europe. He did not immediately impose communist governments, and he restrained communist parties in western Europe.[45] If the United States had been less ideological, a spheres of influence solution may have been possible. The focus of the superpower relationship would have been on external, not internal, identity. Others argue, however, that domestic and foreign policy cannot be separated that neatly. Stalin could not tolerate non-communist governments throughout eastern Europe without their threatening the communist order back in the Soviet Union. Finland was an exception because it was on the periphery of central Europe. But Poland and Czechoslovakia were a different story; the Soviet Union could not be indifferent about whether democracy or communism prevailed in those countries because they were located in the heart of the continent.

Nor could the United States accept Finlandization in eastern Europe. As political scientist Colin Dueck tells us, the liberal democratic culture in the United States was so strong that practically all American policy makers rejected a spheres-of-influence policy that involved closed, authoritarian domestic systems in eastern Europe.[46] It was not because the United States insisted that every country be democratic; it was because the United States could not be comfortable in an international system that sanctioned strict controls and barriers between countries. The international system had to be open, at least for trade and travel; otherwise, understanding and diplomacy would not be possible. The United States feared secrecy and authoritarian power in eastern Europe because this type of system might weaken commitments to freedom and markets in western Europe or even weaken democracy back in the United States.

CAUSAL ARROW: PERSPECTIVES

Undermine cooperation	Prevent spheres of influence	Differing domestic ideologies
LIBERAL	REALIST	IDENTITY

Because of who they were, the United States and the Soviet Union pursued conflicting zero-sum goals in the international system. As Secretary of State James F. Byrnes said in 1945, "There is too much difference in the ideologies of the U.S. and Russia to work out a long term program of cooperation."[47] Even before the Cuban Missile Crisis, President Kennedy acknowledged the same divide. In a letter to Premier Nikita Khrushchev in August 1961, Kennedy observed how differences in philosophies and language (identities) severely complicate efforts to communicate. Notice in his comment that ideas drive communications or interactions, not the reverse as liberal perspectives might expect:

> You and I have already recognized that neither of us will convince the other about our respective social systems and general philosophies of life. These differences create a great gulf in communications because language cannot mean the same thing on both sides unless it is related to some underlying purpose.[48]

(See Table 4-3 for a summary of identity explanations for the origins of the Cold War.)

TABLE 4-3

The Causes of the Origins of the Cold War: The Identity Perspective and Levels of Analysis

Identity perspective		
Systemic	*Structure*	Divergent ideologies: no spheres of influence possible because identities of United States and Soviet Union create relationship of enemies rather than rivals
	Process	"Sovietized" trumps "Finlandized" eastern Europe
Foreign policy		Stalin fears democratic systems in eastern Europe will undermine communist system in Soviet Union
Domestic		U.S. anticommunism as a belief system
		Soviet Union's communist ideology as a belief system (not as embedded historical dialectic, which is a critical theory perspective)
Individual		Kennedy and Khrushchev cannot understand each other because of different philosophies

(Level of analysis — leftmost vertical label)

How Ideas Ended the Cold War

How can a Cold War end peacefully? If ideas can "construct"—cause or constitute—events, how do they change in the course of events? Three possibilities illustrate the identity perspective on the end of the Cold War: convergence of ideas, change of ideas, and triumph of ideas.

Convergence. The first possibility is that opposing systems of ideas eventually converge at the systemic process level of analysis. The United States becomes more postmodern (community oriented), while the Soviet Union becomes more modern (individual oriented). Writing in the late 1960s, Zbigniew Brzezinski, later President Carter's national security adviser, anticipated such a convergence:

> The 1950s were the era of certainty. The two sides—Communist and Western—faced each other in a setting that pitted conviction against

conviction. Stalinist Manicheans [who see the world in terms of good and evil] confronted Dulles's missionaries. That mood quickly gave way to another, with Khrushchev and Kennedy serving as transitions to an era of confusion. Dissension in the communist world prompted an ideological crisis, while the West increasingly began to question its own values and righteousness. Communist cynics confronted liberal skeptics.

There are indications that the 1970s will be dominated by growing awareness that the time has come for a common effort to shape a new framework for international politics. . . . an emerging global consciousness is forcing the abandonment of preoccupations with national supremacy and accentuating global interdependence.[49]

Notice that in Brzezinski's prediction ideas ("an emerging global consciousness") are driving out realist factors ("abandonment of preoccupations with national supremacy") and emphasizing liberal ones ("accentuating global interdependence"). Brzezinski does not fail to take realist and liberal factors into account; he simply sees identity factors as driving or dominating them. The causal arrows run from ideas to power to institutions.

Brzezinski's prediction rested on the expectation that ideas in the East and West would converge. He expected them to converge equally toward the center, but two other identity explanations of the end of the Cold War suggest that Soviet ideas moved more toward the West than vice versa.

CAUSAL ARROW: PERSPECTIVES

Facilitates inter-dependence	Weakens anarchy	Global consciousness
LIBERAL	REALIST	IDENTITY

Soviet Ideas Change. The second way the Cold War ends through ideas is that one side changes and persuades the other side to follow suit. Many constructivist accounts attribute the end of the Cold War to **New Thinking** in the Soviet Union, especially by Mikhail Gorbachev. Influencing outcomes from an individual level of analysis, Gorbachev and his advisers introduced domestic reforms: *glasnost* to open up political debate and *perestroika* to modernize the Soviet bureaucracy and economy. But, equally important, they also formulated new ideas about foreign policy. Soviet officials and western European experts used **peace research studies** and other transnational and intergovernmental contacts initiated with the West under the Helsinki Accords (a secondary emphasis from the systemic process level of analysis) to develop new ideas about security structures in Europe. Gorbachev talked about "a common European home" involving shared identities and less threat or confrontation. He loosened Soviet controls in eastern European countries, and refugees flooded from behind the iron curtain. The Berlin Wall was breached on November 11, 1989, and the Cold War seemed to be on its way to an end.

Now the question became, again, what to do about Germany. Not only the Soviet Union but also France and Britain harbored doubts about German reunification. West Germany, however, under Chancellor Helmut Kohl, acted swiftly to initiate reunification. To keep events from spinning out of control, the allies set up the "two

New Thinking: Gorbachev's ideas of domestic reform known as *glasnost* and *perestroika*.

peace research studies: scholarly inquiry dedicated to the study of the potential for international peace, emphasizing collective and common-humanity approaches rather than balance of power.

plus four" talks, the four World War II allies (United States, Soviet Union, Britain, and France) plus the two German governments. In these talks, according to more agency-oriented constructivist perspectives, the end of the Cold War was decided more by argumentation than by power (as realist perspectives stress) or bargaining (as liberal perspectives stress).[50] Through an authentic and serious conversation, U.S. officials persuaded the Soviet Union to accept a reunited Germany and permit it to join NATO. The key arguments were that Moscow would be better off with a reunited Germany inside NATO than an independent one outside NATO and that Germany, once united, should have the right of self-determination, including the right to decide whether it wanted to join NATO or not. According to one account, Gorbachev accepted the last of these arguments on the spot, stunning members of his own delegation.[51] As identity perspectives see it, "this incident probably constituted one of the most extraordinary cases of arguing in international affairs" and, as social constructivist perspectives see it, vindicated the focus on discourse and dialogue as the most important influences on state behavior.[52]

U.S. Ideas Win. A third explanation from an identity perspective is that the United States and its Western allies won the Cold War through a systemic structural competition of ideas. The Soviet Union changed, to be sure, but it changed more radically than even Gorbachev expected. It ceased to exist altogether and disbanded in December 1991 into fifteen separate republics. Moreover, Gorbachev's New Thinking was not really new but rather a face-saving rationalization to accept the Western ideas of freedom and self-determination. The new European home under the Organization for Security and Cooperation in Europe (OSCE) that Gorbachev envisioned never came about. Instead, NATO expanded to include all of eastern Europe. In 2004, it admitted the Baltic states, three of the former republics of the Soviet Union, even though some Western officials had promised in the negotiations not to extend NATO jurisdiction to the east.[53] Events were being pushed by something more powerful than Soviet New Thinking or promises made in negotiations over German reunification.

And that something, according to this identity account of the end of the Cold War, was the power of ideas—or new thinking—coming from Washington, not from Moscow. When Ronald Reagan took office in January 1981, he rejected containment, which had dominated U.S. thinking since Truman, and called instead for "a crusade for freedom that will engage the faith and fortitude of the next generation." He harked back to the more aggressive American ideological approach at the beginning of the Cold War and predicted prophetically in 1982 that "the march of freedom and democracy . . . will leave Marxism-Leninism on the ash-heap of history as it has left other tyrannies which stifle the freedom and muzzle the self-expression of the people."[54] His first comprehensive statement on U.S. policy toward the Soviet Union, NSDD-75, issued on January 17, 1983, "went beyond what any previous administration had established as the aims of its Cold War approach" and stated explicitly that U.S. policies toward the Soviet Union were "to contain and over time reverse Soviet expansionism . . . [and] to promote, within the narrow limits available to us, the process of change in the Soviet

Union toward a more pluralistic political and economic system."[55] Reagan's policy targeted regime change (identity), not
stability (realist) or détente (liberal). On the fortieth anniversary of the Yalta Conference in 1985, Reagan stated clearly
that his objective was not containment but rollback: "There is
one boundary that can never be made legitimate, and that is the
dividing line between freedom and repression. I do not hesitate to say we wish to undo
this boundary. . . . Our forty-year pledge is to the goal of a restored community of free
European nations."[56]

CAUSAL ARROW: PERSPECTIVES

Increases geopolitical tensions	Makes Yalta unacceptable	Regime change
REALIST	LIBERAL	IDENTITY

Speaking to an audience in front of the Brandenburg Gate in West Berlin on June 12, 1987, with the Berlin Wall visible in the background, President Reagan contrasts freedom and communism and calls on Gorbachev to "tear down this wall."

Reagan's vision included a buildup of American and free-world defense and economic
capabilities, support for freedom fighters in Central America and elsewhere, negotiations
with the Soviet Union to eliminate nuclear weapons, and the rending of the iron curtain.

In a now-famous speech in Berlin in summer 1987, Reagan stood before the Berlin Wall at the Brandenburg Gate and said,

> There is one sign the Soviets can make that would be unmistakable, that would advance dramatically the cause of freedom and peace.
>
> General Secretary Gorbachev, if you seek peace, if you seek prosperity for the Soviet Union and Eastern Europe, if you seek liberalization: Come here to this gate! Mr. Gorbachev, open this gate! Mr. Gorbachev, tear down this wall.[57]

If ideas have power, Reagan's ideas in hindsight proved to be very powerful indeed. The challenge of freedom was too much, and the military division of Europe symbolized by the Berlin Wall and the iron curtain as well as the totalitarian institutions of the Soviet Union and its allies bowed to the march of freedom. When the world was finally able to look behind the iron curtain in 1991, it saw the devastation caused by the defeated set of ideas. Communist ideas had bankrupted and demoralized Eastern societies.[58] No one could question anymore that ideas shaped institutions and power. Or so it is argued from this particular identity perspective. (See Table 4-4 for a summary of identity explanations for the end of the Cold War.)

TABLE 4-4

The Causes of the End of the Cold War: The Identity Perspective and Levels of Analysis

Level of analysis	Identity perspective		
Systemic	*Structure*	U.S. democratic ideas prove superior to Soviet Marxist-Leninist ideas
		United States and Soviet Union construct a new identity as rivals rather than enemies
	Process	Soviet and U.S. ideologies converge toward the center
Foreign policy		Gorbachev accepts the idea of Germany in NATO, to the surprise of his own domestic advisers
Domestic		Soviet ideology mellows
Individual		Gorbachev develops New Thinking
		Reagan revives America's liberal democratic ideas

≫ Liberal Explanations

Liberal interpretations of the Cold War emphasize the role of institutions, interdependence, and diplomatic negotiations. From the systemic level of analysis, the United Nations constituted a second attempt—after the League of Nations—to establish collective security institutions. When the United Nations failed, regional NATO and European institutions cultivated security and economic interdependence and, in the case of European integration, transformed political interests and identities. The information revolution further deepened economic ties. Finally, from the systemic process level of analysis, détente and the Helsinki Accords created an alternative set of relations between the superpowers that gradually supplanted deterrence and crisis escalation. As liberal perspectives see it, the superpowers addressed disputes by communicating and learning from one another rather than by threatening and manipulating the use of nuclear weapons.

United Nations

The United Nations was established in April 1945 even before the official end of World War II. President Franklin Roosevelt was determined to avoid the failure of the League of Nations. He sought, from a foreign policy level of analysis, to balance the external requirements for collective security with the internal requirements of American constitutionalism. He had already, in spring 1942, sketched out his idea of the "four policemen," the three main wartime allies—Britain, the United States, and the Soviet Union—plus China, which would have a special role in monitoring and enforcing the postwar peace. He succeeded where Wilson failed.

The four policemen, plus France, eventually became the permanent members of the UN Security Council. To ensure their participation and avoid the League experience, the UN Charter gave each permanent member of the Security Council a veto (Article 27). The Council was also charged with "primary responsibility" (Article 24) for keeping the peace. The General Assembly, in which all UN member nations participated, could not consider an issue that was before the Security Council unless asked to do so by the Council (Article 12). In Chapter VI of the Charter (Articles 33–38), the Council had at its disposal all the peaceful means of settling disputes that the League had. But, in addition and most important, the Council had the military means to back up its decisions. Chapter VII (Articles 39–51) called on all members to "make available to the Security Council . . . armed forces, assistance, and facilities, including rights of passage, necessary for the purpose of maintaining international peace and security" (Article 43) and to "take such action by air, sea, or land forces as may be necessary to maintain or restore international peace and security" (Article 42). The Military Staff Committee, made up of the chiefs of staff of the veto powers, was to command the UN military forces.

At last, here was a collective security institution worth its salt. It combined liberal and realist features for managing world affairs. The great powers had special privileges, a realist feature. But they had to work together through international institutions (set of common rules) to accomplish their tasks, a liberal feature. If the veto powers disagreed, members retained "the inherent right of individual or collective self-defense" (Article 51). This provision proved to be a big loophole. But if the great powers were not on board, the institution would not be effective anyway. That was certainly one lesson drawn from the League's experience.

The whole scheme depended on great power cooperation. Clearly Roosevelt hoped to continue the wartime cooperation with the Soviet Union. "The essential thing," he believed, "was to build a relationship of trust with Stalin."[59] He decided that Russia was neither innately aggressive, as some realists believed, nor ideologically driven, as some identity perspectives suggested. In discussions held by the allies at the Teheran Conference in Iran in late November 1943, Roosevelt called Stalin "Uncle Joe" and commented, "From that time on our relations were personal. . . . The ice was broken and we talked like men and brothers."[60] Later he told the American people, "I believe we are going to get along very well [with Stalin] and the Russian people—very well indeed."[61] Roosevelt's design for the United Nations depended very much on the relationships and interactions within institutions that would breed trust and cooperation. Compared to containment (a realist approach) and anticommunism (an identity approach), this approach was classically liberal.

CAUSAL ARROW: PERSPECTIVES

Build trust through institutions	Reduce military competition	Overcome ideological differences
LIBERAL	REALIST	IDENTITY

Truman's Blundering Diplomacy

What went wrong? One liberal explanation is that Roosevelt died and was replaced as U.S. president by Harry Truman. Truman was a much less experienced and skilled negotiator than Roosevelt. At his very first meeting with Soviet officials in April 1945, Truman berated Foreign Minister V. M. Molotov over the Soviet failure to hold elections in Poland as promised at Yalta. When Molotov left, he said to Truman, "I have never been talked to like that in my life." Truman replied, "Carry out your agreements and you won't get talked to like that."[62]

CAUSAL ARROW: PERSPECTIVES

Truman's blundering	Disrupts communications	Creates international conflict
INDIVIDUAL	SYSTEMIC PROCESS	SYSTEMIC STRUCTURAL

Hardly a good start, right? Subsequently, at Potsdam in July 1945, Truman used clumsy tactics to impress Stalin with American nuclear weapons. As Churchill noticed, Truman, who was brand new at his job, seemed more self-confident and assertive in his discussions with Stalin once he had received word that Little Boy had been successfully tested in New Mexico.[63] For one week, Truman said nothing to Stalin about the bomb but held intensive discussions with his generals and Churchill to decide whether to use the bomb against Japan. After that decision was made, he "casually mentioned to Stalin that we had a weapon of unusual destructive force."[64] Stalin, well informed by his spy Fuchs, responded offhandedly that he was glad to hear it and hoped the allies would make good use of it against the Japanese.

Baruch Plan: proposal by the United States in 1946 to create a United Nations agency to control and manage nuclear weapons cooperatively.

Whether Truman sought to intimidate Stalin is disputed. But Truman's silence and then assertiveness at Potsdam might have easily seemed to Stalin like American bluster and aggression. And even though the United States subsequently proposed the **Baruch Plan** to establish an international agency under the United Nations to manage nuclear weapons cooperatively, the Soviet Union had every reason to wonder how fair this arrangement would be, given that America remained the only country outside the agency with the know-how to develop atomic weapons on its own should it choose to do so.

At the UN foreign minister conferences held in the fall and winter of 1945, the United States and Soviet Union could not agree on the postwar handling of Germany. The misunderstandings concerned Soviet troops in Iran, reconstruction of Germany, access to Berlin, Soviet policy in Poland, and other issues. Eventually, contacts ended. In 1947, the superpowers discontinued foreign minister meetings, and serious negotiations went into a deep freeze for much of the next two and a half decades.

Notice that in this case the causes of the Cold War come mostly from the individual or small-group, bureaucratic level of analysis and involve problems of relationships and interactions. The Cold War was not preordained by international circumstances (a realist argument) or domestic ideology (an identity argument). It resulted from a breakdown in negotiations. Opportunities to resolve the Berlin and German problems were lost. Stalin proposed German unity and neutralization in 1952, but the West ignored his proposal. By this time, the Western countries had other priorities: supporting the new West German government and building up NATO military forces. President Dwight Eisenhower and Premier Nikita Khrushchev met at the Geneva Summit in July 1955, but the "spirit of Geneva" did not last very long. Communications deteriorated once again, and the Hungarian, Berlin, and Cuban crises followed.

CAUSAL ARROW: PERSPECTIVES

Undermine spirit of Geneva	Leave geopolitical issues unresolved	Mistakes in diplomacy
IDENTITY	REALIST	LIBERAL

NATO and the European Community

The failure of the United Nations leads liberal accounts to turn to regional institutions as the causal source of international order after World War II.[65] These institutions had their origins in the Atlantic Charter, a document signed in August 1941 by Britain and the United States before the United States entered the war. The Atlantic Charter downplayed realist factors (the United States was not a belligerent) and played up liberal and identity factors. Members would participate equally in Atlantic institutions without veto powers (liberal factor), but they would share closer ideological ties than realist versions assumed (identity factor). The common principles acknowledged, for example, pluralist constitutional procedures based on majority rule and protection of minorities and called for an open international political and economic system. After the war, NATO and the institutions of the European Community embodied these principles.

Liberal accounts of the Cold War emphasize that NATO was proposed initially as a political association, not a military alliance, and that the United States was drawn into a military alliance only very reluctantly after the Korean War broke out.[66] As they see it, NATO was a collective security arrangement, because it was directed against threats in general, not against specific threats from the Soviet Union as in the case of an alliance. In testimony before Congress, Secretary of State Dean Acheson, a realist who may have been simply acknowledging strong liberal sentiments in Congress, said in reference to the NATO treaty, "It is not aimed at any country; it is aimed solely at armed aggression."[67] NATO strengthened political commitments to open governments and free markets in western Europe, not military programs to arm the West against Soviet aggression from eastern Europe.

From the liberal perspective, a primary purpose of NATO, therefore, was to back up political and economic integration in western Europe. After a century of war, France and Germany still distrusted one another. Realists had tried various alliance solutions. Now technocrats charged with modernizing the French economy came up with a liberal solution. Jean Monnet, head of the French Planning Ministry, convinced the French foreign minister, Robert Schuman, to create the European Coal and Steel Community (ECSC). This novel economic institution integrated the coal and steel industries of France and Germany, the two industrial sectors most important for war-making, and gradually reoriented these sectors and the two countries toward common non-zero-sum goals of economic growth rather than zero-sum goals of national security. European economic integration was born and became one of the most powerful institutional movements in history.

Integration subsequently transformed the European state system and ended, for all practical purposes, centuries of brutal warfare in Europe. Keep that in mind if you doubt that the liberal perspective has much to offer to the understanding of international affairs. Of course, realists will point out that European unification happened only because, after the Korean War, NATO became a conventional military alliance and protected Europe from the scourge of Soviet power that ravaged eastern Europe after World War II. Even if NATO was the catalyst, however, integration still happened and realists have no explanation for why it happened. Nor do they have a good explanation for why these institutions survive and flourish today even after the Soviet Union disappeared and a realist alliance was no longer necessary.

The ECSC was established in 1951 among France, Germany, Italy, Belgium, the Netherlands, and Luxembourg. It was followed by a failed and premature attempt to integrate the full defense sectors of France and Germany. The European Defense Community (EDC) was designed to accommodate German rearmament and create a European alliance under the protective wing of NATO. But France was not ready to rearm its traditional enemy, and the National Assembly killed the idea in 1954. Germany was rearmed directly under NATO. The United States retained paramount military responsibilities.

In 1958, however, the European states took another big step toward economic integration. The same six ECSC countries created the European Economic Community (EEC) and the European Atomic Energy Community (Euratom). The EEC established a common market in industry—no internal tariffs and common external tariffs—and a common policy in agriculture, which managed prices above market levels. Euratom pooled research and development activities to exploit peaceful uses of nuclear power.[68] The Commission of the EEC was a supranational body that had sole authority to initiate legislation. It became the driving force behind European integration, and in 1968 the

Foreign ministers of six European nations sign the treaty for the European Coal and Steel Community in Paris, France, on April 18, 1951, and set out on the historic path leading to today's European Union.

EEC absorbed the ECSC and Euratom to become the European Communities (EC). Great Britain, Denmark, and Ireland joined the EC in 1973, Greece in 1981, and Austria, Finland, and Sweden in 1986. The European Communities became the European Union in 1993 and extended its economic activities beyond the common market to include monetary and economic union. It also targeted a common foreign and security policy and internal police, judicial, and immigration affairs.

The United States encouraged and supported European integration. The Marshall Plan required European countries to cooperate to receive U.S. aid and led to the creation of the Organisation for European Economic Co-operation (OEEC). The United States and Canada joined the OEEC in 1961, when it became the Organisation for Economic Co-operation and Development (OECD). Although American leaders were always ambivalent about Europe becoming another major power, President Eisenhower actually hoped to make Europe into a "third force" that would relieve the United States of some of the economic and military burdens of protecting Europe.[69] He sought ways to transfer control of nuclear weapons to a European defense force, but these efforts failed and became moribund when France announced in 1966 that it was withdrawing from NATO's military command structure. France and Europe as a whole chafed under American military dominance but never unified to replace it.

Despite many crises, NATO and the EC flourished. They enlarged, and more members became democratic. From the liberal perspective, these institutions illustrate vividly how regularized patterns of interaction can discipline power (for example, make U.S. power, which was dominant after the war, less threatening to the allies), focus countries on non-zero-sum goals of free trade and currency union (create the unprecedented prosperity of postwar Europe), and narrow different conceptions of national interests such that political union eventually becomes a possibility (the prospect of the EU).

CAUSAL ARROW: PERSPECTIVES

Regular economic interactions in the EC	Diminish focus on conflict	Cultivate common rather than national loyalties
LIBERAL	REALIST	IDENTITY

Western institutions alone cannot account for the outcome of the Cold War because they dealt only with Western countries. But when the Cold War ended, Western institutions were ready to assume larger responsibilities. They were strong and, as liberal perspectives see it, had become more than alliances. They existed as the foundations of a global collective security community that the United Nations, and before it the League of Nations, had never been able to provide.

Cuban Missile Crisis from a Liberal Perspective

The breakdown of U.S.–Soviet negotiations after 1945 was the great failing of Western diplomacy, as liberal perspectives see it. It took twenty years to revive that diplomacy and another twenty years for the diplomacy to bear fruit. Until the Cuban Missile Crisis, there were almost no systematic discussions between the United States and the Soviet Union. After the Cuban crisis, President Kennedy remarked about the absence of a process of regular communications and subsequently installed a hotline to Moscow in the White House. In 1963, the United States and the Soviet Union concluded the first arms control agreement, the Nuclear Test Ban Treaty, which limited the size of nuclear tests in the atmosphere.

Liberal perspectives see the causes and lessons of the Cuban Missile Crisis very differently than realist perspectives. They question whether the U.S. threat of escalation from quarantine to full-scale invasion caused the Soviet Union to back down. They argue that beneath the drama of threat and escalation, Kennedy and Khrushchev, operating at the foreign policy and systemic process levels of analysis, actually cooperated to help circumvent domestic pressures from hard-liners. The two leaders engaged in an interdependent process of reassurance and mutual learning that ended in significant compromises on both sides. The United States agreed secretly to remove the Jupiter missiles from Turkey, which the Soviet Union viewed as threatening, if Moscow removed the missiles from Cuba, which the United States viewed as threatening. And if Moscow rejected a secret agreement, the United States was ready to make this commitment public under the United Nations, exploiting a liberal means to resolve a realist confrontation.[70]

On Saturday night, before he knew that the Soviet Union would accept the secret arrangement the next day, Kennedy instructed his secretary of state, Dean Rusk, to contact a professor at Columbia University, Andrew Cordier, and have him ready to ask the UN secretary-general, U Thant, to propose the Jupiter missile exchange publicly. While Kennedy could not accept such a demand directly from Khrushchev, he could accept it from the UN, even though his acceptance would still seriously damage U.S. credibility with its allies by making it look like the United States was abandoning Turkey's defense to save America's skin. Far from being ready to invade Cuba, as realist accounts emphasize, Kennedy was looking for every possible way to compromise, recognizing that he could not control the process of escalation as realists believed.

Whether Kennedy was more serious about this so-called Cordier initiative or about an invasion, which some advisers later denied he ordered, we will thankfully never know.[71] The important point is that the liberal and realist perspectives look at the same facts and make different judgments. Realists emphasize the threat of invasion; liberals emphasize the mutual efforts of leaders to negotiate a compromise. The liberal perspective does not deny the existence and impact of force and deterrence; it just judges that impact to be negative and unhelpful in situations of crisis management. As Richard Lebow and Janice Stein argue, "Deterrence can impede early warning, lead to exaggerated threat assessments, contribute to stress, increase the domestic and allied pressures on leaders to stand firm, and exacerbate the problem of loss of control."[72] By contrast, "crisis resolution is most effective when leaders 'learn' about others' interests as well as their own, when they reorder or modify their objectives in light of the risk of war, and then engage in fundamental trade-offs."[73] (See Table 4-5 for a summary of liberal explanations for the causes of the origins of the Cold War.)

CAUSAL ARROW: PERSPECTIVES

| Learn about others' interests | Overcome suspicions | Willingness to negotiate |
| IDENTITY | REALIST | LIBERAL |

Détente and the Helsinki Accords

The liberal emphasis on diplomacy reached full flower during the **détente** phase of the Cold War. Détente emerged first in Europe in the 1960s. General Charles de Gaulle distanced France from NATO and began diplomatic overtures in Moscow to resolve the lingering postwar issues of Berlin and the territorial borders of central Europe. West Germany signed a much-heralded reconciliation treaty with France in 1963 and also moved toward reconciliation with the East. The Christian Democrats, elected to power in 1948, had put West Germany's integration into NATO and the EEC ahead of negotiations with East Germany and Moscow. In 1966, however, the Social Democrats joined the government and in 1968 took power on their own. The Social Democrats had always favored negotiations with the Soviets. Had they been in power in 1952, they may well have accepted Stalin's offer to unify Germany as a neutral country. Under Foreign Minister and then Chancellor Willy Brandt, the Social Democrats now initiated a series of visits to reconcile Germany with its neighbors in the East and to recognize the East German government.

détente: a phase of the Cold War beginning in the 1960s when the West initiated diplomatic overtures to Moscow.

TABLE 4-5

The Causes of the Origins of the Cold War: The Liberal Perspective and Levels of Analysis

Liberal perspective		
Systemic	*Structure*	Collective security under United Nations and Baruch Plan to centralize control of nuclear weapons fails: • Small collective security: great power veto on Security Council ensures preponderance of power, but United States and Soviet Union clash • Big collective security: unanimity in UN General Assembly but Assembly is subordinate to Security Council; used only once in Korea because Soviets were absent in Council
		NATO and EC develop collective security and free trade at regional level
	Process	Soviet Union sees Marshall Plan (open systems) as threat to authoritarian institutions in eastern Europe
		United States sees closed systems in eastern Europe as threat to pluralist institutions in western Europe
		Diplomacy: differences over Poland, Germany, Greece, and so on could have been negotiated
		Lack of trade and communications between East and West
Foreign policy		Kennedy and Khrushchev cooperate to circumvent domestic hard-liners and settle the Cuban Missile Crisis
Domestic		French parliament rejects European Defense Community
Individual		Truman threatens Stalin
		Roosevelt misinterprets Stalin
		Jean Monnet and French technocrats negotiate ECSC

Level of analysis

The United States, alienated from Europe because of the Vietnam War, joined the rapprochement process late. President Nixon and his national security adviser, Henry Kissinger, concentrated on negotiating an end to the Vietnam War and opening up a new alliance with China. Under pressure from European initiatives, however, the United States and its three wartime allies (Britain, France, and the Soviet Union) signed in 1971 the Berlin Accords, a set of agreements normalizing the situation in Berlin. Although the wall remained in place, East and West Germany recognized one another and Germany accepted the postwar borders in eastern Europe.

Liberal perspectives applauded the SALT and ABM disarmament agreements signed in 1972 and 1979. They did not accept the realist version of escalation dominance, which required capabilities at all rungs of the ladder of escalation, including limited nuclear exchanges, to compel the adversary to back down in a crisis. They strongly supported the ABM Treaty and advocated large further reductions of nuclear arms, including a comprehensive test ban treaty to stop further detonations of nuclear warheads both above- and belowground.

Détente peaked in 1975 with the **Helsinki Accords**. Thirty-five nations from East and West met in Helsinki, Finland, under the auspices of the UN Conference on Security and Cooperation in Europe (CSCE, a regional UN organization that in 1991 became the Organization for Security and Cooperation in Europe) and concluded three baskets of agreements to encourage diplomatic interactions and economic interdependence between the two blocs: arms control, trade, and human rights. SALT II agreements were signed in 1979, although they were never ratified by the United States. Trade restrictions were relaxed, although the Soviet Union never received most-favored-nation status (meaning entry to markets at the lowest tariff rates accorded to the most-favored nations) because it continued to restrict the emigration of Jewish dissidents. And monitoring of human rights (an identity element), especially in eastern Europe, began to open up the closed communist systems, although the Soviet invasion of Afghanistan in 1979 generated new restrictions.

As liberal accounts believe, détente in the 1970s let the genie of cooperation out of the bottle; and despite the resurgence of the Cold War in the late 1970s and early 1980s, the genie could not be put back in the bottle again. The Helsinki Accords proved especially valuable. Even in the midst of renewed Cold War tensions, conferences followed at Belgrade (1977–1978), Madrid (1980–1983), and Vienna (1986–1989). More important, nongovernmental groups established regularized contacts. Arms control groups in the United States (for example, the Union of Concerned Scientists), peace research institutes in western Europe (for example, the Stockholm International Peace Research Institute), social democratic and labor parties in Europe (for example, the Social Democratic Party in Germany), and policy institutes in the Soviet Union (for example, the Institute of the World Economy and International Relations) intensified contacts and developed concepts of common security, interdependence, and conventional arms reduction that reduced the fear of unilateral offensive operations. Some of these groups penetrated government circles, opening up domestic institutions and creating transnational coalitions. They affected in particular Gorbachev and other Soviet new thinkers.[74] Notice how in the liberal perspective ideas follow from rather than cause institutional interdependence. Without regularized institutional processes at both the international and domestic levels, New Thinking might not have emerged. In contrast to identity perspectives, liberal interpretations emphasize the regularity of contacts more than the substance. They emphasize that "ideas do not float freely."[75] They need institutional incubators to sprout and grow.

Helsinki Accords: a series of agreements between East and West in 1975 concerning arms control, trade, and human rights.

CAUSAL ARROW: PERSPECTIVES

Create New Thinking	Decrease security dilemma	Helsinki Accords
IDENTITY	REALIST	LIBERAL

The Information Revolution and the End of the Cold War

From the liberal perspective, another factor came into the picture about the same time as détente and decisively contributed to the end of the Cold War. The information revolution ushered in a whole new age of technological innovation comparable to the industrial revolution. Information technologies tied the world together as never before. Computers created the new global highway of the Internet just as earlier steam engines opened up sea travel, electricity powered telegraph and telephone lines, and combustion engines produced the automobile. Countries that wanted to get on board had to participate in international trade. This positive economic incentive, more than any other, liberal accounts suggest, drove the Soviet Union to reconsider its economic and strategic policies. From a liberal perspective, the information revolution emphasized the pursuit of non-zero-sum economic goals more than the zero-sum military goals of SDI emphasized by realists and undermined the last resistance to ending the Cold War ideological division within Europe and throughout the world.

Gorbachev reacted to rather than caused these developments. His New Thinking helped interpret events, but without the events themselves it would have had little effect. Nor, as realist accounts suggest, was Gorbachev just reacting to military threats. He was casting about for new opportunities to encourage economic change and growth. Firms were beginning to operate all over the world, forming numerous and intricate alliances for the development and production of information-age products, and outsourcing more and more production to foreign shores. The most productive industries were global ones. No country could cut itself off from these developments and keep up with the rest of the world.[76]

In February 1986, Gorbachev noted the importance of these developments. "By the early 1980s," he observed, "the transnational corporations accounted for more than one-third of industrial production, more than one-half of foreign trade, and nearly 80 percent of the patents for new machinery and technology in the capitalist world."[77] The Soviet Union had to become part of this new corporate world, and to make that possible Gorbachev had to reconsider his foreign policy and persuade Western countries to remove Cold War containment restrictions on the export of high-technology goods and information to the Soviet Union. Unlike China, which had no empire, the Soviet Union had to give up its empire first to gain access to global trade and investment markets.

Notice again the direction of the causal arrows in these conclusions. As liberal accounts see it, Soviet military developments during the 1970s and 1980s were all ephemeral. So was the U.S. military buildup in response to Soviet challenges. Underneath all this misplaced military investment, contacts between East and West demonstrated to the Soviet Union that it was falling steadily behind and would have to make major internal reforms to become a part of the new world information economy. Ideology may have mattered in the sense that Gorbachev still hoped he could reform and save the communist system. But the driving

CAUSAL ARROW: PERSPECTIVES

Increasing contacts | Make military buildup irrelevant | Promote internal reforms

LIBERAL | REALIST | IDENTITY

TABLE 4-6

The Causes of the End of the Cold War: The Liberal Perspective and Levels of Analysis

	Liberal perspective		
Systemic	*Structure*	Information revolution elevates non-zero-sum over zero-sum goals	
	Process	Détente and Helsinki Accords deepen interdependence	
	Transnational	Nongovernmental peace research groups emerge between European countries and Soviet Union	
Foreign policy		Gorbachev outmaneuvers hard-liners to initiate East–West rapprochement	
Domestic		Soviet Union needs to become part of globalized world	
Individual		Gorbachev initiates bureaucratic reforms	

(Level of analysis is labeled vertically along the left side of the table.)

forces for change were not new ideas but new technological forces propelling the world toward unforeseen levels of interconnectedness in the twenty-first century. (See Table 4-6 for a summary of liberal explanations for the end of the Cold War.)

≫ Critical Theory Perspective

Mainstream explanations of the origins and the end of the Cold War emphasize the cause and effect of individual variables such as communist belief systems, détente, and power shifts. Critical theory perspectives shift the focus from individual causes acting sequentially to deep-seated historical forces acting in an interconnected manner. Critical theory highlights the dialectical process of social change, driven by a combination of material, institutional, and social forces that lead to a more just and peaceful future.

According to Marxist-Leninism as a historical process (not just a specific belief system), the United States was the leading representative of the capitalist forces and the Soviet Union was the leading representative or vanguard of the communist forces. The two countries were not, primarily, pursuing their own ideologies or interests but were fulfilling their roles in a predetermined historical drama of social and political revolution. Individual leaders and countries are secondary. Causality is cumulative and constitutive, involving a historical consciousness that entraps the participants.

Thus, America's propensity to expand markets, through the so-called open door policy in Asia and the Marshall Plan policy in Europe, was not something it could control. It was a consequence of monopoly capitalism. Listen to the first words of a telegram sent to Moscow by the Soviet ambassador to the United States, Nikolai Novikov, in September 1946: "Reflecting the imperialistic tendency of American monopoly capital, U.S. foreign policy has been characterized in the postwar period by a desire for *world domination.*"[78] Monopoly capital creates the desire for world domination, not specific factors such as the pursuit of power or American ideology. And monopoly capitalism cannot be disaggregated into separate causes or levels of analysis. It is deeply interwoven in the fabric of history and provokes resistance from the disadvantaged or poorer states that the United States seeks to dominate. Capitalist expansion empowers oppressed social classes, and class struggle produces a more just and equitable distribution of wealth. Eventually, socialist institutions based on state property replace liberal market institutions based on private property. Gabriel and Joyce Kolko, among others, develop this type of revisionist or Wisconsin School (see Chapter 3) interpretation of the origins of the Cold War.[79]

As the Cold War turned out, Marx's critical theory perspective proved to be wrong. It was capitalism, not communism, that moved history forward. Marx did not see things clearly, perhaps because he, too, was entrapped in historical consciousness and could not separate himself objectively from the forces that operated around him. But critical theory perspectives would point out that the forces of economic injustice continue to operate today even though communism has all but disappeared. Inequality persists, and underlying tensions between social classes and the forces of production continue to drive history.[80] (See Table 4-7 for a summary of critical theory perspective explanations for the origins and end of the Cold War.)

TABLE 4-7

The Causes of the Origins and End of the Cold War: The Critical Theory Perspective and Levels of Analysis[a]

Critical theory perspective		
Systemic	*Structure*	Historical dialectic of social change drives a class struggle between capitalist and communist societies, leading to a workers' state free of oppression and inequality
	Process	
Foreign policy		
Domestic		
Individual		

(left margin label: Level of analysis)

a. Recall that critical theory perspectives do not separate perspectives and levels of analysis.

SUMMARY

Realist perspectives emphasize power. At the systemic structural level, bipolarity and a power vacuum caused the Cold War, and U.S. power outcompeted Soviet power to end the Cold War. At the systemic process level, Western alliances proved superior. At the domestic level of analysis, either the Soviet Union caused the Cold War because it was aggressive militarily or the United States did because it was aggressive economically; the Cold War ended either because the United States revived its military and economic power or because the Soviet economy collapsed.

Liberal perspectives emphasize institutions, diplomacy, and interdependence. At the systemic structural level of analysis, the Cold War started because the United Nations failed and collective security could be achieved within the Western region only under NATO and the EU. At the systemic process level, it started because the Marshall Plan threatened the Soviet Union, while the spread of Marxist-Leninism in western Europe threatened the United States. And at the individual level, it started because Truman threatened Stalin and Roosevelt misinterpreted Stalin. The Cold War ended, at the systemic structural level, because the information revolution emphasized non-zero-sum goals; at the systemic process level, it ended because détente and Helsinki deepened East–West interdependence; at the foreign policy level, it ended because government bureaucrats formed transgovernmental coalitions; and at the domestic level, it ended because NGOs emerged and opened up domestic institutions in European countries and the Soviet Union.

Finally, identity perspectives emphasize the configuration and construction of ideologies. At the systemic structural level, ideological divergence caused the Cold War. And at the domestic level, it was Soviet ideological zealotry or American anticommunism—take your pick—that caused the confrontation. From this perspective, the Cold War ended at the systemic structural level because U.S. ideology proved superior, at the systemic process level because Soviet and U.S. ideologies converged, at the foreign policy level because Gorbachev was persuaded by Western arguments despite the skepticism of his own advisers, at the domestic level because Soviet ideology mellowed, and at the individual level because Gorbachev developed New Thinking or Reagan revived America's classical liberal democratic identity—again, take your pick.

Critical theory perspectives see both the origins and the end of the Cold War as the unfolding of deeply embedded historical processes that, although they did not end in the triumph of communism, nevertheless continue to widen economic inequalities and injustices in the global system.

Sharpen your skills with SAGE edge at **edge.sagepub.com/nau4e**. **SAGE edge for students** provides a personalized approach to help you accomplish your coursework goals in an easy-to-use learning environment.

KEY CONCEPTS

STUDY QUESTIONS

1. How would you line up the following causes of Soviet behavior in Kennan's analysis in the long telegram: security, ideology, and international institutions?

2. In what way do realist and liberal interpretations of deterrence differ, especially as they relate to the use of force and diplomacy?

3. What led to a resolution of the Cuban Missile Crisis as seen from liberal and realist perspectives?

4. What does *Finlandization* mean, and how did different perspectives interpret it?

5. Do the following causes of the end of the Cold War reflect different perspectives or levels of analysis: information revolution, emergence and outreach of peace research and other nongovernmental groups in Germany and elsewhere, and détente?

On November 9, 1989, the Berlin Wall came down, and the Cold War effectively ended. On September 11, 2001, the twin World Trade Center towers in New York City came down, and a new kind of global terrorist conflict started.

These two events marked the transition to the contemporary international system. How much of today's system is new and how much is a continuation of the patterns of history? Did the attacks of 9/11 change everything? Yes, they did, in the sense that a major conflict loomed once again above the contours of the international system. Terrorism was a global phenomenon, connecting violent cells across national borders and waging war between distant nations. Most ominously, it was supported by rogue nations bent on acquiring and in some cases transferring WMDs, including nuclear materials and weapons. At the same time, terrorism, especially in contrast to World Wars I and II and the Cold War, was a local and less visible phenomenon. Its roots lay deep in the ethnic, religious, economic, and border disputes of divided states, and it struck unexpectedly, making it difficult for those targeted to deter or preempt terrorist attacks because there was no warning, and making it tempting for those who expected to be targeted to prevent such attacks by striking before they could actually occur. So, yes, there were some novel elements to the new threat.

But, no, on the other hand, 9/11 did not change everything. There was much familiar in the drama that unfolded in the decades after the end of the Cold War. In the same year the Cold War ended, an Egyptian jihadist, El-Sayyid Nosair, gunned down a right-wing Jewish rabbi, Meir Kahane, in the Marriott East Side Hotel in New York. At the time, it was a relatively minor event, but Nosair wrote something in his notebook that portended events to come. Jihad, he explained, called for the

breaking and destruction of the enemies of Allah. And this is by means of destroying, exploding, the structure of their civilized pillars such as the touristic infrastructure which they are proud of and their high world buildings which they are proud of and their statues which they endear and the buildings which gather their head[s,] their leaders.[1]

Here was a vision of 9/11 already at the time of 11/9, the fall of the Berlin Wall and end of the Cold War in Europe. And Nosair was not acting in isolation. He maintained regular contact with Sheikh Omar Ahmad Abdel Rahman in Egypt. Known as the Blind Sheikh, Rahman had authorized the assassination of Anwar Sadat, Egypt's leader who made peace with Israel in 1979. With Nosair's help, Rahman settled in the United States and then planned the first assault on "their high world buildings"—the truck (actually, van) bombing of the World Trade Center towers in New York City on February 26, 1993.

Most important, how we think about international relations did not change with 11/9 or 9/11. Perspectives and levels of analysis remain central to our understanding of events and debates about the contemporary world. In Part II, we take a little different tack than in Part I and examine the contemporary world by applying only a single perspective in each chapter and emphasizing what that perspective sees from the different levels of analysis. Thus, we look in Chapter 5 at realist perspectives on today's world from different levels of analysis, in Chapter 6 at liberal perspectives on today's world from different levels of analysis, and in Chapter 7 at identity perspectives on today's world. In each chapter we concentrate on the important events and causal factors that the perspective being examined emphasizes—for example, the balance of power in the case of the realist perspective, international institutions in the case of the liberal perspective, and ideas in the case of the identity perspective. And we look at these primary causal forces at all levels of analysis. So in the case of Chapter 5 and realist perspectives, for example, we are interested in *systemic structural factors* such as American dominance and counterbalancing by rising powers, *systemic process factors* such as the use of force in diplomacy, *foreign policy–level* decision making involving the interplay of foreign and domestic causes, *domestic-level causes* such as interest group power struggles, and *individual-level causes* affecting leadership. In Chapters 6 and 7, we examine the principal liberal and identity events and causes of the contemporary world from each of these levels of analysis. This approach helps us to concentrate on one perspective at a time, whereas in previous chapters we considered all three (or four) perspectives at the same time when investigating World War I, World War II and the Cold War. We pay less attention in Part II to the critical theory perspective, but we devote a whole chapter in Part III, Chapter 10, to that perspective on globalization. So, by the time we finish the book, you will have delved deeply into each of the four perspectives on contemporary international affairs.

Soon to be U.S. president George W. Bush (left), secretary of defense Colin Powell, and vice president Dick Cheney (right) wave to a crowd in Dearborn, Michigan, in November 2000. After the events of September 11, 2001, Powell and Cheney would come to defend different positions within the realist perspectives: power balancing and power transitioning.

REALIST PERSPECTIVES ON TODAY'S WORLD
Dominance, Balance of Power, and State Institutions

5

As we have learned through our study of the landmark cases of World War I, World War II, and the Cold War, world historical events can be analyzed from a range of different perspectives. Each perspective uses a specific set of conceptual tools to help make sense of the causes of those events and to draw certain conclusions about their resolution. More recent political events are of course open to the same range of perspectives, and it's to the contemporary world that we now turn in this part of the book. In this chapter, instead of covering the perspectives in sequence, we'll stand in the shoes of a realist, focusing in a more sustained way on the issues and aspects of international relations that realists pay most attention to, as we address critical events of the post–Cold War era. Subsequent chapters will give the same depth of attention to liberal and identity perspectives; still, in order to help us keep these other perspectives in mind, this chapter provides brief counterpoints to help sharpen some of the differences.

Realist perspectives see the years after the end of the Cold War primarily in terms of the distribution of power, not in terms of institutional or ideological factors. At the systemic structural level of analysis, they see a world that is *unipolar* under American dominance yet increasingly subject to *asymmetric threats* from smaller powers that use technology, such as cyber warfare, to challenge larger foes. The most serious threats are not the occasional terrorist attacks from nonstate actors at the domestic level of analysis but, instead, coordinated efforts by terrorist groups and their state sponsors at the systemic process level to acquire nuclear weapons and undermine stability throughout the world. Weaker but rising states, such as China and Russia, exploit the bewildering blizzard of ethnic and interstate conflicts that resurfaced after the Cold War and use failed and radical states as bases from which to chip away at Western dominance. As realist perspectives see it, domestic-level conflicts are less the consequence of poverty (as liberal perspectives argue) or of the construction and manipulation of group identities (as identity perspectives conclude) than they are the result of ageless struggles among ethnic and national groups to survive, control territory, and redistribute power. Institutions that are grounded in the state, not weaker and more divided international institutions, remain the best way to deal with such conflicts, and a rational approach to foreign policy decision making offers the best calculus for integrating "interests defined in terms of power" with foreign goals of order and stability.

Realist perspectives anticipate the historical cycle of empires and equilibrium. Some, following the power transition school, believe that the United States can preserve its predominance and advocate preemptive measures to forestall challengers. Others, following the power balancing school, anticipate decline and rely on deterrence and containment to contend with rising powers such as China, resurgent powers such as Russia, and wealthy counterweights such as the European Union and Japan. Offensive realists identify with power transition theory; defensive realists identify with power balancing theory. But few realists believe that (as liberal perspectives emphasize) international institutions, courts, and economic development can replace the balance of power; the need remains for unilateral action, flexible alliances including coalitions of the willing, and the use of military force to stabilize world politics and underwrite economic interdependence.

The defining characteristic of the realist perspective from any level of analysis is the direction of the causal arrows. They run from the distribution of relative power to the international jockeying that takes place in international diplomacy and institutions to the self-images that countries develop in competition with one another. Here is one prominent realist scholar making these causal arrows explicit for us:

> Of course, states sometimes operate through institutions and benefit from doing so. However, the most powerful states in the system create and shape institutions so that they can maintain, if not increase, their own share of world power. Institutions are essentially "arenas for acting out power relationships." . . .

. . . Nationalism is probably the most powerful political ideology in the world, and it glorifies the state. . . . Although the members of the European Union have certainly achieved substantial economic integration, . . . both nationalism and the existing states in western Europe appear to be alive and well. . . . But even if . . . western Europe becomes a superstate, it would still be a state, albeit a powerful one, operating in a system of states.[1]

CAUSAL ARROW: PERSPECTIVES

Defines ideas of self and others, such as nationalism	Determines control of institutions	Relative power
IDENTITY	LIBERAL	REALIST

In the sections that follow, we'll focus on the central realist concerns by looking in turn at the nature of American dominance in this newly unipolar world, the mechanics of counterbalancing and the rise of new powers, domestic power struggles in weak states, and the role of state-based institutions in foreign policy decision making.

⟫ American Dominance

Realist perspectives recognized immediately the unique feature of the post–Cold War world. It was not institutional unity or democratic expansion; it was American dominance or unipolarity. For the first time in history, a war among great powers—namely, the Cold War—had ended without a fight. And the country that came out on top not only dominated the postwar landscape but also did so unscathed. The United States had suffered no significant losses in the Cold War, as a victorious England had in World War I or the Soviet Union had in World War II. There was no central Europe to rebuild, although eastern Germany and Europe would require substantial investments for decades to come. And there were no big power threats to parry, as Russia had challenged British power after 1815 and the Soviet Union had challenged U.S. power after 1945. The United States stood at the pinnacle of unchallenged power.

Within the United States, however, realists were themselves divided in their views about the nature of American dominance, as well as about the strategies the United States ought to pursue in order to preserve global order. The decades after the end of the Cold War saw a vigorous and consequential debate take place between power transition realists like Dick Cheney and power balancing realists like Brent Scowcroft and Colin Powell.

Power Transition Realists

Power transition realists believe that American dominance is the safest structure for American security and that dominance can be preserved. They see wars arising from movement *toward* equilibrium, either by the decline of dominant powers or by the rise of challenging powers. They seek, therefore, to preserve hegemony and justify it morally because hegemony fosters peace.

In 1992, in the last year of George H. W. Bush's presidency, power transition realists in the Pentagon, led by Secretary of Defense Dick Cheney, drafted a controversial strategy document that called on the United States to forestall the emergence of any challenger to

American predominance.[2] Although this document was not affirmed as official policy, it later resurfaced following the terrorist attacks of September 11, 2001, in a 2002 national security strategy document under the George W. Bush administration and influenced the U.S. decision to take preemptive action in Iraq, which was believed to be manufacturing weapons of mass destruction. The 2002 document laid out the strategic doctrine of preemption, a policy to use force to head off potential challengers rather than wait to be attacked. The document stated that "while the United States will constantly strive to enlist the support of the international community, we will not hesitate to act alone, if necessary, to exercise our right of self-defense by acting preemptively against . . . terrorists, to prevent them from doing harm against our people and our country."[3]

Preemption implied that the enemy was about to attack. And even if that was not the case, power transition realists thought, action might be necessary, because the terrorist threat was less visible than threats from more traditional enemies. The United States could not wait until it saw "armies gathering at the border"; terrorist "armies" did not appear until after they had already struck. Against terrorists and their supporters, the United States had to prevent, not just preempt, wars.

Thus, the distinction between preemptive and preventive wars blurred. The United States might have to attack whether it saw the other side getting ready to attack now (preemption) or just thought the other side might do so at some unspecified time in the future (prevention). Understandably, other countries viewed this justification of aggressive action with alarm, but power transition realists reasoned that the United States could preempt with impunity since no other nation or even group of nations had the power to oppose it. Compared to previous hegemons, the United States enjoyed in the mid-1990s an extraordinary concentration of power in all categories: national wealth, military expenditures, and composite measures of power. As political scientist William Wohlforth observed, "Never in modern international history has the leading state been so dominant economically and militarily."[4]

For power transition realists, therefore, preventive war became more likely both because of the nature of the threat and because of unipolarity. Notice that, from this realist perspective, policy and the prospects of preventive war are driven by the structure of power, not by the misguided strategies of Pentagon leaders or the ideology of American leaders eager to spread democracy. You could change the leaders, which an individual level of analysis might recommend, or diminish the domestic desire to spread democracy, which a domestic level of analysis might suggest, but the systemic structural pressures would remain and prevail in influencing policy again in the future.

CAUSAL ARROW: LEVELS OF ANALYSIS

Structural pressures → Dominate ideologies → Determine strategies of leaders

SYSTEMIC   DOMESTIC   INDIVIDUAL

Power Balancing Realists

Power balancing realists predicted American dominance would not last. After all, historically, empires have always succumbed to equilibrium. Therefore, Charles Krauthammer, a well-known realist commentator, called the post–Cold War period "the unipolar moment" or, alternatively, "a holiday from history," meaning a brief interlude from conflict and the cycle of empire and equilibrium.[5] But how long would "the moment" or "holiday" last? As Krauthammer suggested, it might be decades. Other realists thought it might be much shorter. For Henry Kissinger, the world of equilibrium or multipolarity was already at hand: "Victory in the Cold War has propelled America into a world which bears many similarities to the European state system of the eighteenth and nineteenth centuries."[6]

Power balancing realists see wars arising from movements *away* from equilibrium. They seek, therefore, to reduce hegemony by accommodating rising powers and advocate equilibrium and coexistence. Power balancing realists took great comfort, for example, in the stability of the bipolar configuration during the Cold War struggle. Bipolar equilibrium nurtured peace, and for all its problems, the bipolar world produced a cold war, not a hot one. Many realist analysts assumed and perhaps even preferred that the Cold War would go on indefinitely.[7]

Stability versus Hegemony

Thus, when the Soviet empire and then the Soviet Union itself disintegrated, power balancing realists advised caution. They saw the same dilemma that President Kennedy had talked about during the Cold War—before you call for independence from one tyrant, be sure you can avoid oppression by another tyrant that may be even worse. George H. W. Bush and his national security adviser, Brent Scowcroft, took this approach in 1991 after fighting broke out in Yugoslavia and an independence movement threatened stability in Ukraine. Bush expressed the dilemma openly when he visited Kiev, Ukraine, in August 1991: "Americans will not support those who seek independence in order to replace a far-off tyranny with a local despotism."[8] Dubbed the "Chicken Kiev" speech (unfairly perhaps, but what journalist can resist that juicy morsel?), the elder Bush's remarks demonstrated clearly the power balancing realist's preference for stability over regime change.

Bush's defense secretary, Cheney, disagreed. He opposed the Bush-Scowcroft line, which was also supported by Colin Powell, then chairman of the Joint Chiefs of Staff. Cheney argued for a more aggressive policy to break up the Soviet Union, whatever the consequences for the spread of democracy. He was expressing the views of an offensive realist. Leading the power transition school, Cheney saw an opportunity to extend America's power advantage. Even "if democracy fails" in the fifteen Soviet republics, Cheney argued, "we're better off if they're small."[9] Notice the realist causal arrows in Cheney's comment: the distribution of power counts more than the spread of democracy. Breaking up the former Soviet Union would increase the relative power of the United States even if democracy, a lesser goal, did not prevail in the now smaller Soviet republics. This subtle emphasis, again a matter of the direction of causal arrows, separates offensive-minded or power transition realists such as Cheney from other analysts, such as power balancing realists who give

CAUSAL ARROW: LEVELS OF ANALYSIS

Dictates diplomacy	Matters more than spread of democracy	Distribution of power
LIBERAL	**IDENTITY**	**REALIST**

In 1990, President George H. W. Bush is joined in the Oval Office by General Colin Powell, Dick Cheney, John Sununu, and Brent Scowcroft.

the advantage to stability over power or more identity-oriented neoconservatives who give the edge to democracy over power.

Vice President Cheney and Secretary of State Colin Powell squared off again twelve years later over the Iraq War, which President George W. Bush initiated in the wake of the 9/11 attacks. Cheney wanted to press America's dominance and decisively shift the balance of power in Iraq and the Middle East; Powell worried about destabilizing the region and winding up with even worse fundamentalist governments. He coined the "Pottery Barn" argument (another catchy metaphor!), warning Bush, "If you break it [meaning Iraq], you own it [for better or for worse]." Brent Scowcroft, who was now in civilian life, agreed with Powell and opposed the American decision to invade Iraq. He warned, quite presciently, that "an attack on Iraq at this time would seriously jeopardize, if not destroy, the global counter-terrorist campaign we have undertaken."[10]

For power transition realists, therefore, 9/11 sparked a new global war on terror and a renewed division of the world into friendly and enemy states. Reflecting this approach shortly after 9/11, President George W. Bush warned the world, "You're either with us or against us in the fight against terror."[11] Power balancing realists, on the other hand, called for regional containment to deter Iraq (and neighboring Iran, another state hostile to the United States) and for more attention to stability rather than aggressive campaigns to force regime change.[12]

Unilateralism versus Multilateralism

From a realist perspective, the **global war on terror** involved both **rogue states** and failing or **failed states** and could not be treated simply as a criminal act by nonstate actors that could be handled through international police action (Interpol) and courts (as liberal perspectives argue, see Chapter 6). Power transition realists suspected a wider conspiracy and reached for the familiar instruments of unilateralism, flexible coalitions, sanctions, and war to terminate financial support for and defeat the global enemy. Power balancing realists saw the threat as limited to Afghanistan, preferred to rely on existing alliances such as NATO, and resisted widening the conflict.

Power transition realists emphasized the intelligence that connected the dots between terrorists and rogue states. In the 1990s, an international smuggling ring, masterminded by A. Q. Khan and headquartered in Pakistan, systematically acquired and transferred nuclear materials and technology to rogue states and terrorist groups. David Albright, a respected nuclear weapons expert, testified about this operation before Congress in May 2006:

> Starting as an ingenious effort to sidestep western sanctions and outfit Pakistan with nuclear weapons, Khan and his ring of smugglers soon went global. The activity of this syndicate straddled four decades and involved countries, companies, secret bank accounts, and agents on four continents. Armed with a catalog filled with everything from whole gas centrifuge factories to nuclear weapon designs, this network helped outfit nuclear weapons programs in Libya, Iran, and North Korea and possibly aided Al Qaeda in its quest for nuclear weapons before the fall of the Taliban. Remnants of the Khan network may yet help other nuclear weapons programs and terrorist groups.[13]

The A. Q. Khan network symbolized the nature of the new global threat that led power transition realists to break away from standing alliances and international institutions. This threat was different from conventional threats from state actors, they believed, and NATO was not equipped to respond to terrorism and conflicts outside Europe. Moreover, NATO after the Cold War was largely an American enterprise. The allies brought few military assets to the table to fight conflicts outside Europe, unlike during the Cold War, when allies fielded large armies to defend Europe's borders against Soviet forces. In Bosnia, where conflict erupted in the early 1990s, the EU took the lead but had insufficient military capabilities to suppress violence and had to turn to the UN and then to NATO forces to end the conflict. The same thing had happened in Kosovo. There, in 1999, the United States fought an air war directed by an institutional committee of allies within NATO. American commanders had to decide each bombing target by consensus among sixteen countries.[14] The United States did not want to repeat

global war on terror: a worldwide military campaign to defeat nonstate terrorist groups such as Al Qaeda and the rogue states that support them.

rogue states: states that seek systematically to acquire nuclear weapons with the possible intent of passing them on to nonstate terrorists.

failed states: states whose domestic institutions have collapsed.

this model in Afghanistan or Iraq, where the terrorist target was more elusive. From a power transition perspective, most conscious of America's advantage in preponderant power, the standing international institutions offered considerably less value to fight the 9/11 attackers. Greater advantage was to be achieved through independent action with ad hoc groups of nations that wished to contribute and undertake specific tasks associated with the immediate threat. The realist causal arrow thus ran from preponderant power to institutions and dictated breakout from reliance on multilateral institutions, even with allies.

CAUSAL ARROW: PERSPECTIVES

Preponderant power	Circumvents existing international institutions	Destroys the terrorist enemy
REALIST	LIBERAL	IDENTITY

Thus, when the European allies invoked Article 5 of the NATO Treaty, the United States declined the offer. Article 5 declared an attack against one NATO member as an attack against all members. Europe relied on this provision during the Cold War to ensure U.S. support to defend Europe. Now Europe invoked it to support the defense of the United States. But the circumstances were different. As power transition realists saw it, the United States was a hegemon and did not need European support as it did during the Cold War. The structure of power dictated a more unilateral approach. NATO was mostly sidelined, although some allies helped individually and NATO subsequently assumed responsibility for security and reconstruction in Kabul and, after 2006, in Afghanistan as a whole.

If the United States was unwilling to accept multilateral help from its closest allies, it was unlikely to accept help from the United Nations. The UN stood behind the United States in Afghanistan and passed several resolutions expressing general support for U.S. actions. But the Pentagon put together an ad hoc alliance or "coalition of the willing" to overthrow the Taliban government in Afghanistan, where most of the 9/11 hijackers had been trained.

The war in Afghanistan went better than expected. By early 2002, U.S. special forces working with Afghan militia opposed to the ruling Taliban government had secured control of the country. Encouraged perhaps by this military success, power transition realists now took on wider aspects of the conflict.

In his State of the Union message in January 2002, President Bush included rogue states supporting terrorism as the enemy, not just Al Qaeda, the nonstate actor that trained the hijackers in Afghanistan and was most directly responsible for 9/11. He called Iraq, Iran, and North Korea the "axis of evil" and in late summer 2002 began to position American military forces in the Persian Gulf to confront this threat. The national security strategy document of September 2002 made clear that the United States might act alone and defined terrorists to include not only "terrorist organizations of global reach" but "any terrorist or state sponsor of terrorism which attempts to gain or use weapons of mass destruction (WMD[s]) or their precursors."[15]

In October 2002, Bush secured congressional authority to use force against Iraq. The vote indicated wider support than did similar votes in the 1991 Gulf War (House 296–133 and Senate 77–23, compared to 250–183 and 52–47, respectively, in 1991). Later developments called into question the primary rationale—namely, that Iraq possessed weapons of mass destruction—but at the time the American public was united behind the call for force. Then, at the urging of Secretary of State Powell, Bush took his case to the United Nations. In November, the UN Security Council agreed unanimously in Resolution 1441 to afford Iraq "one final opportunity" to come clean on its WMD programs or "face serious consequences." Confronting the gathering U.S. invasion force in the Persian Gulf, Saddam Hussein let UN inspectors back into the country for the first time since 1998, when he had kicked them out. Realist perspectives would emphasize

Secretary of State Colin Powell makes the case to the United Nations in February 2003 that Iraq possesses weapons of mass destruction.

here the role played by force in getting the inspectors back in and creating a diplomatic option that did not exist after 1998. But now the presence of the invasion force created incentives to use it; the clock was ticking on diplomatic alternatives. In bitter discussions during the winter of 2002–2003, the United States and the other great powers could not agree on whether Iraq was complying with UN requirements and, more important, on whether force should be used—in short, what "serious consequences" meant.

When France, Russia, and Germany indicated they would not accept the use of force under any conditions, the United States, with Great Britain, Poland, Italy, Spain, and an assortment of smaller allies, acted without UN or NATO authorization. Coalition forces invaded Iraq in March and secured Baghdad by mid-April. Twelve years after its great success in the Persian Gulf War, the UN was sidelined once again by great power conflicts.

What the war ended, it was learned that Iraq did not have any weapons of mass destruction. The Iraq Survey Group, a team of 1,400 weapons specialists sent in by the U.S. government after the successful invasion of Iraq to find nuclear and other weapons of mass destruction, came up empty-handed. Aside from precursor agents, Iraq had no chemical or biological weapons and only aspirations for a nuclear program. Subsequently, other commissions—the 9/11 Commission, which published its report in 2004 on who and what were responsible for 9/11, and the Iraq Study Group, which issued a report in 2006 on future steps in Iraq and the war on terror—confirmed the absence of WMDs and questioned the wisdom of the entire intervention.[16] Nevertheless, American troops remained in Iraq until 2011 and suffered total casualties of nearly 5,000 U.S. soldiers dead and as many as 25,000 wounded; more than 100,000 Iraqi civilians were killed over the course of the war. The Iraq War spawned bitter divisions in the American political system reminiscent of those created by the Vietnam War in the 1970s.

Force and Diplomacy

By 2005 the world began to perceive the United States as dead set on acting alone. George W. Bush's "in your face" diplomatic style did not help. While Bill Clinton had softly rejected the Kyoto Protocol and the International Criminal Court (asking Congress, in the last days of his presidency, to ratify the ICC even though he knew Congress would not do so), Bush seemed to relish denouncing multilateral agreements. He terminated the ABM Treaty with Russia and suspended negotiations to contain nuclear programs in North Korea, both cornerstones of a liberal approach for controlling nuclear weapons (see Chapter 6). Simultaneously, he pulled back from negotiations to settle long-standing political grievances in the Middle East. Although he concluded the Strategic Offensive Reduction Treaty (SORT), a further agreement with Russia to reduce offensive weapon systems, this agreement was not a formal treaty and did not involve the verification procedures called for by previous START agreements.

Was it a mistake for the United States to refuse NATO help in Afghanistan? Liberal perspectives think so (see Chapter 6), and many power balancing realists think so too. NATO's help was eventually needed anyway. If the United States had asked NATO for help in Afghanistan, it might have eased alliance differences later as the allies considered intervening in Iraq. NATO had no forces ready to go into Afghanistan in the winter of 2001–2002, so U.S. forces could have conducted the initial assaults without NATO interference. Then NATO forces might have arrived in the fall of 2002 and created a very different diplomatic atmosphere for the debate about Iraq as well as subsequent developments in Afghanistan.

True, power transition realists concede, but in September 2001 the United States did not know how long it would take to subdue Taliban forces in Afghanistan. The fighting might still be going on by the time NATO forces arrived, and now the United States would have to fight a war again by consensus, as it had in Kosovo. Moreover, NATO helped in Afghanistan for the first few years only in policing and reconstruction activities. The initial combat forces were supplied mostly by U.S. and British troops under a separate non-NATO command. Even after NATO assumed overall command in 2006, some NATO allies, such as Germany, refused to accept combat roles or argued conveniently that there was less need to use military force, advocating civilian construction approaches instead. Even in areas of noncombat support, allies failed to meet their commitments to supply helicopters, transport planes, and other equipment.

Moreover, in the case of Iraq, the United States and Britain positioned 200,000 forces in the Gulf to force inspectors back into Iraq. Without those forces, there would have been no UN inspectors in Iraq and hence no diplomatic option to contain Iraq's nuclear program. France, Germany, and Russia did not contribute to these forces, yet now they wanted to dictate how these forces would be used and how long the inspectors would have to search for WMDs. If the allies had contributed to the invasion forces to begin with, they may have had more right to influence these decisions. And they would have certainly had to answer to their own people about how long they could keep their military forces in the hot desert without eventually using or withdrawing them. Power transition logic says that sharing influence always requires sharing power and danger.

The fundamental problem in a unipolar world, from the realist perspective, is the divorce between capability and responsibility. Smaller powers want responsibility but contribute few capabilities. Weaker countries always use international institutions to tie down stronger countries. The European members of NATO cannot compete with the United States in material capabilities, so, as other weak states have done historically, they use international institutions to restrain larger powers.[17] The European members insist that the United States make decisions only through NATO, while they spend far less on defense capabilities and do not risk the lives of their own troops in combat missions. Allies and other powers use the United Nations for the same purposes.

It's the adage, realists argue: If you have a hammer, you want to use it. If you don't have a hammer, you don't want others to use theirs. The dilemma is a consequence of the distribution of power. Until NATO becomes a more balanced institution in which Europeans contribute significantly to combat capabilities, as they did on the central front in Europe during the Cold War, realist arguments suspect that institutions such as NATO and the UN are more committees to delay action than real capabilities to fight nasty wars. In the end, the European allies have to decide to strengthen their defense capabilities independently, convincing their people not only to pay more for military forces but also to risk the lives of their own sons and daughters in combat, not just in peacekeeping missions.

From a realist perspective, therefore, the U.S. decision not to rely on NATO was the right one. The decision was a consequence of structural realities, unipolarity, not willful choice by the United States or defiance by the allies. Nevertheless, the United States suffered a significant loss of prestige. The nation's standing in the world, measured in terms of credibility and esteem, went down.[18] Realists, especially power balancing realists governed by prudence in the use of force, care about **prestige**, or the reputation for using force wisely to promote stability, not regime change. So, even in realist terms, the costs were substantial.

prestige: a nation's reputation for using force credibly and prudently to stabilize the status quo.

The divorce between the distribution of power and influence in diplomacy is broader than just Afghanistan and Iraq. As power transition advocates see it, it also extends to the broader Middle East conflict and policies toward other rogue states, such as Syria, Iran, and North Korea. Diplomacy can accomplish only what the underlying balance of power permits. And diplomacy was not working because, from a realist perspective, the balance of forces on the ground was moving against the moderate groups that support diplomatic solutions.

After the murder in 1995 of Yitzhak Rabin, the Israeli prime minister and Labor Party leader who had led the Oslo Accords negotiations on the Israeli side, extremists gained ground throughout the Middle East—so much so that Yasser Arafat, the Palestinian leader, conceded that had he agreed to the Camp David talks in 2000, negotiated by President Clinton, he would have been assassinated within a few weeks. In Iran, a more radical leader, Mahmoud Ahmadinejad, won rigged presidential elections in 2005 and again in 2009. And despite the election of a more moderate leader, Hassan Rouhani, in 2013, Iran continues to defy repeated UN resolutions and sanctions to stop its nuclear program, which includes activities, such as enriching uranium, integral to a weapons capability. Palestine became more violent. After Arafat's death in 2004, Hamas, the militant Muslim faction, won parliamentary elections in Palestine, took control of Gaza when Israeli forces withdrew, and launched relentless missile attacks against Israel. In Lebanon, the assassination of the moderate former prime minister Rafik al-Hariri in 2005 sparked renewed conflict between supporters of Syria (which occupied Lebanon in the 1990s and withdrew its forces only under pressure in 2005) and proponents of Lebanese independence. As part of the Lebanese turmoil, Israel invaded southern Lebanon in 2006 and then withdrew without much gain. Finally, in a continuing effort to stabilize Iraq, the United States surged military forces into the country in 2007 to stem the growing insurgency against the new U.S.-supported Iraqi government. But in 2011, U.S. troops left Iraq, and Iran now helps extremists in both Iraq and Syria fight the civil war to preserve the Assad government in Syria.

In Korea, the United States established the Six-Party Talks, engaging a coalition of Japan, South Korea, China, and Russia to pressure Pyongyang multilaterally rather than the United States negotiating bilaterally with North Korea, as it had done in the 1990s. North Korea eventually concluded an agreement in February 2007 that allowed inspectors to return and dismantle its plutonium program, but Pyongyang still refused to document its enriched-uranium program or its nuclear assistance to Syria on the nuclear installation that Israel bombed in 2007. The regime increased repression, concealed a secret enriched-uranium nuclear program (which it subsequently denied), and exploded primitive nuclear bombs in October 2006, May 2009, and February 2013.

Thus, across a broad front, as realists see it, moderate forces were in retreat. Until the balance of forces was altered on the ground, diplomacy could not achieve very much. As Secretary of State Condoleezza Rice once said, "You are not going to succeed as a diplomat if you don't understand the strategic context in which you are actually negotiating."[19] Following this realist logic, George W. Bush delayed diplomacy while trying to improve the balance of forces on the ground. In the early part of the decade, he shunned Arafat and devised the "road map," a framework for peace backed by the United States, Russia, the EU, and the UN (the so-called Quartet) to strengthen moderate forces within the Palestinian Authority and Israel. Eventually, in November 2007, Bush launched a new round of Arab–Israeli peace talks. In all these cases, realist objectives sought to strengthen military positions before negotiating seriously.

Critics from a liberal perspective, on the other hand, blasted the realist strategy for delaying diplomatic solutions while exacerbating military tensions. President Obama came into office in 2009 promising a new focus on diplomacy and less emphasis on the use of force. In summer 2013, he seized upon a Russian-initiated proposal to destroy chemical weapons in Syria, and despite the escalating civil war in Syria and the gains of extremist groups, such as Hezbollah and Hamas, in Lebanon and Gaza, he urged his new secretary of state, John Kerry, to give priority to a Middle East peace settlement between Israel and the Palestinian Authority.

Notice again how the realist and liberal perspectives differ in their emphasis on the use of diplomacy versus force. From the realist perspective, the use of force makes effective diplomacy possible. The Iraq War reduced extremism, eliminating one state that rejected Israel—namely, Hussein's Iraq—and at the same time reinforcing moderate leaders in countries such as Egypt, Jordan, and Saudi Arabia. It set the stage for Middle East democracy and peace initiatives. From the liberal perspective, the use of force undercuts diplomacy (more on this in Chapter 6). The Iraq War diverted attention from peace talks in the Middle East and from fighting terrorism in Afghanistan. And American unilateralism increased rather than decreased extremism in Iran, Syria, and the Palestinian Authority. The difference lies in judgments about whether the use of force makes diplomacy more effective or less effective.

The Iraq debate was bitter and often personal. But, when the situation is viewed from the vantage point of perspectives, there is no need to assume, as each side did—and immediate participants always do—that the other side was acting in bad faith. EU allies and perhaps also Russia looked to international institutions to solve the crisis (the liberal perspective) because they genuinely felt that the moral weight of the international community backed up by sanctions would suffice to contain and deter Iraq. They were a little disingenuous, we might argue, because they did not admit that force was the only way the inspectors got back into Iraq and they did not willingly accept their share of the burden in providing that force. On the other hand, the United States and Britain looked to the balance of power (the realist perspective) because they genuinely felt that diplomatic pressures and economic sanctions, which had been applied for more than a decade, would not suffice to disarm Iraq. They, too, were a bit disingenuous in the sense that they were unlikely to trust any response Saddam Hussein might have made to reveal and give up his WMDs. But, altogether, the disagreement among the allies was substantive and real, not contrived and mean-spirited.

Wars of Choice or Necessity

Were the Iraq and Afghanistan conflicts wars of necessity or choice? This question is answered by level of analysis tools. Was George W. Bush the principal culprit (individual)? Or was it an intelligence failure (bureaucratic), a shift in domestic politics after

9/11 toward more conservative or nationalist elements in Congress (the domestic level of analysis), weaknesses in UN and International Atomic Energy Agency (IAEA) institutions that allowed Saddam Hussein to defy international sanctions (the systemic structural level of analysis), or the requirement for great power consensus in the UN (the systemic process level of analysis)? If variables from the systemic level matter more, the decision to go to war is necessary. If variables from the individual level matter more, the decision is a matter of choice. The answer matters because when you fix something you can't change everything, even if you'd like to.

In 2007, the opposition Democratic Party took control of both houses of the U.S. Congress, and in 2009, Barack Obama, the Democratic candidate, became president. Did this shift at the domestic level of analysis change American foreign policy toward terrorism and the wars in Iraq and Afghanistan? In some respects, it did. President Obama reversed the emphasis of many Bush administration policies. As already noted, he upgraded diplomacy and downgraded the use of force. He withdrew all American forces from Iraq and ended America's combat role in Afghanistan. He reinstated an emphasis on multilateralism and international institution building and, in a multitude of speeches and policy actions in his first term in office, he emphasized collective goods, such as security actions through the UN in dealing with Iran, and common goals or "shared" interests, such as international cooperation in dealing with interconnected material problems of climate, energy, and nonproliferation.[20] By contrast, he de-emphasized "sovereign" or national interests that separate countries along political and moral lines. In Prague, in 2009, he said, "When nations and peoples allow themselves to be defined by their differences, the gulf between them widens."[21] He tacked away from topics that, in his view, divide nations (democracy, national security, competitive markets, and unilateral leadership) and toward topics that help to integrate them (cooperative security, disarmament, economic regulations, and diplomacy).

CAUSAL ARROW: LEVELS OF ANALYSIS

President Obama → De-emphasizes sovereign interests → Emphasizes common interests

INDIVIDUAL   DOMESTIC   SYSTEMIC

At another level, however, Obama perpetuated significant Bush administration policies, suggesting that the causes of behavior may be coming primarily from the systemic rather than the individual or domestic levels of analysis (and reversing the causal arrows above). He did not close the detention center in Guantanamo, Cuba; he continued policies of surveillance on phone calls and e-mails that led to a domestic scandal in 2013, when Edward Snowden, an employee of the National Security Agency (NSA), leaked information about these secret programs; and he escalated drone strikes in Afghanistan, Pakistan, Yemen, and elsewhere that killed American citizens as well as foreign nationals.[22]

So, in this example, what is driving U.S. policy in the struggle against terrorism? Is it primarily domestic-level forces in the United States, or is it domestic-level forces in Afghanistan and Iraq? Or perhaps the primary causes come from the systemic level, where global terrorists and rogue states threaten the West but European allies cooperate only reluctantly to confront these threats. Will America's retreat from Iraq and Afghanistan end those conflicts? Or will terrorists and their supporters in Iran and in the intelligence services of Pakistan keep the pot boiling in the Middle East and Afghanistan? Should the United States use force preventively before it is attacked, as it did in Iraq, or should it wait until the threat of attack is more visible (preemptive war) or an attack has already occurred (defensive war)? All these questions have to do with whether force (realist), diplomacy (liberal), or nation building (democracy) is the most important causal force and whether this causal force is coming from the individual, domestic, or systemic level of analysis. Can you see how perspectives and levels of analysis can be helpful for understanding and interpreting these everyday policy decisions and controversies?

TABLE 5-1

American Dominance: The Realist Perspective and Levels of Analysis

Realist perspective			
Systemic	*Structure*		Unipolarity prompts U.S. preemption to preserve American dominance (power transition)
	Process		U.S. dominant power creates incentive to act unilaterally outside international institutions
Transnational			Al Qaeda employs asymmetric power across states as a nonstate actor
Foreign policy			George W. Bush delays diplomacy to push back against extremists on the ground, while Barack Obama reduces the use of force to restore credibility to American diplomacy
Domestic			Shifts in power in U.S. Congress precipitate changes in global policy
Individual			Defense secretary (later vice president) Cheney gives priority to expanding American power over spreading democracy

Level of analysis

≫ Counterbalancing

Realists emphasize the relative distribution of power. But they disagree about which distribution of power is most desirable and stable. We have just discussed unipolarity and the effort by power transition realists to attain and preserve it through preemption and prevention. The flip side of unipolarity, however, is multipolarity. And power balancing realists anticipate the return of multipolarity. They do not believe that unipolarity can be sustained. They expect other countries to become stronger and eventually counterbalance the United States in the age-old competition for power. Power balancers therefore focus on containing, not preempting or preventing, the rise of powers such as China, Russia, Japan, and the European Union.

Rising Powers

In the 1990s China emerged as a preeminent rising power. In 1979, Deng Xiaoping replaced the leader of China's communist revolution, Mao Zedong, and reoriented China's economy toward growth and world markets. China adopted the strategy of Japan and the smaller Asian "tigers" that used export development to modernize their economies (more about this in Chapter 9). The results were nothing short of spectacular: China grew by 10 percent per year. Its current potential seems unlimited. Here is what a 2012 report by the National Intelligence Council said about China:

> The diffusion of power among countries will have a dramatic impact by 2030. Asia will have surpassed North America and Europe combined in terms of global power, based upon GDP, population size, military spending, and technological investment. China alone will probably have the largest economy, surpassing that of the United States a few years before 2030.[23]

China's strength, as well as its weakness, is the size of its population: 1.35 billion. If the majority of Chinese ever achieve middle-class status—and that's a big if, suggesting how difficult it is to develop a country with a large population—China will dwarf the world, except perhaps for India, which also has a population of more than 1 billion. Although China is nowhere close to that status yet, it is moving rapidly in an upward direction, albeit with some slowdown since 2010 because of the global recession. It is modernizing its military, increasing arms expenditures annually at double-digit rates. It controls a stockpile of several hundred nuclear warheads, an ICBM fleet capable of reaching the United States (a fleet no longer fixed and dependent on liquid fuels, which made it vulnerable and slow to launch, but mobile and fueled by solid propellants), a nuclear-powered ballistic missile submarine force, and a first aircraft carrier to project Chinese naval power beyond its shores. It is also developing so-called anti-access/aerial-denial capabilities to deny U.S. aircraft carriers the ability to roam risk-free through China's coastal waters and the island chains reaching out into the Pacific Ocean.[24]

China has used its military power in the past to occupy Tibet in 1950, fight a border war with India in 1971, and briefly invade Vietnam in 1979. Today it is the primary supporter of the nuclear-touting regime in North Korea and considers Taiwan, an island off the southeast coast of China occupied by nationalist forces in 1949 after the communists defeated the nationalists on the mainland, to be a renegade part of the fatherland and threatens to invade if Taiwan moves toward independence. It has been steadily building up its arsenal of short-range missiles aimed at Taiwan; in March 1996, it fired missiles into the sea around Taiwan, prompting the United States to send two aircraft carrier groups into the area to deter Beijing (the kind of move that will be riskier in the future as China acquires anti-access/aerial-denial technologies). China competes with Japan and other Asian countries for oil resources in the East and South China Seas and now includes the strategic and resource-rich South China

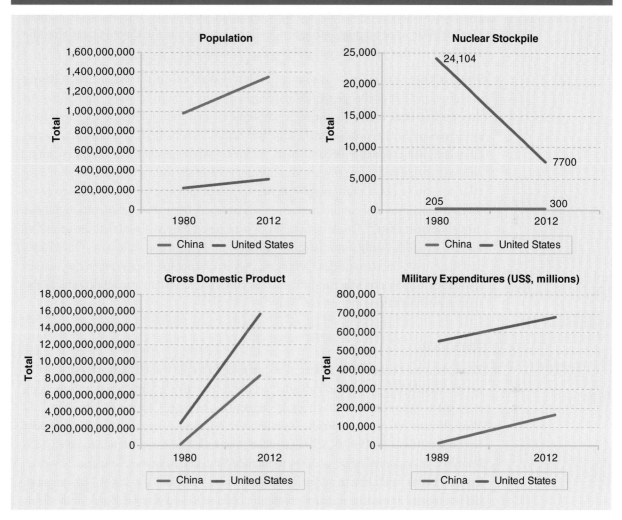

FIGURE
5-1

Rising China

Sources: Data are from the World Bank; the Center for Arms Control and Non-Proliferation; Robert S. Norris and Hans M. Kristensen, "Global Nuclear Weapons Inventories, 1945–2010," *Bulletin of the Atomic Scientists*, July 1, 2010; Stockholm International Peace Research Institute Military Expenditure Database, http://milexdata.sipri.org/files/?file=SIPRI+milex+data+1988-2012+v2.xlsx.

Sea as part of its core interests. It is developing a blue-water navy that could extend its operational capability as far east as the "second island chain," a line beyond Japan and the Philippines; such a fleet would clearly challenge American naval dominance in the Pacific.[25]

Realist perspectives fret about other counterweights to American power, even if these countries are democracies. (Notice how power trumps identity.) In the years immediately after the Cold War, they saw Japan, Germany, and the EU challenging American power. The saying was "The Cold War is over, and Japan has won." America, it was widely feared, had exhausted its treasury in the Cold War and was now in economic decline.[26] Meanwhile, Japan had spent very little on defense, was protected by the United States, and was aggressively exploiting export markets to undercut American preeminence. Germany and the EU were doing the same thing. Together these allies in the Cold War were waging a struggle for supremacy against the United States after the Cold War in what some analysts dubbed the "Cold Peace."[27]

The challenge was mostly economic, or what realists called soft balancing.[28] Rising powers could not challenge the United States directly in hard military capabilities, so they pushed back indirectly through economic rivalry and diplomatic sparring, such as opposition to U.S. policies at the UN. But realists assume that, in time, soft counterbalancing will eventually become hard. As Henry Kissinger warned, "The new international system will move toward equilibrium even in the military field, though it may take decades to reach that point."[29] Better to accept and accommodate than to resist this movement toward equilibrium. Even the prospect of nuclear proliferation did not disturb some realists.[30] Thinking in terms of deterrence, they assumed that the spread of nuclear weapons would automatically produce equilibrium and stalemate. Once states and their opponents had nuclear weapons, they would not use them; rather, they would settle their disputes by other means, such as conventional balances and détente, as the superpowers had done in the Cold War.

Alliances

Russia was another obvious potential counterweight to the United States. From a realist perspective, NATO was always an alliance, not a collective security organization going beyond the logic of alliances, as liberal perspectives see it (see Chapter 6). After the Cold War, it became an insurance policy—or alliance in waiting—to protect against a resurgent nationalist Russia. In 1999 NATO expanded to include Hungary, Poland, and the Czech Republic. It expanded again in 2004 to include Slovakia, Romania, Bulgaria, Slovenia, Estonia, Latvia, and Lithuania. Finally, Albania and Croatia joined in 2009. These regimes did not require immediate military protection because Russia was weak and, under Boris Yeltsin, its president in the 1990s, cooperated with the West. But under Vladimir Putin, who succeeded Yeltsin in 1999, Russia became more assertive and less democratic.

Putin intervened in Ukraine to oppose a reformist government and pressure it by cutting off gas supplies. And in 2008 Russia invaded the sovereign state of Georgia, occupied the provinces of South Ossetia and Abkhazia, and recognized them as independent states (as of 2013 only five other countries had followed suit, including Venezuela, Nicaragua, and Nauru). Dimitry Medvedev, Russia's president from 2008 to 2012 because Putin could not succeed himself, declared a "sphere of privileged interests" in the former Soviet space: "Russia, like other countries in the world, has regions where it has privileged interests. These are regions where countries with which we have friendly relations are located."[31] Reelected as president in 2012, Putin continued the crackdown on Ukraine and neighboring states. Inside Russia, he shut down independent media outlets, threw out elected provincial governors in favor of Moscow-appointed henchmen, arrested political foes, was implicated in the assassination of liberal journalists and human rights activists, and shackled foreign organizations assisting democratic groups in Russia. In realist eyes, NATO is still needed to secure the new democracies in eastern Europe against this newly assertive and otherwise unchecked Russian power.

In addition, offensive realist advocates, such as Dick Cheney and Donald Rumsfeld, campaigned in the 1990s to terminate the ABM Treaty. They sought to develop more robust missile defense systems, as President Reagan had advocated, that might be effective against reduced numbers of offensive missile systems. Such defensive systems might also counter the threat of proliferation from terrorists and rogue states seeking to acquire WMDs and the missile systems to deliver them. In 1998, Rumsfeld, later defense secretary under George W. Bush, chaired the Commission to Assess the Ballistic Missile Threat to the United States. The commission concluded,

> Concerted efforts by a number of overtly or potentially hostile nations to acquire ballistic missiles with biological or nuclear payloads pose a growing threat to the United States, its deployed forces and its friends and allies. These newer, developing threats in North Korea, Iran, and Iraq are in addition to those still posed by the existing ballistic missile arsenals of Russia and China, nations with which we are not now in conflict but which remain in uncertain transitions.[32]

However, President Obama scaled back plans to deploy defensive missiles in Europe against the Iranian threat and worked to reset relations with Russia. He concluded a new START Treaty that reduced nuclear weapons between Russia and the United States but not with China and delayed enhanced NATO missile defense systems to defend against rogue states such as Iran and North Korea.

Asymmetric Warfare

From a realist perspective, threat and warfare took on a different character under unipolarity, or American primacy. The unprecedented asymmetry in the distribution of power put a premium on the use of force to disrupt and disconcert an adversary rather than to counterbalance or defeat it. There was no chance to defeat a vastly superior enemy directly, but there was an opportunity to create fear and spread uncertainty throughout the enemy's extended realm. Barbarian invaders had done this on the borders of the Roman Empire, eventually weakening and ending Roman rule. And revolutionary groups have done it repeatedly over the centuries to undermine subsequent empires. The less powerful therefore have always thought in terms of **asymmetric threat and warfare**, the exploitation of technology and psychology to target the peripheral vulnerabilities of a larger foe and wrestle it to the ground.

asymmetric threat and warfare: the exploitation of technology and psychology to target the peripheral vulnerabilities of a larger foe.

terrorism: the use of violence against innocent civilians to advance political aims.

As Professor Richard Betts tells us, "Terrorism is the premier form of 'asymmetric warfare.'"[33] **Terrorism** is the use of violence against innocent civilians to advance political aims. It is an old art of statecraft, especially for weaker groups fighting against stronger, more established foes. It has been present for some time in the Middle East and in other parts of the world, such as Northern Ireland and the Basque region in Spain. Irgun, for example, was a Jewish terrorist organization that fought the British to secure Israel's statehood. Now Arab terrorist groups fight Israel to achieve Palestinian statehood.

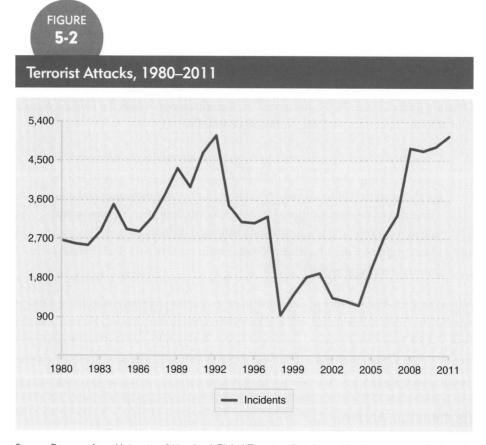

FIGURE
5-2

Terrorist Attacks, 1980–2011

Source: Data are from University of Maryland Global Terrorism Database, http://www.start.umd.edu/gtd.

The rise of terrorism, therefore, is no surprise from a realist perspective. Several factors, however, sharply escalated the threat of asymmetric warfare in the post–Cold War era. First, new information technologies empowered individual terrorist groups not only to communicate more effectively but also to develop strategies on a global scale. After Muslim jihadists defeated the Soviet Union in Afghanistan, Osama bin Laden described the threat now posed by the United States: the "collapse [of the Soviet Union] made the U.S. more haughty and arrogant and it has started to look at itself as a Master of this world and established what it calls the new world order."[34] He determined to set up a global network to confront this new "Master of the world." Al Qaeda emerged just as the Cold War ended and became a full-fledged global NGO with corporate and financial operations all over the world. It runs multinational businesses in construction, manufacturing, banking, leasing, commodities, exporting, and importing. And from its earliest days, its members have included Muslim followers from many nations across the Islamic world—Libyans, Filipinos, Nigerians, Iraqis, Saudis, Yemenis, Jordanians, and Algerians.

THE BIN LADEN TAPE

CNN

UBL: They were overjoyed when the first plane hit the building, so I said to them: be patient.

CNN broadcasts a tape made on December 13, 2001, in which Osama bin Laden discusses plotting the September 11 attacks on the United States. The Bush administration called the tape the "smoking gun" that proved bin Laden's direct responsibility for the attacks.

Terrorist groups also engage in **piracy**, the violent act of seizing people or property at sea to exact ransom or policy changes. Piracy has been around since the earliest days of commerce. It was used in the eighteenth century by Muslim caliphs who raided European and American merchant ships in the Mediterranean Sea and demanded ransom for imprisoned sailors. Today, piracy abounds in the Arabian Sea and the Gulf of Aden, an area known as "Pirate's Alley," where extremists from Yemen, Somalia, and other littoral states operate. The numbers of pirate attacks have grown in recent years, from twenty in 2006 to more than two hundred in 2010, and total extortion from piracy reached more than $200 million in 2010.[35]

Second, modern technology made large powers increasingly vulnerable to the tactics of terrorism. The United States, for example, has almost 600,000 bridges, 170,000 water-treatment systems, more than 2,800 power plants (104 of them nuclear), 190,000 miles of interstate pipelines for natural gas, almost 500 skyscrapers, and hundreds of airports, harbors, sports arenas, and shopping centers, not to mention thousands of miles of open borders—most easily accessible to attack by terrorists. It would be relatively easy for violent groups to target strategic links in these systems and send out ripple effects of physical disruption and fear that would magnify the impacts of relatively specific attacks.

The most vulnerable strategic system, of course, is the Internet itself. **Cyber warfare** emerged in the 1990s as a means, using software, to attack and disable defense and other strategic systems, such as electrical grids, banking and financial networks, and emergency communications systems. China and Russia are two of more than one hundred countries trying daily to break into other nations' defense and other strategic networks. Russia launched cyber attacks against Estonia in 2007 and Georgia, prior to its invasion of that country, in 2008. China operates one of the most extensive cyber threat opera-

piracy: acts of violence at sea carried out to exact ransom or policy changes to support terrorism.

cyber warfare: software attacks against countries' computer systems controlling defense and other strategic operations.

tions in the world. According to Mandiant, a private information security firm, China launches cyber attacks against both corporate and government targets from a facility in Shanghai that "is likely government-sponsored" and houses in the same building a similar operation of the Chinese People's Liberation Army.[36] China and Japan regularly lob cyber attacks at each other, as do Pakistan and India. Iran attacks Saudi Arabian oil companies, and North Korea targets banks in South Korea. Hackers attack NATO headquarters at least a hundred times a day; according to Anders Fogh Rasmussen, the NATO secretary-general, "It's no exaggeration to say that cyber attacks have become a new form of permanent, low-level warfare."[37] Wikileaks, the media Web site dedicated to disseminating classified information, caused a sensation in 2010 by distributing thousands of pages of top-secret classified cables that not only embarrassed governments, such as the United States, but also compromised foreign leaders, often dissidents, who had confided to U.S. diplomats their interest in working with the United States against their own governments.[38]

The United States is no exception. It too designs software to invade and destroy vital systems in other countries. One of the most sensational episodes of cyber warfare in recent years involved Stuxnet, a computer worm that U.S. and Israeli intelligence services deployed in 2010 to cripple Iranian nuclear installations. Stuxnet originated in the George W. Bush administration under the code name Olympic Games and was endorsed in tense White House meetings by the Obama administration. Instead of bombing centrifuge installations that purify uranium for use in nuclear weapons, Stuxnet hacked into the computer systems controlling the centrifuges, temporarily disabling as many as one thousand of five thousand centrifuges.[39]

Third, less powerful groups gained a greater advantage in the element of surprise. Offense holds a huge advantage over defense. In guerrilla wars, it has been estimated that defensive forces need an advantage of personnel as high as ten to one to defeat insurgency groups. Given all the vulnerable systems where guerrillas or terrorists might attack, the cost to defend against terrorism was now much larger. In fact, the need to defend so many vulnerable places at such high costs created an incentive for larger states to preempt or prevent attacks. The money would be better spent on trying to locate and kill the members of terrorist cells through advanced espionage techniques and covert operations than on establishing passive defenses at all the points of vulnerability. On the other hand, aggressive intelligence measures spread fear and concern, especially in democratic societies, that fundamental civil rights were being violated. Terrorist groups could play on this political vulnerability to weaken the pride and resolve of defending democracies.

Fourth, some states became systematic supporters of nonstate terrorism. Rejectionist states—meaning those rejecting Israel—such as Iran, Iraq (before 2003), and Syria had long supported terrorist groups such as Hezbollah in Lebanon and Hamas in Palestine. But now other, failed states, internally divided and vulnerable to outside insurgent groups, became potential safe havens and training centers for terrorism. The hijackers who carried out the 9/11 attacks trained in the 1990s in Afghan camps under the Taliban government, a government that had emerged from the tribal warfare and chaos that ensued in Afghanistan after Soviet troops withdrew in 1989. When bin Laden had his passport taken from him in Saudi Arabia in 1991, he went to Sudan, where an Islamist radical government under Hassan al-Turabi harbored terrorists. From Sudan, Al Qaeda allegedly played a role in attacking American troops in Somalia, at the time another failed and lawless state.[40] Training activities for holy war also take place in Pakistan, the Philippines, Yemen, and potentially Syria, where extremist groups now control substantial real estate.

Fifth, the information age facilitated the spread of WMDs, and rogue states sought systematically to acquire such weapons, primarily to threaten retaliation against the unipolar power should it attack but also with the possible intent of passing WMDs on to nonstate terrorists. After the first Persian Gulf War, Iraq was discovered to be much closer to having a nuclear weapon than the world community had thought. Subsequently, as already noted, the A. Q. Khan network was unraveled. Dr. Abdul Qadeer Khan, the group's eponymous leader, was the top scientist in the Pakistani program to develop nuclear weapons. His network was an elaborate global nongovernmental web of individuals and corporations that, as it later came out, sold nuclear technology and equipment, including possible weapons designs, to rogue states such as Libya, Iran, and North Korea.[41] Thus, possible links between rogue states and nonstate terrorists through shadowy global networks exploiting the new information highways of global commerce and communications were creating a new axis of asymmetric warfare, although little of this was very visible or well understood yet in the early 1990s.

What was increasingly visible was a methodical increase in disruptive violence aimed especially at the predominant power, the United States. After the World Trade Center van bombing in 1993, global terrorists bombed Khobar Towers, a U.S. military barracks in Dhahran, Saudi Arabia, in 1996; U.S. embassies in Kenya and Tanzania in 1998; and a U.S. warship, the USS *Cole*, in the port of Aden, Yemen, in 2000. Plans to blow up a series of U.S. civilian planes in Southeast Asia and to disrupt Los Angeles International Airport in the United States during the millennium celebrations were thwarted. All of these events occurred before the sensational attacks of 9/11 and, from realist perspectives, during a decade when international institutions and economic interdependence expanded significantly and should have, according to liberal perspectives, diminished terrorism. (See Table 5-2 for a summary of realist highlights of the world today from the different levels of analysis.)

⟫⟫ Domestic Power Struggles

Realists see power struggles affecting behavior at all levels of analysis. At the domestic level, ethnic conflicts reproduce the contest for power. Ethnic groups, like nation-states, see themselves as separate and divided. They live in a situation of anarchy and struggle to survive. As realists see it, ethnic identities do not change and serve a necessary purpose. They offer people meaningful associations that make them feel good about their

TABLE 5-2

Counterbalancing: The Realist Perspective and Levels of Analysis

Realist perspective			
Systemic	*Structure*	Rising powers counterbalance to challenge American dominance (power balancing)	
	Process	Small powers use multilateralism and international institutions to constrain great powers	
Transnational		Weak actors use asymmetric warfare to resist powerful actors	
Foreign policy		President George W. Bush exploits the 9/11 attacks to expand the global war on terror and secure reelection	
Domestic		Rogue and failed states spawn violence	
Individual		Bin Laden declares war against United States and West	

(Level of analysis)

group and provide for their safety and welfare.[42] After all, family is the basic ethnic or biological building block of society. It nurtures and protects individual identities. It is not surprising that, since the first recorded political societies in Mesopotamia (today's Iraq), ethnic groups have existed and persisted.

From a realist perspective, politics should accommodate this reality rather than try to reengineer the human family. Historically, accommodation has been achieved through the recognition of multiple actors. To be sure, actors have grown in size as technology has made it possible to expand the scope of governance. But larger groups have their limits. From the realist perspective, they cannot provide cognitive satisfaction for everyone. The family of common humanity may exist, but, if it does, it is mostly rhetoric and too amorphous to galvanize loyalties and, if it is real, it may smother diversity and freedom. Thus, multiple separate groups, however small or large, drive the process of domestic and international politics and indeed prevent the consolidation of dominance by single or hegemonic groups.

Ethnic Conflicts

From this perspective, it makes sense to separate ethnic groups that are hostile toward one another. Separation worked in the case of the fifteen Soviet republics and the Yugoslav republics of Slovenia, Croatia, Macedonia, and Montenegro, all of which became independent after 1991. And, for realist observers, **partition** may still be the best solution for Bosnia-Herzegovina and Serbia. Serbs live separately from Muslims and Catholics in Bosnia, and Muslims live separately from Serbs in Kosovo, a province of Serbia in former Yugoslavia. Bosnia remains united under a loose confederation, but Kosovo became

partition: the separation of hostile ethnic or religious groups into different territories or states.

independent of Serbia in 2008. By 2013, some one hundred nations had recognized Kosovo independence. Forcing hostile people to live together is possible only if one group coerces or dominates the others, as Serbia did in the cases of Yugoslavia and Kosovo and as Russia did in the case of the Soviet Union. It is better, realist perspectives assume, for each group to manage its own affairs.

Ethnic partition and ethnic cleansing involve heartrending displacement of civilians. Here, elderly women and men, children, and wounded evacuees are driven by Bosnian Serbs from the fallen enclave of Zepa to the government-held town of Kladanj.

A case in point is Africa. From a realist perspective, colonialism forced diverse ethnic groups to live together in new African nations, and this legacy contributes, at least in some part, to the many ethnic conflicts in Africa today. State boundaries in Africa followed arbitrary colonial boundaries drawn in Europe. Ethnic groups were forced together, and postindependence unity was possible only through the dominance of one ethnic group or coalition over another. German colonialists in Burundi and Rwanda, for example, relied on Tutsis, an ethnic group that made up only 14 percent of the population, to control the Hutus, who made up 85 percent (the vast majority). They instilled in Tutsi elites theories of racial superiority, which Belgium perpetuated when it took over the German colonies after World War I. As realist perspectives see it, the requirements of governing in such multiethnic situations caused the construction of racial theories to justify the rule of one ethnic group by another.

Notice how in this realist case power does not ignore ideas but shapes them to suit the needs of power! Elite leadership and manipulation may be involved, to be sure, but they are now intervening factors between power and ideas, not independent causes, as liberal perspectives might argue. The cause is the requirement of power to govern an unsustainable mix of ethnic groups, and it is too much to expect the leadership to manage such situations without oppression. Resentment and rebellion by marginalized ethnic groups become endemic.

CAUSAL ARROW: PERSPECTIVES

Shapes ideas of racial and ethnic separation	Influences elite leadership and manipulation	Struggle for power
IDENTITY	LIBERAL	REALIST

African ethnicity, of course, might have been so diverse that it was not possible to accommodate all ethnic differences by partition. And referenda or other means of ascertaining local preferences for national boundaries might have unleashed a wave of violence of their own. Still, it is worth pondering, from a realist perspective, how different Africa's experience over the past fifty years might have been if national boundaries had been drawn with greater attention to ethnic compatibilities. Nigeria, for example, has more than three hundred ethnic groups, including four major ones: Hausa (21 percent), Yoruba (21 percent), Ibo (18 percent), and Fulani (11 percent). In 1965, when oil was discovered in the Ibo region, the Ibos declared independence, calling their region Biafra. A civil war followed. Biafra lost, and more than a million people died. Today, fighting persists in Nigeria between the Muslim-dominated Hausa and Fulani tribes in the north and the Christian-dominated Ibo and Yoruba tribes in the south.

ethnic cleansing: the systematic persecution, torture, and killing or removal of a religious or ethnic group with the intent to take over the territory of that group.

But partition also has its downside. It rewards separatists and creates incentives for ethnic groups to expel one another in what is called **ethnic cleansing**. This is what happened in Bosnia. When Yugoslavia dissolved in 1991, some ethnic groups proceeded to seize territory held by minority groups and drive them out. In 1995 Serbians slaughtered eight thousand Muslim men and boys in Srebrenica, expecting later to annex Bosnian territory to Serbia. Any resolution of borders in Bosnia, thus, either sanctioned the ethnic cleansing that took place during the war or brought refugees back to re-create the same mix of ethnic groups that existed before violence erupted. Partition, therefore, may not resolve conflict but simply displace it. When Slovenia and Croatia separated from Yugoslavia, their separation did not end the conflict. It simply led to more fighting, this time between Serbia and Croatia over the Serbian-inhabited province of Krajina inside Croatia. There, Croatian military leaders committed atrocities for which they now stand trial before a special tribunal in The Hague.

Unless a balance of power exists and works well, which is the realist way to accommodate separation, separation merely stimulates competitive armament and is itself prone to instability. At one point in the Bosnian conflict, for example, some realist solutions advocated arming the Muslims so they could better defend themselves against the Serbs and Croats. If some kind of intervention is necessary to ensure the balance of power, however, maybe that intervention could also incorporate institutional and leadership innovations that might mitigate ethnic antagonisms, as liberal perspectives advocate (more on this in Chapter 6).

Arab–Israeli Conflict: Two-State Solution

ethno-national communities: groups of people in which ethnic and national identities overlap substantially.

The Arab-Israeli dispute offers another example in which partition—that is, a two-state solution—may be the only way to avoid war. Both the Arab and Israeli peoples constitute **ethno-national communities** that have searched for centuries for territorial homelands. Although both have ancient claims to Palestine, neither had established a national home there prior to 1948. After World War I, Britain promised in the Balfour Declaration to work for a Jewish homeland in Palestine. After World War II and the Holocaust, international support for a Jewish nation increased. In 1948, the United States backed a UN resolution that partitioned Palestine between Arabs and Israelis. But the participants in the conflict could not agree, and war ensued.

Indeed, six full-scale wars ensued, the first in 1948 and the most recent in 1982, when Israel invaded Lebanon. In a war in 1967, Israel occupied large portions of Palestinian territory as set by the original partition, including the West Bank (bordering Jordan),

Gaza (bordering on Egypt), and the Golan Heights (bordering on Syria). Since 1982, the region has been afflicted by repeated smaller conflicts, such as Israel's battle with Hezbollah in 2006 and uprisings, or intifadas, such as the one that torpedoed the Camp David agreement in 2001. Palestinian militants launch terrorist attacks and suicide bombings in the occupied territories. Israeli forces impose rigid police controls, establish Jewish settlements in the occupied territories, and destroy Palestinian homes and neighborhoods to suppress terrorist activities.

The most prominent issue is territory. The Palestinians demand a homeland, but some also want to eliminate Israel. Israelis demand secure borders, but some also want to annex the occupied territories and eliminate Palestine. The obstacles to a final settlement include where the borders will be drawn; how Jerusalem, which both sides claim as their capital, will be managed; and what will be done with millions of Palestinian refugees who fled the occupied territories. By 2005, after almost continuous negotiations since the beginning of the conflict, both entities, Israel and the Palestinian Authority (created during the Oslo negotiations in the 1990s to bring together the various Palestinian factions), accepted a two-state solution, but extremists, supported by Iran, Syria, and, before 2003, Iraq, continued to reject it.

What should be done? Observers taking a realist perspective worry most about stability in the area. The Middle East is a strategic piece of real estate, not only because of oil but also because of its location between Europe and Asia and between Christianity and Islam. Great powers have historically intervened and competed in this area. So, the top priority from a realist perspective is to preserve the status quo both regionally and in terms of outside intervention. That was clearly the thrust of U.S. policy during the Cold War. Preventing great power clashes was more important than the negotiation of a final Arab–Israeli settlement or the democratic reform of authoritarian governments in the region. Stability is still the priority goal for realist observers and caused many of them to object strongly to the war against Iraq in 2003, precisely because it threatened to increase extremism and to endanger fragile governments in the region.

Palestinian youths place their national flag on top of a section of Israel's separation fence in the West Bank village of Ramat near Ramallah to protest Israel's military action on the Gaza Strip, on November 19, 2012.

CAUSAL ARROW: PERSPECTIVES

Or democratic reform of dictators	More important than negotiations	Prevention of great power clashes
IDENTITY	LIBERAL	REALIST

Observers taking a liberal perspective worry most about negotiations to achieve a final Israeli–Palestinian peace settlement. President Clinton gave these negotiations top priority in 2000, even though the military initiative was slipping into the hands of hard-liners in both Palestine (the intifada began in September 2000) and Israel (the more hard-line Likud Party replaced the Labor Party in February 2001). To secure this agreement, the United States and other sponsoring governments were ready to pump large amounts of foreign aid into the region. The judgment was that peace would strengthen moderates to reform corrupt governments; instead, unreformed extremists torpedoed the agreement.

Observers taking an identity perspective worry most about reforming the oppressive political regimes in the region. Palestinians are unable to accept negotiated compromises or restrain their military forces until they have stronger and more accountable leadership. Arafat, the Palestinian leader, confessed that, had he signed the 2000 agreement, he would have been dead within a few weeks. He controlled neither the minds nor the might of his own people. Nor was the Likud government in Israel in a position to compromise. It was beholden to settlers who demanded the annexation of the occupied territories.

Thus, as some identity perspectives see it, negotiations and stability awaited the success of democratic reforms (recall the reaction to 9/11 by columnist Jim Hoagland, as discussed in the Introduction). And opportunities for negotiations and stability improved when Arafat died in 2004 and Ariel Sharon, Israel's prime minister, faced down extremist settlers and removed some eight thousand of them when Israel withdrew from the Gaza Strip in 2005. But then democratic elections in the Palestinian Authority in 2006 brought the militant group Hamas to power. Hamas immediately split away from Fatah, the more moderate Palestinian group, took control of Gaza, and initiated daily rocket attacks against Israel. Democracy exacerbated rather than moderated extremism. Will moderates or extremists prevail in the political struggle, and does democratic reform help or hurt the peace process?

TABLE 5-3

Domestic Power Struggles: The Realist Perspective and Levels of Analysis

Level of analysis	Realist perspective		
Systemic	Structure	Colonial powers carve up Africa	
	Process	UN partitions Palestine	
Transnational		Palestinian refugees constitute a transnational movement of discontent	
Foreign policy		Arafat juggles peace negotiations and domestic political survival	
Domestic		Ethnic conflicts in failed states, such as the Taliban government in Afghanistan, provide fertile conditions for the rise of terrorism	
Individual		Leaders reinforce ethnic differences	

>>> State Institutions and Foreign Policy

As we have discussed thus far, realist perspectives focus on the struggle for power among separate actors—states in the international system and ethnic and other groups at the domestic level. Realists focus on states not because they are blind to the growing influence of international institutions or nonstate actors such as terrorists but because states remain the most powerful actors in contemporary world affairs, and realism follows power. States defend their sovereignty and work through ad hoc great power groups to control international institutions. And domestic interest groups acting through bureaucratic and other domestic institutions exert central influences in foreign policy decision making. Let's look briefly at these causal factors in the realist view of today's world.

Sovereignty

States emerged in the seventeenth century partly because they performed functions more efficiently than city-states or city-leagues.[43] City-states were too small to defend against new technologies, particularly gunpowder and the professionalization of the military, and city-leagues based around the Baltic and Mediterranean Seas lost prominence as the development of interior waterways, such as the Rhine River, opened up the vast expanse and resources of continental landmasses. Monarchs finally achieved the upper hand over the pope and the Holy Roman Emperor. Like Louis XIII and his foreign minister, Cardinal de Richelieu, they established borders and defended them, compelling the respect and recognition of other states.

As technology advanced, states, of course, could not dominate all aspects of their external environment and had to enter into interstate or intergovernmental relationships to cope with external exigencies. They met at conferences such as Osnabrück and Münster and concluded treaties such as the Treaty of Westphalia. In the nineteenth century, states convened more conferences, signed more treaties, and established intergovernmental bureaucracies to administer many of them. The Concert of Europe in 1815 created the first expectation of a regular conference process, and the Universal Postal Union in 1874 put in place one of the first expert or functional international institutions to facilitate interdependence, in this case through the delivery of mail. Between 1848 and 1919, states signed treaties that filled 226 thick books. Between 1920 and 1946, they filled 205 more volumes. And between 1946 and 1978, they filled another 1,115 volumes.[44] IGOs grew in numbers and significance. They codified laws and practices, which interfered in the domestic jurisdiction of states.

From a realist perspective, states run IGOs and constrain the influence of NGOs. Recall how Russia under Putin shut down foreign aid agencies in Russia and placed NGOs under tight registration requirements. Even so, IGOs develop lives and often independence of their own. So states, particularly the great powers, look for ways to regain some control over international institutions by establishing less formal "steering committees" made up of big countries, such as the G-7, G-8, and G-20. These **great power groups** meet on a regular basis to influence the international agenda and set directions and tasks for international

great power groups: assorted informal groupings of the major economic and financial powers known as the G-7, G-8, and G-20.

CAUSAL ARROW: PERSPECTIVES

Great powers groups → **Manage IGOs** → **And constrain NGOs seeking to alter domestic politics**

REALIST   LIBERAL   IDENTITY

institutions. As a rule, the great power groups are less formal or bureaucratic than IGOs. They bring world leaders together for face-to-face talks and try to coordinate the work of many international organizations, both governmental and nongovernmental, that are involved in areas such as foreign aid, trade, global finance, the environment, and anti–drug trafficking efforts.

However, from some liberal perspectives, these groups lack the legitimacy of universal organizations. Debate persists as to which countries should be included in these groups. The G-7 included only democratic countries until Russia became a member in 1997 and the G-7 became the G-8. The G-20, established in 1999, includes further great power aspirants such as China, Brazil, and India, while smaller developing countries belonging to the G-77 complain that they are insufficiently represented in the G-20. Do countries gain membership by virtue of power (realist), equality (liberal), or ideology (identity)? Or are these informal great power groups simply additional tools of core-country hegemonism, as critical theory perspectives assert?

President of the European Commission José Manuel Barroso and (left to right) Japanese Prime Minister Shinzo Abe, German Chancellor Angela Merkel, Russian President Vladimir Putin, British Prime Minister David Cameron, U.S. President Barack Obama, French President François Hollande, Canadian Prime Minister Stephen Harper, Italian Prime Minister Enrico Letta, and President of the European Council Herman Van Rompuy arrive for the "family" group photograph at the G-8 venue of Lough Erne in Enniskillen, Northern Ireland, on June 18, 2013. At the two-day summit, hosted by Prime Minister Cameron and held in Northern Ireland for the first time, leaders of the G-8 nations gathered to discuss numerous topics, but the situation in Syria dominated the talks.

Over the years, states have also merged and fragmented. They have voluntarily or involuntarily ceded sovereignty to higher, supranational, or to lower, subnational, authorities. The Prussian state, for example, transferred its sovereignty to the German state. The Czechoslovakian state gained its sovereignty from Austria-Hungary, only to cede it later to the separate Czech and Slovak states. So, new actors are part of the changing landscape of international affairs.

Today, the EU is a new sovereign and independent actor in many sectors, such as trade and monetary policy, and regional organizations in general are gaining greater influence and attention. A big question is whether this process of merger and dissolution of states simply leads to new actors that are just like states, but now larger or smaller, or whether institutions like the EU are novel entities that behave differently than traditional states. Will the world of organizations *above* the nation-state eventually lead to institutions that go *beyond* and are different from the nation-state? Realists doubt it, as we saw in Professor Mearsheimer's comment at the beginning of this chapter.

Foreign Policy

A common approach to international relations taken by realist perspectives is the foreign policy or decision-making approach. It addresses state action as a function of leaders' choices based on the costs and benefits of various foreign policy options mediated by the domestic groups and institutions that determine the political survival of leaders.[45]

A simplifying assumption portrays decision makers as rational actors. They have preset goals or preferences and evaluate those goals against the foreign and domestic circumstances they face to select the courses of action that maximize their goals and minimize their costs. They calculate these costs and benefits mostly in material terms. How much will each action cost and how much will it return? Where do their goals or preferences (identities) come from? They come from previous actions that *reveal* their preferences. The model is not interested in how preferences or identities change. Preferences are simply taken as given. Thus, the United States has a revealed preference for free trade and generally seeks that goal in its foreign policy actions. It weighs the costs and benefits of imports and exports under various options to advance that goal and chooses the one that returns the most and costs the least.

The simplified rational choice model makes other assumptions. The actor is unitary—that is, it makes its decisions as a single actor, not as a composite of multiple actors who engage in bargaining and trade-offs. This unitary actor assumption is frequently valid in situations of national emergency. Under duress, multiple actors pull together as a single unit. So, for example, one of the most widely respected studies of U.S. policy making during the Cuban Missile Crisis employs the rational actor model to analyze the Kennedy administration's assumptions and calculations in that crisis.[46]

A second assumption is that actors have access to complete information. Intelligence is accurate and available to all participants. As we learn in the case of the Iraq War, that is not always the case. Nevertheless, it is true that in 2002 most of the principal participants, both domestic and foreign, agreed that Iraq possessed weapons of mass destruction.[47] Again, in emergencies, participants tend to rally around one another. In more normal circumstances, however, they may have different and often incomplete information.

Rational decision making therefore may be influenced by bureaucratic organization, domestic politics, and group and psychological dynamics. Some of the elements that get drawn into the decision-making equation include bureaucratic infighting, interest groups, the military-industrial complex, political parties, legislatures, and public opinion. Decision making is the outgrowth of a struggle for power, this time at the domestic level of analysis among various subnational actors and institutions. From a realist perspective, what drives these groups are material concerns—security and prosperity at the international level and survival in power and expanding bureaucratic budgets and turf at the domestic level.

Bureaucratic Politics

In a pluralistic society, multiple agencies make up the decision-making system. In the U.S. government, the Defense Department, State Department, Office of the Director of National Intelligence, Trade Representative's Office, Treasury and Commerce Departments, and a slew of domestic agencies vie for attention and policy influence. The president and his executive office coordinate and direct this interagency process. The National Security Council (NSC), created in 1947, meets at the cabinet level and brings together the principal national security agencies. The president chairs the NSC, but multiple subcommittees headed up by staff members of the NSC coordinate interagency officials at lower levels involving assistant secretaries and deputy assistant secretaries. Other offices in the executive branch, such as the Office of Management and Budget, play a critical role in deciding on government expenditures, including defense and foreign assistance budgets.

In all governments, the decision-making process is complex and ongoing. Each agency represents a particular interest—defense agencies represent security interests; foreign ministries, diplomatic interests; treasury and economic or commerce ministries, economic and trade interests; and so on. In a typical case, the Defense Department worries most about what assignments might be given to military forces and whether the mission is clear and adequate resources are available. Foreign ministries press diplomatic initiatives and look for negotiated rather than military solutions. Economic ministries keep track of trade and financial costs and benefits. In the tug-of-war among agencies, final decisions are not always rational or definitive. When I was in government, I once heard the secretary of state exclaim, "Nothing is ever decided around here!" He was decrying the fact that interagency competition is fierce and never stops. A decision made today is opened up for debate again tomorrow. In authoritarian countries, some agencies gain dominance and make decisions that exclude and even eliminate other agencies. Former intelligence agency officials, led by President Putin, constitute such a group in Russia today.

Interest Groups

Government agencies also have close ties to domestic interest groups. Corporate and other for-profit groups, as well as nonprofit groups, organize and lobby to influence executive branch decision making and legislative branch legislation. Businesses and unions are particularly interested in budget and trade decisions, farmers worry about agricultural legislation, consumer groups lobby on environmental and consumer protection issues, and philanthropic and nonprofit groups weigh in on foreign aid and development assistance.

Other major interest groups may include immigrant and ethnic associations. In the United States, Jewish, Turkish, Armenian, Polish, Indian, Cuban, and other "hyphenated" Americans lobby to influence U.S. relations with Israel, the Middle East, eastern Europe, Latin America, and South Asia. In Germany, associations represent the interests of families displaced after World War II; others work to reconcile Germany's past with the Jewish nation of Israel.

Military-Industrial Complex

A key interest group in many countries is the military-industrial complex. It includes the major producers of military weapons, the government and private research institutes that develop new weapons, and the veterans' organizations that lobby on behalf of the armed services. In some countries, such as Egypt and China, the military-industrial complex controls a significant portion of the economy and produces civilian as well as military goods. The international traffic in arms is supported by both legal and illegal sale of arms and ammunition by various countries' military-industrial complexes.

Domestic Politics

Political parties and legislatures play a role in foreign policy in many countries. In democratic countries, they decide, along with the executive branch, the broad outlines of foreign policy and the size and composition of defense budgets. Legislatures control policy directly in parliamentary systems, in which the majority party fills the executive branch positions to decide government policy. In presidential systems, such as the United States, legislative and executive branches share responsibility for foreign policy decision making.

Public opinion exercises broad constraints on foreign policy decision making. Either through free and fair elections or through street protests, the wider public passes judgment on the policies of the leaders in power. Open media, a broad electorate, widespread basic education, and an impartial judicial system are all essential elements of a foreign policy decision-making system that serves and in some measure responds to the will of the people.

Individual Leaders

Perhaps the most important elements of state institutions and foreign policy making are individual leaders. They bring to the table different backgrounds, personalities, political skills and handicaps, and psychological predispositions. They organize their offices and decision-making procedures to reflect their own needs and preferences. American presidents have employed a variety of decision-making systems to make national security policy. President Dwight Eisenhower, a former military general, had one of the most tightly organized and efficient NSC systems. President Franklin Roosevelt was known for having one of the loosest systems, one that depended almost entirely on him. When Roosevelt died in office, his vice president, Harry Truman, knew almost nothing about the state of American military and foreign policy affairs, including the existence of the highly secret atomic bomb program.

Psychological factors clearly affect foreign policy decision making. Leaders are under enormous pressure, especially in emergency situations. They rely heavily on instinct and judgment and in the end make decisions that they are satisfied or comfortable with, rather than the most rational ones. One danger is that they may surround themselves with like-minded advisers. In such a situation, something psychologists call groupthink can take hold, in which the decision-making system encourages conformity and excludes consideration of alternatives that lie outside the group's thinking, producing decisions that are sometimes far less than optimal. Something like this, some analysts believe, affected decision making on Vietnam during the Kennedy and Johnson administrations.

Overall, therefore, foreign policy decision making is often not very rational. But as a first approximation, realist perspectives would argue, it is often better to approach it as if it were than to assume that it is not. Realist perspectives tend to minimize the extent of irrationality in foreign policy making, being less inclined than liberal or identity perspectives to attribute foreign policy to bureaucratic inefficiencies or psychological abnormalities. The external material realities are primary causes and, from the realist perspective, usually penetrate the web of decision-making complexity and confusion sufficiently to produce polices that can be explained in largely rational terms.

TABLE 5-4

State Institutions and Foreign Policy: The Realist Perspective and Levels of Analysis

Level of analysis	Realist perspective		
Systemic	Structure	State sovereignty prevails
	Process	States use great power groups to control international negotiations
Transnational		Interest groups lobby across borders to influence U.S. foreign policy
Foreign policy		In making decisions, state leaders maneuver between domestic agencies and international factors
Domestic		Interest groups compete to decide policy
Individual		Psychological factors reduce rationality

SUMMARY

In today's world, realist perspectives emphasize the role of systemic structural factors that stem from American dominance and the efforts of rising powers to counterbalance that power. Power transition realists advise that the United States try to retain that dominance and preempt or prevent efforts by rising powers to reduce it. Power balancing realists urge that the United States accommodate rising powers and contain or deter rather than preempt or prevent their rise. Asymmetric warfare, especially terrorism and cyber warfare, brings new challenges but does not rise to the level of existential threat. More attention should be paid to ethnic conflict and the resolution of conflict through peaceful means, especially partition; in the case of the Arab–Israeli dispute, a two-state solution, with international security guarantees, should be sought. Finally, realist perspectives look to states to deal with most problems in the contemporary world and assume, at least as a first cut, that states make rational decisions, despite the complexity of domestic agencies and interests involved and the irrationalities of groupthink and psychological bias that affect individual leaders.

Sharpen your skills with SAGE edge at **edge.sagepub.com/nau4e.** **SAGE edge for students** provides a personalized approach to help you accomplish your coursework goals in an easy-to-use learning environment.

KEY CONCEPTS

asymmetric threat and warfare, 217

cyber warfare, 219

ethnic cleansing, 224

ethno-national communities, 224

failed states, 205

global war on terror, 205

great power groups, 227

partition, 222

piracy, 219

prestige, 209

rogue states, 205

terrorism, 218

STUDY QUESTIONS

1. What is the difference between dominance and counterbalancing? Which type of realists supports each?

2. How do realists think about the relationship between force and diplomacy?

3. What is the preferred realist solution to ethnic or indigenous conflict and why? Where has that solution worked, and where has it not worked?

4. What is the rational choice approach to foreign policy decision-making? What are its assumptions?

5. How does the realist perspective see the future of the international system? Do integrated states like the European Union constitute new actors? What about the future of IGOs and NGOs?

Demonstrating the successful use of collective security from the liberal perspective, the United Nations Security Council votes on November 29, 1990, to adopt a resolution authorizing the use of military force against Iraq beginning in January 1991.

6 LIBERAL PERSPECTIVES ON TODAY'S WORLD
Collective Security, International Negotiations, Institutions, and Law

On August 2, 1990, Iraq invaded Kuwait. In contrast to the world's response when Japan invaded Manchuria in 1931 or Hitler annexed the Sudetenland in 1938, international organizations responded to Iraq's actions promptly and decisively—the way they were supposed to. The United Nations immediately condemned the attack, and the United States, supported by all the great powers, mobilized a UN-blessed military force to eject Iraq from Kuwait. As that unprecedented global action took place, President George H. W. Bush proclaimed to Congress a "new world order . . . in which the rule of law supplants the rule of the jungle" and expressed to the UN General Assembly what appeared to be the fulfillment of liberal hopes to replace the balance of power with a collective security system:

> This is a new and different world. Not since 1945 have we seen the real possibility of using the United Nations as it was designed: as a center for international collective security.
>
> The changes in the Soviet Union have been critical to the emergence of a stronger United Nations. . . .
>
> Two months ago, . . . once again the sound of distant thunder echoed across . . . the vast, still beauty of the peaceful Kuwaiti desert. . . .
>
> But this time, the world was ready. The United Nations Security Council's resolute response to Iraq's unprovoked aggression has been without precedent.[1]

Shortly after the end of the Cold War, the world seemed to have at last a global 911, a world police organization to call in the event of international violence.

At the systemic structural level of analysis, liberal accounts of the world today focus on the integrating forces of international institutions and economic interdependence. They highlight the promise of a revived United Nations based on its success in the first Persian Gulf War and, when that promise dimmed, the enlargement of regional institutions such as NATO and the European Union to include former communist countries. They promote international law and stress the expansion of the global trading system through the World Trade Organization (WTO) and the North American Free Trade Agreement (NAFTA) to include China, Mexico, and other developing countries. At the systemic process level, liberal accounts emphasize negotiations, bargaining, and compromise. They pursue efforts to reduce arms and stanch the proliferation of nuclear, biological, and chemical WMDs. At the transnational level they emphasize the role of nongovernmental organizations, and at the domestic level they focus on the peaceful reconciliation of intrastate conflicts through better elite leadership and institutional and economic transformation. As liberal accounts see it, failures of diplomacy and development account in large measure for festering conflicts that spawn ethnic, nationalist, and terrorist hatreds.

In recent years, at the foreign policy and domestic levels, liberal accounts have laid most of the blame for failed diplomacy on the United States. After leading the world to the first successful implementation of collective security in the first Persian Gulf War, the United States retreated from its support of UN intervention in Somalia; did nothing in 1994 when genocide occurred in Rwanda; initially let the European Union take the lead in ethnic conflicts in Croatia, Bosnia, and other former Yugoslavian republics; and belatedly rallied NATO, not the UN, to deal with these conflicts, splitting the veto powers on the UN Security Council and alienating Russia. Even before 9/11, the United States failed to ratify significant international agreements, such as the Comprehensive Test Ban Treaty and the Kyoto Protocol, and did little to support nonproliferation objectives when Saddam Hussein kicked UN inspectors out of Iraq in 1998 and terrorist threats escalated.

FIGURE
6-1

The Growth of Liberal Institutions

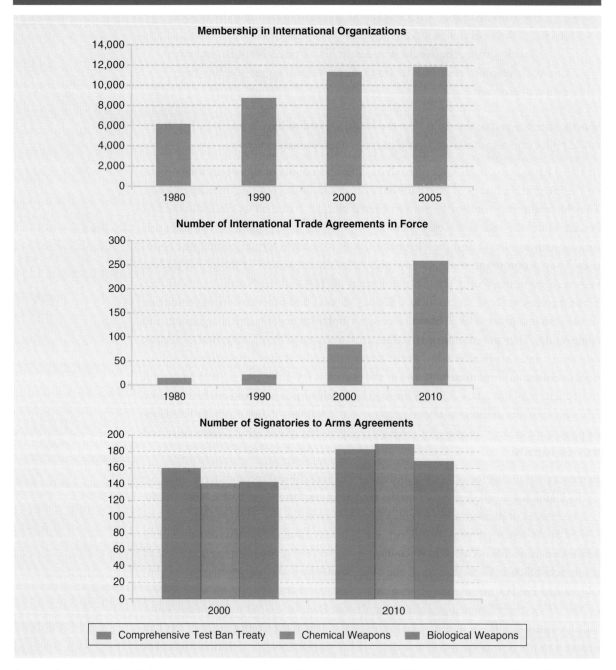

Membership in International Organizations

Number of International Trade Agreements in Force

Number of Signatories to Arms Agreements

Comprehensive Test Ban Treaty   Chemical Weapons   Biological Weapons

Sources: Data on membership in international organizations are from Jon C. Pevehouse, Timothy Nordstrom, and Kevin Warnke, "The COW-2 International Organizations Dataset Version 2.0," http://www.correlatesofwar.org/COW2%20Data/IGOs/IGOv2-1.htm. Data on international trade agreements are from World Trade Organization, "Regional Trade Agreements," http://www.wto.org/english/tratop_e/region_e/region_e.htm. Data on signatories to arms agreements are from Arms Control Association, "Fact Sheets: Treaty Membership and Signatory Status," http://www.armscontrol.org/factsheets/treatymembership.

Perhaps the biggest failure came after 9/11 at the individual level of analysis. President George W. Bush led the world to war in Afghanistan and Iraq and did so without UN or NATO help. From a bargaining calculus emphasized by liberal perspectives, war is always the most costly option, and when it occurs, it is often the result of mistaken choices, not circumstantial necessities. Different leaders and stronger commitments to multilateralism, international law, economic development, and the control of armaments might have avoided war. According to liberal perspectives, President Obama, in contrast to President George W. Bush, put American leadership back on track, upgrading diplomatic initiatives and downgrading military ones. He extended an open hand to the Muslim world, dispatched a swarm of envoys to global hot spots, ended America's involvement in the Iraq War as well as its combat role in Afghanistan, and was very reluctant to intervene militarily in foreign conflicts such as the one in Syria.

This chapter highlights these liberal aspects of the contemporary international system. It focuses on collective security, international negotiations and bargaining, and international institutions, including intergovernmental and nongovernmental institutions as well as legal and economic institutions. Along the way, we will identify the different levels of analysis from which these liberal factors influence international affairs. The focus on interaction leads states and other actors to pay less attention to their material (realist) and ideological (identity) differences and more attention to the "sticky" or habit-forming process of path-dependent problem solving that moves them slowly toward wider cooperation and integration. Again, we do not ignore the realist or identity aspects of international affairs but see them in this chapter as liberal perspectives see them. From time to time, I'll remind you how realist and identity perspectives might disagree, but for more on realist and identity aspects of the world, you'll need to turn to Chapters 5 and 7. From a liberal perspective, the causal arrows run from repeated and intensifying interactions, which focus attention on solving problems, to ideological differences, which become less important, to material outcomes, which benefit all and make power disparities less relevant. Here is how the historian Paul Schroeder draws the causal arrows for a liberal rather than realist interpretation of European history:

> The history of international politics is not one of an essentially unchanging, cyclical struggle for power or one of the shifting play of the balance of power, but a history of systematic institutional change—change essentially linear, moving overall in the direction of complexity, subtlety, and capacity for order and problem-solving. . . . [History consists] of the constituent rules of a practice or civic association: the understandings, assumptions, learned skills and responses, rules, norms and procedures, etc. which agents [actors] acquire and use in pursuing their individual divergent aims within the framework of a shared practice.[2]

Notice how "constituent rules" operating "within the framework [institution] of a shared practice" lead to a greater capacity for cooperation and problem solving *despite* the existence of divergent individual aims (liberal overrides identity).

CAUSAL ARROW: PERSPECTIVES

Decrease importance of material disparities	Narrow ideological differences	Institutions
REALIST	IDENTITY	LIBERAL

>>> Collective Security: United Nations in Operation

As President George H. W. Bush noted, the Persian Gulf War of 1990–1991 was a textbook case of collective security. According to liberal accounts, Bush and Bill Clinton understood the value of strong international institutions. Bush's secretary of state, James Baker, pursued a self-conscious strategy of institution building—that is, the systematic strengthening of international institutions to solve common problems. Baker insisted that Germany be reunified and remain a member of NATO, and he led the first Persian Gulf War effort through the UN. "Men like Truman and Acheson," Baker once said, "were above all, though sometimes we forget it, *institution builders*. . . . I believed we should take a leaf from their book."[3] Clinton's ambassador to the United Nations and later secretary of state, Madeleine Albright, endorsed what she called "assertive multilateralism" or "multilateral engagement and U.S. leadership within collective bodies."[4]

Here we consider how the United Nations works in practice—in the first Persian Gulf War, Somalia, Rwanda, and, most recently, Libya. In following sections, we examine the specific powers, institutions, and reforms of the UN system, as well as legal and economic institutions associated with the UN.

A Collective Security Triumph: The First Persian Gulf War

Iraq invaded Kuwait allegedly for many reasons: to control Kuwait's oil, to alter colonially imposed borders, to gain assets to pay off Iraq's huge debt from its eight years of war with Iran (1980–1988), and so on. But whatever the reasons, the entire world wasted no time in condemning Iraq as the aggressor and taking immediate actions to sanction it. One day after the attack, Iraq's fellow states in the Arab League (founded in 1945) denounced the aggression. On the same day, the UN Security Council unanimously passed Resolution 660, which demanded Iraq's immediate and unconditional withdrawal from Kuwait. Over the next few months, the Security Council passed no fewer than ten additional resolutions that declared Iraq's annexation of Kuwait null and void, demanded release of foreign hostages taken by Iraq, held Iraq liable for war and economic damages, imposed trade and financial embargoes, cut off air cargo shipments, and established a naval blockade. Had the League of Nations acted this decisively in 1931 when Japan invaded Manchuria, who knows how differently things might have turned out in the 1930s?

Despite universal condemnation, however, Saddam Hussein, Iraq's tyrannical ruler since 1979, did not budge. The United States and other UN members began to build up forces in the Persian Gulf, initially to defend Saudi Arabia from further Iraqi assaults in what was called Operation Desert Shield. In late October, they doubled these forces and positioned them to expel Iraq from Kuwait through an invasion code-named Operation Desert Storm. On November 29, 1990, the UN Security Council pronounced the diplomatic words of war, authorizing members "to use all necessary means" if Iraq did not withdraw by January 15, 1991. The U.S. Congress debated the issue and, on January 12, also authorized the president to use "all means necessary." The vote in Congress, however, was close (52–47 in the Senate and 250–183 in the House), suggesting the difficulty of persuading the American public to go to war unless the United States has been attacked directly, even when the UN has approved the war beforehand.

Probably no war in history has been as legitimate as the first Persian Gulf War, if we measure legitimacy by the universal approval of all nations, both democracies and nondemocracies. What produced this consensus? Liberal perspectives see it as the coming of age of international law. Iraq violated the most cherished principle of the interstate system since the Treaty of Westphalia in 1648, namely, the sovereignty of another country, and it did so in such a blatant way as to alienate all its supporters. The world united to declare Iraq's invasion of Kuwait a threat to all countries everywhere and then to isolate and ultimately defeat the country that was defying the most basic rules of the United Nations. Realist perspectives, of course, might stress the importance of oil supplies rather than the rule of law (Iraq's behavior threatened oil supplies that practically all countries needed from the Persian Gulf), or the simple fact that the United Nations could mount a credible collective security operation because the United States dominated it, whereas the League of Nations never included all the great powers. Alternatively, identity perspectives might highlight the converging values of East and West, as communism unraveled in eastern Europe and the former Soviet Union and the international community came together to protect the right of all nations to independence, self-determination, and the rule of law.

After last-minute initiatives to negotiate compromises by both the United States and the Soviet Union failed—the two former adversaries cooperating, albeit not always smoothly—Operation Desert Storm commenced on January 17. Massive aerial assaults hammered Iraq for a month. Then, an invasion force swept across the Kuwaiti border. Some 700,000 UN (including 550,000 U.S.) troops, 2,000 tanks, and 1,700 helicopters participated. It was the biggest battle ever in the deserts of Arabia.

By February 28, Iraqi forces had been driven out of Kuwait. UN resolutions had authorized expelling Iraq from Kuwait but not changing the regime in Baghdad. International consensus was more important than the spread of democracy. Accordingly, the U.S.-led army stopped at the Iraq border. It did not pursue Iraqi forces to Baghdad and unseat Hussein. From a liberal perspective, this was the right decision. The United States did not exceed UN authority. However, from a realist perspective, Saddam Hussein used the reprieve to smash local Shiite and Kurdish rebellions and reestablish his tyrannical control in Baghdad. And from an identity perspective, tyranny in Iraq persisted to spawn another decade of strife and eventually a second Iraq war in 2003.

CAUSAL ARROW: PERSPECTIVES

IDENTITY	REALIST	LIBERAL
Limits spread of democracy and removal of Hussein from power	Restrains use of force	International consensus primary

One unintended consequence of leaving Hussein in power was the longer-term stationing of U.S. and Western troops in Saudi Arabia to protect the oil fields. Western forces now occupied the heartland of Islam. Here is a case, as liberal perspectives see it, of path dependence. The United States did not intend to offend Islam; rather, its intent was to protect an ally. Nevertheless, one step leads to another along a path of events, and the end result is something that no one really anticipated (remember liberal accounts of World War I as an accidental war?). Radical Islamic fundamentalists, such as Osama bin Laden, saw the presence of "infidel" troops in the land of the holy places of Mecca and Medina as a declaration of war against Islam.[5] Bin Laden issued his fatwa, or decree, "Declaration of War against the Americans Occupying the Land of the Two Holy Places" in 1996 and then retaliated against the United States in the attacks of September 11, 2001. In this case, the unintended outcome was more violence. In most but not all cases, the liberal perspective emphasizes desirable outcomes such as greater international cooperation, economic prosperity, and political liberalization.[6]

Collective Security Failures: Somalia and Rwanda

The United Nations rode a crest of acclaim after its success in the first Persian Gulf War. Secretary-General Boutros Boutros-Ghali issued a report in 1992 titled *An Agenda for Peace.* It set out a plan for the use of UN forces not only for **peacekeeping activities**, that is, monitoring cease-fires and separating combatants, which the UN had done during the Cold War, but also for **peace-enforcement activities**, compelling countries to follow the terms of UN resolutions as had just been done in the case of Iraq. For a time, both President George H. W. Bush and President Bill Clinton, who took office in January 1993, supported this plan and held talks with the Soviet Union and then Russia to establish the military staff committee that was intended to assemble and direct UN forces under enforcement actions called for by Chapter VII of the UN Charter. UN responsibilities mounted. By January 1994, the UN was in charge of seventeen military missions around the world, deploying some seventy thousand personnel at an annual cost of more than $3 billion.

But then, almost as quickly as it had risen, the UN fell. The turning point came in Somalia. In December 1992, the United States dispatched forces under UN auspices to provide humanitarian relief to citizens in that country, which was torn by civil war. As in the case of many UN missions, however, it was difficult for the troops to feed and clothe people without also protecting them. And protecting them meant inevitably becoming involved in the local conflicts. That happened in October 1993 in Mogadishu, the capital of Somalia. When one of the Somalian warlords, Aideed, attacked UN troops, the UN authorized U.S. forces to capture him. In the fighting that ensued, a U.S. Black Hawk helicopter was shot down and eighteen U.S. soldiers died (the incident inspired a subsequent nonfiction book and Hollywood movie adaptation). One dead American soldier was dragged through the streets of Mogadishu. With Congress in an uproar, President Clinton ordered American troops to pull out of Somalia by the end of March 1994.

Notice that this explanation comes from the foreign policy level of analysis. In making his decision Clinton tried to balance between domestic forces urging withdrawal and systemic process factors urging support for the UN. In this case, realist perspectives

peacekeeping activities: UN actions devoted to monitoring cease-fires and separating combatants in third-world conflicts.

peace-enforcement activities: UN actions intended to compel countries by force or threat of force to follow the terms of UN resolutions.

might argue that systemic structural factors were too weak because the United States had no material interests in Somalia—no oil or strategic requirement for military bases as in the case of the Middle East. When instability was closer to America's shores in Haiti later in 1994, the United States did intervene to restore a stable government. On the other hand, liberal perspectives might argue that at the domestic level institutional factors within Congress trumped collective or national security concerns. The Somalia lobby in the U.S. Congress was simply weaker than the Haitian lobby. Identity perspectives might lament the lack of moral commitment to sustain U.S. involvement whether significant material and political interests are involved or not. Once again, as in 1919, the open-ended burdens of collective security or global humanitarian commitments proved too much for the United States. The American people were not ready to sacrifice American lives in places where the United States had no material interests.

CAUSAL ARROW: PERSPECTIVES

Overrides moral considerations	Determines national security threat	Domestic institutional pressure
IDENTITY	REALIST	LIBERAL

Recall our discussion of ethics in Chapter 1. While some commentators applauded the original U.S. intervention in Somalia as an example of a purely moral foreign policy—a universalist position motivated by principles independent of circumstances—others condemned it as immoral, meddling in other people's affairs without a sufficient material stake to ensure that the United States would stick it out when the going got tough—a pragmatist position that asks if the intervention helps more than it hurts. Was peace indivisible and hence a collective good available to all or to none, as liberal perspectives envision? Or was it separable, in the sense that no country, however dominant, could be expected practically or morally to intervene in conflicts where it had no significant private goods (national interests) at stake?

Weakened by Somalia, the United States and the United Nations swung to the other extreme in Rwanda in 1994 and did nothing when Hutus killed more than half a million Tutsis in an acknowledged case of genocide, the willful and massive slaughtering of one group by another on purely ethnic or racial grounds. Expectations for the UN receded steadily after this point and ended up a decade later in the ugly debacle of UN division and corruption during and after the Iraq War of 2003.

Collective Security Restored: Libya

After two decades of disuse, collective security reemerged in 2011 in the case of the intervention by Western powers working through the United Nations in Libya. When the Arab Spring broke out (for discussion of democratic movements in the Middle East, see Chapter 7), Tunisia, Egypt, Libya, and most recently Syria suffered internal protests and violence. In Libya civil war threatened the regime of long-standing dictator Colonel Muammar el-Gaddafi and posed the prospect of large-scale civilian casualties. In March 2011, the UN Security Council supported the establishment of no-fly zones to protect endangered civilians and prevent "crimes against humanity," particularly in eastern Libya. The Arab League, a bloc of twenty-two Arab countries, also supported the intervention. Russia and China went along with the decision as long as the UN did not take sides in the conflict.

With both Libyan and French flags flying behind him, a Libyan rebel loads artillery as Gaddafi's forces are hit by a NATO air strike on April 5, 2011. NATO support for the intervention in Libya spotlights the recent reemergence of collective security, but the fact that the United Nations did not get involved also highlights how complicated such activities can be.

As in Somalia, however, that proved difficult to do. While a larger group of nations, including Middle Eastern states such as Saudi Arabia and Qatar, backed the UN effort, NATO took control of the military operations, and Britain and France took the lead within NATO. They accounted for most of the air operations and naval blockade. The United States provided indispensable intelligence and military assets, such as AWACs air surveillance aircraft and precision-guided munitions, such as Tomahawk cruise missiles. Inevitably, NATO operations sided with the rebels seeking to overthrow Gaddafi, and Russia and China vetoed further UN military actions. Gaddafi was killed in October 2011, and NATO's operations in Libya ended, although fighting continued in the country. This situation provoked attacks in September 2012 against the U.S. consulate in Benghazi, where four American diplomats were killed, including the American ambassador to Libya.

The Libyan intervention demonstrates the ongoing difficulties with collective security. All countries, especially the great powers, seldom see their interests in common in such interventions. Russia and China, pressed by the consensus in the Arab League, accepted limited intervention to protect civilians but opposed any actions that would take sides in deciding domestic political outcomes. They feared precedents that might legitimate UN interventions in disputes such as those involving Chechnya (a southern province of Russia bordering Muslim countries where Russia battles separatist elements) and Taiwan (an autonomous island off the coast of China claimed by China), which they consider their own domestic affairs. But protecting civilians against both sides, as in Somalia, is unrealistic and, further, would undoubtedly require a more substantial intervention to quell the violence than Russia, China, or any other country would be likely to support. As a result, the outcome tips in the realist direction of the great powers that wield the most decisive capabilities in the dispute. In this case, that was NATO operating with European countries in the lead, in contrast to American leadership in the Bosnian and Kosovo campaigns.

TABLE 6-1

Collective Security in Today's World: The Liberal Perspective and Levels of Analysis

Level of analysis	Liberal perspective		
Systemic	*Structure*	Success of UN collective security in first Persian Gulf War and then its failure in Somalia	
	Process	Path dependence leads to Osama bin Laden's declaration of war against West	
Foreign policy		President Clinton, caught between international and domestic pressures, decides to pull troops out of Somalia	
Domestic		Domestic conflict makes it difficult for UN to intervene impartially	
Individual		Saddam Hussein defies UN resolutions despite defeat	

≫ International Negotiations

International negotiations build the foundations of collective security by seeking to resolve military conflicts through peaceful conflict resolution and bargaining. When negotiations succeed, as they did temporarily in the Oslo Accords in the mid-1990s, they create hope that peace and economic interdependence may eventually supplant power struggles and war. When they fail, they spawn controversial debates about the legitimacy and necessity of war. NATO interventions in Bosnia and Kosovo restored order to the Balkan region but alienated Russia and China, sidelining the UN and, from some liberal perspectives, violating international law. U.S. wars in Afghanistan and Iraq, which occurred without UN or NATO authorization, raised even more poignant questions about when war is a matter of choice rather than necessity and whether cheaper alternatives to war might be found through improved bargaining processes.

As president Bill Clinton looks on during a ceremony on the White House lawn in September 1993, Israel's Prime Minister Yitzhak Rabin (left) and PLO leader Yasser Arafat share a historic handshake on the peace plan known as the Oslo Accords.

Peaceful Conflict Resolution: Middle East

The first Persian Gulf War sparked the most serious round of Middle East peace negotiations since the 1979 peace agreement between Israel and Egypt. The cause, from the liberal perspective, was path dependence, or the momentum of post–Cold War cooperation between the United States and the Soviet Union/Russia that spilled over into the revival of UN diplomacy. Building quickly on UN success in the Gulf War, the United States convened a conference in Madrid, Spain, in October 1991. The conference brought together all the principal parties to the Arab–Israeli dispute, including Palestinian representatives not affiliated with the Palestine Liberation Organization (PLO). At the time, Israel did not recognize the PLO.

Although formal meetings stalled after Madrid, informal talks started between Israeli and PLO officials outside Oslo, Norway. These back-channel talks allowed the parties to explore options in secret without committing themselves to any option officially and enabled them to deny that the talks were taking place, if necessary. The talks eventually led to public agreements, the Declaration of Principles signed at the White House in September 1993, and then a series of agreements known as the **Oslo Accords**. Israel withdrew troops from Gaza and areas of the West Bank and recognized the PLO as the legitimate representative of the Palestinian people. The PLO, under the leadership of Yasser Arafat, returned to the West Bank from exile in Tunisia and progressively assumed police and other functions over a wider area of the West Bank and Gaza. Palestinians held their first national elections in 1996, and Arafat became president of the new Palestinian Authority (PA), which replaced the PLO. In October 1994, Jordan signed a peace treaty with Israel. For anyone familiar with the travails of the Arab–Israeli dispute, these seemed to be monumental steps toward peace. Resolution of one of the most divisive disputes in the Middle East and third world seemed to be at hand.

Oslo Accords: a series of agreements reached in 1993 between the Palestine Liberation Organization and Israel that Israeli troops would withdraw from Gaza and areas of the West Bank and that the PLO and Israel would recognize one another.

But it was not to be. And from a liberal perspective, there are a variety of explanations from different levels of analysis for the failure to reach peace in the Middle East. Perhaps it was because of the diplomatic inflexibility of individuals such as Arafat—the individual level of analysis—who was unable to give up the mace of revolution for the mantle of peacemaker. Or perhaps it was because domestic coalitions—the domestic level of analysis—shifted in Israel, giving more power to parties that opposed negotiations, while the PLO pursued strategies that weakened moderates and empowered radicals among Palestinians. In Israel in December 1995, Orthodox extremists murdered Yitzhak Rabin, the Israeli prime minister and Labor Party leader who had led the Oslo initiative. The Likud, Israel's more hard-line conservative party, took power under Benjamin Netanyahu. Smaller Orthodox parties, fueled by Zionist immigrants from Russia and eastern Europe, joined government coalitions and advocated the annexation of occupied territories. Israel stepped up construction of new settlements in the West Bank and Gaza. In the Palestinian Authority, Arafat failed to deliver on policing the West Bank, and extremist elements, such as Hamas and Islamic Jihad, seized control of parts of the Palestinian security forces. Through repetitive interactions and feedback, which liberal perspectives emphasize, extremism in Israel fed on extremism in Palestine, and vice versa. The Oslo process, caught in the middle, was the victim.

Or perhaps the Oslo peace process failed because the great powers had other diplomatic priorities—a systemic-level explanation. Once the United States lost its enthusiasm for the UN, Washington's and Europe's attention shifted to NATO and managing disputes in the Balkans and eastern Europe. The United States reacted slowly to the rise of extremism in both Israel and the PA. Most important, little came out of Oslo to improve economic prospects in the Middle East. For millions of young people in the Middle East, zero-sum goals of territorial control and religious zealotry remained more important than non-zero-sum goals of professional education and employment. Egypt had been at peace with Israel since 1979, but there was nothing to show for it in terms of trade or higher standards of living benefiting both countries.

intifada: an uprising of Palestinians in territories occupied by Israel.

Negotiations continued, but the peace process was in deep trouble well before President Clinton made a final futile effort to bring the parties together at Camp David in 2000. That effort failed, and a new **intifada**, involving generalized violence and suicide bombings, broke out in the occupied territories in February 2001.

CAUSAL ARROW: LEVELS OF ANALYSIS

Limit Clinton's role	Undermine Oslo Accords	Shifts in domestic coalitions
INDIVIDUAL	SYSTEMIC	DOMESTIC

Intervention and Legitimacy: Bosnia and Kosovo

The UN was tested by interventions in Bosnia in the early 1990s and Kosovo in the late 1990s, and in both cases, it came up short. In lieu of weak international institutions, therefore, liberal perspectives turned to stronger regional institutions, such as NATO and the EU. These institutions, through spillover and other path-dependent mechanisms, had gathered momentum during the Cold War, and they now stepped into the breach as global institutions faltered in the mid-1990s.

Realist accounts predicted, wrongly thus far, that institutions such as NATO would dissolve once the Soviet threat disappeared.[7] Realists considered these institutions to be alliances against specific threats, not collective security arrangements against general threats. To distinguish the difference, realists referred to NATO as a collective *defense* arrangement, not a collective *security* arrangement. When the threats ended, the defense arrangements were expected to end. Liberal perspectives saw it differently. For them, these institutions were regional collective security arrangements that, although not universal, nevertheless consolidated power and authority on a collective rather than selective (alliance) basis. They invested legitimacy, or the authority to use military power, at a regional level higher than the nation-state. Whereas states decided individually when to form alliances and use force, NATO decided these issues collectively. When was it legitimate, however, to act at a regional or NATO level as opposed to a universal or UN level? From the liberal perspective, how broad did the international consensus have to be to act legitimately?

In spring 1991, civil war broke out in the former Yugoslav republics. Ethnic divisions separated Western, Slavic, Turkish, and Arab peoples. Religious differences further divided Catholics, Orthodox Christians, and Muslims. Of the six provinces in former Yugoslavia, Slovenia and Croatia were mostly Catholic, with a significant Orthodox Serbian minority in Croatia; Serbia, Montenegro, and Macedonia were mostly Slavic and Orthodox, with significant Muslim minorities; and Bosnia-Herzegovina (Bosnia, for short) had roughly equal Orthodox and Muslim populations, with a significant Catholic minority. Bosnia, along with Croatia, became the focus of the conflict.

In the first year, the EC (which became the EU in 1993) took the lead and tried to negotiate a cease-fire and peaceful settlement. By mid-1992, the United Nations had deployed a UN Protection Force (UNPROFOR) in Croatia and Bosnia. UN and EC officials established the International Conference on the Former Yugoslavia (ICFY) to propose cease-fire plans. None worked, and after a mortar round went off in the marketplace of Sarajevo in February 1994, killing 68 people and wounding 197 others, the EU realized it did not have the military power to stop the violence. The United States and NATO were called on to support UNPROFOR with air strikes.

NATO had the power, but did it have the legitimacy to use that power? To be legitimate, as some liberal perspectives see it, NATO needed UN authorization. But working through the UN was ultimately not possible. Russia had veto power on the Security Council and blocked efforts to sanction Serbia, which the other powers perceived to be the primary aggressor. When violence escalated again in summer 1995, NATO acted without UN authority and launched weeklong air strikes against Serb targets in Bosnia. The United States also assumed the diplomatic initiative and called the parties together in Dayton, Ohio, to hammer out what became known as the Dayton Accords. A NATO-led peace Implementation Force (IFOR) replaced UNPROFOR. Eventually, the UN gave its blessing, and NATO, with some sixty thousand troops and related equipment, began its first so-called out-of-area mission—that is, a mission outside the central European area as defined by the Cold War threat.

In 1999, NATO got a second bite at the apple in Yugoslavia. Fighting broke out again, this time in Kosovo, a province of Serbia, after Serbia tried to crush the Muslim majority in that region. When Russia supported Serbia and again prevented UN action, NATO intervened once more and bombed Belgrade, the capital of Serbia. Serbia relented, and NATO and then EU forces policed a cease-fire in Kosovo.

In Kosovo, however, NATO had intervened in a dispute within a sovereign state, not a dispute between sovereign states as in the case of the first Persian Gulf War or one within a failed state as in Bosnia. Fearing intervention in unstable provinces of its own, such as Chechnya, Russia strongly protested this collective security action against a sovereign state and increasingly opposed NATO thereafter.

In summer 1990, U.S. officials had promised the Soviet Union that NATO would not expand its security role eastward. But now in 1999, NATO not only played a key role in stabilizing the Balkans but also expanded its membership to include Poland, Hungary, and the Czech Republic (the western part of the former Czechoslovakia, which had separated peacefully in January 1993 from the eastern part, known as Slovakia). In 2004, NATO expanded again to admit seven more new members—one republic from the former Yugoslavia, Slovenia; three republics from the former Soviet Union, Lithuania, Latvia, and Estonia; and three more eastern European countries, Slovakia, Romania, and Bulgaria. U.S. officials struggled not to alienate Russia. President Clinton made U.S.-Russian relations a centerpiece of his foreign policy and invited Russia to join a NATO-Russian Permanent Joint Council.[8] The idea was to start with regional collective security and eventually expand to include everyone in universal collective security. But when the Kosovo crisis occurred, Russia walked out of the Permanent Joint Council. President George W. Bush, pursuing a more bilateral rather than collective security approach to Russia, reconstituted the Permanent Joint Council in May 2002 as the NATO–Russia Council.

What makes military intervention legitimate? From a liberal position, many in Europe and the United States still believe it requires prior UN authorization. Sovereignty, the capability to maintain domestic order and defend territory, gives all countries the right to decide what is legitimate. But can Russia or other nondemocratic countries, such as China, block actions that democratic countries deem necessary to defend freedom or human rights? Others may argue that democratic countries decide legitimacy because their governments are elected and held accountable by their own people. From an identity perspective, legitimacy derives from democracy, not from sovereignty and universal participation. If the democratic countries in NATO and elsewhere can decide alone, however, won't that eventually cause a new Cold War, or worse, with Russia or China? And what if even the democratic countries in NATO cannot agree on military intervention? Does France or Germany have the right to veto actions that the U.S. Congress considers to be in the national interest of the United States? From a realist perspective, each nation decides what is legitimate. These issues came to a head in the 2003 Iraq War and sharply divided institution-oriented liberal and stability-oriented realist perspectives from more democracy-oriented identity perspectives.

CAUSAL ARROW: LEVELS OF ANALYSIS

Shift legitimacy from unanimity to democracy	Replace universal collective security organizations	NATO and EU
DOMESTIC	SYSTEMIC STRUCTURAL	REGIONAL

Bargaining and War: Iraq

Bargaining provides a liberal perspective on war. It involves a strategic or reciprocal exercise in which two or more parties interact rationally to resolve a dispute (e.g., over territory or trade), each taking into account the reactions of the other parties. Now, the actions of one actor depend on the actions of other actors, with all actors seeking to make credible commitments about the interests they intend to defend and to signal effectively the costs they are willing to accept. As Professor David Lake explains,

"The core idea of bargaining theory is that, because war is costly, there must exist a negotiated outcome that will leave both sides better off than if they actually fight. In this way, war is a failure of bargaining, an inefficient outcome that all parties would avoid in the absence of bargaining imperfections."[9]

In bargaining theory, each actor has a preferred outcome in which the dispute is resolved entirely in its favor. The status quo lies in between. Actors then calculate their respective capabilities to go to war to move the outcome in their preferred direction. If that outcome diverges from the status quo, the actors may have a rational interest in war. But war is costly, calculated in terms of the capabilities lost with respect to the objectives gained. So there is always some range of negotiated outcomes, however narrow, that would leave the actors better off without war. If negotiations fail and they nevertheless go to war, it is because they are unable to make credible commitments because capabilities are shifting (one side is growing weaker and decides to fight now rather than later, the preventive war case) or intentions are uncertain (one actor may fear that the other will defect from its commitments in the future).

In the two Iraq Wars, 1991 and 2003, the United States and Iraq faced off in a geopolitical struggle over influence in the Middle East. By invading Kuwait in 1990 Iraq demonstrated its dissatisfaction with the status quo. The United States, by expelling Iraq from Kuwait and leading the effort over the next decade to box Saddam Hussein in, declared its preference for the status quo. Improving on the status quo was costly. Eventually, the United States paid $3 trillion for the war. The estimates beforehand were much lower, around $50–$60 billion, yet still substantial. Iraq, from its experience in 1990, also saw war as very costly. Given these high costs, there were outcomes that would have left both parties better off without war. The United States might have reached an accommodation with Iraq in which Iraq would raise the price of oil while the United States would continue to protect the sea-lanes through which oil supplies were delivered. In rough fashion, that was the bargain that the United States reached with Saudi Arabia in the 1970s, when Saudi Arabia tripled oil prices and the United States continued to dominate the distribution and security of oil supplies. Alternatively, Saddam Hussein might have accepted exile without retribution and a new Iraq government might have accepted UN inspections to verify the absence of WMDs. One of the great puzzles of the 2003 Iraq War is why Saddam Hussein risked his power, indeed his very life, to defy UN nuclear weapons inspections when he had no nuclear or other weapons of mass destruction.

Bargaining theory offers two explanations. With respect to credible commitments, the United States was simply unable to believe that Saddam Hussein would abide by any negotiated outcome. He had demonstrated for more than a decade that he could not be relied upon to keep his word. And on Iraq's side, Saddam Hussein was unable to provide a costly signal to demonstrate his benign intent, such as admit he had no WMDs, because he feared revealing his weakness to foreign opponents such as Iran and domestic foes more than he feared the response of the United States. Second, bargaining theory points to information deficiencies that precluded a negotiated outcome without war.

Iraq assumed that the United States was bluffing and would not use force without the approval of its major allies and perhaps the UN as a whole. On the other side, the United States convinced itself, sincerely or otherwise, that the costs of war would be low. It ultimately suffered from large information gaps about the real situation in Iraq, especially the postconflict situation, which, after the brief military operation, spiraled out of control and raised the costs of the war beyond what anyone, including the war's opponents, had anticipated.

Bargaining theory suffers from some significant weaknesses, however. Why did the Clinton administration, which experienced the same bargaining circumstances with Iraq, not use military force? One answer may be 9/11. The terrorist attacks led the Bush administration to an entirely different interpretation of Iraq's intent. That is, the 9/11 attacks intervened as a structural variable that changed the deep background conditions of bargaining. As a model based on reciprocal relations rather than structural circumstances, bargaining theory is less capable of handling exogenous events such as structural shifts of power. Similarly, the possibility that states make commitments and then change regimes in the future that do not honor those commitments introduces identity factors that bargaining theory generally omits. (Recall the explanation for World War I that Germany could not trust commitments by Russia because Russia might change regimes in the future and become a less reliable partner to the German monarchy, which of course is exactly what happened when Russia became communist

TABLE 6-2

International Negotiations in Today's World: The Liberal Perspective and Levels of Analysis

Level of analysis			Liberal perspective
	Systemic	*Structure*	9/11 attacks create an entirely new structural setting for interpreting Saddam Hussein's behavior
		Process	Bargaining theory assesses the costs and benefits of war, creating negotiating options that are always less costly than war
		Regional	NATO and EU step in for UN to mediate Bosnia and Kosovo crises
	Foreign policy		Arafat weighs Middle East peace agreement with Israel against the requirements of maintaining his leadership of the Palestinian Authority
	Domestic		Collapse of moderate governments in Israel and Arab states after 1995 undermines Oslo Accords
	Individual		Clinton's efforts to mediate Arab-Israeli dispute in 2000 come up short

in 1917.) Finally, bargaining theory does not handle well psychological factors that distort information and the interpretation of information. What if Saddam Hussein was simply paranoid and unable to make credible commitments with anyone, friend or foe? Or what if George W. Bush was determined to avenge Iraq's attempt to assassinate his father in 1991, whatever the response from Baghdad? Rationalist bargaining theory, focused on the foreign policy and systemic process level of analysis, inevitably shortchanges individual- and domestic-level identity factors as well as structural-level realist factors.

⫸ International Institutions

The preferred way to deal with global conflict from a liberal perspective is to strengthen international regimes and institutions, both intergovernmental and nongovernmental organizations. In this section we discuss IGOs first—principally the United Nations and its role in interventions to keep the peace, deal with terrorism, avoid humanitarian disasters, and control weapons of mass destruction. Then we consider briefly the explosion of NGOs that play an increasingly important role in contemporary world affairs, especially when observed from a liberal perspective.

United Nations

United Nations:
the principal general-purpose intergovernmental organization that deals with collective security, economic and social development, and international law and human rights.

The **United Nations** is the principal general-purpose IGO in contemporary international affairs. It deals with all three major international issues: collective security and peace, economic and social development, and international law and human rights. The UN Security Council has primary responsibility for peace and security. The UN General Assembly coordinates economic and social issues through its Economic and Social Council (ECOSOC). And the International Court of Justice (ICJ) serves as the UN's primary judiciary organ. The UN Secretariat, with a staff of about nine thousand people under its regular budget, provides administrative support led by the secretary-general. A Trusteeship Council set up to administer colonial or non–self-governing territories after World War II is now defunct, although it still exists on the books. In 2013, the UN had 193 member states.

Let's look at the responsibilities of the United Nations in ethnic disputes, cases of terrorism, humanitarian interventions, control of weapons of mass destruction, and reform of the UN system.

Peacekeeping and Ethnic Conflicts. As we learned in earlier chapters, the UN was given enforcement powers under the UN Charter. The five permanent members of the Security Council with veto rights have the authority not only to mediate disputes under Chapter VI but also to enforce UN decisions under Chapter VII. The Cold War between the United States and Soviet Union ended that expectation. Prior to 1990, the Security Council used Chapter VII only twice to enforce mandatory sanctions against Southern Rhodesia (today Zimbabwe) in 1966, when the white minority declared independence, and against South Africa in 1977 in an effort to end apartheid. The UN sent forces

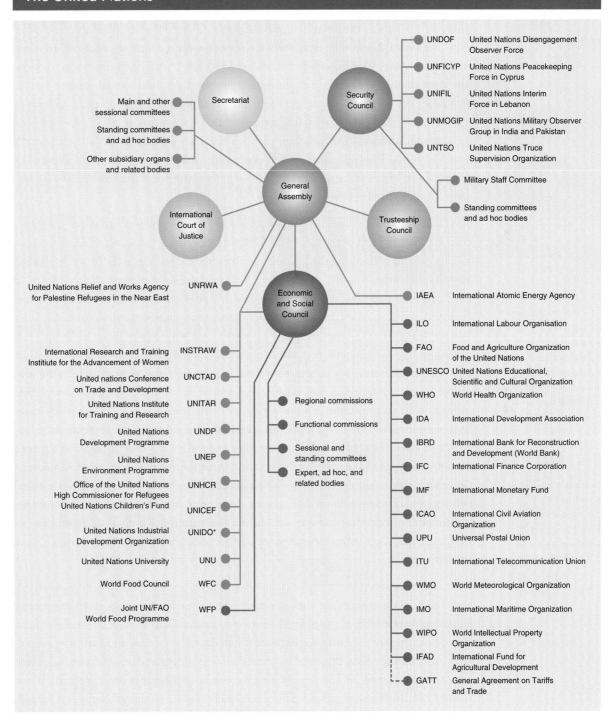

FIGURE 6-2

The United Nations

General Assembly
- Secretariat
  - Main and other sessional committees
  - Standing committees and ad hoc bodies
  - Other subsidiary organs and related bodies
- Security Council
  - UNDOF — United Nations Disengagement Observer Force
  - UNFICYP — United Nations Peacekeeping Force in Cyprus
  - UNIFIL — United Nations Interim Force in Lebanon
  - UNMOGIP — United Nations Military Observer Group in India and Pakistan
  - UNTSO — United Nations Truce Supervision Organization
  - Military Staff Committee
  - Standing committees and ad hoc bodies
- International Court of Justice
- Trusteeship Council
- Economic and Social Council
  - United Nations Relief and Works Agency for Palestine Refugees in the Near East — UNRWA
  - International Research and Training Institiute for the Advancement of Women — INSTRAW
  - United nations Conference on Trade and Development — UNCTAD
  - United Nations Institute for Training and Research — UNITAR
  - United Nations Development Programme — UNDP
  - United Nations Environment Programme — UNEP
  - Office of the United Nations High Commissioner for Refugees — UNHCR
  - United Nations Children's Fund — UNICEF
  - United Nations Industrial Development Organization — UNIDO*
  - United Nations University — UNU
  - World Food Council — WFC
  - Joint UN/FAO World Food Programme — WFP
  - Regional commissions
  - Functional commissions
  - Sessional and standing committees
  - Expert, ad hoc, and related bodies
  - IAEA — International Atomic Energy Agency
  - ILO — International Labour Organisation
  - FAO — Food and Agriculture Organization of the United Nations
  - UNESCO — United Nations Educational, Scientific and Cultural Organization
  - WHO — World Health Organization
  - IDA — International Development Association
  - IBRD — International Bank for Reconstruction and Development (World Bank)
  - IFC — International Finance Corporation
  - IMF — International Monetary Fund
  - ICAO — International Civil Aviation Organization
  - UPU — Universal Postal Union
  - ITU — International Telecommunication Union
  - WMO — World Meteorological Organization
  - IMO — International Maritime Organization
  - WIPO — World Intellectual Property Organization
  - IFAD — International Fund for Agricultural Development
  - GATT — General Agreement on Tariffs and Trade

Source: The United Nations.

to Korea in 1950, but the General Assembly authorized that action, not the Security Council, which the Soviet Union boycotted at the time because the UN refused to seat the new communist government in China.

Nevertheless, as discussed in Chapter 4, UN forces did play a key role during the Cold War under Chapter VI of the Charter, which regulates the peaceful settlement of disputes. In conflicts in the Sinai Peninsula, Cyprus, Golan Heights, Lebanon, and other areas, the United Nations inserted forces to play a peacekeeping, not peace-enforcement, role, to supervise cease-fires and mediate negotiations. These forces intervened to separate combatants, to observe and monitor cease-fire lines, and to maintain or restore civil order. All parties consented to these interventions, and UN forces had to limit or terminate intervention if any party requested that they do so. In 1973, the Egyptian government, before starting another war with Israel, requested that UN forces leave the Sinai Peninsula. They did, and war followed. Even with these limitations, however, UN peacekeeping forces are generally credited with preventing conflicts from escalating into confrontations between the superpowers.

The United Nations and related organizations have been involved in most of the ethnic conflicts since the end of the Cold War. UN peacekeeping or observer missions were or still are present in Burundi, the Democratic Republic of the Congo (DR Congo), Sudan, Somalia, Lebanon, Kosovo, Macedonia, Afghanistan, and numerous other places. In 2013, according to UN reports, the UN had 117,404 military and civilian personnel deployed in fifteen countries or territories across four continents at a cost of $7.5 billion per year.[10] The EU keeps the peace in Bosnia, and NATO is involved in Afghanistan and supports peacekeepers from the African Union in Darfur. The objective of outside intervention in these cases is, first, to separate the belligerents; second, to feed the war-ravaged populations; third, to mediate the disputes; and fourth, to reconstruct in some fashion common institutions and leadership to overcome divisions. These efforts range from simple monitoring and reporting about arms and militia movements to reconstruction and nation building; however, they generally stop short of democracy promotion or regime change. The United Nations champions sovereignty, not democracy. **Federalism**, for example, offers a way to decentralize power to accommodate tribal and regional differences without requiring democracy, and economic development is a more neutral process to create wealth and ameliorate ethnic conflicts. Growth changes the game from a zero-sum struggle over limited resources to a non-zero-sum increase in mutual gains.

federalism:
a method of decentralizing power to accommodate tribal and regional differences.

Liberal perspectives dispute realist claims (see Chapter 5) that ethnic identities are hardwired and require separation. They also resist identity perspective appeals to integrate or assimilate diverse ethnic groups into a single nation (see Chapter 7). Realists, they argue, tend to exaggerate the influence of ancient hatreds on behavior, and identity perspectives overlook the role of domestic institutions in containing and resolving ethnic unrest. Weak or failed states are the principal reason ethnic conflicts get out of control. When domestic institutions fail, ethnic groups face more intense security dilemmas. One side resists disarming because it cannot be sure that the other side will disarm. Thus, anything that reduces distrust lessens incentives toward violence.[11] Domestic institutions offer greater transparency and reduce the level of fear. Liberal perspectives see a positive role for institutions in domestic conflicts, just as they do in international conflicts.

CAUSAL ARROW: LEVELS OF ANALYSIS

Make unnecessary assimilation of ethnic identities	Override elite manipulation	Transparent domestic institutions
INDIVIDUAL	FOREIGN POLICY	DOMESTIC

According to liberal perspectives, **elite manipulation** engenders ethnic conflicts. Leaders exploit people's fears to advance their own personal and group ambitions. In former Yugoslavia, for example, Slobodan Milosevic and other leaders in Serbia incited violence to massacre some eight thousand Muslim men and boys at Srebrenica in 1995. Such violence was not inevitable. The borders of the Yugoslav republics had been drawn in the 1940s and 1950s on the basis of extensive negotiations and consultations, unlike many of the borders in Africa. Most Yugoslav republics had mixed populations that lived peacefully side by side. Some three million people, out of a population of twenty-two million, were the products of ethnically mixed marriages or were themselves married to someone of a different ethnicity.[12] So, violence had to be incited, liberal perspectives contend. But once violence begins, it is self-perpetuating; people grow fearful where before they were tolerant. The extent to which elites incite or respond to mass fear is hard to pin down and ultimately depends on judgment. But the fact that animosity and conflict foster thuggish behavior is undisputed. Look at the behavior of leaders such as Mobutu Sese Seko in DR Congo and Robert Mugabe in Zimbabwe.

elite manipulation: leaders' exploitation of people's fears to wage ethnic conflict for the leaders' own personal and group interests.

International interventions try to stop and reverse destructive elite behavior. Peacekeeping forces have kept the peace in Bosnia and Kosovo, with minor flare-ups, since 1995. They have also stopped the butchery in Sierra Leone and Liberia. Where fighting continues, as in the Darfur region of Sudan and the eastern part of DR Congo, the problem is usually that there are not enough peacekeeping forces. Once fighting stops, international institutions undertake **postconflict reconstruction** activities, resettling ethnic groups back into the areas from which they were expelled, rebuilding infrastructure and homes destroyed in the conflict, and mediating political processes of reconciliation and power sharing. In the Democratic Republic of the Congo, for example, UN mediators facilitated a cease-fire agreement in 1999. Although fighting continued, all parties eventually signed a power-sharing agreement in 2003. In 2010, rival leaders held various posts in a shaky transition government in Kinshasa, while rival tribes, Lendu and Hema, continued to clash in the Ituri region along the Ugandan border far from Kinshasa. A 17,000-strong UN force tried to keep the peace. But the area continues to be filled with thousands of refugees, and the fighting is gruesome. Many of the combatants are youths and even children. They are often high on drugs. They rape, hack people to death, and indulge in primitive rituals such as pulling out the hearts of enemies and wearing women's wigs and dresses to ward off death in battle.

postconflict reconstruction: activities aimed at resettling displaced populations and rebuilding areas ravaged by ethnic conflict.

Thus, international interventions are no panacea either. First, international peacekeeping forces are usually ill trained and insufficiently supported to carry out their missions. For example, when Serbian forces entered Srebrenica in 1995, Dutch UN forces fled in front of them. The Serbian troops actually wore UN uniforms and fooled Muslim inhabitants into cooperating. Second, UN officials and troops may be corrupt. UN peacekeeping forces in DR Congo were reportedly involved in drugs and rape, often abusing their positions of power over local populations.[13] Third, there are limits to international interventions. The further international institutions get into the process of nation building, the more difficult it is for them to remain neutral. Inevitably, domestic groups, particularly minority ones, seek to use these institutions to back their own narrow interests, and the institutions get caught in between. For example, when the Albanian Muslim majority in Kosovo declared independence in early 2008 while the province was still under UN administration, the Serbian minority protested vehemently. Serbian supporters rioted in Belgrade, burning the U.S. embassy, and Russia refused to recognize Kosovo or to cooperate with the UN. As identity perspectives might argue, lasting solutions depend on nation building and eventual reconciliation of ethnic identities, not just peacekeeping and the reconstruction of physical facilities.

Terrorism and Humanitarian Intervention. Terrorism and human rights raise new questions about the responsibility of the United Nations to intervene in the affairs of sovereign states. Without any warning or visible buildup before an attack, a terrorist cell can detonate an atomic weapon and blow up a major city, killing millions of people. Should one state intervene in another if it suspects that state of harboring terrorists or possibly providing them with WMDs? That was the question raised by U.S. intervention in Iraq in 2003. The UN could not reach an agreement. When the Security Council deadlocks, the only other justification for the use of force under the UN Charter is self-defense (Article 51). Some countries, such as the United States and Great Britain, concluded that Iraq was seeking WMDs and might provide them to terrorists. They undertook a preemptive war as an act of self-defense, arguing that such action is justified when the threat is *imminent*—that is, one country is about to attack another. Others concluded that the visible links between terrorism and WMDs were unconvincing and accused the United States of waging a preventive war, a much more controversial act of self-defense mounted against an *immanent* threat—one that is anticipated in the future.

After the start of the Iraq War in 2003, Kofi Annan, then UN secretary-general, convened the High-Level Panel on Threats, Challenges and Change to consider the criteria for legitimate intervention in the face of the new threat of terrorism. The panel identified five criteria: (1) a sufficiently clear and serious threat to warrant the use of force; (2) a primary purpose of stopping the threat, not other motives such as regime change; (3) the use of force as a last resort; (4) the use of proportionate and minimum necessary force; and (5) the use of force only if the consequences of doing so are unlikely to be worse than no action.[14] Notice the liberal prescriptions to use force only as a last resort and not to change regimes but to ameliorate conditions that might be worse than using force. Short of military intervention, the UN also acts to impound the personal assets of known terrorists and requires states to strengthen domestic laws affecting illegal financial transactions and the security of nuclear materials. Even these measures are controversial, however, and reflect different perspectives on security threats. Realist perspectives are generally going to see a bigger threat sooner; liberal perspectives will insist on maximum participation in the decision to intervene, which means Security Council or General Assembly approval; and identity perspectives will distinguish between interventions on behalf of universalist ideas, such as genocide, and those on behalf of purely national interests, such as access to oil. Critical theory perspectives see such interventions as efforts by the hegemonic core country to preempt counterhegemonic challenges.

In 2001, another panel drew attention to a further responsibility of the United Nations. The International Commission on Intervention and State Sovereignty called for "the **responsibility to protect**, the idea that sovereign states have a responsibility to protect their own citizens from avoidable catastrophe—from mass murder and rape, from starvation—but that when they are unwilling or unable to do so, that responsibility must be borne by the broader community of states."[15] This responsibility includes the willingness of the United Nations to prevent such catastrophes if possible, to react to them by means that include military intervention, and to rebuild the afflicted country after such intervention. The commission was an unofficial group, convened by the government of Canada and several major private foundations, but its report found wide resonance. States still disagree, as we will see, about how these protections are defined and whether these rights go beyond physical abuse and also include economic, social, and political rights. But if this trend continues, it implies a shift in the focus of international governance away from the rights of states to the rights of individuals. At least in some substantive areas, states will no longer be sovereign to do whatever they want to their own people. If national governments were to mistreat their own people in areas of basic human rights, they would be subject to sanctions or intervention by global institutions. Global institutions would hold national institutions accountable for more than just control of their territory and mutual respect for sovereignty. The International Criminal Court, as we see in the following, asserts the right to try leaders of national governments on charges of crimes against humanity if national courts refuse to do so.

responsibility to protect: the idea that sovereign states have a responsibility to protect their own citizens from avoidable catastrophe, and, if they cannot or will not, the international community must bear that responsibility.

Since the end of the Cold War, interventions for humanitarian purposes have become more frequent. As Martha Finnemore writes, "Humanitarian claims now frequently trump sovereignty claims."[16] When the international community does not intervene, as in the case of genocide in Rwanda in 1994, states feel the obligation to explain why. President Clinton, for example, visited Rwanda in 1998 and apologized to the Rwandan people for the failure of the United States and the international community to stop the Hutu rebels who slaughtered more than half a million of their Tutsi neighbors.

In 1999, Kofi Annan, the UN secretary-general at the time, spelled out the issues in stark form:

> If humanitarian intervention is, indeed, an unacceptable assault on sovereignty, how should we respond to a Rwanda, to a Srebrenica—to gross and systematic violations of human rights that offend every precept of our common humanity? . . . surely no legal principle—not even sovereignty—can ever shield crimes against humanity.[17]

Many developing countries, not to mention Russia, China, and other authoritarian states, are reluctant to go along with such broad interpretations of basic human rights. Russia opposed UN intervention in Kosovo, blocking action by the UN Security Council and forcing the United States and other countries to act through NATO. It also opposed Kosovo's declaration of independence in 2007, fearing that granting autonomy or independence to minority groups inside a country (in this case, the Kosovar people inside Serbia) might strengthen separatist demands in Chechnya and other parts of Russia to break away from the Russian state. China feared similar separatist demands in Taiwan, Tibet, and its western province of Xinjiang. Russia, China, and France also opposed U.S. intervention in Iraq; regime change, they believed, went too far and interfered in the sovereign affairs of another state.

Recent interventions have been increasingly multilateral rather than unilateral. According to data compiled by Finnemore, thirty-four military interventions took place during the four decades of the Cold War, twenty-one of which were unilateral. Thirteen took place in just the first decade after the end of the Cold War, ten of which were multilateral. Increasingly, as liberal perspectives advocate, interventions are considered legitimate only if they are carried out multilaterally. Many nations considered the intervention in Iraq in 2003, where the United States acted without NATO or UN authorization, to be illegitimate. But several years before, NATO intervened in Kosovo without UN authorization. If the world can act only with the agreement of all great powers, realist perspectives ask, how often will it act? And what if, as identity perspectives ponder, some great powers, such as Russia and China, do not defend human rights as vigorously as others? Won't basic human rights be compromised? On the other hand, if human rights are defined by selected countries that have similar values, intervention becomes a prescription for regime change and for imposing the political ideologies of those particular countries.

Recognizing the seriousness of the issue, Annan asked the International Commission on Intervention and State Sovereignty to come up with an answer to the question of when intervention is justified. The commission compromised on a rather complicated set of threshold criteria. The UN could intervene in cases of

> large scale loss of life, actual or apprehended, with genocidal intent or not, which is the product of deliberate state action, or state neglect or inability to act, or a failed state situation; or large scale "ethnic cleansing," actual or apprehended, whether carried out by killing, forced expulsion, acts of terror or rape.[18]

Not surprisingly, states continue to disagree about whether a large-scale loss of life is actual or "apprehended," meaning anticipated in a given situation, or whether a given state is unwilling or unable to act in that situation to prevent atrocities. The procedural norms of international life are changing. Sovereignty is no longer sacrosanct. But what *basic human rights* or *genocide* means is still disputed. The United States called the Darfur violence in Sudan genocide, but it did not apply the same label to Rwanda, Kosovo, or the killing fields of Cambodia, where the communist Khmer Rouge government killed as many as 1.7 million people—one-fourth of the country's population.

Nonproliferation of WMDs. Liberal perspectives place great stock in controlling and reducing arms, especially weapons of mass destruction. The recent conflict in Syria (see the Introduction to this textbook for details of the Syrian civil war) illustrates the problems of both domestic-level violence spawned by weak or illegitimate governments and the potential spread and use of WMDs. A UN report accused the Syrian government of Bashar al-Assad of using chemical weapons against its own people, killing more than a thousand men, women, and children and increasing pressure on the international community to intervene. The United States threatened a military strike to punish the Assad regime and uphold the international ban against chemical weapons. But Russia, a strong supporter of Assad, accused the rebels of using chemical weapons and opposed UN intervention. When President Obama pulled back from his threat to strike to ask Congress for permission to use force, which the Congress and American public overwhelmingly opposed, Russia stepped forward and offered a proposal to remove and destroy Syria's chemical weapons. No cease-fire was in place, but UN arms inspectors entered the country and began the difficult, perhaps impossible, task of finding and destroying all chemical weapons, which are generally harder to detect than nuclear facilities, while the country remained engulfed in civil war.

The United Nations nominally superintends a host of regimes to control weapons of mass destruction. Since 1957, an international regime has existed to ban the spread of nuclear weapons. The International Atomic Energy Agency, a UN agency headquartered in Vienna, Austria, is the modest successor to the Baruch Plan of 1946, which, as noted in Chapter 4, failed to consolidate all nuclear weapons under the authority of a single international institution. The IAEA accepts the possession of nuclear weapons by the great powers but seeks to prevent the spread of such weapons to other states by fostering peaceful development of nuclear power under international inspections and safeguards. Nonnuclear states can exploit peaceful nuclear power to generate electricity while IAEA inspection teams monitor the storage and use of civilian materials that could be diverted to weapons programs. In 1968, the **Treaty on the Non-Proliferation of Nuclear Weapons (NPT)** strengthened the IAEA system. It solidified the commitment of nonnuclear states not to acquire nuclear weapons and of nuclear states to reduce nuclear arms and to share the technology and benefits of peaceful nuclear energy with nonnuclear states for electricity, medical uses, and other applications. Only five states are not members of the NPT: North Korea, Israel, India, Pakistan, and South Sudan. The NPT was extended indefinitely in 1995, and review conferences are held every five years to address problems of implementation.

The NPT, supplemented by cooperation among the major nuclear suppliers, achieved some notable successes. Brazil, Argentina, South Africa, South Korea, and eventually

Treaty on the Non-Proliferation of Nuclear Weapons (NPT): a 1968 treaty that seeks to prevent the spread of nuclear weapons and materials while fostering the civilian development of nuclear power.

Libya abandoned nuclear weapons programs. Ukraine, Belarus, and Kazakhstan also gave up Soviet nuclear weapons when they became independent. India and Pakistan, however, acquired nuclear weapons in the 1990s. And Pakistan, through an elaborate and illegal global nongovernmental network of individuals and corporations established by A. Q. Khan, a top Pakistani scientist, sold nuclear technology and equipment to other groups and states, including Libya, Iran, and North Korea.[19] Israel is believed to have nuclear weapons. And Israel bombed suspected nuclear weapons sites in Iraq in 1981 and in Syria in 2007. Many nuclear weapons sites in Russia remain inadequately protected. In 1997, Russia acknowledged that it was unable to account for the whereabouts of 84 of some 132 nuclear bombs of suitcase size.[20]

Iraq, North Korea, and Iran became particularly troublesome cases. Iraq's capabilities, as we now know, were substantially gutted by IAEA inspection teams after the first Persian Gulf War. As liberal perspectives see it, UN arms control regimes functioned in this instance just the way they were designed to function. However, Iraq kicked the UN inspectors out in 1998, creating the impression that Iraq was proceeding full speed ahead with its nuclear weapons programs. When the inspectors returned at the end of 2002, they were unable—because of lack of time, lack of access, or both—to verify that Iraq did not have WMDs. North Korea threatened in 1993 to withdraw from the NPT, but then signed an agreement with the United States that placed its plutonium-producing reactor under IAEA surveillance. However, this agreement did not account for the spent fuel (which contains plutonium) previously extracted from this reactor and did not cover other nuclear programs based on enriched uranium, which North Korea later initiated. Iran persists in pursuing a broad-based civilian nuclear program that it claims is permitted under the NPT but includes enrichment of uranium very close to levels designed for use in nuclear weapons. In addition, Iran does not allow IAEA inspectors to visit these facilities, as called for by the NPT.

Chemical Weapons Convention (CWC): international agreement made in 1993 to ban the production and use of chemical weapons.

Biological Weapons Convention (BWC): international agreement made in 1972 to ban the production and use of biological weapons.

The **Chemical Weapons Convention (CWC)** (1993) and **Biological Weapons Convention (BWC)** (1972) ban the production and use of chemical and biological weapons. These weapons are less difficult and less expensive to develop than are nuclear weapons and are, therefore, easier to hide. When the Cold War ended, it was learned that the former Soviet Union had pursued a vast clandestine biological weapons program in direct violation of the BWC. Saddam Hussein in Iraq and Bashar al-Assad in Syria used poison gas against their own people. China, Cuba, Iran, North Korea, and Syria were also suspected of developing biological weapons. To be effective, inspection and compliance procedures need to be extremely stringent. But the United States fears that the procedures proposed thus far, including unannounced inspections, are not adequate to detect weapons violations but intrusive enough to reveal defense secrets. As a result, it has refused to accept new inspection protocols for these weapons. The use of chemical and possibly biological weapons generated widespread alarm when the Aum Shinrikyo group released sarin gas in the Tokyo subway system in 1995 and when, according to the Federal Bureau of Investigation, Bruce Ivins, a scientist at a U.S. weapons laboratory, mailed letters containing anthrax spores to media figures and members of the U.S. Congress in October

2001. In 2010, the same company that sequenced the human genome created a living virus from laboratory DNA, inaugurating the era of "synthetic biology" or the potential creation of deadly living organisms that may be used for civilian (medical) or military (weapons) purposes.[21]

The end of the Cold War offered an unprecedented opportunity to reduce the world's level of strategic and conventional arms. Aside from pooling military power in collective security institutions, liberal perspectives call for reducing arms to the minimum level possible. The Strategic Arms Reduction Talks—START I in 1991 and START II in 1993—lowered by two-thirds the number of offensive ballistic missiles and warheads maintained by Russia and the United States. The ABM Treaty signed in 1992 (discussed in Chapter 4) banned antimissile defense systems except at one location. The 1990 **Treaty on Conventional Forces in Europe (CFE)** reduced and established a roughly equal balance of major conventional weapons systems (tanks, artillery, aircraft, and so on) and troop strength among some thirty countries in Europe. The **Comprehensive Test Ban Treaty (CTBT)**, concluded in 1996, eliminated all testing of nuclear weapons above- and belowground, and the Anti-Personnel Landmine Treaty, which became effective in 1999, outlawed the use of land mines. From a liberal perspective, the way to end violence is to ban or limit arms. If the instruments of violence are not available or are carefully monitored, the destructive consequences of conflicts in the international system can be sharply reduced. Then international trade and development programs can drain the swamp of poverty and ignorance that fosters arms buildups and conflict.

United Nations Reforms. Critics of the United Nations, often from identity and realist perspectives, raise pointed questions about who provides the oversight of international institutions. The UN bureaucracy, unlike domestic bureaucracies, is not subject to immediate scrutiny by parliaments and NGOs. Nondemocratic UN members face no such scrutiny at all, even at home. Liberal perspectives urge reforms to improve accountability, but only at a pace that involves multilateral participation and consent. The UN adopted some reforms in the 1990s, but then the Iraq oil-for-food scandal revealed continuing widespread corruption. In administering sanctions against Iraq, UN officials were accused of influence peddling, taking kickbacks, and other criminal offenses. Another investigation uncovered the loss of some $298 million in UN funds through fraud and mismanagement of UN peacekeeping operations.[22] As identity perspectives lament, international norms governing the behavior of civil servants are weak. Others point out, however, that UN norms may be no weaker than those in some national bureaucracies, where corruption and scandals are also frequent occurrences.

Changing threats, the advent of globalization, and the eruption of scandals led to widespread calls for UN reforms. The principal reforms proposed include expanding the Security Council; trimming down the bureaucracy; improving the UN's ability to cope with new threats such as state collapse, WMDs, and terrorism; and getting serious about human rights and development.

Treaty on Conventional Forces in Europe (CFE): treaty signed in 1990 reducing and establishing a roughly equal balance of major conventional weapons systems and troop strength in Europe.

Comprehensive Test Ban Treaty (CTBT): international agreement reached in 1996 to stop the testing of nuclear weapons both above- and belowground.

It has been suggested that the Security Council be expanded from fifteen to twenty-four members. Brazil, Germany, India, Japan, Egypt, and either Nigeria or South Africa are likely candidates for permanent seats and, hence, veto power. But China opposes Japanese membership, and the United States has expressed skepticism about German membership, which would give the EU three seats on the Council. Adding veto members to the Security Council would make it more representative but not necessarily more efficient. An alternative is to give the new members semipermanent status, with four-year renewable terms instead of the two-year nonconsecutive terms for current nonpermanent members. Under other proposed reforms, the secretary-general's office would gain more powers and responsibility over budgets, and some bureaucracies would be eliminated. The Human Rights Commission, chaired in recent years by some of the worst human rights offenders, such as Cuba, Libya, and Sudan, was replaced in 2006 by the Human Rights Council, which is elected by a majority of the UN Assembly and meets for longer periods than did the previous commission.

CAUSAL ARROW: PERSPECTIVES

Wider and fairer participation	Diminishes role of great powers	Strengthens human rights norms
LIBERAL	REALISM	IDENTITY

The reforms proposed for the UN are controversial and reflect continuing differences among the perspectives. Realist perspectives seek greater accountability by great powers. Liberal perspectives seek wider and fairer representation. Identity perspectives seek stronger democratic norms, particularly in the human rights area. As we note in Chapter 7, when the new Human Rights Council was set up, the United States wanted members to be elected by two-thirds of the Assembly membership, which would have given democratic nations blocking power. But the majority of members, still nondemocratic, insisted on a simple majority vote.

Nonstate or Nongovernmental Organizations

Liberal perspectives pay special attention to nonstate actors. Today, all kinds of nonstate or nongovernmental elites are active within the sovereign domains of states. They create transnational or cross-national groups and institutions that weaken state influence. Some NGOs, such as terrorist groups, seek to destroy state authority directly. Other NGOs act in support of state interests; they project, not weaken, state power. Rogue states, for example, sponsor terrorism to advance their national interests. And some governments use multinational corporations as national champions to secure energy and raw materials for national security. The activities of such state-controlled NGOs raise concerns, as we note in Chapter 8 in the case of Chinese resource companies or the sovereign wealth funds of countries holding huge foreign exchange reserves.

transnational nongovernmental organizations (TNGOs): international commercial or not-for-profit advocacy organizations, typically independent of and not founded by governments.

Transnational nongovernmental organizations (TNGOs) are by far the most numerous actors in international affairs. By some estimates, there are as many as 40,000 such organizations, excluding MNCs, which number separately another 82,000 entities. In comparison, there are fewer than 200 nation-states and some 250 or so IGOs.[23] TNGOs are extensions of the nongovernmental or private lives of individual states into the public life of international affairs. Nongovernmental domestic actors take up international activities and become known as transnational actors because they are neither governmental nor intergovernmental organizations.

Liberal perspectives tend to see this phenomenon as a normal development of technology and specialization expanding the expertise and scope of institutions. Realist perspectives, because they emphasize the role of governmental (not nongovernmental) actors, tend to be more skeptical. They see NGO activities as either extensions of government policies or, if they are independent, unaccountable to anyone and, hence, disruptive of international order. Most countries, for example, expect their MNCs to operate abroad in ways consistent with their home country's security and economic interests. In turn, they are wary of NGOs from other countries because these NGOs may act in ways contrary to their national interests. The United States, for example, worries about NGOs that campaign to eliminate land mines or threaten to use the new International Criminal Court to punish American military personnel overseas because these NGOs do not answer to governments and may interfere with U.S. or UN military missions abroad.

Identity perspectives point out that NGOs may be uniquely the creatures of democratic governments. Nondemocratic governments see NGOs simply as extensions of foreign influence and disallow them. Myanmar and North Korea, for example, do not permit NGOs to operate domestically. They effectively ban international NGOs from entering their borders even when disasters strike, such as after a cyclone hit Myanmar in 2008 or during periodic famines in North Korea. China persecutes religious groups, such as the Falun Gong, and Russia has clamped down harshly on independent media and other activities, particularly in political areas, where NGOs support the promotion of democracy in Russia. Pakistan and authoritarian Muslim countries do not control many of the NGOs within their own borders, particularly the radical fundamentalist groups and madrassas (Muslim schools) that pose direct threats to their authority as well as terrorist threats to Western governments. In 2006, President Pervez Musharraf, at that time Pakistan's authoritarian leader, called the madrassas supported by transnational fundamentalist groups the largest NGO in the world.[24]

Are the existence and role of NGOs, then, largely a Western phenomenon and related to the development of constitutional and then democratic states? As we examine further

CAUSAL ARROW: PERSPECTIVES

Foster global norms → Weaken national sovereignty → Expanding NGOs

IDENTITY   REALISM   LIBERAL

A plainclothes police officer wrestles a female Falun Gong practitioner to the ground in China after she took part in a protest in Beijing's Tiananmen Square in May 2000.

in Chapter 10, critical theory perspectives may think so. Developments such as the Reformation, the industrial revolution, and pluralist competition empower individuals to participate in commerce and politics. In non-European cultures, especially Asian and Islamic societies, individuals matter less; groups and religious communities matter more. Authoritarian and theocratic states foster monolithic NGOs, such as madrassas; democratic states foster independent NGOs.

Democracies not only recognize but also promote NGOs and civil society as fundamental components of political society. From an identity perspective, the spread of NGOs in the world today owes as much to the spread of democracy as to the acceleration of technology and interdependence. Notice the judgment here that ideational or identity factors may be more important than institutional ones. If the international community becomes less hospitable to democracy, NGOs might become less important even if interdependence remains at high levels.

FIGURE 6-3

A Sampling of Transnational NGOs, by Field or Mission Focus

Development	Health	Women's rights	Children's rights	Human rights	Foreign aid	Environment	Anti-corruption
Bill & Melinda Gates Foundation	Amnesty International		International Crisis Group		World Wildlife Fund		Transparency International
Ford Foundation	Pathfinder International	Catholic Relief Services	Human Rights Watch		Ford Foundation	The Nature Conservancy	Partnership for Transparency Fund
Open Society Institute	International Association for Maternal and Neonatal Health		Oxfam		Greenpeace		Open Society Institute
MacArthur Foundation	Doctors Without Borders	International Alliance for Women	Coalition to Stop the Use of Child Soldiers		ActionAid		Global Witness
Forest, Trees, and People Program	Carter Center	Global Alliance Against Traffic in Women	International Save the Children Alliance	Carter Center	MercyCorps	The Jane Goodall Institute	International Initiative on Corruption and Governance

Even today, in a world where nondemocracies remain strong, NGOs are not always independent and tend to be concentrated. A few large NGOs dominate most issue areas, and many do not function on the democratic principles of representation, accountability, and transparency. For example, eight large NGOs account for more than half of the money going into world relief work, and few NGOs provide the public with detailed information about their personnel, operations, budgets, and funding sources.[25] This reality is not surprising, at least from the point of view of some identity perspectives, because some of the states today that spawn these NGOs are also not transparent or democratic.

NGOs exist across the broad spectrum of activities and functions that make up modern life—economics, environment, development, law and human rights, disarmament, politics, society, and the military. Many engage in not-for-profit activities, but others, such as MNCs, are for-profit institutions. Their efforts vary in effectiveness, but a number of them have received Nobel Prizes for their work, among them the International Campaign to Ban Landmines (1997) and, most recently, Doctors Without Borders (1999). Two examples, the World Wildlife Fund and Amnesty International, suggest how NGOs operate in today's international system.

The World Wildlife Fund (WWF) is the largest multinational conservation organization in the world, with activities in one hundred countries and five million members globally. WWF invented and pioneered the use of the debt-for-nature swap. Such a swap enables an indebted developing nation to avoid cutting back on essential environmental projects. Here is the way a debt-for-nature swap works. The International Monetary Fund often counsels debtor developing nations to reduce domestic expenditures to free up resources to repay their debts. Among the first expenditures that such countries are likely to cut are those for environmental projects. If a developing country agrees not to do this, WWF will purchase some of that country's foreign debt at a discount from a commercial bank or other originating source and transfer the title of the debt to the developing country. The developing country then converts the purchased debt into local currency and uses the proceeds to continue to fund essential environmental projects.

WWF carried out its first debt-for-nature swap in Bolivia in 1987. From that year through 2003, WWF negotiated some twenty-two debt-for-nature swaps in ten countries across four continents. Altogether it purchased debt worth around $55 million at a discount price of $23 million, which was then converted into the equivalent of $46 million for conservation purposes. Bolivia developed training programs to improve the management of lowland forests; Costa Rica purchased land for national parks; Madagascar undertook conservation programs to manage protected areas such as natural forests; the Philippines instituted training programs and infrastructure for national parks; Cameroon protected part of the world's second-largest tropical forest, home to elephants, gorillas, hundreds of bird species, and indigenous groups such as the Baka; and Poland funded programs to study and develop river basin resources.[26]

Amnesty International (AI) is among the most famous human rights NGOs and won the Nobel Peace Prize in 1977. The organization was founded in 1961 by Peter Benenson, an English lawyer. Sitting on a train one day in 1960, Benenson read about two Portuguese students sentenced to long prison terms for criticizing Portugal's then dictator António Salazar. He resolved to do something about it and founded AI. Headquartered in London, AI now has offices in eighty countries. Its members include more than 2.2 million people organized into more than fifty sections from around the world. The members are crucial to AI's survival and growth. Individual donations make up the bulk of the organization's income, which in 2009 totaled more than $45 million. Of this amount, only about 1.5 percent came from other sources, such as investments. AI also accepts money from "carefully vetted" businesses, but it is unique among NGOs in that it never takes money from governments or political parties.[27]

AI focuses on eight global goals:

1. Reform and strengthen the justice sector; that is, end the imprisonment of prisoners of conscience, unfair political trials, torture, unlawful killings, and so on.

2. Abolish the death penalty, both in particular countries and internationally.

3. Protect the rights of defenders, that is, those who work on behalf of human rights.

4. Resist human rights abuses in the "war on terror," which AI believes has caused "a widespread backlash against human rights."

5. Defend the rights of refugees and migrants.

6. Promote economic, social, and cultural rights for marginalized communities, such as indigenous peoples and Roma (Gypsies), with a focus on fighting forced evictions such as those that took place around Africa in 2006.

7. Stop violence against women, notably rape and domestic violence.

8. Protect civilians and close the taps that fuel abuses in conflicts in places such as Sudan, Israeli-occupied territories, and Lebanon.

An Amnesty International protester in Thailand holds a sign in support of Burmese human rights at a demonstration against Myanmar's military junta, February 28, 2009.

When AI received the Nobel Prize in 1977, the Nobel Committee cited AI's work on behalf of prisoners of conscience, noting that of the six thousand prisoners that AI "adopted" from 1972 to 1975, three thousand had been released by 1977. It praised in particular the way AI mobilizes thousands of individuals locally to "adopt" and develop close relationships with prisoners, reassuring them that they have not been forgotten. At the time, AI volunteers wrote letters to officials asking about the prisoners and letting governments know that someone was aware of the situation. To remain apolitical, AI assigned prisoners to adoption groups within specific Cold War regions: East, West, and the third world.[28]

265

In AI's early years, neither the UN nor governments welcomed the organization's initiatives. But its grassroots and practical approach scored big. Today, it unmasks human rights abuses in China, Somalia, Myanmar, Congo, and the United States, taking the lead in condemning U.S. practices at places like Guantanamo and Abu Ghraib.

TABLE 6-3

International Institutions in Today's World: The Liberal Perspective and Levels of Analysis

Level of analysis	Liberal perspective		
Systemic	Structure	United Nations is principal IGO in contemporary system	
	Process	United Nations intervenes militarily for humanitarian and other purposes	
Transnational		NGOs such as WWF and AI develop nationally and organize and act across nations	
Domestic		National governments have the "responsibility to protect" or international community may intervene	
Individual		Peter Benenson founds Amnesty International	

≫ International Law

International law among states dates roughly from the Westphalia Treaty in 1648. Sovereignty, not religious belief (whether a state was Catholic or Protestant), adjudicated relations among states. Thereafter, Christian beliefs faded while international law and liberal constitutional ideas, especially at the domestic level (e.g., Britain's constitutional monarchy, America's republican government), flourished. States increasingly accepted more legal obligations toward one another. Early jurists codified the rudimentary body of international laws. Hugo Grotius, a seventeenth-century Dutch jurist, wrote the classic work *On the Law of War and Peace*, and Eméric Vattel, an eighteenth-century Swiss legal scholar, made his contribution in *The Law of Nations*. Between 1581 and 1864, states concluded some 291 international agreements to protect the wounded and innocent in war. The Geneva Convention of 1864 became the basis of the Hague Conventions of 1906 and an expanded Geneva Convention of 1949, which regulate conduct in war to the present day and are points of issue in the contemporary debate on the handling of prisoners in the conflict with terrorism.

Law and Democracy

Did liberal constitutional ideas in democratizing states such as Britain and the United States drive this development of international law, or did international practice gradually shape a legal consensus that embraced sovereignty and eventually certain basic human rights for all peoples? You say both, and certainly you are right. But which was more important overall or in any given situation in time? From a liberal perspective, common practice and procedure shape ideas, while from an identity perspective shared ideas drive practice. Again, it is not a question of one perspective ignoring the other but of which key variable emphasized by each perspective causes the other.

CAUSAL ARROW: PERSPECTIVES

Diplomatic practice	Shapes respect for sovereignty	Encourages common norms
LIBERAL	REALIST	IDENTITY

These differences in perspective shape current debates on international law. Is international law whatever states decide, even if many of those states are not democracies? Whose law is it that governs international relations? Professor Jed Rubenfeld points to a different understanding of law that exists today between Europe and the United States:

> Europeans have embraced international constitutionalism, according to which the whole point of constitutional law is to check democracy. For Americans, constitutional law cannot merely check democracy. It must *answer* to democracy—have its source and basis in a democratic constitutional politics and always, somehow, be part of politics, even though it [politics] can invalidate the outcomes of the democratic process at any given moment.[29]

CAUSAL ARROW: PERSPECTIVES

Inclusiveness	Restrains national sovereignty	Develops international norms
LIBERAL	REALIST	IDENTITY

Democratic norms	Legitimates institutions	Counters nondemocratic groups
IDENTITY	LIBERAL	REALIST

From the European point of view, law must be inclusive of all cultures and check democratic as well as nondemocratic states. The causal arrow runs from law to democracy. Thus, when the United States acts outside the law of the United Nations, which is the most inclusive and therefore legitimate institution in contemporary world affairs, it breaks the law, as many Europeans believe the United States did in invading Iraq in 2003 without UN approval. From the American view, democratic politics legitimates law. Nondemocratic states cannot make legitimate international law. UN law therefore is not as binding as democratic law, as the U.S. administration argued in 2003. The causal arrow runs from democratic ideas to law.

Both arguments have flaws. The danger in the European view is that nondemocratic groups may dominate and then break the law, as the Nazis did domestically in Germany in the 1930s or Russia did internationally by invading Georgia in 2008. The danger in the American view is that one country, even if democratic such as the United States, may decide that it alone, not a majority of other democratic peoples or countries, makes the law and decides whether the invasion of another country is legitimate or not. Can you see that the difference between these two understandings of international law is a function of the direction of the causal arrow running between law (liberal) and democracy (identity)? Many disagreements in international affairs lie behind these subtle distinctions in the causal relationship of variables, which is why we work so hard to understand and use alternative perspectives in this book.

International Courts

International courts also play an important role in liberal approaches. They address legal grievances that frustrate alienated groups. The Hague Conferences at the turn of the nineteenth century established the Permanent Court of Arbitration, a standing panel of jurists from which disputants could pick a panel to arbitrate their dispute. The League of Nations created the Permanent Court of International Justice, and the United Nations supplanted that court with the **International Court of Justice (ICJ)**. The ICJ is made up of fifteen judges elected by a majority of the UN Security Council and General Assembly. Most recently, the **International Criminal Court (ICC)** made permanent the practice of trying individuals for wartime criminal acts started by the ad hoc tribunals for war crimes in World War II, Yugoslavia, and Rwanda. The ICC, like domestic courts, decides cases brought by civilians as well as by governments, although, unlike domestic courts, it does not have independent police power to enforce its decisions.

The objective from a liberal approach to international affairs is ultimately to domesticate international disputes—to eliminate the role of violence in decision making and subject disputes to the same measures of economic redress and rule of law that apply to domestic disputes. Constitutional orders guaranteeing the rule of law replace balance-of-power politics based on violence.[30] Peaceful diplomacy and courts adjudicate where alliances once did.

The ICJ, also known as the World Court, sits in The Hague, the Netherlands. Its fifteen justices are elected for nine-year terms by majority votes in the UN Security Council (acting without a veto) and General Assembly. It has no powers to force parties to appear before the court or to enforce its decisions. Only states, not individuals or NGOs, can bring cases to the court. States can accept ICJ decisions as compulsory, but when Nicaragua accused the U.S. government in 1984 of mining Nicaragua's harbors, the United States rejected the court's ruling and did not comply with the requirements of compulsory jurisdiction. In fifty-five years, the ICJ considered only 107 cases and made 52 judgments. It issued another 24 advisory opinions. None of these dealt with major issues, although the ICJ helped developing countries resolve a number of border disputes—for example, Cameroon and Nigeria—and issues related to fisheries and continental-shelf jurisdiction.

The most controversial case brought before the World Court perhaps illustrates the institution's limitations. In 2000, Belgium issued an arrest warrant for Abdoulaye Yerodia Ndombasi, a former DR Congo foreign minister accused of inciting genocide against Tutsis in Rwanda in 1998. Belgium relied on a legal principle known as **universal jurisdiction**, the claim that some crimes are so heinous every individual country has a right to prosecute them wherever they may occur. DR Congo contested the case

International Court of Justice (ICJ): the UN's main judicial institution to arbitrate disputes among nations.

International Criminal Court (ICC): a permanent tribunal started in 2002 to prosecute war crimes.

universal jurisdiction: the claim of a single state that it can prosecute perpetrators of war crimes anywhere in the world.

Relatives of a victim of the 2010 postelection crisis in Côte d'Ivoire watch the TV coverage of former president Laurent Gbagbo as he appears before the International Criminal Court in The Hague in February 2013. The ICC will decide whether there is enough evidence to try Gbagbo for masterminding a bloody election standoff in 2011. Gbagbo is the first former head of state to come before the court.

in the World Court and won. The court argued that Belgium had no right to interfere in the sovereign domain of other states.[31] Nevertheless, a number of European countries have such laws, and some threatened to try U.S. officials for prisoner abuses during the Iraq War.[32]

Ad hoc tribunals were created after World War II to deal with war criminals in Germany and Japan. The atrocities committed in Rwanda and former Yugoslavia revived interest in such panels. Today, ad hoc international tribunals try war criminals from these conflicts in The Hague and in Arusha, Tanzania. These tribunals respond to individual, not just state, complaints. But they are criticized because they respond to ad hoc situations and are accused of reflecting "victors' justice" rather "impartial justice."

In 1998, the ICC created a permanent court to replace such ad hoc tribunals. The ICC prosecutes individuals, and states party to the court are required to cooperate with ICC investigations. It considers four types of crimes: genocide (the killing of people because of their race, ethnicity, or religion), crimes against humanity (forcible transfer of populations, torture, enslavement, and murder), war crimes, and crimes of aggression (left undefined). Anyone can bring a case to the ICC. The ICC acts as a court of last resort, however, accepting cases only if national courts prove unwilling or unable to act. As of the end of 2013 the ICC had issued no verdicts but had five suspects under arrest with two trials under way. Some indicted individuals, such as President Omar Bashir of Sudan, who was reelected in 2010, remained at large. The ICC was also pursuing investigations into several other situations, such as recent atrocities in Libya and Mali. Some cases have been resolved when those accused have died in prison, as did Slobodan Milosevic, former president of Serbia.

The United States, China, and India, among others, refused to join the ICC. The United States, reflecting realist concerns, argued that the ICC might prosecute U.S. soldiers, saying that U.S. courts are unwilling to do so. A case in point might be the treatment of prisoners by the U.S. military at the Guantanamo Bay detention camp. The United States, more than any other country, has soldiers deployed around the world to protect international peace and security. Anyone who opposes U.S. actions might bring a case against its soldiers, even its president, before the ICC. The U.S.

supports an amendment making the ICC subject to Security Council veto. Critics say that such a veto is overkill; the chances of rogue prosecutions are minimal. In the meantime, because the ICC has already gone into effect, the United States negotiates so-called Article 98 agreements with other countries, committing them not to send Americans to the ICC for prosecution.[33]

Is prosecution of criminal behavior always conducive to peace? At the domestic level of analysis, we usually answer that question in the affirmative. But in international conflicts, the answer is not always so obvious. Justice is complicated in countries that are transitioning from civil war to peace. Some participants regard postconflict tribunals as "victors' justice." Reconciliation may be promoted, they argue, if past leaders are not openly tried and prosecuted. After its revolution against apartheid, for example, South Africa decided not to prosecute individuals responsible for the racist policies of the apartheid government. Instead it celebrated the heroic actions of the new leaders and government, especially its first president, Nelson Mandela. On the other hand, other countries have decided that they cannot clear the decks for future peace until they settle accounts for past atrocities. The ad hoc tribunal for Rwanda, for example, is engaged in such an effort. It has completed fifty trials and convicted twenty-nine defendants, and the trials of eleven more are ongoing.

CAUSAL ARROW: PERSPECTIVES

| Help or hinder reconciliation? | Punish atrocities | Tribunals |
| IDENTITY | REALIST | LIBERAL |

>>> International Economic Institutions

Liberal perspectives strongly promote world trade and economic development. Wealth, although not a pure collective good because growth can be distributed unequally, is nevertheless a prerequisite of greater economic justice and political opportunity. The United Nations, through its Economic and Social Council, nominally superintends the global economic institutions, but the three main international economic institutions—the International Monetary Fund, World Bank, and World Trade Organization—are for all practical purposes independent of the UN system. They are sometimes called the Bretton Woods institutions because of their association with the postwar conference in Bretton Woods, New Hampshire, in 1944 that founded them.

Economic and Social Council

The UN General Assembly plays a general oversight role in the economic and social area. It operates through six committees of the whole (in which all members participate): disarmament, economic, humanitarian, decolonization, budget, and legal.

The Second Committee, dealing with economics, oversees ECOSOC, the UN's principal economic organ. ECOSOC has fifty-four members elected on the basis of geographic representation to three-year terms by the General Assembly. It usually includes the veto powers. ECOSOC oversees a bewildering array of specialized agencies and commissions. First come seventeen specialized UN agencies, including the World Health

Organization, the Food and Agriculture Organization, the IAEA, and the Bretton Woods institutions. Then come the ten functional commissions—the Commissions for Social Development, Human Rights, Status of Women, Sustainable Development, Population and Development, and so on. There are also regional commissions for economic affairs—Europe, Asia, Latin America, and Africa. The UN Economic Commission for Latin America (ECLA) led the opposition against free-market policies to create the UN Conference on Trade and Development (UNCTAD) in 1964. In UNCTAD, developing countries formed the Group of 77, or G-77 (now actually 131 countries), to lobby for a "new international economic order" (NIEO) to replace the Bretton Woods system. Still further UN programs and funds exist, such as the UN Environment Programme (UNEP) and the World Food Programme (WFP).

Even if it had the power, ECOSOC could not oversee such a sprawling bureaucracy—and it has few powers. It can only issue recommendations and receive reports. It has no control over agencies' budgets or secretariats. For years, some members, especially the United States, which pays the largest share of the UN budget, complained about UN expenditures. The United States withdrew from the UN Educational, Scientific and Cultural Organization (UNESCO) in 1984 because of corruption and withheld funding from the UN general budget. In this case, Washington was sharply criticized for impeding UN activities. But the United States argued that there was no other way to enforce accountability.

International Monetary Fund

In 2013, the IMF had 188 member countries. Each country has a representative on the Board of Governors, usually the minister of finance or central bank chairman. The board meets once a year but is too unwieldy to exercise daily control. It designates policy overview to the International Monetary and Finance Committee (IMFC). The IMFC consists of twenty-four governors, five from the top contributing countries (the G-5: the United States, Japan, Germany, France, and the United Kingdom) and nineteen from various geographic groups of countries. The IMFC meets twice a year and delegates daily responsibility to the Executive Board. The Executive Board directors are assigned to permanent duty at IMF headquarters in Washington, D.C. The IMF staff totals about 2,400 civil servants, led by a managing director and three deputy managing directors. By convention, the European members select the managing director, although that could change as members seek more equitable representation for developing countries.

IMF quota: the share of money that each country provides to the International Monetary Fund for lending, which determines its voting power.

Voting in the IMF is based on quotas, and quotas in turn are based on countries' economic power, including gross domestic product (GDP), current account transactions, and official reserves. An **IMF quota** represents the maximum amount of money a country provides to the IMF for lending to correct balance-of-payments problems. When a country enters the IMF, it pays 25 percent of this quota in SDRs (the international paper currency that has been issued in small amounts) or a major currency such as the dollar, the yen, or the euro. It pays the remaining 75 percent in its own currency. IMF resources totaled $477 billion in early 2011.

Not surprisingly, the United States has the largest vote, 16.5 percent (slightly less than its quota of 17.4 percent because all countries start with a base of 250 votes). The G-5 countries have 37.98 percent of the vote, and the G-7 countries (adding Canada and Italy) have 41.2 percent of the vote. Since the G-5 countries are the only permanent members on the Executive Board (the other nineteen countries share representatives), the IMF is essentially run by the major financial countries. They provide the bulk of the financial resources, and they call most of the shots.

IMF quotas are recalculated every five years. Increasing and redistributing quotas are controversial steps that require an 85 percent majority vote. Notice that the United States can block a quota increase or reform. The last two reviews in 2003 and 2008 did not increase the quotas. The IMF needs fewer resources because it plays a smaller role in funding current account deficits; today, commercial banks and other private institutions do most of the financing. The U.S. quota has declined as its relative share of global wealth has declined. When fully implemented, the quota review in 2008 gives China the third-largest quota and places the BRIC countries (Brazil, Russia, India, and China) among the top ten shareholders.

The principal task of the IMF is to encourage sound domestic economic policies to support global growth and economic stability. The IMF conducts annual surveillance studies of member countries' policies, discusses these studies with the authorities in each country, and provides technical assistance to improve fiscal, monetary, exchange rate, banking, and statistical capabilities. If a country requires balance-of-payments assistance, the IMF lends the country money, but it does so on the condition that the country alter its policies to correct its balance-of-payments deficit (for example, by cutting fiscal deficits to reduce domestic demand and hence foreign imports). This conditionality is the most controversial aspect of IMF activities. An international organization run by the major powers, in effect, dictates domestic policies for countries running balance-of-payments deficits. What is worse, the United States, although a deficit country, never has to borrow from the IMF because it can always print dollars to pay its current account deficits. Other countries are willing to hold those dollars and, in effect, lend them back to the United States, as long as these countries have confidence that the U.S. economy is strong and they can invest these dollars in bonds or other U.S. assets. On a few occasions in the past, when the United States ran short of foreign exchange reserves in other currencies, it arranged financing with other countries outside the IMF. Although the IMF criticizes U.S. policies, it has no leverage over U.S. policies through lending, as it does with developing countries.

CAUSAL ARROW: LEVELS OF ANALYSIS

Undercuts local leaders' responsibilities	Dictates national economic policy	IMF conditionality
INDIVIDUAL	**DOMESTIC**	**SYSTEMIC**

Critics charge that IMF policies serve primarily the interests of advanced countries. Like bankers, the G-7 or the G-10 countries (actually eleven countries, adding Belgium, the Netherlands, Sweden, and Switzerland to the G-7) care most about getting their money back. IMF conditionality squeezes developing countries to pay debts, which reduces the resources available for domestic growth. For the first time in 1995, the IMF and

World Bank set up a program to reduce the debts of the heavily indebted poor countries (HIPCs). The HIPC program targeted thirty-nine deeply distressed developing countries for debt relief. As of 2013, thirty-five countries, twenty-nine of them in Africa, had received debt relief totaling $75 billion, and another four were under consideration for candidacy. In 2005, the G-8 countries supplemented the HIPC program with the Multilateral Debt Relief Initiative (MDRI). MDRI cancels 100 percent of the debt owed to multilateral institutions, such as the IMF and the World Bank, as countries fulfill their obligations under the HIPC program.

In 1999, the G-7 began holding a larger meeting involving some developing countries. Known as the G-20, this meeting included key developing countries such as China, India, Indonesia, Brazil, Mexico, Argentina, Turkey, South Korea, South Africa, and Saudi Arabia, as well as Russia, Australia, and the EU. The G-20 assumed center stage during the global financial crisis in 2008–2009, reflecting the greater equality of wealth and power generated by globalization. Although the G-7 and G-20 meet separately, they provide in parallel a better balance of influence between advanced and developing countries in global economic decision making. Still, these great power groups have no formal authority, unlike the IMF.

Whatever its faults, the IMF has nurtured phenomenal growth in developing countries since 1945. The Asian tigers benefited from IMF programs, and despite criticism of the IMF during the Asian financial crisis of the 1990s, many stricken countries (for example, South Korea and Thailand) bounced back quickly from that crisis. The IMF was particularly effective in guiding India through a balance-of-payments crisis in the early 1990s and helping that country make a historic turn toward more open and market-oriented policies. The result is that India, along with China, has joined the world economy, and these two countries (with more than a third of the world's population) are now among the fastest-growing economies in the world. After the financial crisis of 2008–2009, the developing countries recovered quickly and in 2013 were growing more than twice as fast as advanced countries.

World Bank

The International Bank for Reconstruction and Development (IBRD), or World Bank, is the main global institution for promoting development and alleviating poverty. It is part of the World Bank Group, along with four other associated institutions: the International Development Association (IDA), the International Finance Corporation (IFC), the Multilateral Investment Guarantee Agency (MIGA), and the International Centre for Settlement of Investment Disputes (ICSID). While the World Bank makes loans to middle-income countries (some $21 billion in 2013), IDA focuses on the world's eighty-two poorest countries (loans of $16.3 billion in 2013). IFC invests in private enterprises in developing countries. MIGA guarantees foreign direct investment in developing countries against noncommercial or political risks, such as expropriation or war. ICSID helps to settle foreign investment disputes and thus encourages private investment.

In 2013, the World Bank, like the IMF, had 188 member countries; a country has to be a member of the IMF to join the World Bank. The Bank is run by a structure similar to the IMF, with a Board of Governors and a Board of Executive Directors. Eight countries have permanent representatives on the Board of Executive Directors (China, Russia, and Saudi Arabia in addition to the G-5). Bank voting is based on the size of a country's economy. Again, the United States has the largest share of votes—about 16 percent; the G-5 countries control 37 percent, and the G-7 countries 43 percent. Changes in 2010 gave China the third-largest share at 4.4 percent, behind the United States and Japan. The Bank has more than ten thousand employees and is run by a president traditionally selected by the United States.

A fishmonger uses battery-powered portable lamps as she waits for customers at a night market in Yangon, Myanmar, in September 2013. The World Bank recently approved aid for a power plant project in Myanmar aimed at boosting electricity production in one of Asia's poorest countries.

Members pay an initial subscription to the World Bank just as in the IMF. IDA increases subscriptions (called replenishments) every four years. But the World Bank itself, unlike the IMF, raises most of its money by selling World Bank bonds on private financial markets. Because governments back World Bank bonds, these bonds have the highest security rating and therefore sell at a higher price or lower interest rate. The World Bank passes on these lower interest rates to developing countries. If the latter were to borrow directly from private financial markets, they would have to price their bonds at lower levels and pay much higher interest rates.

The World Bank and the IDA make loans for development purposes, from infrastructure projects (dams, roads, ports, and so on) to basic human needs (food, health, education, housing, and so on) to sustainable energy and environmental programs. In 2013, the World Bank was involved in some eighteen hundred projects across virtually all developing countries. The projects included providing microcredit in Bosnia and Herzegovina, raising AIDS-prevention awareness in Guinea, supporting the education of girls in Bangladesh, improving health care delivery in Mexico, and helping East Timor and India rebuild after civil strife and natural disasters. Increasingly World Bank programs have focused on the needs of the poorest people around the world, some 1.2 billion people living on less than $1 per day.

The World Bank faces fewer criticisms of the sort that plague the IMF because it is explicitly focused on poverty. Nevertheless, World Bank projects are faulted for catering to large-scale rather than micro projects (which benefit the poor more directly); for tolerating, even facilitating, corruption; for being ineffectively coordinated; for damaging the environment; and for ultimately failing to reduce inequality. The Bank is also criticized for having a bloated and overpaid staff. World Bank officials travel around the world in comfortable style and earn relatively high bankers' salaries that are exempt from income tax in the United States, where the Bank's headquarters are located. As Table 6-4 shows, while the World Bank's lending has gone down dramatically since the financial crisis of 2008–2009, the institution's administrative expenditures have increased. Does that mean that big bureaucracies are not always the best solutions for encouraging growth or better governance?

TABLE
6-4

Lending and Spending: World Bank Expenditures (in $US millions)

	Lending commitments	Administrative expenses
2009	32,911	1,441
2010	44,197	1,589
2011	26,737	1,564
2012	20,582	1,631
2013	15,249	1,761

Source: World Bank, Finances, "Financial Results," http://web.worldbank.org/WBSITE/EXTERNAL/EXTA
BOUTUS/0,,contentMDK:22669594~menuPK:8336873~pagePK:51123644~piPK:329829~theSite
PK:29708,00.html.

World Trade Organization

The International Trade Organization (ITO) was originally proposed in 1945. But unlike the IMF and World Bank, it was not approved, in part because of the U.S. Congress's objection to the inclusion of agriculture. As a result, only the section of the ITO that dealt with manufacturing trade was put into effect. Known as the General Agreement on Tariffs and Trade (GATT), this institution was the smallest and perhaps most effective of the Bretton Woods institutions (suggesting smaller bureaucracies may be better than big ones?). The GATT led six major rounds of multilateral trade negotiations, reducing tariffs and other barriers to trade and opening up the vast global markets that dominate the world economy today. The last round was the Uruguay Round of trade negotiations, initiated in 1986 and implemented in 1994. It not only expanded trade liberalization beyond manufacturing products to include agriculture, investment, and services but also established the more comprehensive World Trade Organization, which acquired limited powers to overrule national laws and compel offending countries to change their laws or pay penalties and make compensation to offended countries. The United States, Canada, and Mexico also signed NAFTA, taking a first step toward the regional integration of markets in North America. China and Mexico became members of the WTO, and the global community accelerated the provision of technical assistance, foreign aid, and investment capital to the developing world.

The WTO had 159 members in 2013 (GATT started with 23) governed by the Ministerial Conference, which meets at least once every two years. Below the Ministerial Conference is the General Council, which meets several times a year at the headquarters in Geneva, Switzerland. The General Council also meets as the Trade Policy Review Body to critique the trade policies of member countries and as the Dispute Settlement Body to resolve trade disputes. Below the General Council are councils for trade in goods (essentially the updated GATT), services (governed by the General Agreement on Trade in Services, or GATS), and intellectual property (governed by the agreement on trade-related intellectual property issues, or TRIPs). (GATS and TRIPS came out of the conclusion of the Uruguay Round in 1994.) WTO still has the smallest bureaucracy of all the original Bretton Woods institutions, with around 640 personnel. A director-general selected by consensus leads the organization. The director-general in 2013, like most recent directors, came from a developing country (Brazil), suggesting the growing importance of emerging nations such as Brazil, India, China, South Africa, and Indonesia in global markets.

The WTO, unlike the IMF and World Bank, operates on the basis of one country, one vote, not a quota system based on country size or, in this case, share of world trade. Voting is by consensus, which makes WTO politics more equitable but also more cumbersome than that of the IMF or World Bank. In the case of expert panels to resolve trade disputes, however, the consensus rule has been modified. Under the GATT, one government could block a decision by a dispute panel indefinitely; a consensus was needed to approve a panel decision. Under the WTO, a consensus is needed to block a decision. Thus, one country, particularly the country on the losing end of a panel decision, cannot thwart the entire dispute-settlement procedure. An appeals process has been instituted whereby a losing country can challenge a decision on legal grounds, but once the appeals process is completed, the panel decision has to be implemented. The losing government has three choices: change its offending law, compensate the winning country through mutually agreed trade concessions in some other area, or accept retaliation or imposition of equivalent trade barriers by the winning country.

These WTO dispute-settlement provisions are very controversial. For the first time, an international institution can enforce a decision against an advanced country and specifically against the United States. Many members of Congress objected when the process was instituted. But notice that the WTO cannot force the United States to change its laws. The United States has two other choices. In practice, however, the United States usually changes its laws to comply. It did so in a famous case (well, OK, not so famous

that you would have heard about it) when the WTO rejected U.S. legislation that allowed U.S. firms to set up export companies in the Caribbean to avoid federal taxes. Overall, the WTO dispute-settlement process has worked well. The WTO settled some three hundred cases in its first eight years, while the GATT settled three hundred in its entire lifetime.

⟫⟫ Regional Institutions

regional organizations: organizations whose members come from and are limited to specific geographic regions of the world.

The state, subnational, and transnational NGOs and the IGOs compete for the institutional loyalty of actors in international affairs. Increasingly, so do **regional organizations**. Regionalism, in fact, may be, according to some scholars, a stronger force in contemporary international affairs than nationalism (states), fragmentation (NGOs), or globalization (IGOs).[34] Regional organizations have proliferated. During the Cold War, many regional organizations took the form of alliances: NATO, the Western European Union (WEU), the Warsaw Pact, the Rio Pact, the Central Treaty Organization (CENTO, in the Middle East), and SEATO (in Southeast Asia). Others were more economic in nature: the European Common Market (now the EU), the Council for Mutual Economic Assistance (COMECON, in the Soviet economic bloc), the Latin American Free Trade Agreement (LAFTA—now the Latin American Integration Association, or LAIA), the Association of Southeast Asian Nations (ASEAN), and the Central American and Andean Common Markets. Still others constituted regional diplomatic organizations—the Organization of American States (OAS), the CSCE (now the OSCE), and the Organization of African Unity (now the African Union)—or politically inspired institutions, such as the Council of Europe, with its promotion of human rights and democracy in Europe. In the past decade or so, further regional organizations have sprouted, especially in trade and financial relations: NAFTA, Asia-Pacific Economic Cooperation (APEC), the Central American Free Trade Agreement (CAFTA), and various versions of ASEAN, such as ASEAN plus 3 (which adds China, Japan, and South Korea) and plus 6 (which adds Australia, New Zealand, and India). (Table 6-5 presents a summary of current membership in key regional organizations.)

Regional Integration

No regional organization has achieved greater significance in contemporary international affairs than the EU. How did this happen, and what can the case of the EU tell us about how and what kind of new actors might emerge in the world system in the future? The EU built on two ideas: the functionalist thinking of English scholar David Mitrany that working on functional activities such as food and health will not only solve problems but also make political considerations less relevant, and the logic of neofunctionalism that cooperation changes political loyalties themselves.[35] As regional institutions succeed, participants will shift their loyalties (identities) from state institutions to higher-level supranational institutions. This will happen through a combination of institutional processes such as spillover, as envisioned by the liberal perspective, and creative leadership, as envisioned by identity perspectives. Spillover involves path

TABLE
6-5

Membership in Key Regional Organizations

African Union	ASEAN	APEC	European Union	LAIA	NATO
Algeria	Brunei Darussalam	Australia	Austria	Argentina	Albania
Angola	Cambodia	Brunei Darussalam	Belgium	Bolivia	Belgium
Benin	Indonesia	Canada	Bulgaria	Brazil	Bulgaria
Botswana	Laos	Chile	Croatia	Chile	Canada
Burkina Faso	Malaysia	China	Cyprus	Colombia	Croatia
Burundi	Myanmar	Hong Kong	Czech Republic	Cuba	Czech Republic
Cameroon	Philippines	Indonesia	Denmark	Ecuador	Demark
Cape Verde	Singapore	Japan	Estonia	Mexico	Estonia
Central African	Thailand	Korea	Finland	Paraguay	France
Republic[a]	Vietnam	Malaysia	France	Panama	Germany
Chad		Mexico	Germany	Peru	Greece
Comoros		New Zealand	Greece	Uruguay	Hungary
Congo-Brazzaville		Papua New Guinea	Hungary	Venezuela	Iceland
Côte d'Ivoire		Peru	Iceland[b]		Italy
Democratic		Philippines	Ireland		Latvia
Republic of		Russia	Italy		Lithuania
the Congo		Singapore	Latvia		Luxembourg
Djibouti		Taipei	Lithuania		Netherlands
Egypt[a]		Thailand	Luxembourg		Norway
Equatorial Guinea		United States	Malta		Poland
Eritrea			Montenegro[b]		Portugal
Ethiopia			Netherlands		Romania
Gabon			Poland		Slovakia
Gambia			Portugal		Slovenia
Ghana			Romania		Spain
Guinea			Serbia[b]		Turkey
Guinea-Bissau[a]			Slovakia		United Kingdom
Kenya			Slovenia		United States
Lesotho			Spain		
Liberia			Sweden		
Libya			Turkey[b]		
Madagascar[a]			Former Yugoslav		
Malawi			republic of		
Mali			Macedonia[b]		
Mauritania			United Kingdom		
Mauritius					
Morocco[a]					
Mozambique					
Namibia					
Niger					
Nigeria					
Rwanda					
Sahrawi Republic					
(Western					
Sahara)					
São Tomé and					
Príncipe					
Senegal					
Seychelles					
Sierra Leone					
Somalia					
South Africa					
South Sudan					
Sudan					
Swaziland					
Tanzania					
Togo					
Tunisia					
Uganda					
Zambia					
Zimbabwe					

a. Membership suspended or withdrawn.
b. Candidate.

dependence, resolving one common problem that leads to the need to resolve additional ones. Thus, establishing a common market, which the European Community did in 1958 by reducing internal tariffs, created additional needs to reduce nontariff barriers (such as differing regulations) and eventually unify national currencies, which the EC did in the late 1980s and early 1990s. Creative leadership means establishing **supranational institutions**, such as the European Commission, that initiate proposals from the standpoint of common rather than national interests, compelling national governments to reassess their separate interests and upgrade or integrate them at a higher level. As time went on and more issues were subjected to this process, member states identified more and more with the supranational authorities rather than their national authorities.

supranational institutions: institutions above the level of the state, like the European Commission, that are motivated by common, rather than state-specific, goals.

The focus on regional integration and spillover was eventually absorbed by interdependence and globalization studies.[36] Interdependence studies put more emphasis on the increasing number of horizontal interactions among global actors than on the vertical and loyalty-shifting character of regional institutions such as the European Union. In terms of our perspectives, we might say that liberal factors, which emphasize repetitive interactions, became more important than identity factors, which emphasize ideas and the construction of new political identities. Indeed, interdependence studies became known as neoliberal approaches because they focus almost exclusively on institutions, not on values or identities as in earlier classical liberal approaches. Nevertheless, Europe continued to integrate, even debating the idea of a European constitution. Such a constitution, although still disputed, would define a common political identity at the European, rather than national, level (see more in the following discussion).

CAUSAL ARROW: PERSPECTIVES

Supranational institutions and spillover	Reduce focus on separate national interests	Shift state-based identities to regional institutions
LIBERAL	REALIST	IDENTITY

CAUSAL ARROW: LEVELS OF ANALYSIS

Global interdependence	De-emphasizes supranational identities	Emphasizes national sovereignty
SYSTEMIC	REGIONAL	DOMESTIC

Other regions also cultivate regional institutions. The Organization of African States changed its name to the African Union to mimic the EU and put greater emphasis on a common African identity. The Asian states talk about regional relationships not just in terms of efficiency, as liberal perspectives emphasize, but also in terms of Asian values, or what became known as "the Asian Way," as identity perspectives emphasize.

Most regional integration studies adopt rationalist rather than constructivist methods. They hypothesize that creative institutional leadership by actors such as the European Commission *causes* the shift of political loyalties to supranational institutions. Social constructivist studies too are concerned with how political identities change, but they pay little attention to regional integration studies, drawing their inspiration more from sociological than political science studies. Why, we may ask? One reason may be that social constructivist studies employ constructivist, not rationalist, methods. They see identities as *constituting*, rather than causing, events and are more interested in cumulative verbal discourses than in novel institutional devices such as the supranational European Commission. Here is an example of how studies of international relations differ because they adopt different methodological approaches.

Let's look more closely at European integration, which represents one of the most significant developments in post–World War II international relations. The case of the European Union can sensitize us to the interplay of states (power), institutions, and ideas as the international system changes in the future.

European Union

The **European Union** began as a functional activity inspired by postwar leaders in Europe who were determined to end European wars. Jean Monnet, a French economist, was the principal architect of postwar European integration. He envisioned a process that would integrate the coal and steel sectors of France and Germany, taking a vital war-making industry out of the hands of nationalist rivals. As functionalist theory predicts, once these sectors were removed from rival state institutions, political divisions would recede. Monnet convinced Robert Schuman, then French foreign minister, to adopt this idea. In 1951, Schuman proposed the ECSC. As discussed in Chapter 4, the ECSC inspired further integration plans—a proposed European Defense and Political Community (EDPC), which ultimately failed, and the European Atomic Energy Community and European Economic Community, or Common Market, which subsequently succeeded. The EDPC used a direct intergovernmental approach to integrate state interests. It was clearly premature. Wartime adversaries such as France and Germany were not ready to integrate their defense capabilities. But the neofunctional approach used by the ECSC concentrated primarily on economic interests and worked better. Euratom, the EEC, and the ECSC attacked separate but interrelated functional activities under a common legal framework established by the Treaties of Rome. Most important, the Treaties of Rome framework created the supranational leadership organs known as commissions that were given exclusive rights to initiate legislation. This arrangement put community-minded officials in charge of designing policies that integrated and went beyond national interests, pushing separate nation-states toward common solutions.

Spillover. The Common Market succeeded spectacularly by creating a common industrial market, which reduced internal tariffs to zero and established unified external tariffs, and a Common Agricultural Policy (CAP), which subsidized and protected European farmers. In 1967, in a further demonstration of spillover, the commissions of the three communities merged to form the single Commission of the European Communities (EC, no longer EEC). And starting in 1973, the EC expanded six times to include by 2013 a total of twenty-eight members.

The EC also deepened as well as widened. Once tariffs were reduced to zero, different internal regulations became the principal barriers to trade. In a classic example of spillover, the establishment of a common market solved one problem (tariffs at the border) but in the process exposed another (regulations that restricted trade internally). Notice here the work of path dependence emphasized by liberal perspectives. Thus, starting in 1987, the Single Market Act reduced regulatory barriers and converted the Common Market into an economic union, a market with no internal tariff barriers and common nontariff regulations. One means of lowering and integrating

European Union: a supranational organization that in 1993 superseded the European Communities and now unites European democracies in specific policy areas.

mutual recognition: a way of reconciling different regulatory standards across nations by requiring that product standards accepted in one country be recognized by all participants.

internal regulations was the principle of **mutual recognition**, which provided that a product standard applied in one country—say for automobile safety glass—would be recognized in all countries. A second method called on member countries to adopt minimal standards in some areas, such as in pollution controls, that all countries had to meet but then allowed countries to go beyond those standards if they wished. Finally, in a third method, members harmonized regulations, adopting a single standard for all countries. With the regulatory barriers significantly reduced, the EC took the unprecedented step in 1992 of moving toward a monetary union. The cost of exchanging currencies had now become the biggest obstacle to trade. Once again, spillover required widening the EC's jurisdiction. The Maastricht Treaty created the Economic and Monetary Union (EMU) and set in motion the adoption of a single currency, the euro, which was introduced in 1999.

The Maastricht Treaty also created two additional pillars of cooperation, the Common Foreign and Security Policy (CFSP) and common policies on justice and home affairs, and merged them with the EC to form the European Union. The new pillars continued to make decisions through traditional intergovernmental mechanisms rather than supranational authority. But forty years after the failure of the EDPC, foreign policy and domestic law were brought under the umbrella of the new EU, setting the stage for potentially full integration in the future.[37]

Structure of the European Union. EU institutions consist of the Commission, the Council of the European Union, the European Parliament, and the European Court of Justice; the European Central Bank (ECB) is the most important specialized institution. The Council, Commission, and Parliament meet in Brussels, although the Parliament also meets in Luxembourg and Strasbourg (France). The Court of Justice sits in Luxembourg. The ECB has its headquarters in Frankfurt, Germany.

European Commission: the organ of the European Union that has the exclusive authority to initiate legislation and pursue the goals of an ever-closer union.

The **European Commission** is the unique organ of the EU. A supranational body, it has the exclusive authority to initiate legislation and pursue the goals of an ever-closer union. It provides (although not always) the creative leadership envisioned by neofunctionalism. In areas where policies have been integrated, such as trade in goods, the Commission represents the EU. Nonmember countries, such as the United States, negotiate with the Commission, not individual EU member states. In 2013, the Commission had twenty-eight commissioners, one from each member state. Member states select the president of the Commission, who then, in consultation with member states, chooses the other commissioners. Notice that Parliament does not select the Commission, let alone establish the government, which includes the European Council (see the following discussion); in this sense, the European Union is not a parliamentary democracy. But Parliament interviews each commissioner and then votes on whether to approve the Commission as a whole, not individual commissioners. The Commission serves for five years coincident with elections for the European Parliament. The Parliament can dismiss the entire Commission by adopting a vote of censure. Although it has never done so, the threat to do so in 1999 led a scandal-ridden Commission to resign. Some 23,000 civil servants work in the Commission bureaucracy.

FIGURE 6-4

The European Union: Key Institutions

European Court of Justice	**European Central Bank**	**European Council (summit)**
One judge for each member state Interprets and enforces EC treaties and laws	Controls money supply and sets interest rates for the EU	Convenes meetings of prime ministers and presidents up to four times annually

European Parliament	**European Commission**	**Council of the European Union (The Council)**
Legislative body of the EU Directly elected members	Initiates legislation Leadership of EU Commissioners come from member states	Assembly body that represents member states One minister from each member state

Member states

The **Council of the European Union** represents the member states. One minister from each state attends Council meetings. The subject matter of a meeting determines which specific ministers are present—that is, agricultural ministers deal with agriculture, finance ministers with finance, and so on. Up to four times a year, the prime ministers and/or presidents of the member states come together in summit meetings called the **European Council**. Summit meetings deal with overall issues that cut across ministers' jurisdictions and resolve issues that are blocked at lower levels. Under the Treaty of Lisbon, which went into effect in December 2009 (see later in the chapter), the president of the Council rotates every six months among the member states. The Council has its own secretariat, known as the Committee of Permanent Representatives, which often competes with the Commission bureaucracy.

The Council is both an intergovernmental and a supranational body. It represents national governments as an IGO but acts as a supranational body in the context of European treaties. Someday, for example, it might become something akin to the senate of a United States of Europe, representing the separate nation-states of Europe just as the U.S. Senate represents the fifty states of the United States. One major supranational feature of the Council is **qualified majority voting (QMV)**. On some, not all, issues, decisions are made by a majority vote, not by consensus or veto. Member states vote both individually and on the basis of a certain number of votes allocated to each state. Currently, QMV requires a majority of member states (14 out of 28), 74 percent of

Council of the European Union: the assembly that brings together the member states of the European Union.

European Council: summit meetings of the Council of the European Union, involving heads of state and government, that deal with crosscutting and controversial issues.

qualified majority voting (QMV): the principle that decisions by international organizations are made by weighted majority votes, as in the European Union today.

allocated votes (255 out of 345), and at least 62 percent of the EU's total population; these allocations will shift again in 2014 and 2017. The system is complex to make it impossible for big countries to act alone or to block decisions by a majority of other countries.

European Parliament: the only directly elected institution in the European Union.

The only directly elected institution in the EU is the **European Parliament**. It currently has 766 members, although the allocation of seats across EU countries will change with elections in 2014. Members are elected every five years by Europe-wide elections. Seats are not apportioned by population, as they are, for example, in the U.S. House of Representatives. A member from a small state represents a smaller number of people than does a member from a large state. Representatives do not sit in Parliament in national groups but in seven Europe-wide political groups, the principal ones being the conservative European People's Party and European Democrats (EPP-ED), the liberal Party of European Socialists (PES), and a smaller centrist group known as the Alliance of Liberals and Democrats for Europe (ALDE).

democratic deficit: the criticism made of the European Union that it is not directly accountable to the people it represents.

The Parliament has gained wider powers since it was first elected directly in 1979, but its powers still pale in comparison to those of national parliaments. It cannot initiate legislation, and it approves the budget and other legislation only by co-decision with the Council. It is the weakest institution in the EU, and this fact has given rise to the debate in the EU about the **democratic deficit**, a criticism that points to a gap between EU institutions and the people they represent. The Council and Commission, for example, are not elected by the people but are appointed by national governments. And the Parliament, which is elected by the people, can dismiss the Commission as a whole but not reestablish it. Nor can the Parliament seat or dismiss the European Council. Thus, the most powerful common institutions in Brussels operate once removed from the scrutiny of the people, who elect their own governments but not the principal EU leaders. And the EU Parliament is too weak to fully compensate for this gap.

European Court of Justice (ECJ): the judicial body that has the power to interpret and enforce European Union treaties and law.

The **European Court of Justice (ECJ)** has the power to interpret and enforce EU treaties and law. It consists of one judge from each of the twenty-eight member states, but it usually sits in a "grand chamber" of thirteen judges or sometimes in smaller chambers of only three to five judges. It decides on the constitutionality of EU law, offers advisory opinions, and adjudicates disputes not only among EU members and institutions but also between individuals or corporations (NGOs) and the EU. In the latter function, the ECJ goes beyond traditional international courts. Like the European Court of Human Rights under the Council of Europe (see Chapter 7), the ECJ recognizes a right of **individual standing**, which allows individuals to bring cases before the court and thus conveys a sense of European identity or citizenship to the European people independent of national governments.

individual standing: the right of civilians, as well as states, to bring cases before a court, uncommon in international law until recently.

The ECJ superintends the mammoth body of EU law known as the *acquis communautaire*, which new members must accept when they enter the EU. At the last count, since 1952 the ECJ has heard more than 15,000 cases and rendered 26,800 judgments. When we compare that to the ICJ, which has considered only several hundred cases in recent years, we see why some students of international affairs are more impressed by regional organizations than by international ones. Some of the ECJ's most notable rulings include banning the placement of any limit on the number of players from other EU countries that can play on a national soccer team (in other words, all of Germany's national team might, theoretically, come from other EU countries) and declaring parts of the German constitution illegal because they banned women from participating in military combat activities.

The **European Central Bank (ECB)** is one of the most powerful EU institutions, even though only eighteen (Latvia joined in 2014) of the twenty-eight members of the EU currently belong to it; those are the members that use the euro currency. We notice the effect of the ECB immediately when we travel in Europe. There are no more German marks or French francs—these have been replaced by the euro in those countries. But since the United Kingdom still uses pounds and controls its own currency, it does not belong to the ECB. The ECB is run by an executive board consisting of the president, vice president, and four other members, all appointed for eight-year nonrenewable terms by agreement among the presidents and prime ministers of the participating member states. The Governing Council of the ECB, which consists of the executive board and the governors of the seventeen participating central banks, controls the money supply and sets short-term interest rates. The ECB acts independently. It can neither ask for nor accept instructions from any other EU or national body. Yet it controls one of the key levers determining the fate of the national and ultimately the European economies.

We can understand why this institution is both so remarkable and controversial. Member states gave up control of their money supply, a critical instrument of national economic sovereignty, when they created the ECB. And they did so without the usual checks and balances of a strong parliament or fully unified political system in Brussels. In the United States, for example, the Federal Reserve not only acts independently, but it also reports regularly to a very powerful and watchful Congress and consults closely with the Treasury Department on other aspects of economic policy, such as fiscal policy, which the Federal Reserve does not control. The ECB also reports to the European Parliament, but the Parliament, remember, is much weaker than the U.S. Congress. And the ECB consults with finance and economic ministers from the eighteen ECB countries, but the EU has not agreed on a common fiscal policy. In 1997, the European Council adopted the Stability and Growth Pact, which committed member states to keep fiscal deficits below 3 percent of GDP and total national debt below 60 percent. In 2005, however, Germany, France, Portugal, Italy, Greece, and the Netherlands—half of the ECB members at the time—were in violation of one or both limits. In 2010, when the ECB bailed out Greece, Greece's budget deficit and national debt were double the allowed percentages of GDP. Ireland, too, received emergency loans in 2010, as did Portugal and Spain in 2011–2012, two much larger countries with more serious consequences for European economies.

If member states fail to control fiscal deficits, the ECB is left with two choices. It can loosen the money supply to accommodate these deficits, which risks inflation because loose money and loose fiscal policy create more demand for goods than the available

European Central Bank (ECB): the banking institution whose Governing Council controls the money supply and sets short-term interest rates for the European Union.

supply of goods, or it can ignore the deficits and pursue a sound monetary policy, which risks growth because the combination of tight money and loose fiscal policy (government demand for borrowing) raises interest rates and slows growth. The European debt crisis divided member states. Germany and other northern European states wanted ECB loans to include conditions about tighter fiscal constraints, but the indebted countries, mostly in the south, faced street riots from citizens protesting budget cuts and preferred a looser monetary policy. The ECB, we could say, is swimming in uncharted waters (more on this in Chapter 8).

European constitution: a 2004 European Union document, not yet ratified, that significantly increased the extent of European unity.

European Constitution. In 2002, the EU countries held a convention to draft a **European constitution**. The integrating states of Europe were facing a challenge comparable to that in the United States of America in 1787. With enlargement and monetary union, Europe had become so complex it needed a political and, indeed, constitutional overhaul. This constitutional facelift could be seen as another major instance of spillover from economic and monetary to political affairs. The convention, chaired by former French president Valéry Giscard d'Estaing, presented a far-reaching document to an Intergovernmental Conference (IGC) of the European Union. In June 2004, the IGC adopted a somewhat less ambitious yet still substantial document. However, the IGC-approved constitution required ratification by all member states before it could go into effect. In the summer of 2005, popular referenda in France and the Netherlands rejected the constitution. Although the reasons were many and related to local as well as European politics, some wondered if the process of European integration had peaked.

CAUSAL ARROW: PERSPECTIVES

Revival of national sovereignty	Defeated ratification of constitution	Weakened European supranationalism
REALIST	LIBERAL	IDENTITY

Realist observers saw a revival of national sovereignty. Liberal proponents stressed the need for more coherent institutions. And identity perspectives blamed the democratic deficit. The debate demonstrated, again, the influence of perspectives on judgments about institutional movements such as the European Union.

Lisbon Treaty: a 2009 treaty that implements many of the provisions of the unratified European constitution by intergovernmental agreement.

The Lisbon Treaty. After two years of weighing how to proceed, European governments decided to move ahead without popular support, risking further backlash over the democratic deficit. In December 2007, they signed the **Lisbon Treaty**, which implements many of the provisions of the constitution by intergovernmental agreement. Only parliaments have to ratify intergovernmental agreements. Although another public referendum in Ireland in June 2008 also rejected the treaty, parliaments eventually ratified it, and it went into effect in December 2009.

Under the Lisbon Treaty, the European Union now has a longer-term president elected by the European Council serving for two and a half years; a high representative for foreign affairs acting as the chief diplomat of the EU; a more powerful European Parliament enjoying co-decision rights with the Council on almost all legislation (but still no right to initiate legislation, which only the Commission has and retains); more decisions made using QMV, with a simplified QMV formula taking effect in 2014; and a Charter of Fundamental Rights that makes the rights embodied in the European Convention on Human Rights legally binding on all EU institutions and member states.

With all its deficiencies, the European Union represents a remarkable instance of institution building at the regional level, comparable to what the United States undertook in the nineteenth century to bind the states of America together in a single federal government. The final outcome in Europe will be different from that in the United States, to be sure, but the comparative exercise suggests the potential for expanding the scope of governance in international affairs that liberal perspectives have often emphasized.

Asian and Other Regional Institutions

Regional developments in Asia and other parts of the world suggest the limits of global governance. While Latin American institutions share many similarities with North American and European political traditions, Asian and African institutions are more distinct. As Professor Peter Katzenstein tells us, "Asian regionalism is shaped by the character of Asian states."[38] And in at least three ways, Asian states are different from Western states: they rely less on formal institutions and the separation of powers; they transact business and politics more on a personal and familial basis than through the contracts, laws, and courts more familiar in the West; and they place more emphasis on the well-being of the society as a whole than on the freedom or individualism of each citizen. These differences are evident in Asian regional organizations.

ASEAN is the principal Asian IGO. It was founded in 1967 by five countries: Indonesia, Malaysia, the Philippines, Thailand, and Singapore. Brunei joined in 1984, Vietnam in 1995, Laos and Myanmar in 1997, and Cambodia in 1999. ASEAN was established primarily to accelerate economic growth and indirectly to shield Asian countries from Cold War conflicts raging in Indochina. But the approach in ASEAN was never as institutional or centrally directed as in the European Common Market. The originating document contained only five articles, and ASEAN did not start a free-trade area until 1992. While that objective is now more or less in place, ASEAN countries do not have common external tariffs, and free trade is limited to a narrower range of products than in the EU (for example, rice, a principal agricultural product, is excluded). There is no single market with common regulations or currency in ASEAN. And ASEAN avoids legal approaches to dispute settlement, relying on consensus mechanisms rather than on court proceedings.

Still, ASEAN has evolved further. In 1994, it initiated along with other Asian countries the ASEAN Regional Forum (ARF). ARF brings together ASEAN and other countries, including the United States, Australia, China, Russia, Japan, India, and South Korea, to foster constructive dialogue on security and political issues and to contribute to confidence-building measures (such as releasing white papers on defense expenditures) and preventive diplomacy in Asia. The only multilateral security organization in Asia, ARF is based on the strict principle of noninterference in the internal affairs of states. ARF has no secretariat, and its attendees are called participants, not members. China resists such

ASEAN: the Association of Southeast Asian Nations, the principal Asian IGO.

22ND ASEAN SUMMIT
24 - 25 APRIL 2013

DAR SERI BEGAWAN, BRUNEI DARUSSALAM

Southeast Asian leaders (left to right) Philippine President Benigno Aquino, Singapore's Prime Minister Lee Hsien Loong, Thailand's Prime Minister Yingluck Shinawatra, Vietnam's Prime Minister Nguyen Tan Dung, Brunei's Sultan Hassanal Bolkiah, Myanmar's President Thein Sein, Cambodia's Prime Minister Hun Sen, Indonesia's President Susilo Bambang Yudhoyono, Laos's Prime Minister Thongsing Thammavong, and Malaysia's Senate President Abu Zahar Ujang pose for a group photo at the summit of the ten-nation Association of Southeast Asian Nations (ASEAN) in Bandar Seri Begawan, Brunei, in April 2013. The summit was dominated by efforts to defuse tensions over the South China Sea and deepen economic links throughout the region.

institutionalization, preferring to think of international institutions as state-centric actors defending national sovereignty from both other governments and nonstate actors such as NGOs. ASEAN and ARF, for example, do not have any mechanisms to monitor elections or advocate for human rights, as the Council of Europe does in the European region.

APEC is another loose institution that is characteristic of the Asian style of international cooperation. Founded in 1989 through an initiative by Australia, APEC is a forum of some twenty-one Pacific Rim countries concerned with economic activities in the region, such as trade and investment. It meets annually, has a small secretariat, and includes Taiwan. For that reason, its annual gatherings are called leaders' meetings rather than summits, which usually involve heads of state and government (recall that China does not recognize Taiwan as a state entity). APEC prides itself on being the only intergovernmental grouping in the world operating on the basis of nonbinding commitments, open dialogue, and equal respect for the views of all participants.

**TABLE
6-6**

Legal, Economic, and Regional Institutions in Today's World: The Liberal Perspective and Levels of Analysis

Liberal perspective		
Systemic	*Structure*	International courts and Bretton Woods economic institutions establish universal rules and procedures
	Process	ICC and WTO dispute-settlement procedures generate controversy regarding infringement of national sovereignty
	Regional	European Union exercises supranational authority
Foreign policy		National governments subject to strong domestic parliaments give authority to EU institutions subject to weak European parliament, creating a "democratic deficit"
Domestic		Domestic groups view intervention by international tribunals as "victors' justice"
Individual		President Omar Bashir of Sudan defies ICC

Level of analysis

SUMMARY

Liberal perspectives emphasize the causal role of repeated interactions, interdependence, path dependence, and unintended outcomes on international affairs. At the structural systemic level, they highlight the role of collective security and intergovernmental institutions such as the United Nations. At the systemic process level, they zero in on diplomacy, negotiation and bargaining, and the role of nongovernmental groups. From a bargaining perspective, there is always a better option than the use of force, and liberal perspectives seek to reduce the role of armaments and force in international affairs. At the domestic level, liberal perspectives spotlight elite leadership and the building of stronger domestic institutions to contain ideological and material disparities. And at the individual level, liberal perspectives push for better information, more open dialogue, and respect for alternative points of view.

Sharpen your skills with SAGE edge at **edge.sagepub.com/nau4e.**
SAGE edge for students provides a personalized approach to help you accomplish your coursework goals in an easy-to-use learning environment.

KEY CONCEPTS

STUDY QUESTIONS

1. How do liberal perspectives explain the failure
    of the Oslo Accords? Contrast with realist and
    identity perspectives.

2. Why did the United Nations succeed in the first
    Persian Gulf War and fail thereafter? Was it the
    momentary dominance of the United States after
    the Cold War ended, the farsighted foreign policy
    leadership of Presidents George H. W. Bush
    and Bill Clinton, or the religious humiliation
    of fundamentalist Muslims by the presence of
    Western forces in the Gulf? Which perspective
    and level of analysis are involved in each
    argument?

3. From the liberal perspective, when is it legitimate
    to intervene in the domestic affairs of another
    state? Contrast with realist and identity
    perspectives.

4. What is a strategy from the liberal perspective
    for U.S. and Western relations with China? How
    would it differ from a strategy from the realist or
    the identity perspective?

5. Why is the European Union considered to be
    an archetypical institution from the liberal
    perspective, while the UN Security Council is
    considered to be a blend of the realist and liberal
    perspectives?

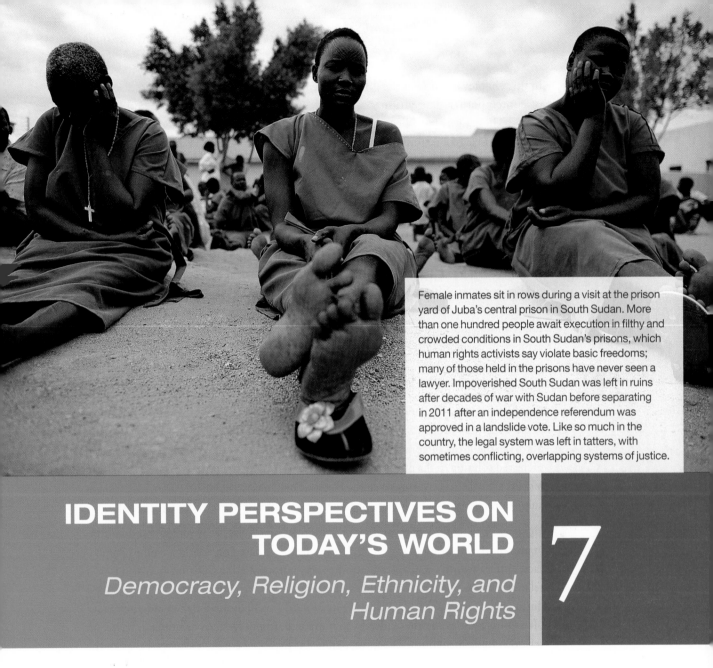

Female inmates sit in rows during a visit at the prison yard of Juba's central prison in South Sudan. More than one hundred people await execution in filthy and crowded conditions in South Sudan's prisons, which human rights activists say violate basic freedoms; many of those held in the prisons have never seen a lawyer. Impoverished South Sudan was left in ruins after decades of war with Sudan before separating in 2011 after an independence referendum was approved in a landslide vote. Like so much in the country, the legal system was left in tatters, with sometimes conflicting, overlapping systems of justice.

IDENTITY PERSPECTIVES ON TODAY'S WORLD

Democracy, Religion, Ethnicity, and Human Rights

7

Identity perspectives see the world through the lens of the competition and construction of ideas. Actors pursue power and participate in diplomatic, trade, and other interactions to advance the self- and shared images they hold. According to identity perspectives, ideas motivate the pursuit of power and the quest for wealth, security, and other collective goods. The causal arrows run from what actors are (identity) to what they acquire (realist) to those with whom they associate (liberal).

In this chapter we look at the different ideas that animate the debates and discourse of contemporary international affairs: democracy, religion, ethnicity, and human rights. These ideas have been around for quite a while and have been reinterpreted by successive generations. Ancient societies relied primarily on ethnicity and religion to motivate human activities and relationships. In later times, religious or moral ideas morphed into the Catholic Church in the West, Confucian values in the East, and Muslim morality in the Middle East. Ethnicity evolved into various cultures and nationalisms, and the territorial nation-state emerged to combine ideas of religion and culture. Secular ideas appeared in ancient Greece, Rome, Mesopotamia, India, and China. The Renaissance in Europe and counterpart movements elsewhere unshackled human reasoning and launched the scientific and industrial revolutions. Political ideologies sprang forth, and the age of "isms" (liberalism, fascism, communism, and so on) was born. In recent decades, the concept of human rights—that is, the basic physical, economic, social, and maybe even political rights of individual human beings—has achieved international prominence. Are any of these ideas universal and capable of spreading to all peoples, or are they all particular and, if not antagonistic, at least agnostic toward one another?

One identity view of the world today emphasizes the spread of democracy. At the systemic structural level of analysis, since the Cold War, the ideas of democracy have won out over the ideas of communism, and democracy is now perceived by many as the preferred solution to the problems of war and peace in eastern Europe, the Balkans, and maybe, after the Arab Spring, even the Middle East. In this argument, democracy trumps culture and becomes a possibility in all countries, not just Western ones.

However, a second identity argument contends the reverse, that religion and culture matter more. Civilization, the highest form of culture based on religion, trumps democracy, and the world is engaged in another clash of ideologies, this time between world religions, Islam and the West, rather than political ideologies as between East and West during the Cold War. A Christian Western world of liberal secular democracy faces off against a series of other cultures that are either non-Western or illiberal, based on religious fundamentalism. The most significant potential conflicts emerge between the Western world on one side and a combination of Confucian China–centered and Muslim Middle East–centered civilizations on the other. For realists, this confrontation is simply the age-old struggle for power, taking place this time between civilizations of broadly similar nation-states rather than between different nation-states within the same civilization, as in the case of earlier Europe. From an identity perspective, however, it is a struggle for power among very different types of actors—civilizations rather than nation-states—whose interactions may lead to different kinds of international systems, some more anarchic than others, depending on how shared identities are constructed.

A third identity perspective emerges at the domestic level. Here ideas emphasize multiculturalism and the shaping of civic identities that embrace tolerance and diversity; in this way, broader identities encompass narrower ethnic identities and even civilizations. They foresee the emergence of a global civilization of multiple traditions, what one political scientist calls a "polymorphic globalism." This global civilization embraces "a loose sense of shared values entailing . . . the material and psychological well-being of all humans."[1]

A fourth identity perspective, operating at the individual level of analysis, champions basic human rights expressed in the United Nations Universal Declaration of Human Rights and offers, for many advocates, the best hope for integrating diverse political ideologies and civilizations. Basic human rights focus first on material protections and benefits—guarantees against torture, starvation, and environmental catastrophes. Broader protections and benefits follow—for reducing economic inequality, eliminating social discrimination, and supporting cultural integrity. At some point, human rights include political rights—the rights to assemble, to speak freely, to vote, and to have access to impartial courts. But a virtue of this perspective is that it tries initially to stake out common ground on nonpolitical human needs.

Again, in this chapter we do not ignore realist and liberal perspectives. Instead, we try to see them as identity perspectives do. Along the way we will point out where realist and liberal perspectives may disagree. The difference once again is a matter of how the causal arrows run. The contradiction and confluence of ideas shape the pursuit of power and the evolution of institutions more than the balance of power and interdependence shape ideas.

Here is how Francis Fukuyama, one scholar who emphasizes the primary causal role of ideas in history, draws the causal arrows in explaining the events since the end of the Cold War:

> What we may be witnessing is not just the end of the Cold War, or the passing of a particular period of postwar history, but the end of history as such: that is, the end point of mankind's ideological evolution and the universalization of Western liberal democracy as the final form of government. This is not to say that there will no longer be events to fill the pages [of journals and newspapers] . . . , for the victory of liberalism has occurred primarily in the realm of ideas or consciousness and is as yet incomplete in the real or material world. But there are powerful reasons for believing that it is the ideal that will govern the material world *in the long run*.[2]

We consider more of this view below. But notice how Professor Fukuyama sees ideas shaping the material world, more so than the reverse. All perspectives are in play, but "in the long run" ideas prevail over power and institutions.

⫸ Democracy

Democracy is a set of ideas about political power and institutions. It revolves around three basic features: (1) opposing political parties rotate peacefully in power through free and fair elections; (2) all institutions in the government, including the military, are subject to the control of elected officials; and (3) individuals have fundamental protections of their civil rights—the rights to assemble, to speak out, to practice their religions, to form and support political parties, to vote, and to adjudicate their griev-ances in impartial courts. These are demanding features. Democracy is much more than elections. The Muslim Brotherhood won elections in Egypt but then proceeded to change the country's constitution to require the government to rule by Muslim law, disenfranchising secular (nonreligious) groups. Then the military, outside the control of the Muslim Brotherhood, stepped in to overthrow the Muslim Brotherhood. Free and fair elections and civilian control of the military may be difficult to ensure in a culture that does not protect individual rights. What if a society values community more than individual values? What if a culture believes that political institutions should reflect the society's religious faith? Can such a society become democratic?

A tension exists between culture, religion, and ethnic identities on one hand and democ-racy and human rights on the other. That tension underlies the discussion in this section and throughout the rest of the chapter.

End of History

In the early 1990s, Francis Fukuyama wrote a book, *The End of History and the Last Man,* that captured for many the meaning of the new era ushered in by the events of the end of the Cold War.[3] Communism has just died a peaceful death in the Soviet Union, and democracy, its ideological adversary for a century, stood unchallenged around the world. Fukuyama asked how this had happened. His answer was that democracy sup-plied something that communism or any other political identity did not, namely, a sense of equal recognition among individuals and groups of human beings that ended the historical quest for domination of one group by another. In international politics, it ended the quest for empire and equilibrium by creating a "democratic peace" in which all countries recognized one another as equal and legitimate, eliminating the struggle for power and status and, hence, the incentive for war.

Fukuyama drew heavily on the work of the German philosopher Georg W. F. Hegel. Hegel developed a nonmaterialist account of history that contrasted with both the mate-rialist account of Karl Marx and the rationalist account of Immanuel Kant, two other German philosophers. He argued that human beings have three parts to their makeup or soul: a desiring (material) part for objects such as food, drink, and shelter to preserve their bodies (realist); a reasoning (rationalist) part that tells them how best to acquire these material objects (liberal); and a "spiritedness" (social) part that seeks recognition from other human beings of the individual's or group's self-worth (identity). The spirited quest for recognition, which Hegel called "thymos," is what drives history. People desire to be recognized by other people, and that spiritedness ignites a struggle for social status to gain recognition by others. Notice that the struggle is primarily for status, not for power or institutional inclusion; hence, Hegel and his pupil Fuku-yama reflect identity perspectives, not realist or liberal perspec-tives. The struggle for status drives the struggle for power and institutions both between lordship and bondage in domestic affairs and between dominance and revolution—or empire and equilibrium—in international affairs.

CAUSAL ARROW: PERSPECTIVES

Struggle for status	Drives struggle for power	Determines institutional outcomes
IDENTITY	REALIST	LIBERAL

MAP
7-1

Freedom in the World

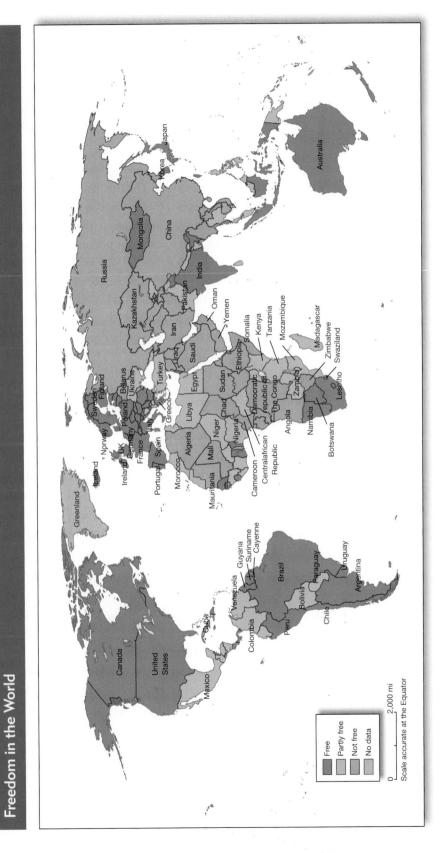

Free
Partly free
Not free
No data

0   2,000 mi
Scale accurate at the Equator

Democracy, unlike other sources of identity such as civilization and religion, was supposed to have ended this struggle because it was based on the universal and equal recognition of all human beings and states. Once societies accepted one another as equals, the struggle for recognition was over; thus, the **end of history** was at hand. War was unnecessary among democracies, and indeed the statistical evidence of the democratic peace, which we discuss in the conclusion of this book, shows that democracies do not go to war with one another.

end of history: an idea advanced by Francis Fukuyama that the spread of democracy had brought an end to the violent struggle among nations for equal recognition.

There was plenty of evidence to support Fukuyama's thesis. Democracy spread steadily after the eighteenth century, albeit in waves.[4] The first wave peaked in the 1920s, then receded in the 1930s and 1940s. The second wave peaked in the 1960s, and the third wave in the 1990s washed away the main vestiges of tyranny in the world. In that decade alone, after the end of the Cold War, sixty-three countries became democratic. Today, ninety countries are rated as free or strong democracies, 1–2.5 on a scale of 1 to 7 using some twenty-five different empirical measures to evaluate democracy. Another fifty-eight countries are rated as partly free, 3–5 on the same scale.[5] While the numbers of free and partly free democracies have gone down since 2005, suggesting the wave is receding somewhat as before, two-thirds of the world's population now live under democracy. See Map 7-1.

Democracy or Culture?

Fukuyama's updating of Hegel's thesis landed on fertile ground. It offered an ideational explanation for the institutional success of NATO and the EU after the end of the Cold War. The institutional processes themselves were not determinative, as liberal perspectives argued; the political ideas behind democracy were the deciding factor. Even some liberal scholars, who stressed the binding and transformational power of institutions, recognized that democracy might be the causal force behind institutions because democracies were more likely than other states to bind themselves in such institutions.[6] In identity perspectives, ideas target and shape the institutions. In liberal perspectives, institutions shape the ideas.

But could a political idea break down cultural and religious barriers? Could democracy transcend Western civilization? It seemed so. Japan and India were non-Western democratic countries, and after the Cold War other non-Western countries, such as South Korea and Taiwan, became democratic. Yet in the Middle East democracy seemed to be excluded. There, Turkey was a struggling to demonstrate that a Muslim party, in power in 2013, might be replaced peacefully by a secular party without the military having to intervene, as the military did in 2013 in Egypt. And only Israel, a Western-oriented nation, was a strong democracy. Even in Israel's case, radical Orthodox Jewish groups advocated the annexation of Gaza and the West Bank, steps that would almost certainly end the Israeli democracy because Palestinians would then constitute a majority of the Israeli population and would have to become second-class citizens if Israel were to remain a Jewish state. It was not surprising, then, from this perspective that the part of the world where democracy failed to take hold was also the center of regional and global conflict.

CAUSAL ARROW: PERSPECTIVES

Absence of democracy	Failure of diplomacy in the Middle East	Growing power of extremists
IDENTITY	LIBERAL	REALIST

From an identity perspective, the absence of democracy, not the failure of Middle East diplomacy or the growing power of extremists, was the cause of such conflict.

Spreading democracy therefore may enable the world to transcend anarchy and war. In his State of the Union message in 1994, President Clinton called "the advance of democracy elsewhere . . . the best strategy to ensure . . . [U.S.] security and to build a durable peace." Invoking the democratic peace, he said, "Democracies don't attack each other, they make better trading partners and partners in diplomacy."[7] Madeleine Albright, secretary of state in Clinton's second term, led the effort to bring democratic countries together in their own institution, the Community of Democracies. Launched in Warsaw, Poland, in 2000, the Community of Democracies strengthens civil societies at the domestic level and encourages cooperation among democratic countries in the United Nations and other organizations at the systemic process level. The European Union became a powerful magnet in the 1990s to strengthen and secure democratic institutions in the former communist states of Europe. Through trade and nongovernmental interactions, the EU helped eastern European countries revitalize the democratic infrastructure that had been destroyed by the oppressive communist system. Think of the difference that a united democratic Europe made in the aftermath of the Cold War. After World Wars I and II, Europe lay shattered and torn. Democracy was weak and markets were riddled by protectionism and state intervention. In the 1990s, after the Cold War, powerful democratic institutions and free markets in western Europe and the world at large surged across the boundaries of eastern Europe to reclaim freedom for the whole of Europe and, for a time, even Russia.

Some realist analysts also agreed with the focus on democracy. Charles Krauthammer, a conservative commentator, called for a realism aimed at democracy, not just stability. He wanted a "democratic realism," a strategic policy that not only went "around the world bashing bad guys over the head" but also "at some point . . . implant[ed] something, something organic and self-developing. And that something is democracy."[8] Secretary of State Condoleezza Rice favored a similar democratic realism when she called for a "balance of power that favors freedom."[9] Notice in these views how democracy (identity) solves security and stability issues (realist) as well as trade and diplomatic ones (liberal).

CAUSAL ARROW: PERSPECTIVES

Stabilizes trade and diplomacy	Improves global security	Democracy
LIBERAL	**REALIST**	**IDENTITY**

Middle East Democracy Initiative

The relatively peaceful and hopeful decade of the 1990s gave way to the much more tumultuous start of the new millennium. From an identity perspective, the terrorist attacks of September 11, 2001, raised anew the debate about the role of democracy and government reform in shaping international behavior, especially in the context of the Middle East. Was the root cause of terrorism the tyranny of corrupt governments in the Middle East and, hence, the solution the long-term reform and transformation of these governments toward greater accountability and democracy? Or was the cause religious fanaticism on the part of fundamentalist Islam that portended a wider, perhaps existential, conflict between Islamic and Western values and, hence, the prospect of ideological and terrorist warfare until one side mellowed or changed, as in the case of the Cold War? Or were both democracy and fundamentalism the wrong construction of identities for the West and Islam, so that the world would have to discover a new discourse as the solution to terrorism, one that offers justice and equality to all identities, whatever their roots in differing civilizations or political ideologies?

President George W. Bush agreed with the view that democratic reform was crucial throughout the world, including in the Middle East, where so few democracies existed. In 2004 he launched his Greater Middle East Democracy Initiative. The expansion of political rights and participation in the Muslim world would combat the tyranny and extremism of fundamentalist religious dogma. Either out of conviction or because he found no WMDs in Iraq, Bush turned to democracy as the solution to terrorism in Iraq and the rest of the Middle East. To get at the roots of terrorism, the United States and the international community had to transform the political regimes in the Arab and Muslim world into democracies.

Notice that, from this perspective, unlike the liberal perspective, the primary sources of terrorism are not economic—poverty, disease, and unemployment. They are political—oppressive regimes that deny their people basic freedoms, such as a practical education, economic ownership, and political opportunity. Instead of allowing basic freedoms, these regimes siphon off millions of dollars in aid and oil revenues to finance corrupt and bloated bureaucracies and to foment foreign conflicts to unite their people and divert them from domestic oppression. Unless these conditions of governance are addressed, this approach contends, opening markets and promoting trade, as liberal perspectives propose, will be like "spitting into the wind." Political reform is a prerequisite of economic growth, reversing the liberal hope that economic growth brings political liberalization.

CAUSAL ARROW: PERSPECTIVES

| Lack of freedom | Increases poverty, disease, unemployment | Generates extremist violence |
| IDENTITY | LIBERAL | REALIST |

George W. Bush pressed for regime reforms in the Palestinian Authority (PA) before supporting further negotiations between the PA and Israel. He gave regime or identity change precedence over negotiations or liberal approaches. In his inaugural address in January 2005, he declared it U.S. policy "to seek and support the growth of democratic movements and institutions in every nation and culture, with the ultimate goal of ending tyranny in our world."[10] And in a speech at the National Defense University in March 2005, he repeated the point: "It should be clear the best antidote to radicalism and terror is the tolerance kindled in free societies."[11]

But many critics disagreed. Does the promotion of democracy, especially in the Middle East, bridge or widen the gap between the West and Islam? Rather than bringing cultures together, democracy may divide them. It may create the very opportunity that radicals seize to win elections and then consolidate power, as happened in Egypt, Pakistan, and elsewhere and could happen in Saudi Arabia. Then what should the West do? Stand by and let extremists take power, as happened in Iran in 1979? Or intervene and keep a nondemocratic but friendly government in power, as France did in Algeria in 1992, when it installed a military government and ousted the Islamic radicals who had just won the elections? This issue became real in spring 2006 when Hamas, the Palestinian group that rejects Israel, won the PA elections and now sits in the Palestinian government, and it happened again in 2013 when the military overthrew an elected Muslim-dominated government in Egypt.

Or would it be better, as social constructivists might argue, to emphasize common human rights, not regime change, and to focus on economic, social, and cultural, not political, rights? President Obama believes that the emphasis on democracy widens rather than bridges differences. In speeches in Cairo and Moscow in 2009, he mentioned democracy only near the end of his talks and emphasized the need to reach out to other cultures and religions and intensify the dialogue among civilizations.[12] In Prague, he dismissed domestic differences among nations: "When nations and peoples allow themselves to be defined by their differences, the gulf between them widens."[13] He extended an open hand of diplomacy to Iran in 2009 even as the regime in Tehran shut down, imprisoned, and executed dissident leaders associated with the "Green Revolution." In sharp contrast to President Bush, he downplayed the role of American democracy or exceptionalism. In France in 2009, he said, "I believe in American exceptionalism, just as I suspect that the Brits believe in British exceptionalism and the Greeks believe in Greek exceptionalism."[14] Again, in a speech at the UN in September 2013, he said: "Some may disagree, but I believe America is exceptional—in part because we have shown a willingness through the sacrifice of blood and treasure to stand up not only for our own narrow self-interests, but for the interests of all."[15] As Thomas Carothers, a sympathetic observer, explains, while Obama has clear commitments to democracy, he mixes "that outlook . . . with strong pragmatic instincts." These include "a wariness of overstatement, a disinclination to lead with ideology, and the desire to solve problems through building consensus rather than fostering confrontation."[16]

Arab Spring

The debate about democracy in the Middle East became an immediate reality in the domestic uprisings known as the Arab Spring. On December 17, 2010, an Arab street vendor in Tunisia set himself on fire and ignited a cascading set of protests and revolutions that rocked authoritarian governments in the Middle East from Morocco to Syria. Mohamed Bouazizi's self-immolation—a desperate act in reaction to a lack of work and the confiscation of his wares by authorities—advertised both the economic stagnation and the political oppression of most of the governments in the Middle East.

Citizens of the Arab and Muslim world have spent much of their history living under repressive regimes. In 2006, out of forty-seven Muslim-majority countries in the world, only three, Mali, Senegal, and Indonesia, lived under "free" regimes.[17] Mali has since experienced a military coup and was invaded in 2012 by Al Qaeda–affiliated terrorists followed by an intervention of French-led Western forces to restore order. Between 2006 and 2013, Sierra Leone was the only other Muslim-majority country to join the

FIGURE
7-1

Freedom in Muslim-Majority Countries versus World Countries

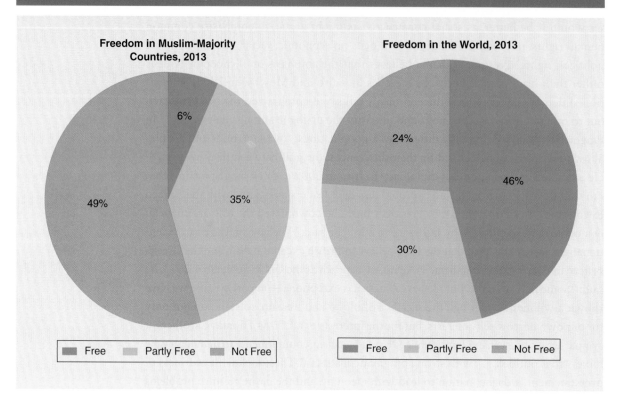

Source: World Values Survey, "Online Data Analysis," http://www.wvsevsdb.com/wvs/WVSAnalize.jsp.

category of "free." The pattern is even starker in the Arab portion of the Muslim world, which lacks a single electoral democracy or "free" country.[18] By contrast, in the non-Islamic world in 2001, 85 countries were "free," 39 were "partly free," and 21 were "not free," while fully 110 of 145 states, or 76 percent, had democratically elected regimes. Moreover, quantitative global analysis reveals a strong statistical relationship between Islam and authoritarianism, even when other demonstrated influences on democracy, such as economic development and ethnic uniformity, are factored in.[19]

Not all analysts are skeptical. Political scientist Larry Diamond believes that the obstacle to democracy in Middle East is not Islam or culture but "authoritarian statecraft . . . the patterns and institutions by which authoritarian regimes manage their politics and keep their hold on power."[20] Notice how he draws the causal arrows: from institutions or liberal factors that trump cultural or identity ones. The people in the Middle East want democracy no less than do people anywhere else. To be sure, Diamond notes, "outside the West, there is a stronger authoritarian temptation, but in no region does it reach a majority preference on average."[21] According to the World Values Survey (which conducts regular polls tapping into value preferences), Muslim and Christian "civilizations" are "virtually identical" in their preference for democratic ideals and "somewhat more democratic than most other cultural groups" on political dimensions (see Figure 7-2). But Muslim and Christian countries display a "staggering difference" on "social issues." Christian countries approve of gender equality, homosexuality, abortion, and divorce and disapprove of having religious standards for political leadership. Muslim countries reverse these preferences. The difference here concerns freedom of religion and whether that freedom is fundamental to democracy. Diamond concludes that religious differences "affect the depth and content of democracy but . . . not necessarily . . . the vigor or vitality of it." He disagrees with those, such as Fareed Zakaria (see below), who believe that democracies that do not protect religious freedom are less durable.

Did the Arab Spring portend a change in these dismal patterns? Tunisian protests were followed in spring 2011 by revolutions in Egypt, Libya, Yemen, and Syria, among others. In the case of Libya and Syria, civil war erupted. Other authoritarian governments in the Middle East, in Jordan, Saudi Arabia, and Qatar, clamped down or scrambled to stay ahead of the protests. Elections in Tunisia and Egypt initially offered promise. The Ennahda Party, Tunisia's main Islamist party, won elections in October 2011 with 41 percent of the vote. It reached out to moderates to form a coalition with Ettakatol, the leading social democratic party. As Rached Ghannouchi, the leader of Ennahda, explains, the government since then has been based on a combination of "a moderate Islamist party and a moderate secular party." It produced a draft constitution in June 2013 that is now before the legislature. Thus far Tunisia has remained on track, but economic conditions in the country continue to deteriorate. Frustrated young men gravitate to Salafist or extremist groups such as Ansar al-Sharia, which gained notoriety in 2012 because of its involvement in the raid in Benghazi that killed the American ambassador.

The situation in Egypt stands in sharp contrast. After ousting dictator Hosni Mubarak, Egypt too held elections in January 2012. The Muslim Brotherhood, Egypt's main Islamist party, won with 51 percent of the vote, narrowly defeating the candidate representing the ousted forces of Mubarak. Mohamed Morsi, the leader of the Muslim Brotherhood, took office as president and pledged to serve the people but also not to betray God. He proceeded to exclude the secular opposition and rammed a constitution through in late 2012 that alienated large segments of the Egyptian population. In June 2013 the matter came to a head. Street violence prompted the Egyptian army to intervene and unseat Morsi. As it had after the Mubarak ouster, the interim military government promised to hold new elections. But now the question is whether the Muslim Brotherhood will see any purpose in new elections if an elected government can be so easily removed by the military. And if the Muslim Brotherhood were to win again in new elections, what would the military do?

FIGURE
7-2

Having a Democratic Regime Is . . .

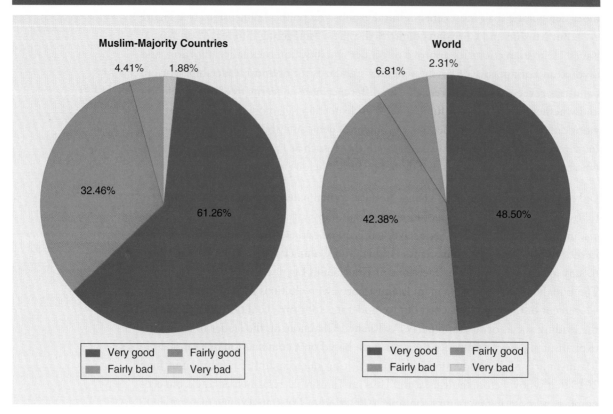

Source: World Values Survey, "Online Data Analysis," http://www.wvsevsdb.com/wvs/WVSAnalize.jsp.

The Arab Spring illustrates the extreme tensions among culture, religion, and democracy. If Islamists win elections and then end democracy, as Nazi and other radical parties have done elsewhere, is the Arab Spring little more than a transition from one authoritarian government to another? Democracy becomes simply one vote *one time*. And the new government committed to a religious rather than a secular order may be more intolerant than the old one. On the other hand, if the military stands guard to protect secular forces—as it has, for example, in Turkey and now in Egypt—is its intervention still not the antithesis of peaceful democratic change? How do societies long repressed by authoritarian rule develop the habits of compromise and reconciliation? How do they refrain from using government to coerce opponents to accept their religious beliefs or to squelch economic opportunity? The Arab Spring of democratic hope has a long way to go if it is going to avoid becoming an Arab Winter of renewed repression.

From the different perspectives, the causes of democracy are multiple. They may derive from the success or failure of elites, economic development, and diplomatic aid (liberal); from power struggles and external intervention (realist); or from conflicting cultural, religious, and civilizational identities. And the causes of democracy may come from the different levels of analysis, as Table 7-1 shows.

Egyptian demonstrators gather next to a concrete-block barricade during confrontations outside Cairo's security headquarters in February 2012. Clashes continued in the Egyptian capital as activists called for civil disobedience across Egypt.

⟫ Religion

Religion has played a role in the political lives of all countries. Roman and Orthodox Catholic churches dominated medieval Europe, and Protestant and Catholic states warred against one another for centuries in early modern Europe. Is religion a more powerful cause of individual and group behavior than democracy? Does democracy in fact derive from the Christian religion, tied closely to the Protestant ethic, which Max Weber, the German sociologist, saw as being the source of Western capitalism and individualism?[22]

TABLE 7-1

Democracy in Today's World: The Identity Perspective and Levels of Analysis

Level of analysis	Identity perspective		
	Systemic	*Structure*	Democracy prevails and history ends
		Process	Democratic nations cooperate through the Community of Democracies
	Foreign policy		George W. Bush launches Greater Middle East Democracy Initiative to rally domestic support for interventions in Iraq and Afghanistan
	Domestic		Moderates and radicals contend in Arab Spring to shape democracy
	Individual		Mohamed Bouazizi, Tunisian street vendor, ignites Arab Spring

If so, it's doubtful that democracy, at least in its Western form of pluralist parties, divided institutions, and individual civil rights, can be transplanted across diverse civilizations.

Clash of Civilizations

Some scholars conclude that religion is the stronger influence. Professor Samuel Huntington, for example, wrote a book a few years after Fukuyama's in which he argued that cultures or civilizations "are far more fundamental than differences among political ideologies and political regimes."[23] Civilizations, according to Huntington, represented the highest form of culture, involving larger groupings of countries than traditional nation-states. They represented enduring differences among peoples based principally on religion but also on other cultural factors, such as language, history, customs, institutions, and the way people subjectively identified themselves. Huntington detected the contours of a future struggle for power along the borders of different civilizations and foresaw the possibility of a **clash of civilizations**.

clash of civilizations: a thesis advanced by Samuel Huntington that past and future global conflicts can be traced along the fault lines between nine major world civilizations.

In a famous article published in 1993 and expanded into a book in 1996, Huntington identified nine major civilizations. As Map 7-2 shows, they include Western (North America and Europe), Orthodox (eastern Europe and Russia), Confucian or Sinic (China), Islamic (North Africa, Middle East, and central, South, and Southeast Asia), Hindu (India), Buddhist (Tibet and Indochina), Shinto (Japan), Latin American, and African (sub-Saharan Africa). He found that historical conflicts proliferated along the fault lines between these civilizations. For example, the Cold War was waged between the Western and Orthodox civilizations. Repeated crusades and wars took place between the Islamic and Western civilizations. China and Japan were historical rivals, reflecting conflicts between the Confucian (Sinic) and Shinto civilizations, as were India and China, reflecting conflicts between the Hindu and Confucian civilizations, and India and Pakistan, reflecting conflicts between Hindu and Muslim civilizations. And so on. Huntington was particularly intrigued by conflicts in the Balkans. Here three religious civilizations—Western, Orthodox, and Islamic—came together. In each province of the former Yugoslavia, as we noted earlier, fighting tended to follow the divisions between religions or civilizations. Huntington asked if these fault lines might not become the locus of future international conflicts. He worried, in particular, about conflicts between the Western civilization (North America and Europe) and Islamic countries in the Middle East and the possibility that Islamic countries, such as Iran, might align with Confucian powers (namely, China) to counterbalance the United States.[24]

At the time, Huntington's analysis was sharply criticized. Some critics accused him of creating a self-fulfilling prophecy—thinking about the world in such contentious terms would make it so. Realist perspectives rejected the idea that ideological divisions were primary, and liberal perspectives rejected the implication that diplomacy was not up to the task of integrating Islam as well as China into the existing Western world order. Huntington, in his defense, did not see the clash as inevitable; he placed a question mark after the phrase "clash of civilizations." But he did offer a lot of evidence to justify his concern.

By suggesting that civilizations were more hardwired in people than the ideological differences that had characterized the Cold War or the cultural and nation-state differences that had divided Europe earlier, Huntington was venturing into the world of changing identities in international affairs. Some analysts therefore interpret his argument as an

MAP
7-2

The Clash of Civilizations

CIVILIZATIONS

- Western
- Latin American
- Islamic
- African
- Orthodox
- Sinic
- Hindu
- Buddhist
- Shinto

In Jerusalem, Israel, many intersecting civilizations are visible. Here we see the Temple Mount (Har haBayit in Hebrew and Haram al Sharif in Arabic), which is considered a holy site by many religions.

identity perspective. On the other hand, Huntington's purpose was not to suggest how ideas change and transcend material (realist) or institutional (liberal) circumstances, but rather to point out that identities, especially at the highest level of civilizations, do not change very much. They are historically rooted and serve to divide the world in ways that might be considered permanent. He expected that the distribution of power in the world would always remain decentralized, whatever the specific sources of identity in any given era. Since realists have always conceded that states can merge or disappear and identities change but anarchy will still persist, Huntington's argument can also be seen as realist.

Huntington anticipated much of what happened after the Cold War. He offered, in particular, a framework for understanding the new threat of terrorism and its eventual targeting of the United States. Osama bin Laden and nonstate actors such as Al Qaeda took the lead, but history suggested this effort might find wider global support among states from different civilizations seeking to counterbalance American power. The subsequent discovery that China had assisted Pakistan in developing nuclear weapons and that Pakistan's A. Q. Khan network had supplied nuclear technology to Libya, Iran, and North Korea even seemed to confirm the Confucian–Islamic alliance that Huntington feared. Altogether, Huntington's thesis generated much debate and raised important questions, even if unintended, about how identities change and shape international events.

Religion Trumps Democracy

From Huntington's analysis, democracy as a political ideology is not likely to spread across the fault lines of different civilizations. It is part of Western civilization, not a universal value.[25] Fareed Zakaria, a journalist and realist foreign policy analyst, was similarly skeptical. He argued that many countries in the Middle East and the third world held elections but did not have civil societies that protected individual rights and nurtured the basic institutions of a free press and independent courts to ensure real competitive political processes. These countries were "illiberal democracies," in the sense that they supported elections but not the underlying civil liberties that ensure the ability of opposing parties to rotate peacefully in and out of power. Hence, democracy in these countries was unstable and easily reversed. Zakaria pointed out that civil societies in Western states developed in parallel with elections over long periods and that similar development would be necessary before other countries could achieve real democracy. Zakaria wanted the United States to go more slowly. "Instead of searching for new lands to democratize and new places to hold elections," he advised, the United States and the international community should work "to consolidate democracy where it has taken root and to encourage the gradual development of constitutional liberalism across the globe."[26] Zakaria's skepticism, some might argue, is borne out by the travails of democracy in the Arab Spring.

Some critics pointed out the hypocrisy of the West's pursuit of democracy in the Middle East. They noted the irony of the United States pulling away from the old democracies in Europe and North America to construct new democracies in Iraq and the Middle East. Some old democracies, like France and Germany, opposed the Iraq War. And if democracy could not hold the Western allies together over Iraq, how could it build bridges between the United States and countries in the Middle East? Perhaps power overrode both democracy and common institutions, as strict realist perspectives argued. The United States had the power to intervene, and therefore it did. Or perhaps the United States would be driven back to common institutions, as liberal perspectives expected. Unilateralism and preemption were simply not sustainable. The debate reflected the continuing need to make judgments, after the examination of as many facts as possible, regarding the relative importance of ideational, power, and institutional factors in determining outcomes and prescribing solutions in international affairs.

Islam and the Muslim World

Islam is a vast and complex religion—and it is now center stage in the contemporary international system. It is just as important that the non-Muslim world understand Islam as it is that Islam understand the non-Muslim world.

Muslims total about 1.5 billion people worldwide, roughly 25 percent of the world's population. They constitute the majority of the populations of a string of countries extending from Morocco across North Africa through the Middle East, to South and Southeast Asia. Indonesia is the largest Muslim country, with more than 200 million people. The center of Islam lies in the Middle East. Saudi Arabia safeguards the holy places of Mecca and Medina; the first is the birthplace of the Prophet Muhammad, who founded Islam, and the second is the city of his famous *Hijra*, or migration, in 622 C.E. (the beginning, by the way, of the Muslim calendar).

Most Muslims are **Sunnis**, members of the branch of Islam that identifies with the caliphs, the elected successors of Muhammad dating back to the seventh century.

Sunnis: members of the majority branch of Islam that identifies with the caliphs, the elected successors of Muhammad dating back to the seventh century.

Shiites: members of the minority sect of Islam that identifies with a seventh-century renegade group that advocated divine rather than elective succession.

A minority are Shia or **Shiites**. They identify with a renegade group that advocated divine rather than elective succession. Their leader was Ali, a paternal cousin of Muhammad and the husband of the Prophet's only surviving daughter. When the third caliph, Uthman, was assassinated in 656, Ali became caliph. But in 661, he too was assassinated. His son, Husayn, tried to retrieve the caliphate in 680 but was massacred at Karbala and his head sent to Damascus. Later, this tragic slaying of the Prophet's grandson became the inspiration of the Shia movement, which divided Islam between orthodox (Sunni) and radical (Shiite) camps.

Today the center of Shia Islam is located in the town of Qum in Iran, a Persian country, although many holy sites, such as Najaf and Karbala, are located in Iraq, an Arab country. Sunni Islam was centered initially in Syria (Ummayad dynasty) and then in Iraq (Abbasid dynasty), and by the thirteenth century it had splintered into various dynasties in Egypt and elsewhere.

jihad: war waged for holy or religious reasons.

Other radical branches of Islam developed over the centuries. When the Mongols stormed the Middle East in the thirteenth century, Taqi al-Din Taymiyya, a revered Sunni Muslim scholar, elevated **jihad**, or holy war, to the same level of doctrine as the five pillars of Islam—prayer, pilgrimage, alms, declaration of faith, and Ramadan (the Muslim holy days). He authorized holy war not only against infidels, or the "far enemy" (at that time the Mongols and Turks), but also against apostate rulers within Islam, or the "near enemy." Islam had to purify itself internally as well as defeat the infidels externally.

Holy war was not unique to Islam, of course. For two centuries before Taymiyya, Christian warriors had crusaded against Muslims to conquer their holy land of Jerusalem and surrounding territories. The Knights Templar and Hospitallers were Christian orders whose members were both priests and warriors called to wage their own version of holy war against Muslim infidels.[27] Schismatic wars within Christianity were also hardly unknown. Popes and emperors excommunicated and, indeed, executed or poisoned one another during the Middle Ages, and Protestants and Catholics fought the cataclysmic Thirty Years' War in the seventeenth century.

Why did the Islamic world fade in the fifteenth century and Christian Europe rise? "What went wrong?" as the Princeton scholar of Islam Bernard Lewis puts it.[28] For one thing, the Reformation and Enlightenment in Europe passed Islam by. The reasons are many and disputed: no separation of church and state in Islam, no concept of competitive politics or markets, the second-class status of Muslim women, and so on. But one consequence (and perhaps, after 1500, also a cause) emphasized by critical theory perspectives was Western imperialism, the breakout of European energies and avarice that sent sailing ships around the world, Western armies into Egypt under Napoleon in 1798, and then Western colonialists into the Middle East in the nineteenth century. The experience of Western imperialism and then, on top of that, Israel's creation and the imperialist ambitions of some Israelis to annex the West Bank and Gaza seared the Muslim mind and seeded the ground for a broad-based suspicion, if not hatred, of Western life and values.

Saudi Arabia, the land of Islam's holy places, escaped imperialism, which made the presence of U.S. troops there in the 1990s all the more intolerable. This intolerance was based on a virulent version of Islam. In the eighteenth century, Muhammad ibn Abd al-Wahhab, a spiritual descendant of Taymiyya, teamed up with Muhammad Ibn Saud, then ruler of parts of Arabia, to unite the whole of Arabia. Al-Wahhab preached a rigid and puritanical form of Islam known as **Wahhabism**, which harkened back to the radical ancient men, or Salafis, of the early caliphates. Today, the alliance between Wahhabism and the royal family of Saud creates a situation in Saudi Arabia that exists in many other Muslim countries, such as Pakistan. Governments control the wealth and, in Saudi Arabia's case, oil and promote trade and other links with Western societies, while religious leaders, the clerical establishments, control the society and educate the young people and wider citizenry to reject modern values and take up jihad against the Western infidels. Elites balance domestic and systemic requirements at the foreign policy level of analysis, suggesting that if the elites are toppled major changes may follow, driven by domestic-level (Wahhabist radicals in Saudi Arabia) or systemic-level (Iranian intervention in Saudi Arabia) forces.

Wahhabism: a rigid and puritanical form of Islam originating in the eighteenth century with the Arabian spiritual leader Muhammad ibn Abd al-Wahhab.

Hassan al-Banna, an Egyptian worker with the Suez Canal Company, founded the Muslim Brotherhood in 1928. The Brotherhood advocates a return to the Koran and sharia, or Islamic law, as the basis of a proper Muslim society. The Brotherhood addresses social as well as political needs and offers the most effective infrastructure of economic and social services (education, health, banking, and so on) of any organization in Islam. It spread rapidly to other countries in the 1930s and 1940s but went underground in the 1950s when postwar military and authoritarian governments in the Middle East suppressed religious groups. Today it has resurfaced as a result of the Arab Spring and constitutes the largest and most effective political organization in Egypt and several other Muslim countries. Repressed again in Egypt following the military coup in 2013, the Brotherhood remains a wild card in the evolution of peaceful Islam.

Sayyid Qutb, an Egyptian writer and former government official, brought many of the radical strands of Islam together in the mid-twentieth century and focused them on the United States. He came to the United States in 1948 and studied at Northern Colorado Teachers College, where he developed a strong distaste for American culture and values. His puritanical view rejected not only Western consumerism and usury (the charging of interest for the use of money, which earlier Christianity also condemned) but also the liberation of women, sexual license, and the breakdown of the family associated with Western culture. Qutb saw the West as the enemy and urged Islam to go back to its seventh-century roots.

Qutb is the prophet of contemporary Islamic fundamentalism. Omar Rahman (the Blind Sheikh), who was behind the first World Trade Center attack, and Osama bin Laden, who was behind the second, were both disciples of Qutb. Can these radical proponents of contemporary Islamic fundamentalism lead the rest of Islam to a worldwide confrontation with democracy and the West, much as Lenin and Stalin led radical Marxist forces to a global confrontation between the Soviet Union and the United States? Judgments differ.

Whither the West and Radical Islam?

Fundamentalist Islam is the most radical version of Islam. It advocates a theocratic world order or caliphate (the governmental form of earlier Islamic empires) that revives the purist values of ancient Islam and rules by religious law, which systematically discriminates against women and excludes most of the secular and market mechanisms of modern societies. If fundamentalist Islam spreads and acquires the technological and military power that communism commanded during the Cold War, it would pose a significant threat to democracy, challenging the thesis that the end of history is at hand.[29]

Tensions between Islamic reformers, who favor increasing modernization and secularism, and Islamic fundamentalists, who want to see political institutions and laws that are based on religious precepts, lie at the heart of political divisions in the Middle East and will affect future relations between those states and the West. Today, Egypt and Turkey represent more moderate Sunni branches of Islam, as does Indonesia. But the struggle persists in these countries also, which is why the Arab Spring has attracted so much attention.

Iran represents a militant Shiite branch of Islam and is the leading advocate of a restoration of the medieval Muslim caliphate. Shiites are a majority in Iraq and a minority in Syria, where they have ruled under the Assad family and Alawite sect since 1970. The rebels in Syria are mostly Sunni but split between moderate and radical elements. Afghanistan and Pakistan are majority-Sunni societies but deeply divided between moderate and extremist elements, such as Al Qaeda, headquartered in the frontier regions of Pakistan. Islam extends across East and North Africa, mostly Sunni, where radical groups such as al-Shabaab in Somalia, Boko Haram in Nigeria, and Al Qaeda in Islamic Maghreb are active. Militant groups also exist in Southeast Asia, such as the Moro National Liberation Front in the Philippines.

Most Muslims are not fundamentalists, and most fundamentalists are not terrorists. Still there is, as Daniel Benjamin and Steven Simon point out, a "strong connection between the subculture of terrorism and a broader culture in which the basis of terrorist values is well established and legally unassailable."[30] Islam does not openly condone terrorism, but neither does it openly condemn it. In that sense, much of Islam is on the sidelines in the global struggle against terror. Which way Islam swings between the reformers and the fundamentalists—toward increasing modernization and secularism or toward religious fervor and martyrdom—will determine how Islam relates to the West and whether that relationship becomes one of enemy, the case earlier with communism; one of rival, the case today between the West and China; or one of friend, the case among Western countries. As we recall from Chapter 1, identity perspectives emphasize the extent to which we shape the nature of anarchy and international affairs by our ideas and discourse.

For identity perspectives that emphasize the relative distribution rather than the social construction of identities, radical Islam produced militant crusades against Europe in the past and, given the deep-seated resentments and absence of secular modernization, might do so again in the future. Much depends on which way the rest of Islam swings. Some believe that there is enough resentment in Islamic countries to swell the ranks of holy warriors for a long time to come. Abdurrahman Wahid, former president of Indonesia, the world's largest Muslim country and a generally moderate one, says, "Wahhabi/Salafi ideology has made substantial inroads throughout the Muslim world. . . . [It is] a well-financed, multifaceted global movement that operates like a juggernaut in much of the developing world, and even among immigrant Muslim communities in the West."[31] Estimates are that some sixty thousand warriors trained in Afghanistan alone when it was under Taliban control. If we count the thousands trained elsewhere and the additional thousands who sympathize with and finance jihadism, sleeper cells may well proliferate everywhere in the industrialized world.[32] That these time bombs provide the potential for a long-term global war that will eventually undermine Western stability and confidence is certainly not out of the question. Especially troubling is the possibility that terrorists may join up with state power. What if Saudi Arabia, with its oil wealth, and Pakistan, with its nuclear capability, should fall into the hands of Islamic radicals? Both countries, but especially Pakistan, suffer from political uncertainty. From this perspective, it would not be wise to underestimate the internal values and convictions that drive radical Islam. Without full modernization, the values of radical Islam may not be enough to succeed. But, don't forget, the Soviet Union never fully modernized, yet it produced an enormous challenge for the West and caused untold suffering and death.

CAUSAL ARROW: PERSPECTIVES

Reduces counter-balancing by rising powers	Makes possible trade and development	Tempering of radical Islam
REALIST	**LIBERAL**	**IDENTITY**

Others, taking a more liberal perspective that emphasizes feedback and modernization, disagree. They see radical Islam as no worse than Christian fundamentalism and worry that Jewish fundamentalism (for example, Orthodox demands for annexation of the West Bank and Gaza) is just as bad and provokes much of the deep-seated Arab resentment. From this perspective, it is better to downplay the ideological causes of the conflict and pursue trade and development to get at the roots of the poverty and despair that breed terrorism. The ranks of radical Islam may not be so great. The 9/11 hijackers were educated Arabs who were uprooted from their own societies and disaffected with their experiences in the Western societies where, like their mentor Qutb, they studied. According to some reviews of the biographies of known terrorists, three-quarters of them come from the upper or middle classes.[33] Only a small percentage come out of madrassas, or Muslim religious schools, some of which teach hatred and holy war toward the West. So perhaps, as Oliver Roy, a British author, argues, the number of terrorists is much smaller than the estimated totals.[34] Those who make up this smaller number may be better educated, but they are apparently educated for no purpose in that there are few jobs at home to absorb their energies except in corrupt bureaucracies or oil-sodden royal families. Thus, if education alone is not the answer to terrorism, modernization may still be. Diversifying Persian Gulf countries away from oil and opening up manufacturing, investments, and exports might not only create more jobs but also reorient incentives so that religious schools teach more practical subjects.

Shanghai Cooperation Organization (SCO): group of Asian nations led by China and Russia to resist U.S. power.

Analysts taking a realist perspective see a more systemic phenomenon of power balancing at work. Rising powers use terrorism and Islam to chip away at American dominance. Although China and Russia cooperated with the United States in Afghanistan, their interest was to restrain terrorist radicals in their own countries. From a realist perspective, they have larger systemic interests in opposing U.S. hegemony. Even before 9/11, Russia and China created the Shanghai Five, which included Kazakhstan, Kyrgyzstan, and Tajikistan, renaming it in 2001 the **Shanghai Cooperation Organization (SCO)** and adding Uzbekistan as a member and other countries as observers—Mongolia, Iran, Pakistan, and India. The SCO promotes cooperation, including joint military exercises, to defend common interests and counter U.S. dominance. Russia and China also resist hard-line U.S. policies toward Iran and North Korea. And in 2007 Russia suspended its participation in the Treaty on Conventional Forces in Europe and vigorously opposed U.S. plans to deploy missile defenses in the Czech Republic and Poland to defend against Iranian missiles. China has cultivated governments in the Middle East and Africa (for example, Iran and Sudan) as well as in Latin America (for example, Cuba and Venezuela), both to gain access to oil and to counterbalance American influence. Radical Islam has become a pretext for a wider campaign to reduce American hegemony and influence. Although Huntington's anticipation of a Confucian–Islamic alliance to counterbalance Western power may not yet be fully visible, realist perspectives see disturbing developments in that direction. Table 7-2 summarizes the influence of religion from the different levels of analysis.

≫ Ethnicity and Nationalism

How do identities change at the local level and various ethnic groups acquire a sense of nationhood? This is a central question from an identity perspective. As we learned in the introduction to this text, when identities converge or are shared, common institutions

TABLE 7-2

Religion in Today's World: The Identity Perspective and Levels of Analysis

Level of analysis		Identity perspective	
Systemic	Structure	Clash of civilizations
	Process	Confucian and Islamic countries resist the Western liberal order
Foreign policy		Muslim Brotherhood navigates to expand Islam abroad and to end military rule at home
Domestic		Shiites and Sunnis contend to shape Muslim identity
Individual		Taymiyya, al-Banna, and Qutb found radical Islamic sects

arise and collective benefits multiply. A peaceful liberal order prevails. When identities diverge or conflict, cooperation is much more difficult and anarchy tends to create a struggle for resources and survival. A balance-of-power realist order prevails. Notice in these cases how identities shape institutions and the distribution of resources (power). The causal arrows run

CAUSAL ARROW: PERSPECTIVES

REALIST	LIBERAL	IDENTITY
Which distribute resources	Shape common or separate institutions	Ethnic loyalties

from ethnicity or nationalism to common or divided institutions to collective or competitive allocation of material wealth. And the emergence of order or anarchy occurs at any level of analysis. In this section, we consider these forces at the domestic level of analysis.

Nationhood involves reordering the priority of the manifold identities held by individuals. At any one time, people feel loyalty to their families, their local communities, their religious organizations, and their national communities. In a strong state, individuals may identify with their ethnic or religious groups in private life, but they tend to associate more with the nation or state in public life. As *Financial Times* columnist Krishna Guha writes, "Ethnic and religious identity may define values, but citizenship must define attitudes to law and political process."[35] Citizenship involves a **civic identity**, as opposed to an ethnic one, and that means people are willing to submit to the laws of a common government rather than those of separate ethnic or religious groups. They entrust their physical safety to a set of institutions that go beyond their specific group and that they consider to be legitimate.

A key determinant of group identity, therefore, is the authority that people turn to and consider legitimate to make and enforce the law. Which group or institution has this legitimate authority and can use force against the people if they break the law or can use force on their behalf if some other group attacks the people? When threats emerge, do people turn to their ethnic group to defend them or to a local or national government? This can be a wrenching choice. For example, at the outbreak of the American Civil War, General Robert E. Lee was asked why he had joined the Confederacy even though he was a West Point graduate and believed the Union was right on the question of preserving national unity. He said it was because he could not draw his sword against his own family and the state of Virginia. At that moment, he was saying that his family and regional ties were stronger than his national ones.

Civic Identity

Family or ethnic ties are always strong. If a nation is to be constructed or preserved, however, national memories and allegiance need to be stronger. Bosnian Serbs and Croats need to see themselves as more distinct from the Croats in Croatia and the Serbs in Serbia than from the Serbs, Croats, and Muslims living inside Bosnia. Chechens eventually have to trust Moscow more than their own provincial leaders. Non-Arabs in Sudan have to look to the capital, Khartoum, for help rather than to their own tribal leaders. Protestants in Northern Ireland have to trust Dublin more than London, and ethnic Chinese who reside in Indonesia or Malaysia have to rely more on the governments of

nationhood: a status acquired by states strong enough to protect their borders and command the loyalty of their citizens.

civic identity: identity constructed when people are willing to submit to the laws of a common government rather than those of separate ethnic or religious groups.

those countries to protect them than on the prospect of flight to Hong Kong or some other foreign refuge when trouble arises.

Setting out the requirements of nationhood in this fashion suggests how difficult nationhood may be to achieve and why so many analysts are skeptical about **nation building**. Still, this is the process throughout history by which ethnic groups have evolved toward nationhood and, in some cases, such as the EU, beyond nationhood. It is a long-term process. It may be important to start people moving in a collective direction without knowing the exact destination, as liberal perspectives would emphasize. But eventually people have to figure out where they want to wind up. What kind of people do they want to be? Do they want a religious or a secular state? Do they want a democratic government or an authoritarian one?

For many who view ethnic conflict from an identity perspective, democracy promotion becomes the goal and the long-term solution to ethnic conflict. Indeed, as political scientist Amitai Etzioni argues, ethnic separation is justified only in cases where ethnic groups are fighting against oppression: "Only when secessionist movements seek to break out of empires—and only when those empires refuse to democratize—does self-determination deserve our support."[36] From an identity perspective, the moral or normative claim to democracy may be the only way to adjudicate ethnic conflicts.

nation building: the process through which ethnic groups evolve toward nationhood.

CAUSAL ARROW: PERSPECTIVES

Democratic reforms	Achieve stable state institutions	Justify territorial separation
IDENTITY	LIBERAL	REALIST

Liberal perspectives are more skeptical. As Raymond C. Taras and Rajat Ganguly argue, "Liberals may sympathize with the motives and moral claims [such as democracy] that separatist movements embody, but they insist that other ways are available to satisfy their demands short of recognizing their right of secession."[37]

This is a classic case of a difference in judgment between identity and liberal perspectives looking at ethnic conflicts. An identity perspective emphasizes the importance of ideational forces over institutional ones and justifies ethnic secession if it leads to more democracy. The liberal perspective emphasizes processes within existing institutions despite separate moral claims and expects to find ways to accommodate moral differences short of secession.

Thus, international interventions to deal with ethnic conflicts through the reconstruction of identities also have their limits. At some point, unless all outside parties share similar political values, they will disagree about the political form that nation building should take. Russia, for example, is skeptical about democracy in the Balkans and in Iraq. China is equally skeptical about democracy in Taiwan and in North Korea (for example, through unification with a democratic South Korea). Some African countries are fragile and vulnerable. One-party rule based on the dominant ethnic group may not be democratic, but it is potentially more stable, especially in countries where ethnic and family ties are stronger than national ones. The Kikuyu tribe, which ruled Kenya since its independence in 1963, maintained stability but in the process alienated the minority Luo and other tribes, which ignited violence in late 2007 after disputed elections. Constructing new identities is as political as it gets. Little wonder that talk about regime change, especially by force, sparks controversy. But even softer versions of regime change trigger widespread disagreement. It may seem self-evident to Americans that a multiethnic society is to be preferred over a partitioned society and that democracy is the best, perhaps only decent, way to construct a multiethnic society. But it is certainly easy to understand why communist societies saw that goal for many years as objectionable and why fundamentalist and deeply divided societies today find it not only dangerous but also immoral.

Nation Building: Iraq and Afghanistan

Iraq and Afghanistan illustrate many of the classic features of ethnic and religious divisions and efforts to resolve them through the construction of a national identity. Iraq has a proud history that evokes memories of self-governance and grandeur. Baghdad was once the imperial center of the Abbasid dynasties that ruled Islam at the peak of its Golden Age. Subsequently Iraq was part of the Ottoman Empire, where until 1924 Turkish dynasties served as the last caliphates of the Muslim world. Iraq also experienced colonialism. During World War I, Britain encouraged the Arabs to revolt against the Ottoman Turks, who were aligned with Germany. When the Ottoman Empire dissolved after the war, Britain secured a League of Nations mandate to create and administer Iraq. The new territory was an artificial agglomeration of Kurdish and Arab ethnic groups and of Sunni and Shiite religious sects. Sunnis, who dominate in most Arab countries, were a minority in the new Iraq, around 20 percent. Shiites, whose religious center was outside Iraq in the neighboring, non-Arab, Persian territory of Iran—also a British mandate—were the majority, around 60 percent. Kurds, who are mostly secular, make up the remaining 20 percent and tend to have more in common with Turkish tribes in Turkey, Syria, and Iran than with the Sunni or Shiite Arabs in Iraq. In 1932, Iraq became formally independent under a Hashemite king, but it was never stable. After a series of military coups, it became a republic in 1958 and then in 1968 fell under the rule of the Baath Party, an Arab Sunni group that made up only 20 percent of the population and advocated secular nationalism. In 1979, Saddam Hussein took control of the Baath Party and proceeded to crush Shiite and Kurdish opposition and fight wars against Iran (1980–1988), Kuwait (1990), the United Nations (1991), and the United States (2003).

Afghanistan is a similarly proud and beleaguered country. Founded in 1747, the country was colonized and contested for a century or more as a buffer between the British and Russian empires. It became independent in 1919, but it never had a strong central government or sense of nationhood. The Soviet Union invaded and occupied the country in 1979. When the Soviet Union left in 1989, civil war ensued, eventually resulting in a takeover of the government by the Taliban, an extremist Muslim sect that allowed Al Qaeda to establish training camps in Afghanistan and attack the United States on 9/11.

Pakistani paramilitary soldiers escort a truck loaded with a container full of with supplies for NATO and U.S.-led forces in Afghanistan at the Pakistani border town of Jamrud on November 17, 2008. The troubled Khyber Pass border crossing was the site of frequent attacks by Taliban militants during the U.S.-led operations in the region.

The country is divided along tribal lines. The Pashtun, who have traditionally ruled the country, make up 42 percent of the population and occupy the eastern and southern regions. Tajik tribes make up another 27 percent and, together with Hazara and Uzbek tribes at 9 percent each of the population, occupy the northern and western parts of the country. Pashtuns are also prominent in Pakistan, and the Taliban forces that ruled the country before the U.S. invasion roam back and forth across a disputed border and frontier between Afghanistan and Pakistan. The Obama administration has referred to the Afghanistan problem as AfPak, suggesting the two countries are a single region in the fight against Al Qaeda and the Taliban.

Can Iraq and Afghanistan be governed by any force other than elite oppression or partition? After invading and overthrowing governments in both countries, the United States has tried to develop a centralized government along constitutional and democratic lines. It spent three years in Iraq cobbling together a federalist and constitutional government that, after three closely contested elections in 2005, 2009, and 2013, is still very divided and fragile. It did the same in Afghanistan only to witness elections in 2009 that were widely considered to be fraudulent. The Kabul government is rife with corruption and indecision, and presidential elections take place again in 2014. Attempts in both countries to train local military, police, and civil servants to take over security and reconstruction efforts and allow U.S. and other foreign forces to leave the two countries are hindered by numerous obstacles. Nevertheless, U.S. forces left Iraq in 2011 and planned to leave Afghanistan in 2014. The United States left no troops stationed in Iraq because Iraq refused to conclude a status of force agreement that would protect American forces from local prosecution. As of late 2013 it was not clear whether any U.S. forces would be left behind in Afghanistan.

Skeptics believe that any effort to fashion a national, let alone democratic, identity in either of these countries is unlikely to succeed. Already in 2006, then senator Joseph Biden and foreign policy expert Leslie Gelb were calling for the soft partition of Iraq, by which they meant creating autonomous zones (as in Bosnia) in which Kurds,

Sunnis, and Shiites could run their own affairs, with a central government that would manage only common interests.[38] The best we can hope for in Iraq, the skeptics argue, is a government of oligarchs who will divide up the spoils of the country's oil and maintain stability under the loose supervision of international institutions. More recently, similar proposals have been made for Afghanistan. One idea, known as reconciliation, is to let the Kabul government negotiate power-sharing deals with Taliban forces in the country. Indeed, in 2012 the United States initiated separate discussions with the Taliban under the good offices of the Arab country Qatar, creating further suspicions in Kabul that a U.S. exit will result in a return of the Taliban government. Richard Haass, president of the Council on Foreign Relations, called in 2010 for the "de facto partition of Afghanistan." Realists, as before, favor hard partition, the separation of ethnic groups along ethno-nationalist lines. Under this approach, as Haass wrote, "the United States would accept Taliban control of the Pashtun-dominated south so long as the Taliban did not welcome back Al Qaeda and did not seek to undermine stability in non-Pashtun areas of the country. If the Taliban violated these rules, the United States would attack them with bombers, drones, and Special Forces."[39] This alternative was described as a counterterrorism strategy focusing on suppressing terrorist attacks rather than a counterinsurgency strategy focusing on building a national government.

What do you think will happen? Can you see the different perspectives at work: partition (realist), nation building (identity), and reconciliation (liberal)? Which perspective will prove to be right? You, too, have to decide.

≫ Human Rights

Today's world may be witnessing a transition from norms of state sovereignty to norms of human rights. For four hundred years, sovereignty defined the state as the principal actor in international affairs; it guaranteed the rights of states, not the rights of individuals or human rights more generally. Sovereignty means simply noninterference in the internal affairs of other states. States can decide for themselves how to organize their domestic life and treat their own people. Notice that the emphasis here is on the autonomy of the state, not its anatomy or what its constitution or political makeup may be. The state is sovereign whether it is organized by democratic, despotic, or doctrinal (religious) rules. Governments can define themselves in any way they choose—Protestant or Catholic, Orthodox or Roman, Muslim or Jewish, authoritarian or pluralistic—and what they decide is nobody else's business. The substance, or anatomy, of the actor matters less than the independence, or autonomy, of the actor. Sovereignty conceals the question of who or what is sovereign. Is it a monarch, an aristocracy, a class of merchants or workers, or an elected and representative government of the people as a whole? This is a substantive question that became more important as nationalism and the idea of democracy spread. Sovereignty portrays the state more as an institutional shell than as a substantive commitment. As we will see, however, sovereignty is challenged by a new idea: universal human rights.

Universal Human Rights

As noted earlier, for centuries empires considered their own people (mostly just the elites) to be civilized and the rest of the world to be barbarians. That changed when the Westphalian states began to recognize one another as equals regardless of race or religion. It changed further in the nineteenth century when states abolished the slave trade and then eventually slavery itself. The Geneva Convention of 1864 and subsequent elaborations in the 1920s and 1940s mandated humane treatment for captured military personnel during war and established certain protections for civilians as well; and the International Committee of the Red Cross, a Swiss NGO, began its long history of visiting and monitoring the treatment of prisoners around the world. Surprisingly, the Covenant of the League of Nations was silent on human rights, and the United States opposed incorporating the principle of racial equality advocated by Japan. Nevertheless, the League itself developed refugee and other assistance programs that promoted human rights.

universal human rights: rights inherent in all human beings that are often expressed and guaranteed by law in the forms of treaties, customary international law, general principles, and other sources of international law.

The United Nations Charter was the first treaty in world history to recognize **universal human rights.** In Article 1, the Charter states that one of the purposes of the United Nations is "to achieve cooperation in solving international problems of an economic, social, cultural or humanitarian character, and in promoting and encouraging respect for human rights and for fundamental freedoms for all without distinction as to race, sex, language, or religion." The United Nations had legally binding authority to act only in security areas, however, although the Security Council later recognized the possibility that violations of human rights might lead to security crises, as in the cases of racism in South Africa and Southern Rhodesia (now Zimbabwe). Security was being interpreted increasingly in terms of the consequences for individual human beings. The objective was the human security of people, not just the national security of states. After World War II, special tribunals tried and executed war criminals in Germany and Japan. And the Holocaust during World War II led to the UN Convention on the Prevention and Punishment of the Crime of Genocide. Decolonization after World War II effectively eliminated the right of states to govern foreign subjects, replacing it with the right of *self*-determination.

Universal Declaration of Human Rights: a UN declaration approved in 1948 prescribing the obligations of states to individuals rather than of individuals to states.

Gradually, the emphasis was shifting from the rights and responsibilities of states to the rights and responsibilities of individuals and groups within states. In 1948, the United Nations adopted the **Universal Declaration of Human Rights.** A nonbinding declaration, this document covered the panoply of rights long advocated by Western states: the right to political participation and civic freedom; entitlements to adequate food, clothing, shelter, and health care; and the right to freedom from fear of bodily harm. No state voted against the declaration; however, the Soviet Union and seven other states, all communist except South Africa and Saudi Arabia, abstained. And it was not until almost twenty years later, in 1966, that the UN codified these rights in two binding treaties: the International Covenant on Economic, Social and Cultural Rights (ICESCR) and the International Covenant on Civil and Political Rights

(ICCPR). Together with the Charter, these documents constitute what amounts to an international or global bill of rights, identifying certain common obligations all states have toward civil society or their individual citizens.

States disagree about which rights are more fundamental. Authoritarian states such as China emphasize social and economic rights; liberal democracies such as the United States emphasize civil and political rights. China never ratified the ICCPR, and the United States never ratified the ICESCR. The ICCPR set up a Human Rights Committee that monitors the Covenant and can consider individual cases. The ICESCR receives only state reports.[40] (For some key indicators of human rights, see Table 7-3.) Still, a consensus has grown that the most basic rights, such as freedom from physical abuse, torture, and genocide, should be protected, and implementation of such protection has shifted incrementally from national to international institutions such as the permanent International Criminal Court, established in 1999. The ICC has the right to accept cases brought by individuals or global citizens, not just by states or national governments.

To be sure, implementing, let alone enforcing, these norms has not been easy. Realist perspectives might say that this is because powerful states, such as China and the United States, simply ignore them. Liberal perspectives would say it is because international institutions are not yet strong enough. In the past, countries such as Cuba, Libya, and Sudan chaired the UN human rights committees and made a mockery of the UN deliberations. Nevertheless, identity and liberal perspectives point to some significant successes. UN sanctions worked against apartheid South Africa to bring down that regime. And human rights discussions under the auspices of the Helsinki Accords in 1975 opened up eastern Europe and the Soviet Union to political reforms that contributed to ending communism in Europe.

CAUSAL ARROW: PERSPECTIVES

Restrain national behavior	Shape international law	Human rights norms
REALIST	LIBERAL	IDENTITY

Let's look more closely at the successes and controversies of implementing basic human rights through the UN Universal Declaration of Human Rights, the European Convention on Human Rights, and human rights regimes in other regions.

UN Human Rights Commission/Council

During the Cold War, the United Nations intervened in military or humanitarian conflicts only with the consent of the rival superpowers and often that of the local authorities as well. When the Cold War ended, numerous internal or intrastate conflicts erupted—in Somalia, Cambodia, and Bosnia, to name a few. The UN Security Council expanded its definition of what constitutes a threat to international peace and security under Chapter VII to include intrastate conflicts. As human rights specialist David P. Forsythe points out, "Security could refer to the security of persons within states, based on human rights, and not just to traditional military violence across international frontiers."[41] The office of the secretary-general became more active. Supported by developing nations that became

TABLE 7-3

Human Rights: Key Indicators, 2012

Total number of displaced persons (refugees) worldwide	45.2 million
Percentage of refugees under the age of 18	46%
Percentage of refugees who are female	48%
Country of origin of the greatest number of refugees	Afghanistan
Country hosting the most refugees	Pakistan
Percentage of women in legislatures, worldwide average	21%
Gender wage gap, OECD countries	15%
Gender wage gap, Korea	37%
Ratio of maternal deaths worldwide per 100,000 live births	210
Ratio of maternal deaths in developed regions per 100,000 live births	16
Ratio of maternal deaths in developing regions per 100,000 live births	240
Ratio of deaths worldwide of children under age 5 per 1,000 live births	48
Ratio of deaths in sub-Saharan Africa of children under age 5 per 1,000 live births	98
Number of children involved in child labor	168 million
Number of children involved in hazardous labor	85.3 million
Incidence of child labor in low-income countries	22.5%
Incidence of child labor in upper-middle-income countries	6.2%

Sources: United Nations High Commissioner for Refugees, *Displacement: The New 21st Century Challenge,* UNHCR Global Trends 2012 (Geneva: UNHCR, 2013), http://www.unhcr.org.uk/fileadmin/user_upload/pdf/UNHCR_Global_Trends_2012. pdf; Inter-Parliamentary Union, "Women in National Parliaments," http://www.ipu.org/wmn-e/world.htm; OECD, "Gender Equality: Gender Wage Gap," http://www.oecd.org/gender/data/genderwagegap.htm; World Health Organization, UNICEF, UN Population Fund, and World Bank, *Trends in Maternal Mortality: 1990 to 2010* (Geneva: WHO, 2012), http://whqlibdoc.who.int/ publications/2012/9789241503631_eng.pdf; International Labour Organization, "Global Child Labour Trends 2008 to 2012," http:// www.ilo.org/ipec/Informationresources/WCMS_IPEC_PUB_23015/lang--en/index.htm.

UN Human Rights Commission: the commission that drafted and implements the Universal Declaration of Human Rights.

new members of the United Nations after decolonization, Secretary-General Boutros Boutros-Ghali appointed the first UN high commissioner for human rights in 1993. The idea was to broaden the attention focused on human rights.

The traditional center of UN diplomacy on human rights was the **UN Human Rights Commission.** Prominent in drafting the Universal Declaration of Human Rights, the commission consisted of representatives of states elected by the **UN Economic and Social Council (ECOSOC)**, a major organ of the UN General Assembly. Initially, because it represented states, most of which are reluctant to interfere in sovereignty, the commission did not entertain specific complaints about human rights abuses. But after the late 1960s, under pressure from developing countries, it began to discuss human rights abuses in Israel, South Africa, Haiti, and Greece. Based on resolutions passed by ECOSOC, the commission was also able to consider complaints from NGOs, not just states. However, ECOSOC decides which NGOs have consultative status in the UN—that is, which can attend meetings and submit documents to the commission. ECOSOC denied consultative status to some legitimate human rights NGOs. As Margaret Karns and Karen Mingst point out, delegations feared that NGOs might eventually weaken or eliminate the monopoly of states in global decision making.[42] In addition, ECOSOC elects commission representatives on the basis of equitable geographic representation. This provision, along with the fact that many UN members are still authoritarian or even, in some cases, totalitarian regimes, severely politicized the Human Rights Commission. Cuba, which approximates a totalitarian regime, was elected to the commission, and at one point Libya, an oppressive monarchy, became president of the commission.

Eventually, the commission was disbanded and replaced in 2006 by the **UN Human Rights Council**. Members of this council are now elected by a majority of UN members voting by secret ballot and taking into account "the contribution of candidates to the promotion and protection of human rights." Seats are still apportioned by geographic area, but the General Assembly can suspend membership in the council by a two-thirds majority vote if a member "commits gross and systematic violations of human rights." The United States had sought a two-thirds vote to elect members, rather than to suspend them, and wanted to identify specific human rights violations that would disqualify a candidate. But in the interest of moving ahead, the United States accepted the compromise. Thus far, the council continues to politicize and in some cases to trivialize human rights.[43] At a 2009 UN human rights conference in Durban, South Africa, the president of Iran delivered a tirade against Israel, prompting a walkout by multiple countries including the United States, whose president called the speech "appalling and objectionable."[44]

The United Nations human rights regime includes other conventions. Two important ones are the UN Convention on the Elimination of All Forms of Discrimination against Women (CEDAW) and the UN Convention on the Rights of the Child (CRC).

Convention on Women's Rights

The **UN Convention on the Elimination of All Forms of Discrimination against Women (CEDAW)** was developed by the Commission on the Status of Women, initially a subcommission of the UN Human Rights Commission. Passed by the General Assembly in 1979, CEDAW prohibits all discrimination against women, defined as

UN Economic and Social Council (ECOSOC): a major organ of the UN General Assembly that until 2006 elected members of the UN Human Rights Commission based on geographic representation.

UN Human Rights Council: the organization that replaced the UN Human Rights Commission in 2006.

UN Convention on the Elimination of All Forms of Discrimination against Women (CEDAW): the 1979 UN convention broadly prohibiting all discrimination against women.

any distinction, exclusion or restriction made on the basis of sex which has the effect or purpose of impairing or nullifying the recognition, enjoyment or exercise by women, irrespective of their marital status, on a basis of equality of men and women, of human rights and fundamental freedoms in the political, economic, social, cultural, civil or any other field.[45]

A total of 187 countries are parties to the convention. They elect a committee of twenty-three experts in the field of women's rights to receive and investigate reports from the member states submitted every four years.

Member states have applied numerous reservations to CEDAW. Muslim countries, for example, do not recognize provisions of the convention inconsistent with religious law (sharia). Saudi Arabia emphasizes the harmony and complementarities between men and women but not equality. The United States is one of eight countries yet to ratify the convention. Ratification has been stalled since 1980 in the Senate, where critics argue that the convention infringes on U.S. sovereignty, promotes abortion, interferes with the notion of family, and will legalize prostitution.

In 2000, CEDAW adopted an optional protocol that permits individual women and women's groups to submit complaints. Fewer than half the member parties subscribe to this protocol, reflecting the reluctance of states to give women the right to appeal to an international body over national authorities if women feel their country is not respecting their rights.

Convention on the Rights of the Child

UN Convention on the Rights of the Child (CRC): the UN convention adopted in 1989 to protect the rights of children.

The **UN Convention on the Rights of the Child (CRC)** was adopted by the General Assembly in 1989. It seeks to protect the rights of every child—defined as anyone under eighteen years of age, unless adult status has been attained earlier under national law—to life, to freedom from abuse, and to food, shelter, education, conscience (including religion), and participation in the community. It too developed initially out of the Universal Declaration of Human Rights, and, like CEDAW, it functions through a committee of experts (in this case, eighteen) elected by 193 member parties. Member parties are required to report to the committee of experts every five years.

CRC does not have provisions to hear complaints from individual children or their representatives. Optional protocols seek to prevent children from being used in warfare or subjected to sale, prostitution, or pornography. The United States has not signed CRC, arguing, as it has in other cases, that the convention does not bind oppressive countries that abuse the rights of not only children but also adults and that U.S. law provides greater real protection for children's rights than the does the law of any other country.

The United Nations is clearly hampered by the fact that there is still no clear consensus on the substance of basic human rights. Are basic human rights universal or are they cultural? Is the UN human rights regime just another form of Western cultural imperialism? Countries such as Cuba, Libya, and Zimbabwe contend that the United States and other Western countries violate the human rights of blacks, Muslims, the poor, and other minorities. The basic rights to health care and education, they claim, are more essential than rights to political and civil liberties, and the Western nations, through their control of multinational corporations and wealth, systematically deprive developing nations of the most basic human needs. The United States and European countries counter that these charges are merely a smoke screen for repressive regimes that not only deny their people the freedom to acquire property and wealth but also systematically bleed their countries of resources and capital through corruption and favoritism.

CAUSAL ARROW: PERSPECTIVES

Help or hinder Western imperialism	Shape common or separate rules	Universal or culturally based human rights
REALIST	LIBERAL	IDENTITY

European Human Rights Regime

Regional bodies such as the European Commission on Human Rights and the European Court of Human Rights set even higher standards for human rights, including the political rights to assemble and to vote. These human rights regimes increasingly prescribe the obligations of states to individuals rather than just of individuals to states. Perhaps human rights are best managed at the regional level, where countries share greater cultural affinity.

The development of a human rights regime has progressed furthest in Europe. Created in the late 1940s, before economic integration began under the European Coal and Steel Community, the **Council of Europe (CE)** guarantees not only human rights but also rights to political participation. In 2013, forty-seven countries belonged to the Council of Europe. The early treaties of the European Communities did not mention human or political rights, but the Maastricht Treaty in 1992, which transformed the European Communities into the European Union, committed the EU to respect the rights guaranteed by the Council of Europe. The European Court of Justice administers EU law.

The centerpiece of Europe's human rights regime is the **European Convention on Human Rights and Fundamental Freedoms**, adopted by the CE in 1950. Drawing on the UN's 1948 Universal Declaration of Human Rights, the convention establishes basic protections that block governments from violating citizens' rights to due process (legal rights, trial by jury, and so on) and political participation. The convention is enforced by the Council of Ministers (usually foreign ministers) and by the **European Court of Human Rights**, located in Strasbourg, France.

The innovation of the European Convention on Human Rights was not only to create an intergovernmental body to monitor the human rights behavior of governments but also to allow private parties (such as individuals, NGOs, and associations of people), not just governments, to petition the court. Originally, a separate European Commission of Human Rights screened these private petitions and represented the petitioners if their cases went forward to the Court of Human Rights or Council of Ministers. But subsequent changes enabled private parties to appear directly before a special chamber of the court.

This move to give individuals, not just states, legal standing in international human rights proceedings was controversial. First, after ratifying the convention, a member state still had the right to accept or reject the jurisdiction of the European Court of Human Rights as well as the option of allowing private parties from that state to petition the court. Eventually, all member states accepted these provisions. But for many years the Commission of Human

Council of Europe (CE): organization founded in 1949 to promote human rights in Europe.

European Convention on Human Rights and Fundamental Freedoms: the convention adopted by the Council of Europe in 1950 to protect citizens' rights to due process and political participation.

European Court of Human Rights: the court that administers European human rights law.

A Kurdish woman reacts to the May 2005 decision by the European Court of Human Rights to uphold a ruling in favor of jailed Kurdish leader Abdullah Ocalan, saying that a Turkish court that had sentenced him to death in 1999 had tried him unfairly. The court, whose ruling is not binding, recommended that Turkey retry Ocalan, but it declined to do so. Ocalan's sentence was commuted to a life sentence, which he is serving in the prison island of Imrali.

Rights approved very few of the private petitions that it screened, and states as a rule did not often choose to take one another to court over human rights. Only eight cases had been brought to the court by states as of 2005. By contrast, the number of private petitions continued to increase, despite the early rejection rates, and the commission began to approve a larger percentage of them. To improve efficiency, the commission was eventually replaced by a chamber of the court made up of several judges. Private parties could now go directly to the Court of Human Rights for preliminary hearings. As of 2013, the court had rendered more than sixteen thousand judgments, and every year it receives more than fifty thousand applications from parties wishing to have their cases heard.

Of the private cases heard by the court, one concerned the complaint of a couple from Slovenia that their son died in a hospital in 1993 as a result of medical negligence. After eleven years of legal proceedings, Slovenian courts had rejected their claim. The couple brought the case to the European Court of Human Rights, and in June 2007, the court decided that it would hear the case. The plaintiffs alleged that the legal proceedings in the Slovenian courts were excessively lengthy and unfair. They relied, in particular, on Articles 2 (right to life), 6 (right to a fair hearing), and 13 (right to an effective remedy) of the European Convention on Human Rights. The plaintiffs won their case and were awarded the modest sum of 7,540 euros.

A second case concerned a group of Turkish nationals who contested a decision by the Turkish courts to declare a parcel of land that the plaintiffs said had been in their family for three generations as belonging to the state forest. Relying on Article 1 of Protocol 1 (protection of property) to the European Human Rights Convention, the applicants contended that the Turkish courts' decision constituted a disproportionate interference with their right to the peaceful enjoyment of their possessions. A third case involved a television station in Norway that aired commercials for a political party despite a Norwegian law that prohibits political commercials on TV. The television station had been fined and, after losing an appeal to Norway's Supreme Court, brought the case to the European Court.[46]

These cases suggest how deeply European law is reaching into the domain of national law. Remember that the states that belong to the Council of Europe are for the most part liberal democracies. Why are their citizens petitioning a European court for rights that presumably their national courts ensure? One reason is that national laws are not in all cases fully democratic, and, even among democracies, nations may differ in the degree to which they protect human rights. Russia, for example, is a member of the Council of Europe but hardly qualifies as a liberal democracy. And although human rights are fully protected in the United Kingdom, some rights are protected by custom rather than by formal laws. In 1997, UK citizens brought four hundred petitions to the European Court of Human Rights. More generally, the experience of the European Court of Human Rights suggests that people are becoming more comfortable identifying with regional as well as national authorities to protect their basic rights. As one human rights expert notes, "Even with liberal democracy at the national level, there [is] still a need for regional monitoring of human rights—there being evident violations by national authorities."[47]

Do states comply with the European court's judgments? As a rule, yes. But there are still instances of noncompliance. Earlier, Britain and Italy were the most frequent violators of the court's decisions. By 2005, the bulk of violations came from Turkey and Russia. In cases of noncompliance, the Council of Europe's Council of Ministers can order that compensation be paid. But, unlike domestic courts, the European Court of Human Rights cannot turn to a police force to arrest violators.

The Council of Europe has passed other human rights conventions. The European Social Charter, originally developed in 1961, was revised in 1996 and as of 2013 had been signed by forty-seven members and ratified by forty-three members. The Social Charter covers basic rights to housing, employment, health, education, legal and social protections, freedom of movement, and nondiscrimination. As such, it is more expansive and intrusive on national prerogatives. Social rights cannot be adjudicated by the Court of Human Rights, although there is some talk about making social rights part of the European Convention on Human Rights in the future. Nevertheless, from 1998 to 2012 the European Committee of Social Rights, charged with implementing the Social Charter, received eighty-eight complaints from collective private parties (such as trade unions and human rights groups), heard eighty-two of them, and decided seventy-two on the merits.[48] In one such case in 2012, the committee ruled against the authorities in France for discrimination against Romanies (Gypsies) from Romania and Bulgaria who were illegally deported from France.

In 1986, the Council of Europe also passed the European Convention for the Prevention of Torture and Inhuman or Degrading Treatment or Punishment. All members ratified this convention. It is implemented by a committee of uninstructed (meaning independent of government) individuals who can make ad hoc visits to detention centers with minimal advance notice to investigate prisoners' treatment. In recent years, the committee has ruled against France for abuse of a suspected drug dealer and against Turkey and Russia for a variety of abuses. The fact that European states are accustomed to monitoring one another on the treatment of detainees may explain their outrage at the U.S. abuses of detainees at Guantanamo, Abu Ghraib, and secret CIA detention centers around the world, some in Europe. The United States does not participate in such regional human rights regimes and, hence, is not accustomed to such oversight.

Other Regional Human Rights Regimes

Latin America and Africa have human rights regimes that are similar to those in Europe, but numerous states in these regions have systematically violated the standards of basic human rights. Asia established a human rights regime for the first time in 2009, while Arab and broader Islamic countries use human rights issues primarily to vilify Israel. The limits of the acceptance of basic human rights remind us that the world is not yet a community of common humanity, if we understand the latter to mean that a consensus exists on such rights.

Latin America's human rights regime is centered in the Organization of American States. The OAS has a regional convention for the protection of human rights and the Inter-American Commission and Court of Human Rights to implement it. The **American Declaration on the Rights and Duties of Man** dates from 1948, the **Inter-American Convention on Human Rights** from 1969, and the **Inter-American Court of Human Rights** from 1979. Although the declaration and convention have content similar to that of the European regime, only twenty-four of thirty-five states in the region accept the jurisdiction of the Inter-American Court of Human Rights. As a result, the court for many years had a small caseload; as of 2004, it had handed down only 45 binding and 17 advisory opinions.[49] In 2010, however, some 1,600 complaints were filed, and 128 cases were before the court.

Only the Inter-American Commission appointed by states and the states themselves can bring cases to the court. Nevertheless, in 1998, Brazil and Mexico, two of the region's most important states, accepted the court's jurisdiction. The United States still does not, for fear that membership will subject U.S. defendants to all sorts of frivolous lawsuits.

Africa too has a Charter on Human and Peoples' Rights, which went into force in 1986. But Africa's charter sets up only an advisory commission to implement its provisions; until 2004, there was no court to hear cases. In that year, the African Court on Human and Peoples' Rights was created, and in 2006 the court's first judges were elected. But only states can bring cases, unless they explicitly accept the right of individuals to petition. Few are expected to do so.

Asia created its first human rights charter in 2009. The **ASEAN Intergovernmental Commission on Human Rights (AICHR)** is the product of fifteen years of efforts by nongovernmental groups to establish governmental responsibility for human rights. The record of Asian governments continues to lag behind. Only nine Asian states subscribe to the International Covenants on Civil and Political Liberties and Economic and Social Rights. By contrast, dozens of states subscribe to the UN CEDAW and CRC.

American Declaration on the Rights and Duties of Man: the world's first international human rights instrument of a general nature, adopted by the nations of the Americas in April 1948.

Inter-American Convention on Human Rights: an international human rights instrument adopted by the nations of the Americas in 1969.

Inter-American Court of Human Rights: the court charged with implementing the Inter-American Convention on Human Rights.

ASEAN Intergovernmental Commission on Human Rights (AICHR): Asian human rights commission established in 2009.

The rights of oppressed groups, such as minorities, indigenous groups, peasant and working-class groups, and the disabled, and the rights to political participation are not widely recognized by Asian states. Asian states see these rights as a threat to state interests and sovereignty. Most of them view rights as being granted by the state rather than as being protected from the state. Thus, social stability and the preservation of the state take precedence over the enforcement of human rights. Some states, such as China, Singapore, and Malaysia, argue unabashedly for Asian values that give priority to society rather than to individuals.

The Arab and broader Islamic worlds have similar disregard for basic or—as they see them—Western human rights. The Arab League has a Human Rights Commission that focuses largely on what it perceives to be Israeli atrocities in occupied territories, and the Organization of the Islamic Conference (OIC), which consists of fifty-seven Muslim countries spread across four continents, created a Commission on Human Rights in 2012, which states that it will promote rights "in conformity with Islamic values." For the past decade, the OIC has campaigned at the UN Human Rights Commission/Council to restrict the right of freedom of expression, urging the council to report on instances, such as public statements against the Islamic religion, where freedom of expression involves religious blasphemy. As the International Humanist and Ethical Union (an umbrella NGO for human rights organizations advocating a humanist rather than a religious or democratic definition of human rights) lamented, the OIC's position "would turn the [Council's] mandate on its head." "Instead of promoting freedom of expression," the Council "would be policing its exercise."[50] In 2009, the United States cosponsored a resolution with Egypt to condemn "negative religious stereotyping," a formulation that critics fear will be used to prosecute domestic dissidents in Egypt and other Islamic countries who protest against religious oppression. (See Table 7-4 for a summary of identity explanations for nation building and human rights.)

TABLE
7-4

Nation Building and Human Rights in Today's World: The Identity Perspective and Levels of Analysis

Identity perspective			
Systemic	*Structure*	Universal Declaration of Human Rights	
	Process	UN Human Rights Council legislates on human rights	
	Region	European Court of Human Rights	
Foreign policy		Russia resists international human rights interventions for fear of implications for domestic separatist movements, such as in Chechnya	
Domestic		Civic, ethnic, and religious identities clash in nation building	
Individual		Individuals bring cases to human rights courts	

(Left vertical label: **Level of analysis**)

SUMMARY

To explain events in the contemporary world, identity perspectives appeal to the convergence and clash of ideas and self-images. At the structural level they give most attention either to expanding democracy, human rights, and international courts or to the emerging clash of civilizations between Islam and the West. At the systemic process, domestic, and individual levels, identity accounts point to the spread of transnational networks such as Al Qaeda and the Community of Democracies, the clashes between secular, moderate and fundamentalist groups within individual nations, and the leadership role of individuals such as Osama bin Laden and Sayyid Qutb.

 **for CQ Press** Sharpen your skills with SAGE edge at **edge.sagepub.com/nau4e.** **SAGE edge for students** provides a personalized approach to help you accomplish your coursework goals in an easy-to-use learning environment.

KEY CONCEPTS

American Declaration on the Rights and Duties of Man, 324

ASEAN Intergovernmental Commission on Human Rights (AICHR), 324

civic identity, 311

clash of civilizations, 302

Council of Europe (CE), 321

end of history, 294

European Convention on Human Rights and Fundamental Freedoms, 321

European Court of Human Rights, 321

Inter-American Convention on Human Rights, 324

Inter-American Court of Human Rights, 324

jihad, 306

nation building, 312

nationhood, 311

Shanghai Cooperation Organization (SCO), 310

Sunnis, 305

Shiites, 306

UN Convention on the Elimination of All Forms of Discrimination against Women (CEDAW), 319

UN Convention on the Rights of the Child (CRC), 320

UN Economic and Social Council (ECOSOC), 319

UN Human Rights Commission, 318

UN Human Rights Council, 319

Universal Declaration of Human Rights , 316

universal human rights, 316

Wahhabism, 307

STUDY QUESTIONS

1. What is the difference between Fukuyama's forecast of the end of history and Huntington's forecast of the clash of civilizations? Why is Fukuyama's perspective considered to be identity and Huntington's realist?

2. Is freedom a universalist or a Western value?

3. What is the difference between civic and ethnic identities, and which perspective emphasizes each?

4. Are human rights political or economic? If both, which comes first, democratic governance or economic development?

5. Which courts allow individuals, not just states, to bring cases for review? Should international courts take precedence over national courts even among democratic countries?

Recorded history began five thousand years ago, but a world economy involving trade and finance across the entire globe began only about five hundred years ago. For the first four and a half millennia, people lived primarily on the land and produced everything they needed in local villages and communities. Then around 1500 C.E., the world exploded economically. European nations led this development, even though China and the Islamic world were more advanced only a few centuries before. As Bernard Lewis, the well-known Middle East historian, writes, "Medieval Europe was a pupil and . . . a dependent of the Islamic world."[1]

What happened to explain this phenomenon? In his best-selling book *The World Is Flat*, Thomas Friedman identifies three historical phases of globalization, the knitting together of the world into a single market economy:[2]

globalization 1.0: early period of globalization, from 1492 to 1800, driven by mercantilism and colonialism.

globalization 2.0: later period of globalization, from 1800 to 1950, driven by global market institutions such as multinational trading and manufacturing corporations.

globalization 3.0: latest period of globalization, starting in the second half of the twentieth century, driven by the flattening of the global playing field and the knowledge economy rather than by imperialism or manufacturing conglomerates.

- **Globalization 1.0** lasted from 1492 to 1800 and "shrank the world from a size large to a size medium." This was the age of mercantilism and colonialism. The driving force was brawn, not brains—"how much muscle, how much horsepower, wind power, or, later, steam power—your country had and how creatively you could deploy it." As Paul Kennedy tells us (see the introduction to Part I), ships and firepower led the parade, not motives or institutions.

- **Globalization 2.0** ran from 1800 to the mid-twentieth century; it was ended by World War II. It "shrank the world from a size medium to a size small." This was the age of British hegemony, or Pax Britannica. The driving force was new institutions, particularly the emergence of private global actors such as multinational banks and

corporations. Global megacompanies exploited the dramatic drop in transportation and then communications costs to weave the world together into a seamless web of interconnected products, capital, and labor. They operated global trading and shipping companies, mined raw materials, and developed worldwide agribusiness and manufacturing conglomerates.

- **Globalization 3.0** arrived during the second half of the twentieth century and "is shrinking the world from a size small to a size tiny and flattening the playing field at the same time." This is the age of American hegemony, or Pax Americana, and the driving force is the Internet, "the newfound power for *individuals* to collaborate and compete globally." Individuals now communicate, innovate, form groups, conduct business, and move money worldwide just the way MNCs do. Brains, not brawn or institutions, shape the world economy. And that world is now increasingly flat, meaning that every country and civilization can take part. China, India, and, potentially, Muslim countries—"every color of the human rainbow"—can participate in the globalization chat room. Neither power disparities nor institutional advantages matter as much as the ability to think creatively.

Notice how Friedman's three versions of globalization can be understood in terms of our three principal perspectives on international relations. In globalization 1.0, physical power mattered most (the realist perspective). In globalization 2.0, multinational institutions drove the process (the liberal perspective). And in globalization 3.0, innovations and ideas matter most (the identity perspective). But Friedman, of course, is making judgments. Maybe the ships and firepower of globalization 1.0 were the products of the Reformation and Protestant ideas (the identity perspective), which gave a divine blessing to the acquisition of wealth. Or maybe the MNCs that drove globalization 2.0 were simply artifacts of Britain's dominant power (the realist perspective) or of Enlightenment ideas embracing free markets and private property (the identity perspective). And perhaps globalization 3.0 is not about brains and flattening but about *American* brawn and imperialism (the realist perspective) and unprecedented global interdependence (the liberal perspective). Friedman sees technological change as the rocket booster behind all three versions of globalization. And he sees the impact of technological change as leveling or flattening the playing field for all individuals and all civilizations, regardless of ideological differences. In all these respects, his perspective on globalization is quintessentially liberal.

In Part III we address these realist, liberal, and identity aspects of contemporary globalization as well as a critical theory perspective on globalization. Chapter 8 focuses on the material and institutional aspects of globalization, the relative (realist) and liberal (absolute) gains that result from worldwide economic activities. It examines the mechanisms that make globalization work—the domestic and international economic policies (trade, investment, and finance)—and create the prosperity and crises of a globalized world.

Chapter 9 addresses more directly identity aspects of the global economy and the environment. Identity perspectives ask about the values that motivate economic gains: Gains for whom (which countries and cultures) and for what (consumerism or environmentalism)?

Finally, Chapter 10 takes a critical theory look at development. It asks whether there is anything useful that can be learned from the history of a world economy that is scarred by pervasive Western imperialism, inequality, and injustice. From 1500 C.E. on, Western countries rigged world markets and created the so-called free-market conditions of comparative advantage and foreign investment companies. Free markets then systematically exploited poor countries and locked them into the peripheral status that has characterized their existence ever since. Why would this history contain anything that might be of use in the future? Chapter 10 fleshes out the important downsides of globalization, issues that are not always accounted for by the principal perspectives. It examines the marginalization of indigenous peoples, women, and children and explores dependency and world systems studies that seek to raise the world's self-consciousness about the pervasive power and perfidy of Western imperialism.

Kerim Muhammet poses with his two new smartphones after waiting in line overnight to be among the first to purchase the latest generation of the smartphone in Glendale, California, September 2013. Do the economic policies that make his purchases possible make the countries of the world increasingly interdependent—and more vulnerable?

REALIST AND LIBERAL PERSPECTIVES ON GLOBALIZATION

8

Trade, Investment, and Finance

How does globalization actually work? What policies and institutions govern it? Too many scholars and commentators write about globalization without saying anything about how the actual economic mechanisms of globalization work.

In this chapter we consider the domestic economic, trade, investment, and financial policies that make the international economy work or not work. Domestic policies provide the ballast for the world economy. Most of the economic activity in which a country engages still takes place inside that country. Foreign trade (exports and imports) constitutes only 20–25 percent of total national production in the United States and Japan; in the case of the EU as a whole, foreign trade dependence is considerably smaller. Domestic savings, even in the poorest countries receiving the most foreign aid, still account for more than 90 percent of all savings. So the policies that affect domestic economies are crucial and constitute, so to speak, the ground floor of the world economy. The more open international markets are and, therefore, the more layers or floors are added to domestic markets, the more important domestic or ground-floor policies become. They act as the foundation of the global economic edifice, supporting or weakening the upper floors.

Trade and investment are the principal upper floors of the world economy. To switch metaphors, they are the meat and potatoes of the global market. When they function properly, the health of the world economy flourishes. Economists refer to trade and investment markets as the *real economy*. Finance provides the money to pay for trade, investment and savings. It is the wine or beverage of the world economy. It supplies the liquidity that enables the world economy to digest the meat and potatoes and to invest in the next meal of meat and potatoes. Economists refer to saving and lending markets as the *financial economy*.

When trade and investment markets go bad, financial markets lose their anchor and slosh around with plenty of speculation and much instability. They act like diners who have had too much wine and too little meat and potatoes. Perhaps that's what happened to the world economy in 2008–2009. International bankers and investors sold and swapped mountains of mortgage and credit card debt and related derivatives that were less and less tied to the real economy of property and productive investment. On the other hand, if the world economy does not have enough liquidity or wine, markets stagnate or choke on meat and potatoes. That's probably what happened in the 1970s when government financing became insufficient to cover oil debts and private capital markets were not yet liberalized. Global lending was relatively scarce, and factories and farms did not invest enough to break bottlenecks and move new products to market. For the world economy to work properly, the real and financial economies have to work in sync. Meat, potatoes, and wine—trade, investment, and finance—need to reinforce one another.

In this chapter we focus largely on realist and liberal aspects of the global economy. Realist perspectives view the world economy primarily in terms of relative gains, the expectation that global markets require security and that security is inevitably a function of the relative distribution of power. Recall that from a realist perspective, relative power is the primary causal variable and anarchy requires self-help. So security relations lead economic ones, such that extensive global markets in which governments reduce barriers to economic exchanges do not emerge except under the aegis of a hegemonic power. The hegemonic power dominates security relations, has little to fear from rivals, and therefore supports and gains most from extensive economic relations. That's why globalization accelerated under British and American hegemony and may be sustained, according to realist perspectives, only if the United States or another hegemon exercises dominance in world affairs. Otherwise, under conditions of equilibrium, states worry more about their security and limit their economic ties primarily to allies. During periods of multipolar security relations, such as in the seventeenth century before British hegemony and in the 1930s between the British and American hegemonies, global markets slowed or contracted. They became mercantilist, not laissez-faire, with governments seeking to intervene more in economic exchanges rather than to reduce government barriers to trade.

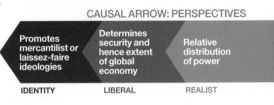

Liberal perspectives, by contrast, focus on absolute or collective gains. They stress the joint benefits that can be obtained through comparative advantage in trade, investment, and finance and expect that over time growing wealth will temper security competition and create a world of satisfied powers. Such satisfied powers, despite the existence of equilibrium in power relations with one another, will seek to preserve economic interdependence and avoid the disruptions of security conflicts and war. Unlike realist perspectives, where security leads economic ties, liberal perspectives see economic interdependence eventually dominating security competition. International institutions such as the Bretton Woods institutions set up after World War II will diminish the significance of national institutions and establish more global standards of security. Once again the direction of the causal arrows is key to distinguishing between realist and liberal perspectives.

CAUSAL ARROW: PERSPECTIVES

Establishes global norms → Reduces security competition → Economic interdependence

IDENTITY   REALIST   LIBERAL

≫ Snapshot of Globalization

Let's begin by looking at globalization and how it affects you directly through the various domestic and international economic policies that make up the world economy. Let's assume you buy a new smartphone. What are the policies that affect your purchase?

- *Domestic economic policies:* Maybe you purchased the smartphone because you got a new job, received a tax cut, or were able to borrow money cheaply. Government policies lie behind each of these options. Most jobs are created by the private sector, but government regulations affect those jobs indirectly, and government spending or tax cuts may stimulate the creation of new jobs directly. Interest rates may be low because the Federal Reserve System is also trying to stimulate the economy. Government spending and tax policy we call fiscal policy; Federal Reserve policy we call monetary policy. Taken together, fiscal and monetary policies constitute *macro*economic policy—that is, broad policy that affects the domestic economy as a whole. Government regulations constitute *micro*economic policy—specific policy that affects only targeted sectors or industries, such as antitrust policy toward the telecom companies handling your smartphone calls.

- *Trade policies:* The smartphone you bought was probably imported from overseas. It may have been assembled in China with components made in Taiwan and Singapore. Production on such a global basis cannot be profitable unless government policies are in place to reduce barriers to trade. Lower barriers mean that when items move across national boundaries they are not subjected to excessive tariffs or limited by quotas and other regulations called nontariff barriers. If the United States imports more goods and services from China and other countries than it exports to them, it runs a trade deficit. And if net government transfers (for example, foreign aid) and net interest and dividend earnings on foreign investment (earnings from previous U.S. investments abroad minus earnings of previous foreign investments in the United States) are added, it runs a **current account** deficit in its balance of payments (more on these accounts later).

- *Investment and savings policies:* If a country spends more than it earns in the international economy—that is, runs a current account deficit because it imports more than it exports—it has to borrow from abroad to pay for those extra imports. Where does that money come from? Workers and companies in Taiwan, Singapore, and China save more than do workers in the United States. They do not spend all their wages and profits from producing your smartphone. Because their governments provide fewer retirement and health care benefits, workers have to save more for their own future. Chinese workers, for example, put 40 percent of their earnings in the bank.

  Developing countries use some of those savings for domestic investments. But if savings are larger than domestic investments, those savings go abroad. The outflow—or inflow for the other country—of those savings equals what we call the **capital account** of a country's balance of payments. This account includes **portfolio investment,** the transfer of money to buy stocks and bonds, and **foreign direct investment (FDI),** the transfer of money in that year to build factories or purchase real estate abroad. Since the 1980s, barriers to capital flows have been reduced, just like those for trade flows. Companies can now move whole factories to other countries without heavy fees or restrictions and, as our example suggests, invest easily in other countries' stock or bond markets. This liberalization of capital markets is the distinctive feature of globalization 3.0 (see the introduction to Part III).

- *Financial and exchange rate policies:* The capital account and current account taken together constitute the **balance of payments.** The balance of payments records all economic transactions with other countries, and these international transactions involve the use of foreign currencies. Net supply and demand for a country's currency yields its **exchange rate,** that is, the value of the country's currency in terms of a foreign currency. One U.S. dollar may equal one

current account: the net border flows of goods and services, along with government transfers and net income on capital investment.

capital account: the net flows of capital, both portfolio and foreign direct investment, into and out of a country.

portfolio investment: transfers of money to buy stocks, bonds, and so on.

foreign direct investment (FDI): capital flows to a foreign country involving the acquisition or construction of manufacturing plants and other facilities.

balance of payments: a country's current and capital account balances plus reserves and statistical errors.

exchange rate: the value of a country's currency in terms of a foreign currency.

hundred Japanese yen, for example. Exchange rates have a powerful impact on the prices of imports and exports. A higher exchange rate makes exports more expensive, and a lower exchange rate makes imports more expensive. Thus, exchange rate movements are controversial among countries.

In a system of floating exchange rates, the current and capital accounts more or less offset one another because exchange rates go up or down to clear accounts. In a system of **fixed or managed exchange rates**, however, a country may lose or accumulate foreign currencies, called foreign exchange reserves, as the country buys or sells its currency to maintain a fixed or targeted rate for its currency. If countries hold large foreign exchange reserves, they may target a lower value for their exchange rate, which helps them sell more exports than they would if market forces prevailed. China has been accused of doing this in recent years. Meanwhile, countries with surplus foreign exchange reserves invest in sovereign debt funds that buy assets abroad. China today owns more than $1 trillion in U.S. Treasury bonds.

If, on the other hand, a country runs consistent current account deficits and its foreign exchange reserves are low or exhausted, it has to borrow an equivalent amount from abroad, which shows up on its capital account. If foreign lenders doubt that the country will be able to pay back such loans, foreign lending dries up and the country's currency plummets, because without loans the currency has to go down to make exports cheaper and imports more expensive. This is the stuff of which foreign debt and currency crises are made, such as the Eurozone crises in recent years that afflicted the currency (euro) and heavily indebted countries in the European Union, including Ireland, Greece, Spain, and Portugal. Theoretically, the United States could face such a crisis as well, and indeed it did in 2008–2009. It has run current account deficits for most of the past forty years, and there is always the possibility that foreign countries might start selling the dollars they have accumulated. But because many international trade (such as oil) and financial transactions are paid for in dollars, countries are willing to hold large reserves of dollars. As long as they are willing to do so, the United States can cover its debt by simply printing more dollars—that is, until dollars become worth less due to inflation in the United States or foreign governments begin to sell dollars for political reasons, as France did during the Cold War and China may do in the future. The crisis in 2008–2009 was not a run on the U.S. dollar as much as it was a drying up of liquidity in the global, private-sector banking system, which came into existence only in the 1970s and 1980s. Concerned about bad loans, private banks everywhere—in Europe, Asia, and the United States—suddenly began to lend less. With all banks drawing back, private-sector lending froze up. Governments had to step in big time.

All of these policies interact with one another. For example, when the United States uses monetary policies to lower interest rates, as it has done since the financial crisis of

fixed or managed exchange rates: exchange rates that are fixed by governments to gold, another currency, or a basket of currencies.

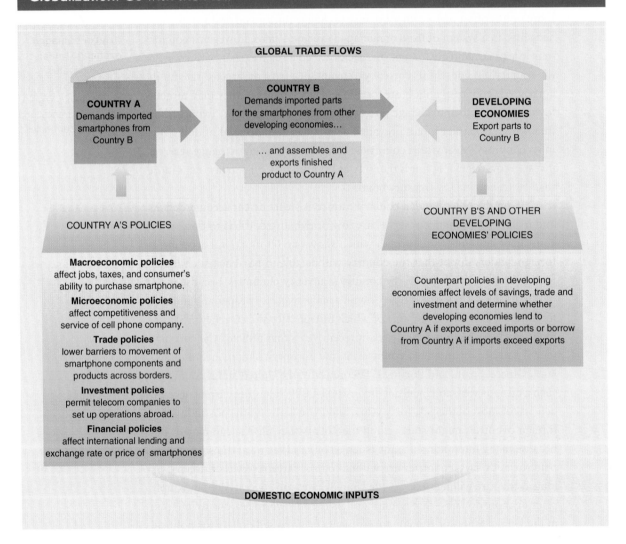

FIGURE
8-1

Globalization: Go with the Flow

2008–2009, dollar assets such as bonds yield lower returns and investors are encouraged to buy bonds or other assets in foreign currencies, such as the yen, to earn higher interest rates abroad. The demand for foreign currency drives up the exchange rates of those countries and makes their exports more expensive. Countries such as Brazil and South Korea have complained bitterly that easy U.S. monetary policy has had a detrimental effect on their economic growth. When European countries facing debt crises tightened fiscal policies in recent years, the United States complained because it wanted Europe to increase demand for U.S. exports and stimulate U.S. recovery.

Countries are increasingly interdependent. If they want to retain the economic benefits of international markets, they have to give up a certain amount of control over their domestic policies. Liberal perspectives generally assume that they will do so and coordinate their policies on a more common basis. Realist perspectives are not so sure. For example, what if China decides for political reasons not to lend its savings to the United States anymore? When it stops, U.S. interest rates will rise, U.S. housing and growth will slow, and companies may cut back production and employment. American housing and jobs did decline in 2008–2009, and so did Chinese lending. Of course, Chinese exports to the United States also slowed. Both sides paid a price, and that's why liberal perspectives assume they will continue to cooperate. Nevertheless, others believe it makes no sense and may even be immoral to take savings out of poor countries like China and give it to rich countries like the United States. From this moral (identity) perspective, the world is supposed to help poor countries grow rich, not help rich countries indulge their insatiable consumer appetites. It's not surprising therefore that globalization, just like the balance of power, looks different from the standpoints of different perspectives.

CAUSAL ARROW: LIBERAL PERSPECTIVES

And overrides security concerns	Reduces control of domestic policies	Interdependence increases benefits
REALIST	IDENTITY	LIBERAL

CAUSAL ARROW: REALIST PERSPECTIVES

Which preserve national autonomy	Lead to cutbacks in interdependence	Security concerns
IDENTITY	LIBERAL	REALIST

OK, that's a first cut at the way globalization works. Take a deep breath now, and we will look more slowly and systematically at each of these mechanisms.

⋙ Domestic Economic Policies

There are basically two types of domestic economic policies: macroeconomic policies, which include fiscal and monetary policies, and microeconomic policies, which include regulatory policies of all sorts.

Macroeconomic Policies

Fiscal policy, as we have noted, is the national budget. If it is balanced, the budget's influence on the economy is neutral. If the budget is in deficit, however, the government is spending more in the economy than it is taking out of the economy in taxes or revenues. In that case, fiscal policy is stimulating the economy, creating more net demand. Keynesian policies call for such a stimulus whenever the economy has unused resources, that is, when unemployment and unused industrial capacity are high. In the financial crisis of 2008–2009, all governments, including the United States, adopted stimulus packages to revive economic growth. As the economy then revives, according to Keynesian logic, production and employment increase, people and businesses earn and spend more, tax revenues go up, and the budget comes back into balance. If the budget is in surplus, the government is taking more resources from the economy by taxing than it is providing by spending. Thus, the government is contracting or slowing down the growth of the economy. Governments are seldom eager to do that, so Keynesian logic usually works in only one direction, to stimulate an economy and eventually contribute to overheating and inflation when industrial production cannot keep up with consumer demand.

Monetary policy seeks to control the money supply. In open-market operations, central banks buy and sell short-term government securities, thereby pushing up or lowering the prices of these securities. Changes in short-term interest rates then indirectly affect long-term interest rates. When short-term interest rates fall close to zero and can't be reduced any lower, central banks may buy long-term securities to lower long-term interest rates directly; this action is called quantitative easing. The U.S. central bank has taken this step several times in recent years: during the financial crisis of 2008–2009 and again in fall 2010 and fall 2012.

Now, consider how fiscal and monetary policy interact with one another and with the world economy. If fiscal policy is stimulative—that is, in deficit—the government is borrowing from domestic savings. Domestic savings consist of what the government saves (public savings, which are negative if the government runs a deficit) and what private households and industries save after they finish spending and investing (private savings). If the government absorbs total private savings to finance its fiscal deficits, additional savings have to come from abroad. That creates an inflow or surplus on the capital account. Now, as we know, if the capital account is in surplus, the current account has to be in deficit. In this way, a budget deficit may lead to a current account deficit, and economists frequently speak, especially in the case of the United States, about the "twin deficits," namely, a budget deficit linked with a current account deficit. Notice, however, that a budget deficit does not have to cause a current account deficit. If private savings are huge, the government can run a deficit and not have to borrow from abroad. The country can still run a current account surplus. That's exactly what Japan has done in recent decades; the government ran chronic budget deficits, but Japan continued to show a current account surplus. The Japanese people and companies save an enormous amount compared to their counterparts in the United States, and the Japanese government was able to finance its budget deficits entirely from domestic savings.

Now, what if, in addition to a budget deficit, the government is running a tight monetary policy? It is trying to absorb local currency, or liquidity, by selling bonds and raising interest rates. Higher interest rates attract foreign capital or savings. The bigger the budget deficit (loose fiscal policy encouraging imports) and the higher the interest rate (tight monetary policy encouraging foreign deposits), the larger the capital inflow. This inflow creates a capital account surplus and, as its flip side, a current account deficit. All of this assumes no change in private savings. But what if the budget deficit stimulates more consumption and business spending? After all, that's what it is designed to do. Private savings then also go down. Now the inflow of foreign savings has to be even greater to cover not only public spending but also private spending and investment. This describes the flow of foreign savings to the United States in the early 1980s, caused by U.S. fiscal deficits and tight money policy. No wonder, at the time, European leaders like German chancellor Helmut Schmidt complained about "the highest interest rates since Jesus Christ." He meant the enormous squeeze that U.S. policies of big budget deficits and tight money were putting on capital resources (savings) and, hence, interest rates in Europe.

L 106.68 +0.13 BRENT CRUDE 122.69 +1.14 RBOB GAS 3.0586 +0.0185 NATURAL GAS 2.523 +0.004 HEATING OIL 3.2258

LEVATED, LONG-TERM UNEMPLOYMENT
S STILL NEAR RECORD LEVELS AND

SQUAWK ON THE STREET HD

KING NEWS
KE: FUNDAMENTALS TO SUPPORT
G CONTINUE TO BE WEAK

NASDAQ
+6.88 +0.23
2,993.64

Intel (INTC) 1K@27.10 0.14 Apple (AAPL)

Often governments combine a loose monetary policy with budget deficits. They are trying to revive an economy and avoid deflation, a downward spiral of prices. Stimulating both fiscal and monetary policies creates two bangs for every buck—higher spending and more money. This combination of domestic macroeconomic policies, however, generates large debts, both at the treasury department and at the central bank. From 2009 on, the U.S. government added $1 trillion to the federal deficit with its stimulus program, and the Federal Reserve added another $2.5 trillion to its balance sheet by printing money to buy long-term securities from banks and other financial institutions. In 2013 it bought $85 billion per month, or another $1 trillion for the full year. The danger is that such a stimulus may not work if there are other bottlenecks in the economy, such as excessive regulations and price controls (the case in the United States in the 1970s) or bad existing loans inhibiting banks from making new loans (the case in the United States in 2009–2012). And if the stimulus does work, it may create another danger (inflation) if the government and the Fed do not withdraw the excess money from the economy in a timely way. Demand will rise faster than supply, prices will go up, exports will become less competitive (because they are now more expensive), imports will become more attractive (because they are now relatively cheaper than domestic goods), and the country will incur a growing current account deficit. If interest rates are low and inflation is rampant, a country may find it difficult to attract foreign savings. Indeed, capital may go in the opposite direction. Anticipating that the growing current account deficit may lead to a depreciation of the currency to correct the deficit, local investors may try to get their money out of the country. This scenario all too often afflicts poor developing countries that have lost control of their domestic policies and offer few good opportunities to attract foreign investment. But it also

In February 2012, traders at the New York Stock Exchange watch a monitor showing Federal Reserve Chairman Ben S. Bernanke giving his semiannual monetary policy report to the U.S. Congress. Bernanke said that continuing the monetary stimulus is warranted even as the unemployment rate falls and rising oil prices may cause inflation to rise temporarily.

affected the United States in the 1970s and could do so again in the aftermath of recent stimulus policies if investors flee a weakening dollar.

Realist perspectives expect countries to pursue different macroeconomic policies and rely on competition and fluctuating exchange rates to coordinate or narrow differences in fiscal and monetary policies. They resist coordinating policies internationally. This was the approach used by the United States in the early 1980s to drive inflation down by driving U.S. interest rates and the dollar up, thereby leading other countries to raise their interest rates too (and reduce inflation) or see their currencies decline.

CAUSAL ARROW: REALIST PERSPECTIVES

Differing macroeconomic policies	Use market forces to coordinate policy	Lead to similar approaches across countries
REALIST (WILLIAMSBURG SUMMIT)	LIBERAL	IDENTITY

CAUSAL ARROW: LIBERAL PERSPECTIVES

International policy coordination	Intervenes in national markets	Creates similar approaches across countries
LIBERAL (TOKYO SUMMIT)	REALIST	IDENTITY

Liberal perspectives urge the direct coordination of macroeconomic policies through international summits and institutions. In the preparations for the Tokyo Summit in 1986, the United States and other major industrial countries agreed to reduce interest rates together to bring the dollar down. If the United States had reduced interest rates unilaterally, the dollar might have gone down too rapidly (because money would have flowed into other currencies offering higher interest rates), and if Europe or Japan had reduced interest rates without the United States, the dollar might have gone up and not down. Identity perspectives urge the adoption of similar macroeconomic policies by all countries. At the Williamsburg Summit in 1983, the G-7 countries agreed to pursue similar policies of sound money, disciplined spending, low inflation, and deregulation. This consensus, which spread throughout the 1980s and became known in the 1990s as the Washington Consensus, advocated low inflation and market reforms in developing as well as developed countries. Eventually, strong opposition developed to these free-market ideas, and in the recent financial crisis, the world buzzed about the need for a new policy direction, the Beijing Consensus, reflecting more statist or government-mandated economic policy ideas.

Microeconomic Policies

Fiscal and monetary policies influence supply and demand, and supply and demand influence prices. So, a big factor for any country is how well supply and demand structures respond to macroeconomic policy. That depends on domestic labor and capital markets and whether individual workers and firms are sensitive to price changes and market forces. A government's microeconomic policies have a lot to do with the flexibility of domestic capital and labor markets. Are those markets free to adjust to changes, or are there significant bottlenecks in various sectors that resist change?

Microeconomic policies come in many forms. The principal ones are regulations, subsidies, price controls, competition or antitrust policies, and labor union laws. These policies may apply to specific sectors of the economy, such as agriculture or telecommunications; specific industries, such as steel or semiconductors; or specific firms, such as General Motors, which the U.S. government took over temporarily during the financial crisis of 2009. As a rule, such policies do not apply to the economy as a whole, and that is how they are distinguished from macroeconomic policies.

Regulations establish health, safety, environmental, labor, and other standards for domestic products and services. They apply to traded products through various qualitative restrictions, such as the requirement that imported windshields for automobiles meet domestic crash standards. Obviously, a point of conflict arises when domestic and trade regulations differ. A big task of international trade negotiations is to narrow these differences. In the Single Market Act of 1987, the European Community rationalized domestic regulations among its member countries to create a single integrated market with compatible regulations, not just a customs union with zero internal tariffs. Although regulations serve good purposes, they also involve costs and, if excessive, reduce market flexibility and efficiency.

Subsidies come in the form of grants and loans at below-market interest rates. Boeing, the U.S. aerospace company, has long complained that the European Union subsidizes Airbus, the European aerospace company that competes with Boeing. The EU, on the other hand, argues that the U.S. government does the same thing for Boeing by procuring large defense systems from the company. Such purchases create a large guaranteed market for Boeing, enabling it to reduce costs for commercial aircraft. Japan and the Asian tigers subsidized domestic industries to jump-start their development and then subsidized the exports those industries produced.

Price controls are used to keep prices down, and price supports are used to keep them up. The United States introduced price controls in 1973 to contain inflation, but at the same time it stimulated the economy with loose fiscal and monetary policies, which drove prices up. The government was heating up the economy—in effect, creating steam—while freezing relative prices that might have redirected resources toward scarce supplies—allowing no place for the steam to go. Eventually, the kettle exploded. Conflicting policies produced goods that were not scarce and put unbearable pressure on the prices of goods that were scarce. Both stagnation and inflation resulted. The EU's Common Agricultural Policy is a prominent example of the use of price supports. CAP sets domestic prices for agricultural products above market levels. It then imposes import quotas to keep cheaper foreign products out and provides export subsidies to encourage the sale of more expensive domestic surpluses abroad. Notice that all these microeconomic policies, like the macroeconomic ones, affect trade and hence globalization.

Competition policies deal with monopolies. Sometimes they authorize monopolies. For example, in former communist countries, practically all industries were state monopolies. Until the 1980s, the telecommunications sectors in many Western countries were monopolies as well; in the United States, a private monopoly, AT&T, dominated the telecom sector. Today, utility sectors in most countries are still monopolies, although that's beginning to change.[1] For years, however, and particularly since the end of communism, governments have deregulated or privatized many monopolies. Antitrust policies in the United States broke up the Rockefeller Standard Oil empire in 1911 and AT&T in 1984. Eastern European countries sold numerous state monopolies in the 1990s. The EU investigated the U.S. firms Microsoft and Intel on charges of monopoly practices in the computer operating system and computer chip industries.

Labor union laws set minimum wages and working conditions for factory and other workers. Labor unions in advanced countries complain bitterly that these laws are so lax in developing countries such as China, where unions are forbidden, that these countries have unfair trade advantages. Immigrants from Mexico and other developing countries undermine labor laws more directly, taking jobs below minimum wage and working illegally in advanced countries. Unions, on the other hand, restrict layoffs and push expensive compensation packages that reduce competitiveness and cause companies to invest abroad or in equipment to eliminate, rather than create, jobs at home. European countries have much stronger unions than does the United States. In past decades, they also have had much higher unemployment than the United States—roughly twice as high. European companies are reluctant to hire new workers because they can never get rid of them. On the other hand, many workers in the United States lose their jobs, and those who find new ones often work for lower wages or fewer benefits than they received previously.

≫ Trade

Trade policy affects the prices of goods and services when they cross borders, either by taxing or subsidizing the prices or by restricting the quantity or quality of the goods and services. Taxes on goods and services crossing national borders are called **tariffs**. The price of an import may be increased by a certain percentage, customs fees and duties collected, and export taxes (for example, the United States taxed soybean exports in the 1970s to protect short supplies at home) or subsidies imposed (for example, to boost exports of aircraft, large industrial machinery, or food products).

tariffs: taxes on goods and services crossing borders.

Trade policy also involves **nontariff barriers (NTBs)** such as quotas and qualitative regulations. Quotas are quantitative limits on imports and exports regardless of price. An embargo reduces imports or exports to zero; for example, the Arab members of the Organization of the Petroleum Exporting Countries (OPEC) embargoed oil in 1973. Qualitative regulations involve restrictions on traded products to protect safety, health, labor standards, and the environment. Imported toys have to meet certain safety standards, agricultural products certain health requirements, imported clothing basic labor standards (for example, no slave labor), and car mufflers approved environmental standards. Trade policies also include domestic laws that allow companies to appeal for relief from import surges, dumping practices (a foreign producer's sale of a product abroad at a price below domestic production costs), subsidies, and other unfair trade policies pursued by foreign producers. Sometimes governments use domestic trade laws to protect products through the back door. For example, other countries often accuse the United States, whose tariffs are low, of using antidumping laws to restrict imports.

nontariff barriers (NTBs): policy instruments other than price, such as quotas and qualitative restrictions, designed to limit or regulate imports and exports.

Seventeen seventy-six was an eventful year. For Americans, it was the year Thomas Jefferson wrote the Declaration of Independence—the inspiring manifesto of political freedom stating that all people are created equal. In the same year in London, Adam Smith published another manifesto, this one dealing with economic freedom. In his book *An*

Inquiry into the Nature and Causes of the Wealth of Nations, Smith traces the wealth of nations to the principle of specialization—the more specialized nations are, the wealthier they are. "The division of labour," he writes, "occasions, in every art [activity], a proportionable increase of the productive powers of labour. The separation of different trades and employments from one another . . . is generally carried furthest in those countries which enjoy the highest degree of industry and improvement."[2]

Specialization and the Division of Labor

Smith gives the example of the manufacture of pins. One person draws the wire, another straightens it, a third cuts it, a fourth points it, a fifth grinds it at the top for receiving the head, and so on. Altogether, making a pin in Smith's day involved eighteen distinct operations. As workers specialized, they became more proficient, saved time, and discovered easier and readier means to accomplish their individual tasks. Workers can also specialize to make different products rather than components. Smith spoke about the butcher, the baker, and the brewer, each of whom could specialize and become more proficient in making a particular product. Then all of them could exchange their products and have more of everything than they would if they had produced each product for themselves.

Notice that, to specialize, workers must be free to exchange the products of their labor with one another. If the butcher's meat is taxed or embargoed, he cannot purchase the baker's bread. Thus, specialization brings with it the idea of unimpeded exchange or integration of economic activities. Factories integrate such specialized exchanges vertically, while markets integrate them horizontally. Obviously, factories and markets may work under different rules. Communist economies organize factories and markets based on direct political control and government plans. Bureaucracies set multiyear production and consumption quotas and dictate direct exchanges of resources and final products. Capitalist economies organize production based on opportunity costs and market competition. Numerous independent managers calculate the **opportunity costs**, or the costs of alternative uses of resources based on competitive prices, and decide to buy or sell products based on the most efficient use of those resources.

opportunity costs: the costs of alternative uses of resources based on competitive prices.

If markets are truly competitive, meaning no one producer or consumer is large enough to influence price, benefits increase for all by what Smith calls the "invisible hand." Producers and consumers act independently against competitive forces that are beyond their control, and the net result is an increase in the wealth and well-being of all participants. Does Smith then believe that there is no role for domestic or international government—that is, for the *visible* hand? No, he devotes one of the five parts of his treatise to the role of government. He sees defense and education as government tasks. He even anticipates the drudgery of factory work, or what he calls the "mental mutilation" induced by specialization—boredom from repetitive activities in a production process—and calls on the government to encourage public diversions (such as recreation and parks).[3] But the government must leave the butcher, baker, and brewer free to exchange their products on a wider competitive basis so that they are not dealing just with friends, which restricts the size of markets, or being told what to charge, which distorts the efficiency of markets. Specialized businesses need access to a relatively free marketplace in which prices are determined by impersonal competition rather than by friends or government connections and, hence, possibly corruption.

Comparative Advantage

comparative advantage: a relationship in which two countries can produce more goods from the same resources if each specializes in the goods it produces most efficiently at home and the two trade these goods internationally.

Comparative advantage in international trade derives from the same principles of specialization and division of labor. Countries have different talents, resources, institutions, and people. They are better at doing some economic activities than other economic activities. Even if they are more advanced and better at doing everything—mining, manufacturing, and farming—they are still comparatively better at doing one of these activities and letting others do the rest. Think of Tiger Woods, the professional golfer. He plays golf a lot better than he sews shirts or produces food. It pays for him to focus on golf, even if he is just as good at sewing and farming as someone else. His comparative advantage derives from his *relative* talents, not from his *absolute* talents. The same is true for countries. If they can specialize in what they do relatively best, they can be more productive. Thus, poor countries do not have to produce something more efficiently than rich countries; they just have to produce one thing more efficiently than some other thing that they produce themselves.

In 1817, David Ricardo, another English economist, demonstrated Smith's principle of specialization for international trade. He took two countries, Portugal and England, and considered their relative talents in producing two goods: cloth and wine. As Table 8-1 shows, Portugal can produce both products more efficiently than England. It can produce a bolt of cloth in 90 days of labor, while England requires 100. And it can produce a barrel of wine in 80 days, while England requires 120. Portugal has an absolute advantage in both products, meaning it can produce both products more efficiently than England. The benefits of comparative advantage are easier to show when each country is better at producing one product, but Ricardo wanted to take the hard case, when one country is better at producing both products.

At first glance, then, why should countries specialize and trade if they can produce both products more efficiently? But look again at Table 8-1. In Portugal, one bolt of cloth should exchange for 9/8 barrels of wine. Why? Because it takes exactly the same number of days of labor—or input—to make these two quantities. In England, one bolt of cloth will exchange for 5/6 barrels of wine. Thus, one bolt of cloth buys more wine in Portugal (9/8 barrels) than it does in England (5/6 barrels). Conversely, one barrel of wine buys more cloth in England (1⅕ bolts) than it does in Portugal (8/9 bolts). So, if Portugal and England could trade cloth (where 1C stands for one bolt of cloth) for wine (where 1W stands for one barrel of wine) at any ratio between 1C = 9/8W and 1C = 5/6W, both countries would gain. To see this, look again at Table 8-1. With 1,000 days of labor invested, half in each product, Portugal and England together produce 10⅚ bolts of cloth and 10⁵⁄₁₂ barrels of wine. With 1,000 days of labor invested in only the product each produces more efficiently, England produces 10 bolts of cloth and Portugal 12½ barrels of wine. They have not used more resources, yet they have produced almost the same amount of cloth (10 compared to 10 5/9 bolts) and 20 percent more wine (12½ compared to 10 5/9 barrels). The reason is comparative advantage—Portugal is comparatively more efficient at making wine, even though it is better than England at making both products, and England is comparatively better at making cloth, even though it is less efficient than Portugal at making both products.

This is a simplified example. More is involved in making wine and cloth than labor, and exchange rates may distort costs and push the exchange ratios outside the range where trade is beneficial (in the example, between 1C = 9/8W and 1C = 5/6W). But the result holds even if we include other costs: land, capital, and knowhow. Whatever it takes to make a bolt of cloth, we compare that to the costs of making wine, or the opportunity costs. What is the cost of the opportunity I forgo if I make cloth instead of wine, or vice versa? The more alternative uses of resources that are involved, meaning the more products and countries involved, the bigger the gains. Comparative advantage offers all countries the opportunity to create more wealth without using additional resources, including the poorest countries. Trade, in short, is a powerful multiplier of wealth for all countries, just like technology. (Critical theory perspectives see comparative advantage as coerced and exploitative, not free and mutually beneficial; see Chapter 10.)

TABLE 8-1

Comparative Advantage

	Days of labor required to produce	
	Cloth (1 bolt)	*Wine (1 barrel)*
Portugal	90	80
England	100	120
	1,000 days of labor without specialization produces	
	Cloth (500 days)	*Wine (500 days)*
Portugal	5 5/9 bolts	6¼ barrels
England	5 bolts	4 1/6 barrels
Total	10 5/9 bolts	10 5/12 barrels
	1,000 days of labor with specialization produces	
	Cloth (Portugal, 0 days; England, 1,000 days)	*Wine (England, 0 days; Portugal, 1,000 days)*
Portugal	0 bolts	12½ barrels
England	10 bolts	0 barrels
Total	10 bolts	12½ barrels

Source: Data on "days of labor required to produce" are from James C. Ingram and Robert M. Dunn Jr., *International Economics*, 3rd ed. (New York: John Wiley, 1993), 29.

Exceptions to Unrestricted Trade

If unrestricted trade is so wonderful, we might ask, why then is it so disputed? Well, there are obvious limitations to liberalizing barriers to trade. One involves products critical to a nation's defense. A nation may wish to have national security export controls to limit trade in military and dual-use (having both commercial and military applications) products and technology. Adam Smith recognized this limitation, and all nations and economists since have drawn the line at liberalizing barriers if national security interests might be compromised. They impose limits not only on critical military weapons materials, parts, and designs but also on imports of vital products crucial to the overall economy, such as energy, food, and potentially scarce resources, such as copper or bauxite.

The difficulty with national security exceptions to free trade is where to draw the line. In some sense, every product may be essential for national security. As a rule, exceptions apply more to new products and technologies than to widely used ones and more to WMDs than to conventional weapons. Still, the United States frets about dependence on foreign oil, and Japan worries about excessive dependence on food imports. Diversifying suppliers of crucial imports and stockpiling reserves, such as oil, are alternative ways to minimize the national security risks of trade dependence.

infant industries: developing industries that require protection to get started.

A second exception to unrestricted trade is protection for **infant industries**. How do countries develop new industries to compete in international markets if from the get-go those industries are wide open to imports from more advanced industries in foreign countries? Thus, infant industries, it is argued, warrant initial trade protection until they develop the scale and experience to compete effectively with imports. This was the rationale for the **import substitution policies** of developing countries right after World War II. These policies sought to substitute domestic industries for imports—hence the term *import substitution*— to protect them from imports until they could compete at world standards. As we will discuss in Chapter 9, Latin American countries pursued such policies, as did late-developing industrialized nations in the nineteenth century like the United States, Germany, and Japan.

import substitution policies: policies developed in Latin America that substitute domestic industries for imports.

Infant industry protection seems logical enough. The problem, of course, is to know when the "infant" has grown up. Too often, protected industries get used to protection and never grow up. They compete only against local counterparts, which are also infants, while industries in other countries that compete in foreign markets face stiffer competition and develop new and better products. Larger countries, such as Brazil, Argentina, and Mexico, are more tempted by import substitution strategies than are small ones, such as the Netherlands and Singapore, because large countries have big internal markets for local industries to supply. But even large countries run into limitations and eventually shift to more open trade policies. The United States did so in the early twentieth century, Germany and Japan came around after World War II, and the large Latin American countries followed suit in the 1990s.

Strategic Trade Theory

A more serious challenge to the theory of comparative advantage developed in the 1980s and 1990s. Until World War II, most international trade involved the exchange of complementary products, such as food products for manufactured goods. Trade was mostly inter-industry trade, in which complementary products were exchanged by different industries and often by countries at different stages of development. In colonial regimes, for example, imperial powers exported manufactured goods and imported agricultural products and commodities. Even as late as the early 1950s, two-thirds of all trade took place between advanced and developing countries. In this case, comparative advantage seemed to explain trade patterns quite well. Colonial territories were mostly southern countries with climates and populations suitable for agriculture and mining. Advanced countries were northern

countries with less arable land and more industry and technology. Each country traded products that it produced relatively more efficiently than other countries.

After 1950, however, trading patterns began to shift. By 1990, three-quarters of all trade was among advanced countries and only one-quarter between advanced and developing countries. And the trade among advanced countries was in competitive, not complementary, products. Advanced countries shipped automobiles, aircraft, cameras, machine tools, and semiconductor chips to one another, not agricultural or raw material products. And they often shipped products to one another within a single industry; for example, some exported the semiconductor chips for computers while others shipped central processing units. Trade was mostly intraindustry trade, in which components from the same product or industry were traded. What explained this type of trade? Did countries have different capabilities (that is, talents) within industries (for example, within the cloth industry) as well as between them (cloth and wine)?

Yes, in one sense, specialization had advanced now to differentiating tasks within industries as well as between industries. If Japan could specialize in semiconductor chips and produce them in sufficient volume to cover the U.S. and European as well as the Japanese markets, it could exploit **economies of scale**, whereby the larger the amount of anything produced, the lower the average cost of production. The United States might do the same in customized chips or sophisticated central processing units. OK, but what explains the fact that Japan specialized in computer chips and the United States in central processing units? Or that the United States dominated the international aircraft market? How did comparative advantage work in these cases of economies of scale?

Workers unload imported unprocessed sugar at the Dhampur Sugar Mill in Asmoli, India, in August 2009. Sugar jumped to a twenty-eight-year high in New York as low monsoon rainfall in India threatened to limit cane yields and excess precipitation delayed harvesting in Brazil, prolonging a global production deficit. India is the world's biggest consumer of sugar.

economies of scale: cost advantages whereby the larger the amount of a good that is produced, the lower the average cost of production.

It might be argued that the United States simply had more sophisticated workers in the computer central processing and aircraft industries. But did it have more sophisticated workers because it already had a dominant share in computer and aircraft sales around the world, or did the existence of more sophisticated workers create the dominant market share? Which came first, the sophisticated workers or the dominant market share? And, as discussed earlier in the case of Boeing and Airbus, did governments help their industries gain dominant market share?

Seeking to explain this conundrum, economists developed a new trade theory called strategic trade, starting from the premise that in markets for some products the economies of scale are so large that only one firm or country can make a profit in that product in world markets. If another firm enters the market, profits drop below costs and neither firm can gain. In such markets, the firm exploits what economists call monopoly rents. Lacking competition, it sets prices higher than they would otherwise be.

Thus, the firm that gets to the market first wins, whether its product is more efficient or not. Think of the keyboard for the typewriter and now the computer. The placement of the keys on the typewriter is neither logical nor efficient. But the so-called QWERTY keyboard became the standard. It got to the market first and everyone learned to type using it. Another example may be Microsoft, which dominated the market in operating software systems for computers with Windows, which, some believe, was actually inferior to others, such as Apple's Macintosh. But Microsoft got to the market first and captured monopoly rents. Now it is hard for other companies to challenge Microsoft. In 2009, the EU moved to break up Microsoft's monopoly by demanding that it separate parts of the Windows operating system before it can compete in European markets. Here is a classic example of path dependence, a result that no one consciously intends. Because it costs a lot of money to get into monopoly markets, what economists call "high barriers to entry," governments may be the only actors with sufficient resources and authority to help companies compete.

competitive advantage: a trade advantage created by government intervention to exploit monopoly rents in strategic industries.

So, this theory of trade assumed that comparative advantage did not just exist naturally to be exploited; it had to be created. And only governments had the deep pockets to create it. Thus, rather than reducing government intervention to encourage comparative advantage, governments intervened in the case of strategic trade to create what became known as **competitive advantage.** Competitive advantage calls for governments to protect and subsidize key industries and technologies, whereas comparative advantage calls for governments to lower protection and subsidies for trade. Japan was thought to have a special advantage in strategic trade because it had a highly trained bureaucracy and a relatively weak parliament. Government could pick industries and technologies for the long term and not be besieged by special interests promoting this or that industry important to some legislator's constituency. Japan, it was said, had patient capital—that is, money invested by the government or government-directed banks over the long term to develop dominant industries for the future. By contrast, the United States was short-term oriented, with a Congress dominated by special interests and industries expected to earn profits on a quarterly basis.

What about this new trade theory? Does it invalidate comparative advantage and call for governments to intervene in trade markets rather than withdrawing from them by lowering barriers to trade? Realist perspectives tend to favor strategic trade because they focus on relative gains and view markets as zero-sum. Monopoly in markets, like hegemony in international politics, may be the best alternative. Identity perspectives see strategic trade as suggesting how different economic cultures—a more consensus-oriented Japanese culture versus a more individualistic American culture—distort and limit comparative advantage.

CAUSAL ARROW: REALIST PERSPECTIVE

| Promotes national autonomy | Creates strategic trade | Monopoly |
| IDENTITY | LIBERAL | REALIST |

Liberal perspectives tend to be skeptical of strategic trade because it limits common gains. Indeed, liberal economists who came up with the idea also suggested that strategic trade theory may have some limitations. Although theoretically valid, it is very difficult to implement in practice.[4] The reasons? First, very few industries actually have the features that permit one company or country to dominate. And second, if there are such industries, it is very difficult to know in advance which ones are critical for the future. Bureaucrats may be good, but if they were that good they would have a better track record. Japan's Ministry of International Trade and Industry (MITI), now the Minis-

CAUSAL ARROW: IDENTITY PERSPECTIVE

| Increase national wealth | Distort comparative advantage | Different cultures |
| REALIST | LIBERAL | IDENTITY |

CAUSAL ARROW: LIBERAL PERSPECTIVE

| Narrows national differences | Limits strategic trade | Comparative advantage |
| IDENTITY | REALIST | LIBERAL |

try of Economics, Trade and Industry (METI), made many choices about industry development in Japan that proved to be wrong, especially as Japan caught up with Europe and the United States.[5] And now that Japan is no longer catching up in world markets, its economy has slowed dramatically, and its strategic trade model seems to offer no special advantages.

Identifying future technologies and industries and targeting them using government programs are easier to do when countries are catching up. Japan was catching up in the 1960s and 1970s, as China is doing today. While catching up, a government can look at competitive world markets and see where its industries are behind. It can then subsidize and protect those industries until they achieve global competitiveness. In this situation, strategic trade theory is a form of the infant industry argument applied to catching up with world standards in high technology. But guessing which completely new industries will dominate markets in the future is another matter. Nanotechnology, which exploits the property of materials at very small dimensions, is a new technology for the future. But its uses are vast and still in many cases unknown. Sorting out what aspects to focus on and particularly what aspects to develop first is difficult and best left perhaps to a competitive process of trial and error in the marketplace among multiple participants. Government policies for research and development (R&D) and procurement still play a role, but this role is more one of supporting broad infrastructure for an economy (for example, funding multiple research projects and educating qualified engineers), similar to developing an efficient transportation and communications system, than one of picking specific winners in the technology and industry sweepstakes of the future.

Trade and Jobs

Does trade create jobs or destroy them? This is the biggest controversy related to trade. As we will see, it does both. It destroys relatively less skilled or low-wage jobs and creates relatively more skilled or high-wage jobs. In this sense, trade acts as a jobs escalator, moving people up to higher levels of skills and wages, assuming they can acquire the required training and education. On balance, trade creates *better* jobs but not necessarily *more* jobs.

From a realist perspective, which emphasizes exports, taking in more imports than exports may be seen as substituting foreign jobs for domestic jobs. After all, any product imported in excess of exports involves a foreign job to service domestic demand, not a domestic job. This is what led Latin American countries to embrace import substitution policies. They sought to substitute domestic jobs for the foreign jobs producing imports. Realists tend to see trade as a zero-sum game. But this reasoning, according to the liberal perspective, looks too narrowly at trade. It ignores broader interconnections (interdependence). Much more is going on in domestic policies and overall relations between importing and exporting countries than in trade.

CAUSAL ARROW: PERSPECTIVES

Lost domestic jobs (REALIST) → Warrant import restrictions (LIBERAL) → Increase domestic autonomy and self-esteem (IDENTITY)

Remember from our earlier discussion that more imports than exports also means that foreign countries are lending money to the importing country. Now, if that money goes into luxury consumption or corruption, it is wasted. But if it goes into productive uses, it helps the importing country develop and grow. Poorer countries are expected to import more than they export; they need machinery and capital equipment to build new factories. Richer countries such as the United States are expected to export more than they import; they then lend money to developing countries. But the United States imports more than it exports and thus borrows from developing countries like China. Is such lending perverse? Not necessarily. It depends on what the United States does with the borrowed money. If it invests the foreign money to develop new service and high-tech industries, where it has a comparative advantage, it contributes to U.S. and world growth. Whether the United States or any other net-importing country actually uses capital inflows for such purposes is a function of its domestic policies, not its trade policies.

CAUSAL ARROW: PERSPECTIVES

Foreign capital inflows (LIBERAL) → Go into productive (unproductive) domestic investments (REALIST) → Strengthen (weaken) national confidence (IDENTITY)

Identity perspectives emphasize the ideas governing domestic policy more than net exports (the realist perspective) or the specialization and comparative advantage driving trade policy (the liberal perspective). For example, a developing country may pursue domestic policies that encourage elites to import luxury goods, not machinery. Domestic policies support an elite culture, not economic efficiency. Or, as another example, the United States might be pursuing inflationary domestic policies, as it did in the 1970s. Higher prices encourage imports for consumption, not investment, because consumers buy now before prices go up while industries wait to invest until prices stabilize. Economic policies serve a consumer, not investor, culture. If domestic policies encourage savings and investment rather than luxury or inflation-driven consumption, a trade deficit does not cost jobs but, instead, creates the right kind of jobs. Developing countries need to import more than they export because they

CAUSAL ARROW: PERSPECTIVES

Domestic policy choices (IDENTITY) → Favor domestic consumption (investment) (REALIST) → Weaken (strengthen) economic efficiency (LIBERAL)

are developing. But they also need to import the right products that will enable them to grow in the future and later pay back the money they borrowed for excess imports.

What about trade with low-wage countries? If such trade doesn't cost jobs, doesn't it lower wages and reduce standards of living in advanced countries if they try to compete with low-wage countries? An economic theory known as the Hecksher-Ohlin theory suggests it might. Over time, trade will equalize prices for products from different countries. That's the effect of creating a single world market with converging prices. But economists Eli Hecksher and Bertil Ohlin argued that it will also equalize prices eventually for labor and other inputs or factors of production. As prices for final products become more competitive through trade, so will prices for factors of production such as labor. Thus, some critics of free trade worry that, with unlimited supplies of labor in developing countries, trade will eventually drive wages in advanced countries down to levels prevailing in developing countries. After all, in the late 1990s, the average worker in manufacturing in China cost only $730 per year, while in Germany the average worker cost $35,000 per year and in the United States $29,000 per year.[6]

The critics are right that wages for low-skilled jobs will move down in advanced countries, at least relative to higher-skilled wages in advanced countries. But they are wrong that wages in developing countries will never move up relative to wages in advanced countries. Wages in developing countries are lower because productivity is lower. **Productivity** is measured by how much output is produced by a given input. A worker in a developing country takes longer to do a job than a worker in an advanced country because of lesser skills and poorer health. So, the worker in China who makes $730 a year produces annually only $2,900 worth of value-added (that is, output minus inputs), while the German worker who is paid $35,000 a year produces $80,000 worth of value-added and the American worker paid $29,000 produces $81,000 of value-added.[7] For trade to drive wages down, productivity would have to go down. Yet, as we learn in this chapter, trade increases efficiency and hence productivity in both advanced and developing countries. Thus, if trade equalizes wages, it does so at higher, not lower, levels in both countries.

productivity: output per unit of input.

The data in Figure 8-2 suggest that as imports from developing countries increase, wages in developing countries move up toward levels in advanced countries. In 1960, developing countries that traded with the United States paid their manufacturing workers only 10 percent of the wages paid to American workers. By 1992, that figure had jumped to 30 percent.[8] Wages for workers in industrial countries that traded with the United States rose even faster, exceeding U.S. wages in 1992. Productivity and, hence, wages in manufacturing go up, not down, as developing and industrial countries trade more with one another. Wages today in China are going up, not down, causing Chinese officials to worry about developing higher value-added export industries.

So, if manufacturing wages are converging, as the Hecksher-Ohlin theory predicts, they are converging toward the top, not the bottom. Moreover, trade with developing countries permits advanced countries like the United States to shift employment to the high-tech and service sectors, where more than two-thirds of the workforce is employed. These sectors dominate U.S. exports, and export jobs pay 5–15 percent more than the national average.[9]

FIGURE
8-2

Wages of U.S. Trading Partners as a Share of U.S. Wages, Manufacturing

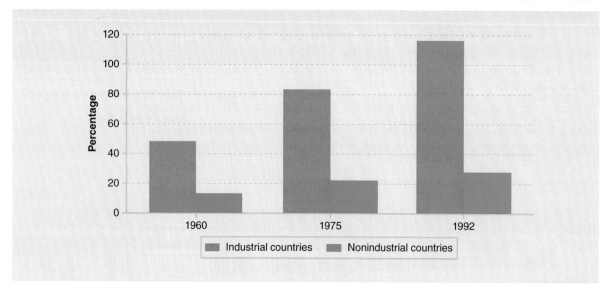

Source: Gary Burtless, Robert Z. Lawrence, Robert E. Litan, and Robert J. Shapiro, *Globaphobia: Confronting Fears about Open Trade* (Washington, DC: Brookings Institution, 1998), 69. Used with permission.

Thus, trade shifts jobs from lower productivity and wage levels to higher ones. This movement is, after all, the story of industrialization and development. Map 8-1 shows this story as told by employment or jobs data. In the nineteenth century, before the industrial revolution took off in the United States, 80 percent of the American people earned their living on the land. Today, less than 2 percent are engaged in agriculture; jobs moved into the manufacturing sector. By 1950, more than 40 percent of American workers were employed in manufacturing. Then, the next phase of the industrial revolution began. Jobs moved into the service sectors. Today, less than 10 percent of American workers are employed in manufacturing, while more than two-thirds are employed in service sectors. Jobs moved into retail, transportation, banking, data processing, software, finance, marketing, and other information-related activities. In recent decades, for example, United Parcel Service (UPS), a major U.S.-based delivery service, added on average several hundred thousand jobs per year to its workforce. We read about the loss of steel and automobile jobs but seldom about the creation of new jobs in service industries, such as UPS. This is another reason we need to know more about international events than just what newspapers tell us.

Think about this statistic. In 2005, when the U.S. economy was growing, just over twenty-nine million jobs were lost and thirty-one million jobs were created.[10] Jobs are churning every day. Why don't we read about that? What perspective or special

MAP
8-1

Labor Patterns Worldwide

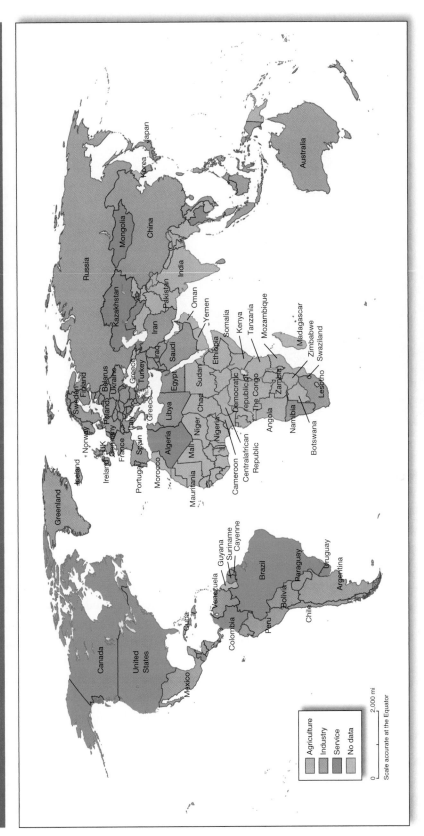

Agriculture
Industry
Service
No data

0   2,000 mi
Scale accurate at the Equator

Source: Central Intelligence Agency, "The World Factbook," https://www.cia.gov/library/publications/the-world-factbook.

Note: Data for percentage of labor force by occupation come from different years, but most are from within the past ten years. For labor force data, agriculture, fishing, forestry, and mining are considered agriculture. Government, public works, construction, trade, tourism, commerce, utilities, and the like are considered services. Any processing of raw materials beyond agriculture, mining, fishing (e.g., food processing, oil refining, or canning tuna) is considered manufacturing. In cases where employment in manufacturing is less than 15 percent, that country is classified according to which other sector claims the greatest share. That accounts for some industrializing countries, such as Brazil, Algeria, and Mongolia, being classified as service economies when they are still developing manufacturing industries. Data are not available for some countries; those countries are not shaded.

The Jin Mao Tower (center left) and the Oriental Pearl Tower (background center right) stand among other commercial buildings, seen from the Shanghai World Financial Center, in Shanghai, China. Urbanization has swelled in China as government efforts to revive demand have driven a rebound in industrial output, retail sales, and the housing market.

interest is driving the news coverage? Jobs changing on a massive scale is the mark of a growing and robust economy. The former communist countries tried to save jobs by not participating in free international trade—and they did save jobs. They saved the same old jobs in the same old industries that became obsolete and uncompetitive and eventually went bankrupt. Then everyone lost and had to change jobs, all at once. By contrast, throughout the cycles of job loss and creation over the past century, per capita incomes in the United States and other capitalist countries rose. And during the periods of greatest prosperity in this century—before World War I and after World War II— world trade markets were open and expanding. In the interwar period, when trade was restricted, the country suffered a severe depression. Certainly no one would argue that free trade hinders growth. U.S. citizens are far better off today than they were a century ago. Developing countries also gain from trade if they pursue sound domestic policies and world markets remain open to their products. In fact, in recent decades, as globalization exploded, developing countries such as China, India, Brazil, and Mexico grew twice as fast as advanced countries.

Opponents of free trade say, yes, but trade involves job losses by the least-skilled workers in a society, those least capable of finding new jobs. These workers become marginalized and inequality increases. And the critics are right. As we have learned, trade shifts jobs from activities in which countries are less efficient into those in which they are more efficient. That means the less efficient or least-skilled workers are displaced.

(By reporting only jobs lost, the media clearly act as advocates for these workers.) This happens in both developing and advanced countries. Think of the enormous displacement going on today in the Chinese countryside. Millions of Chinese laborers are no longer needed on the farm, where machinery and better farming know-how are increasing production with less labor. They migrate to the cities, a strange and disorienting environment for people used to a traditional rural culture. Today, 51 percent of China's people live in cities, compared to 18 percent in 1978. At least thirteen million make the shift every year. They are the least educated and the most vulnerable Chinese citizens. Similarly, high school–educated steel and automobile workers in the United States, whose families have worked in these industries and lived in the same communities for generations, suddenly lose their jobs and have to move to new and unfamiliar areas.

These are serious issues, and past remedies have been inadequate. Many countries offer **trade adjustment assistance** in the form of cash benefits or programs to retrain workers displaced by trade. But these programs often discourage workers from searching for new jobs by paying them what they earned before and do little to help workers overcome the psychological effects of losing a job and moving a family. Newer plans call for wage insurance that would encourage displaced workers to take new jobs at whatever level of pay. The insurance would then make up the difference between the old and new wages. But is a remedy pegged specifically to jobs lost through trade the answer, or should the problem, like an excess of imports over exports, be viewed in a broader perspective? Data show that job loss for workers without high school diplomas is just as great in industries that are not affected by trade as in those that are.[11] Something larger is going on.

trade adjustment assistance: cash benefits or retraining programs for workers displaced by trade.

From a liberal perspective, the fundamental cause of change in jobs is not trade but technological development. Farmers in China and steelworkers in the United States lose jobs primarily because new machinery does their old jobs more efficiently, not because trade takes place. Technological development is a function of education and domestic economic policies. So, doing a better job generally of educating and retraining workers and of pursuing domestic policies to sustain healthy growth may be more important than specific trade assistance programs. Domestic policies, in short, play a bigger role than trade policies. Notice the primary level of analysis here. In Chapter 10, we discuss trade from the critical theory perspective, which emphasizes systemic over domestic levels of analysis. One thing is certain. Stopping trade ends the possibility of using resources more efficiently and, thus, stops or reduces growth. On the other hand, neglecting displaced workers creates powerful forces to stop trade. So, dealing with the transition of the least-skilled workers displaced by technology and trade in both developing and advanced countries is part of the global effort to continue open trade and spread the benefits of growth.

CAUSAL ARROW: LEVELS OF ANALYSIS

| Increase average incomes | Facilitate open trade markets | Domestic policies |
| INDIVIDUAL | SYSTEMIC | DOMESTIC |

Finally, what about **unfair trade**? A catchall complaint is that countries at different stages of development cannot trade with one another because their standards are too different. Identity perspectives are particularly concerned about this aspect of trade. It is not just that wages are lower in developing countries but also that labor, environmental, health, and other regulatory standards that reflect different values are lower. Think about the

unfair trade: trade that violates an international trade agreement or is considered unjustified, unreasonable, and discriminatory.

controversy that arose in the United States in 2007 concerning the import of toys from China. Some four million toys from China sold as Aqua Dots were recalled because children swallowed beads in the toys containing a dangerous chemical.[12] If industries can export products that are unsafe, that are produced with child labor or with few concerns for pollution and the health or safety of their own workers, and that are subject to lower taxes or higher subsidies, their exports are not fairly priced and therefore undercut the higher labor, environmental, and other standards in the importing countries. Numerous trade rules exist in domestic legislation and international agreements to safeguard against these abuses. But differences will always exist unless countries become identical to one another. In that case, however, there would be no basis for comparative advantage and mutually beneficial trade. From a liberal perspective, managing regulatory differences by rules that meet minimal levels of fairness and raise standards as countries develop is probably the best way to proceed. As we see next, that's increasingly the job of the World Trade Organization.

Global Trade Negotiations

In the nineteenth century, Great Britain applied free-trade policies unilaterally. It simply removed tariffs on corn (grain) imports and reduced barriers on other imports as well. Why didn't farmers resist? They lost jobs as agricultural products from abroad flooded British home markets. Moreover, because Britain was liberalizing trade unilaterally, export interests did not immediately gain. So why did Britain do it? The realist answer from the domestic level of analysis is that farmers were simply too weak politically to stop the free-trade movement. Technology had shifted the advantage to manufacturing activities. Exporters had gained the upper hand earlier by shipping manufacturing goods to colonial territories. Now, once other industrializing countries such as France and the Netherlands followed Britain's lead to liberalize unilaterally, manufacturing exporters gained access to industrial markets as well.

In the 1930s, when the United States took the lead in trade negotiations, it did not liberalize imports unilaterally but reduced barriers through bilateral negotiations. It negotiated so-called reciprocal trade agreements; each country lowered tariffs and opened markets. Now, although importers lost, exporters in the same country gained. As long as export interests dominated, free-trade agreements went forward. Consumers gained because of lower prices, and workers gained new jobs in the export sector but lost others in the import sector. So, the politics of trade liberalization depended on whether export interests outweighed import-competing interests. Consumers are usually not a significant factor in trade politics because they are affected only indirectly—through incremental price increases on imported products—and do not organize nationally to protect their wallets as labor unions do to protect their jobs.

most-favored-nation (MFN) principle: a principle under which nations that negotiate tariff reduction offer the same low tariff to all nations that they offer to the most favored nation, meaning the nation that pays the lowest tariffs.

Protectionism dominated through World War II. In 1947, more than two hundred bilateral quota agreements limiting imports by specific amounts carved up markets in Europe. The liberalization process to reduce these barriers was slow. Gains from bilateral trade agreements between just two countries were not enough to generate much enthusiasm. Moreover, the United States applied the **most-favored-nation (MFN) principle** to these agreements. The MFN principle gives all countries, including those that do not participate in the bilateral negotiations, the same benefits as the countries participating. Some way had to be found to get more countries involved directly in negotiations if trade liberalization was to become more significant.

This was the rationale for the initiation of **multilateral trade rounds**, in which multiple countries negotiated simultaneously. The GATT, which dealt only with manufactured goods, organized the first such round in 1947, which lowered tariffs by an average of 20 percent. Even among twenty-three countries, however, these negotiations went slowly. As more countries joined the GATT, the process became more difficult still. The next four rounds accomplished less, although free trade moved forward in the OEEC (the Marshall Plan) and the European Common Market.

By the sixth round in the 1960s, known as the **Kennedy Round,** a broader approach was undertaken, called across-the-board trade negotiations. Countries agreed to lower tariffs by a certain average across all manufactured products, rather than product by product. The Kennedy Round reduced tariffs on average by about 35 percent. This was the first round in which the EC countries negotiated as a group. They had consolidated their common market in 1962 and now had a common external tariff toward outside countries.

Few developing countries participated in the GATT rounds, and few of the products, such as agriculture and commodities, for which the GATT was not responsible were included. Nevertheless, some developing countries in Asia that emphasized exports exploited the MFN principle to get a foothold in advanced-country markets.

The participation of developing countries increased in the next two rounds. The **Tokyo Round** in the 1970s moved trade liberalization forward even as developing countries challenged the GATT and other Bretton Woods institutions. The Tokyo Round accepted a proposal from UNCTAD, the developing countries' preferred trade organization, to grant developing countries tariff preferences. Known as the Generalized System of Preferences (GSP), these preferences violated MFN rules by applying tariff reductions discriminatorily. For approved products, GSP granted exports from developing countries duty-free access, while similar exports from advanced countries faced tariffs. Developing countries were also not required to reciprocate. Notice the realist premise of GSP (as compared to the liberal premise of MFN), skewing relative gains toward developing countries. GSP, however, was severely limited by restrictions. Many exports did not qualify, such as textiles, steel, and footwear. These products were being increasingly restricted by quotas, and GSP exports lost duty-free access if they exceeded a de minimis level, which was usually set fairly low. Nevertheless, the Tokyo Round recognized the need to bring developing countries increasingly into the world trading system. Overall, the Tokyo Round lowered tariffs on average by another 30–35 percent. Tariffs were now so low that other restrictions or NTBs, such as domestic regulations, were becoming more important and attention was shifting to product sectors that the GATT was never intended to address, such as services, agriculture, and investment.

The **Uruguay Round** was the first round to bear the name of a developing country and the first to involve significant participation by developing countries. Initially,

---

multilateral trade rounds: trade negotiations in which multiple countries participate and reduce trade barriers simultaneously.

Kennedy Round: the sixth round of trade talks, under which across-the-board trade negotiations took place, reducing tariffs by an average of 35 percent.

Tokyo Round: the seventh round of trade talks, in which tariffs were reduced further across the board and developing countries were granted tariff preferences.

Uruguay Round: the eighth round of trade talks and the first to bear the name of a developing country; it extended free trade to services, investment, agriculture, and intellectual property.

developing countries blocked the round. They broke up a GATT ministerial meeting in Geneva in 1982 because they feared that a new focus on services and investment would divert attention from their concern with manufactured goods, especially the quota restrictions on textiles in the Multi-fiber Agreement, and other low-technology exports.[13] Domestic reforms in the 1980s changed their minds. Countries such as Mexico and India shifted toward more market-oriented policies and followed Asian countries to focus more on exports. The Uruguay Round was finally launched in 1986 and ended successfully in 1994.

The Uruguay Round lowered tariffs further, but its big accomplishment was to extend the principle of free trade beyond manufactured goods to services, investment, agriculture, and intellectual property. The new General Agreement on Trade in Services was signed, and steps were taken to convert agricultural barriers to tariffs for future liberalization and to create common rules for investment and intellectual property. The widened agenda for liberalization was incorporated into the WTO, which superseded the GATT as the principal international trade organization. The GATT continued as a part of WTO, along with GATS and other agreements. Advanced countries agreed to remove quantitative restrictions on textiles and other products. The infamous Multi-fiber Agreement, which had existed since the 1960s, terminated over the next ten years, ending in early 2005. And developing countries looked ahead to the next round, which would deal for the first time with the liberalization of agricultural products, an area of potentially enormous benefit for large and small developing countries alike.

The ninth round of multilateral trade negotiations commenced in Doha, Qatar, in November 2001. As in the case of the Uruguay Round, the first attempt to launch the **Doha Round** failed. In 1999, hundreds of NGOs turned out in Seattle to protest the spread of free trade. Nevertheless, known as the Developing Country Round, Doha puts key objectives of developing countries at the top of the agenda, such as reducing agricultural subsidies in the European Union and United States, liberalizing patents for high-priced medical drugs for AIDS and other diseases in the third world, and strengthening trade capacity-building infrastructure and procedures in the most vulnerable developing countries. At the same time, the Doha Round also calls for further measures that benefit advanced countries, such as lower barriers on industrial, service, and investment flows.

Doha Round: the ninth and most current round of trade talks, which offers significant potential benefits to developing countries in agriculture, medicines, and infrastructure.

Regional Trade

Multilateral trade rounds are complex and difficult to manage. Free trade on an MFN basis is a collective good. All countries can enjoy it even if they don't contribute to it. In these circumstances, many countries become free riders; they wait to see what other countries will contribute, thereby hoping to get the benefits without contributing much themselves.

The WTO currently has 159 members. Recall that the GATT and WTO operate on a one-country, one-vote basis, unlike the IMF and World Bank, which have weighted voting (see Chapter 6). Decisions in trade areas require consensus, a time-consuming process. The Uruguay Round took eight years to complete. In 2013, the Doha Round was in its twelfth year and still not concluded. Countries become impatient and seek alternative trading arrangements at the bilateral or regional level, even though such trade is theoretically less beneficial than global trade.

Article 24 of the GATT makes an exception to the MFN principle for discriminatory regional trade blocs that agree to reduce their internal tariffs to zero. A common market then establishes a common external tariff, while a free-trade area allows members to retain different external tariffs. This was the basis for the creation in the 1950s of the European Common Market and the European Free Trade Area (EFTA). The countries that founded EFTA eventually joined the European Union, Britain being the most important one in 1973. Many developing countries also tried regional trade arrangements. Examples included the Central American Common Market (El Salvador, Nicaragua, Costa Rica, Guatemala, and Honduras), the Andean Common Market (Peru, Bolivia, Ecuador, Colombia, and Venezuela), the East African Common Market (Kenya, Tanzania, and Uganda), and the Latin American Free Trade Association (LAFTA).

U.S. Undersecretary of Commerce for International Trade Christopher Padilla (center) plays with a melon next to Nicaraguan Minister of Promotion, Industry and Trade Orlando Solorzano (right) on February 27, 2008, in Managua. Padilla was on an official visit to Nicaragua to check on the implementation of the free-trade agreement among the United States, the Dominican Republic, and Central America.

Through the Tokyo Round, however, the emphasis remained on global trade liberalization. Then, in the early 1980s, the United States, frustrated by its failure to launch a new global round in 1982, turned more to bilateral and regional arrangements. It signed bilateral trade agreements with Israel and Canada, and then it negotiated NAFTA, bringing Mexico into the U.S.-Canadian bilateral agreement. President Clinton extended this idea to a free-trade area for all of Latin America, the Free Trade Area of the Americas (FTAA). But major countries such as Brazil and Argentina objected, and FTAA stalled. Brazil and Argentina had formed their own regional trade organization, known as Mercosur, fearing dominance by a North American trade bloc. The United States negotiated a smaller regional pact with five Central American countries plus the Dominican Republic, known as the Central American Free Trade Agreement, and concluded further bilateral agreements with, among others, Chile, Morocco, Australia, Colombia, Panama, Peru, and South Korea.

Regional agreements proliferated elsewhere. ASEAN initiated regional trade arrangements in Asia. Then, in the late 1980s, Australia and, subsequently, the United

States launched APEC. Bringing together the countries of the Pacific Rim, APEC is a consultative mechanism rather than a free-trade area. Nevertheless, it reflects the enormous growth of trade in the Asian region, especially since China became a member of the WTO in 1999. China, South Korea, and Japan also pursue the "ASEAN plus three" forum, which excludes the United States. And "ASEAN plus six" adds Australia, New Zealand, and India and negotiates a Regional Comprehensive Economic Partnership (RCEP), which also excludes the United States. To counter these exclusive initiatives, the United States launched the Trans-Pacific Partnership (TPP), which brings together the United States, Japan, and ten other Asian and Latin American countries. Meanwhile, bilateral free-trade agreements proliferate. Japan and China have bilateral trade agreements with countries in Southeast Asia, the United States has a bilateral agreement with South Korea, and the EU too has special regional trading arrangements with Mediterranean countries and the so-called Lomé countries in Africa.

From 1948 to 1994, the GATT reported 123 regional trade agreements. Since 1995, the WTO has reported more than 575, of which 379 are in force. Most of these agreements are small and insignificant. But, as regional and bilateral trade arrangements proliferate, a big debate arises as to whether these arrangements are "stepping-stones" or "stumbling blocks" to global free trade. Regional arrangements inherently give preference to members over nonmembers. The increasing number of regional blocs therefore increases discrimination and reduces the benefits compared to MFN trade. On the other hand, bilateral and regional ties spark emulation. Brazil lowers tariffs with its neighbor Argentina to better compete with the United States, which lowers tariffs with its neighbor Mexico. Countries compete to lower tariffs, albeit within competitive regional blocs. As long as bilateral and regional agreements move in a liberalizing direction, they may develop momentum that might recharge negotiations at the global level, unlike the protectionist pacts of the 1930s, when countries competed to raise tariffs. But current bilateral and regional free-trade arrangements add to the complexity of international trade, what trade specialists call a "spaghetti bowl" of deals that distort investment by creating incentives to get behind the external tariff walls of regional common markets.[14] And as countries narrow their focus to regions, they may become more alienated from one another politically. Global free trade still offers greater benefits, and the completion of the Doha Round remains the test of whether regional pacts have stimulated global liberalization or substituted for it. Table 8-2 summarizes the realist and liberal aspects of trade issues from the different levels of analysis.

≫≫ Investment

As noted earlier, foreign direct investment involves the transfer of physical assets or facilities to a foreign country (factories, warehouses, real estate purchases, back-office activities such as accounting, and the like). It may be accomplished through mergers and acquisitions across borders, in which a foreign firm takes over an existing local firm, or through so-called greenfield investments, in which a foreign firm builds a new facility on an open "green field." FDI is usually long-term and brings into play what is now a major nonstate international actor—the multinational corporation, such as IBM or Royal Dutch Shell.

TABLE
8-2

Key Issues in Trade: The Realist and Liberal Perspectives and Levels of Analysis

Perspective		
Systemic	*Structure*	Realist: Hegemony facilitates integration of global markets; equilibrium encourages competition Liberal: Wider markets (comparative advantage) benefit all
	Process	Realist: Alliance or regional trade is preferable Liberal: Multilateral trade rounds facilitate freer trade
Foreign policy		Realist: Strategic trade uses export markets to catch up domestically Liberal: Open markets promote technological leadership in future products
Domestic		Realist: Protectionism substitutes domestic production for imports (import substitution and infant industry) Liberal: Domestic policies (education and technology) are more important than trade policies
Individual		Realist: Low-skilled labor suffers; high-skilled labor gains Liberal: Specialization benefits all individuals

Level of analysis

Realist perspectives regard international investment from the standpoint of gaining access to resources and markets and protecting defense industries to safeguard national military and economic security. In 2005, the United States blocked a bid by the Chinese oil company CNOOC to take over the American oil company Unocal. In 2009, Australia nixed a bid by the Chinese metals company Chinalco to buy the Australian mining firm Rio Tinto. Countries resist foreign investment in security areas and use their economic clout to gain access to critical supplies, such as energy, or to put pressure on other countries' domestic and foreign policies. In recent years, China has used foreign aid aggressively to secure resources around the world, while Russia has twice cut off gas supplies to Ukraine and used gas price reductions to secure a new lease for the Russian naval base located in Ukraine at Sevastopol. In 2010, in a spat over control of uninhabited islands in the East China Sea, China cut off supplies of rare earth minerals, used in products from cell phones to precision-guided munitions, first to Japan and later to the United States and Europe.

CAUSAL ARROW: PERSPECTIVES

Increase distrust between countries	Discourage foreign investments	Safeguards on national security industries
IDENTITY	**LIBERAL**	**REALIST**

Liberal perspectives acknowledge the security and economic dependence created by foreign investments but prefer broader measures to diversify investments and strengthen international rules to protect national interests. They support the inclusion of resource

CAUSAL ARROW: PERSPECTIVES

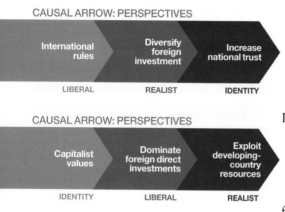

CAUSAL ARROW: PERSPECTIVES

and service industries in the WTO to settle investment conflicts, much the way the WTO does in trade. And they hope investment links, like trade ties, will become so intense that states will no longer contemplate the use of military threats or force to affect investments.

Identity perspectives see problems with unlimited investment flows. They worry that powerful capitalist corporations and banks use liberalized capital markets to dominate and exploit developing-country cultures. Some advocate strict limits on private international capital flows and urge more foreign aid and public or government sources of international financing. Critical theory perspectives see FDI as one of the principal tentacles by which core countries maintain their stranglehold on peripheral developing countries.

Resource-Based Foreign Investments

Until 1960, most FDI went into resource-based industries (mining and agriculture) and infrastructure (roads, railroads, public utilities, and so on). In the last quarter of the nineteenth century, British firms invested heavily in mines, public utilities, and railroads in North and South America, India, Australia, and South Africa. American firms followed with major investments in plantation crops in Latin America: tobacco, cotton, sugar, coffee, bananas, and fruit of all sorts. During and after World War II, American firms accelerated overseas investment in critical raw materials such as copper, tin, and bauxite, often with the encouragement of and subsidies from the U.S. government.

Resource-based foreign industries were often oligopolies, or concentrations of a few firms that were integrated both vertically (that is, they did their own shipping and marketing, as well as production) and horizontally (that is, they produced raw materials, as well as agriculture and processed goods). Oligopolies were highly profitable. At one point before World War I, returns on FDI supplied about 10 percent of Britain's national income.[15] This early FDI took place within colonial empires or along North–South lines and left a legacy of exploitation and ill will that persists today (more on this in Chapter 10).

resource curse: a phenomenon in which an abundance of natural resources inhibits development in other sectors.

For the countries that have them, abundant resources often prove to be a mixed blessing. In fact, economists call this phenomenon the **resource curse**. Where resources are abundant, corruption is easy and local elites fight one another to grab resources. Diamonds in Angola and oil in Nigeria led to civil wars. Moreover, resource-based extraction often does little to develop the interior of a country and sometimes ravages the landscape and environment. The delta region in Nigeria experienced repeated oil spills. Moreover, resource demand is cyclical and declines over time, compared to manufacturing. This causes wide price fluctuations and drives up the value of the local currency, which then costs more than it should and discourages foreign investment and exports in nonresource areas. In Saudi Arabia, for example, oil still makes up 45 percent of GDP, 90 percent of export earnings, and 80 percent of government revenues. After more than fifty years of development, the country's non-energy-related manufacturing sector remains minuscule.

Resource-based MNCs have considerable leverage when they first begin operations in a country. Local governments need the MNCs' resources and expertise. After a while, however, foreign companies become more subject to local government influence as it becomes easier for governments to impose taxes and other regulations. Firms with a lot of capital already invested cannot pick up and leave a country as easily as they entered it. In addition, host countries gradually learn the technology and business of the MNCs and may nationalize foreign firms, as OPEC did in the case of the big "Seven Sisters" oil companies. In recent years, nationalist governments in Venezuela and Bolivia imposed new taxes and nationalized some parts of foreign companies that were developing oil and natural gas in those countries.

The rapid development of China and India has added enormous new pressure on natural resource markets in the Middle East, Africa, and Latin America. With a fifth of the world's population, China now consumes half of the world's cement, a third of its steel, and more than a quarter of its aluminum. And Chinese firms are scouring the world from Canada to Indonesia to Kazakhstan to secure additional resources. In late 2007, the government of the Democratic Republic of the Congo announced that Chinese state-owned firms would invest $12 billion to build or refurbish railroads, roads, and mines in that country in return for the right to mine copper ore of equivalent value. The size of the deal is the equivalent of DR Congo's entire foreign debt, three times its annual budget, and ten times the amount of foreign aid the country receives. China is also guzzling oil and investing in the oil-rich states of the Persian Gulf to secure oil imports. In 2013, it imported 5.6 million barrels of oil per day, a figure

In early February 2012, South Africa's Eastern Cape Premier Noxolo Kiviet (third from left) stands with Jin Yi, vice president of First Automobile Works (FAW), a Chinese company, during a ceremony marking the start of construction at a state-of-the-art truck and passenger car plant in the Coega industrial development zone in Port Elizabeth, South Africa. FAW is set to invest 600 million rand toward the plant.

that is expected to rise steadily over the next twenty years. China's growing influence promises to make MNC expansion into resource development increasingly important in world politics, reviving the role that resource development played in the colonial era of Western expansion.

Manufacturing Foreign Investments

By the mid-1950s, however, resource-based investments were less significant than booming manufacturing investments. Some manufacturing companies became multinational before World War II. The Singer Sewing Company set up operations in Europe in the late nineteenth century, and Ford and General Motors established factories in Europe during the interwar period. FDI in manufacturing, however, did not expand in a big way until the late 1950s and 1960s. The Bretton Woods economic system established after World War II did not liberalize foreign investment and other capital flows across national borders, so investing abroad had to come primarily from the Eurodollar market or dollars accumulated in foreign banks.

By the late 1960s, American MNCs were a strong presence in western Europe, concentrated in growth sectors and under the control of a relatively few American companies. U.S. firms, for example, accounted for 25–30 percent of the automobile market, 60–70 percent of the aircraft and tractor markets, 65 percent of the computer market (industrial computers; there were no personal computers as yet), 30 percent of the telephone market, and 25–30 percent of the petroleum products market. Three companies—Esso (now ExxonMobil), General Motors, and Ford—accounted for 40 percent of all U.S. investments in France, Germany, and Britain, and just twenty-three firms controlled two-thirds of all U.S. investments in western Europe.

These investments sparked European complaints that U.S. companies, concentrated in high-tech sectors, impeded European technological development. This so-called technology gap controversy sparked new interest in the causes of FDI.[16] Did investment flows increase efficiency as trade flows did? If so, should FDI, and perhaps capital flows more generally, be liberalized as the GATT was liberalizing trade flows?

Theoretically, investments should flow to countries that provide the highest rates of return. And returns should be higher where capital is scarcest and in greatest demand. That suggests that investments should flow primarily from advanced countries to developing countries. In past years, that has not been the case. But, as Figure 8-3 shows, with improvements in the investment climate in many developing countries, more than half of FDI inflows in 2012, for the first time ever, went to developing, not advanced, countries. Of a total of $1.35 trillion in global direct investment, $703 billion, or 52 percent, went to developing countries; $561 billion, or 42 percent, went to developed ones; and $82 billion, or 6 percent, went to the Commonwealth of Independent States (CIS).[17] Still, developed countries host most existing foreign investment. At the end of 2012, the stock of FDI in developed countries was twice that in developing countries. U.S. investment position in Europe was nearly four times larger than corporate America's investment position in all of Asia. Why is this so?

FIGURE
8-3

Foreign Direct Investment Inflows: Global and by Group of Economies, 1984–2012

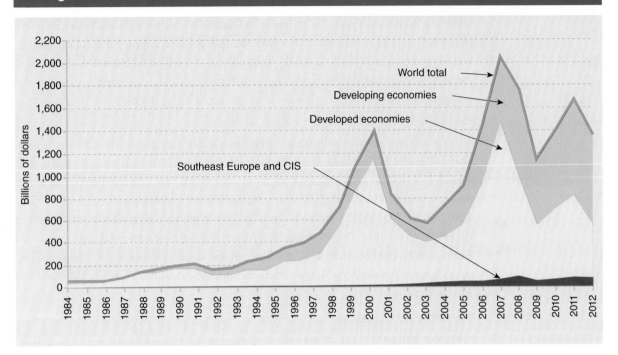

Sources: Data are from UNCTAD, *World Investment Report 2013: Global Value Chains, Investment for Development* (New York: United Nations, 2013), 19, http://unctad.org/en/PublicationsLibrary/wir2013_en.pdf; UNCTAD, "Interactive Database," http://unctad.org/en/Pages/DIAE/FDI%20Statistics/Interactive-database.aspx.

One explanation was developed by economist Raymond Vernon.[18] Known as the product life cycle, it argues that high-tech product development goes through various stages. In the first stage, when the product is first created, the company operates close to home, where R&D facilities are located and new products can be tested and adapted to consumer needs. American firms had an advantage at this stage because U.S. research and consumer markets were highly advanced. Thus, U.S. firms produced at home and exported to other advanced markets where there was a demand for sophisticated products. In the second stage, as the technology matures and other costs—labor and shipping—become more important, it is advantageous to shift production to European markets. Once the European Common Market existed, tariffs were lower inside Europe, and by producing the product closer to the final consumer, a company avoided paying the external tariff and helped meet local competition. Finally in the third stage, when production has become fully routine, production shifts to developing countries, which have the lowest labor costs. Developing countries then export the product back to the United States and Europe. Thus, the expansion of U.S. investments to Europe in the 1960s reflected the second stage of the product life cycle, when FDI displaces exports in advanced markets, and the expansion of MNCs to Asia in the 1970s and 1980s reflected the third stage, when FDI moves to developing countries, which export back to more advanced countries. According to the product life cycle theory, FDI seemed to follow demand (consumers) more than supply (labor), and thus most of it went to advanced countries where demand was high and changing.

A second explanation is that, initially, few developing countries welcomed FDI in manufacturing. As noted in previous chapters and again in Chapter 9, Latin American countries were intent on developing their own industries through import substitution policies, and many newly independent developing countries feared neocolonial influences from the MNCs. They advocated technology transfer without the accompanying capital and management, but that approach was neither accepted by MNCs nor terribly effective for mastering new technologies.

Some Asian developing countries bucked the trend. Starting in the 1950s the four tigers—Taiwan, Hong Kong, South Korea, and Singapore—focused on exports and welcomed FDI. As the product life cycle theory predicted, investments began to flow to these countries in labor-intensive and standardized technology products. In the 1970s, a second wave of MNCs expanded to Asia, this time including European as well as American companies. The success of the Asian tigers encouraged emulation, and other Asian nations opened up to FDI: the Philippines, Thailand, Indonesia, Malaysia, and later China and India. Some Latin American and African countries, such as Mexico and Tanzania, did so as well.

The GATT did not deal with investments, so the expansion of MNCs was negotiated on a country-by-country and, often, contract-by-contract basis. Bilateral investment treaties proliferated, much the way bilateral trade agreements did in the 1940s. These treaties were often discriminatory and involved numerous restrictions that affected trade. Developing countries set up free-trade export-processing zones in which they gave foreign companies profitable concessions, such as low or no taxes, lenient labor laws, and duty-free imports, as long as these companies produced for export. Foreign investors found such zones attractive for importing components and assembling final products for export. However, export zones produced limited local benefits. Often the value-added to production (the difference between the value of the inputs and the value of outputs from these zones) was relatively small, and while foreign firms employed local workers, they created enclave communities rather than linking up with internal markets and developing local resources. In some ways, manufacturing export zones resembled the natural resource enclaves of earlier resource-based multinational investments.

Proliferating export zones and the oil crisis accelerated interest in liberalizing capital markets. In the 1970s, the United States began to negotiate bilateral investment treaties that contained clauses requiring national treatment. National treatment meant that, rather than offering special treatment for FDI in selective export zones, host countries treated foreign investors the same as local or national investors in the rest of the economy. This reduced the discrimination inherent in export zones. The GATT began to discuss and negotiate rules to govern investment and technology restrictions that distorted trade, so-called trade-related investment measures (TRIMs) and trade-related intellectual property measures (TRIPs). The GATT also discussed a Multilateral Agreement on

Investment (MAI), and the WTO acquired jurisdiction over investment as well as trade issues when it superseded the GATT in 1994.

As technological development quickened and FDI became freer, the product life cycle collapsed. That is, countries had very little time to recoup their R&D costs between the development of a product and the shifting of its production overseas. Investments spread simultaneously to many markets at once. It was essential for companies to be invested in all these markets from the outset and to develop comparative advantage in high technology by encouraging networks of universities, entrepreneurs, and financiers to create new products. Strategic trade theory suggested that comparative advantage was no longer based on fixed factors, such as lower labor costs, but depended increasingly on getting to markets first and dominating those markets as quickly as possible. Once a company had a large market share, it could reap monopoly profits or rents and recoup development costs.

The next, or fourth, wave of MNC expansion reflected this emphasis on investing in the most advanced markets simultaneously. First Japan in the 1980s and then European countries in the 1990s invested massively in the U.S. market. Some developing countries—Brazil, Mexico, and South Africa—also developed their own MNCs. In 2008, 28 percent of 82,000 transnational corporations came from developing countries. Some countries are friendlier to FDI than others. China welcomed FDI primarily for export, while FDI in Japan remains a small share of the value of total sales or employment compared to the United States or Europe. Overall, FDI spread, and world markets became intensely competitive. Companies were now truly global, often decentralizing to run operations from regional headquarters abroad rather than from the home countries.

Service-Sector Foreign Investments

A further step in this evolution became visible in the early 2000s. Companies expanded abroad not just to manufacture products but also to provide services. Historically, services such as entertainment were more homebound enterprises catering to local cultures, languages, and tastes. But advances in transportation and communications now shrank the service world. Financial companies—banks, insurance companies, and mutual, pension, and hedge funds—set up operations overseas. Retail (for example, Wal-Mart and McDonald's), telecommunications (AOL and Google), and entertainment companies (Disney and Bertelsmann) did so as well.

The latest expansion of multinational service industries comes in areas of data processing, back-office accounting services, software development, and call centers. This phenomenon is known as foreign outsourcing. Whereas in earlier expansions MNCs continued to do payroll, data services, and R&D activities at the home headquarters, they now exploited the Internet to outsource these tasks to foreign firms. Payroll and other forms of accounting and data processing could be sent to firms in India or China for completion and shipped back via the Internet to the home company within a day or two. Even research tasks could be outsourced. An R&D firm in Dalian, China, might be asked to develop a new software program for a cell phone chip. The task could be done entirely online, without the need to transfer physical facilities.

Textile workers, steelworkers, and their unions have long decried foreign or offshore investment in manufacturing. As they see it, each investment offshore subtracts from U.S. jobs onshore. More recently, highly skilled labor has raised similar concerns about outsourcing. Silicon Valley software operations are being outsourced to Egypt, India, and Ireland, where engineers work for much less pay. FDI, like trade, involves job displacement, and job displacement is disruptive. But the issue is also what the alternative might be. If foreign outsourcing is banned, companies will become less competitive or have to invest in more advanced technology at home. The latter, too, results in job losses, as machines replace labor. More textile jobs have been lost in the United States because of the modernization of local plants than because of trade or offshore investments.

Perhaps the next service to be outsourced will be education. Training by corporations as well as instruction by universities may be done online from offshore locations. Professors may lose their jobs or at least have to compete with instructors abroad who specialize and teach online courses in specific topics. Then we'll get a chance to see how much professors—especially economics professors—really favor free trade.

The problem with restricting foreign investments is the same as that with restricting foreign trade. Restrictions by one country can be matched by restrictions by another country. If the United States blocks U.S. firms from investing in Japan, Japan will retaliate by blocking Japanese investments in the United States. Today, Japanese companies operate in forty-nine U.S. states and employ approximately 600,000 Americans. What happens to these jobs if the United States tries to save other jobs by preventing U.S. firms from investing abroad? Won't Japanese unions insist that those jobs created in the United States be brought back home to Japan? Everyone loses. Remember, trade does not necessarily increase jobs; it just promotes better jobs. The same is true of foreign investment. In 2007, U.S. MNCs and foreign MNCs based in the United States created jobs that paid on average 20 percent more than all other jobs in the U.S. economy. These same firms undertook $665.5 billion in capital investment, which constituted 40.6 percent of all private-sector nonresidential investment. They exported $731 billion in goods, 62.7 percent of all U.S. goods exported. And these firms also conducted $240.2 billion in R&D, a remarkable 89.2 percent of all U.S. private-sector R&D.[19] Offshore firms are the most advanced in any economy. Cut them off and world growth will shrink.

Multinational Corporations

Yes, but aren't these MNCs too big, and don't they, like their resource predecessors, abuse local economies and cultures, especially in less advanced countries? In 2012, world sales (domestic and exports) of foreign affiliates totaled $26 trillion, up from $2.7 trillion in 1982. Their world exports in 2012, by comparison, equaled only $7.5 trillion, up from $2.2 trillion in 1982. The gross domestic product of foreign affiliates—the sales of foreign affiliates minus the cost of production, or the value-added—totaled $6.6 trillion in 2012 compared to the world GDP of $70.0 trillion.[20] Thus, in 2012, foreign affiliates, some 770,000 worldwide, accounted for about 10 percent of world production, while their total sales were almost four times as large as their world exports. Moreover, MNCs themselves accounted for over 33 percent of world exports. And they employed some 72 million workers, or about 4 percent of the world's workforce. FDI has integrated the world economy far more than trade. Because FDI takes place primarily among advanced countries, this integration is more extensive among advanced countries than between them and developing countries. Nevertheless, MNCs headquartered in developing countries now account for about one-quarter of all MNCs.

If we use total sales as a measure, in 2000, MNCs made up fifty-one of the world's one hundred largest economies. But this measure compares the total sales of MNCs with the GDP of countries, and recall that GDP is measured by total sales (output) minus total costs (inputs), or value-added. When corporations are measured by value-added, only twenty-nine companies appear among the top one hundred economies, and only two of these—ExxonMobil at forty-five and General Motors at forty-seven—rank in the top fifty.[21] Still, that is a large number. Few developing countries appear in the top one hundred economies. So, twenty-nine MNCs are much larger than the economies of many developing countries, certainly of the poorest countries.

Doesn't this give them enormous clout? Yes and no. Yes, they control large amounts of capital and labor, and, as realist perspectives point out, that gives them real power. But no, they also must compete, and recipient countries can play them off against one another, certainly more so than they could fifty years ago, when MNCs were fewer in number and highly concentrated in specific sectors such as resources.

MNCs usually pay higher wages than local firms but not as high as they pay in their home countries. Yet international human rights groups find numerous instances of labor abuses, especially among sweatshops in export-processing zones. That wages and conditions can be improved is beyond doubt, but applicable standards need to be proportionate. Workers in developing countries are less productive than their counterparts are in advanced countries. If they were paid the same wages as workers in developed countries, no firm would invest in or trade with developing countries. The relevant standard is what they were paid before they went to work for foreign firms. In almost all cases, workers—especially women and children—do better where MNCs are present. Most women are unemployed before the MNCs arrive; children work because parents often require it, and they would be working anyway if they stayed on the farm. Children also worked during the early stages of development in advanced countries; at that time, abuses occurred and had to be corrected. The same holds true today in developing countries. For a dissenting view on the impact of MNCs, see the critical theory perspective developed in Chapter 10.

Immigration Policies

The movement of people across national boundaries is a relatively new feature of globalization. Immigration, of course, has always existed, but people flows accelerated after the end of the Cold War and the adoption by developing countries, such as Mexico, of more open and market-oriented economic policies.

Migrant farmworkers from Mexico harvest organic spinach at the Grant Family Farms Wellington, Colorado, in September 2010. The farm, the largest organic vegetable farm outside California, hires some 250 immigrant workers during the peak harvest season. Owner Andy Grant lamented that the issue of illegal immigration has become politicized nationally. "They feed America," he said of immigrant workers. "They should not be victimized." Grant said his workers start at $7.25 per hour, which is the minimum wage in Colorado.

Most countries limit immigration. The United States is one of the most open. The European Union concluded the Schengen Agreement, which opened borders within the EU but maintained restrictions toward immigrants from outside the EU, especially from Muslim countries. Other countries, such as Japan, control immigration to fill specific and usually less desirable jobs in the economy. Germany admits guest workers, principally from Turkey and the Balkan states that made up former Yugoslavia, but its laws make it difficult for such workers to become German citizens. Some immigrants also represent security threats, which have escalated in the era of terrorism.

When people are free to move, wages are the principal economic factor driving them. Wages in the United States are some five times higher on average than wages in Mexico. This disparity drives labor north, so much so that it comes in illegally as well as legally. Although the United States has admitted some twenty-three million immigrants since 1965, mostly from Latin America, another eleven million—three to four million from

Mexico alone—have slipped in illegally. How to treat these immigrants is a perennial and heated issue in U.S. politics and U.S.–Mexican relations, and illegal immigration is also a problem in many other countries. Immigrants make up 15 percent of the population in more than fifty countries worldwide, suggesting that flows of people are becoming as common as flows of goods and capital.

Skilled immigrants have become more important as globalization has affected the information industries. Software engineers from India populate Silicon Valley and other high-tech centers in the United States. Skilled laborers in the United States worry about the outsourcing of other service jobs to India and Egypt. With the Internet, people don't have to move. The jobs are brought to them. People located in India, not the United States, often do data processing and handle customer service calls for companies located in the United States.

CAUSAL ARROW: REALIST PERSPECTIVES

Strengthens national identity — Influences immigration — Population is power

IDENTITY — LIBERAL — REALIST

CAUSAL ARROW: LIBERAL PERSPECTIVES

Increases material well-being — Exploits cultural differences — Open immigration

REALIST — IDENTITY — LIBERAL

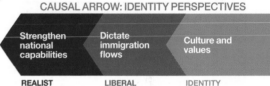

CAUSAL ARROW: IDENTITY PERSPECTIVES

Strengthen national capabilities — Dictate immigration flows — Culture and values

REALIST — LIBERAL — IDENTITY

Realist perspectives tend to see population as an important ingredient of national power and are reluctant to liberalize immigration flows unless doing so offers relative national advantage. Liberal perspectives emphasize the opportunities to match labor skills and economic needs across national boundaries and increase common material benefits. Identity perspectives tend to view immigration flows in the context of preserving cultural homogeneity or encouraging cultural diversity. They might also emphasize basic human rights and treat immigration issues largely as refugee problems. Table 8-3 summarizes investment aspects of the global economy fromm the different levels of analysis.

>>> Finance

Since the liberalization of financial markets in the early 1980s, finance (portfolio investments), including currency transactions, has become by far the biggest component of global markets, dwarfing trade and FDI. In 2007, global financial stock, which includes bank deposits, government and private debt securities, and equities, reached a grand total of $194 trillion, up from $12 trillion in 1980 and $53 trillion in 1993. During this period global capital markets grew faster than world GDP, topping out in 2007 at almost four times the global GDP. That trend was broken by the global financial crisis of 2008–2009. The global capital stock fell in 2008 by $16 trillion to $178 trillion. Another $12 trillion was lost in the first half of 2009. Global households save about $1.6 trillion per year, so the decline equaled about eighteen years of global household savings. Capital flows (annual) as opposed to stock (cumulative) cratered from $10.5 trillion in 2007 to $1.9 trillion in 2008.[22]

What happened to cause this crisis? To understand that, we need to know more about how global finance functions. Global finance involves exchange rates, currency

TABLE 8-3

Key Issues in Investment: The Realist and Liberal Perspectives and Levels of Analysis

Level of analysis		Perspective
Systemic	*Structure*	Realist: Competition for resources and markets Liberal: Common rules to expand and diversify foreign investment
	Process	Realist: Use MNCs to support foreign policy goals Liberal: Expand WTO to include investment
Foreign policy		Realist: Export zones exploit foreign markets to develop local industries Liberal: Encourage immigrants to fill domestic economic needs
Domestic		Realist: Foreign or offshore investment in Country B by Country A costs jobs in Country A Liberal: Foreign investment in Country B by Country A is reciprocated by foreign investment in Country A by Country B, which creates jobs in Country A
Individual		Realist: Screen immigrants to promote national security Liberal: Allow immigrants to promote national wealth

markets, balance-of-payments accounting, debt financing, and financial crises, such as the Asian financial crises in the 1990s, the banking crash of 2008–2009, and the ongoing European Union debt crisis.

Exchange Rates

The exchange rate is the price of one country's currency in terms of another country's currency. Change it, and you have changed the relative prices of everything that moves across the borders between these two countries. Let's say we import a Chinese shirt today that costs 12 renminbi and we pay $2 for it because the exchange rate (in 2013) is roughly $1 to 6 renminbi. Tomorrow the value of the renminbi goes up (fewer renminbi buy the same amount of dollars); the exchange rate changes to $1 to 4 renminbi. The shirt still costs 12 renminbi, but we now pay $3 instead of $2 to import it. Notice how powerfully the exchange rate affects trade. A country can in effect subsidize all its exports by maintaining an undervalued exchange rate. That's why exchange rates are so controversial and why the U.S. Congress in recent years threatened China with tariffs if it did not raise its exchange rate so U.S. consumers would pay more for Chinese imports and hence buy fewer of them. U.S. consumers might then buy more domestic goods and create more domestic jobs, or so it is thought. Consequently, exchange rates are often the first thing that governments have to coordinate when they want to create a stable world economy. If they don't, they get the beggar-thy-neighbor policies that destroyed world markets in the 1930s, when every country tried to cheapen its export prices by devaluing its currency and no country succeeded because imports became more expensive and export demand dried up.

What should the exchange rate be? Sometimes governments fix exchange rates, called a fixed exchange rate system, as under the Bretton Woods system right after World War II. But how do governments know what the correct price should be? It's a tough call. Because many factors affect prices, such as unemployment and trade policy, it matters what the general conditions in a country are when the exchange rate is fixed. For example, employment was low and trade restricted in 1945 when exchange rates were set at Bretton Woods. As restrictions and other conditions changed, more than twenty countries, including Great Britain, had to alter their exchange rates in 1949. Economists talk about equilibrium exchange rates in terms of purchasing power parity—that is, what a general basket of goods in one country costs compared to the same basket in another country. This measure eliminates the influence of different inflation rates on exchange rates. Often purchasing power parity rates are used to compare total output in one country to that in another. But using any particular measure to set exchange rates is not very reliable.

So, maybe the best policy is to let the marketplace decide the exchange rate, just watch to see how much of the currency for a particular country is supplied and how much is demanded by all the exporters and importers in the world economy. To some extent, that's the system that exists now. Except for some developing countries such as China, which peg their rates either to the dollar or to a basket of currencies, exchange rates float. That means, of course, they may be volatile because markets are sometimes volatile, especially if short-term capital flows are not restricted. And if rates are volatile, trade and investment become unpredictable, and then the world economy shrinks. So, most governments today watch their exchange rates carefully, and sometimes they intervene to keep them from falling or going up too much. In the midst of the world financial crisis in 2010, Japan, China, Brazil, and South Korea all intervened to influence the value of their currencies. The governments feared that a higher currency value would make their exports more expensive just at a time when these countries were trying to increase domestic production and jobs and to recover from the economic recession. To prevent such undesired exchange rate movements, governments intervene to keep their exchange rates within certain ranges or to have them go up or down gradually. Economists call this system a managed float or dirty float because governments often intervene secretly.

Currency Markets

How do governments affect exchange rates? Central banks buy or sell their own countries' currency in large enough quantities to affect its price. That's called exchange market intervention. But global currency markets today are so deep that even government purchases or sales amount to only a small proportion of the market and therefore may not have much effect. Transactions of roughly $4 trillion take place every day in currency markets. Over a year, that adds up to $1 quadrillion. Compare that with annual global output of around $70 trillion, and you can see that the world economy is getting pretty heady, with a lot of wine flowing across national boundaries compared to a significantly smaller amount of meat and potatoes.

Thus, timing becomes very important. Central banks act secretly and try to catch the markets off guard. On other occasions, central banks may coordinate their interventions. If they all buy or sell a currency at the same time, chances are they will have a bigger impact. Even better is when central banks coordinate their short-term interest rates to support currency changes. If the United States is trying to weaken the dollar, it lowers its interest rates while European countries do not lower their rates as much or keep them the same. Now currency traders demand more European currencies with higher interest rates and fewer dollars with lower interest rates. This is what the G-7 countries did in 1985 when they acted to bring the high dollar down. Now you know why investors and financial markets pay so much attention to G-7 and G-20 meetings and to what central bankers say. Often central bank officials try to affect markets just by what they say, knowing that the best way to affect the market, given the small part that governments affect directly, is to get private actors to move in a certain direction. For example, in the 1990s a strong dollar was important to ease the Asian financial crisis. Why? Because a strong dollar encouraged U.S. imports and helped Asian economies export more and recover sooner. Thus, the U.S. secretary of the Treasury, Robert Rubin, repeated over and over again during this period that a high dollar was in U.S. interests.

Intervening to alter exchange rates can change other policies, such as monetary policy. Let's say the New York Fed, one of the regional banks of the Federal Reserve System, acting under instructions from the U.S. Treasury Department—which has exchange rate authority in the U.S. government—sells dollars to keep the price from going too high. It acquires foreign currencies and puts them into its foreign exchange reserves. Now there are more dollars in circulation. In effect, the intervention has expanded the money supply. If the Fed does not want to expand monetary policy, it has to reabsorb those dollars. It does so by selling U.S. Treasury securities and sponging up excess dollars. That's called sterilization. Now the dollar supply is back to where it was before. But if that's the case, the price of the dollar cannot be affected much, right? Well, maybe it can be affected in the short term until the market figures out what the Fed is doing. But, generally, economists believe it is not possible to change exchange rates significantly through intervention unless monetary authorities are willing to let the money supply expand or contract—in other words, unless they do not sterilize the intervention. In recent years when the Bank of Japan intervened to prevent a rise in the yen, it maintained an extremely loose monetary policy involving interest rates only fractionally above zero.

Liberal perspectives tend to favor G-7 and G-20 coordination to maintain exchange rates within relatively narrow ranges, believing that exchange rate volatility encourages protectionism and capital flight. Realist perspectives tolerate greater exchange rate competition, believing that it is hard enough to get agreement on policy choices domestically, let alone among numerous countries internationally. And without underlying agreement on policies, coordination is, at best, a short-term fix and, at worst, a long-run inflationary threat, because when politicians meet in public gatherings they like to cut interest rates, not raise them. Finally, identity perspectives are eclectic, favoring stable exchange rates if they serve the right goals and flexible rates if they don't. For example, labor groups tend to favor flexible rates because they oppose the budget austerity that is sometimes required to maintain fixed rates, whereas investor and management groups tend to favor fixed rates, which create a more stable environment for savings and investments.

CAUSAL ARROW: LIBERAL PERSPECTIVES

Minimizes protectionism	Fosters similar policy approaches	Exchange rate coordination
REALIST	IDENTITY	LIBERAL

CAUSAL ARROW: REALIST PERSPECTIVES

Maximizes material gains	Concentrates attention on domestic policies	Exchange rate competition
REALIST	IDENTITY	REALIST

CAUSAL ARROW: IDENTITY PERSPECTIVES

Increase relative gains	Favor flexible or fixed rates	Different actors
REALIST	LIBERAL	IDENTITY

Balance of Payments

Border flows of goods and services plus government transfers and net income on capital investments constitute a country's current account. Government transfers involve foreign aid and military expenditures. Net income on capital investments includes the interest and dividends earned by one country on its foreign investments in all other countries minus the interest and dividends earned by all other countries on foreign investments in the first country. Notice that trade of goods and services is only one part of the current account. Merchandise trade is an even smaller part because it excludes trade in services, which in the information age is becoming larger. Thus, trade deficits and current account deficits are not the same thing. For twenty-five years after World War II, the United States ran trade surpluses that were large enough to offset its foreign aid and military expenditures. But after 1970 the trade surplus declined and then disappeared altogether. America's current account went into deficit and has stayed there ever since, except for seven years. The United States has been borrowing from other countries for a long time, although only more recently from poor countries such as China. This borrowing (and lending for China) comes through the capital account and includes portfolio investments (stocks, bonds, and cash) and FDI (plants and other facilities). Taken together, the current and capital accounts make up the country's balance-of-payments account. People flows do not appear in the balance of payments, although any money that immigrants remit to their home countries does appear as remittances in the current account. Table 8-4 shows the balance of payments for the United States in the calendar year 2008.

One way to think about the balance of payments is as your country's checkbook at a bank known as the World Economy. If you spend more than you earn, you have a deficit in your checkbook, a current account deficit, and have to borrow an equivalent amount, a capital account surplus or inflow, from the World Economy bank. If you spend less than you earn, you have a surplus in your checkbook, a current account surplus; if you don't draw it out, you in effect lend that amount, a capital account

TABLE 8-4

U.S. Balance of Payments, 2008 (in billions of dollars)

Current account			Capital account		
Goods and services					
Exports	1,826.6		Net capital transfers	0.953	
Imports	−2,522.5		U.S.-owned assets abroad	−0.106	
(Subtotal)		−695.9	Foreign-owned assets in the United States	534.1	
			Net financial derivatives	−41.2	
			Capital account balance		**493.7**
Income on investments					
Income	761.6		Reserve account	4.8	
Payments	−636.0		Statistical discrepancy	200.1	
(Subtotal)		125.6	(Subtotal)		204.9
Government transfers		−128.4			
Current account balance		−698.7	**Capital account balance + reserves + statistical discrepancy**		698.7
Balance of payments (current account balance + capital account balance + reserve account + statistical discrepancy)					0

deficit or outflow, back to the World Economy bank, which pays you interest on your checking or savings account. Notice that any checkbook surplus is offset by a loan to the bank and any checkbook deficit by borrowing from the bank. Similarly, any current account surplus is offset by loans to other countries, or a capital account deficit. And any current account deficit is offset by borrowing from other countries, or a capital account surplus. The current and capital accounts are mirror images of one another with opposite signs (if one is negative, the other is positive). As Table 8-4 shows, after increases or decreases in foreign exchange reserves held by central banks and statistical discrepancies, the balance of payments equals zero. Like your checkbook, it's just an accounting device.

Nevertheless, realist perspectives often see a checkbook or current account surplus as desirable. In the mercantilist era, such a surplus meant that a country accumulated gold, and that was a good thing because gold could be used to buy the instruments of national military and economic power. In today's global economy, it means that a country accumulates loans or lends to other countries. Is that good or bad? Realist outlooks say it's good because it's better to be a lender than a borrower. And they have a point. During financial crises in the late 1990s, Asian countries resented the policies that the IMF and United States imposed on their economies as conditions for new loans. Subsequently, they formed their own lenders' club, the Chiang Mai Initiative, to make loans to one another in future crises and avoid IMF conditionality. Similarly, in 2010, Greece resented conditions tied to loans made by the IMF and European Union to help that country survive a financial crisis.

CAUSAL ARROW: PERSPECTIVES

Maximizes national influence	Increases lending to other countries	Surplus in current account
IDENTITY	LIBERAL	REALIST

But how big an advantage is it to be a lender? What if the borrower can't pay the loan back? You know the old saw: If I owe the bank $100, I'm in trouble; if I owe the bank $100 million, the bank is in trouble. Neither the IMF nor the United States could afford to let the Asian countries go bankrupt. Nor could the EU simply cut Greece loose without jeopardizing the financial well-being of other countries such as Spain and Portugal. So there is risk in international lending, just as in any other type of lending. Liberal perspectives tend to emphasize mutual dependency between lender and borrower and see current account surpluses and deficits as normal and inevitable given the high levels of trade and capital interdependence. Chronic balance-of-payments and debt imbalances, however, are a problem because they threaten the sustainability of trade and capital flows.

CAUSAL ARROW: PERSPECTIVES

Equalizes national influence	Causes shifting (not chronic) current account surpluses and deficits	Mutual dependency
IDENTITY	REALIST	LIBERAL

Debt Markets

The expansion of financial markets was inevitable once trade and FDI were liberalized. Current account deficits and surpluses grew and had to be financed by lending from surplus countries to deficit ones. As liberal perspectives see it, it was a classic case of spillover or path dependence. If corporations operated worldwide, so must banks, insurance companies, investment houses, pension funds, mutual and hedge funds, and stock, bond, and currency exchanges. After all, companies have to borrow, invest, and work in multiple currencies. They have to insure trade and financial transactions, hedge against currency and interest rate risks, and diversify their assets across country markets.

Global banks and financial institutions mobilize world savings and make them available for investment opportunities worldwide. As we learned earlier, countries that save more than they invest accumulate current account surpluses and then make loans to other countries by running capital account deficits. Countries that invest more than they save do the reverse. Overall, this financial intermediation function is good for everyone.

If global financial institutions did not exist, countries that saved more than they invested would have to bury the extra savings in the ground. No country could invest more than it saved. Local resources and opportunities would be wasted.

But open financial markets also bring global problems. Whereas capital flows in the earlier Bretton Woods system came largely from governments and intergovernmental institutions, such as the IMF and World Bank, private sources (commercial banks, investment houses, and pension, mutual, and hedge funds) now provide the bulk of capital flows in world markets. These flows are not only large; they are also volatile. In 2008, as we have noted, annual global capital flows dropped by more than $8 trillion, or 80 percent. These are huge sums and shifts. Short-term capital flows are particularly volatile. Some economists advocate restricting short-term flows. For these economists, the problem is speculation and international regulation. Others believe the problem lies in weak banking systems in developing countries. For them, the solution is domestic reforms to make local banks more competitive. Can you see the tension here between domestically led and internationally led economic approaches, between the domestic and systemic levels of analysis? Do you start at the domestic end of the problem or the international one? And if you do both, which takes the lead?

CAUSAL ARROW: LEVELS OF ANALYSIS

| Foreign speculation | Encourages capital outflows | And weakens domestic economy |
| SYSTEMIC | INDIVIDUAL | DOMESTIC |

CAUSAL ARROW: LEVELS OF ANALYSIS

| Weak banking systems | Encourage speculation and corruption | And create international financial crises |
| DOMESTIC | INDIVIDUAL | SYSTEMIC |

derivatives market: the market that exchanges instruments derived from existing loans and financial assets, hedging them against future changes in prices, earnings, or interest.

Now derivatives markets come into the picture. A **derivatives market** involves the exchange of financial claims against future earnings by households, corporations, and financial institutions. An example of a derivative is a stock option. The option derives from the stock, hence the term *derivative*. You buy an option, however, not the stock. The option is a right to purchase or sell a stock at a given strike price within a given time period. You may be hedging against the rise or fall of a stock that you own, or you may just be speculating against price changes. Derivatives can be created for any asset: commodities, loans (including mortgages), insurance policies, and so on. Parties in global financial markets often swap or package financial assets to spread risks. They also sell insurance to cover risks on regular assets as well as derivatives assets.

Creating derivatives doesn't create new wealth, as in the case of new loans, equity investments, or FDI, but it does serve the useful business purposes of hedging against changes in future earnings, prices, or interest rates. If you are in business and need raw materials in the future (say, oil), you may wish to purchase future contracts, an option or derivative to buy those commodities at a given price in the future. You are anticipating that prices may go up, and you want to lock in a price now. Someone on the other end of the contract sells you that option because he or she may hold the commodities and anticipate that the price will go down. Market participants make opposite sides of a trade and make these sorts of guesses about future prices all the time. It's a part of normal business activity.

The derivatives market grew phenomenally and then collapsed spectacularly in the financial crisis. In 2006, the notional value of the derivatives market was $477 trillion. That was more than thirty times the size of U.S. GDP, which was around $15 trillion, and roughly three times the size of all global financial assets of $167 trillion in 2006. This market was not only huge, but, because it was new, it was also largely unregulated by international and, in many cases, national authorities. Let's take a closer look at how these elements of global finance came together in the 1990s and 2000s to create the financial bubble that burst in 2008.[23]

Global Financial Crisis

In 1998, bankers at J. P. Morgan (which became JPMorgan Chase in 2000 when it merged with Chase Manhattan Bank) packaged the first collateralized debt obligations (CDOs), or what were then called Bistro deals. They pooled into a single security or CDO some three hundred loans on the books of J. P. Morgan worth about $9.7 billion. They intended to sell these loans as securities based on the income stream or interest payments of the loans. Normally, when a bank sells securities, it has to keep a certain amount of capital in reserve in case the loans go sour. In this case, J. P. Morgan calculated that it needed to hold only $700 million in reserve against the nearly $10 billion worth of securities it wanted to sell. Some bank regulators signed off on that, but others urged J. P. Morgan to reserve or insure against the missing $9 billion as well.

Enter American International Group (AIG), the London firm that became notorious during the financial meltdown. AIG was a regular client of J. P. Morgan and had a division that specialized in derivatives. AIG decided that it would sell J. P. Morgan insurance on the extra $9 billion of the CDO package. Because it operated out of London and was an insurance company, AIG did not face the same requirements to hold reserves as banks did. Thus, it sold the insurance, known as credit default swaps (CDSs), for a tiny but steady stream of income, assuming that the deal was essentially risk-free and that AIG would never have to pay out the $9 billion. In time, these CDSs became very valuable. Remember, they were insurance policies that paid off if the loans went sour. For the moment, however, the loans seemed good and the insurance seemed to be as worthless as insurance against the end of the world. International rating agencies, such as Moody's, which grade loan instruments in terms of riskiness, essentially agreed that such deals were low risk and gave the securities package a triple-A rating, the highest possible.

The die was cast for rolling out literally trillions of dollars worth of these types of security packages over the next decade. J. P. Morgan was followed by every other big bank and investment house around the world—in Europe and Asia as well as the United States. All kinds of loans, including housing, credit card, and car loans, began to be packaged and sold as CDOs, covered in many cases by insurance policies or CDSs. It was not only private banks that joined the party. Two of the biggest mortgage lenders were government agencies, Fannie Mae and Freddie Mac, created by Congress to encourage home ownership. They borrowed money in private markets on the basis of tax-supported government guarantees to finance home loans for middle-class families. They packaged and sold mortgage loans to the tune of $5 trillion. Because home ownership is considered a good thing, Fannie Mae and Freddie Mac pushed loans that many people could not afford, called subprime loans. As long as housing prices went up, everything was fine. Owners

In September 2008, the stock market ticker in New York's Times Square flashes that the Dow has plunged 777 points after the U.S. Congress failed to pass a proposed bailout bill.

could always sell the house for a profit or borrow more against the increased equity to keep up their payments. In all these cases, the assumption was that if one loan went bad, others would remain good. In fact, securities were broken down into tranches, with the riskier tranches bearing higher interest rates, precisely to insulate less risky loans from more risky ones. The chance that defaults in any given pool of loans might be interconnected in such a way that one bad loan might trigger another one, a problem known as correlation, was considered minuscule.

But you guessed it—that's exactly what happened. Once housing prices began to decline, the riskier tranches went bad first. But then investors began to fear that the less risky tranches were also worth less. Rating agencies downgraded the less risky securities. Not knowing exactly who held the loans, how many of the loans were bad, and what the real prices of these assets were, the markets panicked and began to pull back from making any loans at all. Eventually debt markets froze up completely. Interest rates spiked even for overnight loans, which are the lubricant of daily banking. Government central banks in the United States, Britain, and other countries had to step in. They bought debt to make cash available to the banks to keep them afloat. Not only the commercial banks were involved. For the first time, the Federal Reserve Bank intervened to keep an investment house from going under. Bear Stearns, a Wall Street investment company, was taken over by JPMorgan Chase, with substantial financial assistance from the Federal Reserve Bank. But the Fed was unlikely and unable to save every financial institution. When a second investment house, Lehman Brothers, went under in September 2008, the Fed did not step in, and the global contraction of credit cascaded.

Make no mistake—some people made money. Investors who bought the CDSs or insurance policies on the securitized loans saw the value of their insurance policies rise dramatically or received payment in full for the loans that went bad, which they had insured against. That's the nature of markets. For every trade that turns out bad, there is another one that turns out good. The question is whether governments should step in to make the bad loans good again. If they don't, will markets implode, as they did in the 1930s? Are financial institutions, especially big private banks and investment houses, too big to fail? So far, governments have not decided that they are.

Altogether, by buying debt assets from private institutions, the Federal Reserve Bank added more than $2 trillion to its balance sheet, tripling the amount it carried before. In addition, Congress authorized a $700 billion bailout package for the banks, the Troubled Asset Relief Program, known as TARP. This money was initially intended to buy bad debt from the banks, the so-called toxic assets of CDOs and CDSs that were now worth much less. If these assets were valued at market prices, the capital assets of banks would be drastically reduced, compelling them to do still less lending. But because it was too difficult to figure out how much the toxic assets were worth (there were no buyers), the money was used instead to recapitalize the banks—that is, to buy their stock to replenish their capital reserves. Much of the bad debt still remains on the balance sheets of banks, not only in the United States but abroad as well, and may be a factor reducing the capacity of banks to lend for a long time to come. But private bank stocks have recovered, and by selling the stock it acquired, the U.S. government has recovered more than 90 percent of the money involved in the bailout.[24]

Here is a classic case of how global markets sometimes outpace the capacity of both national and global governments to manage them. At about the same time in 1998 that J. P. Morgan was packaging its first CDO, Fed and U.S. Treasury regulators met to consider a proposal by the Commodity Futures Trading Commission (CFTC) to regulate the derivatives market. Robert Rubin, then U.S. Treasury secretary, Alan Greenspan, chairman of the Federal Reserve System, and Lawrence Summers, who succeeded Rubin as Treasury secretary, agreed that the markets understood more about risk than any federal regulator did and refused to intervene. Over the next decade, Treasury and White House officials of both parties reaffirmed this decision even as the derivatives market exploded. According to one observer, "Stopping this [CFTC proposal] let the momentum build and led to subprime as well as soaring commodity prices today because unregulated derivatives trading soared after that."[25]

So, who regulates the derivatives markets? Even inside countries, the regulators are not clearly designated. In the United States, regulations are dispersed among a whole series of alphabet-soup agencies, including the Fed, the U.S. Treasury, CFTC, and the Securities and Exchange Commission (SEC). In the midst of the subprime crisis, the U.S. Treasury Department unveiled a comprehensive proposal to revise and restructure banking and financial regulations, and the IMF reviewed a report by the Financial Stability Forum, a commission of banks and regulators from the major industrial countries, which recommended the strengthened surveillance of international banking and derivatives markets.

Since the liberalization of financial markets began in the 1970s, central banks meeting at the Bank for International Settlements (BIS) in Basel, Switzerland, have regulated global capital markets through what are called the Basel Accords (also known as the Basle Accords, using the British spelling). In 1988, central banks issued Basel I, a set of minimal guidelines for banks in terms of how much capital they must hold to back up loans and what qualifies as capital (for example, equity such as stocks or corporate bonds and other debt instruments). The ratio of loans to capital reserves is called the leverage ratio and has been generally set in the case of domestic banks at about 8 to 1. Basel II was adopted in 2004 to tighten and link required reserves to the riskiness of the loans being made. But banks became adept at defining the riskiness of both loans and assets to foster expanded lending, and neither Basel 1 nor Basel II prevented leverage ratios from rising during the recent financial crisis, at some financial institutions to 100 to 1 and more. After the financial crisis, Basel III was concluded in 2010. It sets strict requirements on what qualifies as capital but phases the requirements in over a decade. Regulators fear that being too strict in the middle of the global recovery from the financial crash might squeeze lending even more and delay new investment and growth.

More regulation seems to be in the cards, but bear in mind that if regulations become too tight, banks and other financial institutions will reduce lending. If they reduce lending, they take in fewer deposits. In short, they mobilize fewer savings. And if private and public institutions cannot put their savings in the bank, they have to bury them in the sand. So, banking is not a rogue activity, although some banks may engage in rogue activities. Banking is an essential function that lubricates expanding international trade and investment markets and makes sure that the meat and potatoes of the world economy—namely, trade and investment—stay on the table, not just for the next meal but for future ones as well.

Eurozone Crisis

Financial markets bring to the fore the sensitive interrelationships between domestic policies and international trade and investment. When the financial crisis hit in 2008–2009, companies and consumers got fewer loans and drastically curtailed production and spending. Not far behind came drastic cutbacks in jobs and freezes on new hires. Growth and employment contracted more sharply than in previous recessions, in part because they had started at higher levels after three decades of solid global growth. (In terms of unemployment and inflation, the 2008–2009 recession was not as bad as the 1981–1982 recession.) As already noted, governments reacted to this downturn with massive stimulus programs.

But now questions arose as to how governments and central banks should manage all this debt and easy money as economies recovered. The European countries faced a particularly tricky situation. As we discussed in Chapter 6, some eighteen of the twenty-eight EU member states, called the Eurozone countries, had unified their currencies in a common currency known as the euro. They established the European Central Bank, like the U.S. Federal Reserve Bank, to set interest rates and manage this new currency. Eurozone states no longer exercised their own independent monetary and exchange rate policies. But what happens now when some members—like Ireland, Greece, Portugal, and Spain—get into balance-of-payments and debt problems? A traditional way for countries to cope with this situation is to lower interest rates and the value of their currency. That increases the price of imports and decreases the price of exports, reducing imports, increasing exports, and cutting the current account deficit. Governments are very reluctant to cut spending programs and deficits because that slows growth and causes domestic political protests. In the Eurozone, however, they no longer control their own monetary policy. They have to persuade the European Central Bank to offer generous terms to finance and reschedule their debt to avoid cutbacks in government spending. If the central bank is too generous, however, investors lose confidence in the currency and capital flees the Eurozone, creating a wider financial crisis.

Who provides the financing for this Eurozone rescue? Unless the EU turns to outside lenders such as China or the IMF, the surplus countries in the Eurozone have to come up with the financing. In the EU that's principally Germany. So Germany is now calling the shots as to how generous or strict the EU will be with the Eurozone countries in default on their debts. That doesn't sit well with citizens in Greece or Portugal. The Eurozone countries do not have a common fiscal policy, so there is no safety net such as a government normally provides when a section of a country experiences high unemployment. In effect, by keeping money tight with no offsetting spending, Germany and the European Central Bank force the indebted countries to cut their own spending. Germany now emerges as an imperialist power forcing them into austerity programs. In spring 2010, the EU decided it was time to trim fiscal deficits and rein in spending. Riots broke out across Europe, and the United States, fearing a double-dip recession, complained that such austerity measures were inappropriate. The United States wanted the European Central Bank to lower interest rates further by expanding the central bank's balance sheet (quantitative easing) as the Fed had done in the United States. Economic policies in Europe and the United States were now working at cross-purposes to one another, one contracting and the other expanding. Currencies in emerging markets also came under strain. China, long accused of holding down the value of its currency, the renminbi, was called on again to let it appreciate. If money could not flow into China, it flowed into other emerging markets, raising the value of currencies in Brazil and South Korea and causing Brazil's finance minister to declare that a "currency war" was under way.[26]

In these situations, there are only so many actions that countries can take. These actions reflect the use of the policies discussed at the beginning of this chapter by which countries manage their relationships with the world economy: exchange rate, macroeconomic (fiscal and monetary), microeconomic, trade, and financial policies. One, countries can let their currency float, risking higher prices for their exports and the loss of jobs. The Eurozone countries, which have given up independent monetary policy, cannot do that. Two, they can intervene in the exchange markets to keep their currency down, as China does, or up, as the EU does. If they do the former, they accumulate further foreign exchange reserves. At the end of 2013, China held some $3.7 trillion in reserves, giving it a massive treasure chest to invest around the world ($1 trillion or more in U.S. Treasury bonds). Three, they can alter their macroeconomic policies, as the United States and Europe did in late 2010 when the United States expanded its monetary policy and Europe contracted its fiscal policy. Four, they can undertake domestic structural reforms (change their microeconomic policies) to boost spending in surplus countries (China, Germany, Japan, and some OPEC countries) and savings in deficit countries (United States, Britain, France, Canada, and Australia). Five, they can impose restrictions on trade, as the U.S. Congress threatened to do in recent years. And six, they can impose capital controls to stem the inflow of money, as Brazil and Thailand did in 2010 by taxing capital inflows.

The interrelationships of all the instruments of international economic policy are summarized in Figure 8-4. Who bears responsibility for coordinating these instruments at the international level? This is the governance question. Do you start with domestic or international actions? For years, the United States pressed China to revalue its currency

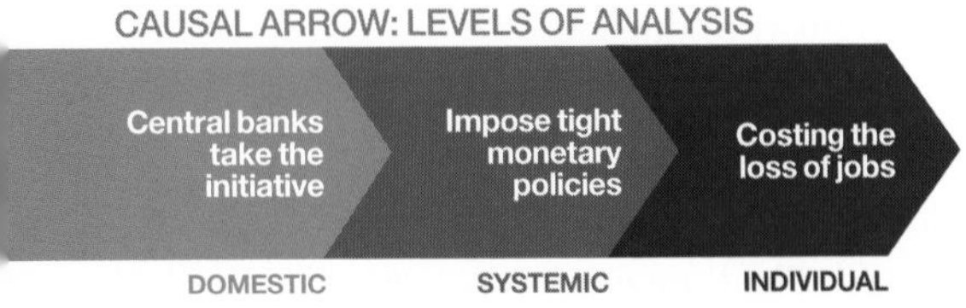

CAUSAL ARROW: LEVELS OF ANALYSIS

| Central banks take the initiative | Impose tight monetary policies | Costing the loss of jobs |
| DOMESTIC | SYSTEMIC | INDIVIDUAL |

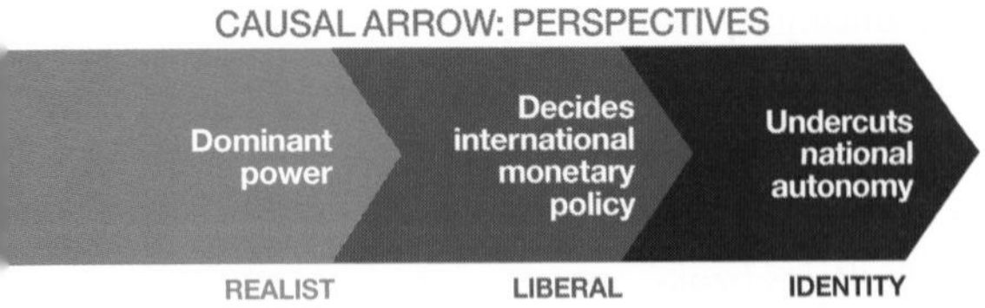

CAUSAL ARROW: PERSPECTIVES

| Dominant power | Decides international monetary policy | Undercuts national autonomy |
| REALIST | LIBERAL | IDENTITY |

unilaterally—that is, to take a domestic approach to solve the problem. Then, in late 2010, it proposed a global or systemic approach that set a limit on current account surpluses or deficits for all countries of 4 percent of GDP by 2015. And who leads? Domestically, central banks control the punch bowl and rein in the party when financial liquidity, the wine-induced merrymaking, becomes excessive. But central banks are secretive and usually independent of elected authorities. Congress and other political authorities often resent the power of the central banks. Think of all the unhappiness in the United States over the recent bank bailouts, even though the government has gotten back most of this money. No one is terribly eager to give this kind of power to central bankers in the global economy. By default, therefore, as realist perspectives might expect, power flows to the dominant country. In the early 1980s, the United States acted single-handedly as the world's central bank to end the

FIGURE 8-4

Instruments of International Economic Policy

COUNTRY X	INSTRUMENTS	ALL OTHER COUNTRIES
Foreign security policies	**International security institutions** (UNSC, alliances, informal coalitions)	**Foreign security policies**
Foreign economic policies	**International economic institutions** (IMF, World Bank, WTO, G-7, G-20)	**Foreign economic policies**
Exchange rates	Fixed or floating exchange rates	Exchange rates
Trade	Current account	Trade
Investment and lending	Capital account Current account + Capital account = Balance of payments	Investment and lending
Immigration	Labor and refugees flows	Immigration
Domestic economic policies	**Interactions of domestic policies**	**Domestic economic policies**
Macroeconomic policies: fiscal and monetary		Macroeconomic policies: fiscal and monetary
Microeconomic policies: regulation, infrastructure		Microeconomic policies: regulation, infrastructure
Social welfare		Social welfare

TABLE 8-5

Key Issues in Finance: The Realist and Liberal Perspectives and Levels of Analysis

Perspective			
Systemic	*Structure*		Realist: Bretton Woods initially established a fixed exchange rate system and imposed capital controls
			Liberal: Basel Accords set common rules for global banks
	Process		Realist: Prefers flexible exchange rates
			Liberal: Favors coordinating exchange rates
Foreign policy			Realist: Germany sets Eurozone policy to maintain domestic competitiveness
			Liberal: U.S. officials decide that domestic banks know more about managing international risk than governments do
Domestic			Realist: Domestic banks are too big to fail and receive taxpayer bailout funds
			Liberal: Labor unions riot in Greece, Spain, and Portugal to protest austerity measures to repay debt
Individual			Realist: Buyers of credit default swaps benefit from crash
			Liberal: Bystanders benefit because government bailout prevented worse catastrophe

Level of analysis

inflationary party of the 1970s. Today, in the Eurozone, Germany is in effect acting as the EU's central bank as the Fed may be acting once again as the world's central bank, this time to ease the supply of money, inflate the world economy, and avoid what some Fed economists fear could be a deflationary spiral. Table 8-5 summarizes financial aspects of the world economy from the different levels of analysis.

SUMMARY

Trade, investment, and finance create the opportunity for specialization and comparative advantage in the global economy. All other things being equal, comparative advantage results in the more efficient use of resources; with the same input, countries can produce more output. In the real world, however, all other things are seldom equal. Thus, trade and investment advantage some workers, industrial sectors, and countries while disadvantaging others. The least-skilled workers, sectors, and economies lose

benefits; the most-skilled gain them. To preserve the benefits of trade, investment, and financial markets, therefore, countries have to find ways, both domestically and internationally, to smooth the transition from less skilled to more skilled workers. Better education, wage insurance, and the accountability of MNCs, banks, and local governments are necessary; or the backlash from the less skilled workers and countries may shut down trade, investment, and banking activities. If nothing is done, nations may be bypassed or may collapse, as happened in communist countries with outdated workers and industries.

Realist perspectives raise important questions about who gains and who loses, relatively, from international trade and investment. Liberal perspectives raise equally important questions about competition, accountability, and institutional arrangements to achieve better outcomes at the domestic and international levels. And identity perspectives focus on the changes in policy ideas and traditional cultures that are inevitable when growth occurs. Change is a constant that alters identities. That fact becomes even more evident as we turn in the next chapter to a discussion of the development process in Asia, Latin America, Africa, and the Middle East.

 Sharpen your skills with SAGE edge at **edge.sagepub.com/nau4e.** **SAGE edge for students** provides a personalized approach to help you accomplish your coursework goals in an easy-to-use learning environment.

KEY CONCEPTS

balance of payments, 332

capital account, 332

comparative advantage, 342

competitive advantage, 346

current account, 332

derivatives markets, 376

Doha Round, 356

economies of scale, 345

exchange rate, 332

fixed or managed exchange rates, 333

foreign direct investment (FDI), 332

globalization 1.0, 327

globalization 2.0, 327

globalization 3.0, 327

import substitution policies, 344

infant industries, 344

Kennedy Round, 355

most-favored-nation (MFN) principle, 354

multilateral trade rounds, 355

nontariff barriers (NTBs), 340

opportunity costs, 341

portfolio investment, 332

productivity, 349

resource curse, 360

tariffs, 340

Tokyo Round, 355

trade adjustment assistance, 353

unfair trade, 353

Uruguay Round, 355

STUDY QUESTIONS

1. What is the difference between absolute and comparative advantage? Give examples of each using the scenario of wine and cloth discussed in this chapter.

2. Does trade increase, decrease, or shift jobs? Which jobs gain and lose from trade? What are the remedies for job losses? Which is the more important cause of job shifts, trade or technology?

3. Which perspective emphasizes the following approaches to trade and why: multilateral trade rounds; trade and investment conditioned on the same environmental, labor, and other standards; and strategic trade?

4. In which sequence did the following types of FDI evolve: resource, manufacturing, and service-sector investments? Which perspective is reflected in each of the following approaches to FDI: national security export controls, reducing TRIMs and TRIPs, and requiring all countries to implement the same cultural standards to regulate labor and capital?

5. Which is greater in the world economy, trade and FDI or portfolio and currency transactions? Describe what the world economy would look like if, first, trade and FDI were banned and, second, portfolio and currency transactions were banned.

A group of children from the town of Kabo in northern Central African Republic (CAR) line up to be vaccinated against measles after eight cases were reported at a hospital in the area. CAR is one of the world's poorest and most neglected countries, with an average life expectancy of thirty-nine years. Decades of fighting various rebel factions in the north of the country have resulted in hundreds of deaths and more than 200,000 internally displaced people. Outside the capital, Bangui, there are no paved roads and no electricity, and banditry is extensive.

IDENTITY PERSPECTIVES ON GLOBALIZATION
9
Development and Environment

Development is about wealth, but even more so it is about wealth for whom and at what cost to the environment. In this chapter, we focus on the identity aspects of development and the environment. There are four aspects to development: Where do countries start in the process? What are the human measures of development and change in terms of jobs and social interactions? What are the consequences for the environment? And, finally, what are the values that development serves, and what constitutes social justice in the age of globalization?

development: the process of material, institutional, and human progress in a particular country or region.

Map 9-1 shows the distribution of national income measured by gross domestic product per person in purchasing power parity (PPP), which takes account of the fact that goods are cheaper in poorer countries and a dollar buys more there than elsewhere. North America, western Europe, Israel, Qatar, Kuwait, Oman, Japan, Taiwan, South Korea, Hong Kong, Singapore, Australia, and New Zealand are the principal areas of the world where the average annual income exceeds $25,000 per person. By contrast, in most countries in Africa incomes average less than $5,000 per person. A few countries in eastern Europe, Latin America, the Middle East, and Asia, such as Poland, Russia, Mexico, Brazil, Chile, Saudi Arabia, and Malaysia, have incomes over $10,000 per capita, but the majority of countries in these areas have incomes that fall below $10,000.

But while wealth remains unevenly distributed today, that's not the whole picture. Over the past forty years, development has brought about greater income *equality* in many parts of the world. Since 2000 we have seen significant growth in the middle class across regions that once showed major disparities between the rich and poor, notably in Latin America and parts of Asia. Still, much of Africa suffers the highest levels of inequality. Map 9-2 tracks changes between 2000 and 2011, expressing the GDP per capita for each country as a ratio to world GDP.

Development takes place through work and social change. The type and location of jobs migrate from less to more sophisticated levels. Look back at Map 8-1, which shows the employment side of development. Influenced by technological change, development involves the movement over generations of the bulk of jobs from agriculture to manufacturing and eventually to high-skilled service activities. The least developed countries still have most of their populations employed in agriculture (or in low-skilled service jobs in tourism or government). More developed and industrializing countries have a substantial proportion of their workforces employed in manufacturing. Some, such as France and Germany, are downsizing jobs in manufacturing and moving them into services; others, such as China, are increasing jobs in manufacturing and moving them out of agriculture. The most advanced countries, such as the United States, have completed the transition from manufacturing to services. They have entered the information age. Their workforces are employed predominantly in high-skilled service activities, such as finance, telecommunications, software, and consulting. This employment transition does not mean that the most advanced countries have lost their manufacturing or agricultural sectors. The United States remains a leader in both sectors, and manufacturing output in the United States today equals the same share of GDP that it did fifty years ago—between 20 and 25 percent. It's just that U.S. companies produce manufactured and agricultural goods with far less labor than they used to. The United States needs less than 2 percent of its workforce in agriculture and less than 10 percent in manufacturing to produce these products.

Development also has major implications for the environment. The world's environment or ecosystem is complex. Development's impacts start with population growth, as crowding limits the amount of land available for the cultivation of crops, exhausts resources such as energy and water, and threatens the diversity of animal and plant life. This is compounded by industrial and agricultural growth that pollutes the atmosphere and waterways, damages the ozone layer, and arguably warms the Earth. The ecosystem

Global Development: Country GDP (PPP) per Capita

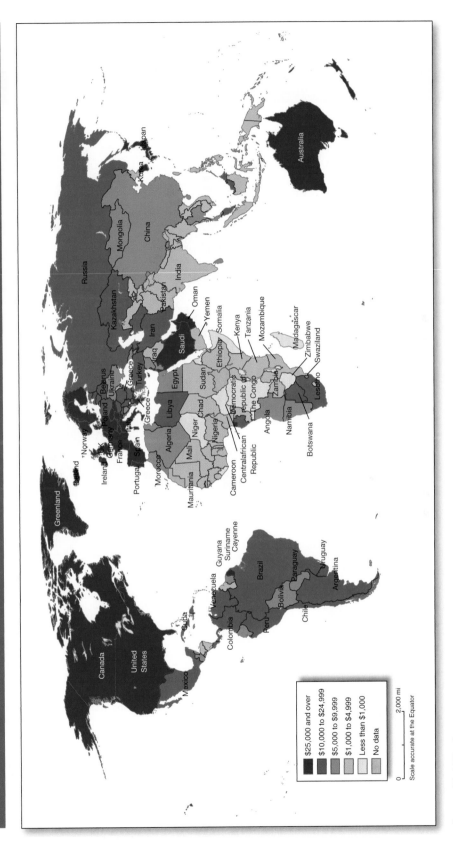

Source: World Bank.

387

MAP 9-2

Income Distribution: Persistent Inequalities and New Opportunities

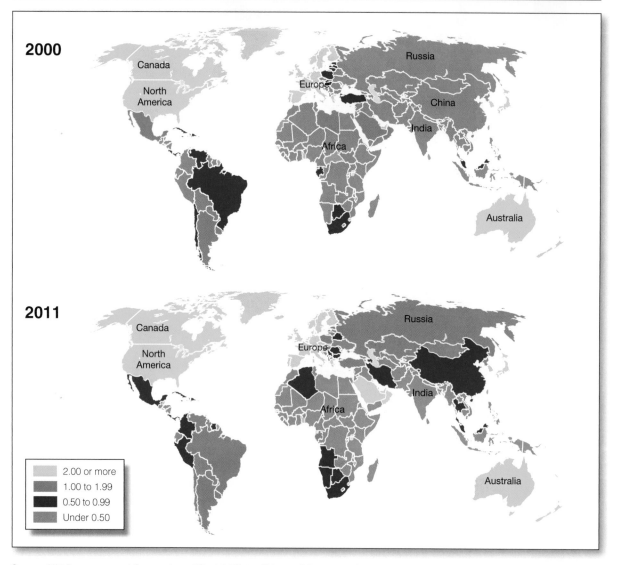

Source: UN Department of Economic and Social Affairs, "National Accounts Main Aggregates Database," http://unstats.un.org/unsd/snaama/selbasicFast.asp.

Note: The numbers in the legend measure each country's GDP expressed as a multiple of the average world GDP. Countries with scores of 1 to 2 or more have GDPs above the average world GDP for the years shown. Countries with scores of less than 1 are below the world average. Notice the changes in Latin America and Asia in particular as many of those countries have moved from lower to higher GDPs and into the middle class. No data are available for French Guiana and Western Sahara.

is the medium that transmits deadly diseases and pandemics and causes natural disasters such as hurricanes and earthquakes. These natural disasters, in turn, contribute to massive refugee movements that catalyze trafficking in drugs and human beings. (See Map 9-6 later in the chapter for a snapshot of climate vulnerability.)

Most of all, development is about values and identity. Who or what is it that develops? Is it an ethnic or tribal group, a religious sect, a social class, a nation, a civilization, or a world? What kind of people are we? How are we alike and how do we differ? Today's developing countries have different roots, come from different cultures and religions, and face different circumstances from those of advanced countries when the latter were developing. Emerging from colonization by the Western world, developing nations seek independent futures and fear neocolonialism, or dependence on global markets that embody historical oppression. Moreover, while they recognize that their development has costs for the environment, they resent the idea that they must share equally with advanced countries the burdens of climate change. They expect advanced countries to bear the costs of developing renewable energy sources and either subsidize such sources in the developing world or do the lion's share of reducing carbon emissions in the advanced world. Many in both the developed and the developing worlds believe the world needs a new self-image, one that emphasizes a common destiny rather than separate national interests. They argue that the world has many players but only one stage, and that stage is planet Earth. The environment—the Earth's surface, the materials below it, and the atmosphere and space above it—is the world's common home. It is the classic example of a collective good. It will be preserved for all peoples or it will be preserved for none.

Issues of identity and justice therefore lie at the root of the development process. Most analysts agree that wealth disparities cannot be ignored, especially in an age of globalization. But is the goal perfect equality and social solidarity? Or is the goal

Ecuadoran women from the Amazon region march through the streets of Quito, the capital city, to protest the federal government's recent decision to exploit the oil reserves of the Yasuni National Park, a move that will affect the lands of many indigenous communities.

maximum freedom, a solid floor for everyone, and then space for individual, community, and national achievement and differentiation through competition? In some countries, such as Russia, people assume that if their neighbors get ahead they must be corrupt. Hence, fewer incentives exist for individuals to take the initiative and get ahead. In other countries, such as Haiti, elites do take the initiative and get ahead, but then they forget about their neighbors. What is the right mix of incentives to help oneself and to help others? Without individual initiative, development does not occur, as many communist countries learned. And without social solidarity, communities divide and development becomes oppression, as many failed states have experienced.

Identity perspectives highlight the separate and common values of a globalizing world. Advanced countries, which are mostly Western, hold the advantage and both help and hinder the development of poorer countries, which are mostly non-Western. Western countries tend to see their civilizations as superior and urge developing nations to adopt Western policies and standards. The Western identity embraces free markets, dating back to the Reformation, which blessed worldly efforts as a way to please God. Other identities see free markets as degrading and blasphemous in the eyes of their religion. Evidence suggests that global markets do indeed offer appealing prospects for acquiring material wealth. Since World War II, countries in Asia, which exploited global markets early, fared best, while those in Latin America, which pursued more protectionist policies, floundered. Some countries in the Middle East and North Africa got rich on oil, but most remained poor in terms of industrialization, suffering from what is called the resource curse. Conditions in sub-Saharan Africa stagnated, although prospects improved in recent years as China, India, and other rapidly developing countries scrambled for African resources to fuel globalization. So, growth has accelerated and spread over the past fifty years, a remarkable, if uneven, achievement. Yet growth also raises poignant identity issues, especially for countries with non-Western religions and cultures. One big shared value of all cultures and peoples of the Earth is the environment. The shared identity of planet Earth implies the need to adopt more common approaches to problems of globalization and social justice.

CAUSAL ARROW: PERSPECTIVES

Separate or common values	Shape conflict and cooperation	Yield material benefits or losses
IDENTITY	LIBERAL	REALIST

In this chapter, we examine and compare the development experiences of developing countries in four regions: Asia, Latin America, the Middle East and North Africa (MENA), and sub-Saharan Africa (SSA). In each region, we look at four aspects of development: domestic and regional stability, macro- and microeconomic policies, trade strategies, and the role of domestic and regional culture and values. At the end, we summarize and compare the regions' development experiences using this framework. Then we address the major issues of the environment and development. As always, we consider all perspectives but highlight identity aspects in contrast to the realist and liberal aspects of development emphasized in the previous chapter.

⟫ Asia

Asia has been the most successful developing region since World War II, far more successful than Latin America, which is the next-best-performing area. Even after Asia experienced severe financial crises in 1997–1998 and again in 2008–2009, the region grew by an average of 9 percent per year through the year 2010, more than doubling its wealth and lifting millions of people out of poverty.[1]

In a report on the phenomenon known as the **East Asian Miracle**, the World Bank notes that "from 1965 to 1990, the twenty-three economies of East Asia grew faster than all other regions of the world." Most of the gains, the report points out, were "attributable to seemingly miraculous growth in just eight economies: Japan; the 'Four Tigers'—Hong Kong, the Republic of Korea [South Korea], Singapore, and Taiwan, China; and the three newly industrializing economies (NIEs) of Southeast Asia, Indonesia, Malaysia, and Thailand."[2] (See Map 9-3 for Asia's regions.) These eight countries grew twice as fast as the rest of Asia, three times as fast as Latin America and South Asia, and five times as fast as sub-Saharan Africa. In the last decade of the period covered by the World Bank report, China joined the growth parade, followed by India in the 1990s. From 1990 to 2010, China and India, where 40 percent of the world's population resides, grew by 10 and 8 percent per year, respectively. No country in the world grew as fast as China, and no country with the same poverty rates and population, except China, grew as fast as India. As a result, 400 million people in China and some 200 million in India have been lifted out of poverty into the middle class. Asia shows that both high growth and greater equity are possible in global markets. Since the financial crisis, Asian growth has slowed—China at 9.3 percent (2011) and 7.8 percent (2012), and India at 6.3 percent (2011) and 3.2 percent (2012)—but it still remains above the rate of growth in most other countries, including the advanced ones.

Why did East Asia grow three times faster than Latin America? And why are China and India growing faster even today? Asia and Latin America make a good contrast because Asian countries pursued export-oriented development strategies that exploited economic competition in open international markets, while Latin American countries, for the most part, adopted import substitution strategies that counted on protected domestic markets for development. Both regions learned something from their different experiences. By the turn of the millennium, Latin American countries moved toward more export-oriented strategies, while some Asian countries questioned the value of completely open markets, especially for short-term capital flows.

Economic Miracle

The tigers of East Asia—Hong Kong, Singapore, Taiwan, and South Korea—pioneered export-led development and achieved a development status that, for all practical purposes, put them in the same class as developed countries. With annual per capita income around $30,000, South Korea, for example, is now a member of the OECD, the economic organization of industrial countries. The tigers were followed by a second wave of newly industrializing countries (NICs) in Southeast Asia: Malaysia, Philippines, Thailand, and Indonesia. These countries boast per capita incomes between $4,400 and $17,000, roughly halfway between developing and industrialized countries. The most recent wave of Asian export tigers includes China and India, countries that alone account for 40 percent of the world's population and 80 percent of the world's poor people. On a nominal basis, China now has a per capita income of approximately $9,233 and India of $3,876.[3]

MAP
9-3

Asia's Regions

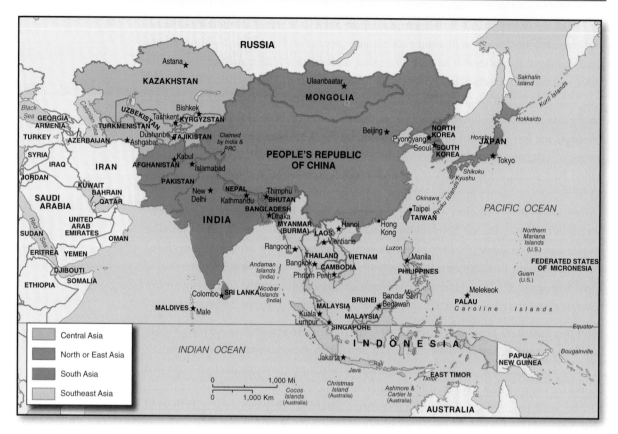

Note: North or East (sometimes called Northeast) Asia includes China, Hong Kong (now part of China), Taiwan (claimed by China), the two Koreas, and Mongolia; it also includes Japan, which is, however, an industrialized country. Southeast Asia includes the ten nations that make up ASEAN. South Asia includes India, Pakistan, Bangladesh, Afghanistan, and the small island or mountain states of Sri Lanka, Bhutan, and Nepal. Central Asia consists of the former republics of the Soviet Union: Kazakhstan, Kyrgyzstan, Turkmenistan, Tajikistan, and Uzbekistan. Together, Asian countries have about 3.5 billion people, or 55 percent of the world's population, and about one-third of world GDP.

What is more, these countries not only grew, but they also witnessed a dramatic reduction in inequality. In the 1970s and 1980s, Indonesia, Malaysia, Singapore, and Thailand reduced the proportion of people living below the poverty line by 25–40 percentage points. As noted earlier in this chapter, China and India achieved similar reductions in the 1990s and 2000s. Each of the four tigers and three of the four NICs (Malaysia is the exception) had a relative inequality ratio (that is, the ratio of the income share of the top 10 percent, or decile, of the population to that of the bottom decile) of less than 10, well below that of almost all other developing countries. In short, development in Asia did not increase domestic inequality. One reason may be that Asian countries, such as South Korea, invested in rural areas and general education rather than in urban development and elite universities, as did many Latin American countries.

Stable Governments/Unstable Region

Domestic political stability helps development, and Asia had domestic political stability in spades. After World War II, authoritarian or stable one-party governments (as in China) held power for long periods throughout the region. However, international unrest was a major factor in Asia. Two major wars took place there—Korea (1950–1954) and Vietnam (1961–1975). And China continues to reunify its territory—at least as China defines it—peacefully in the case of Hong Kong and Macao but increasingly with threats and a buildup of military force in the case of Taiwan. North Korea pursues nuclear weapons and could start another war of major proportions in the region.

So, it is hard to argue that overall stability, taking into account the international as well as the domestic environment, is the secret to Asian development success. What is more, democracy has spread in Asia, particularly since the mid-1980s. And democracy, while it aids development in some ways, often brings with it greater political disputes, scandals, and uncertainties that also impede economic policy.

Military governments in South Korea repressed labor groups for three decades, including engaging in violent crackdowns that remain issues in South Korean politics today. In 1987, the military finally turned the government over to civilian leaders, but the conservative political party that initially controlled the government was still supported by the military. It was not until ten years later that the liberal opposition party not beholden to the military won office. In 2007–2008, the government (both presidency and legislature) switched back again to the conservative parties, reflecting a peaceful rotation of parties in power that even Japan did not achieve in the first forty-five years of its postwar existence. Today, South Korea has a robust multiparty system and wrestles with the legacy of past authoritarian governments (complete with trials of former presidents and military leaders) as well as the delicate problem of living side by side with North Korea and its threat of another devastating war.

Taiwan, too, is now a democracy that rotates power peacefully between opposition parties, complicating the issue of reunification with mainland China, which remains an authoritarian communist country. A civilian government supported by the military took power in 1987. Then in 2000, a liberal opposition party not identified with the military won the presidential elections and, in 2001, a plurality in the legislature as well. In 2007–2008, power rotated back to the conservative parties. Taiwan's parties differ on relations with mainland China. The conservative Kuomintang, or Nationalist Party, accepts the notion of "one China" and supports eventual unification with China. The liberal Democratic Progressive Party leans more toward national self-determination and independence for Taiwan. Because Taiwan's economic life is closely tied up with trade and investment on the mainland, these political differences add uncertainty to economic policies.

Democracy also made inroads in Southeast Asia. In 1986, the Philippines ousted dictator Ferdinand Marcos. Thailand held competitive elections in 1988. And Indonesia held its first parliamentary elections in thirty years in 1999 and its first direct elections for the presidency in 2004. All these democracies are weak. The Philippines remains vulnerable to military coups (six attempts from 1986 to 1992 alone and the most recent one in

Myanmar's prodemocracy leader Aung San Suu Kyi arrives at her National League for Democracy headquarters on November 14, 2010, in Yangon, Myanmar. Suu Kyi had been held under house arrest for the majority of the past fifteen years but has now finally been released by the country's military leaders. After the first elections in twenty years, the military-backed Union Solidarity and Development Party was reported to have won.

early 2006). Thailand, too, suffered military coups, most recently in September 2006. Indonesia lost one province in 1999 when East Timor separated from it violently, and it faces secessionist struggles in other provinces such as Aceh, the scene of the tsunami disaster in 2004.

What is more, unlike the situation in Europe, Asian democracies still live with totalitarian neighbors. Three of the four remaining communist governments in the world—China, Vietnam, and Laos—are in Asia (Cuba is the fourth). Brutal military governments rule in North Korea, Bhutan, and Myanmar (formerly Burma), although since 2011 some relaxation of military restrictions has occurred in Myanmar, where a courageous woman, Aung San Suu Kyi, leads the democratic opposition. Even successful small states, such as Singapore (which separated from Malaysia in the 1960s) and Malaysia, have repressive governments. Beijing has been slowly squeezing democracy in Hong Kong since the former British territory reverted to China in 1997.

A bright spot for democracy in Asia is India. The largest but also the poorest democracy in the world has recently opened up to trade and foreign investment. Its growth prospects now rival China's. But India, too, has hostile and unstable neighbors. India and Pakistan possess nuclear weapons and face off against one another over the disputed province of Kashmir. India and China have border disputes. Pakistan has an unstable government and fights in a troubled relationship with the United States against Taliban terrorists in Afghanistan and within its own borders. Afghanistan fights for its modest democratic life surrounded by right-wing theocrats in Iran and military generals in

Pakistan. Bangladesh and Sri Lanka struggle against separatist movements. Maoist guerrillas toppled the Nepalese monarchy in 2008.

What about Asia's colonial legacy? Western European countries colonized much of Asia in the eighteenth and nineteenth centuries, and in the twentieth century the United States, China, and Japan followed suit. Only Thailand, like Saudi Arabia in the Middle East, escaped colonialism. Colonial rule was harsh and left lasting grievances. China resents Western and American hegemony. South Korea and China harbor bitter memories of Japanese occupation. French colonialism in Indochina spawned the Vietnam War and left lingering communist governments in Laos and Vietnam. Nevertheless, colonialism did not cripple development in Asia to the extent that it may have in Latin America, Africa, and the Middle East. Why? Some might say, from a realist perspective, that it is because Asia geopolitically was farther away from the Western powers than Latin America, the Middle East, or Africa and benefited from Cold War conflicts that poured American aid money into South Korea and Taiwan. Others might say, from a liberal perspective, that it's because the region was more central to commerce and shipping than landlocked countries in other regions (countries close to the Suez and Panama Canals being exceptions). Still others might argue, from an identity perspective, that it's because Asia had a more unified and resilient regional culture based in Confucianism, or what people today call "Asian values."

CAUSAL ARROW: PERSPECTIVES

| Exploited global market opportunities | Overcame consequences of colonialism | Confucian values |
| LIBERAL | REALIST | IDENTITY |

Sound Economic Policies

In its study of the Asian economic miracle, the World Bank praised the sound domestic economic policies of the eight high-performing Asian economies (HPAEs):

> Macroeconomic management was unusually good and macroeconomic performance unusually stable, providing the essential framework for private investment. Policies to increase the integrity of the banking system, and to make it more accessible to nontraditional savers, raised the level of financial savings. Education policies that focused on primary and secondary schools generated rapid increase in labor force skills. Agricultural policies stressed productivity and did not tax the rural economy excessively. All the HPAEs kept price distortions within reasonable bounds and were open to foreign ideas and technology.[4]

As a result of sound domestic policies, inflation was only one-tenth as great in the HPAEs as it was in other developing countries and only one-twentieth the levels in Latin America. Because inflation rates remained under control, interest rates were more stable and real interest rates, which subtract out inflation, stayed positive, encouraging long-term savings and investments. Asian countries had savings and investment rates twice as high as those of other developing countries—40 percent compared to 20 percent. Money stayed at home rather than fleeing into foreign currencies, as happened so often in Latin American countries. One reason inflation stayed low is that governments restrained fiscal policy and kept fiscal deficits in line. The average annual budget deficits in South Korea as a share of GDP ran one-fifth the levels of many Latin American countries.[5]

Microeconomic policies focus on land reform, primary education, small enterprises, and housing and health services.[6] Indonesia and Thailand traditionally had widespread land-ownership, but South Korea and Taiwan, as well as Japan, did not and instituted **land reform** after World War II. Taiwan seized land from landlords and compensated them with shares in state enterprises. In South Korea, U.S. occupation forces redistributed land confiscated from Japanese landowners, and then the South Korean legislature, after lengthy debate, seized the properties of Korean landlords, paid them nominal compensation, and parceled out the properties to 900,000 tenants. Hong Kong and Singapore had no agricultural sector. Land reform in the Philippines and elsewhere lagged behind, and so did economic development.

Land reform created a sense of participation on the part of rural areas and formed the basis for successful education programs. Asian governments poured money into public education. Compared to other developing countries, Asian governments concentrated on primary and secondary education. South Korea, for example, put 85 percent of its investment into basic education and only 10 percent into higher education and universities. Venezuela, by contrast, put 45 percent into higher education. Education in Asia served the masses, not just the elites. South Korea and Taiwan developed educated labor forces, which then took jobs in the urban and industrial sectors. Educated workforces, in turn, developed demand for higher education, which was supplied in good part by private universities and capital.

Asian governments absorbed educated labor forces by supporting small and medium-size enterprises. In all economies, these firms account for most of the employment. As government policies stimulated the broad economy, specific programs provided preferential credits and specific support services for smaller companies.

Why didn't Korean and Taiwanese peasants coming to the big cities to find jobs wind up, like Latin American peasants, living in slums on the outskirts of affluent neighborhoods? A big reason is the investment that Asian governments made in housing and health services. Hong Kong and Singapore, besieged by migrants from China and Malaysia, built massive public housing projects. By 1987, more than 40 percent of the population in Hong Kong and 80 percent in Singapore lived in public housing. Most of the inhabitants owned their own units. South Korea and Indonesia had similar public-supported housing programs.

For decades, Asian workers were not free. Governments suppressed radical activity in the labor sector. But the political discontent was managed and did not result in coups or revolutions, as often was the case in Latin America, because the governments provided generous education, housing, and other benefits, such as land reform, that sustained a sense of participation in national prosperity.

Export-Led Development

Throughout the region, therefore, governments played a crucial role in Asian development. The issue was not the government's role per se, but what kind of role the

land reform: domestic policies to redistribute land for the purposes of equity and development.

government played. Did government provide incentives to support market-oriented and competitive development, or did it give special privileges to cronies and corrupt industrial and technological elites, and suppress market competition? The debate intensified between those who urged reliance on market or comparative advantage and those who emphasized government intervention to create market or competitive advantage. This was the same debate, now in the development arena, that divided advocates of comparative advantage and advocates of strategic trade in the trade arena (discussed in Chapter 8).

One point is certain: Asian high performers geared their development toward foreign markets. They relied primarily on export-led development to exploit foreign markets, not on import substitution policies to protect domestic markets. Governments intervened domestically to create internationally competitive industries; they did not intervene internationally to coddle inefficient domestic industries. They created export zones for selected industries, usually industries at the lower end of the technological spectrum, where the countries possessed a labor cost advantage. For example, the Asian tigers first exported toys and handicrafts and later textiles, shoes, radios, and black-and-white television sets. Eventually, they graduated to the heavy manufacturing industries, including steel, chemicals, and shipbuilding, and thereafter to more sophisticated components and consumer products such as semiconductor chips, automobiles, computers, and electronic games.

The key point, then, is that Asian governments took their development signals from international markets and intervened in domestic markets to achieve international competitiveness. This strategy required a disciplined bureaucracy. Here Asia had another advantage over Latin America. By tradition, the best and the brightest in Asia went into government service, and government bureaucrats were motivated more by technical expertise than by political or personal gain. Governments were not immune to corruption, as scandals in Japan, South Korea, and Taiwan repeatedly demonstrated. And bureaucrats were often closely connected to business interests, leaving government posts at some point to take up second careers in the corporate sector. But the process was motivated by a sense of national pride and duty, not the rent-seeking and resource-stripping policies that afflicted many elitist Latin American governments.

Later studies showed that Asian development was not necessarily a result of greater efficiency or productivity—that is, getting higher output out of the same level of capital and labor inputs. It was mostly a consequence of investing more capital and labor to achieve higher output.[7] Asian countries did a better job than other developing countries of mobilizing domestic savings (capital) and a well-educated, healthy workforce (labor). A part of the secret at least was the sound underlying domestic policies that created stable prices and exchange rates to guide and sustain resource mobilization. At some point, however, growth by accumulation involving the addition of more and more labor and capital resources to achieve higher output reaches its limits. Further growth requires higher productivity, or getting more outputs with the same inputs, and that requires innovation and industrial restructuring toward higher-technology or value-added industries.

Limits to Export-Led Growth

By the late 1990s, Asian export-led development reached its limits in three areas. The first was the rapid expansion of international markets. More and more countries were pursuing export-led growth. Recall that the end of the Cold War brought the former communist countries into world markets. Trade markets were becoming increasingly crowded. Countries had to run faster to stay in place. Before Japan had mastered the shipbuilding industry, South Korea was building ships and taking away market share. And before South Korea had mastered shipbuilding, China was building ships. As suppliers multiplied and each sought to protect its own home market, consumers relatively dwindled. In a small way, export-led development, after many countries adopted it, replicated the market squeeze that occurred in the 1930s when everyone wanted to export and no one wanted to import—export markets became saturated. By the mid-1990s, Asia was awash in excess production capacity for electronic products, steel, automobiles, and shipbuilding.

The second area limiting export-led performance was that, as Japan and other Asian high performers caught up with world standards, they had to rely more on innovation to develop future markets. Asian bureaucracies may have been better at imitating existing industries, but they were not necessarily better at inventing and creating future ones. As one critic noted in the case of Japan, "Funding concentrated on a 'catch-up' targeting of known technologies was much easier than having to push out along an unknown technological frontier." Once a country caught up, "it was no longer clear where and how to spend the money since future technologies by definition did not exist."[8]

Much of Asian development also depended on a single market, the United States. In 1999, the United States still absorbed 24 percent of Hong Kong's exports, 31 percent of Japan's, 30 percent of the Philippines's, 21 percent of South Korea's, 25 percent of Taiwan's, and 22 percent of Thailand's.[9] As the dollar soared in the 1990s, so did the currencies of a number of Asian countries that tied their currencies to the dollar, such as South Korea and Hong Kong. So, currency appreciation also hurt export performance. Finally, protectionism in the United States was growing. As country after country, including now the titan of China, grew by exporting to the U.S. market, Congress called for protection against imports. In a real sense, the open U.S. market gets a good deal of the credit for the success of Asian development strategies, and now for development strategies in Mexico and elsewhere. But, like export markets overall, the U.S. market reached a saturation point, at least in the political sense of being willing to absorb more and more foreign imports.

The third limit on the Asian export-led model was in the financial area. Finance or banking was the sector in Asian countries that was least efficient. Governments dominated credit markets through postal savings systems and then disbursed loans to support government industrial and technological development. There was little competition from private sources. Japan and South Korea restricted foreign investment; and private equity markets, where companies raise money directly by selling stocks and bonds, were relatively small in most Asian countries. As a result, the allocation of loans became routine and hard to change. Banks invested in the same companies, and companies invested in the same industries, developing cozy relationships, in what subsequently became known as **crony capitalism**. As a result, industries built up excess capacity. They added new steel or automobile plants when none was needed or more roads and bridges when existing ones were not being used. Many of these loans later went sour.

crony capitalism: noncompetitive lending and investment relationships between government financial institutions and private industry.

China pursues policies similar to those of the earlier Asian fast growers. It bases its growth on exports, it channels loans to industry largely through state banks, and it maintains an undervalued exchange rate to gain a foreign market advantage. But there is one major exception. Unlike Japan and South Korea, which initially discouraged FDI, China welcomes it. In 2006, FDI inflows into China totaled $69 billion.[10] In 2012, it totaled $253 billion. The accumulated stock of FDI in China amounts to more than $1.8 trillion. In addition, China saves an enormous percentage of its GNP, around 49 percent. So, China is not dependent on foreign capital, although it does need the foreign expertise that comes with FDI. Indeed, it exports capital, using its surpluses on current account to buy U.S. Treasury bonds and finance the twin deficits of the United States, as discussed in Chapter 8.

The problem in China is massive inefficiency. The country is accumulating bad loans at an astonishing rate. It uses four to five times more energy to produce a unit of output than the industrialized countries. Although it has privatized many sectors, it maintains large numbers of inefficient state enterprises to preserve the jobs they provide. And it wrestles with the rural and urban disruption that moves thirteen million people per year from farms to cities, looking for work. At the moment, investment in transportation, energy, and business infrastructure takes precedence over investment in housing and health care. In the future, China may have to spend more on housing and health services, thereby co-opting the working classes the way Hong Kong, Singapore, and Taiwan did.

India is moving in the same direction, but it is probably twenty years behind China. While China has reduced average tariffs from 35 percent to 13 percent and its trade—exports plus imports—accounts for 70 percent of GDP, India still has average tariffs above 28 percent and its trade accounts for only 45 percent of GDP. India is much less open to foreign investment, with a total FDI stock of $206 billion, compared to China's $1.8 trillion. Enforcing a contract in India takes 1,420 days, compared to 406 in China, while shutting down a bankrupt business takes seven years, compared to twenty months in China.[11] Illiteracy in India tops 38 percent, against just 5 percent in China. In 1999–2000, only 47 percent of children passed through five years of primary school in India, while 98 percent did in China. In India 68 percent of the people still live in the countryside; in China, 48 percent. Industrial activities employ less than 20 percent of the labor force in India, but nearly 30 percent and rising in China.

microfinancing: the provision of small loans to individuals in developing countries, especially women.

Microfinancing, or the provision of small loans to individual entrepreneurs, especially women, originated in South Asia. Muhammad Yunus, a Bangladeshi who won the

A man makes chapatis as an Air India passenger jet flies over the Jari Mari slum before landing at nearby Mumbai Airport in Mumbai, India. The redevelopment of the Jari Mari slum, along with that of the nearby Dharavi slum, stalled during the global economic financial crisis.

Noble Peace Prize in 2006, started the Grameen Bank in 1976 with $27. Today it serves more than 6.7 million borrowers, and microfinancing worldwide topped $8.1 billion in 2012. As microlending has grown, however, so have microlenders' problems with defaults and corruption. Like all development initiatives, microfinancing is only one of many instruments to combat poverty.[12]

Asian Values

Successful Asian societies are more ethnically homogeneous than Latin American or African countries. China is mostly Han, with a small but restive Muslim population in the western part of the country. Japan, except for minuscule Korean and indigenous minorities, is, as Edwin Reischauer, Harvard professor and onetime U.S. ambassador to Japan, observed, "the most thoroughly unified and culturally homogeneous large bloc of people in the world, with the possible exception of the Northern Chinese."[13] Both North and South Korea are ethnically unified, although the peninsula was divided historically into three separate regional kingdoms. South and Southeast Asian countries are more diverse. Overseas Chinese constitute a majority in Singapore and significant minorities in Malaysia, Indonesia, and other countries. The overseas Chinese often dominate commercial life and create resentment among indigenous populations, for example, among the Malays and Indonesians. Four major religions divide the region: Islam in Pakistan,

Bangladesh, and Indonesia; Hinduism in India; Buddhism in China, Tibet, and Japan; and Shintoism in Japan.

Asia's success sparked a debate about **Asian values**. Was it widespread Confucian values that contributed to domestic stability and motivated bureaucratic and commercial success? Confucianism gives priority to family and society over the individual. Nowhere in Asia is individualism celebrated as it is in the United States; instead, authority patterns infuse all levels of society—in the family, business, and the state. This authority is patrimonial, personalized, and less institutional or accountable than authority in the West. It creates extended family ties that infiltrate formal institutions and are difficult for outsiders, especially foreigners, to access. *Quanxi,* the Chinese word for close personal relationships, ties markets together rather than legal contracts. Japanese business practices too are notoriously exclusive and discriminatory. While much of this is changing, Asian societies are still comparatively more cohesive than societies in other regions of the world. As Mahathir Mohamad, the former president of Malaysia, put it bluntly, "The group and the country are more important than the individual."[14]

> **Asian values:** the Confucian ideas emphasizing authority over individualism that motivated economic success in Asia.

Asian values may also help explain the less formal and less institutionalized nature of economic integration in Asia and the continued political divisions that make Asian international affairs more unstable. There is no common market in Asia as there is in Europe. APEC is a forum rather than a legal institution like the European Union. China, to be sure, is more open to FDI than are Japan and South Korea. Nevertheless, much of this integration is a function of the relocation of investments from Southeast Asia and Hong Kong to mainland China, where products are assembled from imported components and shipped to the United States and other world markets. (Remember the story in Chapter 8 about the purchase of your smartphone.) Asian integration is still more vertical and outward-oriented than European integration, which is more horizontal—competitive—and inward-oriented. The European Union, for example, exports only 10–15 percent of its trade outside Europe, whereas Asian countries, as we have noted, depend heavily on U.S. markets.

Paradoxically, Asian values may also explain the greater rivalry that permeates the Asian region. Because Asian societies are ethnically insulated from one another, especially in East Asia, they have been less willing to forgive and forget wartime or historical wrongs. Bitter memories linger between Japan and China and between Japan and South Korea, breaking out periodically in ugly violence, such as anti-Japan demonstrations in China in spring 2005. Cultural homogeneity strengthens development within a country, but it impedes integration among countries or gives this integration a less institutional and stable character. Reconciliation in Asia lags well behind that in Europe, where a common European culture of multilateral institutions and law is slowly supplementing national cultures. China's looming dominance may also deter integration in Asia; in contrast, relatively equal partners developed the EU. Table 9-1 summarizes the key features of Asian development, which we now contrast with Latin American development.

TABLE
9-1

Key Factors in Asian Development: The Identity Perspective and Levels of Analysis

	Identity perspective		
Systemic	*Structure*	Western interference through colonial and regional wars National cultural homogeneity and common Asian values compete	
	Process	*Quanxi* relationships exploit policies of export-led growth	
Foreign policy		Authoritarian governments navigate between domestic political stability and regional geopolitical instability	
Domestic		Asian values encourage competent bureaucracies, stable macro- and microeconomic policies, land reform, and primary education	
Individual		Asian values de-emphasize individualism	

(Left vertical label: **Level of analysis**)

≫ Latin America

Latin America's development experience contrasts sharply with that of Asia. Except for Chile, Latin American countries deliberately opted out of the GATT free-market trading system after World War II and based their development strategies on import substitution rather than on export-led growth. This model facilitated some initial industrial development in Brazil, Argentina, Mexico, and other countries, but it actually made Latin America more, rather than less, vulnerable to international markets. Industries served domestic markets only and did not stay competitive in the absence of foreign competition. They developed little export capacity to finance vital imports. When the oil crisis hit in the 1970s, Latin American countries had to borrow heavily to finance higher-priced oil imports, and when interest rates went up in the 1980s, they could no longer service their loans. Latin America experienced a *lost decade* while East Asia experienced an economic miracle.

Lost Decade

From 1950 to 1973 Latin American countries grew on average by 2.5 percent per year in real GDP per capita. This performance was slightly below the average for all developing countries (2.7 percent per year) but less than half the growth rate in South Korea and Taiwan and one-third the growth rate later in China and Thailand. Brazil and Mexico did best, growing at about 3.8 percent and 3.1 percent per year, respectively. These were the years of domestic-oriented import substitution policies in Latin America, and the performance was not that bad. So, it is incorrect to say that protectionist policies never pay.

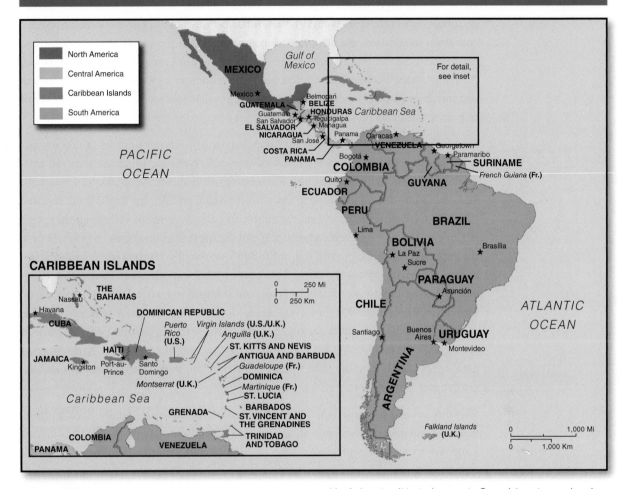

Latin America's Regions

North America
Central America
Caribbean Islands
South America

Gulf of Mexico

MEXICO

For detail, see inset

Mexico ★

Belmopan
BELIZE
GUATEMALA
HONDURAS *Caribbean Sea*
Guatemala ★
San Salvador ★ ★ Tegucigalpa
EL SALVADOR ★ Managua
NICARAGUA
San José
COSTA RICA
PANAMA

Panama
Caracas ★
VENEZUELA Georgetown
Paramaribo
SURINAME

PACIFIC

OCEAN

Bogotá ★
COLOMBIA
Quito ★
ECUADOR

GUYANA

French Guiana (Fr.)

PERU

Lima ★

BRAZIL

BOLIVIA
★ La Paz
Sucre ★

Brasília ★

CARIBBEAN ISLANDS

PARAGUAY
Asunción ★

ATLANTIC

OCEAN

THE
BAHAMAS
Nassau
Havana
CUBA

DOMINICAN REPUBLIC

0   250 Mi
0   250 Km

CHILE

Santiago ★

Buenos
Aires ★
URUGUAY
Montevideo

Puerto
Rico
(U.S.)
Virgin Islands (U.S./U.K.)
Anguilla (U.K.)

HAITI
JAMAICA
Kingston
Port-au-
Prince
Santo
Domingo

ST. KITTS AND NEVIS
ANTIGUA AND BARBUDA
Guadeloupe (Fr.)
DOMINICA
Martinique (Fr.)
ST. LUCIA

ARGENTINA

Montserrat (U.K.)

Caribbean Sea

GRENADA

BARBADOS
ST. VINCENT AND
THE GRENADINES

Falkland Islands
(U.K.)

0   1,000 Mi
0   1,000 Km

COLOMBIA
PANAMA

VENEZUELA

TRINIDAD
AND TOBAGO

Note: As this map shows, Latin America encompasses one country in North America (Mexico), seven in Central America, and twelve in South America. Strictly speaking, not all are "Latin" (or Spanish and Portuguese)—some are English, Dutch, and French—and eight small Caribbean countries also belong to the developing countries of the Western Hemisphere. Together these twenty-eight principal countries account for about 589 million people, or 8.2 percent of the world's population.

Notice, however, that these policies paid off mostly in big countries, such as Brazil and Mexico, which had large domestic markets to support import substitution industries.

The issue is, at what price do such policies pay? The next decade and a half, from 1973 to 1987, suggested the price was pretty high. Known as the **lost decade,** this period saw average real per capita growth in Latin America plummet to 0.8 percent per year. It held up best in Brazil at 2.2 percent, dropped dramatically in Mexico to 0.9 percent, and was negative for the entire period in Argentina at –0.8 percent. What happened? Well, Latin America went through a very difficult transition period occasioned in part

lost decade: a period of economic stagnation in Latin America brought on by domestic policies, the oil crises, and high debt, lasting from the early 1970s to the late 1980s.

by oil crises, which ran up the region's external debt. The debt of six major countries—Argentina, Brazil, Chile, Colombia, Mexico, and Peru—increased from $35 billion to $248 billion in less than a decade. But import substitution policies also played a role. They fueled inflation and did nothing to reduce inequality. Inflation rates soared to an average of more than 100 percent per year, compared to 20 percent in the earlier decades, ten to thirty times higher than inflation rates in Asia and the industrialized countries. In addition, the disparity of incomes between the top 10 percent of income earners and the bottom 20 percent was twice as high in Latin America as in Asia and the industrialized countries.[15] Chile was the only country to weather the oil crises and continue to grow, and it was also the only country that followed export-led rather than import substitution policies.

Starting in the late 1980s, almost all Latin American countries undertook market-oriented policy reforms. Following the Washington Consensus, which emphasized free-market economics, they stopped accommodating inflation, liberalized domestic markets, and opened trade and investment ties with foreign firms. As the World Bank reports, "Policies were better in nearly *every* country in Latin America in 1999 than they were in Chile in 1985."[16] And remember, Chile had the most liberal policies in 1985. At first, the expected economic growth did not follow. Although growth in the region accelerated in the early 1990s—reaching 7 percent in 1992—it tailed off badly after 1995, when Mexico underwent a financial crisis, and slumped to zero in 1998, where it stayed through 2002.[17] After 2002, however, Mexico and the rest of Latin America rebounded smartly. From 2003 to 2008, the region grew by more than 5 percent per year, the best record since the early 1970s. Even after the financial crisis of 2008–2009, Latin America grew again in 2010 by more than 5 percent, but the crisis took a longer-term toll, and the growth rate slowed down to 2.5 percent in 2013.[18]

Was this belated performance the result of free-market policies finally paying off, or was it a consequence of soaring oil, agricultural, and commodity prices, which benefited Latin American energy producers such as Mexico and Venezuela and beef producers such as Argentina? Some analysts see changes in Latin America largely as a product of U.S. neocolonialism and intervention (realist). Others see them as the consequences of insufficient market interdependence and weak national and regional institutions (liberal). And still others see them as the outcomes of conflicting ideologies and class and ethnic warfare (identity).

The World Bank suggests that four "syndromes"—that's diplomatese for "causes"—account for Latin America's failure to match the better performance of Asian developing countries: (1) governments that are dominated by elites, are unstable, do not protect property rights, and engage in corruption; (2) macroeconomic policies that cause inflation, fiscal deficits, volatile exchange rates, and high debt; (3) external policies that restrict trade and investment; and (4) financial systems that are dominated by state-owned banks and legal institutions that do not enforce contracts. The World Bank also adds a fudge factor—bad luck. This covers geography (landlocked countries), disease susceptibility, and the "curse" of resources (remember from Chapter 8 the problems of resource-based industries?).[19]

Whatever the syndromes or causes, here are the results. In 1800, Argentina had a per capita income equal to that of the United States; today, its per capita income is less than one-third that of the United States. Similarly, in 1800, Brazil, Mexico, Chile, and Peru had per capita incomes at 40–50 percent of the U.S. level. Today, Chile is still at about 40 percent, and all of the others are closer to 25 percent. Let's look more closely at the four "syndromes" associated with this dramatic divergence in living standards between the United States and Latin America. They correspond to the four dimensions of the comparative regional framework we use in this chapter—geopolitics, internal policies, external policies, and cultural values. (For a summary of the discussion that follows, see Table 9-2.)

Early Decolonization/Unstable Governments

Colonized by European powers after 1500, Latin America had already secured its independence in the early nineteenth century. After that, South American countries, such as Brazil and Argentina, remained largely free of outside interference—with a few exceptions, such as British intervention in the Falkland Islands in 1833. But Mexico, the Caribbean, and Central American countries endured American expansion and periodic intervention for the next one hundred years. Mexico lost roughly half of its territory to American conquest, and American troops occupied Cuba, Nicaragua, Honduras, the Dominican Republic, and other neighbors for extended periods of time. In most cases, the pretexts for intervention were instability and the threat of interference by outside powers, principally the former European colonial powers. In 1823, the Monroe Doctrine (named for James Monroe, who was U.S. president at the time) declared the Western Hemisphere to be America's sphere of influence, and U.S. forces intervened in Colombia to create the state of Panama and build the Panama Canal. Thus, while Latin American countries, unlike other developing countries, escaped early from direct colonialism, they labored under the continuing presence and sometimes direct intervention of the "colossus to the north." Puerto Rico and the Virgin Islands, of course, became and remain American territories.

Military rule and political instability characterized Latin American politics throughout much of the nineteenth and twentieth centuries. Interruptions of constitutional power were common. In the seventy-five years after 1900, only Colombia and Costa Rica had fewer than ten years of nondemocratic rule. All the other countries clocked at least two decades of dictatorial rule. Some, such as Argentina, Brazil, Ecuador, Bolivia, Mexico, the Dominican Republic, and all of the Central American countries except Honduras, clocked four decades or more. A few, such as Haiti, never experienced a peaceful transfer of power from one party to another. The only exceptions to this experience of authoritarian rule are the small English-speaking islands of the Caribbean.[20]

Today, most Latin American countries, with the exceptions of Cuba and Venezuela, are democracies. But they are weak democracies. Although elections take place, the continuous, stable transfer of power between opposing political parties is less common. Instead, Latin America has experienced waves of democratization and then reversals. After World War II, democracy spread to all Latin American countries except five: Paraguay, El Salvador, Honduras, Nicaragua, and the Dominican Republic. By 1954, however, this wave had been reversed, and only four countries remained democratic: Uruguay, Costa Rica, Chile, and Brazil.[21] Then, in 1964, Brazil succumbed to a military coup; Chile did likewise in 1973. Critics blamed U.S. policies for this rollback. Fearing communist governments in the region, U.S. intelligence agencies assisted coups in Guatemala (1954) and Chile (1973) and fought Castro's takeover in Cuba (1959).

Another wave of democratization began in 1978. Some thirty elections occurred over the next sixteen years in fifteen countries that had previously been under authoritarian rule. Half of these elections represented second, third, or fourth elections, and four-fifths of them involved peaceful transitions to opposing parties.[22] Latin America seemed to be on the way to a more stable pattern of pluralist politics. Mexico's democratic turn in 1997 provided further encouragement. Opposition parties took control of the National Assembly for the first time, and a center-right party, the National Action Party (Partido Acción Nacional, or PAN), won the presidency in 2000, taking that office from the Institutional Revolutionary Party (Partido Revolucionario Institucional, or PRI), which had ruled Mexico for seventy years. The PAN retained the presidency in elections in 2007, but the office was returned to the PRI in 2012 with the election of Enrique Peña Nieto.

Nevertheless, Latin America also endured some democratic reversals. A dictator, Alberto Fujimori, ruled Peru for a decade before he was driven into exile in Japan. Venezuela succumbed in 1999 to the populist military dictator Hugo Chávez, whose successor (after Chávez's death in 2013), Nicolás Maduro, continues his policies. Colombia and Ecuador fought debilitating civil wars against drug lords and guerrillas. Bolivia experienced riots, threats of secession by individual provinces, and unstable governments. Argentina flirted with a populist and potentially extraconstitutional regime. And Cuba, even after Castro stepped down in 2008 in favor of his brother Raúl, remained an outpost of authoritarian and quixotic rule in the region. A so-called pink tide seemed to engulf parts of Latin America.

CAUSAL ARROW: PERSPECTIVES

| Turn to left | Reintroduced statist policies | Exacerbated conflict over resources |
| IDENTITY | LIBERAL | REALIST |

Political instability is undoubtedly a major cause of the disappointing economic performance in Latin America. It is also a reason that governments in this region tend to centralize and control economic policies and institutions. When politics and markets are unstable, economic resources do not grow, and the political game becomes zero-sum. Governments pursue dirigiste or neo-Marxist policies to keep economic resources under tight political control and thereby marginalize the opposition. The only way the opposition can gain economic advantage is by seizing political power; there is no independent marketplace of any significance. In a reversal of the causal arrows above, realist considerations (struggle for wealth) trump institutional (dirigiste) and ideological (democratic) factors.

Import Substitution Policies

Latin American countries were the "poster children" for import substitution policies. These policies called for developing local industries to substitute for imports. Even before World War II, elites in Brazil, Mexico, and other Latin American countries found

President Nicolás Maduro greets a crowd of people on election day, April 14, 2013, in Caracas, Venezuela.

such centralized economic policies congenial for political control. Import substitution policies meant protected and, hence, highly profitable domestic markets. The governments doled out licenses to political supporters, who then ran companies either as state-owned enterprises or as private companies with generous state subsidies.

State policies encouraged a massive and rapid reallocation of capital from agriculture and rural areas to industry and urban areas. State marketing boards bought and sold major food products. They set food prices very low to feed the urban population, in effect extracting savings from the rural sector by not paying market prices for agricultural output. Economists call this policy **financial repression**, forcing savings from rural areas at below-market rates of return. State entities also controlled and developed natural resources, such as oil, selling these products at subsidized prices at home and profiting from their export abroad. Pemex, the state-owned oil company in Mexico, dominated all aspects of energy supply, including electricity. State-run or state-dependent companies controlled most industries. During World War II, Brazil created state companies in steel, iron ore, airplane engines, tractors, trucks, automobiles, soda ash, caustic soda, and electricity. Other licenses went to private companies. These companies then lobbied to limit competition. They were what economists call **rent-seekers**, hoping to exploit monopoly rents from markets that had limited or no competition. If the markets were large enough

financial repression: a policy in which states extract savings from one sector, such as agriculture or labor, to benefit another sector, such as industry.

rent-seekers: firms that lobby to limit competition, extracting monopoly rents by producing at low costs while selling at high prices.

to support significant volumes of output, as they were in Brazil and other big Latin American countries, companies could make high profits. They achieved low costs from economies of scale while setting high prices in the absence of competition. Best of all, they faced no foreign competition and could get cherished import licenses, if needed, to purchase foreign equipment or technology that was not available locally.

Governments controlled the commanding heights of the economy. To finance industrial development, they extracted savings by tapping natural resources and holding wages down. Financial repression worked as long as labor and natural resources remained plentiful and local industries expanded. From 1940 to 1982, the large Latin American countries grew at rates of 6–8 percent per year. But the government budgets were always under strain; the tax base of the economy was small, and industry absorbed more taxes in the form of government subsidies than it paid. Savings and natural resources eventually became more difficult to extract. Meanwhile, expenditures soared, mostly to accommodate privileged elites and to build infrastructure—universities, hospitals, and electrical power—that catered to urban needs. Budget deficits became chronic, and monetary policies expanded to accommodate government deficits. Central banks, controlled by finance ministries, printed money to pay the bills. Too much money chased too few goods, and inflation soared and encouraged debtors, who repaid loans in currency that was worth less. By 1986, the per capita debt in Latin America was three times as high as that in Asia.[23] Inflation also encouraged **capital flight**; money moved out of the local currency and country. If you're holding a local currency that is declining in value daily due to inflation, it makes sense to convert it into a foreign currency that is appreciating.

capital flight: the movement of money out of the local currency and country because of inflation and economic or political instability.

External shocks ended the party. The oil crises of the 1970s hit oil importers such as Brazil hard, although they benefited oil producers such as Mexico and Colombia and were fairly neutral for self-sufficient oil producers such as Argentina, Chile, and Peru. The real crunch came from higher interest rates in the 1980s. The one thing someone in debt does not want is higher interest rates. When Great Britain and the United States decided to attack the inflation of the 1970s by raising interest rates, Latin America's debt mountain creaked and then collapsed. With massive debt burdens, high interest rates raised debt-servicing costs dramatically. Because most of the debt was in dollars, Latin America had to export more. But import substitution policies had done little to develop exports. Latin American exports in 1986 were only 13 percent of GDP, compared to 22 percent in 1929.[24] Exports had gone backward. Thus, Latin American countries first paid only the interest on their loans and rolled over the principal. Then they could not pay the interest either, and they defaulted altogether. Mexico was the first to do so in 1982, and others followed. Latin American countries spent the next decade rescheduling debt and trying to reverse domestic policies that had reached a dead end.

Opening Markets

Chile was the first Latin American country to try export-led development policies. Under a repressive but stable military government, which the United States helped to bring into power, Chile moved in the late 1970s toward more competitive market-oriented policies. It attacked inflation by disciplining the growth of the money supply, reduced fiscal deficits, converted a portion of foreign debt into equity (an early form of privatization), deregulated the domestic economy, and opened markets to foreign trade and investment. Such sweeping changes had their costs, but Chile weathered the lost decade better than other Latin American countries and became the model in the 1990s when other Latin American countries adopted more market-oriented policies.

Mexico made the decisive breakthrough. In the late 1980s, it abandoned 150 years of **economic autarky,** or a closed domestic economic system; shut down the notorious citadel of Mexican economic nationalism, the Ministry of Commerce and Industry; and joined the GATT and the world trading system. It reduced tariffs and integrated markets with its developed neighbors in NAFTA. Over the next decade, Mexico abolished seven hundred of its twelve hundred state enterprises, introduced more realistic market prices for previously subsidized commodities, made large cuts in bloated public-sector bureaucracies, and established an independent central bank and more competitive private banks. Mexico also became a major oil exporter, although the government retained exclusive control of the energy sector.

economic autarky: a closed domestic economic system based on protectionism and state-owned industries.

The returns were not immediate or spectacular. The Mexican economy overheated, and Mexico suffered another financial crisis in 1994. It devalued the peso, reallocating resources from domestic use to exports. The devaluations squeezed domestic demand and hurt small consumers and entrepreneurs. Nevertheless, with the help of NAFTA, Mexico bounced back quickly. It paid off its emergency loans sooner than required. On balance, as the World Bank concludes, NAFTA "had positive effects on trade, foreign direct investment, technology transfer, and growth, and is also associated with productivity improvements in manufacturing."[25] Mexico grew eightfold from 1993 to 2013, more than doubled its ratio of trade to GDP, and absorbed more FDI than any other Latin American country except Chile. Except for the financial crisis in 2009, when GDP dropped by 6.5 percent, Mexico continued to grow at around 4 percent per year, tripling its GDP in purchasing power terms from 1993 to 2012.

Other Latin American countries followed suit. Argentina, Colombia, Costa Rica, El Salvador, Guatemala, and Nicaragua lowered tariffs by 10–20 percent, and exports and imports soared 1.5–2 times as a ratio of GDP. Brazil and Argentina formed a free-trade community of their own in 1991, known as Mercosur, which Paraguay and Uruguay also joined, and Chile and others became associate members. Again, the transition was not smooth. Argentina's experience suggests the risks of opening markets when domestic institutions are weak. The central government lost control of fiscal policy, and Argentina's provinces went on a spending spree, issuing dollar-denominated bonds to finance debt. External obligations mounted until the currency collapsed in 2002. Argentina defaulted on its debt, and it signed new agreements with the IMF to reform its fiscal policy. Eventually, it reached an agreement with most of its private foreign bank creditors to forgive three-quarters of its debt. But, as with personal credit records, a history of default bedevils Argentina's future access to credit.

The business climate in many of these countries improved, not just for foreign investment but, more important, for domestic investment as well. Microeconomic policies impede local as well as foreign investment. Unreliable infrastructure (ports, roads, telephone systems, and so on), legal problems with contract enforcement, crime, bribes, and regulations add 15 percent to the costs of doing business in Brazil, and upward of 25 percent in other Latin American countries. More than 40 percent of Brazil's roads, which transport 60 percent of all cargo in the country, are essentially unusable because of large potholes.[26] Some 50 percent of Brazilian firms lose money, and 40 percent express a lack of confidence that the courts will uphold their property rights. In Guatemala, 70 percent of businesses express the same concern. Regulations ensnare entrepreneurs in red tape. In Venezuela it takes 144 days to register a new business; in Brazil, 119; in Haiti, 105; in Chile, 27; and in Panama, 7. As a result, entrepreneurs operate outside the law. The **informal sector** in many Latin American countries, in which businesses operate without legal documents and pay no taxes, is huge. In Mexico, it accounts for about 30 percent of GDP and in Peru more than 50 percent.[27] In urban areas alone throughout Latin America and the Caribbean, 56 percent of all jobs are in the informal sector.[28]

informal sector: business activities that take place outside the legal system of a country because of excessive regulations.

Mexico privatized commercial banks in 1991, after nationalizing them in 1982. While privatization was considered a technical success, subsequent bank lending to politically powerful groups contributed to the financial crisis in 1994. After the crisis, Mexico permitted foreign banks and investment firms to enter and increase competition. But banking and financial markets in other countries remain underdeveloped, largely because of a lack of competition and foreign expertise. Most loans still go to those with close connections to the lenders rather than to the most profitable ventures. Equity and bond markets, where firms can raise money independent of government influence, are weak.[29] Nevertheless, in the 1990s, many governments established independent central banks. By the early 2000s, Brazil, Chile, Colombia, Peru, and Mexico had taken away the printing presses that finance ministries used to finance debt and fuel hyperinflation.

From liberal perspectives, market-oriented reforms clearly moved Latin American countries in the right direction. Exports not only grew but also diversified away from commodities, for which prices were declining, and toward manufactured goods, for which prices were rising. For Latin America and the Caribbean as a whole, the share of manufactured exports to total exports tripled from 15.4 percent in 1970 to 46.6 percent in 2000.[30] From realist and identity perspectives, however, trade and other reforms did not measurably reduce inequality, although they did not increase it either. Unlike China and India, Latin America did not see a large reduction in the number of people living below the poverty line.

Social Inequality

Inequality in the mainly middle-income Latin American region is among the highest in the world, with the richest 10 percent of the population receiving 41 percent of total income and the poorest just 1 percent. Poverty reduction has stagnated in recent years, leaving forty-seven million people in the region—more than 8 percent of the population—mired in extreme poverty.[31] Why is inequality in Latin America so resistant to change? Is it culture and the long history of oppression of native populations by European (Spanish and Portuguese) elites, as identity perspectives might argue?

Is it the unholy alliance between U.S. foreign policy interests and local elites that maintains political stability, exploits Latin American resources, restricts Latin American exports such as textiles and agricultural products, and floods Latin American markets with U.S. manufactured exports, as realist perspectives contend?

Is it the failure of social and economic reforms that fuels populist and revolutionary resentment and creates the damaging cycle of political revolution and instability that defeats sustained economic growth, as liberal perspectives might see it?

From a critical theory perspective, it is probably all these things and more (see Chapter 10). But, in comparison to Asian countries, three factors stand out: the absence of large-scale land reform, the relative lack of primary education, and a culture of paternalism and clientelism. Let's look at these factors in sequence.

In Latin America, some 5–10 percent of the population, depending on the country, owns 70–90 percent of the land. Yet more than half the population still earns its living in the countryside. There have been periodic attempts at land reform. Mexico redistributed some land to peasants under the *ejido* **system,** but the plots were owned collectively, not individually, and depended on government development banks for financing. The U.S. aid program in the 1960s known as the Alliance for Progress pushed land reform, and nearly one million peasant families acquired plots. But another ten to fourteen million families did not and continued to work the land as tenant farmers.[32] In Colombia, which until recently was torn by the narcotics trade and crime, large landowners ruled whole tracts of the countryside as feudal fiefdoms and even employed paramilitary forces to protect their territories. In Ecuador, 45 percent of the people live on the land, while 86 percent of the land is owned by the wealthiest 20 percent of the population.[33] Nothing contributes more to the inequality of income in Latin America than the absence of land reform. The richest 10 percent of the people control almost twice as much wealth in Latin America as in the United States, 47 percent compared to 28 percent.

Investment to sustain **basic human needs**—such as education and health care—has improved steadily in Latin America, but primary and elementary school education still lags behind other regions. Much of the problem lies in the fact that so many people still live in the countryside or in urban slums on the edges of gargantuan cities such as São Paulo in Brazil. In Haiti, for example, 50 percent of the population lives outside the urban areas. The earthquake that struck Haiti in 2010 not only killed 300,000 people and displaced another million but also revealed the primitive rural life of many

CAUSAL ARROW: PERSPECTIVES

Yields poverty	Distorts domestic institutions	Culture of oppression
REALIST	LIBERAL	IDENTITY

CAUSAL ARROW: PERSPECTIVES

Weakens local autonomy and pride	Co-opts local elites	U.S. intervention
IDENTITY	LIBERAL	REALIST

CAUSAL ARROW: PERSPECTIVES

Defeats material gains	Fuels populist ideology	Failure of reforms
REALIST	IDENTITY	LIBERAL

ejido **system:** Mexican land reform project that redistributed some land to peasants.

basic human needs: necessities such as clothing, shelter, food, education, and health care.

Destroyed buildings cover the landscape after a massive earthquake devastated Port-au-Prince, Haiti, on January 16, 2010. Is the plight of Haitian citizens mostly a consequence of scarcity (realist perspective), bad government (liberal), culture (identity), or imperialism (critical theory)?

paternalism: a system in which institutions such as the church or state provide for the needs of individuals or groups while stifling individual initiative and entrepreneurship.

Haitians under normal circumstances. Haitians in rural areas lack access to basic sanitation, housing, and health care. In rural ghettos, families need children to scratch a living from the land. When these children lack employment, they are drafted into drug gangs and criminal activities such as those that plague Mexico and Central America and that contribute to the general political discontent and violence throughout Latin America. Discrimination also plays a role. Large portions of the populations of Latin American countries are black or of mixed race (in Brazil, 43 percent; in Colombia, 72 percent). These groups do not receive the same opportunities for education and employment as those of European ancestry. The problems are interconnected. The education problem is part of the land reform problem, which in turn is part of the problem of industrial development, which, if it could happen, might spur education and employment of the rural masses.

Industrial development in Latin America is held back by a paternalistic and clientelist culture in which family and fraternal ties suffocate initiative and entrepreneurship. Individual initiative is not lacking; that's evident in the robust informal sectors in most Latin American countries, which by one estimate account for anywhere from 15 percent to 70 percent of economic activity in these countries.[34] But economic and political institutions do not welcome individual initiative and entrepreneurship. A tradition of **paternalism** prevails, grounded in part in the Catholic Church, which dominates the region. At one point, the church owned 60 percent of the land in Latin America. The heavy weight of the church on society led some Catholic priests and laity to rebel and fight the state openly. They preached a hard-left type of liberation theology and allied with Marxist guerrillas to fuel many of the rebellions in Latin American countries during the Cold War. When institutions stifle the masses long enough, revolutions follow. Democracy is caught in the middle, a desirable but dangerous alternative, as President Kennedy said, if it entails the prospect of fascist populism or paternalistic communism, as we see today in Venezuela and Cuba.

TABLE 9-2

Key Factors in Latin American Development: The Identity Perspective and Levels of Analysis

Identity perspective		
Systemic	*Structure*	Fear of neocolonialism and anti-American resentment abound
	Process	Neo-Marxist ideologies lead to import substitution policies
Foreign policy		Military elites exploit regional stability to gain and maintain domestic power
Domestic		Class divisions among European, mixed-race, black, and native populations create clientelism, corruption, and instability, impeding economic stability, land reform, and wider education
Individual		Informal sector flourishes as only place for entrepreneurship

Level of analysis

⟫ Sub-Saharan Africa

Sub-Saharan Africa (SSA) is part of the larger region of Africa and the Middle East. This region possesses abundant resources, and indeed the Middle East has developed oil resources to become the world's dominant supplier of energy. Those resources, of course, were first developed under colonial rule. Western intervention is a fact of life in these two regions, more so than in parts of Asia—such as Japan—or most of South America. Africa and the Middle East are also the poorest regions of the world, with the largest youth populations and the most deeply embedded discrimination against women. In some Muslim countries, women are largely banned from public places, let alone public life, although change is coming. Liberia elected the first woman ever to serve as an African head of state, Ellen Johnson Sirleaf; women hold one-third of the cabinet posts and 56 percent of parliament positions in Rwanda; and several Arab countries, such as

Morocco, Egypt, and Jordan, now mandate a number of seats for women in national parliaments. Parts of the Middle East are oil rich but industrially poor. Heavy dependence on oil discourages the development of manufacturing and services, and economic fortunes rise and fall with world oil demand. Meanwhile, the fortunes of Africa, which still has little trade or foreign investment, are largely divorced from the world economy. Not surprisingly, these two parts of the developing world face massive obstacles to achieving sustained industrial growth and human development.

Although we speak informally of Africa and the Middle East, what we actually have are two regions divided by the Sahara, a vast desert that stretches across the upper third of the African continent. As Map 9-5 shows, sub-Saharan Africa encompasses the forty-eight states that are located south of the Sahara, and the region referred to here as the Middle East and North Africa, or MENA, is made up of the band of African countries along the Mediterranean and Red Seas, the countries of the Arabian Peninsula and Persian Gulf, the countries of the Levant (Israel, Lebanon, Syria, and Jordan), and Turkey. SSA is non-Arab and draws deeply from earlier African civilizations with largely indigenous and, after colonization, Christian religions. MENA is Arab—Israel, Iran, and Turkey are the main exceptions—and draws deeply from the cultural and spiritual legacies of ancient Egypt and the Golden Age of Islam. We deal with SSA in this section and MENA in the following one.

Poor and Divided Continent

Real income in SSA is one-third less than that in South Asia, the next-poorest region. SSA's total income is just a little more than that of Belgium, and its median income (half the countries are below and half above this level) is the equivalent of the output of a town of sixty thousand people in a rich country. Some 48 percent of the people of SSA live below the poverty line of $1.25 per day.

But SSA is not only the poorest continent; it is also one of the most divided. It consists of forty-eight (or forty-seven if you're not counting Western Sahara, a disputed territory bordered by Morocco, Mauritania, and Algeria) countries with 165 borders, thirteen countries with fewer than 5 million people, and six more with fewer than 1 million people. Many of these small countries are landlocked and far too small to develop independently. Nigeria, with about 169 million people, is the most populous country by far, just about double the population of the next-largest state (see Map 9-5). The wealthiest country by far is South Africa, with more than four times the gross national income per capita (PPP) of Nigeria (US$11,190 compared with US$2,420). (Look back at Maps 9-1 and 9-2 for the distribution of wealth in sub-Saharan Africa.)

Africa was completely colonized, except for Liberia and Ethiopia. The boundaries in Africa were drawn by colonialists in Europe with little regard for ethnic or cultural homogeneity. Arguably, it may not have mattered. Africa is home to so many tribes and ethnic groups that it may have been impossible to create coherent states. Some two thousand tribes exist throughout the continent. They speak some 750 different languages.

MAP
9-5

Sub-Saharan Africa (SSA) and the Middle East and North Africa (MENA) Regions

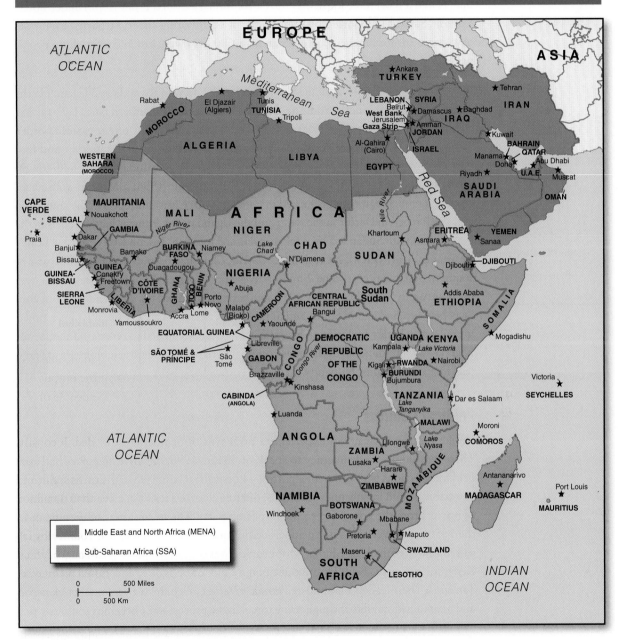

Only four states can claim ethnic homogeneity: Botswana, Lesotho, Somalia (although it is divided by clans), and Swaziland. By contrast, DR Congo alone has 75 distinct languages. Thus, the continent sags under the triple legacy of unfavorable geography, colonial rule, and indigenous divisions.

Since the countries of SSA became independent in the 1950s and 1960s, fighting has been incessant somewhere on the continent. In 2001, civil and interstate wars raged in western Africa, central Africa, and eastern Africa. In western Africa, Sierra Leone was caught up in a savage conflict between local elites in cahoots with Lebanese diamond miners and a rebel force known as the Revolutionary United Front (RUF) under Foday Sankoh. Sankoh, supported by then leader of neighboring Liberia Charles Taylor, set new standards for butchery: an estimated 75,000 lives were lost and 4.5 million people were displaced.

In central Africa, a civil war in the Congo eventually drew in Rwanda and Uganda in the eastern part of the country and Angola and Namibia in the southern part. The war has claimed 5 million lives since 1998 and continues to simmer today on the eastern border, where Rwanda intervenes periodically to attack Rwandan rebel sanctuaries and loot the rich mineral resources in the region. In eastern Africa, Rwanda and Burundi fought wars that culminated in the genocide of the Tutsi tribe in 1994; a Muslim-dominated government in Sudan remains locked in conflicts with Christian rebels in the south and non-Arab rebels in Darfur in the west; and the Ugandan government battles rebels in the border area with Sudan led by a self-proclaimed messiah, Joseph Kony, and his Lord's Resistance Army (LRA). Next door to Darfur, Chad has been destabilized. The war in southern Sudan has cost some 2 million lives and displaced 4 million more people over the past twenty years. In January 2011 southern Sudan voted for independence, but conflicts between Sudan and South Sudan persist. In western Africa, Côte d'Ivoire erupted in civil war. Charles Taylor, from his exile in Nigeria, threatened to return to Liberia, but Nigeria and international authorities cooperated to seize him and send him off to stand trial for crimes against humanity.

Political Reforms

Unlike Latin America, SSA experienced no waves of democracy and then reversals. There was simply no democracy to speak of. Before 1990, only five countries had ever held free elections with competing parties—Botswana, Gambia, Mauritius, Senegal, and Zimbabwe—and in only one, Mauritius, did free elections result in a peaceful transition of power from the governing to the opposing party. The norm after independence in the 1950s and 1960s was not democracy but one-party rule under a strongman, such as Kwame Nkrumah in Ghana, Mobutu Sese Seko in Zaire (now DR Congo), Jomo Kenyatta in Kenya, Felix Houphouet-Boigny in Côte d'Ivoire, and Julius Nyerere in Tanzania. These leaders manipulated ethnic loyalties much the way colonial powers had and maintained stability through brute force. In the process, they became fabulously rich and used state resources to build vast networks of clients. In most cases the strongman's particular ethnic group dominated, but these leaders also built alliances across ethnic groups by lavishing cash awards and other benefits on cooperative groups. Governments were rife with corruption, and ethnic divisions seethed beneath the surface. The United States and the Soviet Union, as part of their Cold War rivalry, lavished foreign aid on client states and reinforced corrupt and authoritarian rule.

The end of the Cold War brought the first real outbreak of democracy in Africa. From 1989 to 1997, forty-four of the forty-eight SSA countries held competitive elections—the exceptions being Nigeria, Somalia, Swaziland, and DR Congo. As you might imagine, many of these elections left much to be desired, given the weakness of political institutions and civil society, such as a free press and independent courts. Of some fifty-four elections between 1990 and 1994, only thirty were free and fair by international election standards. Nevertheless, eleven involved the peaceful transfer of power from an incumbent to an opposing party, something only Mauritius had achieved prior to 1990. The most important peaceful transfer took place in South Africa, the wealthiest and most controversial African country, at least during its apartheid days. This transition was remarkable and stands as a testament to the way democracy can begin even in the most difficult racial or ethnic circumstances. Other peaceful transitions took place in Benin, Burundi, Cape Verde, the Central African Republic, Congo, Madagascar, Malawi, Niger, São Tomé and Príncipe, and Zambia. Three other countries—Lesotho, Mali, and Namibia—installed new governments through elections, but no incumbents chose to run.

Elections in fifteen additional countries took place between 1994 and 1997. They were disappointing. None met international standards. Eleven were boycotted by the opposition and only one, in Sierra Leone, involved a peaceful transfer to an opposing party, although no incumbent ran. In most cases, ruling military leaders ran as civilians, which testified to their growing need to legitimate power by at least nominally seeking the approval of the people. But subsequent military coups in Burundi, Sierra Leone, DR Congo, Gambia, and Niger reversed election results before second elections could be held. Sierra Leone and DR Congo descended into civil war, as we have noted, and fragile governments exist in these countries today under precarious cease-fire arrangements monitored by UN peacekeeping forces.

Second elections in seventeen new democracies from 1995 to 1997 also yielded disappointing results. In only two countries did power change hands—Madagascar and Benin—and in Zambia and Mali incumbents rigged the elections. Kenya remained under one-party rule until the early 2000s, when fragmented opposition groups, mostly based on ethnic ties, came together to unseat the long-reigning Kenya African National Union (KANU) party of Kenyatta and his successor, Daniel arap Moi. Ghana and Senegal followed similar courses to end one-party rule. Uganda remains under one-party rule, although its leader, Yoweri Museveni, is considered by some observers to be progressive.

Since the turn of the millennium, Africa's democratic fortunes remain troubled. Nigeria, the continent's most populous country, held elections in 1999, 2003, and 2007, but each was "less fair, less efficient, and less credible" than the one before.[35] Kenya defeated a referendum in 2005 to expand the powers of the long-ruling government, but disputed elections in 2007 left the country in turmoil under a fragile power-sharing arrangement worked out by Kofi Annan, the former UN secretary-general. Museveni in Uganda overturned constitutional restrictions to stay in power, as did governments in Ethiopia, Eritrea, Cameroon, and Rwanda. Mali succumbed to a military coup and then invasion by Muslim extremists. Some countries, such as Ghana, Sierra Leone, and Liberia, made progress, but, as one student of democracy in Africa reports, "the political struggle in Africa remains very much a conflict between the rule of law and the rule of a person."[36]

Perhaps the most egregious example of bad government in Africa is Zimbabwe. A former British colony—once known as Rhodesia—it inherited a thriving agricultural economy when it became independent. The largely white landowner community stayed on. For a time, Zimbabwe's future looked at least hopeful, but today the country is desperate. The strongman leading the country, Robert G. Mugabe, systematically routed the white landowners out of the countryside and indeed the country, redistributed the land to squatters, and ruined a thriving commercial agricultural sector. Lack of exports and hence foreign currency sent the exchange rate plunging—from a ratio of 55 Zimbabwe dollars to 1 U.S. dollar in 1999 to a ratio of 150,000 Zimbabwe dollars to 1 U.S. dollar in 2005—encouraging inflation and capital flight. By 2008, Zimbabwe had the world's highest official rate of inflation at 100,500 percent per year, and by 2009 it had abandoned its national currency altogether.[37] Almost everything is in short supply. In 2006, Mugabe, whose staple political trick is to find someone else to blame for Zimbabwe's troubles—mostly former colonialists—turned on street merchants operating in the informal sector, blaming them for the short supplies. Although defeated by opposition groups led by Morgan Tsvangirai in early 2008, Mugabe refused to give up power and initiated a campaign of intimidation against the opposition, accusing it of trying to return the country to British colonialists. A regional group, the South African Development Community (SADC), seeks to mediate the conflict, but the international community has taken no decisive action to end Mugabe's reign of ruin.[38]

Is democracy the right formula for development under the circumstances that prevail in Africa? It's a fair question because democracy opens up political competition to all groups, and, if these groups identify with opposing ethnic backgrounds and have little else in common, competition can easily lead to open conflict. Maybe strongman rule, if it is progressive, is a better approach. Perhaps. But what ensures that it is progressive? It certainly isn't in Zimbabwe. Even if it is, what gives one ethnic group the right to rule over another? As realist perspectives might argue, if it's just a matter of who can use force more brutally, why speak of a country at all? Let the various groups establish their own governments and eventually achieve some kind of a balance of power, as states do internationally. This is basically the situation that prevailed in 2010 in Somalia among various clans. That might mean, of course, as liberal perspectives warn, much less interdependence and many more small African states that are more uneconomical and dysfunctional than the existing ones. So democracy, identity perspectives insist, may offer a better way. Even in primitive form, electoral politics compels diverse groups to take one another into account. Over time, or so the cosmopolitan moral view argues, groups in any culture can find ways to reconcile differences through competitive but peaceful means under the rule of law.

CAUSAL ARROW: PERSPECTIVES

Democratic reform	Compels rival groups to cooperate	Yields better material outcomes
IDENTITY	LIBERAL	REALIST

Thus, political stability in Africa remains elusive. It is without doubt one of the major reasons for the region's lack of economic progress. Nevertheless, stability begins with small steps. And compared to the situation before 1990, SSA on the whole has been moving in the right direction. Political change has created an opening for economic reforms, and some African countries are seizing the opportunity.

Economic Reforms

Since 1980 only five SSA countries have achieved a real per capita growth rate above 2 percent per year: Botswana, Cape Verde, Mauritius, Seychelles, and Swaziland. Notice that, except for Swaziland, these are the same countries that score high on political stability and accountability. Botswana has the best record, comparable to that of some East Asian high performers from 1965–1990—8 percent per year GDP growth. But the same party has won every election in Botswana since 1965, and Botswana and the other four countries are extremely small. They hardly qualify as representative of the whole of Africa.

A man buys groceries in Zimbabwe in March 2008 with an armload of Zimbabwe dollars, 25 million of which equal a single U.S. dollar, reflecting the chaos of the economy under the presidency of tyrant Robert Mugabe.

Since the mid-1990s, more countries have exceeded 2 percent per year real (taking out inflation) per capita growth rates. In the 2000s, some eighteen countries, including Ghana, Mali, Mozambique, Tanzania, and Uganda, grew at average rates of more than 5.5 percent per year, more typical of Asian than of African countries. Overall, the proportion of Africans living on less than $1.25 per day fell from 58 percent in 1990 to 51 percent in 2005, but because of population growth, the absolute number of poor people actually rose from 296 to 388 million. Some twenty countries remained trapped in poverty.[39] Oil-producing countries, such as Angola, Cameroon, Chad, DR Congo, Equatorial Guinea, Gabon, and Nigeria, enjoyed the best performance. DR Congo used oil price increases to boost public investments in electricity consumption and school enrollments. But the narrow focus on oil led to a failure to develop other non-resource-based sectors and left the country exposed to a fall in world oil prices. By 2000, real per capita income in the DR Congo had dropped to $900, from $1,000 in the mid-1980s. Sustained growth requires productivity improvements—that is, improvements in efficiency or more output from the same inputs—and those have been uniquely lacking in SSA.[40]

Nevertheless, macroeconomic policies have improved. Except in Zimbabwe, where it reached 100,000 percent in 2008, inflation in SSA is at historic lows. In 2000–2003, only six countries—Angola, Eritrea, Liberia, Nigeria, Zambia, and Zimbabwe—reported inflation rates of more than 10 percent a year. Fiscal policies have seen less improvement. The IMF works with countries to improve the transparency of their fiscal spending. In most countries, few people have access to reliable information about the government budget, and many of the data that are available are not reliable. Weak fiscal constraints facilitate both graft and waste. In Nigeria under military rule, it is estimated that some $40 billion was siphoned off from the fiscal budget, much of it leaving the country. Chronic fiscal shortages then increase pressures to print money and weaken monetary control. Few countries in SSA have independent central banks; South Africa is one that has an independent central bank, and its economic performance ranks among the best.

Microeconomic policies in Africa, as in Latin America, constrain growth. The electricity supply is unreliable. Losses from power interruptions average 6–7 percent of sales in Ethiopia and Zambia, and 10 percent or more in Eritrea, Kenya, and Senegal. Because of red tape, starting a company costs more than five times as much in SSA as it does in South Asia and thirty times as much as in industrialized countries. According to World Bank surveys of the investment climate in various countries, sixteen of the twenty countries with the greatest regulatory obstacles are found in SSA.[41] Transferring a piece of property takes more than a year in Ghana and Rwanda. In Senegal, the costs of transfer equal one-third of the property's value. Courts, too, are slow, and gaining access to them is expensive. To enforce a commercial or loan contract, creditors have to take more than thirty steps and pay more than 43 percent of an average person's annual income. Small businesses in the informal sector, which provide in many cases 70 percent of the nonagricultural jobs in SSA countries, are simply squeezed out of the picture.

Labor laws in SSA countries are among the strictest in the world. In Burkina Faso, for example, companies have to hire people permanently unless the jobs are seasonal, and minimum wage is relatively high. If you cannot lay off workers, you do not hire them; high mandated wages also discourage employment. Only a few SSA countries have credit bureaus to screen private borrowers. Hence, lending to the private sector is rare. Multilateral institutions and foreign aid try to fill this gap with microfinancing, small loans to individual farmers and merchants, especially women, who would not otherwise have access to credit. Microlending is important, but as noted above, alone it cannot override numerous other restrictions on businesses.

Trade and investment played a small role in African development through the mid-1990s. SSA countries' share of world trade dropped by two-thirds—from 2.1 percent in 1975 to 0.7 percent in 1995.[42] The small foreign investment that occurred went mostly into resource extraction—mainly oil—and did little to develop other sectors of the economy. Three major obstacles impeded SSA access to world markets. The first was geography; with so many landlocked countries and conflicts, access across national boundaries was prevented. The second was local government policies that discriminated against agriculture in favor of urban priorities. African governments made generous use of marketing boards that monopolized the purchase of agricultural products in the countryside and sold food to the urban population at subsidized prices and on world markets to enhance tax revenues. Farm income suffered badly, precisely in the areas where poverty was most concentrated.

The third and most inexcusable obstacle consisted of the policies of the industrialized countries, which protected their agricultural markets. The United States, Japan, and particularly the European Union, through its Common Agricultural Policy, not only imposed barriers on agricultural imports but also subsidized the domestic production of food products at much higher prices. Farmers in developing countries suffered, but so did consumers in industrial countries, who paid far more for food products than they would have otherwise. To top it all off, the industrialized countries then sold their surpluses of food products, generated by the artificially high domestic prices, on world markets at subsidized prices or gave away food as foreign aid, keeping the world market prices lower than they would have been otherwise. Thus, developing-country marketing boards got less for their exports than they should have. Farmers and governments in developing countries lost, as did consumers in industrial countries and their governments that paid out the high subsidies. The only winners were the already well-off farmers, usually large ones, in the industrialized countries.

For a while, it appeared that this sham might be ended. In the Uruguay Round in 1994, the international trade community agreed to convert quotas and other NTBs on agricultural trade to tariffs that might then be lowered through trade negotiations. Liberalizing agricultural tariffs was placed at the top of the agenda in the new Doha Round that began in 2001. Unfortunately, as of this writing (in late 2013) that trade round is stalled and likely going nowhere. Resistance from farm communities in the industrialized countries is fierce. Globalization opponents of the WTO and other international institutions rightly criticize the hypocrisy of industrialized countries on farm policy, but many of them also oppose trade liberalization and the Doha Round, which might end this hypocrisy.

Developing countries have higher trade restrictions on manufactured than on agricultural goods. Industrial countries have higher trade restrictions on agricultural than on manufactured goods. If they could bargain lower agricultural barriers in industrialized countries for lower industrial barriers in developing countries, a huge opportunity to exploit comparative advantage would emerge. Because trade barriers have been coming down since 1995, developing-country exports are already rising. Even SSA countries have increased their share of world trade from 0.7 percent in 1995 to 0.9 percent in 2003. Once trade flows more freely, foreign investment follows because MNCs often locate abroad, at least initially, to service other foreign, rather than local, markets. With proper governance, a good climate for foreign investment translates into a good environment for domestic investment. Obviously, much work needs to be done on the business climate, as we have noted. But competition among MNCs, many now from developing countries such as Brazil and India, is much greater today than in the era of import substitution. Developing countries have greater bargaining leverage than they did when MNCs were concentrated in a few advanced countries and interested primarily in resource extraction.

Human Development

Africa is at the beginning stages of industrial development. As Map 8-1 in the previous chapter shows, two-thirds of the people still live in the countryside and work in agriculture. That was also the case in India and China, but there it is changing rapidly. More and more people are moving into cities and industry. By contrast, two-thirds of the people in Latin America already live in cities, although often in squalid slums on the outskirts of big cities. Thus, while human deprivation exists in all poor countries, Africa deals with it at its rural roots. The biggest problems are disease and poor health more generally and discrimination against women, especially in education.

According to the latest report, 22.5 million people in SSA are living with AIDS, about half of them women. The incidence of the disease has declined since its peak in the 1990s, and between 2000 and 2009 infections decreased by 25 percent in about half the countries in the region.[43] There are numerous obstacles to dealing effectively with AIDS in SSA, but three stand out. The first is the difficulty in catching the disease early in high-risk populations, such as sex workers and intravenous drug users, before it is spread, often by roving militias, to the broader community. A few countries in SSA, such as Senegal, have done well in this regard. Others, such as South Africa, have not done as well. For a time South Africa's president, Thabo Mbeki, refused to acknowledge the disease, and precious time was lost. Once the disease has spread, the main defense is education, and providing that education is the second obstacle. To be effective, AIDS education programs require forthright national leadership, widespread public awareness campaigns, and intensive prevention efforts, including advocating the use of condoms and abstinence.

The third obstacle is that of treating existing HIV/AIDS cases, which requires expensive antiretroviral drugs. Here, the global pharmaceutical companies come in for heavy criticism. Some of this criticism is justified; some is not. These companies do an enormous amount of research, which is very expensive. They generally develop new drugs for advanced markets and introduce them in developing markets only after the drugs have been tested and approved for use and sale in advanced countries. They seek to recoup their large and growing research expenses by demanding patent protection, which delays competition and results in high prices for medicines. Indeed, if they could not charge high prices for a time to recoup investment costs, they would stop the research altogether—then there would be no new drugs, unless governments and NGOs picked up the research, manufacturing, and marketing costs. Companies survive on profits, meaning they finance their operations by retaining earnings in the form of profits or by borrowing funds, which they have to repay with future earnings. So it is probably unjustified to criticize their need for profits, unless we are opposed to profit-making organizations altogether.

Where the companies go too far is in exploiting monopoly circumstances when they face no counterbalancing forces. If they own a patent, of course, they face no direct competition, although other companies always produce similar products. So, it seems appropriate that governments and NGOs exercise some scrutiny over company operations and provide assistance if they wish companies to move faster toward the production of cheaper generic drugs or to offer their drugs at discounted prices. New partnerships are emerging in this area. Governments, foundations such as the Bill and Melinda Gates Foundation, and major pharmaceutical companies such as Wyeth, GlaxoSmithKline, and Merck have contributed tens of billions of dollars to fight AIDS in recent years.

Water sanitation and broader health services remain critical deficiencies in SSA countries. Bad water and poor sanitation are responsible for 90 percent of the diarrheal diseases and as much as 8 percent of all diseases burdening poor countries. Ghana, Senegal, South Africa, and Uganda have improved clean water supplies and sanitation services. A key problem is developing sanitation services that can be sustained. Such services have to be paid for by taxes or user fees. Experiments in Senegal, and also India, have demonstrated that on-site sanitation facilities run by local communities and financed by user fees do more to improve sanitation on a sustained basis than do municipal-run toilets, which deteriorate rapidly and are difficult to maintain.

Gender inequality is another major deficiency. In SSA countries, enrollment of girls in primary-level schools is still less than 90 percent that of boys, and the completion rate for girls is 15 percent below that for boys. Girls and women endure inequalities in families, tribes, and villages that stem from centuries-old traditions and superstitions. In some countries, girls are subjected to the painful and often life-threatening mutilation of their female organs, and village women in Malawi, Zambia, and Kenya submit to a ritual in which a woman whose husband has died is required to have sex with one of her husband's relatives to break her bond with her dead husband's spirit. Conflicts in Africa often involve the widespread rape and humiliation of women. Many of these practices contribute directly to the spread of AIDS.

The biggest constraint in dealing with many of these health and educational problems is the lack of adequately trained teachers and health care providers. Money can help to address this problem, but not quickly. Many of the practices that discriminate against education for all, especially for women, would have to be changed to create a larger pool of people who might then be trained for such services. And often the training that is available is not relevant to the conditions in the countryside, as physicians still serve predominantly urban areas. This type of **brain drain** affects numerous countries in Africa (and the Middle East).

brain drain: the emigration of educated people from developing countries.

Despite the obstacles, some African countries have made notable progress. Ghana, Mozambique, Tanzania, and Uganda have accelerated growth and reduced poverty; Malawi has achieved particular success in boosting agricultural productivity; Ghana, Kenya, Tanzania, and Uganda have increased primary school enrollment; Niger, Togo, and Zambia have made progress in combating malaria; Senegal and Uganda have increased access to water and sanitation; Niger has promoted reforestation; and Rwanda has achieved an impressive recovery from conflict. Because these countries start from far behind, however, they remain most vulnerable. The financial crisis of 2008–2009 hit SSA countries the hardest.[44]

Millennium Initiative and Foreign Aid

The Millennium Declaration was signed at the United Nations in September 2000 by 189 countries, including 147 heads of state. The declaration outlined the **Millennium Development Goals.** These goals were very ambitious. By 2015, the international community pledged to eradicate extreme poverty and hunger; achieve universal primary education; promote gender equality and empower women; reduce infant mortality; improve maternal health; combat HIV/AIDS, malaria, and other diseases; ensure environmental sustainability; and develop a global partnership among governments, private companies, and NGOs to increase aid, employment, trade opportunities, debt relief, and affordable medicines for developing countries.

The Millennium initiative stressed the link between international aid and local policies. This link was considered crucial. Too often in the past, it was argued, aid did not influence domestic spending patterns. Governments, for example, did not use aid for health services to improve conditions in rural areas, where the majority of the poor lived; instead, they continued to finance urban priorities, such as state-of-the-art hospitals, that involved heavy administrative costs and often poor and corrupt implementation. On the other hand, aid-donating countries and multilateral agencies attached so many restrictions to projects that there was no sense of ownership by local elites and institutions; local governments felt left out. The Millennium approach stressed country-owned and -led poverty reduction strategies. These strategies aimed at both overall growth and growth of the poorest populations and regions. Multilateral development banks, donor countries, and NGOs were asked to coordinate their aid with country-specific poverty plans.

Official development assistance (ODA), or aid from governments, is rising. In real terms, aid to SSA countries is higher now than it was in 1990 and represents a higher percentage of total worldwide aid (about one-third). Most of this aid is in grants that do not have to be paid back, while the multilateral development banks provide highly **concessional loans,** or loans at subsidized interest rates. Some donors, such as the United States, want the banks to switch to grant aid only, but the banks fear that this step may deplete their resources and that they may not get timely and adequate replenishments. The United States provides the major share of aid to SSA (20 percent). The International Development Association (the so-called soft or concessional loan window of the World Bank) is the next largest provider of aid, followed by France and the European Union.

In 1996, the IMF and World Bank established a debt reduction program for heavily indebted poor countries; thirty of the thirty-six countries assisted under the program since then are in Africa. **Debt relief** involves rescheduling loans and stretching them out over longer periods or forgiving loans altogether. It is probably best applied to the poorest countries that do not yet depend on private bank financing, because once countries start borrowing from private banks debt relief can be just as harmful as it is helpful. Private banks are reluctant to lend to countries after they have previously defaulted. Argentina, which defaulted on its private debt, encountered this difficulty. Moreover, relieving the debts of even the poorest countries requires care, because doing so when corruption is high and local leadership is lacking only encourages more fraud and waste.

The Millennium initiative estimates that SSA countries will need another $75 billion to $100 billion of total aid per year to meet the Millennium Development Goals by 2015. That is four times the current level of official aid and, realistically, not likely to be reached. It is roughly the amount that developing countries could gain by that date through trade if the Doha Round succeeds. Still, we could make the case that the time for aid has never been better. Whereas before 1990 aid was provided largely without a willingness on the part of the donor or recipient communities to consider seriously the quality of domestic policies, today the global community is focused on domestic policies. Development success in Asia and elsewhere has made it unmistakably clear that countries cannot succeed unless they have local leadership that is committed to clean and fair government, growth through sound economic policies, a better investment climate for both domestic and foreign entrepreneurs, and poverty reduction that gives all groups a stake in national prosperity. Table 9-3 summarizes development factors in SSA countries from the different levels of analysis.

TABLE 9-3

Key Factors in Sub-Saharan African Development: The Identity Perspective and Levels of Analysis

Level of analysis	Identity perspective		
Systemic	Structure	Completely colonized by West except for Liberia and Ethiopia Enormous ethnic and cultural diversity	
	Process	Millennium initiative provides foreign aid for better governance Global drug companies help and hinder progress in health Global open-market ideology promotes boom for African commodities	
Foreign policy		Tribal elites, such as Museveni in Uganda, play off foreign countries to maintain domestic divisions	
Domestic		Corrupt governments impede economic and human development Democracy offers opportunity for ethnic conflict and division Statist economic policies foster zero-sum competition for wealth	
Individual		Leaders like Mugabe in Zimbabwe use neo-Marxist ideologies to divide ethnic groups	

≫ Middle East and North Africa

MENA is a paradox. On one hand, the region is very rich in resources, young people, and aid. Oil flows abundantly in many, although not all, of the countries. The workforce is highly educated, compared, for example, to the population in SSA. And countries such as Egypt and Jordan receive large amounts of aid because of the Arab–Israeli conflict. On the other hand, the region is very poor in jobs, skilled manufacturing and service industries, trade, foreign investment, and technology. Compared to other developing countries, MENA countries have small manufacturing sectors, and their share of non-oil merchandise exports is small. In a sense, the entire region suffers from what economists call a resource curse—the abundance of oil diverts attention from non-oil investments, contributes to an overvalued exchange rate, and discourages the development of non-oil investments and exports.

The region also constitutes a strategic piece of real estate that has endured invasions and conflicts since the earliest times. The Philistines and Greeks, Sparta and Athens, Rome and Carthage, Israelites and Babylonians, Catholic and Orthodox Christians, Christians and Muslims, and European colonialists and Ottoman Empire all fought over this land for centuries. The Middle East was Europe's gateway (via the Suez Canal) to China and India, Russia's outlet to the Mediterranean, and Asia's destination on the old trading route known as the Silk Road. The region was a hot spot in the Cold War between the United States and the Soviet Union, and it has been a seedbed of division and terrorism—torn between Arabs and Israelis, Arabs and Persians (Iranians), secular and sectarian governments, and authoritarian government elites and mass publics.

On top of it all, since the 1920s the area has been the richest source of oil and natural gas deposits in the world. The Gulf countries—Iraq, Iran, Saudi Arabia, Kuwait, Bahrain, Qatar, United Arab Emirates (UAE), and Oman—are the oil titans of the region. The Levant countries—Israel, Jordan, Syria, and Lebanon—and the Palestinian Authority (still a nonstate entity until a final Arab–Israeli settlement) have no oil. Their borders and development fortunes center inextricably on Israel, the most fully modernized state in the region. Of the remaining countries—Morocco, Algeria, Tunisia, Libya, Egypt, Yemen, Djibouti, and Turkey—a few (including Libya and Algeria) have oil, but most rely on exports of agricultural and light manufacturing products to Europe. Apart from Israel, Turkey is the most advanced country, with a population of seventy-four million, about the same as Iran, but a per capita income that is about 65 percent higher. Map 9-5 shows the geographic layout of the region; Maps 9-1 and 9-2 show the economic development.

Except for its strategic location and resources, MENA would probably not be considered a separate region, certainly not on a scale with SSA, Latin America, or Asia. It contains only 6 percent of the world's population and accounts for 2 percent of the world's income. And in terms of development, as noted earlier in this chapter, it ranks at the bottom with SSA and South Asia. From 1980 to the early 2000s, per capita income in MENA countries grew annually at a slower rate (0.9 percent) than that of SSA.[45] Since 2000 and the explosion of oil prices, the region has done better, with output growing at more than 5 percent per year. Human development in the region is also significant, with an average life expectancy of seventy-one years, a primary education completion rate of 91 percent, and a mortality rate for children under five years old of forty-eight per thousand. Absolute poverty is low, with around 2.4 percent of the population living on less than $1.25 per day, but vulnerability is high because sizable proportions of the population live on the edge of poverty.[46] Inflation is rising rapidly, and some of the region's major economies, such as Egypt and Saudi Arabia, are fragile. The exception, of course, is Israel, but its economy also suffers from heavy defense expenditures and the political uncertainties of the region. The geopolitical significance of the region attracts global attention, both for good and for bad. Constant turmoil and intervention breed cautious and defensive governments in the region. Leaders lack the confidence to alter the status quo, fear foreign trade and investment, and seem paralyzed by the enormous pressures building up in labor markets, where a growing pool of unemployed people who are young and better educated clamor for economic opportunities and political participation. The outbreak in early 2011 of massive public protests in Tunisia, Egypt, Jordan, and other MENA countries illustrated the problem.

If development is to take place, it will require three ingredients: domestic political reforms and regional peace settlements, an opening up of MENA markets to greater foreign trade and investment, and a more egalitarian and tolerant social order that resolves the religious issues constraining modernization and women's participation in society. Let's look more closely at each of these three areas.

Political Reforms/Regional Peace Settlements

For decades, Cold War rivalries and the Arab-Israeli conflict focused attention on diplomatic and alliance arrangements in the region and neglected, comparatively, domestic reforms. Political settlements and security were considered to be prerequisites of MENA economic development, as the realist perspective might predict. Peace did emerge between Egypt and Israel after 1979, but economic interdependence did not follow. Instead, as the peace process accelerated in the early 1990s under the Oslo Accords, economic development seemed to go in the opposite direction. Oil prices declined in the 1990s, cutting into public revenues, and countries in the region had few alternative private-sector activities to fall back on. Clearly something else was holding back development, something in addition to the political turbulence of the region (realist) and the economic volatility of oil (liberal).

That something else was poor and unaccountable domestic governance, as identity perspectives might expect. World Bank studies documented that, "when compared with countries that have similar income and characteristics . . . , the MENA region ranks at the bottom on the index of overall governance quality."[47] MENA countries have a lower quality of administration in the public sector than would be expected from their incomes, and they measure particularly low on the index of public accountability, which assesses the openness of political institutions and participation, respect for civil liberties, transparency of government, and freedom of the press. By available measures, no MENA government except Israel's reaches even the middle of the scale of democratic features. All the others are lumped together at the authoritarian end of the spectrum. Eleven of these regimes are autocratic republics, and nine are monarchies ruled by kings or emirs. All feature strong executives, corrupt public administrations, nonexistent (Qatar, UAE, and Saudi Arabia) or very weak parliaments (the strongest ones are in Morocco and Bahrain), fragile and in some cases politically dependent courts, and civil societies that are underdeveloped and largely disenfranchised by lack of political and media competition. The result is a development process heavily dependent on inbred political elites, unresponsive to domestic and international markets, and yoked to the price and volatility of oil, as well as worker remittances from abroad and foreign aid. When oil prices soared from 1970 to 1985, the region grew, albeit very wastefully. When oil prices tanked between 1985 and 2000, growth shriveled. Today, higher oil prices again offer hope, and some reforms are under way. But without a fundamental restructuring of domestic institutions, the MENA region is stuck in a poor governance trap.

MENA countries suffer from arbitrary policy making, corrupt administration, and poor public services. The transparency of government is minimal. In some countries, detailed budget information is not available at all, and in most, the absence of a free press means that budget numbers are discussed only inside the government. Tax assessments are ambiguous, and tax collectors, unchecked by parliamentary or civil society groups, exercise virtually unlimited powers.

Corruption is endemic at all levels. Bureaucrats can help you find your land title but then explain that this will take a lot of time and unfortunately they will not be compensated for the extra work, a hint that they expect a tip.[48] Nepotism is also widespread. Public officials dole out jobs and other government favors to ethnic and tribal relations. Favoritism in contracts and tax evasion are highest in Saudi Arabia, Lebanon, Jordan, Egypt, and Tunisia.[49]

Poor governance means that public services are often deficient. Phones, roads, and power facilities are lacking. MENA countries tend to do pretty well in providing access to water and sanitation services—90 percent of urban and 71 percent of rural areas have safe water, and 96 percent and 73 percent, respectively, have improved sanitation facilities. But electric power is in short supply and often interrupted. Each year, according to World Bank estimates, MENA countries lose 13 percent of national output because of power losses. Electric power is unavailable for as much as three months out of the year in some countries, such as Algeria, Morocco, and Yemen. Telephone service has improved. MENA countries now have twice as many phone lines as they did in 1980. But the ratio of unsuccessful phone connections is still extraordinarily high—35 percent in Tunisia, 50 percent in Lebanon, 57 percent in Morocco, and 60 percent in Jordan. The region is far behind Asia in the deployment of mobile phones.

Resource (Oil) Curse

Economic policies are often another casualty of poor governance. They are shaped to extract rents from state-owned resources and government-awarded licenses. Political leaders and bureaucrats channel resources to state-owned enterprises and political clients in the private sector. They set exchange rate, trade, and investment policies to protect these groups. A system of entrenched interests develops and prevents any flexibility. The economy rides up and down on the exogenous fluctuation of oil prices. Social programs appease a disenfranchised civil society but create growing financial burdens and debt, especially when oil or export prices decline. The economy never diversifies, and the MENA countries develop an increasingly educated workforce that finds few jobs or opportunities. Skilled labor leaves the country for Europe or the United States or works in wealthier Gulf oil states and sends back remittances to sustain family members. Foreign aid fills the financing gap rather than stimulating self-sustaining investments and jobs.

Over the past three decades, virtually all the MENA countries followed either de facto or formal fixed exchange rate regimes. Their exchange rates, determined by the reliance on resource exports, were significantly overvalued—by 30 percent in the early decades and by more than 20 percent in the last decade. Oil and resource exports are less sensitive to overvalued exchange rates because they are priced globally and do not face immediate substitutes. But manufactured exports are highly sensitive. If the exchange rate is overvalued by 25 percent, manufactured exports cost 25 percent more than they should. The result, in the case of MENA countries, is a loss of export competitiveness. The ratio of manufactured exports to GDP fell by 18 percent per year. Manufactured exports averaged 4.4 percent of GDP during the previous three decades; they would have averaged 5.2 percent without the overvaluation.[50] This is an enormous albatross around the neck of economies that need to diversify from resource-based to more highly skilled manufacturing and service industries. Why do countries follow such policies? Again, their focus is on resource exports, not manufactured exports. Few domestic interests benefit from exporting manufactured goods; many, especially the state, benefit from exporting oil.

Trade protection is higher in MENA countries than in any other developing region aside from Latin America—the poster child of import substitution policies. Thus, it is very profitable to produce manufactured goods for the domestic market but not for export. If a manufacturer gets a license from the government, he (not many women own businesses) can charge very high prices for domestic products without having to worry about competition from imports. Consumers bear the cost. They buy inferior goods at higher prices. There are no Wal-Marts or dollar stores. Those in power have no incentive to change the system, and those out of power have no influence to change it.

Without competition, the business environment is abysmal. In Egypt, it takes seventeen procedures and 202 days to register a business, even after you get the license. In Jordan, it takes three months. In Lebanon, it takes 721 days to enforce a contract through the court system, in Syria 596 days, in UAE 559 days, and in Algeria 387 days.[51] For the average business, it costs 62 percent of the average person's annual income to register and enforce a business contract. Is it any wonder that many businesspeople don't bother or just pay off a public servant to avoid the courts?

The domestic business environment also limits FDI. In 2000, FDI accounted for only 5 percent of gross capital formation in the MENA countries, compared to 26 percent in Singapore. Again, despite peace between Israel and Egypt for more than thirty-five years and enormous sums of foreign aid given to these countries, no significant trade and investment take place between them. Obviously, peace is necessary to ignite widespread development in the region, but this alone is not enough. Domestic policy reforms are also necessary.

Some reforms are under way. Tunisia and Morocco started trade reforms in the 1980s, including export-processing zones for light manufacturing such as textiles and garments. Jordan cleaned up its fiscal mess and signed a trade agreement with the EU in 1997 and with the United States in 2002. Lebanon ran up huge reconstruction deficits after the civil war ended in 1990, but it is now reforming (albeit in the face of renewed violence from Hezbollah). Algeria, Iran, Yemen, and Syria reformed later and more sporadically. The six Gulf Cooperation Council (GCC) countries—the oil titans Saudi Arabia, UAE, Qatar, Bahrain, Kuwait, and Oman—are the most integrated into the world economy, having developed sophisticated financial systems to manage their investments around the world. They also encourage large inflows of skilled and unskilled workers to service the domestic economy. But the largest one, Saudi Arabia, is still poorly diversified, using its oil revenues to protect a large, inefficient, domestic non-oil sector that is mostly publicly owned. Although Saudi Arabia finally joined the WTO in 2005, it faces the need for continuing reforms to liberalize trade, privatize state companies, and increase FDI.

Women in Muslim Societies

Women benefit from improved social services in MENA countries, from access to safe water and sanitation to opportunities for primary and secondary school education to significantly reduced rates of infant mortality. But women remain far behind the standards prevailing in other countries, with the exception perhaps of those in SSA. Saudi Arabia is the only country in the world that denies women the right to drive.[52]

Four factors impede the full entry of women into MENA development and politics. First, the family rather than the individual constitutes the main unit of society. The centrality of the family is considered a cultural asset and implies that women will marry early and devote themselves to children and household affairs. Second, the man is still seen as the sole breadwinner, and the idea of a two-income household is unwelcome. Third, a modesty code shields the reputation of women, on which family honor rests, and restricts the opportunities for women to enter the workplace and other public spaces. And fourth, family religious laws dictate a radically unequal balance of power between men and women in the family. These cultural and religious factors, more than legal factors, limit employment possibilities.

Women are becoming better educated, with rates of completion of primary school now on par with those of men. The literacy rate among women has gone up from 16.6 percent in 1970 to 75.5 percent today. Women make up 49 percent of the population, but they account for 63 percent of university students.[53]

Female Muslim students study at Da'wi College in the Gaza Strip, but they will likely struggle to find jobs after graduation in the impoverished Palestinian economy.

The difficulty is that women are being better educated but not more widely employed. Women make up only 26 percent of the workforce in MENA countries. That's up by 50 percent since 1960 but still well below what we would expect from the education levels, fertility levels, and age structure of the female population. If employment reached those levels, household earnings would increase by 25 percent. As the World Bank notes, "These increased earnings are the ticket to the middle class."[54] Because women and many young people (men and women) are unemployed, one working person supports more than two other people, the highest ratio in the world and slightly above that for SSA.

Six out of ten people in the region are under twenty-five years of age. This is the time bomb ticking away for MENA governments—young people, including women, are being better educated and prepared to contribute to society, but the countries' and region's economies cannot employ them. Now, armed with smartphones, they take to the streets calling for political change. Interestingly, the resource-poor countries, such as Egypt and Lebanon, do slightly better at employing women than do the resource-rich ones, such as Algeria and Iran. The reason for this, aside from gender discrimination, is that the focus on resources distorts incentives to invest in capital rather than in labor, where more women workers might benefit.

Women are also underrepresented in the political system, but times are changing. Today, 13 percent of parliamentarians in MENA legislatures are women, compared to 19 percent worldwide (and 17 percent in the United States). In 2002, Bahrain set aside five of the thirty seats in its Shura council for women. And in Morocco in the same year, thirty-five women entered the parliament after political parties agreed on a 10 percent quota. Today, both Israel and Iraq have legislatures that are more than 20 percent female. (Table 9-4 presents a summary of key factors in MENA development.)

TABLE 9-4

Key Factors in MENA Development: The Identity Perspective and Levels of Analysis

Level of analysis	Identity perspective		
	Systemic	*Structure*	Strategic battleground between religions and ideologies
		Process	Resource (oil) curse leads to overdependence on exports
	Foreign policy		Military uses foreign aid to sustain authoritarian rule
	Domestic		Inbred authoritarian and religious ideologies cripple public services and discriminate against women
	Individual		Radical individuals become terrorists

Environment

Development both improves and stresses the global environment. Anyone who knows a little history understands that nature in the past was anything but idyllic. Rural life, even with abundant resources, was backbreaking. City life, even with fewer people, was fetid. The atmosphere was virgin but carried deadly diseases and massive storms that wiped away dwellers on land and sea alike. Carbon dioxide was no threat but increased dramatically in prehistoric times as the result of natural occurrences (e.g., volcanic eruptions), not human influence. At the same time, development since industrialization has clearly stressed the environment. Population crowds the Earth; resources are exhausted, at least at affordable prices; pollution, especially that caused by the burning of fossil fuels and emission of carbon dioxide gases, threatens the atmosphere; and pandemics, aided by by modern commerce and travel, spread around the world in a matter of days if not hours. Realist perspectives embrace the competition that drives development and creates the innovations to address environmental issues. Liberal perspectives favor cooperation that treats environmental issues as collective goods. And identity perspectives wonder if the problem requires new identities, national identities that give less emphasis to consumerism and global identities that give less emphasis to nationalism. We look briefly next at the population, resource, pollution, and pandemic aspects of the global environment.

CAUSAL ARROW: PERSPECTIVES

New global and national self-images
Reduce consumerist markets
Preserve planet's environment
IDENTITY
LIBERAL
REALIST

Population

The world's human population lies at the center of the world's environment. Land constitutes about 30 percent of the Earth's surface. As the human population increases, the land becomes crowded; resources are exploited, including animal and plant life; and nutrition and health suffer. Already in the eighteenth century, Thomas Malthus, a British economist and clergyman, predicted that population would outstrip the Earth's ability to feed itself, and famine and disease would follow. Malthus was living through the early days of the Industrial Revolution and might be forgiven for not seeing the potential of technology. Industrialization brought new ways to increase the food supply, but it also added new burdens on the environment. Industrial processes consumed raw materials in large quantities, not only minerals such as iron ore and copper but also, and most important, energy resources such as coal and, later, oil and gas. By spewing chemicals into the air, the human population began to exhaust or destroy other natural resources such as clean air and the protective ozone layer in the Earth's atmosphere. Today, *Malthusian* is a term applied to those who worry about human activity creating environmental burdens that will go beyond the carrying capacity of nature; they call for a limit to human population and industrial growth.

In 2013, there were some 7.2 billion people in the world, and global population is still growing. It is expected to reach 9 billion by 2050 and stabilize thereafter, although some estimates go as high as 15 billion and climbing. Even if it stabilizes, however, population changes will be unevenly distributed around the world. Almost all of the population growth will take place in the developing countries and in already crowded and polluted urban, rather than rural, areas. What is more, because of the way population size changes as living standards improve, most of the population increase will take place in the poorest parts of the developing world, creating throngs of young people with no education, jobs, or future. Youth bulges in the Middle East and Africa will add to political instability, while population declines and aging in the industrialized world may slow growth and create a declining global economic pie. This age gap could build up intolerable tensions and, like an electrical discharge across a voltage gap, spark new streams of immigrants and refugees across national borders, disrupting trade and other global economic activities.

Demographic transitions are periods of accelerating population growth even as living standards increase. Death rates decline first as food supplies increase and access to health care expands. Birthrates change only later as people leave rural areas where more children are needed, the workforce becomes better educated, and the status of women improves. During the interim transition, which can last 50–150 years, the population continues to increase. Only when lower birthrates eventually catch up with lower death rates do population increases stabilize at a lower level.

demographic transitions: periods of accelerating population growth as living standards increase because death rates decline faster than birthrates.

Industrial countries completed this transition a century ago and now face declining population trends. Developing countries fall into two groups: some started the transition forty to fifty years ago and are beginning to see a significant decline in birthrates; others are just starting the transition and face rapid population growth in the near term. East and Southeast Asian nations such as South Korea, Taiwan, Thailand, and, increasingly, China fall into the first group. Sub-Saharan Africa, South Asia, and, to a slightly lesser extent, the Middle East and North Africa fall into the second group. The second group, the poorest countries, like India, will experience the most rapid population increases.

The outcome under these conditions is likely to be demographic disaster caused by starvation, disease, or both.

What is worse, in terms of international implications, population increases in the developing world will be largely among young people, while populations in industrialized nations and some late-transition countries, such as China and Russia, will shift disproportionately to older people. The **youth bulge** is already present in Africa and the Middle East, where in many countries 30–50 percent of the population is under fourteen years of age. The **graying population** of the industrial world is also apparent. In Europe, for example, the number of working-age people will decline over the next twenty-five years by 7 percent, while the number older than sixty-five will increase by 50 percent. This divergence between age groups in industrial and developing countries may both weaken growth and increase violence. Industrial countries may not be able to sustain growth as a larger percentage of their people leave the workforce. And Middle Eastern and African youths who have no jobs may migrate to cities or neighboring countries, where they may stir up unrest and violence.

Studies show that youth bulges are associated with increases in civil and ethnic conflicts. In the 1990s, three demographic factors correlated closely with the likelihood of civil conflict in a country: a youth bulge, rapid urban growth, and exceptionally low levels of cropland and/or freshwater per person.[55] Population imbalances thus spawn conflicts, which in turn induce immigration flows that spread unrest to developed nations. In the early 2000s, legal and illegal immigrants accounted for more than 15 percent of the population in more than fifty countries. By 2015, several million migrants are expected to move annually to North America from Latin America and Asia, to western Europe from MENA as well as eastern Europe, and to richer developing countries from poorer ones. What is more, immigration and refugee flows often mix easily with the drug and sex trades and human trafficking. Population problems, therefore, are a highly mobile and degrading factor for the quality of human life everywhere.

What do we do about population problems? Realist perspectives tend to see population as a factor contributing to national power. Increasing population means more people to work on farms, toil in industries, and fight in armies. In contrast to Europe, for example, the United States has a growing population because it allows freer immigration. Thus, one well-known realist commentator concludes that "it is reasonable to assume that we have only just entered a long era of American hegemony" because "demographic trends show the American population growing faster and getting younger while the European population declines and steadily ages."[56] Large poor countries, of course, might see it differently. China, for example, has pursued a determined policy to reduce its population by enforcing, ruthlessly at times, a one-child-per-couple law. Whether national interests dictate an increase or decrease of population, national governments bear the principal responsibility, as realist perspectives see it, because population is a critical factor in national competition and one-size-fits-all institutions or policies, such as China's one-child policy, do not fit all national situations.

youth bulge: a demographic pattern in which a substantial percentage of the population in a given country is young, typically below the age of fifteen.

graying population: a demographic pattern in which the percentage of a country's population older than sixty-five increases.

Liberal perspectives see the consequences of population increases spilling out over national boundaries and threatening the carrying capacity of the planet itself, not unlike pollution in the atmosphere. Conflict, migration, and refugees carry consequences around the globe like convection currents in the environment. Population growth therefore is a collective, not national, good. It has to be stopped by common institutional efforts to reduce fertility rates, improve nutrition, and control disease. Liberal causes champion global population control through contraception, family planning, and, when necessary, abortion. Planned Parenthood and a host of other NGOs lead the campaign. Foreign aid and international development institutions make major contributions.

Identity perspectives focus on the ideas that lie behind policies to deal with global population problems. Classical liberal and social constructivist perspectives emphasize the emancipation and role of women. They suspect institutions such as nation-states and religious institutions that have oppressed and controlled women and their reproductive rights for centuries. Feminist movements support new concepts of human security to reduce local and domestic violence, where women are more often affected, rejecting old ideas of national security that privilege male-centered institutions such as the nation-state. Faith-based identity groups, such as the Catholic Church, oppose contraception and family planning policies and prefer to educate young people about abstinence and the sanctity of marriage and conception. Ideologically oriented states, such as China, justify abortions and enforce birth control because communist and nationalist ideology takes precedence over women's rights. Finally, deeply religious Muslim states justify oppression in terms of religious law (sharia) that subordinates women to imams, who are exclusively men, and takes precedence over democratic or social constructivist ideologies calling for equal rights for women.

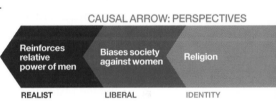

CAUSAL ARROW: PERSPECTIVES

Reinforces relative power of men — **REALIST**

Biases society against women — **LIBERAL**

Religion — **IDENTITY**

Resources

Population and industrial pressures exhaust croplands and food, consume limited energy and water supplies, and destroy animal and plant life. About 600 square meters, or 0.06 hectares, of land—an area roughly the size of a hockey rink—are needed to produce enough food to sustain one person. When countries cannot meet this level of food production, they import food or people move. In Bangladesh, for example, overcrowding in the late 1970s, accompanied by several years of flooding, reduced croplands and forced massive migration across the border into India. By 1990, more than seven million Bangladeshis had made the trek, swelling the population of the Indian state of Assam by more than 50 percent and causing land shortages and conflicts throughout the border regions. We can anticipate large flows of refugees in East Africa, which is already rife with ethnic conflicts. In Pakistan, people flock to urban areas, such as Karachi, and become tinder for popular unrest, violence, and terrorism against local as well as distant governments. Urban sprawl further reduces the availability of needed cropland.

In 2008 and again in 2010, world food prices spiked after more than twenty years of stability. Fears of food shortages led some countries, such as Russia, to embargo grain exports and others, such as Saudi Arabia, to buy up large portions of cropland in countries like Ethiopia, where three-quarters of the arable land is not in use. Kenya leased 100,000 acres of farmland to Qatar, and Tanzania leased 400 square miles to South Korea. The search for farmland focuses on Africa, where the Earth's last large reserves of underused land constitute the billion-acre Guinea Savannah zone, a crescent-shaped swath that runs east across Africa all the way to Ethiopia and southward to DR Congo and Angola. While promising to increase world food supplies, the farmland rush also raises potential threats of agro-imperialism.[57]

Poor people scavenge the Earth for wood to cook their food, and rich nations devour the world's energy resources, especially fossil fuels, to keep their industries going. The loss of forested land contributes to global warming, but equally as important for those who live close by, it reduces the capacity of the land to hold water and contributes to desertification. The Sahara, which stretches across the northern half of Africa, expands annually as many of the world's poorest people strip wooded areas to eke out a paltry existence. The hillsides in Haiti and North Korea are stripped clean of trees. Rich countries, of course, don't need wood for fuel, but they still harvest trees for commercial purposes. And, more important, they mine and burn fossil fuels and use other mineral resources in enormous magnitudes to fire the engines of industrialization.

fossil fuels: coal, oil, and natural gas.

The principal raw materials for industrialization are fossil fuels, iron ore, copper, nickel, zinc, tin, bauxite, platinum, manganese, and chromium. **Fossil fuels**—coal, oil, and natural gas—have the largest consequence for international affairs because they provide 95 percent of world energy consumption and are unevenly distributed. Oil and gas reserves are concentrated in the Middle East, a strategic and unstable part of the world; on the other hand, industrialized countries and rapidly rising countries such as China use the vast majority of all oil and natural gas resources. The existence of massive oil and gas shale deposits, many of which are found in oil-consuming countries such as the United States, might change this picture. But exploiting these resources involves the process of hydraulic fracturing, or fracking—the injection of water under high pressure to break up the rock in which these deposits are trapped—which might have negative environmental consequences. Thus, for the time being, international trade in oil and gas remains enormous and vital.

Moreover, energy use continues to grow. Recent estimates put the world consumption of oil at 88.9 million barrels per day, and consumption is expected to grow anywhere from 100 to 116 million barrels per day by 2030.[58] Consumption of natural gas—the cleanest-burning fossil fuel—will double by 2015 and may account for one-third of energy supply by 2025. It will require a whole new network of tanker and port facilities to transport liquefied natural gas.[59] Oil and gas development, as well as other resource mining, scars and damages the environment, causing periodic oil spills in lakes and oceans and interfering with wildlife in parkland and natural habitats. The 2010 spill in the Gulf of Mexico dumped more than five million barrels of oil into the ocean and onto neighboring shores. As Figure 9-1 shows, between 2003 and 2030 total energy consumption (in BTUs, British thermal units) is expected to more than double in developing (non-OECD) countries while

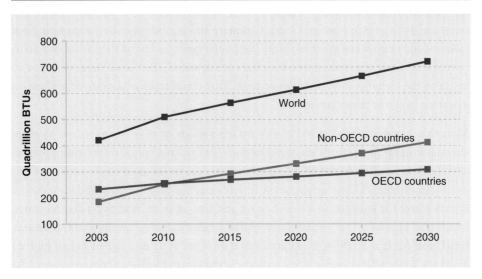

FIGURE 9-1

Projected Energy Consumption, 2003–2030

Source: Data are from the U.S. Department of Energy, Table A1, "World Total Energy Consumption by Region, Reference Case, 1990–2030," http://www.eia.doe.gov/oiaf/ieo/pdf/ieoreftab_1.pdf.

increasing another 30 percent in advanced (OECD) countries. Altogether world energy consumption is predicted to increase by nearly 72 percent.

Other resources are more evenly distributed, although Japan and Europe are generally more dependent on mineral imports than the United States. South Africa controls three-quarters of the world's supplies of manganese and chromium. When it was a pariah in the international community because of its apartheid practices, interest developed in mining manganese and other minerals from the ocean's deep seabed out beyond the territorial claims of littoral states. The Law of the Sea Treaty, negotiated in the 1980s, called for an International Seabed Authority, which would mine manganese and other deep-seabed resources on behalf of all nations. But interest declined after South Africa abandoned apartheid, and early enthusiasm for global commodity agreements to regulate raw material production and trade waned. Nevertheless, resource scarcities were a big concern at the height of the oil crises in the 1970s and have continued to flare up periodically since then.

Water is an old and new resource concern. Civilization began close to rivers and shorelines. Today water disputes are escalating. Water use grew twice as fact as the population during the past century. So, water became more valuable as it became increasingly scarce. One-fifth of the world's population does not have safe drinking water, and

40 percent has no sanitation. Some of the problem arises from nature and the distribution of water, but some is also the result of mismanagement. Water is often subsidized in the same countries where it is scarce.[60] Eighty or more countries suffer water shortages. **Water tables,** or aquifers under the Earth's surface, are sinking, especially in heavily populated countries. In parts of China water levels are falling by five feet per year; throughout India, they are falling at the rate of three to ten feet per year. Lakes and rivers are drying up in western China. Cities are sinking because they're pumping out their underground water reserves. India uses water twice as fast as supplies accumulate, or recharge. Once the underground aquifers are depleted, the use of water will have to be cut to the recharge rate, or by 50 percent. That could reduce harvests dependent on irrigation by as much as one-fourth.

More than one-half of the world's land surface consists of river basins shared by more than one country, and more than thirty nations get one-third of their water supply from outside their borders. In the Middle East and Africa, rivers are a major source of disputes. The Euphrates River originates in Turkey and runs through Syria and Iraq. Turkey diverts water for various uses, which Syria and Iraq oppose. And Syria diverts water, which Iraq opposes. The Jordan River sparks similar disputes among Syria, Lebanon, Israel, and Jordan. In 1964, Israel attacked dams that Syria and Lebanon had built to divert the Jordan River, and in 1967 it captured the Golan Heights, in part to control the upper reaches of the Jordan. Egypt, Sudan, and Ethiopia fight over water from the Nile. China is damming the rivers on the Qinghai-Tibetan plateau, diverting water that would otherwise flow to India and parts of central and South Asia.

Biodiversity refers to the diversity among the multiple species of plant and animal life in nature. Population growth and resource use reduce biodiversity in two ways. First, they lead directly to overhunting, overfishing, and the transplantation of species to areas where they don't belong. Second, they contribute indirectly by eliminating the natural habitats of various plant and animal species, principally through the destruction of rain forests, pollution of rivers and streams, and elimination of agricultural lands, especially wetlands, to accommodate urban sprawl and commercial development. Because the preservation of biodiversity is location-specific, national governments exercise the most control in this area. For example, the United States restricted logging in the U.S. Northwest to save the natural habitat of the northern spotted owl.[61] But international agreements also seek to regulate biodiversity. UN treaties and conventions regulate trade in endangered species and encourage the preservation of such species' natural habitats. Some environmentalists are particularly concerned about whales and dolphins. The International Whaling Commission sets limits on the hunting of certain types of whales, but Norway, Japan, and other countries periodically flout the agreement. Efforts to protect dolphins also affect tuna fishing, restricting fishing methods that catch a lot of dolphins in tuna fishing nets. Under laws to prevent this, the United States banned tuna from Mexico and Venezuela, which reduced Venezuela's tuna fleet to less than one-third of its original size. Mexico and Venezuela complained to the WTO about the U.S. ban, arguing that it was discriminatory. The WTO agreed, sparking a loud outcry

water tables: the aquifers below the Earth's surface that supply freshwater.

biodiversity: the diversity among the multiple species of plant and animal life found in nature.

During a multiyear drought in the early 2000s, women in a village in the Indian state of Gujarat fetch water from a murky water hole shared with animals.

from environmental groups who see the free-trading system running roughshod over environmental concerns.

Pollution and Global Warming

Pollution of the world environment comes in many forms. First, there is **smog**, the belching bile of factories and vehicle exhaust that chokes industrial cities and damages the health of urban residents. While the United States and Europe have curtailed this form of pollution, efforts to reduce smog have only started in the developing world. As one visitor writes, "Smog in Beijing, Shanghai, and other cities reduces visibility most summer days to less than half a mile: when you drive along the elevated highways that cut through Shanghai, office and apartment towers emerge sporadically from the haze and then dissolve away."[62] Second, there is **acid rain**, which results from pollutants that travel in the upper atmosphere and descend in rain, despoiling distant lakes and the plants and wildlife that live in them. Canada complained for years about acid rain caused by pollutants released in the United States. Eventually the two countries signed an agreement to address this transborder pollution problem, but acid rain persists and afflicts numerous other areas. Third, there is **river and ocean pollution**. Industrial effluents, garbage and human sewage, and runoff from agricultural pesticides and fertilizers kill fish and plant life in streams and estuaries, and even in large bodies of water. The Great Lakes and Chesapeake Bay in the United States were badly polluted for years, although they are somewhat improved today; the Mediterranean Sea is still severely polluted.

smog: air pollution, especially as a result of vehicle exhaust and industry.

acid rain: condensation-borne pollutants that may be transported through the upper atmosphere over long distances.

river and ocean pollution: waterway contaminants from industrial and agricultural runoff, garbage, and human sewage.

toxic and hazardous wastes: pollutants from the disposal of petrochemicals, nuclear waste, and other dangerous materials.

Toxic and hazardous wastes constitute the fourth and growing source of pollution. More than 70 percent of China's rivers and lakes are reportedly contaminated with toxic pollutants. In 2005, a petrochemical plant in Jilin, China, northeast of Beijing, exploded and dumped one hundred tons of chemicals into the Songhua River, which then flowed north as a fifty-mile-long toxic slick through other Chinese cities and into Russia.[63] The 1986 nuclear accident at Chernobyl in the former Soviet Union created radioactive pollutants that reached Italy and Sweden and made an entire region in what is now Ukraine uninhabitable for a decade or more. The Aral Sea in the former Soviet Union, now bordering on Kazakhstan and Uzbekistan, shriveled up by 50 percent because a massive Soviet agricultural project to grow cotton diverted and polluted the inland rivers that flowed into the sea. Environmentalists have given up on reclaiming it; it was once the fourth-largest inland sea in the world.

ozone layer: the outer layer of the Earth's atmosphere that protects the planet from solar radiation.

global warming: the heating up of the Earth's atmosphere caused by greenhouse gas emissions.

Altering the outermost blanket of the Earth's atmosphere is the fifth and perhaps most serious form of pollution. Two threats exist. One is destruction of the **ozone layer**, which protects the Earth from harmful solar radiation. The second is contamination of the Earth's atmosphere with greenhouse gases, principally carbon dioxide, which trap heat and, assuming we can control for all the other factors affecting climate, cause **global warming**. The two threats tell different stories. The world community, including top corporations, pulled together to establish a common approach to deal with ozone depletion. The liberal and perhaps identity perspectives seemed to prevail, reflecting common regimes and perhaps a new global civil society of corporations and NGOs demanding more accountability. By contrast, the world community is still divided over the causes and solutions to global warming. Developing countries, such as China and India, see it primarily as an advanced-country problem. Advanced countries, including the United States, worry that if the developing countries don't participate in efforts to reduce carbon emissions, the reductions achieved by advanced countries alone will do little good. Let's look at these threats more closely.

chlorofluoro-carbons (CFCs): chemicals that break down the ozone layer.

Montreal Protocol: an international agreement reached in 1987 that set the specific goal of reducing the use of chlorofluorocarbons by 50 percent by 1998.

The ozone layer is depleted by certain chemicals once used widely by industrial countries in refrigeration and aerosol sprays. These chemicals, primarily **chlorofluorocarbons (CFCs)**, rise to the top of the atmosphere and interact with ozone, breaking it down and reducing the ozone layer. The thinning of the ozone layer leads to increases in human diseases such as skin cancer and disruptions in plant and animal life. For a time, the evidence linking CFCs to ozone depletion was disputed, but the costs of doing something about CFCs were far less than the costs associated with eliminating greenhouse gases. Thus, by the mid-1980s the world community, including major MNCs such as DuPont and Dow Chemical, began to move toward consensus and action. The Vienna Convention for the Protection of the Ozone Layer was adopted in 1985; this international agreement provided a general framework for the adoption of more substantive protocols. In 1987, twenty-two states negotiated the **Montreal Protocol**, which set the specific goal of reducing CFCs by 50 percent by 1998. In 1990, the timetable was accelerated, and eighty-one states agreed to eliminate all CFCs by 2000. When it was discovered in the early 1990s that an actual hole in the ozone layer had emerged above Antarctica, the timetable was accelerated once again. The advanced countries agreed to phase out CFCs by 1995 and to provide aid to third-world countries to do the same by 2010. Advanced countries met the deadline and gave developing countries some $2 billion to help them meet their deadline. But, because of time lags, even the reduced levels of CFCs will not show immediate results. The real verification of the science linking CFCs and ozone depletion won't come until ozone depletion actually begins to recede in line with the elimination of CFCs.

The science and costs of global warming are considerably more controversial.[64] The problem first received widespread international attention in the 1980s. The United Nations invited the UN Environment Programme, which had been created in 1972, and the World Meteorological Organization to form the Intergovernmental Panel on Climate Change (IPCC), a gathering of some two thousand climate experts, to investigate the problem. The panel reported in 1990 that the Earth was indeed gradually warming and that human activity, specifically the production of **greenhouse gases** from burning fossil fuels—mostly carbon dioxide, the rest methane, CFCs, and nitrous oxide—was the contributing cause. The UN Conference on Environment and Development took up the issue in Rio de Janeiro, Brazil, in June 1992. It launched the UN Framework Convention on Climate Change, which called for holding emissions of greenhouse gases to 1990 levels. Meeting later in Japan in 1997, the participating countries adopted the **Kyoto Protocol**, which set deadlines of 2008–2012 for industrial countries to cut average emissions per year by 5 percent below 1990 levels. The developing countries were exempted. The United States, which accounts for about 35 percent of industrial-country emissions, initially signed but then withdrew from the protocol. The protocol entered into force in 2005, after Russia ratified it and the signatories reached the required number of states accounting for 55 percent of all greenhouse gases produced by industrialized countries.

In 2007, when it won the Nobel Peace Prize, the IPCC asserted that human activity or the increase in greenhouse gases was "very likely," at a 90 percent confidence level, to be the principal cause of global warming.[65] In 2013, it upped its confidence level to 95 percent.

Initially the United States led the opposition to the Kyoto Protocol, arguing that the evidence on the dangers of greenhouse gases was incomplete and that a market-based incremental approach would be better than a top-down regulatory agreement. In 2009, however, the Obama administration joined talks in Copenhagen, Denmark, to negotiate a successor agreement to Kyoto. Based on amendments negotiated in 2012, thirty-seven countries accepted binding commitments for the 2013–2018 period to lower carbon emissions, but the United States was not one of them. Complicating matters, the climate talks were marred in 2009–2010 by a scandal involving leaked e-mails purporting to show efforts by IPCC scientists to conceal or water down evidence conflicting with dire warnings of global warming.[66]

greenhouse gases: emissions from fossil fuels and other sources that can cause climate change.

Kyoto Protocol: an agreement reached in 1997 that set deadlines of 2008–2012 for industrial countries to cut their greenhouse gas emissions.

Two arguments are made against a new and more stringent protocol requiring the reduction of carbon emissions: the scientific evidence contains many uncertainties, and the solution of reducing greenhouse gases to 1990 levels is too costly and will be ineffective if it excludes developing countries. The evidence that the Earth is warming is accepted, and the increase in greenhouse gas emissions is also well documented. The scientific dispute is about the link between the two factors. Is the correlation between warming and carbon emissions causal or coincidental? In the case of the depletion of the ozone layer, as physicist Lisa Randall tells us, "chemists were able to detail the precise chemical processes involved in the destruction of the ozone layer, making the evidence that chlorofluorocarbon gases (Freon, for example) were destroying the ozone layer indisputable." But in the case of global warming, she writes, "even if we understand some effects of carbon dioxide in the atmosphere, it is difficult to predict the precise chain of events that a marked increase in carbon dioxide will cause."[67] The Earth's climate has warmed and cooled in cycles for centuries. Ice core samples show warming and cooling trends every 1,500 years going back long before industrialization.[68] In the short run, too, fluctuations occur. The Earth was cooling before 1970, but it has been warming since then, although temperatures leveled out over the past decade. Today, the ice pack around Antarctica is growing and set a record for coverage in 2007, while the ice pack in the Arctic is shrinking.[69]

The climate system is extraordinarily complex. According to a report by the nonpartisan Council on Foreign Relations, uncertainties in climate science include the role of clouds, some of which warm the environment while others cool it; the sun's activity and changes in the Earth's magnetic field, which shields the Earth from solar radiation; the many natural processes that cycle carbon between its different forms (for example, carbon sinks such as rain forests absorb carbon dioxide and then release it when they are destroyed); the still rather coarse resolution of computer models that assign the same temperature to large areas; the possibility of abrupt changes as the result of feedback effects, such as alterations in the circulation of the oceans; and, finally, the weighing of human factors, such as politics, law, and institutions, that involve trade-offs with future generations and the costs of losing species.[70] Many scientists admit that computer climate models are still very crude, yet they believe that the dangers are sufficient to warrant action.[71] The uncertainties divide industries as well as governments. ExxonMobil, like many corporations in the energy industry, opposes an abrupt shift away from fossil fuels. But Royal Dutch Shell and British Petroleum support heavy investments in alternative fuels.[72]

Even if science demonstrates a link between human activity and global warming, at least in the judgment of many scientists, the next issue concerns how much we are willing to pay to solve the problem. On the basis of purely economic costs and benefits, one panel of leading world experts ranked the probable dangers of global warming below that of other critical problems such as HIV/AIDS, malaria, and lack of sanitation.[73] To keep temperatures from rising by 2 degrees Celsius would require a global tax on carbon

emissions that might cost the world as much as $40 trillion a year by the end of the twenty-first century. What are the opportunity costs here? What else must be sacrificed to achieve this goal? China and India discount the dangers of global warming if addressing the issue will slow down their economic growth. They see the Kyoto Protocol, as future generations might see it, as a way of transferring the costs to them for the carbon sins of their predecessors, in this case the industrialized countries.

Small island nations like the Maldives (shown here) are working together to prepare a common strategy to fight rising sea levels that threaten to submerge them.

The problem of global warming illustrates the complexity of integrating scientific knowledge and social preferences. If the Earth warms up significantly, the consequences could be catastrophic. Ice caps will melt; ocean levels will rise; whole island complexes, such as the Maldives off the coast of India, where the highest point is only eight feet above sea level, could disappear; gulf streams will shift and affect temperatures; crops and wildlife will be decimated across wide swaths of existing continents; and weather patterns will change, causing more frequent and increasingly violent hurricanes and other storms. (Map 9-6 shows which areas of the world are most vulnerable to the damage that climate change could bring.) But the probability of these events is smaller than the likelihood of pandemics, wars, or other natural and human-created catastrophes. It would be nice to safeguard against every danger, but the world of policy making, no less than the world of understanding international relations, requires priorities, selection, perspective, and judgment.

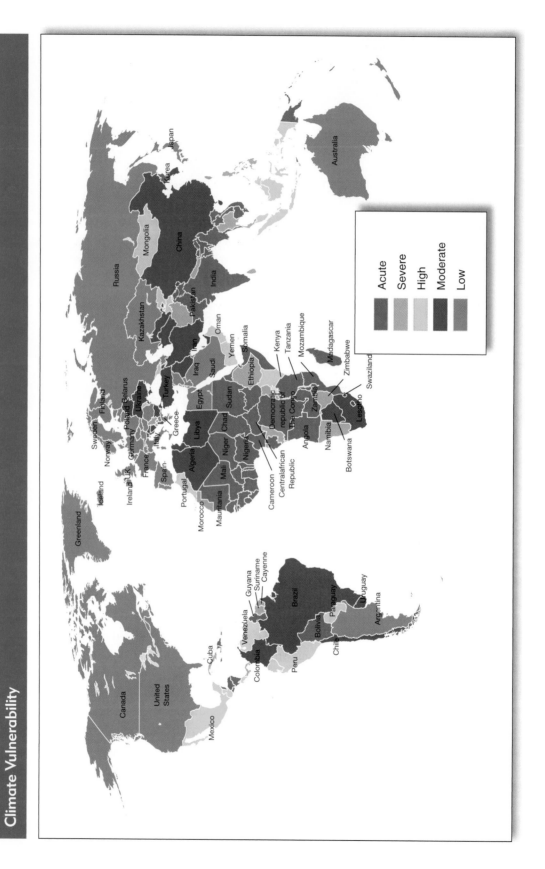

MAP
9-6

Climate Vulnerability

Acute
Severe
High
Moderate
Low

Greenland

Canada

United States

Mexico

Cuba

Venezuela
Colombia
Guyana
Suriname
Cayenne
Peru
Brazil
Bolivia
Paraguay
Chile
Uruguay
Argentina

Iceland
Ireland
UK
Norway
Sweden
Finland
Poland
Belarus
Germany
France
Italy
Spain
Portugal
Greece
Ukraine
Turkey

Russia

Kazakhstan

Mongolia

China

Korea

Japan

India

Pakistan

Iran

Iraq

Saudi

Oman

Yemen

Egypt

Sudan

Ethiopia

Somalia

Libya

Chad

Niger

Mali

Nigeria

Mauritania

Morocco

Algeria

Cameroon

Centralafrican
Republic

Democratic
republic of
The Congo

Kenya

Tanzania

Mozambique

Madagascar

Zimbabwe

Zambia

Angola

Namibia

Botswana

Lesotho

Swaziland

Australia

Pandemics

Diseases are closely interconnected with the human and natural environment. There are about 1,500 known infectious diseases, 60 percent of which affect both animals and humans. The rest infect animals only but carry the potential to affect human beings and could eventually mutate so that they can be passed from human to human. AIDS, which is now transmitted by human sexual activity, originated among primates in Africa, and the avian flu virus originated in domesticated birds and has infected human beings.

The world has long battled infectious diseases. The World Health Organization (WHO), a UN specialized agency, was established in 1948 and led postwar campaigns to eradicate smallpox, polio, and tuberculosis. It succeeded in the case of smallpox, but tuberculosis and polio have since made a comeback. Each year almost 12 million people contract tuberculosis and 990,000 people die from it. An outbreak of polio in Syria in late 2013 triggered massive vaccination campaigns targeting children. Estimates indicate that malaria kills 660,000 people annually and about 219 million people are infected.[74] In recent decades, more than three dozen new infectious diseases have appeared, including hemorrhagic fevers caused by the Ebola virus; severe acute respiratory syndrome, or SARS; and influenza caused by the H5N1 "bird flu" virus.

Pandemics are not new. The Black Plague killed 25 million people, or one-third of the European population, in the fourteenth century. In 1918–1919, the Spanish flu killed 40–50 million people in eighteen months, with some estimates going as high as 100 million. That's many times more than the number of people who died in the fighting in World War I. It's easy to see why pandemics may qualify as national security threats. Two lesser flu epidemics in 1957–1958 and 1968–1969 killed 70,000 and 34,000 people, respectively, just in the United States. One institute estimates that a mild bird flu epidemic as virulent as the flu epidemic in 1968 would kill 1.4 million people and cost $330 billion; an epidemic as severe as the 1918 flu would kill 142 million people and cost $4.4 trillion.[75]

pandemics: outbreaks of infectious diseases such as AIDS, avian flu, and SARS that spread or threaten to spread worldwide.

Each year, a WHO committee decides which flu strains should be included in the annual flu vaccine. More than a dozen international drug companies are researching new vaccines, but only a limited number of companies currently produce vaccines. The number has shrunk from two dozen in 1980 to a handful today. NGOs such as the Global Alliance for Vaccines and Immunization, sponsored by the Bill and Melinda Gates Foundation and others, have stepped up efforts to develop new vaccines and drugs, especially for diseases prevalent in developing countries.

MNCs also contribute. Pharmaceutical and biotechnology companies have launched some sixty projects in recent years to develop new treatments.[76] Merck, the U.S. pharmaceutical giant, donated drugs to eradicate river blindness, a scourge that affected tens of millions of Africans living near rivers (the disease is caused by parasitic worms that work their way through the skin behind the eyes and blind the victims). GlaxoSmithKline, AstraZeneca, and Novartis have built new research centers focusing on neglected diseases. MNCs spend millions of dollars to develop new drugs and then, not surprisingly, file patents and charge high prices to recoup their costs. These high prices in turn—for example, for the antiretroviral drugs used in the treatment of AIDS—often deny help to millions of poor people in developing regions. WHO and NGOs such as the Treatment Action Campaign (sponsored by Oxfam, Africa Action, and others) have lobbied drug companies to reduce their prices on drugs needed in developing countries. Brazilian and Indian companies have also introduced cheap generic versions of some drugs. Prices have gone down, but tensions persist.

Drug companies can't operate without profits and fear the additional liability associated with manufacturing vaccines. When the United States faced a swine flu scare in 1976, Congress asked pharmaceutical companies to manufacture vaccines in haste. The companies, in turn, asked Congress to assume liability, and Congress wound up paying out $90 million to claimants who had received the vaccine and suffered side effects; twenty-five people died.[77] Although Congress vowed never to assume such liability again, the Bush administration passed legislation in 2006 that granted liability protection to manufacturers whose products are used in public health emergencies.[78] Still, manufacturers have never made more than 400 million doses of vaccine in any single year. If an outbreak of avian flu were to become an epidemic, some 5–6 billion doses might be needed.

WHO is one of the largest and most technical international institutions. It has laboratories all over the world and works closely with the Food and Agriculture Organization (FAO), another UN specialized agency, which monitors flu epidemics in animals and advises governments on vaccinations and on culling infected flocks or herds. But can expertise suffice, or will an epidemic involve major political stakes? The World Health Assembly, WHO's main decision-making body, has three delegates from each country—one from the scientific community, one from a professional organization, and one from the nongovernmental community. These delegates then select thirty-two members to sit on the assembly's executive board. By convention, the board is supposed to include at least three members from the UN Security Council, not necessarily from the veto powers. Thus, WHO comes close to being a purely technical institution that tries to pay as little attention to power and politics as possible. It succeeds in part, but it also remains relatively small, with a budget of about $4 billion a year (less than half of the city of Chicago's annual budget).

"Synthetic genomics" presents a new challenge to the world community. Laboratory researchers can now create deadly viruses from genetic code. In 2011 Erasmus Medical Center in Rotterdam, the Netherlands, created a strain from the H5N1 avian flu virus that transmits the disease from human to human. Up to that point, only 565 human cases of H5N1 were known, all infected by birds; 59 percent of those infected died. If the disease becomes able to jump from human to human, millions might be affected. WHO convened summits to address such "dual use research of concern," biological research that, like nuclear or chemical research, has both beneficial and potentially catastrophic effects.[79]

CAUSAL ARROW: LEVELS OF ANALYSIS

National priorities	Impede work of international institutions	Override common humanity concerns
DOMESTIC	SYSTEMIC	INDIVIDUAL

But are expert groups such as the delegates of WHO up to the task of leading the world in dealing with a major epidemic? Realist perspectives doubt it. They believe that countries threatened by a major epidemic will put the interests of their own people first. The countries will isolate those who become infected and quarantine visitors who might spread the disease. Such measures will likely close borders and interrupt trade. If vaccines are in scarce supply, individual countries will treat their own people first. The United States already has contracts that will allow it to buy up at least 600 million of the 1 billion doses of flu vaccine that might be produced in an emergency.[80] Tamiflu, the only antiviral drug available against the avian flu virus, is being hoarded by some groups and was manufactured in 2005 by only one company in Switzerland. And there might be shortages of other supplies, such as mechanical ventilators, respiratory protection masks, and even hospitals. As Laurie Garrett points out, "In the event of a deadly influenza pandemic, it is doubtful that the world's wealthy nations would be able to meet the needs of their own citizenry—much less those of other countries."[81] The reality, according to realist perspectives, is that pandemics are now, in terms of the numbers of dead that might be involved, the equivalent of military attacks. They are matters, therefore, of the highest national security concern and cannot be entrusted to international institutions any more than the nation's defense might be. Domestic priorities take precedence over international institutions and common humanity concerns.

Identity perspectives lament the fact that this national security picture is precisely the problem. People continue to see themselves divided into separate nation-states and ignore the larger reality that they are affected by what happens in other countries and cannot solve these problems by barricading themselves off from one another. Poor nations are especially at risk. If nothing else, national security interests have to be recast to address collective security issues. Nations need a sense of common human purpose and destiny and have to reconstitute their loyalties to take into account human, not just national, security.

CAUSAL ARROW: PERSPECTIVES

Facilitates common approach to pandemics	Overrides national security concerns	Common human purpose
LIBERAL	REALIST	IDENTITY

The instinct is certainly laudable, but on the basis of which ideas do common institutions decide? Do they decide on the traditional basis of "one nation, one vote," regard-

TABLE 9-5

Key Factors in the Environment: The Identity Perspective and Levels of Analysis

Level of analysis	Identity perspective		
	Systemic	*Structure*	Planet Earth, pandemics invite a common outlook
		Process	IPCC studies and reports regularly on the state of climate change
	Foreign policy		Elites play off environmental obligations to foreign countries against development objectives of domestic constituents
	Domestic		Fearful countries stockpile vaccines and other equipment to fight pandemics
	Individual		Individuals carry infectious diseases across national boundaries

less of how much individual nations contribute or whether they govern in a manner accountable to their citizens? Or do they decide on the basis of "one person, one vote," which would require more accountable and transparent governments? When the SARS epidemic broke out in China in 2002, Chinese officials at first concealed vital information, which impeded a rapid response to the epidemic. In a nondemocratic society and a world of separate nation-states, who disciplines this kind of behavior? Table 9-5 summarizes key environmental developments from the different levels of analysis.

SUMMARY

Development, or the spread of material, institutional, and human progress, is necessary but not easy. Poorer countries start from traditions and historical legacies that are different from those that influenced development in today's advanced countries. But the record suggests that progress is possible and countries are not doomed by colonialism or oppression. Asian countries experienced more recent colonialism and more frequent regional wars than Latin American countries,

yet they grew faster over the past fifty years, and today China and India, the two most populous countries in the world, are leading the development competition. The reasons for their outperformance of the Latin American countries are multiple, but open world markets and responsible domestic policies played key roles. Foreign aid mattered much less. (See Table 9-6 for comparisons of the development experiences of the four regions discussed in this chapter.)

TABLE 9-6

Comparing Development Experiences

SUB-SAHARAN AFRICA Dependence on aid	LATIN AMERICA Independence
• Little trade • Bad governance • Lots of economic aid	• Little trade—import substitution • Unstable governance • Less aid
NORTH AFRICA AND THE MIDDLE EAST Dependence on oil	ASIA Interdependence
• More trade—resource curse • Oppressive governance • Lots of geopolitical aid	• Export-led growth • Good governance • Least aid

Environment and development go together, both as causes and as solutions. As advanced countries age and developing countries experience a youth bulge, population pressures build up to slow economic growth and increase immigrant and refugee flows. Industrial pressures on natural resources now come

from rapidly developing countries such as China and India, as well as from advanced countries, and accelerate the world's dependence and interdependence on oil and gas trade. Pollution further integrates the world community, despoiling the air, rivers, lakes, and even the oceans. Most important, chemicals released by human activity deplete the ozone layer and arguably warm the planet, creating a threat to planet Earth equivalent to an invading extraterrestrial force. Add to that the growing prospects of pandemics as large as the 1918 Spanish flu, which killed more people than the fighting in World War I, and the planet has ample reason to address its future cooperatively if it is going to survive.

 Sharpen your skills with SAGE edge at **edge.sagepub.com/nau4e**. **SAGE edge for students** provides a personalized approach to help you accomplish your coursework goals in an easy-to-use learning environment.

KEY CONCEPTS

acid rain, 439

Asian values, 400

basic human needs, 411

biodiversity, 438

brain drain, 423

capital flight, 408

chlorofluorocarbons (CFCs), 440

concessional loans, 424

crony capitalism, 399

debt relief, 424

demographic transitions, 433

development, 386

East Asian Miracle, 391

economic autarky, 409

ejido system, 411

financial repression, 407

fossil fuels, 436

global warming, 440

graying population, 434

greenhouse gases, 441

informal sector, 410

Kyoto Protocol, 441

land reform, 396

lost decade, 403

microfinancing, 399

Millennium Development Goals, 424

Montreal Protocol, 440

official development assistance (ODA), 424

ozone layer, 440

pandemics, 445

paternalism, 412

rent-seekers, 407

river and ocean pollution, 439

smog, 439

toxic and hazardous wastes, 440

water tables, 438

youth bulge, 434

STUDY QUESTIONS

1. What are the different meanings of and ways to measure development?

2. Contrast the different perspectives on development. Which perspective emphasizes each of the following factors: market forces, culture and democracy, and monopolies or rent-seekers? Explain why.

3. What were the main differences in policies pursued by Asian, Latin American, MENA, and African countries? What were the strengths and weaknesses of each approach?

4. What are the differences between the world community's success in dealing with the problem of ozone depletion and its failure thus far to deal with the problem of global warming?

5. In what sense are natural resources, energy, and raw materials exhaustible? Which perspectives emphasize markets, regulations, and ideology as the causes and solutions of resource use?

In June 2013, thousands of protesters march in Frankfurt, Germany's financial district in a "Blockupy" demonstration against capitalism, European Central Bank debt policy, and the exploitation of textile workers in third-world countries, among other issues.

10 CRITICAL THEORY PERSPECTIVES ON GLOBALIZATION

Inequality, Imperialism, and Injustice

In the previous two chapters our discussion of globalization focused primarily on the contemporary era—globalization 3.0. Let's begin this chapter on critical theory perspectives on globalization by rewinding to globalization 1.0, starting with the observation that, while recorded world history is about five thousand years old, the world economy is only about five hundred years old. This allows us to circle back to a key question that this fact raises: What happened around 1500 that suddenly drove the world together and produced modern-day globalization? Why did much of the West in particular see a surge in trade and development?

The mainstream perspectives on international relations have some answers. The identity perspective attributes the rapid development of Europe relative to the rest of the world largely to Renaissance, Reformation, and Enlightenment ideas that inspired the Protestant ethic of scientific, technological, and commercial achievement. As Max Weber, the well-known German sociologist, points out, prior to the Reformation the activities of invention and making money were not looked on as worthy callings in Europe or anywhere else in the world.[1] Protestantism made them acceptable. Not surprisingly, from this perspective, Protestant—not Catholic, Muslim, or Confucian—countries led the process of modernization. Britain launched the industrial revolution, and the United States, its offspring, later pioneered the information revolution.

The realist perspective attributes Europe's ascendance primarily to demography, geography, and the decentralized distribution of power. Europe's population dipped in the tenth and eleventh centuries as a result of the Viking and other invasions and dipped again in the fourteenth century as a result of the Black Plague. But thereafter Europe's population grew vigorously. It fanned out to find more space to grow grain and raise animals. China's agriculture, by contrast, was based on rice and required less space. Thus, China had less motive to expand. According to Pulitzer Prize–winning author Jared Diamond, Europe had a number of environmental advantages over other continents: larger choice of wild plants and animals available for domestication, which enhanced food production and released people to pursue the kinds of specialty crafts that help develop technology; denser population more conducive to the development of resistance to virulent germs; and orientation of its continental axes predominantly from east to west rather than north to south, which accelerated the spread of food production and other technologies.[2] Another favorable factor, emphasized by Paul Kennedy, was the decentralized competition for "ships and firepower."[3] When Columbus sought resources to sail around the world, he was turned down by one monarch after the other. After many years, the Spanish monarchs, Ferdinand and Isabella, finally supported him. By contrast, when a Chinese explorer, Wang Chin, applied in 1479 to explore the Indochinese kingdom of Annam (now Vietnam), he was turned down by the Chinese emperor and had no other monarch to go to. Separate powers—the pope and the Holy Roman Emperor initially, and later multiple states—always struggled to control Europe. Rivalry among the many European monarchs and states spurred progress and enabled Europe to colonize and exploit more centralized, less dynamic empires in other parts of the world.[4]

The liberal perspective traces Western success to technology, specialization, and institutional innovations, such as the modern factory, markets, and domestic and international bureaucracy. Technology was an exogenous factor that multiplied the output of human and animal labor. Its impact, although initially disruptive, was generally progressive over the longer run. Specialization, or the division of labor in which parties specialize to make common or different products, offered unique advantages. From a liberal perspective, which emphasizes relationships and repetitive interactions, such specialization meant that workers became more efficient. By dividing tasks so that each person concentrated on only one component of a product, they produced more together than any individual could produce by trying to make all the components. It also meant that workers could exchange products on a relatively open basis. Specialization became the basis for the emergence of more sophisticated systems of exchange or markets. By contrast, realist perspectives see specialization more in terms of hierarchy and control of exchanges through domestic bureaucracies (e.g., factories) and the international structure of power, while identity perspectives emphasize the ideologies, such as capitalism and Marxism, that motivate specialization.

Trade institutionalized the practice of specialization at the international level and created the attendant need to lower transaction costs. According to economic historian Douglass North, increasing specialization and trade initially raised the transaction costs of exchanges. When trade takes place over longer distances, people do not know one another, as they do in villages. They have to spend more money to find out who owns a particular piece of property, what a fair price for that item might be, and how they might ensure its delivery. From the fifteenth century on, state and international institutions emerged in part to handle these tasks and lower the transaction costs of long-distance trade. As a result, Europe developed "more complex forms of organization" than the traditional exchanges in the Middle East (the souk or bazaar) and Asia (the caravan trade).[5]

When and what kind of state institutions took shape also mattered. A country started on a certain path and accumulated advantages or disadvantages along that path, what liberal perspectives call path dependence. England, for example, got an early start toward decentralized institutions when English lords forced King John to sign the Magna Carta in 1215. It passed these institutions on to the United States. By contrast, Spain, when it united, adopted Castile's centralized bureaucratic system rather than Aragon's decentralized merchant system, and France compounded already centralized Capetian institutions with policies of economic nationalism advocated by Jean-Baptiste Colbert in the seventeenth century. Out of their decentralized institutions, England and the United States went on to create innovative societies that started the industrial and information revolutions. A more centralized France developed later and never quite as efficiently, while Spain and its colonies in Latin America developed even more centralized, paternalistic institutions, such as a large, landowning church, which were less friendly to change and innovation.

What's wrong with these mainstream answers to the question of why the West developed faster than the rest? Remember that the purpose of mainstream perspectives is to understand objectively—that is, independent of the observer or scholar—how the world works by designing propositions or hypotheses (perspectives) about what causes events and then testing these hypotheses against the facts. If the propositions are not falsified, mainstream perspectives try to take this knowledge from the past and apply it to improve or predict the future.

Now comes the rub. Think for a minute about what mainstream conclusions are doing when they are applied to future world development. They establish the West, which has been dominant since 1500, and its experiences as the standard for thinking about and shaping the future of other societies. First, according to identity perspectives, if other countries want to become modern, they have to adopt the Western ideas of the Renaissance, Reformation, and Enlightenment. Second, according to realist perspectives, they may not be able to develop independently because geography and demography appear to favor the Western countries. To the extent that they can develop at all, they may have to do so under the hegemonic rule and stability offered by Western powers. Third, according to liberal perspectives, developing countries have to implement the Western rules and institutions of specialization, comparative advantage, multinational corporations, open markets, and pluralist political systems. In short, the mainstream perspectives suggest that development is a universalistic process that follows a single course initially set by Western ideas, power, and institutions.

Critical theory roundly rejects this conclusion. It contends that Western development is not a product of internal Western ideas, institutions, and competition that can serve as models for future development. Rather, it is a consequence of the systematic *exploitation* of other countries. This exploitation involves military *imperialism* and

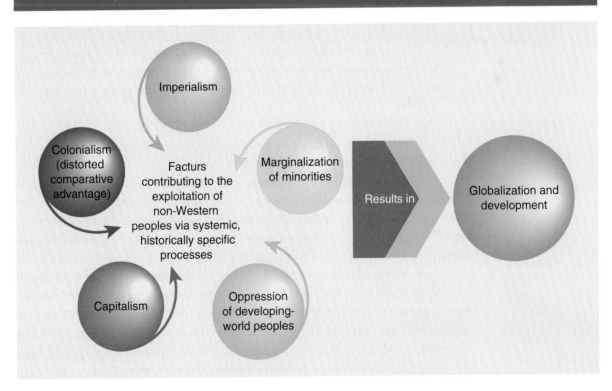

FIGURE 10-1

Critical Theory Perspective on Globalization: Globalization as Consequence, Not Cause

colonialism, which began around 1500 and continue to the present day. It involves, further, the cultural *marginalization* of foreign societies, creating two categories of countries: countries that are Western and advanced, and all the other countries, which are non-Western and undeveloped, primitive, savage—indeed, uncivilized. In addition, it imposes the economic institutions of *capitalism,* in particular the unique oppressive mechanism of the factory and now MNCs, which extract profits from local labor to finance the cosmopolitan consumerism of elite classes. Most of all, Western development was achieved on the backs of women and minorities, who were literally slaves in the colonial era and remain practically so today—oppressed and disenfranchised in the sweatshops and squalid slums spawned in developing countries by globalization. (Each of the concepts italicized above is defined further in the discussion that follows.)

What is more, this exploitation was not carried out piecemeal by individual countries such as Spain and England acting independently or through isolated forces such as Western ideas, institutions, and military forces causing specific outcomes. It was carried out through systemic and historical processes deeply rooted in the structures of particular eras. What made the globalization of the world economy so encompassing and relentless was the fact that it stemmed not just from material circumstances but from cultural, social, institutional, and even spiritual conditions of capitalism. Karl Marx marveled at the power of the bourgeoisie movement that ignited globalization. As John Micklethwait and Adrian Wooldridge observe,

> In less than a hundred years, Marx argued, the bourgeoisie had "accomplished wonders far surpassing Egyptian pyramids, Roman aqueducts and Gothic cathedrals"; had conducted "expeditions that put in the shade all former exoduses of nations and crusades"; and had "created more massive and more colossal productive forces" than all the preceding generations put together.[6]

Thus, as critical theory perspectives see it, globalization is driven by a totalistic (not sequential) logic that cannot be steered or stopped. But it can be understood within a historical period, and the consciousness of the people can be raised to oppose it. As Robert Cox, a respected critical theorist, writes, "Positivism [that is, Western rationalist or mainstream perspectives] can be useful but only within 'defined historical limits.'"[7] Critical studies help unpack specific historical periods and reveal the contradictions and conflicts driving events at a deeper level. These contradictions and conflicts locate marginalized voices and, most of all, demonstrate that another future is possible. Critical theory does not see the future constructed from a set of propositions tested against the past and applied to the future. Rather, it sees a future without the past or other than the past. That future is one in which marginal and minority voices are emancipated, global inequities are lessened, and inclusive institutions prevail. Such a future must be imagined, and therein lies the normative, even utopian, element of critical theories.

>>> Colonialism and Imperialism

From a critical theory perspective, it is hardly a coincidence that Western development began at the same time as Western colonialism. European voyages to discover and colonize other parts of the world began in the fifteenth century. Portugal led the way, capturing Cueta (today a part of Spain) on the northern coast of Africa across from Gibraltar in 1415. By the end of that century, Portuguese explorers had worked their way down the western coast of Africa and initiated voyages around the Cape of Good Hope to the Far East, reaching India and China in the early decades of the sixteenth century. Along the way, they established bases in the Persian Gulf and Malacca, on the west coast of the Malay Peninsula.

colonialism: conquest and exploitation by the European states of poorer peoples and lands in Latin America, Africa, and Asia.

Meanwhile, Spain carved out an empire in another direction. Columbus's voyage in 1492 opened up the Americas, initially the various islands of the Caribbean and then the vast interiors of Central and South America. It was not that Western technology and ideas were that superior to those of the countries colonized. Chinese navigating techniques were as advanced as Portuguese techniques; Chinese ships had already reached the eastern shores of Africa in the early 1400s.[8] And Western ideas that brought slavery and the righteous wrath of Christianity to colonial shores were hardly the liberating forces of the Renaissance or Reformation. Rather, from a critical theory perspective, it was historical happenstance and the unusual cunning of Western adventurers that made the difference. When Spain joined Portugal to contest foreign lands, the two monarchies literally divided the world into two parts rather than fight one another over its boundless resources. At the Treaty of Tordesillas in 1494, they drew a straight line south of the tip of Greenland (370 leagues west of the Cape Verde Islands) across the middle of the Atlantic Ocean, hiving off the easternmost section of South America. Portugal took the territories east of this line, essentially today's Brazil, Africa, and Macau. Spain took everything west of the line, essentially the rest of the Americas and the Philippines. The audacity of partitioning the then-known universe illustrated the Western mind-set of **imperialism** that carved up the world to dominate other societies, militarily, economically, and politically.

imperialism: the forceful extension of a nation's authority to other peoples by military, economic, and political domination.

When the English and Dutch, under the impetus of the Reformation, revolted against Spain and the Hapsburg Empire in the sixteenth and seventeenth centuries, these two sea powers challenged and eventually supplanted Spain and Portugal. France, too, although more of a land power, joined the colonization effort. The later colonial powers transformed the character of colonization. Whereas Spain and Portugal conquered in the name of their monarchs, England and Holland did so in the name of commercial companies, the East India companies, that presaged the age of MNCs. In all cases, however, the motives and methods of conquest were the same. Early colonizers bought cotton cloth in India, exchanged it for slaves in Africa, shipped slaves to Central and South America to mine gold and silver, and used gold and silver to purchase spices and silks in the Far East. The imperialists ransacked the gold and silver in colonial territories and enslaved the human population to work the mines and later the plantations—sugar, cotton, tobacco, and rubber—that did the plundering. Altogether, some ten million slaves were transported from Africa to the New World. Untold millions more died en route or in the local wars among rival tribes in Africa that supplied the slaves.

exploitation: the extraction of profits from the resources and labor of others in an unjust way.

Eventually, as Map 10-1 shows, the West colonized the entire world. The devastation done to the cultures and institutions of local societies was severe and long lasting. At the core, according to critical theory perspectives, was the phenomenon of **exploitation**. Growth was not a process of mutual benefit and gain, a non-zero-sum game; rather, it was a zero-sum game, a process by which a dominant country or class systematically extracted profits from a subordinate country or class and drew that country/class into a tight system of global interconnections from which it was impossible to escape. These connections made it possible for the dominant country/class to strip the subordinate of its just returns and transfer these returns systematically to the dominant center. With the coming of the industrial revolution, the phenomenon of exploitation took on even more sinister dimensions. It led subsequently to the developments of dependency and world systems dynamics that continue to characterize the world economy to the present day.

≫ Dependency

From a critical theory perspective, colonialism was not just a historical phenomenon. It cut deeply into the fabric of local societies and established patterns of dependency and integration that permanently yoked those societies to the objectives and needs of the advanced world. The inequity and indeed brutality of these patterns were best expressed by one of the leading colonizers of Africa, the Englishman Cecil Rhodes, who founded the colony of Rhodesia (now Zimbabwe) and endowed one of today's top prizes for academic achievement, the Rhodes Scholarship (notice how colonialism continues to influence and distort contemporary life):

> We must find new lands from which we can easily obtain raw materials and at the same time exploit the cheap slave labor that is available from the natives of the colonies. The colonies would also provide the dumping ground for surplus goods produced in our factories.[9]

dependency theory: theory developed by critical theorists that explains lack of development in terms of colonialism and oppression.

Here, as critical theorists see it, are the trading and political patterns that characterize globalization today, a set of dynamics they refer to as **dependency theory**. Comparative advantage is not some God-given distribution of resources that confers advantages on each country that it can then exploit in free and uncoerced trading relationships. Rather, it is a pattern of historically determined and dominant relationships shaped by colonial governments and raw power.

Colonial powers not only stripped the colonies of precious metals and other material resources; they also converted and reorganized resources to produce cash crops that paid off handsomely year after year. Agriculture became another large "gold mine" that colonial powers exploited. In Gambia, colonizers replaced rice farming for local consumption with peanut plantations for European consumption. All over Africa, the local foodstuffs that had been grown were replaced: in Ghana and other parts of the Gold Coast of West Africa by cocoa, in Liberia by rubber plantations, in Uganda by cotton, in Dahomey and Nigeria by palm oil, and in Tanganyika (now Tanzania) by sisal. The same patterns prevailed in Asia. Under French rule, rice became the dominant export crop in

MAP 10-1

Colonialism in the Modern World, circa 1900

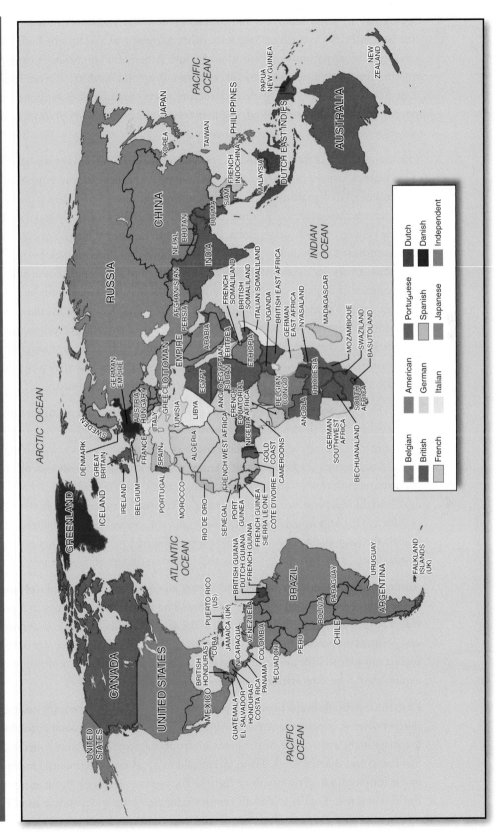

Note: This map shows the global extent of Western colonialism, which originally included Latin America, although Latin America was largely independent by 1900.

457

Indochina, rubber in Malaysia, and coffee in Indonesia. And the great fruit companies, like United Fruit Company, along with other agricultural and mining conglomerates, replicated these patterns in Central and South America. Plantations became the first multinational "factories" in colonial countries, diverting production from local to foreign demand; usurping the best infrastructure, such as land and water, for commercial purposes; and forcing the peasantry onto marginal soil or into work at slave wages in the new enterprises servicing metropole markets.

One consequence of this coerced allocation of comparative advantage was that developing countries lost the capacity to feed themselves. As Frances Moore Lappé and Joseph Collins note, "Colonialism destroyed the cultural patterns of production and exchange by which traditional sectors in 'underdeveloped' countries previously had met the needs of their people."[10] To this day, global trade incentives favor Western agriculture, which dumps surpluses generated by domestic protectionist programs onto global markets and undercuts prices for agricultural products produced in developing countries. Another consequence of coercive comparative advantage is that most local enterprise and production activity is forced into the informal sector—that is, the part of the economy in developing countries that is not globalized and exists without the protection of law, subsidies, and other privileges that flow to the formal sector. Local production in both agriculture and industry is marginalized and can never get hooked up in a beneficial way with the globalized economy, which dashes further and further ahead.

So indelible and enduring were these patterns of plundering that critical theorists developed a more elaborate dependency theory, drawn from the experience of Latin America. Latin America actually had the earliest and least recent encounters with colonialism. By the mid-nineteenth century, most of Central and South America was independent. The Bolivarian revolutions of the early part of that century severed colonial ties with Europe and brought independence to Latin America a century or more before it arrived in Asia or Africa. Yet Latin America's experience is relevant, critical theorists believe, because it reveals the long-lasting effects of colonialism. Despite the hundred years or more since colonialism, Latin America still shows the deep-seated scars of dependency.

metropole: the metropolitan (political, commercial, and military) center of imperial power.

According to dependency theory, the advanced country, or metropole, relates to the developing colonial country or satellite in the same way that a city relates to the countryside. The **metropole**, like the city, organizes the satellite, or countryside, to serve its social and political purposes. The metropole becomes an all-encompassing center of economic, social, and political life and in the process also becomes an all-encompassing center of exploitation. The exploitation derives from five factors.

First, the metropole is independent, but the satellite or dependent country never becomes independent. It is permanently subordinated. The proof of this point for dependency theorists is the experience of the great metropolitan areas of Latin America such as São Paulo and Buenos Aires. These metropolitan areas enjoyed nominal independence in the nineteenth and twentieth centuries. They grew significantly during this period but still at the end of the twentieth century remained largely dependent on the outside metropolis—first the European powers and then the United States.

In 1915, bananas are loaded for export onto a train on the Northern Railway in Costa Rica. The railway was owned by the United Fruit Company and was part of its extensive infrastructure.

Second, Latin America's experience suggests that the satellite grows fastest when it is isolated from the metropole. The greatest industrial development in Argentina, Brazil, Mexico, and other countries such as Chile occurred precisely during those periods when Europe and the United States, the metropoles, were weak and hence less dominant in the international economy. These periods included the European wars of the early seventeenth century, the Napoleonic Wars, World Wars I and II, and the Great Depression of the 1930s. In each of these periods, large Latin American countries enjoyed significant economic growth.

Third, this autonomous development of satellite regions is choked off the minute the metropole recovers and reasserts its oppressive role in the world economy. For example, British-led economic liberalism in the eighteenth and nineteenth centuries undercut incipient manufacturing development in Latin America. Foreign investment destroyed local competition, the export economy absorbed the best lands and other resources, and **systematic inequality** increased both between rural and urban areas and between metropole and satellite countries.

Fourth, the plantation or hacienda (*latifundium*) is a direct result of metropole-satellite relationships. It is not a reflection of the natural stage of agricultural development that subsequently leads to industrial development, as in the evolution of feudalism to capitalism in Europe. Rather, it exists and survives solely at the will of the metropole. Plantations produced products for the metropole country, which in turn supplied food to the satellite country. The development of agriculture did not produce food for industrial and urban development in the satellite country.

Fifth and finally, the proof of this dependence lies in the fact that, as industrialization proceeds, the demand for agricultural and raw material products relatively declines. The

systematic inequality: deep-seated disparity in the distribution of wealth and/or power generated by colonialism and dependency.

terms of trade: relative price of exports and imports.

terms of trade—what is paid in exports for imports—turns against the satellite countries. Because the metropole spends more on industrial goods and less on foodstuffs and raw materials, the satellite economy produces products of declining relative value and slowly dries up. This pessimistic view of the capability of world markets to provide the demand that could spark development in the satellite regions led Latin American countries after World War II to reject export-led growth strategies and turn to strategies based on developing local industries to substitute for industrial imports. In effect, this strategy was an attempt to break completely with the world economy in which the ancient patterns of colonial exploitation were so irreversibly embedded.

⋙ World Systems

world systems: theories (updating Marxism) that explain how colonialism reinforced capitalism and enabled capitalism to survive by exploiting the peripheral countries of the world.

Other work by critical theorists formalized dependency theory into a **world systems** model. Building on Marxism, world systems analysts emphasized the totality of social and economic phenomena in the world economy. Consistent with critical theory perspectives, they rejected the idea of sequential or rationalist causation. As Georg Lukács, a Marxist, once wrote, "It is not the primacy of economic motives in historical explanation that constitutes the difference between Marxism and bourgeois thought, but the point of view of totality."[11]

The world economy—globalization—must be seen as a whole. It is a system or total structure whose unifying metric is the division of labor. Firms and workers existed long before the world economy expanded in 1500. But they did not exist in a total system of multiple states and a global market. The capitalist world system dates from that moment when multiple states and a global market came together for the purpose of accumulating capital. The system, as Marx made clear, is driven by the desire for more profit and capital. This desire persists today, as illustrated by the television commercial featuring a stockbroker who says he never thinks about how well he has done on the last trade, only about how he can do better on the next trade. The accumulation of profits and capital, raw greed, is the raison d'être of the system.

Ideally, any individual or country in the global marketplace would prefer to have a monopoly, because a monopoly generates the greatest differential between the sales price and the cost of production. However, the presence of multiple actors/states makes the establishment of perfect monopolies difficult. Still, larger or leading actors/states can create quasi-monopolies using patents and other market restrictions. Quasi-monopolies last long enough to accumulate considerable profit, but they are eventually challenged by other actors/countries and become less profitable. Once patents expire and innovations arrive in the trailing states, the profits are far less. (There are some similarities here with the product life cycle discussed earlier in this book, but, according to mainstream perspectives, developing countries eventually catch up, as Japan did after World War II and the East Asian tigers, such as South Korea, did thereafter.)

division of labor: the division of world markets into core, peripheral, and semiperipheral areas.

core states: large and leading countries that produce most of the innovative products, which enjoy an initial monopoly.

Thus, the world systems dynamic creates a **division of labor** between leading sectors that generate high profits and lagging products that generate little or no profits. Large and leading countries constitute the **core states** of the world economy; they produce most of the leading products, which enjoy an initial monopoly. Smaller and less developed countries constitute the **peripheral states,** which produce most of the low-profit or lagging products after the monopoly qualities of these products have been substantially diminished. Some countries fall in between. They are **semiperipheral states,** which produce a nearly even mix of monopoly and competitive products.

A Bangladeshi boy works in a recycling facility in Dhaka, Bangladesh. Plastics recycling workers in Bangladesh, one of the world's poorest countries, labor in primitive working conditions and are paid $2 per day. The waste plastics are cut in smaller pieces and then melted in a furnace to make various products.

peripheral states: smaller and less developed countries that produce most of the competitive or lagging products after the monopoly qualities of these products have been substantially diminished.

semiperipheral states: states that produce a nearly even mix of monopoly and competitive products.

The global economy is thus stratified and fixed. Core states have a permanent advantage in producing monopoly products and use their clout in global markets to protect patents and other privileges that produce disproportionate profit. Peripheral states are at a permanent disadvantage because the dynamic of global markets makes available to them only those products for which competition has lowered the available profit. Semiperipheral countries have the greatest difficulty. They struggle to keep from falling back into the peripheral zone while using government intervention (protection, subsidies, and so on) to attempt to advance into the core group. Unless they are of substantial size, like India, Brazil, or China, they have little chance of succeeding.

According to world systems theorists, therefore, a global division of labor is inevitable and largely static. There will always be the need for a division of labor. And while some countries may rise in the hierarchy of core and peripheral states, others will fall. The advantages lie with already developed countries. Thus, as critical theory perspectives see it, global divisions and inequalities persist. Whereas earlier the industrial countries produced textiles, the developing countries now do so. The same is true of steel, automobiles, consumer electronics, and so on. Yet industrial countries retain their lead by producing an endless stream of new products fueled by the profits of earlier products and the protection of patents and other market restrictions. Meanwhile, peripheral states industrialize and some even make it into the semiperipheral class of states, but they can never leap forward far enough financially and technologically to reverse the capitalist world order. Indeed, in return for exports of competitive (low- or no-profit) products to core countries, peripheral countries must continue to accept the exports of core countries in monopoly products. At the heart of Doha Round trade negotiations today, for example, is a trade-off between, on one hand, advanced (core) countries seeking to reduce barriers to trade in developing countries for their highly profitable products in the high-technology, pharmaceutical, and service industries and, on the other hand, developing (peripheral) countries receiving in return reduced barriers in advanced countries for their lower-profit agriculture and low-technology products.

>>> Multinational Corporations and Exploitation of Labor

A large reason for the frozen economic hierarchy of global markets is the MNCs. Like the trading and plantation corporations during the colonial era, the MNCs internalize the division of labor and structure global markets to perpetuate the advantages of the core states. Because of global dependence, states are no longer effective agents that control the MNCs. The states lose a measure of autonomy and cannot reverse the dynamics of capitalist world systems. MNCs hold "sovereignty at bay" and make it more difficult for states to accomplish their domestic and foreign policy objectives.[12]

Although protected by the law, MNCs, critical theorists argue, operate outside the law. They circumvent laws in advanced countries by relocating factories to developing countries. And they circumvent the laws in developing countries by exploiting the desperate conditions of the local poor. If MNCs don't violate the laws directly, they frequently do business with local enterprises and entrepreneurs who are little more than common criminals. The most egregious offenses involve child labor and discrimination against women.

An oft-cited example is a brave young Pakistani boy named Iqbal Masih. Iqbal was indentured to work in a locally run carpet factory at age four for a payment, essentially a loan, of $16 to his parents. Shackled to a loom for twelve hours a day, seven days a week, Iqbal earned so little that at the end of six years his parents owed $400 rather than the $16 for his original servitude. At age ten, Iqbal, learning that **bonded labor** was no longer permitted, stole away one day to attend a rally sponsored by an NGO known as the Bonded Labour Liberation Front. He returned to the factory to free his fellow laborers, infuriating the factory owner, and then became a spokesman on behalf of more than 100 million children under the age of fifteen who worked in peripheral countries in 1994 essentially as slaves. Three years later, he was killed, many suspect by henchmen of the Pakistani carpet industry.[13]

bonded labor: a form of unfree or indentured labor, typically a means of paying off loans with direct labor instead of currency or goods.

Through Iqbal's efforts and NGOs such as the college student organization United Students Against Sweatshops, corporate codes have improved labor conditions in a range of low-tech developing-country industries such as textiles, apparel, footwear, forest products, coffee, and toys. RugMark, a consortium of carpet manufacturers and exporters in India, Nepal, and Pakistan, inspects factories and certifies with the RugMark label rugs that are made without child labor. Reebok, Nike, and other apparel firms have developed similar codes. However, abuses continue and, from some critical theory perspectives, abound. From this perspective, exploitation lies at the heart of the global development process; when confronted in one area, such as slavery, it pops up again in another area, such as child labor.

From the point of view of mainstream perspectives, abuses by MNCs can be corrected and even abolished. From a critical theory perspective, however, MNCs are not the primary cause. There is no single cause; the global system itself is at fault. Competitive processes compel all states to remain open, including core states. Consider the following. If countries want to survive in a highly competitive global economy, they can't tax their MNCs more than other countries do, impose pension and welfare costs that disproportionately burden their industries, or pile up regulations that prevent their firms from adapting to rapid changes in technology and other market conditions. If they do, the MNCs will cut back operations at home and relocate them abroad, where costs and regulations are less onerous. The system, in short, gives MNCs carte blanche.

Countries also lose control of fiscal and monetary policies. They may expand government spending to create jobs and exploit resources, but if they import a large percentage of their consumption, as many developing countries do, much of this added domestic spending goes into imports. It leaks out, in effect, to foreign

firms and does not increase domestic jobs. So, domestic spending has to be increased even more to create jobs. Thus, profligate spending and fiscal deficits in developing countries are not the consequences primarily of bad governance, corruption, or incompetent leaders in those countries; rather, they are the consequences of world system constraints. Local government officials have to pump more and more fiscal gas into the domestic economic car because the gas line of the car is leaking fuel out to foreigners on its way to the engine. Or consider monetary policy. As we have noted in earlier chapters, governments raise interest rates to slow money growth. But raising interest rates more than other countries only attracts capital from abroad, requiring local central banks to raise interest rates still more by selling bonds (reducing bond prices and raising interest rates) to absorb the excess money coming in from abroad.

Iqbal Masih, the twelve-year-old boy who won international acclaim for highlighting the horrors of child labor in Pakistan, was shot dead in 1995, allegedly because of his campaign against child labor.

Mainstream perspectives focus on only specific aspects of this phenomenon of globalization. Liberal perspectives, for example, which emphasize interactions rather than power or ideology, conclude that, because of spillover, governments have no choice but to integrate monetary policies and coordinate fiscal policies, as EU members, for example, are doing today. Their only other alternative is to leave their countries at the mercy of the biggest central banks and government spenders in the global economy—today these are in the United States and the EU. The effect of expanding the reach of globalization to more and more sectors, however, is ultimately beneficial. The scope of governance expands, and global society as a whole becomes more like domestic societies.

But from the critical theory perspective, the situation is actually much worse and cannot be easily corrected by any one measure. There is no way to escape the dependence and relentless division of labor that lies behind these global inequities. The effects of globalization are total. They go well beyond economic policies and weaken the psychological and political will of peripheral countries. Countries lose control of their national media and entertainment industries and, indeed, of their local languages and cultures. Small countries, in particular, are defenseless. McDonald's golden arches descend on these countries, and Hollywood movies and music dominate their airwaves. Slowly, local-language broadcasts and artistic opportunities dwindle. Ancient languages disappear. Cultural diversity is the victim, and the whole world is the loser.

Except perhaps for the big countries. The United States, Japan, and the MNCs of the advanced world may be the winners. As Thomas Friedman explains, the Lexus (representing the culture of modernity) drives out the olive tree (representing the culture of tradition). "Olive trees," Friedman writes, "represent everything that roots us, anchors us, identifies us and locates us in this world—whether it be belonging to a family, a community, a tribe, a nation, a religion or, most of all, a place called home."[14] The Lexus, built for export with ultramodern robots, on the other hand,

> represents all the burgeoning global markets, financial institutions and computer technologies with which we pursue higher living standards today. The biggest threat today to your olive tree is likely to come from the Lexus, from all the anonymous, transnational, homogenizing, standardizing market forces and technologies that make up today's globalizing economic system.

Friedman, however, is a mainstream analyst, seeing the world, as we have noted previously, largely from a liberal perspective. Unlike some critical theory perspectives, he can imagine that globalization has a liberating side:

> There are some things about this system that can make the Lexus so over-powering it can overrun and overwhelm every olive tree in sight. . . . But there are other things . . . that empower even the smallest, weakest political community to actually use the new technologies and markets to preserve their olive trees, their culture and identity.

Witness the upsurge of ethnicity, nationalism, religion, local pride, and interest in personal roots that belie the notion that globalization homogenizes culture. Maybe, as Friedman concludes, the Lexus and the olive tree need one another.

That's the mainstream view of globalization, that it benefits, not destroys, national sovereignty and culture. Countries choose to join the global economy, and globalization gives them more options. No country has developed in isolation. The communist countries were the last to try, and they did not preserve their sovereignty and cultures but eventually lost them. Modernization has been going on for a long time, yet people have retained their identities, their homes, and their communities. Technology benefits local languages and arts by making people aware of diversity and, through the Internet and other information technologies, better able to defend their cultural heritage.

Some critiques of conventional ways of thinking about social movements in the contemporary world have emerged. Sociologist Kevin McDonald argues that Western thinking leads us to analyze social movements, such as protest groups or religious sects, in terms of antagonistic relationships, dialectical processes, and individuals versus the collectivity. McDonald bypasses even constructivism in favor of a more radical alternative that liberates oppressed groups in the future but does not threaten other groups. The alternative he proposes is resonance, where groups that are different resonate or feed off one another rather than conflict with one another. He writes that

> An older international context, where social life largely took place within the borders of nation-states, and where states were the main actors on the international stage, is increasingly giving way to a context involving new global actors, from NGOs, organized crime, or terror networks, and with it, to a whole series of debates attempting to interpret the nature of this emerging global world.
>   . . . We need to grapple with forms of sociality transforming the relationship between individual and collective; with grammars of movement that are better understood in terms of cultural pragmatics . . . and personal experience . . . than organization building and collective identity; with new forms of complexity and fluidity.

He goes on to advocate "a radical paradigm shift" that emphasizes "embodiment and the senses." Instead of action among separate or disembodied groups, in which one group encounters or confronts another, he wants to talk about actions that resonate among groups and reinforce them such as we experience when we encounter "dance, music, drumming, bicycle riding, experiences of vulnerability." These experiences, he writes, "allow us to break out of often repeated debates framed in terms of individual versus the community." He then studies protest and religious groups (NGOs), such as the Falun Gong movement in China, that are searching for more fluid and resonating ways to deal with global differences that do not automatically separate people into disembodied and, hence, antagonistic groups.[15]

≫ Marginalized Minorities: Global Injustice

From a critical theory perspective, nothing is more evident from the assault of globalization than the **marginalization** of indigenous peoples and women. Colonialism, imperialism, and then open world markets ran roughshod over native peoples and forced women into what are in effect ghettos. Think of the plight of the Native Americans, who fell like weeds beneath the scythes of white men expanding across the American continent. Land, the most cherished possession of indigenous peoples, was systematically appropriated or, more accurately, stolen from them. Indigenous tribes were stripped of their livelihood and, even worse, of their culture, identity, and dignity. They were dismissed as primitive,

marginalization:
the social process of making unimportant or powerless certain groups within a society, especially indigenous peoples and women.

uncivilized, and uneducable. The indigenous peoples of Latin America and Asia suffered no less. And the legacy of such material and moral looting goes on to the present day.

Let's listen to Subcomandante Marcos, a leader of the indigenous people of the southeast Mexican state of Chiapas, as he talks about his eviscerated homeland:

> Chiapas loses blood through many veins: . . . petroleum, electricity, cattle, money, coffee, banana, honey, corn, cacao, tobacco, sugar, soy, melon, sorghum, mamey, mango, tamarind, avocado, and Chiapaneco blood all flow as a result of the thousand teeth sunk into the throat of the Mexican southeast. These raw materials, thousands of millions of tons of them, flow to Mexican ports, railroads, air and truck transportation centers. From there they are sent to different parts of the world—the United States, Canada, Holland, Germany, Italy, Japan— . . . to feed imperialism. . . .
>
> In 1989 these businesses took 1.2 trillion pesos from Chiapas and only left behind 616 million pesos worth of credit and public works. More than 600 million pesos went to the belly of the beast.
>
> In Chiapas . . . Pemex [the Mexican state oil company] has eighty-six teeth sunk into the townships of Estacion Juarez, Reforma, Ostuacian, Pichucalo, and Ocosingo. Every day they suck out 92,000 barrels of petroleum and 517 billion cubic feet of gas. . . .
>
> Chiapas also bleeds coffee. Thirty-five percent of the coffee produced in Mexico comes from this area. . . . 53 percent is exported abroad. . . . more than 100,000 tons of coffee are taken from the state to fatten the beast's bank accounts: in 1988 a kilo of pergamino coffee was sold abroad for 58,000 pesos. The Chiapeneco producers were paid 2,500 pesos or less.
>
> Three million head of cattle wait for middlemen . . . to take them away to fill refrigerators in Arriasga, Villahermosa, and Mexico City. The cattle are sold for 400 pesos per kilo by the poor farmers and resold by middlemen and businessmen for up to ten times the price they paid for them.
>
> The tribute that capitalism demands from Chiapas has no historical parallel. Fifty-five percent of national hydroelectric energy comes from this state, along with 20 percent of Mexico's total electricity. However, only a third of the homes in Chiapas have electricity. . . .
>
> The plunder of wood continues in Chiapas' forests. Between 1981 and 1989, 2,444,777 cubic meters of precious woods, conifers, and tropical trees were taken . . . to Mexico City, Puebla, Veracruz, and Quintana Roo. . . .
>
> The honey that is produced in 78,000 beehives in Chiapas goes entirely to the United States and European markets.
>
> Of the corn produced in Chiapas, more than half goes to the domestic market. . . . Sorghum grown in Chiapas goes to Tobasco. Ninety percent of the tamarind goes to Mexico City and other states. Two-thirds of the avocados and all the mameys are sold out of state. Sixty-nine percent of the cacao goes to the national market, and 31 percent is exported to

the United States, Holland, Japan, and Italy. The majority of the bananas produced are exported.[16]

The indictment is total. And Chiapas is but one example. In the Philippines, indigenous peoples totaling 16–18 percent of the population, mostly Muslims, face expulsion from their native lands to accommodate forty-nine major new hydroelectric dams. The proposed energy supply is to encourage foreign investment, not local entrepreneurs. In Peru, Colombia, and elsewhere in Latin America, landless peasants join guerrilla movements to reclaim land and natural resources. In Cuba and Venezuela, Fidel Castro and Hugo Chávez and their successors have championed a new revolutionary-style politics to empower the poor and indigenous peoples. In southern Africa, the Sari, an indigenous people, were evicted from land that became the Central Kalahari Game Reserve, one of the largest such reserves in the world.

Altogether, the United Nations estimates that some 370 million indigenous people live in more than seventy countries around the world. Through efforts by NGOs, the Africa Commission on Human Rights, and the first United Nations International Decade of the World's Indigenous People (1995–2004), the United Nations adopted in September 2007 the landmark Declaration on the Rights of Indigenous Peoples, emphasizing their rights to culture, identity, language, employment, health, education, and other benefits and outlawing discrimination against them. Canada, Australia, New Zealand, and the United States voted against the declaration, arguing that the language was unclear and the negotiating process had not been transparent.

Women are the other main victims of marginalization. Globalization has marginalized women in four principal ways: through low wages to fuel export zones; through neglect of the informal economy, where most women work; through increased unpaid labor by women in the household sector; and through damage to the environment where most women live.

Women constitute most of the workforce of the globally oriented trade activities imposed on developing countries by colonialism. Export sectors have to maintain low wages to service metropole markets, and women are the cheapest source of labor and fill most of the jobs in export-processing zones throughout the developing world. Women constitute up to 90 percent of the workforce in such export zones. They assemble garments, electronics, and other items that require tedious and repetitive manual skills. Women, it is argued, have the natural dexterity and nimble fingers needed to carry out repetitive tasks at very high rates of speed. In export zones, women work fifty to eighty hours a week and earn less than $1 per hour, generally 30–40 percent less than men are paid for comparable work. They enjoy few basic job or social protections and are sometimes subjected to physical and sexual abuses. The practices used in recruiting and housing the women needed to work in these industries have led in some cases to kidnapping and prostitution rings. Women have been lured to fill jobs and then forced into prostitution either directly or indirectly to pay off loans. A sex trade has developed in emerging countries, often associated with other low-wage service industries such as tourism and hotels.[17]

Migrant Bangladeshi women and children haul stones in a quarry in the northeastern Indian state of Assam, earning less than $1 per person per day.

The systematic marginalization of women in developing countries was dramatized in 2012 by the shooting of a fifteen-year-old Pakistani girl, Malala Yousafzai, for seeking an education. While riding the bus home from school, she was shot in the head at point-blank range. In this case, Muslim extremists are the culprits. They consider it an affront to their religion to educate girls and regard Malala as a pawn of Western imperialists who seek to destroy their culture. Miraculously, Malala recovered and initiated a global campaign to promote education for women. She wrote a book, spoke at the United Nations, and became a symbol of the battle against discrimination of women throughout the world.[18]

Discrimination, on a smaller and less exploitative scale, also affects women in industrialized countries. In these countries, the employment of women is concentrated in the garment and low-wage sectors, and these sectors are usually the first affected by job losses when consumers buy the still-cheaper garment and toy imports produced by women in developing countries. When jobs are lost in advanced countries, women, families, and sometimes whole regions are devastated.

Exploited and then just as quickly neglected by the global economy, women work mostly in the informal sector of developing countries. They do jobs that mimic housework, such as cleaning, sewing, and cooking, and are paid far less than even the low wages they would get in the formal sector. For this reason, some mainstream perspectives argue that the formal, or export-centered, global economy is still a step up for women. But critical theory perspectives emphasize the few opportunities that women have to move up within, or to break out of, the export-oriented global economy. Women in developing countries and among the poor in advanced countries are either exploited by the global (modern) economy or left to work in a ghettoized informal economy where there is little support in the form of credits (loans), child care, educational incentives, or health care. As in the case of developing countries more broadly, the patterns of global dependency and world systems involve a dynamic that does not lift individuals, especially women and minorities, from the bottom to the top but rather exploits them for the benefit of those who are already at the top.

Globalization further de-emphasizes the valuable work that women do in the home, even in the most advanced economies. By stressing modernization and the transformation of traditional tasks and communities, globalization values home care even less than traditional societies do. Bearing children and caring for them, maintaining a household that often takes care of elderly members, and sustaining village and community relations are all tasks that are invaluable, indeed priceless, for any society. Yet they are unacknowledged and unpaid in a modern globalized world. The United Nations recently estimated that the unpaid work that women in Mexico did in the home in a year amounted to about $200 billion—a full 23 percent of Mexico's GDP.[19] Even that estimate seems low, because the value of raising healthy, educated children cannot really be measured.

Finally, globalization has devastating impacts on the environments in which most women live. As Manisha Desai points out,

> Whether it is the destruction of the rainforest in Latin America, the felling of trees in the Himalayan Mountains in India, desertification in Africa, or toxic dumping in the United States, the environmental desecration caused by global economic policies has led to increasing material and cultural hardships for women.[20]

Women, who have the primary responsibility for home care, have to work harder to fetch wood, find drinking water, feed cattle, and care for children afflicted by poisons and deprivation. And they do so while seldom owning the land. Only 1 percent of the world's landowners are women. They work the land with less and less help because globalization not only strips the environment of natural resources but also strips the village of their husbands and children. These vital human resources are drawn increasingly from the countryside into the urbanized and globalized economy. This movement of human beings from rural to urban areas (at least thirteen million each year in China alone) creates transient and often impoverished communities where criminal organizations lure young men and women into the sex industry and drug trafficking.

≫ Persisting Global Inequality

Despite all the development of the past five hundred years, why do all these shocking inequalities still exist? Mainstream perspectives answer this question in separate parts.

From a realist perspective, for example, the key question is, Who gains most? Does globalization spread economic benefits or concentrate them? Does the hegemon stay on top, or do other countries—China, India, and oil-producing states—gain more and counterbalance the hegemon? Or, at the individual and domestic levels of analysis, do individuals and minorities eventually work their way up the income ladder? Or are workers and minority groups stuck at the lower end and capitalist managers and financiers ensconced at the upper end?

As we've noted, realist perspectives don't always agree with one another. The power transition school believes hegemons endure because movement toward balance is dangerous and brings war. They agree, in effect, with critical theory perspectives that some kind of hierarchy is necessary to promote development. But power transition realists do not necessarily believe that this hierarchy is rigid or static. The same hegemons, classes, or individuals may not endure. Different countries and classes may rise and fall. Nevertheless, realist accounts do believe that global development is greatest when hegemons rule because hegemonic stability favors growth, as recounted in Chapter 8. So, inequalities are inevitable from this power transition perspective, even though the winners and losers in the inequality sweepstakes change.

The balance-of-power realist school sees it differently. It expects other states or classes and individuals to rise eventually and counterbalance the hegemon. It sees inequalities as dangerous and destabilizing. Thus, at the individual, domestic, and systemic levels of analysis, power balancing realists accept, if they don't seek, relative balance or equality as the norm. They see markets and politics as competitive exercises and trust that increasing equality will stabilize and maximize benefits in the same way that perfectly competitive markets maximize growth. They assume, however, that a balancing of military capabilities preserves stability and peace. If not, power balancing realists favor a world that discriminates between friendly and enemy states. Development is pursued to reduce inequalities among friends, but in relations with adversaries development is a zero-sum game and not recommended.

Liberal perspectives don't have a single answer either. Let's listen first to economists who fear that globalization increases inequalities. According to Joseph Stiglitz, a Nobel Prize–winning economist,

> A growing divide between the haves and the have-nots has left increasing numbers in the Third World in dire poverty, living on less than a dollar a day. Despite repeated promises of poverty reduction made over the last decade of the twentieth century, the actual number of people living in poverty has actually increased by almost 100 million. This occurred at the same time that total world income increased by an average of 2.5 percent annually.
>
> In Africa, the high aspirations following colonial independence have been largely unfulfilled. Instead, the continent plunges deeper into misery, as incomes fall and standards of living decline. The hard-won improvements in life expectancy gained in the past few decades have begun to reverse. While

the scourge of AIDS is at the center of this decline, poverty is also a killer. Even countries that have abandoned African socialism, managed to install honest governments, balanced their budgets, and kept inflation down find that they simply cannot attract private investors. Without this investment, they cannot have sustainable growth.[21]

On similar grounds, economist Dani Rodrik agrees and notes that globalization is leading to a new "digital divide, . . . a deep fault line between groups who have the skills and mobility to flourish in global markets" and groups that don't, "such as workers, pensioners, and environmentalists."[22] The information age, in short, has opened up further inequalities, a **digital divide** between advanced and developing countries in terms of access to computers, cell phones, and other telecommunication devices.

digital divide: the gap between advanced and developing countries in terms of access to the digital devices of the information age.

But now let's listen to an economist who sees globalization as reducing inequalities. According to Martin Wolf, a distinguished economist and journalist at the *Financial Times* in London,

> Between 1980 and 2000, India's real GDP per head more than doubled. . . .
>
> . . . China . . . achieved a rise in real income per head of well over 400 per cent between 1980 and 2000. China and India, it should be remembered, contain almost two-fifths of the world's population. . . .
>
> Never before have so many people—or so large a proportion of the world's population—enjoyed such large rises in their standards of living. Meanwhile, GDP per head in high-income countries (with 15 per cent of the world's population) rose by 2.1 per cent a year between 1975 and 2001 and by only 1.7 per cent between 1990 and 2001. . . . the incomes of poor developing countries, with more than half the world's population, grew substantially faster than those of the world's richest countries. . . .
>
> What . . . has this progress to do with international economic integration? . . . the World Bank divided seventy-three developing countries . . . into two groups, the third [or twenty-four countries, including China, India, Brazil, Bangladesh, Mexico, the Philippines, and Thailand, which alone make up 92 percent of the population of the twenty-four countries] that had increased ratios of trade to GDP, since 1980, by the largest amount and the rest. . . .
>
> The average incomes per head of these twenty-four globalizing countries rose by 67 per cent . . . between 1980 and 1997. . . . the other forty-nine countries managed a rise of only 10 per cent . . . over this period. . . .
>
> . . . the notion that international economic integration necessarily makes the rich richer and the poor poorer is nonsense.[23]

Are these economists talking about the same planet? Some see more people living in poverty than ever before; others see more people climbing out of poverty than ever before. Can both views be right? Well, yes, they can. It depends on which statistics economists use and what they emphasize. The absolute number of people living on less than $1 per day did go up between 1990 and 1998. But, as a ratio of total population over a longer period of time, this number has gone down from 50 percent in 1950 to 32 percent in 1980 to 24 percent in 1992.[24] By more recent estimates, the ratio dropped to 18 percent in 2004 and will drop to an estimated 12 percent in 2015.[25] Thus, Wolf looks at ratios, a longer time period, and the populated countries of India and China. Stiglitz and Rodrik focus on absolute numbers, the most recent period, and the poorest countries of Africa. Reality is different depending on the perspective you bring to bear on it.

Measuring inequality is also very tricky. Are we talking about inequality between countries or within them? For example, between 1820 and 1980 global inequality increased among countries but inequality actually went down within countries.[26] So, from 1960 to 1997, the ratio of incomes of the 20 percent of the world's population living in the richest countries to that of the 20 percent living in the poorest countries went up from 30:1 in 1960 to 74:1 in 1997, while it increased from 7:1 to only 11:1 in the previous era of globalization before World War I (1870–1913).[27] During the same period, however, a burgeoning middle class reduced income differences within countries, ending the appeal of class warfare ideologies such as Marxism and communism. Are we talking about ratios or absolute numbers? From 1980 to 2000, Chinese average real income per head rose by 440 percent; U.S. income per head rose by 60 percent. But the absolute per capita income gap between China and the United States increased from $20,600 to $30,200 per head. China grew faster than the United States but from a much smaller base. It would have had to grow thirty, not seven, times faster to reduce the absolute gap.[28] Closing relative gaps thus takes time and accelerates only toward the later phases of catch-up. Moreover, are we talking about just incomes or the quality of life, which includes life expectancy, education, and health care? Life expectancy and other measures of the quality of life in most developing countries grew steadily from 1950 to 2000, even as incomes grew less in some countries or stagnated in others.

What governs these interpretations and methodological preferences among economists who generally favor a liberal perspective? Perhaps their views are determined not just by wealth and markets (relational or liberal aspects of reality) but also by substantive or ideational issues such as what they consider to be the rate of sustainable development, the preferred quality of life, or the best mechanism for political life—redistributive versus decentralized political practices. In short, identity factors may trump liberal or realist factors. Is it ideologically acceptable that some people remain poor and perhaps even get poorer, at least relatively, as long as more (other) people leave poverty and get richer? Is it acceptable that some people become many times richer than others as long as still others also get richer? For example, is it immoral for Bill Gates to make billions while average middle-class incomes have gone up much less? After all, Gates did create a whole new industry and millions of jobs. Would anyone take such big risks if he or she could not reap big rewards? Should limits be applied to multiples of wealth until every individual, group, or state in the world has reached a certain minimal level of development? If so, what is that minimal level for all participants, what is the multiple limit of wealth that must be enforced until everyone reaches the minimal level, and how do we know what degree of redistribution of resources is still consistent with overall growth and does not result only in the redistribution of the wealth that already exists? These are not easy questions to answer—or they are questions that can be answered only from different ideational, material, institutional, or critical perspectives.

SUMMARY

Critical theory perspectives remind us that questions of causality may not be answered at all given the totality of the world in which all participants, including scholars, are trapped. Our perspectives and preferred methods (including levels) of analysis are themselves the products of the social reality that we seek to examine. We can't escape that reality. Today's world is a legacy of deep and powerful historical forces that emerged around five hundred years ago and produced a developed world economy dominated by western European institutions (states), ideas, and power. An understanding of development and the world economy cannot be pursued apart from this legacy because that history represents only one alternative that privileged Western peoples and subjugated and marginalized non-Western peoples. We cannot apply it to the future without perpetuating the legacy of Western dominance. From a critical theory perspective, we need to search continuously for other alternatives by listening to the narratives and voices of the dispossessed. The purpose of scholarly research has to be not problem solving in terms of applying existing perspectives to present and future issues but a broader, more holistic understanding of the historical structures that have brought us to the present point. That understanding will raise human consciousness about the marginalized groups that have borne the brunt of historical imperialism and bring them into the dialogue, emancipating them to participate and lead the world toward future policies of greater global justice and harmony.

TABLE
10-1

The Causes of Globalization and Development: The Critical Theory Perspective and Levels of Analysis[a]

Critical theory perspective		
Systemic	*Structure*	Globalization and development are results of powerful, interconnected historical forces and social processes connected with Western growth and imperialism that benefit "first-world" peoples at the expense of people in the developing world
	Process	
Foreign policy		
Domestic		
Individual		

Level of analysis

a. Recall that critical theory perspectives do not separate perspectives and levels of analysis.

 Sharpen your skills with SAGE edge at **edge.sagepub.com/nau4e.** **SAGE edge for students** provides a personalized approach to help you accomplish your coursework goals in an easy-to-use learning environment.

KEY CONCEPTS

bonded labor, 462

colonialism, 455

core states, 460

dependency theory, 456

digital divide, 471

division of labor, 460

exploitation, 456

imperialism, 455

marginalization, 465

metropole, 458

peripheral states, 461

semiperipheral states, 461

systematic inequality, 459

terms of trade, 460

world systems, 460

STUDY QUESTIONS

1. How do critical and mainstream perspectives differ on the causes of and solutions for globalization? How do they see the past as it relates to the future?

2. How has colonialism affected today's trading patterns among advanced and developing countries in the agriculture and high-tech industrial sectors?

3. What perspective does the following analysis reflect? "The mercantilists compelled their subjects to sell many goods only to them, paying the colonies less than world market prices for crops and raw materials. . . .

Mercantilist policy also required the colonies to buy many products from the mother country, ensuring that the homeland could sell to its subjects at above world market prices."[29]

4. In what ways are multinational corporations like the raw materials plantations of the colonial era? How have they marginalized indigenous peoples and women?

5. Has global inequality increased or decreased? What is the difference between changes in inequality within countries and changes in inequality between countries?

A group of Kurdish people assemble in the southeastern town of Diyarbakir, Turkey, on September 1, 2013, to celebrate Independence Day and the ongoing struggle for democracy in Turkey.

CONCLUSION

Applying Perspectives and Levels of Analysis: The Case of the Democratic Peace

In an interview with the *Wall Street Journal* in April 2006, George Shultz, secretary of state under President Reagan, spoke about the U.S. effort "to spread open political systems and democracy":

> I recall President Reagan's Westminster speech in 1982—that communism would be consigned "to the ash heap of history" and that freedom was the path ahead. And what happened? Between 1980 and 1990, the number of countries that were classified as "free" or "mostly free" increased by about 50 percent. Open political and economic systems have been gaining ground and there's good reason for it. They work better.[1]

In the 1990s, President Clinton and Madeleine Albright, ambassador to the United Nations during Clinton's first term in office and secretary of state during his second, went one step further. In his State of the Union message in 1994, Clinton tied the spread of democracy directly to national security interests: "The best strategy to ensure our security and to build a durable peace is to support the advance of democracy everywhere. Democracies don't attack each other. They make better trading partners and partners in diplomacy."[2] In 2000, Albright, who had fled Czechoslovakia as a small girl when German forces invaded in 1939, helped establish the Community of Democracies, a group of some one hundred democracies that meets biannually at the ministerial level to promote the core values of democracy. In 2010, the Community of Democracies celebrated its tenth anniversary in Warsaw, Poland, where it also began.

democratic peace: the theory that democratic nations for the most part do not go to war with one another, making the spread of democracy desirable.

Is this support for what some call the **democratic peace** just American chauvinism and idealism? Critical theory perspectives might think so. Or is there something to Reagan's and Clinton's belief that the spread of democracy is a national security interest because democracies do not fight one another? The mainstream perspectives investigate correlations between democracy and war and test for various causes. The evidence that democracies don't fight one another began to emerge in the late nineteenth century when the United States and Great Britain, then the two dominant powers, did not go to war with one another despite several serious conflicts, such as the boundary dispute in 1895 between Venezuela and what was then British Guiana. Was this an accident? Perhaps. It was only one case. But as the number of democracies and opportunities for conflict multiplied, gathering evidence tended to support the proposition that democracies rarely if ever go to war with one another. Nevertheless, the proposition remains contentious, subject to debate even among adherents and open to critique from skeptics. In this conclusion we'll look at the evidence for the democratic peace, including some of the statistical problems associated with it, and explore the major explanations that researchers have offered.

The democratic peace is a good topic for us to address in wrapping up our discussion of international relations because it illustrates nicely the perspectives, levels of analysis, and causal arrows we have studied throughout this book. It also illustrates methodological issues and, hence, the potential as well as the limits of social science when we study human subjects, who are self-conscious and change their minds. Last, it reminds us that all knowledge is biased and incomplete in the sense that we select certain facts and cannot know all the facts, so we have to make judgments and trust our values. The democratic peace argument may be self-centered and perhaps even self-righteous for those of us who live in democracies. But do we dismiss the facts because we want to be tolerant of all values, including nondemocratic ones? Or do we test the facts further because we believe democracy may offer a better way to organize human life? Either way, we admit that knowing something is an exercise of both our intellect and our values.

>>> Evidence

Statistical findings about relations among democracies over the years demonstrate a regularity that, as the political scientist Jack Levy concludes, "comes as close as anything we have to an empirical law in international relations."[3] Democracies do not, or at least only rarely, go to war with one another. They are also slightly less inclined than other states to go to war with any state, whether democratic or nondemocratic. To be sure, democracies still fight frequently against nondemocracies, but they are somewhat less inclined to do so than nondemocracies are to fight among themselves. This empirical finding, if it holds up, has revolutionary implications for international affairs because it suggests that, even if countries remained separate and sovereign, war could be eliminated through the spread of democracy. Anarchy persists, but democracy trumps the security dilemma. That conclusion might seem convenient for political scientists and politicians who believe in democracy. But it may also be true. The best explanation to date of this democratic peace points to the internal characteristics of democracies as they interact with one another in the international system. Reviewing democratic peace studies in 2002, Levy concludes that ideational causes—the joint practice of democracy, that is, a dyad or two democracies interacting at the process level of analysis—appear to trump liberal and realist causes in accounting for the absence of war:

> This empirical regularity cannot be explained by the geographic separation of democratic states [a realist factor], by extensive trade among democratic dyads [a liberal factor], by the role of American hegemonic power in suppressing potential conflicts between democracies in the period since the Second World War [a realist factor], or by other economic or geopolitical factors correlated with democracy. . . . There is a growing consensus that the pacifying effects of joint democracy are real [an identity factor].[4]

Despite Levy's confidence, consensus is no more complete in political science than in physical science. (Remember the controversy over global warming?) Debates about the findings of democratic peace studies continue. The criticisms cluster in two areas: (1) technical factors associated with the definitions of *democracy* and *war* and the validity of the statistical correlation between them, and (2) theoretical factors dealing with explanations of this correlation. As we noted in the introduction to this volume, a correlation is not an explanation. It tells us only that two variables appear together with a certain regularity over a large number of cases. War does not appear in relations among democracies, but such a correlation does not tell us *why* war does not occur among democracies. Democracies might not go to war with one another because they share internal democratic norms and practices—identity factors. Or they may not go to war because they trade, participate in lots of international institutions, and negotiate with one another in unique ways—liberal factors. Or they may act peacefully toward one another because they are allies and avoid war among themselves in order to balance power against other alliances—realist factors. In addition, each of these explanations may come from a different level of analysis.

sample size: the number of cases used for testing correlations.

One of the problems confronting democratic peace studies is that relatively few democracies existed before World War II, limiting the total number of cases available for study. The larger the number of cases—the **sample size**, as scientists say—the stronger and more reliable the statistical correlation. Large numbers of cases enable researchers to discover stronger patterns among the variables. If we have only five cases, for example, the chance that no war may occur is greater than if we have fifty cases. With fewer cases, the finding is less reliable and may be a product of chance, a statistical anomaly that would wash out over time in a larger sample.

How do researchers deal with this problem? One way is to define democracy and war more loosely in order to obtain more cases. If the proposition then still holds, the evidence is more persuasive. For instance, let's relax the definition of *democracy* to include young or weak democracies. Now we find more wars among democracies, such as the War of 1812 between Great Britain and the United States. The correlation is weaker, but so is democracy. Neither country could be characterized at the time as a particularly robust democracy. In Great Britain, less than 20 percent of white males were eligible to vote, while in the United States almost all white males could vote, even though two-thirds of the adult population—slaves and women—still could not. Similarly, if we relax the definition of *war* to include any border incident that involves violence rather than any border conflict that leads to significant numbers of battlefield deaths (say, one thousand, the number used in many democratic peace studies), again we find more wars between democracies, such as the border skirmishes between British Canada and the United States in the late 1830s. Researchers loosen definitions and multiply cases to test the democratic peace proposition more and more rigorously.

As this discussion reminds us, however, the labeling or definition of variables can be very important and may not be completely divorced from biases introduced by the scholar. This is why constructivist scholars remain skeptical of rationalist methods used in democratic peace studies. They doubt whether it is possible to identify separate dependent and independent variables and say that one variable in a correlation causes the other. Maybe the two variables, instead, constitute or mutually cause one another. Causation is continuous and interactive, not segmented and sequential. Critical theory perspectives go one step further. Not only are the variables inseparable, but the historical evolution of capitalism obscures the unrelenting power that spreads democracy by coercion, not consent. As one critical theorist writes, "'Democratic' in this context can only be a code word designating anyone who can be bought or persuaded to work with the penetrating power's foreign policy."[5] The democratic peace is the peace of the democratic hegemon, which in turn is a product of historical circumstances.

Nevertheless, democratic peace researchers are not deterred and have gone on to show that strong democracies not only do not go to war with one another but also do not enter into militarized disputes that threaten war. When studies distinguish along a continuum between strong and weak democracies, they find that new or relatively weak democracies do, in fact, go to war more often with one another.[6] Still, strong

At the headquarters building (known as Berlaymont) of the European Union in Brussels, Belgium, a regional grouping of strong democracies pioneers the way to a democratic peace.

democracies do not, and even weak democracies go to war with one another less often than nondemocratic states do. And when democratic peace studies differentiate between wars and militarized disputes—conflicts in which the threat of violence is raised but there is no actual violence (another way to relax the definition of *war*)—they conclude that "pairs of democracies are much less likely than other pairs of states . . . to threaten each other in militarized disputes less violent than war."[7]

>>> Explanations

What about explanations of the democratic peace? Because a sufficient number of strong democracies have existed only since World War II, the fact that they do not go to war or engage in militarized disputes with one another may be a lingering effect of their Cold War alliance against the Soviet Union. If this realist explanation holds, we may be right back to square one, and the democratic peace would have no significant implications for the future of international relations.

Let's look at different possible mainstream explanations of the democratic peace. By this point (now comes the payoff for all of our efforts) you should be able to detect the primary perspective and level of analysis reflected in each explanation. Three major independent variables are involved: democracy, trade and international organizations, and alliances. They correspond with the causes emphasized by our three mainstream perspectives: identity, liberal, and realist. And three major levels of analysis are involved: systemic structure, systemic process, and domestic. In each explanation, we identify both the primary perspective and the primary level of analysis, showing how the causal arrows run between them. (Once you've read the explanations below, see Map Conclusion-1 for a graphic representation of these variables.)

Explanation 1: Democracies are more peaceful than all other states.[8]

The statement that democracies are more peaceful than all other states clearly suggests that democracy or identity factors are the cause of the peaceful behavior. Democracies are not only more peaceful toward one another, but they are also more peaceful toward nondemocratic states. So, the cause does not derive from the interactions between countries (systemic process) because interactions between democracies alone and between democracies and nondemocracies produce the same results. Nor does it derive from how countries are positioned ideologically with respect to one another (relative identity at the systemic structure level) because democracies are more peaceful toward both other democracies and nondemocracies. Relative identities, in other words, also cannot be the cause. Instead, the primary cause comes from inside the democratic country itself and affects that country's behavior in all interactions and all relative ideological configurations—with democracies and nondemocracies. Hence, the level of analysis is domestic.

CAUSAL ARROW: PERSPECTIVES

Democracy	Creates peaceful behavior toward all countries	Ends war
IDENTITY	LIBERAL	REALIST

CAUSAL ARROW: LEVELS OF ANALYSIS

Democracy inside one country	Predisposes that country toward peace with all countries	Overrides whether countries are positioned as democratic or not
DOMESTIC	SYSTEMIC PROCESS	SYSTEMIC STRUCTURAL

Explanation 2: Democracies do not go to war with one another because they share common domestic norms and institutions.[9]

With its emphasis on common norms and institutions, this statement again suggests that identity factors are the cause of the democratic peace, but this result now requires at least two states that are both democratic. It's not enough that just one state is democratic. So, the primary cause is no longer coming from inside one country alone, or the domestic level of analysis. It is coming from the systemic level. But is it the process or the structural level? The statement tells us how the two countries are positioned with respect to one another—they share common democratic norms and institutions. It does not tell us how they interact with one another and whether democratic norms matter most in that process. Thus, the explanation is from the systemic structural level of analysis, not the systemic process level. It depends on the countries' relative or shared identities as democracies.

CAUSAL ARROW: PERSPECTIVES

Sharing common norms	Creates peaceful behavior	Eliminates war
IDENTITY	LIBERAL	REALIST

CAUSAL ARROW: LEVELS OF ANALYSIS

Position between democracies	Causes peaceful behavior between countries	Overrides national security concerns
SYSTEMIC STRUCTURAL	SYSTEMIC PROCESS	DOMESTIC

Explanation 3: Democracies do not go to war with one another because they trade more with one another and do not want to forfeit the mutual gains from trade.[10]

Now the explanation shifts from an identity to a liberal perspective. The statement says democracies do not fight not because they share common values but because they trade more with one another than with other countries. More trade creates a stake in non-zero-sum gains and a reluctance to forfeit those gains through war. Why democracies trade more with one another is another question that may have something to do with their democratic nature. But it is also possible that trade

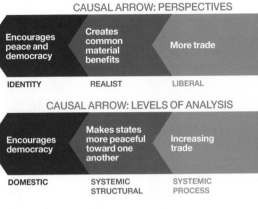

creates peace and that peace then encourages democracy. Democracy may be a consequence, not a cause. (Notice, again, the importance of the direction of causal arrows.) The level of analysis is clearly systemic process because countries have to trade or interact a lot with one another before they experience the outcome of peace.

Explanation 4: Democracies do not go to war with one another because they belong to the same international institutions, whose laws and practices they follow.[11]

Again the explanation is liberal because the outcome depends on interactions, this time within international institutions rather than through trade. The level of analysis is systemic process if the outcome depends on processes within international institutions or systemic structural if it depends on the rules of the institutions or the specialized roles that states play within these institutions.

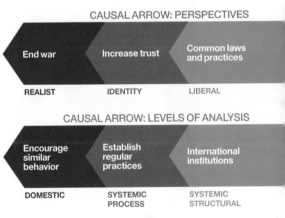

Explanation 5: Democracies do not go to war with one another because they have unique contracting or negotiating advantages that allow them to settle disputes without war.[12]

This explanation suggests that negotiations or diplomatic efforts (liberal factors) cause the outcome, although it still doesn't explain why democracies have such unique negotiating advantages. If we argue that democracies have these advantages because they are democracies, identity factors become the primary independent variable and diplomacy is an intervening variable. But negotiating skill may be the primary independent variable producing peaceful outcomes, which in turn encourage democracy. Once again, the direction of the causal arrows matters. The level of analysis is systemic process because diplomacy involves interactions and democracies achieve peace only

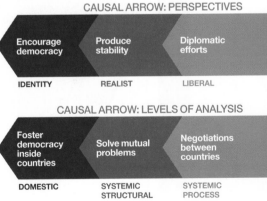

through these interactions, not alone or as a result of their relative or shared positions.

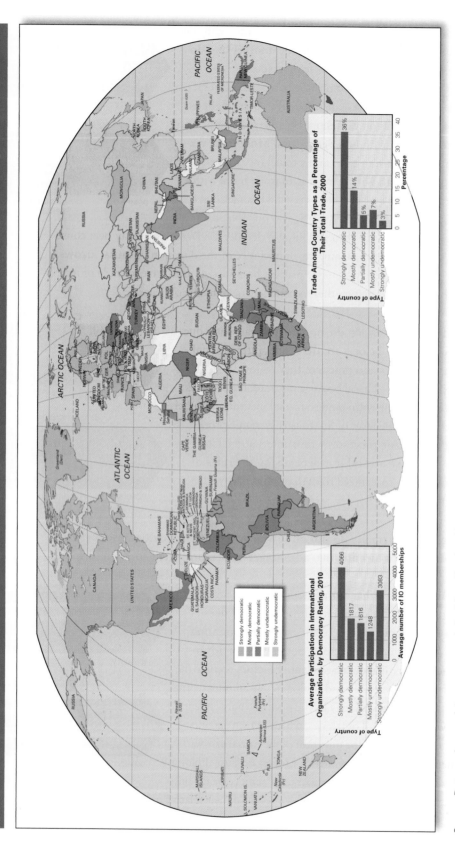

Measures of the Democratic Peace: Democratization, Trade, and Participation in International Organizations

Trade Among Country Types as a Percentage of Their Total Trade, 2000

Strongly democratic — 36%
Mostly democratic — 14%
Partially democratic — 5%
Mostly undemocratic — 7%
Strongly undemocratic — 3%

Type of country

Percentage

Average Participation in International Organizations, by Democracy Rating, 2010

Strongly democratic — 4066
Mostly democratic — 1817
Partially democratic — 1616
Mostly undemocratic — 1248
Strongly undemocratic — 3083

Type of country

Average number of IO memberships

Strongly democratic
Mostly democratic
Partially democratic
Mostly undemocratic
Strongly undemocratic

Source: Data on degree of democracy are derived from Freedom House's *Freedom in the World 2013 Survey,* http://www.freedomhouse.org/template.cfm?page=594. Data on membership in international organizations are from Jon C. Pevehouse, Timothy Nordstrom, and Kevin Warnke, "The COW-2 International Organizations Dataset Version 2.0," *Conflict Management and Peace Science* 21, no. 2 (2004): 101–19. Version 2.3, on which this figure is based, is available at http://www.correlatesofwar.org. All trade data are derived from Kristian S. Gleditsch's "Expanded Trade and GDP" data set, http://privatewww.essex.ac.uk/~ksg/exptradegdp.html.

Note: Data for membership in international organizations (IOs) for the year 2005 include all three types of membership coded for in the Correlates of War database: full, associate, and observer. Differences would be more pronounced but for the fact that the data weigh IOs and the quality of participation by each state in IOs equally, even though some IOs are more important than others and strong democracies clearly play a more important role in the most important IOs. Trade data given here show the amount of trade that countries in each democracy category do with one another, expressed as a percentage of the total trade those kinds of countries conduct. For instance, strongly democratic countries conduct 36 percent of all their total trade worldwide with other strong democracies, whereas strongly undemocratic countries conduct only 3 percent of their total trade with other strongly undemocratic countries. This result suggests that trade may also be a cause of peace among strongly democratic countries because these countries risk a greater loss of trade, and hence wealth, by going to war with one another.

Explanation 6: Democracies do not go to war with one another because they belong to the same alliances counterbalancing or fighting other alliances.[13]

Now the explanation shifts to a realist perspective. Alliances and the balance of power explain the outcome, not democracy, trade, or diplomacy. The level of analysis is systemic structural if we emphasize the relative positioning of opposing alliances within the system or systemic process if we emphasize the interactions by which alliances form and change.

Explanation 7: Democracies do not go to war with one another because they successfully use balance-of-power politics to avoid war.[14]

Perhaps democracies do not go to war with one another because they are effective at balancing power and avoiding war. This is a realist explanation because peace is a product of balance-of-power politics, not of democracy or institutional factors. Of course, the question remains why democratic states are so good at balancing power that they seem to avoid war more often than nondemocratic states. If the answer is because they are democratic, the explanation becomes identity and policies to balance power become intervening variables. On the other hand, if the peaceful behavior is a product of policies to balance power and peaceful behavior in turn leads to more democracy, the explanation is realist. The level of analysis is systemic process because the outcome is achieved through policy interactions between democracies, not through their relative positions or internal attributes.

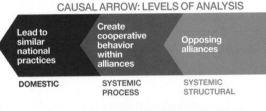

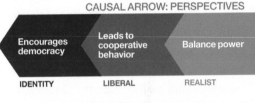

SUMMARY

As you can tell, sorting through so many variables and explanations from democratic peace studies is difficult, to say the least. Analysts change their minds as the work proceeds. Bruce Russett, a pioneer of democratic peace studies, concludes in an early work that "even when controls for physical distance, alliance, wealth, economic growth, and political stability are incorporated into the analysis, an independent explanatory role for democracy remains."[15] In a later study, however, he finds that trade and international organizations also make democracies more reluctant to go to war.[16] As Map Conclusion-1 shows, compared with nondemocracies, democracies tend to trade more with one another and to participate more fully and aggressively in international organizations. But do trade and international organizations affect the outcome independently, or do they affect peace because democracies are more inclined than other states to trade and to join international organizations?[17] Russett, who believed domestic norms and institutions were the best explanation in his early work, now concludes that all three factors—domestic norms and institutions, trade, and international organizations—shape the outcome of the democratic peace. Russett combines identity factors (democracy) and liberal factors (trade and institutions) while rejecting realist explanations of the democratic peace. His explanations come primarily from the domestic and systemic process levels, not the systemic structural level of analysis.[18]

In his conclusion, Russett acknowledges that overlapping and multiple explanations of the democratic peace can lead to an **overdetermined outcome**. Political scientists worry about the interaction of independent variables, or what they call colinearity (two variables) and multicolinearity (multiple variables). We can't say which variable may be the most important; they all seem to be necessary to produce the outcome. Critical theory perspectives and constructivist methodologies might respond, "I told you so." The causes are interactive and cumulative. Peace is not caused by democracy but by the overweening presence of hegemony (critical theory perspective). Or peace is an appropriate or more persuasive outcome associated with social discourse among democracies (constructivist methodology). Notice that this issue is our old problem of the need to select facts and make judgments without ever having all the facts in hand to make a definitive judgment. If everything causes something, nothing does. Or, at least, we can't know what does. Science has reached its limits.

CODA

Well, we've finished our introductory exploration of the field of international relations. The short excursion through the studies of the democratic peace brings together many of the factors stressed throughout this book: the roles of perspectives, levels of analysis, causal arrows, methodological issues, judgment, history (compiling historical cases of relations among democracies), and, ultimately, moral values. Why do we study the democratic peace? Are we being neutral and unbiased, or are we perhaps hoping that the democratic peace is true and that we may work, therefore, toward a world in which democratic values and a democratic way of life prevail? Would we be as enthusiastic if the evidence showed that nondemocracies were more peaceful toward one another than democracies? But, then, maybe we are just taking the facts as we can best assess them. George Shultz says democracies work better, and the most advanced countries, if wealth is one measure of what works, are indeed all democracies.

And President Clinton felt strongly that democracies not only work better but are also more peaceful.

overdetermined outcome: an outcome caused by multiple independent variables, the separate and interactive effects of which are not clear.

Take two thoughts away with you as you put this book on the shelf for future reference. The ability to know things for sure is very difficult. Science encourages us to think rationally and test our perspectives against the facts as systematically and objectively as possible. That's good. But critical theory cautions us against such rationalist approaches, and science is not an answer; it is a method. Always be modest about what you think you know. Take a course in the philosophy of science, and you'll learn that even natural scientists, who study inanimate objects without minds of their own, can never know the way the natural world really works. They can only know, when their model tests out positively, that the world works in ways consistent with that model. But the world may also work in ways consistent with other, totally different models that have yet to be (and may never be) discovered. So, at a minimum, be prepared to spend the rest of your life learning. Keep an open mind, listen to others, be modest enough not to impugn others who disagree with you as being stupid or evil. They may be both (happy thought, right?)—ignorance and evil do exist. But they may also be emphasizing another perspective that is also consistent with the facts. We should be aware of our own ignorance and potential for evil if we wish to work for a better world.

And that's the second thought. You still have to make judgments, almost always without complete information or knowledge. Don't shy away from making decisions. If you fail to choose—if you always wait for more information—the world may pass you by. Develop trust in your own judgment. Learning and growing, as someone reminded me early in my teaching career, are a full body exercise. You need your head, but you also need your heart and maybe, most of all, your spirit and values. Because we are dealing with other human beings, not just with physical phenomena, we need a basis that goes beyond physical phenomena even if we ultimately find out that we humans—our minds, spirits, and even our humanity itself—can be understood in purely physical (chemical, biological, and electrical) terms. How will we treat one another if and when we discover that? And if it depends on which electrode we stimulate or which drug we take, who decides what must be done and who administers these remedies? If no one does, if we are all simply products of our physical sensations, what does it mean to be human?

Think now, at the end of this book, about where we began—the situation in Syria. We can't act responsibly until we know something about Syria. But we can't read everything about Syria because that would require too much time and we may never act, especially in a timely way to affect events while they are still fluid. So, we study with diligence and act with modesty using what we know, being aware that we don't know it all, and maintaining a reverence for what we all are—human beings who think and change even as we study and seek to influence one another.

 Sharpen your skills with SAGE edge at **edge.sagepub.com/nau4e.** **SAGE edge for students** provides a personalized approach to help you accomplish your coursework goals in an easy-to-use learning environment.

KEY CONCEPTS

democratic peace, 476

overdetermined outcome, 484

sample size, 478

STUDY QUESTIONS

1. What is the primary level of analysis of these two statements? (a) Democracies rarely fight one another compared to other states. (b) Democracies fight less against all states.

2. How would constructivist methodology and critical theory critique democratic peace studies?

3. How do researchers generate more cases to test the correlation between democracy and no war?

4. Give an explanation of the democratic peace from each perspective and level of analysis.

5. Why, in your judgment, should the evidence of the democratic peace either play a role or not play a role in American foreign policy?

NOTES

Introduction, pages 1–24

1. Quoted in Douglas Martin, "Kenneth Waltz, Foreign-Relations Expert, Dies at 88," *New York Times*, May 19, 2013, A22.

2. Charles Tilly, *Coercion, Capital, and European States, A.D. 990–1992* (Cambridge, MA: Blackwell, 1990), 35.

3. Ronald Steel, "The Weak at War with the Strong," *New York Times*, September 14, 2001, A27.

4. Caryle Murphy, "A Hatred Rooted in Failings," *Washington Post*, September 16, 2001, B1.

5. Jim Hoagland, "The Mideast's Political Pygmies," *Washington Post*, August 1, 2002, A27.

6. Noam Chomsky, *Failed States: The Abuse of Power and the Assault on Democracy* (New York: Metropolitan/Owl Books, 2006), 14.

7. The labels sometimes differ. Some scholars call rationalist methods naturalist, positivist, or scientific. For a clear introductory discussion, see Jonathon W. Moses and Torbjørn L. Knutsen, *Ways of Knowing: Competing Methodologies in Social and Political Research*, 2nd ed. (New York: Palgrave Macmillan, 2012).

8. See John Gerard Ruggie, "Continuity and Transformation in the World Polity: Toward a Neorealist Synthesis," in *Neorealism and Its Critics*, ed. Robert O. Keohane (New York: Columbia University Press, 1986), 131–57.

9. For more on the debate regarding whether one perspective is better or more objective than another, see David A. Lake, "Why 'Isms' Are Evil: Theory, Epistemology, and Academic Sects as Impediments to Understanding and Progress," and my response, Henry R. Nau, "No Alternative to 'Isms,'" *International Studies Quarterly* 55, no. 2 (June 2011): 465–80 and 487–91, respectively.

10. Sean Wilentz, *The Age of Reagan: A History, 1974–2008* (New York: HarperCollins, 2008), 11.

11. A former Central Intelligence Agency official, who was in the intelligence community in spring 2003 and became a sharp critic of the administration after he left government, wrote, "The Bush administration was quite right: its perception of Saddam's weapons capacities was shared by the Clinton administration, congressional Democrats, and most other Western governments and intelligence services." Paul Pillar, "Intelligence, Policy, and the War in Iraq," *Foreign Affairs* 85, no. 2 (March–April 2006). See also Mortimer B. Zuckerman, "Foul-ups—Not Felonies," *U.S. News & World Report*, November 14, 2005.

12. Jim Hoagland, "Little Help Going Forward," *Washington Post*, July 29, 2004, A23.

13. Quoted in James MacGregor Burns, *Roosevelt: The Lion and the Fox* (New York: Harcourt, Brace, 1956), 157.

14. "The Man Who Beat Communism," *The Economist*, June 12, 2004, 13.

15. These three views are labeled variously by international relations scholars, but they represent the same basic points of view. Michael W. Doyle calls the three views revolutionary (universalist), realist (relativist), and rationalist (pragmatist). Joseph S. Nye Jr. calls them cosmopolitan (universalist), state skeptics (relativist), and state moralist (pragmatist). See Doyle, *Ways of War and Peace* (New York: Norton, 1997), 3; Nye, *Understanding International Conflicts: An Introduction to Theory and History*, 5th ed. (New York: Pearson-Longman, 2005), 23–28.

16. Kofi Annan, "Two Concepts of Sovereignty," *The Economist*, September 18, 1999, 49–50.

17. The story comes from Nye, *Understanding International Conflicts*, 25.

Chapter 1. How to Think about International Relations, pages 25–80

1. Thomas Risse, "'Let's Argue!': Communicative Action in World Politics," *International Organization* 54, no. 1 (Winter 2000): 3.

2. The prisoner's dilemma story comes from game theory, a rational choice approach to the study of international affairs. The rational choice approach emphasizes interactions or the liberal perspective. We use the story here not as a rigorous exercise within that perspective, but to show how changes in assumptions lead to different perspectives and interpretations of the same facts.

3. In the original prisoner's dilemma game, the actors have mixed motives, meaning they have both conflicting (can't go free together) and common (avoid worst outcome of twenty-five years) interests. Changing the goal to frustrating the warden gives the prisoners a dominant interest in common goals and converts the game to a no-conflict situation. Now each actor prefers to cooperate, the upper left box, regardless of what the other actor does. See Arthur A. Stein, *Why Nations Cooperate: Circumstances and Choice in International Relations* (Ithaca, NY: Cornell University Press, 1990), 29.

4. Making the lower right box (DD) least desirable for both prisoners converts the situation from a prisoner's dilemma game to a game of chicken, in which two drivers speed toward one another, risking death unless one or both swerve to avoid the collision. See Glenn H. Snyder and Paul Diesing, *Conflict among Nations: Bargaining, Decision Making, and System Structure in International Crises* (Princeton, NJ: Princeton University Press, 1977), 43–44.

5. Dates herein use the notations B.C.E., for "before the common era" (rather than B.C.), and C.E., for "of the common era" (rather than A.D.).

6. Kenneth N. Waltz, *Theory of International Politics* (New York: Random House, 1979), 131.

7. Robert Gilpin, *War and Change in World Politics* (Princeton, NJ: Princeton University Press, 1981).

8. Hans J. Morgenthau, *Politics among Nations: The Struggle for Power and Peace*, 6th ed., ed. Kenneth W. Thompson (New York: Alfred A. Knopf, 1985), 5.

9. For examples of defensive and offensive realist accounts, see Charles Glaser, *Rational Theory of International Politics: The Logic of Competition and Cooperation* (Princeton, NJ: Princeton University Press, 2010); John Mearsheimer, *The Tragedy of Great Power Politics* (New York: Norton, 2001).

10. Robert Kagan, *The World America Made* (New York: Alfred A. Knopf, 2012), 90.

11. Winston S. Churchill, *The Second World War: The Grand Alliance* (Boston: Houghton Mifflin, 1950), 370.

12. Randall L. Schweller, *Deadly Imbalances: Tripolarity and Hitler's Strategy of World Conquest* (New York: Columbia University Press, 1997).

13. Waltz, *Theory of International Politics;* Mearsheimer, *Tragedy of Great Power Politics.*

14. Dale C. Copeland, *The Origins of Major War* (Ithaca, NY: Cornell University Press, 2000).

15. Daniel S. Geller and J. David Singer, *Nations at War: A Scientific Study of International Conflict* (Cambridge: Cambridge University Press, 1998), 117.

16. See Charles A. Kupchan, *No One's World: The West, the Rising Rest, and the Coming Global Turn* (New York: Oxford University Press, 2012), 185.

17. Paul Kennedy, *The Rise and Fall of the Great Powers: Economic Change and Military Conflict from 1500 to 2000* (New York: Random House, 1987).

18. Morgenthau, *Politics among Nations,* 12.

19. Robert O. Keohane, "Reciprocity in International Relations," *International Organization* 40, no. 1 (Winter 1986): 1–29.

20. See Joseph S. Nye Jr. and David A. Welch, *Understanding Global Conflict and Cooperation: An Introduction to Theory and History,* 9th ed. (New York: Pearson, 2012).

21. Robert O. Keohane, *International Institutions and State Power: Essays in International Relations Theory* (Boulder, CO: Westview Press, 1989), 10.

22. David A. Lake, "Relational Authority and Legitimacy in International Relations," *American Behavioral Scientist* 53, no. 3 (November 2009): 332. See also David A. Lake, *Hierarchy in International Relations* (Ithaca, NY: Cornell University Press, 2011).

23. David A. Lake, "Two Cheers for Bargaining Theory: Assessing Rationalist Explanations of the Iraq War," *International Security* 35, no. 3 (Winter 2010–2011): 7–52.

24. See Stephen D. Krasner, ed., *International Regimes* (Ithaca, NY: Cornell University Press, 1983).

25. Ernst B. Haas, *When Knowledge Is Power: Three Models of Change in International Organizations* (Berkeley: University of California Press, 1990).

26. See Michael N. Barnett and Martha Finnemore, "The Politics, Power, and Pathologies of International Organizations," *International Organization* 53, no. 4 (Autumn 1999): 699–732.

27. G. John Ikenberry, "Introduction: Woodrow Wilson, the Bush Administration, and the Future of Liberal Internationalism," in *The Crisis of American Foreign*

Policy: Wilsonianism in the Twenty-First Century, by G. John Ikenberry, Thomas J. Knock, Anne-Marie Slaughter, and Tony Smith (Princeton, NJ: Princeton University Press, 2009), 16.

28. Michael Steiner, "The Legitimacy to Succeed," *Washington Post,* May 18, 2003, B7 (emphasis in original).

29. Jürgen Habermas, *The Theory of Communicative Action,* vol. 1, *Reason and the Rationalization of Society,* trans. Thomas A. McCarthy (Boston: Beacon Press, 1984); Jürgen Habermas, *The Theory of Communicative Action,* vol. 2, *Lifeworld and System: A Critique of Functionalist Reason,* trans. Thomas A. McCarthy (Boston: Beacon Press, 1987).

30. See Mark L. Haas, *The Ideological Origins of Great Power Politics, 1789–1989* (Ithaca, NY: Cornell University Press, 2005); John M. Owen IV, *The Clash of Ideas in World Politics: Transnational Networks, States, and Regime Change, 1510–2010* (Princeton, NJ: Princeton University Press, 2010); Jeffrey W. Legro, "Whence American Internationalism," *International Organization* 54, no. 2 (Spring 2000): 253–89.

31. Richard Ned Lebow, *A Cultural Theory of International Relations* (Cambridge: Cambridge University Press, 2010).

32. See Edward Hallett Carr, *The Twenty Years' Crisis, 1919–1939* (New York: Harper Torchbooks, 1964), 8.

33. John Gerard Ruggie, *Constructing the World Polity* (London: Routledge, 1998), xi.

34. See, for example, Joshua S. Goldstein and John C. Pevehouse, *International Relations,* 10th ed. (New York: Pearson, 2012), 97.

35. Martha Finnemore, *The Purpose of Intervention: Changing Beliefs about the Use of Force* (Ithaca, NY: Cornell University Press, 2004).

36. See Alexander Wendt, *Social Theory of International Politics* (Cambridge: Cambridge University Press, 1999), 1.

37. Risse, "'Let's Argue!,'" 10.

38. Ibid., 23–28.

39. Alexander Wendt, "Anarchy Is What States Make of It: The Social Construction of Power Politics," *International Organization* 46, no. 2 (Spring 1992): 391–425.

40. Thomas Risse-Kappen, "Collective Identity in a Democratic Community: The Case of NATO," in *The Culture of National Security: Norms and Identity in World Politics,* ed. Peter J. Katzenstein (New York: Columbia University Press, 1996), 367.

41. Michael N. Barnett, "Identity and Alliances in the Middle East," in Katzenstein, *Culture of National Security,* 412.

42. Owen, *Clash of Ideas in World Politics.*

43. Haas, *Ideological Origins of Great Power Politics.*

44. Peter J. Katzenstein, "Introduction," in Katzenstein, *Culture of National Security,* 24.

45. See Matthew Evangelista, "The Paradox of State Strength: Transnational Relations, Domestic Structures, and Security Policy in Russia and the Soviet Union," *International Organization* 49, no. 1 (Winter 1995): 1–39.

46. See Martha Finnemore, *National Interests in International Society* (Ithaca, NY: Cornell University Press, 1996).

47. Alastair Iain Johnston, *Social States: China in International Institutions, 1980–2000* (Princeton, NJ: Princeton University Press, 2008), 199.

48. Emanuel Adler and Michael Barnett, eds., *Security Communities* (Cambridge: Cambridge University Press, 1998).

49. Peter M. Haas, ed., *Knowledge, Power, and Policy Coordination* (Columbia: University of South Carolina Press, 1992).

50. Barnett, "Identity and Alliances in the Middle East," 407.

51. Joseph S. Nye Jr., *Soft Power: The Means to Success in World Politics* (New York: Public Affairs, 2004).

52. See, for example, Judith Goldstein and Robert O. Keohane, eds., *Ideas and Foreign Policy: Beliefs, Institutions, and Political Change* (Ithaca, NY: Cornell University Press, 1993).

53. See Robert Jervis, *Perceptions and Misperceptions in International Politics* (Princeton, NJ: Princeton University Press, 1976). For a survey of psychological approaches to international relations, see James M. Goldgeier and Philip E. Tetlock, "Psychology and International Relations Theory," *Annual Review of Political Science* 4 (2001): 67–92.

54. This approach is called prospect theory. For discussion of its application to international affairs, see Jack S. Levy, "Prospect Theory and International Relations: Theoretical Applications and Analytical Problems," *Political Psychology* 13, no. 2 (June 1992): 283–310.

55. J. Ann Tickner, *Gender in International Relations: Feminist Perspectives on Achieving Global Security* (New York: Columbia University Press, 1992), 130.

56. Robert W. Cox, with Timothy J. Sinclair, *Approaches to World Order* (Cambridge: Cambridge University Press, 1996), 90.

57. Gramsci wrote three volumes of notes while imprisoned by the fascist government in Italy from 1926 to 1935. See Antonio Gramsci, *Selections from the Prison Notebooks,* ed. and trans. Quintin Hoare and Geoffrey Nowell Smith (New York: International, 1971).

58. See, among others, Jacques Derrida and Alan Bass, *Positions* (Chicago: University of Chicago Press, 1982); Michel Foucault, *The Archeology of Knowledge* (New York: Vintage, 1982).

59. Kenneth N. Waltz, *Man, the State, and War: A Theoretical Analysis* (New York: Columbia University Press, 1959).

60. Peter Trubowitz, *Politics and Strategy: Partisan Ambition and American Statecraft* (Princeton, NJ: Princeton University Press, 2011), xiii, 1.

61. Robert D. Putnam, "Diplomacy and Domestic Politics: The Logic of Two-Level Games," *International Organization* 42, no. 3 (Summer 1988): 427–61.

62. Bruce Bueno de Mesquita, *Principles of International Relations: People's Power, Preferences, and Perceptions* (Washington, DC: CQ Press, 2003), 7.

Part I. Historical Patterns, pages 81–82

1. Paul Kennedy, *The Rise and Fall of the Great Powers: Economic Change and Military Conflict from 1500 to 2000* (New York: Random House, 1987), 27–28.

2. Paul W. Schroeder, *The Transformation of European Politics, 1763–1848* (New York: Oxford University Press, 1994), xiii.

3. John M. Owen IV, *The Clash of Ideas in World Politics: Transnational Networks, States, and Regime Change, 1510–2010* (Princeton: Princeton University Press, 2010), 9.

Chapter 2. World War I, pages 83–112

1. For relevant excerpts of the Willy-Nicky telegrams, see Robert K. Massie, *Nicholas and Alexandra* (New York: Dell, 1967), 269–74.

2. John J. Mearsheimer, *The Tragedy of Great Power Politics* (New York: Norton, 2001), 213.

3. Quoted in Hans W. Koch, *A History of Prussia* (New York: Dorset Press, 1978), 341.

4. Relative wealth is measured in terms of iron/steel production and energy consumption. See Mearsheimer, *Tragedy of Great Power Politics,* 66–71.

5. Ibid., 187.

6. Ibid., 72.

7. Fareed Zakaria, *From Wealth to Power: The Unusual Origins of America's World Role* (Princeton, NJ: Princeton University Press, 1998).

8. Stephen R. Rock, *Why Peace Breaks Out: Great Power Rapprochement in Historical Perspective* (Chapel Hill: University of North Carolina Press, 1989).

9. For the relevant paragraph of Crowe's long memorandum, see Joseph S. Nye Jr., *Understanding International Conflicts: An Introduction to Theory and History,* 4th ed. (New York: Longman, 2003), 70.

10. Mearsheimer, *Tragedy of Great Power Politics,* 71.

11. Quoted in Dale C. Copeland, *The Origins of Major War* (Ithaca, NY: Cornell University Press, 2000), 63–64.

12. Some German officials, such as von Schlieffen, did advocate preventive war in 1905. See Marc Trachtenberg, *History and Strategy* (Princeton, NJ: Princeton University Press, 1991), 60–61.

13. Copeland, *Origins of Major War,* 90, 93.

14. This is Copeland's conclusion in ibid., 117.

15. Jack Snyder, *Myths of Empire: Domestic Politics and International Ambition* (Ithaca, NY: Cornell University Press, 1991), 66–67.

16. Ibid., 99.

17. Ibid., 67.

18. For example, Henry Kissinger writes, "Though Bismarck's style of diplomacy was probably doomed by the end of his period in office, it was far from inevitable that it should have been replaced by a mindless armaments race and rigid alliances." Kissinger, *Diplomacy* (New York: Simon & Schuster, 1994), 165. He admits earlier in this book, however, that "the requirements of Realpolitik became too intricate to sustain" (160).

19. Quoted in Otto Pflanze, *Bismarck and the Development of Germany,* vol. 1 (Princeton, NJ: Princeton University Press, 1990), 489.

20. Robert K. Massie, *Dreadnought: Britain, Germany, and the Coming of the Great War* (New York: Random House, 1991).

21. Here is another of many examples where scholars interpret the same facts differently. No one disagrees

with the fact that Germany issued a blank check, but some analysts believe Germany intended the blank check to encourage an immediate limited action by Austria against Serbia, while others believe it encouraged Austria to delay and provoke a wider war. See Jack S. Levy, "Preferences, Constraints, and Choices in July 1914," *International Security* 15, no. 3 (Winter 1990–1991), 171.

22. Quoted in Massie, *Dreadnought*, 875.

23. Trachtenberg, *History and Strategy*, 59.

24. This history has personal significance for me. My grandfather, then a German citizen, marched into Belgium with the German advance. My father, a four-year-old boy at the time, thinks—because memories usually don't start that early—he remembers his dad's leaving the family in Chemnitz arrayed in battlefield uniform and gear.

25. Trachtenberg, *History and Strategy*, 91–92.

26. See Kier A. Lieber, "The New History of World War I and What It Means for International Relations Theory," *International Security* 32, no. 2 (Fall 2007): 157.

27. Ibid., 156.

28. Trachtenberg, *History and Strategy*, 90.

29. Fritz Fischer, *The War of Illusions* (New York: Norton, 1975), viii.

30. Norman Angell, *The Great Illusion* (London: Heinemann, 1912).

31. Quoted in Kissinger, *Diplomacy*, 161.

32. Robert E. Osgood and Robert W. Tucker, *Force, Order, and Justice* (Baltimore: Johns Hopkins University Press, 1967), 51, 52.

33. Stephen van Evera, *Causes of War: Power and the Roots of Conflict* (Ithaca, NY: Cornell University Press, 1999).

34. See Michael W. Doyle, *Ways of War and Peace* (New York: Norton, 1997), 253.

35. Quoted in Snyder, *Myths of Empire*, 83.

36. Quoted in Walter A. McDougall, *Promised Land, Crusader State: The American Encounter with the World since 1776* (Boston: Houghton Mifflin, 1997), 105.

37. Quoted in Fritz Fischer, *Germany's Aims in the First World War* (New York: Norton, 1967), 33.

38. Quoted in ibid., 33, 59.

39. Quoted in Asa Briggs, *The Age of Improvements, 1783–1867* (London: Longman, 1959), 351. Henry Kissinger, a realist, cites Palmerston's realist quotation

from Briggs but not the second, identity-oriented quotation. Kissinger, *Diplomacy*, 96.

40. Mearsheimer, *Tragedy of Great Power Politics*, 214.

41. Levy, "Preferences, Constraints, and Choices," 186.

42. Snyder, *Myths of Empire*, 71.

Chapter 3. World War II, pages 113–148

1. The Hossbach memorandum raises another problem in the analysis of international affairs—the authenticity of documents. Hossbach drafted it five days after the meeting. Why did he wait so long? Were bureaucratic games being played and memos written to tilt the record? Some German generals—for example, General Werner von Fritsch—objected to Hitler's plans at the meeting. Air force and army generals were battling behind the scenes for resources to build up German arms. Hitler never reviewed the Hossbach memorandum, although he was asked to do so twice. So, how official or important was it? Subsequently, the original memo disappeared. It was found in 1943 by a German officer, Count Kirchbach, and copied for the Hossbach German archives. Later, the Americans found it and copied it again for presentation at the Nuremberg trials. Hossbach and Kirchbach subsequently said the Nuremberg copy was shorter than the original and did not include criticisms expressed at the meeting. Did the Americans edit the document to pin blame for the war more squarely on the German leadership? The original document was never found. In this case, there is probably enough other evidence to confirm the general thrust of the meeting. But not everyone agrees. See A. J. P. Taylor, *The Origins of the Second World War* (New York: Atheneum, 1961), xxiii. One side note: my wife and I lived in Bad Godesberg, Germany, in 1969–1970, in the downstairs apartment of the home of Freiherr von Fritsch, a nephew of the general who attended the Hitler meeting. (And you think history doesn't really touch us?) My one regret: I was not yet sufficiently interested to know enough about the Hossbach memorandum to ask the nephew what he or his father (the general's brother) might have known about this controversial document. Don't make my mistake. Get interested now!

2. John Mueller, *The Remnants of War* (Ithaca, NY: Cornell University Press, 2007), 5.

3. Margaret MacMillan, *Paris 1919: Six Months That Changed the World* (New York: Random House, 2002).

4. Quoted in Henry Kissinger, *Diplomacy* (New York: Simon & Schuster, 1994), 127.

5. See Woodrow Wilson's address to Congress, April 2, 1917, History Matters, http://historymatters.gmu.edu/d/4943.

6. Quoted in Kalevi J. Holsti, *Peace and War: Armed Conflicts and International Order, 1648–1989* (Cambridge: Cambridge University Press, 1991), 184.

7. Quoted in Inis L. Claude Jr., *Swords into Plowshares: The Problems and Progress of International Organization*, 4th ed. (New York: Random House, 1971), 52.

8. Quoted in Margaret P. Karns and Karen A. Mingst, *International Organizations: The Politics and Processes of Global Governance* (Boulder, CO: Lynne Rienner, 2004), 283.

9. Quoted in Kissinger, *Diplomacy*, 281.

10. Quoted in Joseph S. Nye Jr., *Understanding International Conflicts: An Introduction to Theory and History*, 5th ed. (New York: Pearson-Longman, 2005), 93.

11. John J. Mearsheimer, *The Tragedy of Great Power Politics* (New York: Norton, 2001), 71, 305.

12. Ibid., 71.

13. Kissinger is one realist who disagrees: "The destruction of Czechoslovakia made no geopolitical sense whatsoever . . . because Czechoslovakia was bound to slip into the German orbit, and . . . Germany would eventually emerge as the dominant power in Eastern Europe." But that begs the questions why Germany had to be dominant in eastern Europe in the first place and why the other powers could not accept this dominance. Maybe structural forces were at work after all. See Kissinger, *Diplomacy*, 316.

14. According to Mearsheimer, Germany was already the wealthiest country in Europe by 1930, but it did not convert this wealth into superior military power until 1939–1940. See Mearsheimer, *Tragedy of Great Power Politics*, 71, 316–17.

15. Robert Conquest, *The Great Terror: Stalin's Purge of the Thirties* (New York: Macmillan, 1968); Robert Conquest, *The Great Terror: A Reassessment* (New York: Oxford University Press, 1990).

16. Kissinger, *Diplomacy*, 367–68.

17. Mearsheimer, *Tragedy of Great Power Politics*, 73.

18. Eric Nordlinger, *Isolationism Reconfigured: American Foreign Policy for a New Century* (Princeton, NJ: Princeton University Press, 1995).

19. Quoted in Nye, *Understanding International Conflicts*, 104.

20. Mearsheimer, *Tragedy of Great Power Politics*.

21. Peter Lieberman, *Does Conquest Pay? The Exploitation of Occupied Industrial Societies* (Princeton, NJ: Princeton University Press, 1996).

22. Jack Snyder, *Myths of Empire: Domestic Politics and International Ambition* (Ithaca, NY: Cornell University Press, 1991), 105.

23. Ibid., 108.

24. Randall L. Schweller, *Deadly Imbalances: Tripolarity and Hitler's Strategy of World Conquest* (New York: Columbia University Press, 1998).

25. Dale C. Copeland, *The Origins of Major War* (Ithaca, NY: Cornell University Press, 2000), chap. 5.

26. Stephen M. Walt, *The Origins of Alliances* (Ithaca, NY: Cornell University Press, 1987).

27. See, for example, Michael N. Barnett, "Identity and Alliances in the Middle East," in *The Culture of National Security: Norms and Identity in World Politics*, ed. Peter J. Katzenstein (New York: Columbia University Press, 1996), esp. 403–13.

28. Taylor, *Origins of the Second World War*, 219.

29. Ibid., 216.

30. Thomas J. Christensen and Jack Snyder, "Chain Gangs and Passed Bucks: Predicting Alliance Patterns in Multipolarity," *International Organization* 44 (1990): 137–68.

31. Copeland, *Origins of Major War*, 238–39.

32. Mark L. Haas, *The Ideological Origins of Great Power Politics, 1789–1989* (Ithaca, NY: Cornell University Press, 2005), chap. 4.

33. Alexander Keyssar, *The Right to Vote: The Contested History of Democracy in the United States* (New York: Basic Books, 2000).

34. Mearsheimer, *Tragedy of Great Power Politics*, 255, 320. A year later, after Roosevelt began a deliberate effort to strengthen the United States, the nation's army had grown to 1,460,998.

35. Samuel P. Huntington, *The Third Wave: Democratization in the Late Twentieth Century* (Norman: University of Oklahoma Press, 1991), 17–18.

36. Again, a personal aside to show why history is interesting: my father was a small boy, eight to ten years old,

in Berlin at the time and remembers being asked by his mother to forage through garbage cans at the army barracks nearby for potato peelings for the family to eat.

37. Conquest, *Great Terror: A Reassessment.*

38. Taylor, *Origins of the Second World War,* 51. Others disagree. See Copeland, *Origins of Major War,* 123.

39. Copeland, *Origins of Major War,* 120.

40. Haas, *Ideological Origins of Great Power Politics,* 113.

41. Charles A. Beard and Mary R. Beard, *The Rise of American Civilization,* vol. 2 (New York: Macmillan, 1930), 344–45.

42. Charles A. Beard, *President Roosevelt and the Coming of War, 1941* (New Haven, CT: Yale University Press, 1948).

43. Quoted in Kissinger, *Diplomacy,* 341–42.

Chapter 4. The Origins and End of the Cold War, pages 149–186

1. George F. Kennan, *Memoirs: 1925–1950* (Boston: Little, Brown, 1967), 292–93. All quotations in these opening paragraphs are excerpts from the long telegram as reprinted in Kennan's memoirs, 547–59.

2. In later writings, Kennan made explicit that "ideology is a product and not a determinant of social and political behavior." John Lewis Gaddis, *Strategies of Containment: A Critical Appraisal of Postwar American National Security Policy* (New York: Oxford University Press, 1982), 34.

3. [George F. Kennan,] "The Sources of Soviet Conduct," *Foreign Affairs* 26, no. 2 (July 1947): 581. For security reasons, Kennan signed the article "X."

4. Henry Kissinger, *Diplomacy* (New York: Simon & Schuster, 1994), 173, 172.

5. Quoted in Milovan Djilas, *Conversations with Stalin,* trans. Michael B. Petrovich (San Diego, CA: Harcourt Brace Jovanovich, 1962), 114.

6. Quoted in Marc Trachtenberg, *A Constructed Peace: The Making of the European Settlement, 1945–1963* (Princeton, NJ: Princeton University Press, 1999), 38. Truman made this statement in a letter to Secretary of State James Byrnes in January 1946. The letter was apparently never sent, because Byrnes denied receiving it.

7. Ibid., 41.

8. Ibid.

9. Winston Churchill, "The Sinews of Peace" speech, in *Winston S. Churchill: His Complete Speeches,* *1897–1963,* vol. 7, *1943–1949,* ed. Robert Rhodes James (New York: Chelsea House, 1974), 7285–93.

10. William Stueck, *Rethinking the Korean War: A New Diplomatic and Strategic History* (Princeton, NJ: Princeton University Press, 2002).

11. Ratio drawn from Gordon Wright, *The Ordeal of Total War: 1939–1945* (New York: Harper & Row, 1968), 263–65.

12. Trachtenberg, *Constructed Peace,* 44–46. At Potsdam, Stalin said of Germany divided by war zones: "Germany is what has become of her after the war. No other Germany exists." Quoted in David McCullough, *Truman* (New York: Simon & Schuster, 1992), 426.

13. Another personal aside: My parents were close friends with an American soldier, Ray Twork, who was at Torgau when the two armies met. In civilian life, Ray was a graphics designer, so he was given the assignment to design the poster that was used the next day when the meeting of the two armies was replayed officially for the military brass and news reporters from all over the world.

14. David P. Calleo, *The German Problem Reconsidered: Germany and the World Order, 1870 to the Present* (New York: Cambridge University Press, 1978).

15. Winston S. Churchill, *Triumph and Tragedy: The Second World War,* vol. 6 (Boston: Houghton Mifflin, 1953), 227.

16. Quoted in McCullough, *Truman,* 537.

17. Graham Allison and Philip Zelikow, *Essence of Decision: Explaining the Cuban Missile Crisis,* 2nd ed. (New York: Longman, 1999), 92–93.

18. Richard Ned Lebow and Janice Gross Stein, *We All Lost the Cold War* (Princeton, NJ: Princeton University Press, 1994), 25.

19. Nikita Khrushchev, *Khrushchev Remembers,* trans. and ed. Strobe Talbott (Boston: Little, Brown, 1970), 493.

20. Not everyone agrees on the importance of Berlin to the Soviets. Allison and Zelikow conclude that Berlin and closing the missile gap are the most satisfactory explanations of Soviet motives in Cuba; Allison and Zelikow, *Essence of Decision,* 107. Lebow and Stein believe the defense of Cuba was more important than Berlin; Lebow and Stein, *We All Lost the Cold War,* 48.

21. Quoted in Allison and Zelikow, *Essence of Decision,* 104.

22. In an interview on October 29, one day after the Soviets conceded, Kennedy said, "We had decided Saturday

night [October 27] to begin this air strike on Tuesday [October 30]. And it may have been one of the reasons why the Russians finally did this [giving in]." Quoted in ibid., 128. We don't know whether this was just postcrisis bravado. Robert McNamara, Kennedy's secretary of defense, insisted that Kennedy did not order an air strike on Saturday night. "If President Kennedy were going to strike on Monday or Tuesday, then he would have told *me* about it so that we could make the necessary preparations. He hadn't told me, so I don't think he *was* going to strike." Quoted in Lebow and Stein, *We All Lost the Cold War,* 128. (Now do you see why it is so hard, in some cases, for scholars even to know the facts, let alone interpret them in the same way others do?)

23. Lebow and Stein, *We All Lost the Cold War,* 294–95.

24. Kennedy cabinet officials told Congress in January 1963, when speculation arose about secret understandings, that there was no deal or trade. McGeorge Bundy, Kennedy's national security adviser, later said, "We misled our colleagues, our countrymen, our successors, and our allies." Quoted in ibid., 123. What is truly mysterious is why the Soviet Union did not leak these secrets. McNamara ordered the Jupiter missiles removed on October 29, confirming that they were part of the deal. They came out six months later, while Khrushchev was still in office. Now he had every reason to reveal the secrets because they would have made the outcome of the crisis look much better for him and the Soviet Union. He didn't and was subsequently driven out of office, in part because of Moscow's humiliation in the Cuban Missile Crisis. Now, there is a mystery that could stand further research.

25. David Coleman, "After the Cuban Missile Crisis: Why Short-Range Nuclear Weapons Delivery Systems Stayed in Cuba," *Miller Center Report* 13, no. 4 (Fall 2002): 36–39.

26. Allison and Zelikow, *Essence of Decision,* 129.

27. I was a member of the 82nd Airborne Division forces that landed in the Dominican Republic in April/May 1965. OK, I'm an imperialist!

28. Quoted in Tony Smith, *America's Mission: The United States and the Worldwide Struggle for Democracy in the Twentieth Century* (Princeton, NJ: Princeton University Press, 1994), 226.

29. Paul Kennedy, *The Rise and Fall of the Great Powers: Economic Change and Military Conflict from 1500 to 2000* (New York: Random House, 1987).

30. Gary Becker and Kevin Murphy, "Do Not Let the 'Cure' Destroy Capitalism," *Financial Times,* March 19, 2009, http://www.ft.com/intl/cms/s/0/98f66b98–14be-11de-8cd1–0000779fd2ac.html#axzz2kpV3ZT00.

31. Martin Anderson and Annelise Anderson, *Reagan's Secret War: The Untold Story of His Fight to Save the World from Nuclear Disaster* (New York: Crown Books, 2009).

32. Quoted in Stephen G. Brooks and William C. Wohlforth, "Power, Globalization, and the End of the Cold War," *International Security* 25, no. 3 (Winter 2000–2001): 29.

33. Ibid., 24.

34. Ibid., 44–49.

35. Quoted in Mark L. Haas, *The Ideological Origins of Great Power Politics, 1789–1989* (Ithaca, NY: Cornell University Press, 2005), 178.

36. Gaddis, *Strategies of Containment.*

37. Quoted in Lou Cannon, *President Reagan: The Role of a Lifetime* (New York: Simon & Schuster, 1991), 286.

38. Quoted in McCullough, *Truman,* 547.

39. Kissinger, *Diplomacy,* 462.

40. Dean Acheson, "Threats to Democracy and Its Way of Life," address to the American Society of Newspaper Editors, Washington, D.C., April 22, 1950, *Department of State Bulletin* 22, no. 565 (May 1, 1950): 675.

41. Quoted in Kissinger, *Diplomacy,* 553.

42. Walter Lippmann, *The Cold War: A Study in U.S. Foreign Policy* (New York: Harper, 1947), 60.

43. Thomas Risse-Kappen, "Collective Identity in a Democratic Community: The Case of NATO," in *The Culture of National Security: Norms and Identity in World Politics,* ed. Peter J. Katzenstein (New York: Columbia University Press, 1996), 373.

44. Ibid., 374.

45. See Stalin's Soviet colleague Roy A. Medvedev, *Let History Judge: The Origins and Consequences of Stalinism,* trans. Colleen Taylor (New York: Alfred A. Knopf, 1971), 474–75. Kissinger agrees; see Kissinger, *Diplomacy,* 443.

46. Colin Dueck, *Reluctant Crusaders: Power, Culture, and Change in American Grand Strategy* (Princeton, NJ: Princeton University Press, 2006).

47. Quoted in Trachtenberg, *Constructed Peace,* 16.

48. Quoted in Haas, *Ideological Origins of Great Power Politics,* 13.

49. Zbigniew Brzezinski, *Between Two Ages: America's Role in the Technetronic Era* (New York: Viking Press, 1970), 274–75.

50. Thomas Risse, "'Let's Argue!': Communicative Action in World Politics," *International Organization* 54, no. 1 (Winter 2000): 1–41.

51. Philip Zelikow and Condoleezza Rice, *Germany Unified and Europe Transformed: A Study in Statecraft* (Boston: Harvard University Press, 1995), 278.

52. Risse, "'Let's Argue!,'" 27.

53. Secretary of State James Baker made this offer to Gorbachev but later backtracked. See Zelikow and Rice, *Germany Unified and Europe Transformed,* 184.

54. Excerpts from Reagan's address before the British Parliament in June 1982, quoted in Cannon, *President Reagan,* 315.

55. Paul Lettow, *Ronald Reagan and His Quest to Abolish Nuclear Weapons* (New York: Random House, 2005), 63–70. For a summary of NSDD-75, see Jack F. Matlock Jr., *Reagan and Gorbachev: How the Cold War Ended* (New York: Random House, 2005), 53–54.

56. Quoted in Paul Kengor, *The Crusader: Ronald Reagan and the Fall of Communism* (New York: HarperCollins, 2006), 220.

57. Quoted in Cannon, *President Reagan,* 774.

58. I had a second cousin who lived in East Germany and came to the West a few years before the wall came down. He later learned, after secret police records were opened up, that the state had used his own children to collect information on him and his wife.

59. Trachtenberg, *Constructed Peace,* 17.

60. Quoted in Frances Perkins, *The Roosevelt I Knew* (New York: Viking Press, 1946), 84–85.

61. Quoted in Kissinger, *Diplomacy,* 413.

62. Quoted in McCullough, *Truman,* 376.

63. Ibid., 432.

64. Ibid., 536.

65. See G. John Ikenberry, *After Victory: Institutions, Strategic Restraint, and the Rebuilding of Order after Major Wars* (Princeton, NJ: Princeton University Press, 2001).

66. See ibid., 184; Trachtenberg, *Constructed Peace,* 119.

67. Quoted in Kissinger, *Diplomacy,* 459.

68. Euratom was the topic of my first book. OK, I know, who cares? See Henry R. Nau, *National Politics and International Technology: Peaceful Uses of Nuclear Power in Western Europe* (Baltimore: Johns Hopkins University Press, 1974).

69. See Robert E. Osgood, *NATO: The Entangling Alliance* (Chicago: University of Chicago Press, 1962).

70. For a liberal critique of realist versions of the Cuban Missile Crisis, see Lebow and Stein, *We All Lost the Cold War.*

71. See note 22.

72. Lebow and Stein, *We All Lost the Cold War,* 325.

73. Ibid., 323.

74. For a full account emphasizing these events, see Matthew Evangelista, *Unarmed Force: The Transnational Movement to End the Cold War* (Ithaca, NY: Cornell University Press, 1999).

75. Thomas Risse-Kappen, "Ideas Do Not Float Freely: Transnational Coalitions, Domestic Structures, and the End of the Cold War," in *International Relations Theory and the End of the Cold War,* ed. Richard Ned Lebow and Thomas Risse-Kappen (New York: Columbia University Press, 1995), 187–223.

76. In his memoirs, former U.S. secretary of state George P. Shultz discusses his extended conversations with Gorbachev about the requirements of the information age. See Shultz, *Turmoil and Triumph: My Years as Secretary of State* (New York: Charles Scribner's Sons, 1993), chap. 30.

77. Quoted in Brooks and Wohlforth, "Power, Globalization, and the End of the Cold War," 38.

78. Nikolai Novikov, "Telegram from the Soviet Ambassador to the United States, to the Soviet Leadership," in *International Relations in Perspective,* ed. Henry R. Nau (Washington, DC: CQ Press, 2010), 270–80 (emphasis in original).

79. Gabriel Kolko and Joyce Kolko, *The Limits of Power: The World and United States Foreign Policy, 1945–1954* (New York: Harper & Row, 1972); William Appleman Williams, *The Tragedy of American Diplomacy* (Cleveland, OH: World, 1959).

80. Robert W. Cox, with Timothy J. Sinclair, *Approaches to World Order* (Cambridge: Cambridge University Press, 1990), 177–79.

Part II. The Contemporary International System, pages 197–198

1. Drawn from El-Sayyid Nosair's notebook, quoted in Daniel Benjamin and Steven Simon, *The Age of Sacred Terror: Radical Islam's War against America* (New York: Random House, 2003), 6.

Chapter 5. Realist Perspectives on Today's World, pages 199–233

1. John J. Mearsheimer, *The Tragedy of Great Power Politics* (New York: Norton, 2001), 364–66.
2. Patrick E. Tyler, "U.S. Strategy Plan Calls for Insuring No Rivals Develop," *New York Times,* March 8, 1992, A1.
3. White House, *The National Security Strategy of the United States of America* (Washington, DC: White House, September 2002), chap. 3, http://georgewbush-whitehouse.archives.gov/nsc/nss/2002.
4. William C. Wohlforth, "The Stability of a Unipolar World," *International Security* 24, no. 1 (Summer 1999): 13.
5. For these phrases, see, respectively, Charles Krauthammer, "The Unipolar Moment," *Foreign Affairs* 70, no. 1 (1990–1991), 23–33; Charles Krauthammer, "Holiday from History," *Washington Post,* February 14, 2003, A31.
6. Henry Kissinger, *Diplomacy* (New York: Simon & Schuster, 1994), 805.
7. Henry Kissinger wrote in 1976, for example, that the Soviet challenge "will perhaps never be conclusively 'resolved.'" See Kissinger, *American Foreign Policy* (New York: Norton, 1977), 304.
8. Quoted in George Bush and Brent Scowcroft, *A World Transformed* (New York: Alfred A. Knopf, 1998), 515.
9. Quoted in ibid., 541.
10. Brent Scowcroft, "Don't Attack Iraq," *Wall Street Journal,* August 15, 2002, A12.
11. See "Bush Says It Is Time for Action," CNN, November 6, 2001, http://edition.cnn.com/2001/US/11/06/ret.bush.coalition/index.html.
12. Richard N. Haas, *War of Necessity, War of Choice: A Memoir of Two Iraq Wars* (New York: Simon & Schuster, 2010).
13. Testimony by David Albright, president, Institute for Science and International Security, before Subcommittee on International Terrorism and Nonproliferation of the Committee on International Relations, House of Representatives, 109th Congress, Second Session, May 25, 2006.
14. See the account by then NATO supreme commander Wesley K. Clark, *Waging Modern War: Bosnia, Kosovo, and the Future of Combat* (New York: Public Affairs, 2001).
15. White House, *National Security Strategy,* 6.
16. National Commission on Terrorist Attacks upon the United States, *The 9/11 Commission Report*(New York: Norton, 2004); Iraq Study Group, *The Iraq Study Group Report* (New York: Vintage Books, 2006).
17. Robert Kagan, *Of Paradise and Power: America and Europe in the New World Order* (New York: Alfred A. Knopf, 2002).
18. See American Political Science Association, *US Standing in the World: Causes, Consequences, and the Future,* Long Report of the Task Force on U.S. Standing in World Affairs (Washington, DC: American Political Science Association, September 2009), http://www.apsanet.org/media/pdfs/apsa_tf_usstanding_long_report.pdf.
19. Quoted in Neil King Jr., "Rice's Perplexing Use of History," *Wall Street Journal,* January 19, 2007, A4.
20. See Scott Wilson, "Shared Interests Define Obama's World," *Washington Post,* November 2, 2009, A1.
21. Barack Obama, "Remarks by President Barack Obama," Hradcany Square, Prague, Czech Republic, April 5, 2009, http://www.whitehouse.gov/the_press_office/Remarks-By-President-Barack-Obama-In-Prague-As-Delivered.
22. Charlie Savage and Peter Baker, "Obama, in a Shift, to Limit Drone Strikes," *New York Times,* May 23, 2013, A1.
23. National Intelligence Council, *Global Trends 2030: Alternative Worlds* (Washington, DC: Government Printing Office, December 2012), iv.
24. Office of the Secretary of Defense, *Military Power of the People's Republic of China 2009* (Washington, DC: U.S. Department of Defense, March 2009).
25. Edward Wong, "Chinese Military Seeks to Extend Its Naval Power," *New York Times,* April 24, 2010, A1.

26. I disagreed. See Henry R. Nau, *The Myth of America's Decline* (New York: Oxford University Press, 1990).

27. Jeffrey E. Garten, *A Cold Peace: America, Japan, Germany, and the Struggle for Supremacy* (New York: Times Books, 1992).

28. Robert A. Page, "Soft Balancing against the United States," *International Security* 30, no. 1 (Summer 2005): 7–45.

29. Kissinger, *Diplomacy*, 23.

30. John J. Mearsheimer, "Back to the Future: Instability after the Cold War," *International Security* 15, no. 1 (Summer 1990): 5–56. In this article, Mearsheimer is thinking like a power balancer, assuming that equilibrium in nuclear capabilities equates with stability. In his later book, he thinks like a power transition realist and argues that states will always seek maximum power and disrupt stability based on equilibrium. See Mearsheimer, *Tragedy of Great Power Politics*.

31. Quoted in Andrew E. Kramer, "Russia Claims Its Sphere of Influence in the World," *New York Times*, September 1, 2008, A6.

32. Commission to Assess the Ballistic Missile Threat to the United States, "Executive Summary of the Report of the Commission," Washington, D.C., July 15, 1998, http://www.fas.org/irp/threat/bm-threat.htm.

33. Richard K. Betts, "The Soft Underbelly of Primacy: Tactical Advantages of Terror," *Political Science Quarterly* 117, no. 1 (Spring 2002): 24.

34. Quoted in Daniel Benjamin and Steven Simon, *The Age of Sacred Terror: Radical Islam's War against America* (New York: Random House, 2003), 106.

35. Rick "Ozzie" Nelson and Scott Goossens, "Counter-piracy in the Arabian Sea: Challenges and Opportunities for GCC Action," Gulf Analysis Paper, Center for Strategic and International Studies, May 2011, http://csis.org/files/publication/110509_GulfAnalysis_Counter_piracy_inthe_ArabianSea.pdf.

36. See Mandiant, *APT1: Exposing One of China's Cyber Espionage Units* (Alexandria, VA: Mandiant, 2012), http://www.mandiant.com.

37. Quoted in Siobahn Gorman and Stephen Fidler, "Cyber Attacks Test Pentagon, Allies and Foes," *Wall Street Journal*, September 25, 2010, http://online.wsj.com/article/SB10001424052748703793804575511961264943300.html.

38. James Kirchick, "Wikileaks' Collateral Damage," *Wall Street Journal*, December 31, 2010, 13.

39. David E. Sanger, *Confront and Conceal: Obama's Secret Wars and Surprising Use of American Power* (New York: Random House, 2012).

40. National Commission on Terrorist Attacks upon the United States, *9/11 Commission Report*, 59–60.

41. William J. Broad and David E. Sanger, "As Nuclear Secrets Emerge, More Are Suspected," *New York Times*, December 26, 2004, 1; David E. Sanger, "Pakistan Leader Confirms Nuclear Exports," *New York Times*, September 13, 2005, A8; Joby Warrick, "Smugglers Had Design for Advanced Warhead," *Washington Post*, June 15, 2008.

42. A school of psychology known as social identity theory finds that people separate themselves into groups that discriminate against one another for no apparent reason. Thus, "unless the group encompasses all of humanity—and this is improbable at least in part because group cohesiveness decreases as it becomes more abstract—humans will always form groups. And with groups come social comparison and competition." This group dynamic creates anarchy, which realists see as the root cause of ethnic competition. Jonathan Mercer, "Anarchy and Identity," *International Organization* 49, no. 2 (1995): 250–51.

43. Hendrik Spruyt, *The Sovereign State and Its Competitors* (Princeton, NJ: Princeton University Press, 1996).

44. Martin Rochester, *Between Peril and Promise: The Politics of International Law* (Washington, DC: CQ Press, 2006), 42.

45. Bruce Bueno de Mesquita, *The War Trap* (New Haven, CT: Yale University Press, 1983); Charles L. Glaser, *Rational Theory of International Affairs: The Logic of Competition and Cooperation* (Princeton, NJ: Princeton University Press, 2010).

46. Graham Allison and Philip Zelikow, *Essence of Decision: Explaining the Cuban Missile Crisis*, 2nd ed. (New York: Longman, 1999).

47. Paul R. Pillar, an intelligence officer at the time and later a sharp critic of the Iraq War, wrote, "The Bush administration was quite right: its perception of Saddam's weapons capacities was shared by the Clinton administration, congressional Democrats, and most other Western governments and intelligence

services." Pillar, "Intelligence, Policy, and the War in Iraq," *Foreign Affairs* 85, no. 2 (March/April 2006), http://www.foreignaffairs.com/articles/61503/paul-r-pillar/intelligence-policyand-the-war-in-iraq. See also Mortimer B. Zuckerman, "Foul-ups—Not Felonies," *U.S. News & World Report,* November14, 2005.

Chapter 6. Liberal Perspectives on Today's World, pages 235–288

1. For excerpts of President Bush's "New World Order" speech to Congress on September 11, 1990, see George Bush and Brent Scowcroft, *A World Transformed* (New York: Alfred A. Knopf, 1998), 370. For the UN speech, see President George H. W. Bush, Address before the 45th Session of the United Nations General Assembly, New York, October 1, 1990, transcript, http://bushlibrary.tamu.edu/research/papers/1990/90100100.html.

2. Paul W. Schroeder, *The Transformation of European Politics, 1763–1848* (New York: Oxford University Press, 1994), xiii.

3. James A. Baker, *The Politics of Diplomacy: Revolution, War, and Peace, 1989–1992* (New York: G. P. Putnam's Sons, 1995), 605–6 (emphasis in original).

4. Madeleine K. Albright, "U.S. Participation in United Nations Peacekeeping Activities," statement made at hearings before Subcommittee on International Security, International Organizations and Human Rights, House Committee on Foreign Affairs, 103rd Congress, Second Session, June 24, 1994, 3–21.

5. Daniel Benjamin and Steven Simon, *The Age of Sacred Terror: Radical Islam's War against America* (New York: Random House, 2003), 106.

6. For more on the pathologies of interdependence, see Michael N. Barnett and Martha Finnemore, "The Politics, Power, and Pathologies of International Organizations," *International Organization* 53, no. 4 (Autumn 1999): 699–732.

7. John J. Mearsheimer, "Back to the Future: Instability after the Cold War," *International Security* 15, no. 1 (Summer 1990): 5–56.

8. Bill Clinton, *My Life* (New York: Alfred A. Knopf, 2004), 750.

9. David A. Lake, "Two Cheers for Bargaining Theory: Assessing Rationalist Explanations of the Iraq War," *International Security* 35, no. 3 (Winter 2010–2011): 10.

10. United Nations Peacekeeping, "Peacekeeping Fact Sheet," September 30, 2013, http://www.un.org/en/peacekeeping/resources/statistics/factsheet.shtml.

11. See the discussion in Jack Snyder and Robert Jervis, "Civil War and the Security Dilemma," in *Civil Wars, Insecurity, and Intervention,* ed. Barbara F. Walter and Jack Snyder (New York: Columbia University Press, 1999), 24–27.

12. Susan L. Woodward, *Balkan Tragedy: Chaos and Dissolution after the Cold War* (Washington, DC: Brookings Institution, 1995), 36.

13. Mark Turner, "Under Fire: The United Nations Struggles to Meet the Challenges of a Changed World," *Financial Times,* June 6, 2005, 11.

14. United Nations, *High-Level Panel on Threats, Challenges and Change, A More Secure World: Our Shared Responsibility* (New York: United Nations, December 2005).

15. International Commission on Intervention and State Sovereignty, *The Responsibility to Protect: Report of the International Commission on Intervention and State Sovereignty* (Ottawa: International Development Research Centre of ICISS, 2001), viii.

16. Martha Finnemore, *The Purposes of Intervention: Changing Beliefs about the Use of Force* (Ithaca, NY: Cornell University Press, 2003), 79.

17. Kofi Annan, Annual Report of the Secretary-General to the General Assembly, SG/SM/7136 GA/9596 (New York: United Nations, September 20, 1999).

18. International Commission on Intervention and State Sovereignty, *Responsibility to Protect,* 32.

19. William J. Broad and David E. Sanger, "As Nuclear Secrets Emerge, More Are Suspected," *New York Times,* December 26, 2004, 1; David E. Sanger, "Pakistan Leader Confirms Nuclear Exports," *New York Times,* September 13, 2005, A8.

20. James Hoge, "Counting Down to the New Armageddon," *New York Times Book Review,* September 5, 2004, 8.

21. Laurie Garrett, "Biology's Brave New World," *Foreign Affairs,* 92, 6 (November/December 2013), 28–53.

22. Mark Turner, "Wrongdoing Costs UN up to $298m," *Financial Times,* January 24, 2006, 3.

23. Union of International Associations, *Yearbook of International Organizations 2009/2010: Guide to Global Civil Society Networks* (Munich: De Gruyter Saur, 2010).

24. Salman Masood, "Pakistanis Back Off Vow to Control Madrassas," *New York Times,* January 2, 2006, A6.

25. See Margaret P. Karns and Karen A. Mingst, *International Organizations: The Politics and Processes of Global Governance* (Boulder, CO: Lynne Rienner, 2004), 245–46.

26. For details, see World Wildlife Fund, "Conservation Finance," http://www.worldwildlife.org/what/howwe doit/conservationfinance/item7065.html.

27. See Amnesty International, "Financial Reports and Accounts," http://www.amnesty.org/en/who-we-are/ accountability/financial-reports.

28. Ann Marie Clark, *Diplomacy of Conscience: Amnesty International and Changing Human Rights Norms* (Princeton, NJ: Princeton University Press, 2001).

29. Jed Rubenfeld, "The Two World Orders," *Wilson Quarterly* (Autumn 2003): 29 (emphasis in original).

30. For one such liberal argument, see G. John Ikenberry, *After Victory: Institutions, Strategic Restraint, and the Rebuilding of Order after Major Wars* (Princeton, NJ: Princeton University Press, 2001).

31. For details of this case, see Ian Hurd, *International Organizations: Politics, Law, Practice* (Cambridge: Cambridge University Press, 2011), chap. 8.

32. Craig Whitlock, "European Nations May Investigate Bush Officials over Prisoner Treatment," *Washington Post,* April 22, 2009, A4.

33. I'm indebted to Professor Alan Buckley for advice on the ICC.

34. Peter J. Katzenstein, A World of Regions: Asia and Europe in the American Imperium (Ithaca, NY: Cornell University Press, 2005).

35. The father of neofunctionalism is Ernst B. Haas. See, among other sources, his *The Uniting of Europe: Political, Social, and Economic Forces, 1950–1957* (Palo Alto, CA: Stanford University Press, 1958); and *Beyond the Nation-State: Functionalism and International Organization* (Palo Alto, CA: Stanford University Press, 1964).

36. See my review essay examining this shift from integration to interdependence studies. Henry R. Nau, "From Integration to Interdependence: Gains, Losses and Continuing Gaps," *International Organization* 33, no. 1 (Winter 1979): 119–47.

37. For thorough and lucid treatment of the EU, see two books by Roy H. Ginsberg: *Demystifying the European Union: The Enduring Logic of European Integration,* 2nd ed. (Lanham, MD: Rowman & Littlefield, 2010); and *The European Union in International Politics: Baptism by Fire* (New York: Rowman & Littlefield, 2001).

38. Katzenstein, *World of Regions,* 223.

Chapter 7. Identity Perspectives on Today's World, pages 289–326

1. Peter Katzenstein, ed., *Sinicization and the Rise of China: Civilizational Processes beyond East and West* (London: Routledge, 2012), 242. See also Katzenstein's edited volumes *Civilizations in World Politics: Plural and Pluralist Perspectives* (London: Routledge, 2010); and *Anglo-America and Its Discontents: Civilizational Identities beyond West and East* (London: Routledge, 2012).

2. Francis Fukuyama, "The End of History," *National Interest,* no. 16 (Summer 1989): 4.

3. Francis Fukuyama, *The End of History and the Last Man* (New York: Avon Books, 1992). Fukuyama drew wide acclaim for his earlier article on this topic (cited in note 2).

4. Samuel P. Huntington, *The Third Wave: Democratization in the Twentieth Century* (Norman: University of Oklahoma Press, 1993).

5. Arch Puddington, *Freedom in the World 2013: Democratic Breakthroughs in the Balance* (New York: Freedom House, 2013), http://www.freedomhouse .org/sites/default/files/FIW%202013%20Booklet_0 .pdf.

6. G. John Ikenberry, *After Victory: Institutions, Strategic Restraint, and the Rebuilding of Order after Major Wars* (Princeton, NJ: Princeton University Press, 2001). See my comment on Ikenberry's book in "Correspondence," *International Security* 27, no. 1 (Summer 2002): 178–82.

7. President Bill Clinton, "State of the Union," January 25, 1994, http://www.let.rug.ln/usa/P/bc42/speeches/ sup94wjc.htm.

8. Charles Krauthammer, "In Defense of Democratic Realism," *National Interest,* no. 77 (Fall 2004): 15–26.

9. White House, *The National Security Strategy of the United States of America* (Washington, DC: White House, September 2002), chap. 1, http://georgewbush-whitehouse.archives.gov/nsc/nss/2002.

10. "The Inaugural Address," *New York Times,* January 21, 2005, A16–17.

11. Jim VandeHei, "Bush Calls Democracy Terror's Antidote," *Washington Post,* March 9, 2005, A16.

12. For texts of these speeches, see Barack Obama, "Remarks by the President on a New Beginning," Cairo University, June 4, 2009, http://www.whitehouse.gov/the_press_office/Remarks-by-the-President-at-Cairo-University-6–04–09; and "Remarks by the President at the New Economic School Graduation," Gostinny Dvor, Moscow, July 7, 2009, http://www.whitehouse.gov/the_press_office/Remarks-By-The-President-At-The-New-Economic-School-Graduation.

13. See Barack Obama, "Remarks by President Barack Obama," Hradcany Square, Prague, Czech Republic, April 5, 2009, http://www.whitehouse.gov/the_press_office/Remarks-By-President-Barack-Obama-In-Prague-As-Delivered.

14. Quoted in James Kirchick, "Squanderer in Chief," *Los Angeles Times,* April 28, 2009, http://articles.latimes.com/2009/apr/28/opinion/oe-kirchick28.

15. Barack Obama, "Remarks by President Obama in Address to the United Nations General Assembly," New York, September 24, 2013, http://www.whitehouse.gov/the-press-office/2013/09/24/remarks-president-obama-address-united-nations-general-assembly.

16. Thomas Carothers, *Democracy Policy under Obama: Revitalization or Retreat?* (Washington, DC: Carnegie Endowment for International Peace, 2012), 12. For a more critical view of Obama's policy toward democracy promotion, see Joshua Muravchik, "The Abandonment of Democracy," *Commentary,* July/August 2009, http://www.commentarymagazine.com/viewarticle.cfm/special-preview—the-abandonment-of-democracy-15185.

17. Daniel Philpott, "Explaining the Political Ambivalence of Religion," *American Political Science Review* 101, no. 3 (August 2007): 505–25.

18. Adrian Karatnycky, "Muslim Countries and the Democracy Gap," *Journal of Democracy* 13 (January 2002): 101–4.

19. See M. Steven Fish, "Islam and Authoritarianism," *World Politics* 55 (October 2002): 4–37. See also Magnus Midlarsky, "Democracy and Islam: Implications for Civilizational Conflict and the Democratic Peace," *International Studies Quarterly* 42 (September 1998): 485–511; Daniela Donno and Bruce Russett, "Islam, Authoritarianism, and Female Empowerment: What

Are the Linkages?," *World Politics* 56 (July 2004): 582–607.

20. Larry Diamond, "Why Are There No Arab Democracies?," *Journal of Democracy* 21, no. 1 (January 2010): 99.

21. Larry Diamond, *The Spirit of Democracy: The Struggle to Build Free Societies throughout the World* (New York: Holt, 2008), 20 (quotes below in this paragraph, 33, 35). See also Thomas Carothers, *Aiding Democracy Abroad: The Learning Curve* (Washington, DC: Brookings Institution Press, 1999).

22. Max Weber, *The Protestant Ethic and the Spirit of Capitalism,* trans. Talcott Parsons (London: Routledge, 1992). Weber's thesis was first published in articles in 1904–1905 and then as a book in 1930.

23. Samuel P. Huntington, "The Clash of Civilizations?," *Foreign Affairs* 72, no. 3 (Summer 1993): 25; see also Samuel P. Huntington, *The Clash of Civilizations and the Remaking of World Order* (New York: Simon & Schuster, 1996).

24. Huntington, "Clash of Civilizations?," 25.

25. Samuel P. Huntington, "The West Unique, Not Universal," *Foreign Affairs* 75, no. 6 (November–December 1996): 28–47.

26. Fareed Zakaria, "The Rise of Illiberal Democracy," *Foreign Affairs* 76, no. 6 (November–December 1997): 42.

27. Stephen Howarth, *The Knights Templar* (New York: Barnes & Noble Books, 1982).

28. Bernard Lewis, *What Went Wrong? Western Impact and Middle Eastern Response* (Oxford: Oxford University Press, 2002).

29. See Francis Fukuyama, "The Neoconservative Moment," *National Interest,* no. 76 (Summer 2004): 57–69.

30. Daniel Benjamin and Steven Simon, *The Age of Sacred Terror: Radical Islam's War against America* (New York: Random House, 2003), 85.

31. Abdurrahman Wahid, "Right Islam vs. Wrong Islam," *Wall Street Journal,* December 30, 2005, A16.

32. Benjamin and Simon, *Age of Sacred Terror,* 452.

33. Marc Sageman, *Understanding Terrorist Networks* (Philadelphia: University of Pennsylvania Press, 2004).

34. Oliver Roy, *Globalized Islam: The Search for a New Ummah* (New York: Columbia University Press, 2004).

35. Krishna Guha, "Ethnic Communities Can Be Devout as Well as Good Citizens," *Financial Times,* July 16–17, 2005, 7.

36. Amitai Etzioni, "The Evils of Self-Determination," *Foreign Policy* 89 (Winter 1992–1993): 35.

37. Raymond C. Taras and Rajat Ganguly, *Understanding Ethnic Conflict: The International Dimension* (New York: Longman, 2006), 57.

38. Joseph R. Biden Jr. and Leslie H. Gelb, "Unity through Autonomy," *New York Times,* May 1, 2006, http://www.nytimes.com/2006/05/01/opinion/01biden.html.

39. Richard N. Haass, "We're Not Winning. It's Not Worth It," *Newsweek,* July 18, 2010, http://www.newsweek.com/2010/07/18/we-re-not-winning-it-s-not-worth-it.html.

40. Hans Peter Schmitz and Kathryn Sikkink, "International Human Rights," in *Handbook of International Relations,* ed. Walter Carlsnaes, Thomas Risse, and Beth Simmons (London: Sage, 2002), 517–36.

41. David P. Forsythe, *Human Rights in International Relations,* 2nd ed. (Cambridge: Cambridge University Press, 2006), 60.

42. Margaret P. Karns and Karen A. Mingst, *International Organizations: The Politics and Processes of Global Governance* (Boulder, CO: Lynne Rienner, 2004), 233.

43. See Judith Sunderland (Human Rights Watch), "Will the UNHRC Fulfill Its Promise?," openDemocracy, April 10, 2008, http://ourkingdom.opendemocracy.net/2008/04/10/will-the-unhrc-fulfill-its-promise.

44. Quoted in Neil MacFarquhar, "Iranian Calls Israel Racist in Geneva," *New York Times,* April 20, 2009, A4.

45. For the text of the convention, see United Nations, UN Women, "Convention on the Elimination of All Forms of Discrimination against Women," http://www.un.org/womenwatch/daw/cedaw/cedaw.htm.

46. For more details on these and other cases, see European Court of Human Rights, "Factsheets," http://www.echr.coe.int/Pages/home.aspx?p=press/factsheets&c=#n1347890855564_pointer.

47. Forsythe, *Human Rights in International Relations,* 127.

48. European Committee of Social Rights, *Activity Report 2012* (Strasbourg, France: Council of Europe, April 2013), 11–12, http://www.coe.int/t/dghl/monitoring/socialcharter/Presentation/ActivityReport2012_en.pdf.

49. Forsythe, *Human Rights in International Relations,* 144.

50. See Roy W. Brown, "Vote on Freedom of Expression Marks the End of Universal Human Rights," International Humanist and Ethical Union, March 29, 2008, http://iheu.org/story/vote-freedom-expression-marks-end-universal-human-rights.

Part III. Globalization and Change, pages 327–328

1. Bernard Lewis, *What Went Wrong? Western Impact and Middle East Response* (Oxford: Oxford University Press, 2002), 7.

2. Thomas L. Friedman, *The World Is Flat: A Brief History of the Twenty-First Century* (New York: Farrar, Straus and Giroux, 2005), quotations from 9–11.

Chapter 8. Realist and Liberal Perspectives on Globalization, pages 329–384

1. I live in Maryland. In 2004, for the first time, I and other power customers could choose from more than one utility to purchase electricity.

2. Adam Smith, *An Inquiry into the Nature and Causes of the Wealth of Nations,* ed. Kathryn Sutherland (Oxford: Oxford University Press, 1993), 13.

3. Ibid., 393–464.

4. This is the conclusion of one of the economists credited with developing the theory. See Paul Krugman, *Peddling Prosperity: Economic Sense and Nonsense in the Age of Diminished Expectations* (New York: Norton, 1994), chaps. 9, 10.

5. Scott Callon, *Divided Sun: MITI and the Breakdown of Japanese High-Tech Industrial Policy, 1975–1993* (Stanford, CA: Stanford University Press, 1995).

6. Martin Wolf, *Why Globalization Works* (New Haven, CT: Yale University Press, 2005), 175.

7. Ibid.

8. Gary Burtless, Robert Z. Lawrence, Robert E. Litan, and Robert J. Shapiro, *Globaphobia: Confronting Fears About Open Trade* (Washington, DC Brookings Institution, 1998), 68.

9. Ibid., 46.

10. George P. Shultz and John B. Shoven, *Putting Our House in Order: A Guide to Social Security and Health Care Reform* (New York: Norton, 2008), 12.

11. Burtless et al., *Globaphobia,* 80.

12. M. P. McQueen and Jane Spencer, "U.S. Orders New China Toy Recall," *Wall Street Journal,* November 8, 2007, A3.

13. I attended this meeting while serving in the White House. I witnessed some very bitter discussions between developed and developing countries.

14. Jagdish N. Bhagwati, *Termites in the Trading System: How Preferential Agreements Undermine Free Trade* (New York: Oxford University Press, 2008).

15. A. K. Cairncross, *Home and Foreign Investment, 1870–1913* (Cambridge: Cambridge University Press, 1953), 3, 23.

16. Henry R. Nau, "A Political Interpretation of the Technology Gap Dispute," *Orbis* 15, no. 2 (Summer 1971): 507–28. I wasn't making history, but I was commenting on it. This was the first article I published as a young scholar.

17. UNCTAD, *World Investment Report 2013: Global Value Chains, Investment for Development* (New York: United Nations, 2013), 217, http://unctad.org/en/PublicationsLibrary/wir2013_en.pdf. The CIS is a group founded in 1991, consisting of eleven former Soviet republics: Armenia, Azerbaijan, Belarus, Georgia, Kazakhstan, Kyrgyzstan, Moldova, Russia, Tajikistan, Ukraine, and Uzbekistan. Turkmenistan discontinued permanent membership as of August 26, 2005, and is now an associate member.

18. Raymond Vernon, *Sovereignty at Bay: The Multinational Spread of U.S. Enterprises* (New York: Basic Books, 1971).

19. Matthew J. Slaughter, "How to Destroy American Jobs," *Wall Street Journal,* February 3, 2010, http://www.cfr.org/publication/21370/how_to_destroy_american_jobs.html.

20. UNCTAD, *World Investment Report 2013,* 23–24.

21. Wolf, *Why Globalization Works,* 222.

22. McKinsey & Company, *Global Capital Markets: Entering a New Era* (Washington, DC: McKinsey & Company, September 2009).

23. If you want to read more about these events, consult Gillian Tett, *Fool's Gold: How Unrestrained Greed Corrupted a Dream, Shattered Global Markets, and Unleashed a Catastrophe* (New York: Free Press, 2010).

24. David Wessel, "Lessons of the Rescue: A Drama in Five Acts," *Wall Street Journal,* September 9, 2013, A1.

25. Nelson D. Schwartz and Eric Dash, "Where Was the Wise Man?," *New York Times,* April 27, 2008, http://www.nytimes.com/2008/04/27/business/27rubin.html?pagewanted=1&_r=2.

26. "How to Stop a Currency War," *The Economist,* October 16–22, 2010, 13.

Chapter 9. Identity Perspectives on Globalization, pages 385–449

1. World Bank, *Robust Recovery, Rising Risks: East Asia and Pacific Economic Update* (Washington, DC: World Bank, 2010). *Asia* here refers to China, Taiwan, South Korea, Singapore, Hong Kong, Indonesia, Thailand, Philippines, Vietnam, Malaysia, and smaller economies, including the Pacific island economies.

2. World Bank, *The East Asian Miracle: Economic Growth and Public Policy,* World Bank Policy Research Report (New York: Oxford University Press, 1993), 1.

3. See Central Intelligence Agency, "The World Factbook," https://www.cia.gov/library/publications/the-world-factbook.

4. World Bank, *East Asian Miracle,* 5.

5. Ibid., chap. 3.

6. Ibid., chap. 4.

7. Paul Krugman, "The Myth of Asia's Miracle," *Foreign Affairs* 73, no. 6 (November–December 1994): 62–79.

8. Scott Callon, *Divided Sun: MITI and the Breakdown of Japanese High-Tech Industrial Policy, 1975–1993* (Stanford, CA: Stanford University Press, 1995), 170.

9. See Henry R. Nau, *At Home Abroad: Identity and Power in American Foreign Policy* (Ithaca, NY: Cornell University Press, 2002), 181 (table).

10. U.S.-China Business Council, "Foreign Investment in China," February 2007, http://www.uschina.org/info/forecast/2007/foreign-investment.html.

11. Data are from the World Bank and from CIA, "World Factbook."

12. Neil MacFarquhar, "Banks Making Big Profits from Tiny Loans," *New York Times,* April 14, 2010, A1.

13. Edwin O. Reischauer, *The Japanese Today: Change and Continuity* (Cambridge, MA: Belknap Press, 1988), 33.

14. Quoted in Kazuo Ogura, "A Call for a New Concept of Asia," *Japan Echo* 20, no. 2 (2002): 40.

15. Data in the preceding two paragraphs are from Angus Maddison, *The World Economy in the 20th Century*

(Paris: Development Centre of the Organisation for Economic Co-operation and Development, 1989), 35, 69–72, 90–97.

16. World Bank, *Economic Growth in the 1990s: Learning from a Decade of Reform* (Washington, DC: World Bank, 2005), 34 (emphasis in original).

17. Ibid., 36–37.

18. Data are from the World Bank.

19. World Bank, *Economic Growth in the 1990s,* 50.

20. Edward L. Gibson, "Conservative Party Politics in Latin America: Patterns of Electoral Mobilization in the 1980s and 1990s," in *Constructing Democratic Governance: Latin America and the Caribbean in the 1990s,* ed. Jorge I. Domínguez and Abraham F. Lowenthal (Baltimore: Johns Hopkins University Press, 1996), 26–42.

21. Leslie Bethell, "From the Second World War to the Cold War: 1944–1954," in *Exporting Democracy: The United States and Latin America,* ed. Abraham F. Lowenthal (Baltimore: Johns Hopkins University Press, 1991), 41–71.

22. Tom Farer, "Collectively Defending Democracy in the Western Hemisphere," in *Beyond Sovereignty: Collectively Defending Democracy in the Americas,* ed. Tom Farer (Baltimore: Johns Hopkins University Press, 1996), 2.

23. Maddison, *World Economy in the 20th Century,* 92.

24. Ibid., 94.

25. World Bank, *Economic Growth in the 1990s,* 147.

26. Geraldo Samor, "Brazil Is Driven to Bad Roads," *Wall Street Journal,* May 25, 2005, A10.

27. Data in this paragraph are from World Bank, *World Development Report 2005: A Better Investment Climate for Everyone* (Washington, DC: World Bank, 2005), overview, 1–20; Matt Moffett and Geraldo Samor, "In Brazil, Thicket of Red Tape Spoils Recipe for Growth," *Wall Street Journal,* May 24, 2005, A1.

28. World Bank, *Informality: Exit and Exclusion* (Washington, DC: World Bank, 2007), 4.

29. World Bank, *World Development Report 2005,* overview, 1–20.

30. World Bank, *Economic Growth in the 1990s,* 68.

31. World Bank, "Latin America and the Caribbean Regional Brief," October 2010, http://www.worldbank.org.

32. Tony Smith, "The Alliance for Progress: The 1960s," in Lowenthal, *Exporting Democracy,* 71–90.

33. Harvey F. Kline, "Colombia: Building Democracy in the Midst of Violence and Drugs," in Domínguez and Lowenthal, *Constructing Democratic Governance,* 20–42; Anita Isaacs, "Ecuador: Democracy Standing the Test of Time," in Domínguez and Lowenthal, *Constructing Democratic Governance,* 42–58.

34. On the role of the informal sector, see Hernando de Soto, *The Other Path* (New York: Harper & Row, 1989); for the estimate, see Guillermo Vuletin, *Measuring the Informal Economy in Latin America and the Caribbean,* IMF Working Paper WP/08/102 (Washington, DC: International Monetary Fund, April 2008), http://www.imf.org/external/pubs/ft/wp/2008/wp08102.pdf.

35. Richard Joseph, "Progress and Retreat in Africa: Challenges of a 'Frontier' Region," *Journal of Democracy* 19, no. 2 (April 2008): 96.

36. Larry Diamond, *The Spirit of Democracy: The Struggle to Build Free Societies throughout the World* (New York: Times Books, 2008), quoted in Joseph, "Progress and Retreat in Africa," 100.

37. "Zimbabwe Law Gives Business Control to Blacks," *Wall Street Journal,* March 10, 2008, A4.

38. Michael Wines, "Zimbabwe, Long Destitute, Teeters toward Ruin," *New York Times,* May 21, 2005, A1.

39. World Bank, *Global Monitoring Report 2010: The MDGs after the Crisis* (Washington, DC: World Bank, 2010), 15.

40. World Bank, *Global Monitoring Report 2005: Millennium Development Goals: From Consensus to Momentum* (Washington, DC: World Bank, 2005), 25–26.

41. Ibid., 44.

42. Ibid., chap. 4.

43. University of California, San Francisco, HIV InSite, "Sub-Saharan Africa," http://hivinsite.ucsf.edu/global?page=cr09–00–00.

44. World Bank, *Global Monitoring Report 2010,* chap. 2.

45. World Bank, *Better Governance for Development in the Middle East and Africa: Enhancing Inclusiveness and Accountability,* MENA Development Report (Washington, DC: World Bank, 2003), 8.

46. Data are from World Bank, "Data: Middle East & North Africa (developing only)," http://data.worldbank.org/region/MNA.

47. World Bank, *Better Governance for Development,* 6.

48. Ibid., 64.

49. Ibid., 98.

50. World Bank, *Trade, Investment and Development in the Middle East and North Africa: Engaging with the World,* MENA Development Report (Washington, DC: World Bank, 2003), 110.

51. Ibid., 93.

52. Faiza Saleh Ambah, "Saudi Women See a Brighter Road on Rights," *Washington Post,* January 31, 2008, A15.

53. World Bank, *Gender and Development in the Middle East and North Africa: Women in the Public Sphere,* MENA Development Report (Washington, DC: World Bank, 2004), 2–6.

54. Ibid., 4.

55. Richard P. Cincotta, Robert Engelman, and Daniele Anastasion, *The Security Demographic: Population and Civil Conflict after the Cold War* (Washington, DC: Population Action International, 2003).

56. Robert Kagan, *Of Paradise and Power: America and Europe in the New World Order* (New York: Vintage Books, 2004), 88–89.

57. Andrew Rice, "Is There Such a Thing as Agro-Imperialism?," *New York Times Magazine,* November 22, 2009, MM46.

58. Robert J. Samuelson, "Geopolitics at $100 a Barrel," *Washington Post,* November 14, 2007, A19. For recent projections taking into account the 2008–2009 economic slowdown, see International Energy Agency, "World Energy Outlook," http://www.worldenergy outlook.org.

59. Amy Myers Jaffe, "How Shale Gas Is Going to Rock the World," *Wall Street Journal,* May 10, 2010, R1.

60. Fiona Harvey, "A Costly Thirst: Proper Pricing of Water Could Ease Shortages," *Financial Times,* April 4, 2008, 7.

61. The irony is that after more than ten years of no logging on some twenty-four million acres in Washington, Oregon, and California, the spotted owl population continues to decline by 7 percent per year. Biologists think that this may be due to the presence of another owl species that kills or mates with the spotted owl. Kimberly A. Strassel, "Owls of Protest," *Wall Street Journal,* October 19, 2005, A12.

62. Horace Freeland Judson, "The Great Chinese Experiment," *Technology Review* 108, no. 6 (December 2005–January 2006): 52.

63. Edward Cody, "Toxic Slick Contaminates Water Supply of Chinese City," *Washington Post,* November 25, 2005, A1.

64. I am indebted to my colleague and former vice president for academic affairs at George Washington University, physicist Donald R. Lehman, who advised me on this section.

65. For IPCC reports, see http://www.ipcc.ch.

66. David A. Fahrenthold and Juliet Eilperin, "In E-mails, Science of Warming Is Hot Debate," *Washington Post,* December 5, 2009, A1.

67. Lisa Randall, "Dangling Particles," *New York Times,* September 18, 2005, WK13.

68. S. Fred Singer and Dennis T. Avery, *Unstoppable Global Warming: Every 1,500 Years* (Lanham, MD: Rowman & Littlefield, 2007).

69. John R. Christy, "My Nobel Moment," *Wall Street Journal,* November 1, 2007, A19. Christy was a member of the IPCC at the time.

70. David G. Victor, *Climate Change: Debating America's Policy Options* (Washington, DC: Council on Foreign Relations, 2004), 12–16.

71. Daniel B. Botkin, "Global Warming Delusions," *Wall Street Journal,* October 17, 2007, A19.

72. Thomas Catan, "Oil Chiefs Disagree on Global Warming Strategy," *Financial Times,* July 7, 2005, 3.

73. See Copenhagen Consensus Center, "Copenhagen Consensus 2004," http://www.copenhagenconsensus.com/projects/copenhagen-consensus-2004. See also Bjorn Lomborg, "Time for a Rethink on Global Warming," *Wall Street Journal,* January 29, 2010, A13.

74. World Health Organization, "Annex 4: Global, Regional and Country-Specific Data for Key Indicators," in *Global Tuberculosis Report 2012* (Geneva: World Health Organization, 2012), http://www.who .int/tb/publications/global_report/gtbr12_annex4.pdf; World Health Organization, "Malaria," Fact Sheet 94, March 2013, http://www.who.int/mediacentre/factsheets/fs094/en.

75. Michael T. Osterholm, "Unprepared for a Pandemic," *Foreign Affairs* 86, no. 2 (March–April 2007): 48.

76. Justin Gillis, "Cure for Neglected Diseases: Funding," *Washington Post,* April 25, 2006, D1.

77. Kimberly Kindy, "Officials Are Urged to Heed Lessons of 1976 Flu Outbreak," *Washington Post,* May 9, 2009, A4.

78. Trevi Troy, "Now Bush Prepared for the Outbreak," *Wall Street Journal,* April 28, 2009, A13.

79. Laurie Garrett, "Biology's Brave New World," *Foreign Affairs* 92, no. 6 (November–December 2013): 28–46.

80. David Brown, "Vaccine Would be Spoken For," *Washington Post,* May 7, 2009, A6.

81. Laurie Garrett, "The Next Pandemic?," *Foreign Affairs* 84, no. 4 (July–August 2005): 17.

Chapter 10. Critical Theory Perspectives on Globalization, pages 450–474

1. Max Weber, *The Protestant Ethic and the Spirit of Capitalism,* trans. Talcott Parsons (London: Routledge, 1992).

2. Jared Diamond, *Guns, Germs, and Steel: The Fates of Human Societies* (New York: Norton, 1999).

3. Paul Kennedy, *The Rise and Fall of the Great Powers: Economic Change and Military Conflict from 1500 to 2000* (New York: Random House, 1987), 28.

4. Immanuel Wallerstein, *The Modern World-System: Capitalist Agriculture and the Origins of the European World-Economy in the Sixteenth Century* (New York: Academic Press, 1976).

5. Douglass C. North, *Institutions, Institutional Change and Economic Performance* (Cambridge: Cambridge University Press, 1990), 122. On the development of property rights, see also John Gerard Ruggie, "Continuity and Transformation in the World Polity: Toward a Neorealist Synthesis," *World Politics* 35, no. 2 (January 1983): 261–85.

6. John Micklethwait and Adrian Wooldridge, "The Hidden Promise: Liberty Renewed," in *The Globalization Reader,* 3rd ed., ed. Frank J. Lechner and John Boli (Malden, MA: Blackwell, 2008), 11.

7. Robert W. Cox, with Timothy J. Sinclair, *Approaches to World Order* (Cambridge: Cambridge University Press, 1996), 7.

8. Gavin Menzies, *1421: The Year China Discovered America* (New York: HarperPerennial, 2004).

9. Quoted in Robin Broad, "Part II: The Historical Context," in *Global Backlash: Citizen Initiatives for a Just World Economy,* ed. Robin Broad (Lanham, MD: Rowman & Littlefield, 2002), 66.

10. Frances Moore Lappé and Joseph Collins, "Why Can't People Feed Themselves?," in *Food First: Beyond the Myth of Food Scarcity* (Boston: Houghton Mifflin, 1977), 75.

11. Georg Lukács, "The Marxism of Rosa Luxemburg," in *History and Class Consciousness* (London: Merlin Press, 1967), 27.

12. Raymond Vernon, *Sovereignty at Bay: The Multinational Spread of U.S. Enterprises* (New York: Basic Books, 1971).

13. Robin Broad, "Part IV: Challenging Corporate Conduct," in Broad, *Global Backlash,* 177.

14. Thomas L. Friedman, *The Lexus and the Olive Tree: Understanding Globalization* (New York: Farrar, Straus and Giroux, 1999), this quotation and those below, 27–29.

15. Kevin McDonald, *Global Movements: Action and Culture* (London: Blackwell, 2006), quotations above, 3, 4, 18.

16. Subcomandante Marcos, communiqué titled "The Southeast in Two Winds, a Storm and a Prophecy." Marcos's writings are collected in *Our Word Is Our Weapon: Selected Writings of Subcomandante Insurgente Marcos* (New York: Seven Story Press, 2002). Subcomandante Marcos is a pseudonym adopted by this Zapatista leader.

17. Nicholas D. Kristof and Shirley WuDunn, "The Women's Crusade," *New York Times Magazine,* August 23, 2009, MM28.

18. Malala Yousafzai with Christina Lamb, *I Am Malala: The Girl Who Stood Up for Education and Was Shot by the Taliban* (London: Weidenfeld & Nicolson, 2013).

19. Patrice Stephens, "The Policy Imperatives and Implications of the Valuation of Women's Unpaid Work: Making Valuation Count and Support Women's Empowerment," presentation to the United Nations, 2013, http://unstats.un.org/unsd/statcom/stat com_2013/seminars/Measuring/Presentation_of_ UN%20Women.pdf.

20. Manisha Desai, "Transnational Solidarity: Women's Agency, Structural Adjustment, and Globalization (2002)," in *The Globalization and Development Reader: Perspectives on Development and Change,* ed. J. Timmons Roberts and Amy Bellone Hite (Malden, MA: Blackwell, 2007), 410.

21. Joseph E. Stiglitz, *Globalization and Its Discontents* (New York: Norton, 2002), 5–6. Copyright © 2002 by Joseph E. Stiglitz. Reproduced by permission of W. W. Norton & Company, Inc. and Penguin Books Ltd.

22. Dani Rodrik, *Has Globalization Gone Too Far?* (Washington, DC: Institute for International Economics, 1997), 2.

23. Martin Wolf, *Why Globalization Works* (New Haven, CT: Yale University Press, 2004), 141–43.

24. Ibid., 158.

25. Fareed Zakaria, *The Post-American World* (New York: Norton, 2008), 3.

26. Ibid., 150–51.

27. Robert Wade, "Winners and Losers" and "Of Rich and Poor," *The Economist*, April 28, 2001, 72–74, 80.

28. Wolf, *Why Globalization Works*, 149.

29. Jeffrey A. Frieden, *Global Capitalism: Its Fall and Rise in the Twentieth Century* (New York: Norton, 2006), 2.

Conclusion, pages 475–485

1. Quoted in Daniel Henninger, "Father of the Bush Doctrine," *Wall Street Journal*, April 29–30, 2006, A8.

2. Quoted in Bruce Russett and John R. Oneal, *Triangulating Peace: Democracy, Interdependence, and International Organizations* (New York: Norton, 2001), 218.

3. Jack S. Levy, "Domestic Politics and War," *Journal of Interdisciplinary History* 18 (Spring 1988): 662.

4. Jack S. Levy, "War and Peace," in *Handbook of International Relations*, ed. Walter Carlsnaes, Thomas Risse, and Beth A. Simmons (London: Sage, 2002), 358–59.

5. Robert W. Cox, with Timothy J. Sinclair, *Approaches to World Order* (Cambridge: Cambridge University Press, 1996), 490.

6. On the relationship between new democracies and war, see Edward D. Mansfield and Jack Snyder, "Democratization and the Danger of War," *International Security* 20 (Summer 1995): 5–38. Russett and Oneal dispute this conclusion; see *Triangulating Peace*, 51, 120.

7. Russett and Oneal, *Triangulating Peace*, 46.

8. R. J. Rummel, "Democracies ARE Less Warlike than Other Regimes," *European Journal of International Relations* 1 (December 1995): 457–79.

9. Bruce Russett, *Grasping the Democratic Peace: Principles for a Post–Cold War World* (Princeton, NJ: Princeton University Press, 1993).

10. Russett and Oneal, *Triangulating Peace*, chap. 4.

11. Ibid., chap. 5.

12. Charles Lipson, *Reliable Partners: How Democracies Have Made a Separate Peace* (Princeton, NJ: Princeton University Press, 2003).

13. Joanne Gowa, *Ballots and Bullets: The Elusive Democratic Peace* (Princeton, NJ: Princeton University Press, 1999).

14. Christopher Layne, "Kant or Cant: The Myth of the Democratic Peace," *International Security* 19 (Fall 1994): 5–49.

15. Russett, *Grasping the Democratic Peace*, 30.

16. Russett and Oneal, *Triangulating Peace*, chap. 2.

17. John Ikenberry argues, for example, that democracies are better able than nondemocracies to bind themselves in international institutions. See G. John Ikenberry, *After Victory: Institutions, Strategic Restraint, and the Rebuilding of Order after Major Wars* (Princeton, N.J.: Princeton University Press, 2001). See also my comment on Ikenberry's book in "Correspondence," *International Security* 27, no. 1 (Summer 2002): 178–82.

18. Russett, *Grasping the Democratic Peace*, 400.

GLOSSARY OF KEY CONCEPTS

A

acid rain: condensation-borne pollutants that may be transported through the upper atmosphere over long distances.

Afghan War: costly war fought by both the Soviet Union in the 1980s and the United States in the 2000s.

agent-oriented constructivism: an identity perspective that allows for greater influence on the part of independent actors in shaping identities.

alliances: formal defense arrangements wherein states align against a greater power to prevent dominance.

American Declaration on the Rights and Duties of Man: the world's first international human rights instrument of a general nature, adopted by the nations of the Americas in April 1948.

anarchy: the decentralized distribution of power in the international system; no leader or center to monopolize power.

Anti-Ballistic Missile (ABM) Treaty: a 1972 treaty between the United States and Soviet Union limiting antiballistic missiles.

appeasement: a policy of making concessions to a stronger foe because one is unwilling to consider the use of force.

arms race: the competitive buildup of weapons systems.

ASEAN: the Association of Southeast Asian Nations, the principal Asian IGO.

ASEAN Intergovernmental Commission on Human Rights (AICHR): Asian human rights commission established in 2009.

Asian values: the Confucian ideas emphasizing authority over individualism that motivated economic success in Asia.

asymmetric threat and warfare: the exploitation of technology and psychology to target the peripheral vulnerabilities of a larger foe.

B

balance of payments: a country's current and capital account balances plus reserves and statistical errors.

balance of power: the strategy by which states counterbalance to ensure that no single state dominates the system, or an outcome that establishes a rough equilibrium among states.

balance of terror: a situation in which two or more countries use the threat of nuclear weapons to deter conflicts.

bandwagoning: the aligning of states with a greater power to share the spoils of dominance.

bargaining: negotiating to distribute gains that are zero-sum (that is, what one side gains, the other loses).

Baruch Plan: proposal by the United States in 1946 to create a United Nations agency to control and manage nuclear weapons cooperatively.

basic human needs: necessities such as clothing, shelter, food, education, and health care.

beliefs: ideas about how the world works as emphasized by identity perspectives.

belief systems: ideas about how the world works that influence the behavior of policy makers.

Berlin Blockade: the first physical confrontation of the Cold War, taking place in 1948–1949, in which Stalin blocked the land routes into Berlin.

biodiversity: the diversity among the multiple species of plant and animal life found in nature.

Biological Weapons Convention (BWC): international agreement made in 1972 to ban the production and use of biological weapons.

bonded labor: a form of unfree or indentured labor, typically a means of paying off loans with direct labor instead of currency or goods.

brain drain: the emigration of educated people from developing countries.

buckpassing: a free-riding strategy wherein a country allows other countries to fight conflicts while it stays on the sidelines.

C

capital account: the net flows of capital, both portfolio and foreign direct investment, into and out of a country.

capital flight: the movement of money out of the local currency and country because of inflation and economic or political instability.

causal arrow: an indicator of which perspective or level of analysis influences the other perspectives and levels of analysis more than the reverse.

causation: explaining events in terms of one another rather than just describing them.

chain-ganging: the creation of a rigid defensive alliance.

Chemical Weapons Convention (CWC): international agreement made in 1993 to ban the production and use of chemical weapons.

chlorofluorocarbons (CFCs): chemicals that break down the ozone layer.

civic identity: identity constructed when people are willing to submit to the laws of a common government rather than those of separate ethnic or religious groups.

civil society: the nongovernmental sector.

clash of civilizations: a thesis advanced by Samuel Huntington that past and future global conflicts can be traced along the fault lines between nine major world civilizations.

Cold War: the global, putatively bloodless (hence cold, not hot) conflict between the United States and the Soviet Union that resulted in massive arms buildups, international conflicts, and proxy wars.

collective goods: benefits, such as clean air, that are indivisible (they exist for all or for none) and cannot be appropriated (their consumption by one party does not diminish their consumption by another).

collective security: the establishment of common institutions and rules among states to settle disputes peacefully and to enforce agreements by a preponderance, not a balance, of power.

colonialism: conquest and exploitation by the European states of poorer peoples and lands in Latin America, Africa, and Asia.

communicative action: an exchange of ideas free of material and institutional influence to establish validity claims.

comparative advantage: a relationship in which two countries can produce more goods from the same resources if each specializes in the goods it produces most efficiently at home and the two trade these goods internationally.

compellence: the use of force to get another state to do something rather than to refrain from doing something.

competitive advantage: a trade advantage created by government intervention to exploit monopoly rents in strategic industries.

Comprehensive Test Ban Treaty (CTBT): international agreement reached in 1996 to stop the testing of nuclear weapons both above- and belowground.

concessional loans: loans made to developing nations at subsidized interest rates.

construction of identities: a process of discourse by which actors define who they are and how they behave toward one another.

constructivism: a perspective that emphasizes ideas, such as the content of language and social discourse, over institutions or power.

constructivist methods: methods that see events as a whole as mutually causing or constituting one another rather than causing one another sequentially.

containment: the policy of the United States during the Cold War that checked aggressive Soviet actions through military alliances.

cooperation: working to achieve a better outcome for some that does not hurt others.

core states: large and leading countries that produce most of the innovative products, which enjoy an initial monopoly.

correlation: a situation in which one fact or event occurs in the same context as another fact or event but is not necessarily linked to or caused by it.

Council of Europe (CE): organization founded in 1949 to promote human rights in Europe.

Council of the European Union: the assembly that brings together the member states of the European Union.

counterfactual reasoning: a method of testing claims for causality by asking what might have happened if one event had not occurred.

critical theory perspective: a perspective that focuses on deeply embedded forces from all perspectives and levels of analysis.

crony capitalism: noncompetitive lending and investment relationships between government financial institutions and private industry.

cult of the offensive: a belief in the advantage of using military power offensively.

current account: the net border flows of goods and services, along with government transfers and net income on capital investment.

cyber warfare: software attacks against countries' computer systems controlling defense and other strategic operations.

D

debt relief: the rescheduling of loans to developing nations to stretch the loans over longer periods of time or the forgiving of the loans altogether.

decolonization: the UN-led process by which former colonies in the third world gained their independence.

defense: the use of force to defend a country after an attack.

defensive realism: a school of realism that says states seek enough power to be secure.

democratic deficit: the criticism made of the European Union that it is not directly accountable to the people it represents.

democratic peace: the theory that democratic nations for the most part do not go to war with one another, making the spread of democracy desirable.

demographic transitions: periods of accelerating population growth as living standards increase because death rates decline faster than birthrates.

dependency theory: theory developed by critical theorists that explains lack of development in terms of colonialism and oppression.

derivatives market: the market that exchanges instruments derived from existing loans and financial assets, hedging them against future changes in prices, earnings, or interest.

détente: a phase of the Cold War beginning in the 1960s when the West initiated diplomatic overtures to Moscow.

deterrence: the use of threatened retaliation through force to deter an attack before it occurs.

development: the process of material, institutional, and human progress in a particular country or region.

digital divide: the gap between advanced and developing countries in terms of access to the digital devices of the information age.

diplomacy: discussions and negotiations among states as emphasized by the liberal perspective.

distribution of identities: the relative relationship of identities among actors in the international system in terms of their similarities and differences.

division of labor: the division of world markets into core, peripheral, and semiperipheral areas.

Doha Round: the ninth and most current round of trade talks, which offers significant potential benefits to developing countries in agriculture, medicines, and infrastructure.

domino theory: a theory held by the superpowers that if one country in a developing region went over to the other side, other countries in the region would follow, falling like dominoes.

E

East Asian Miracle: a period of unprecedented economic growth and development in East Asia between 1965 and 2010.

economic autarky: a closed domestic economic system based on protectionism and state-owned industries.

economies of scale: cost advantages whereby the larger the amount of a good that is produced, the lower the average cost of production.

***ejido* system:** Mexican land reform project that redistributed some land to peasants.

elite manipulation: leaders' exploitation of people's fears to wage ethnic conflict for the leaders' own personal and group interests.

end of history: an idea advanced by Francis Fukuyama that the spread of democracy had brought an end to the violent struggle among nations for equal recognition.

endogenous variables: causal variables that are included in a theoretical model or framework.

Entente Cordiale: an agreement signed in 1904 between Great Britain and France that settled colonial disputes between them and ended a century of British isolation from conflicts on the continent.

epistemic communities: communities of individuals or countries that share a broad base of common knowledge and trust.

ethics and morality: standards of good conduct for human behavior.

ethnic cleansing: the systematic persecution, torture, and killing or removal of a religious or ethnic group with the intent to take over the territory of that group.

ethno-national communities: groups of people in which ethnic and national identities overlap substantially.

European Central Bank (ECB): the banking institution whose Governing Council controls the money supply and sets short-term interest rates for the European Union.

European Commission: the organ of the European Union that has the exclusive authority to initiate legislation and pursue the goals of an ever-closer union.

European constitution: a 2004 European Union document, not yet ratified, that significantly increased the extent of European unity.

European Convention on Human Rights and Fundamental Freedoms: the convention adopted by the Council of Europe in 1950 to protect citizens' rights to due process and political participation.

European Council: summit meetings of the Council of the European Union, involving heads of state and government, that deal with crosscutting and controversial issues.

European Court of Human Rights: the court that administers European human rights law.

European Court of Justice (ECJ): the judicial body that has the power to interpret and enforce European Union treaties and law.

European Parliament: the only directly elected institution in the European Union.

European Union: a supranational organization that in 1993 superseded the European Communities and now unites European democracies in specific policy areas.

exceptionalism: the view that a particular state, and especially the United States, is distinct from others because of its specific history and unique institutions.

exchange rate: the value of a country's currency in terms of a foreign currency.

exogenous variables: autonomous factors that come from outside a theoretical model or system and that cannot be explained by the system.

exploitation: the extraction of profits from the resources and labor of others in an unjust way.

extended deterrence: a strategy of deterrence in which one country uses nuclear weapons to deter an attack on the territory of an allied country.

external identity: the identity of a country that is determined by its historical and external dialogue with other states.

F

failed states: states whose domestic institutions have collapsed.

federalism: a method of decentralizing power to accommodate tribal and regional differences.

feminism: a theory that critiques international relations as a male-centered and -dominated discipline.

financial repression: a policy in which states extract savings from one sector, such as agriculture or labor, to benefit another sector, such as industry.

fixed or managed exchange rates: exchange rates that are fixed by governments to gold, another currency, or a basket of currencies.

foreign direct investment (FDI): capital flows to a foreign country involving the acquisition or construction of manufacturing plants and other facilities.

fossil fuels: coal, oil, and natural gas.

freedom fighters: U.S. term for local forces resisting communist revolution in developing countries.

G

genocide: the systematic persecution and extermination of a group of people on the basis of their national, ethnic, racial, or religious identity.

geopolitics: a focus on a country's location and geography as the basis of its national interests.

global governance: the system of various international institutions and great powers groups that in a loose sense govern the global system.

globalization 1.0: early period of globalization, from 1492 to 1800, driven by mercantilism and colonialism.

globalization 2.0: later period of globalization, from 1800 to 1950, driven by global market institutions such as multinational trading and manufacturing corporations.

globalization 3.0: latest period of globalization, starting in the second half of the twentieth century, driven by the flattening of the global playing field and the knowledge economy rather than by imperialism or manufacturing conglomerates.

global warming: the heating up of the Earth's atmosphere caused by greenhouse gas emissions.

global war on terror: a worldwide military campaign to defeat nonstate terrorist groups such as Al Qaeda and the rogue states that support them.

graying population: a demographic pattern in which the percentage of a country's population older than sixty-five increases.

great power groups: assorted informal groupings of the major economic and financial powers known as the G-7, G-8, and G-20.

greenhouse gases: emissions from fossil fuels and other sources that can cause climate change.

H

hegemony: a situation in which one country is more powerful than all the others.

Helsinki Accords: a series of agreements between East and West in 1975 concerning arms control, trade, and human rights.

human rights: rights concerning the most basic protections against human physical abuse and suffering.

human security: security concern that focuses on violence within states and at the village and local levels, particularly violence against women and minorities.

I

ideal types: perspectives or simplified characterizations of theories that emphasize the most important aspects of reality, not all of its intricacies and variations.

identity perspective: a perspective that emphasizes the causal importance of the ideas and identities of actors, which motivate their use of power and negotiations.

IMF quota: the share of money that each country provides to the International Monetary Fund for lending, which determines its voting power.

imperialism: the forceful extension of a nation's authority to other peoples by military, economic, and political domination.

import substitution policies: policies developed in Latin America that substitute domestic industries for imports.

individual standing: the right of civilians, as well as states, to bring cases before a court, uncommon in international law until recently.

infant industries: developing industries that require protection to get started.

informal sector: business activities that take place outside the legal system of a country because of excessive regulations.

Inter-American Convention on Human Rights: an international human rights instrument adopted by the nations of the Americas in 1969.

Inter-American Court of Human Rights: the court charged with implementing the Inter-American Convention on Human Rights.

interdependence: the mutual dependence of states and nonstate actors in the international system through conferences, trade, tourism, and the like.

intergovernmental organizations (IGOs): formal international organizations established by governments.

internal identity: the identity of a country that derives from its unique national self-reflection and memory.

International Court of Justice (ICJ): the UN's main judicial institution to arbitrate disputes among nations.

International Criminal Court (ICC): a permanent tribunal started in 2002 to prosecute war crimes.

international institutions: formal international organizations and informal regimes that establish common rules to regularize international contacts and communications.

international law: the customary rules and codified treaties under which international organizations operate; covers political, economic, and social rights.

international regime: a network of international institutions or groups not under the authority of a single organization.

intifada: an uprising of Palestinians in territories occupied by Israel.

iron curtain: a metaphor for the political, ideological, and physical (no-man's land) separation of the Soviet Union and Western countries during the Cold War.

iron-rye coalition: a domestic coalition of military and agricultural interests that dominated German politics before World War I.

J

jihad: war waged for holy or religious reasons.

judgment: the broader assessment of what makes sense after one accumulates as many facts and tests as many perspectives as possible.

K

Kennedy Round: the sixth round of trade talks, under which across-the-board trade negotiations took place, reducing tariffs by an average of 35 percent.

Korean War: a proxy war on the Korean Peninsula in the early 1950s between Soviet-backed North Korean and Chinese forces and a United Nations force led by the United States.

Kyoto Protocol: an agreement reached in 1997 that set deadlines of 2008–2012 for industrial countries to cut their greenhouse gas emissions.

L

land reform: domestic policies to redistribute land for the purposes of equity and development.

League of Nations: a universal institution, founded after the Paris Peace Conference in 1919, that embodied the collective security approach to the management of military power.

Lebensraum: Hitler's expansionist ideology that proposed a larger living space for the German racial community.

legitimacy: the right to use power in international affairs.

level of analysis: the direction, or "level," from which the primary cause of events is coming.

liberal nationalism: a form of nineteenth-century nationalism that focused on political ideologies and called for wider participation and the rule of law in both domestic and international politics.

liberal perspective: a perspective that emphasizes repetitive relationships and negotiations, establishing patterns or institutions for resolving international conflicts.

Lisbon Treaty: a 2009 treaty that implements many of the provisions of the unratified European constitution by intergovernmental agreement.

long telegram: George Kennan's diplomatic telegram of 1946 outlining the U.S.–Soviet conflict and arguing for the policy of containment.

lost decade: a period of economic stagnation in Latin America brought on by domestic policies, the oil crises, and high debt, lasting from the early 1970s to the late 1980s.

M

marginalization: the social process of making unimportant or powerless certain groups within a society, especially indigenous peoples and women.

Marshall Plan: the Western plan to rebuild Germany and the rest of Europe after World War II.

Marxism: a theory that emphasizes the dialectical or conflictual relationship between capitalist and communist states in the international system, leading to the triumph of communism, not democracy.

massive retaliation: the strategy of threatening to unleash a general nuclear war.

maximum deterrence: a strategy that relies on many nuclear weapons to deter both conventional and limited nuclear attacks.

methods: the formal rules of reason (rationalist) or appropriateness (constructivist) for testing perspectives against facts.

metropole: the metropolitan (political, commercial, and military) center of imperial power.

microfinancing: the provision of small loans to individuals in developing countries, especially women.

militant nationalism: a form of nineteenth-century nationalism that focused on cultural and racial differences and advocated an aggressive, heroic approach to international relations.

Millennium Development Goals: UN program initiated in 1996 to achieve ambitious development objectives by 2015.

minimum deterrence: a strategy of deterrence that relies on a few nuclear weapons to retaliate and inflict unacceptable damage on the adversary.

modernization: the transformation of human society from self-contained autarchic centers of agrarian society to highly specialized and interdependent units of modern society.

Montreal Protocol: an international agreement reached in 1987 that set the specific goal of reducing the use of chlorofluorocarbons by 50 percent by 1998.

most-favored-nation (MFN) principle: a principle under which nations that negotiate tariff reduction offer the same low tariff to all nations that they offer to the most favored nation, meaning the nation that pays the lowest tariffs.

multicollinearity: a statistical situation in which multiple variables are all highly correlated with one another.

multilateralism: the inclusion of all states in international diplomacy.

multilateral trade rounds: trade negotiations in which multiple countries participate and reduce trade barriers simultaneously.

mutual assured destruction (MAD): the nuclear deterrence strategy that called for the dominance of offensive over defensive weapons.

mutual assured protection (MAP): nuclear strategy, proposed by Reagan, to build up defensive systems and reduce offensive weapons.

GLOSSARY OF KEY CONCEPTS

mutual recognition: a way of reconciling different regulatory standards across nations by requiring that product standards accepted in one country be recognized by all participants.

N

national wars of liberation: Soviet term for proxy wars against Western colonialism in developing countries.

nation building: the process through which ethnic groups evolve toward nationhood.

nationhood: a status acquired by states strong enough to protect their borders and command the loyalty of their citizens.

New Thinking: Gorbachev's ideas of domestic reform known as *glasnost and perestroika.*

nonaligned movement: a coalition led by India, Yugoslavia, and Egypt that stressed neutrality in the Cold War.

nongovernmental organizations (NGOs): nonstate actors such as student, tourist, and professional associations that are not subject to direct government control.

nontariff barriers (NTBs): policy instruments other than price, such as quotas and qualitative restrictions, designed to limit or regulate imports and exports.

norms: ideas that govern the procedural or substantive terms of state behavior, such as reciprocity and human rights.

North Atlantic Treaty Organization (NATO): western alliance in the Cold War.

nuclear triad: the combination of nuclear land-, sea-, and air-based retaliatory weapons.

O

offensive realism: a school of realism that says states seek dominant power.

official development assistance (ODA): aid from advanced governments to developing nations.

opportunity costs: the costs of alternative uses of resources based on competitive prices.

Oslo Accords: a series of agreements reached in 1993 between the Palestine Liberation Organization and Israel that Israeli troops would withdraw from Gaza and areas of the West Bank and that the PLO and Israel would recognize one another.

overdetermined outcome: an outcome caused by multiple independent variables, the separate and interactive effects of which are not clear.

ozone layer: the outer layer of the Earth's atmosphere that protects the planet from solar radiation.

P

pandemics: outbreaks of infectious diseases such as AIDS, avian flu, and SARS that spread or threaten to spread worldwide.

partition: the separation of hostile ethnic or religious groups into different territories or states.

paternalism: a system in which institutions such as the church or state provide for the needs of individuals or groups while stifling individual initiative and entrepreneurship.

path dependence: a process emphasized by liberal perspectives in which decisions in a particular direction affect later decisions, accumulating advantages or disadvantages along a certain path.

peace-enforcement activities: UN actions intended to compel countries by force or threat of force to follow the terms of UN resolutions.

peacekeeping activities: UN actions devoted to monitoring cease-fires and separating combatants in third-world conflicts.

peace research studies: scholarly inquiry dedicated to the study of the potential for international peace, emphasizing collective and common-humanity approaches rather than balance of power.

peripheral states: smaller and less developed countries that produce most of the competitive or lagging products after the monopoly qualities of these products have been substantially diminished.

perspective: a statement or hypothesis that explains the primary cause of what is happening—for example, a struggle for power causes conflict and sometimes wars.

piracy: acts of violence at sea carried out to exact ransom or policy changes to support terrorism.

polarity: the number of states—one (unipolar), two (bipolar), three (tripolar), or more (multipolar)—holding significant power in the international system.

portfolio investment: transfers of money to buy stocks, bonds, and so on.

postconflict reconstruction: activities aimed at resettling displaced populations and rebuilding areas ravaged by ethnic conflict.

postmodernists: theorists who seek to expose the hidden or masked meanings of language and discourse in international relations in order to gain space to imagine alternatives.

Potsdam Conference: the meeting among wartime allies in July 1945 that produced no agreement on the unification of Germany and other issues.

power: the material capabilities of a country, such as size of population and territory, resource endowment, economic capability, and military strength.

power balancing: a school of realism that sees hegemony as destabilizing and war as most likely when a dominant power emerges to threaten the equilibrium of power among other states.

power transition: a school of realism that sees hegemony as stabilizing and war as most likely when a rising power challenges a previously dominant one and the balance of power approaches equilibrium.

pragmatism: the idea that morality is proportionate to what is possible and causes the least harm.

preemptive war: an attack by one country against another because the second country is preparing to attack the first.

prestige: a nation's reputation for using force credibly and prudently to stabilize the status quo.

preventive war: a war by one country against another that is not preparing to attack the first country but is growing in power and may attack in the future.

prisoner's dilemma: a game in which two prisoners rationally choose not to cooperate in order to avoid even worse outcomes.

process tracing: a method of connecting events in sequence to identify cause and effect.

productivity: output per unit of input.

proxy wars: conflicts in peripheral areas in which nuclear powers tested each other's military capabilities and resolve.

psychological studies: studies that emphasize ideas that define actor personalities, although the ideas may not be conscious but subconscious and sometimes irrational.

Q

qualified majority voting (QMV): the principle that decisions by international organizations are made by weighted majority votes, as in the European Union today.

R

rationalist methods: methods that disaggregate and explain events sequentially as one event preceding and causing a second event.

realist perspective: a perspective that sees the world largely in terms of a struggle for relative power in which strong actors seek to dominate and weak actors seek to resist.

reciprocity: the behavior of states toward one another based largely on mutual exchanges that entail interdependent benefits or disadvantages.

regional organizations: organizations whose members come from and are limited to specific geographic regions of the world.

relative identities: identities that position actors' self-images with respect to one another as similar or dissimilar.

relativism: a position that holds that truth and morality are relative to each individual or culture and that one should "live and let live."

rent-seekers: firms that lobby to limit competition, extracting monopoly rents by producing at low costs while selling at high prices.

resource curse: a phenomenon in which an abundance of natural resources inhibits development in other sectors.

responsibility to protect: the idea that sovereign states have a responsibility to protect their own citizens from avoidable catastrophe, and, if they cannot or will not, the international community must bear that responsibility.

revisionist interpretation: an interpretation of the origins of the Cold War that emphasizes American ideological or economic aggression against the Soviet Union and its allies.

river and ocean pollution: waterway contaminants from industrial and agricultural runoff, garbage, and human sewage.

rogue states: states that seek systematically to acquire nuclear weapons with the possible intent of passing them on to nonstate terrorists.

rollback: John Foster Dulles's policy in the 1950s of liberating the eastern European countries from Moscow's control.

S

sample size: the number of cases used for testing correlations.

Schlieffen Plan: Germany's mobilization plan that called for an attack on France first, by way of Belgium, followed by an attack on Russia.

security dilemma: the situation that states face when they arm to defend themselves and in the process threaten other states.

self-determination: nations' right to autonomy in deciding their own domestic identities.

self-help: the principle of self-defense under anarchy in which states have no one to rely on to defend their security except themselves.

semiperipheral states: states that produce a nearly even mix of monopoly and competitive products.

Shanghai Cooperation Organization (SCO): group of Asian nations led by China and Russia to resist U.S. power.

shared identities: identities that overlap and fuse based on norms and images that cannot be traced back to specific identities or their interrelationships.

Shiites: members of the minority sect of Islam that identifies with a seventh-century renegade group that advocated divine rather than elective succession.

smog: air pollution, especially as a result of vehicle exhaust and industry.

social constructivism: an identity perspective in which states and other actors acquire their identities from intersubjective discourses in which they know who they are only by reference to others.

Social Darwinism: a nineteenth-century worldview that saw a struggle among nations for survival of the fittest.

socialist nationalism: a form of nineteenth-century nationalism that sought greater economic equality and social justice, especially in class and colonial relationships.

soft power: the attractiveness of the values or ideas of a country as distinct from its military and economic power or its negotiating behavior.

sovereignty: an attribute of states such that they are not subordinate to a higher power either inside or outside their borders and they agree not to intervene in the domestic jurisdictions of other states.

spheres of influence: areas of contested territory divided up and dominated by great powers, which agree not to interfere in one another's areas.

states: the actors in the contemporary international system that have the largest capabilities and right to use military force.

Strategic Arms Limitation Talks (SALT): U.S.-Soviet talks held in the 1970s to limit offensive weapon systems.

Strategic Arms Reduction Talks (START): U.S.-Soviet talks held in the 1990s to reduce offensive weapons systems.

Strategic Defense Initiative (SDI): the space-based anti-missile systems that formed the core of Reagan's program to enhance U.S. missile defenses.

Sunnis: members of the majority branch of Islam that identifies with the caliphs, the elected successors of Muhammad dating back to the seventh century.

supranational institutions: institutions above the level of the state, like the European Commission, that are motivated by common, rather than state-specific, goals.

systematic inequality: deep-seated disparity in the distribution of wealth and/or power generated by colonialism and dependency.

T

tariffs: taxes on goods and services crossing borders.

technological change: the application of science and engineering to increase wealth and alter human society.

terms of trade: relative price of exports and imports.

terrorism: the use of violence against innocent civilians to advance political aims.

Tokyo Round: the seventh round of trade talks, in which tariffs were reduced further across the board and developing countries were granted tariff preferences.

toxic and hazardous wastes: pollutants from the disposal of petrochemicals, nuclear waste, and other dangerous materials.

trade adjustment assistance: cash benefits or retraining programs for workers displaced by trade.

transnational nongovernmental organizations (TNGOs): international commercial or not-for-profit advocacy organizations, typically independent of and not founded by governments.

transnational relations: relations among nongovernmental, as opposed to governmental, authorities.

Treaty on Conventional Forces in Europe (CFE): treaty signed in 1990 reducing and establishing a roughly equal balance of major conventional weapons systems and troop strength in Europe.

Treaty on the Non-Proliferation of Nuclear Weapons (NPT): a 1968 treaty that seeks to prevent the spread of nuclear weapons and materials while fostering the civilian development of nuclear power.

Triple Alliance: an alliance formed first between Germany and Austria-Hungary in 1879, then joined by Italy in 1882, that accounted for 50 percent of all European wealth in the early twentieth century.

Triple Entente: an agreement signed in 1907 in which Great Britain and France expanded the Entente Cordiale to include Russia.

Truman Doctrine: U.S. policy that defined the Cold War in ideological terms.

U

unanimity: a principle in international affairs that all nations, regardless of size or identity, participate in global institutions and decision making.

UN Convention on the Elimination of All Forms of Discrimination against Women (CEDAW): the 1979 UN convention broadly prohibiting all discrimination against women.

UN Convention on the Rights of the Child (CRC): the UN convention adopted in 1989 to protect the rights of children.

UN Economic and Social Council (ECOSOC): a major organ of the UN General Assembly that until 2006 elected members of the UN Human Rights Commission based on geographic representation.

unfair trade: trade that violates an international trade agreement or is considered unjustified, unreasonable, and discriminatory.

UN Human Rights Commission: the commission that drafted and implements the Universal Declaration of Human Rights.

UN Human Rights Council: the organization that replaced the UN Human Rights Commission in 2006.

unilateralism or minilateralism: action by one or several states but not by all states.

United Nations: the principal general-purpose intergovernmental organization that deals with collective security, economic and social development, and international law and human rights.

Universal Declaration of Human Rights: a UN declaration approved in 1948 prescribing the obligations of states to individuals rather than of individuals to states.

universal human rights: rights inherent in all human beings that are often expressed and guaranteed by law in the forms of treaties, customary international law, general principles, and other sources of international law.

universalism: a position that holds that truth and morality are universal and cannot be adjusted to specific circumstances.

universal jurisdiction: the claim of a single state that it can prosecute perpetrators of war crimes anywhere in the world.

Uruguay Round: the eighth round of trade talks and the first to bear the name of a developing country; it extended free trade to services, investment, agriculture, and intellectual property.

V

values: ideas that express deep moral convictions.

Vietnam War: costly war fought by the United States in Southeast Asia to contain communism.

W

Wahhabism: a rigid and puritanical form of Islam originating in the eighteenth century with the Arabian spiritual leader Muhammad ibn Abd al-Wahhab.

Warsaw Pact: communist alliance in Cold War.

water tables: the aquifers below the Earth's surface that supply freshwater.

world systems: theories (updating Marxism) that explain how colonialism reinforced capitalism and enabled capitalism to survive by exploiting the peripheral countries of the world.

Y

Yalta Conference: a wartime conference held in February 1945 where the United States, Soviet Union, and Great Britain agreed on the unconditional surrender of Nazi Germany and postwar occupation of Europe, including a Soviet sphere of influence in eastern Europe.

youth bulge: a demographic pattern in which a substantial percentage of the population in a given country is young, typically below the age of fifteen.

Z

Zollverein: a customs union created by Prussia involving other German states that lowered barriers to trade and ignited rapid industrial development beginning in the 1830s.

PHOTO CREDITS

Chapter 9: Identity Perspectives on Globalization

Chapter 10: Critical Theory Perspectives on Globalization

Conclusion: Applying Perspectives and Levels of Analysis

INDEX